OXFORD HISTORY OF
EARLY MODERN EUROPE

General Editor: R. J. W. EVANS

DIVIDED KINGDOM

DIVIDED KINGDOM

IRELAND 1630–1800

S. J. CONNOLLY

OXFORD
UNIVERSITY PRESS

Great Clarendon Street, Oxford OX2 6DP

Oxford University Press is a department of the University of Oxford.
It furthers the University's objective of excellence in research, scholarship,
and education by publishing worldwide in

Oxford New York

Auckland Cape Town Dar es Salaam Hong Kong Karachi
Kuala Lumpur Madrid Melbourne Mexico City Nairobi
New Delhi Shanghai Taipei Toronto

With offices in

Argentina Austria Brazil Chile Czech Republic France Greece
Guatemala Hungary Italy Japan Poland Portugal Singapore
South Korea Switzerland Thailand Turkey Ukraine Vietnam

Oxford is a registered trade mark of Oxford University Press
in the UK and in certain other countries

Published in the United States
by Oxford University Press Inc., New York

British Library Cataloguing in Publication Data

Data available

Library of Congress Cataloging in Publication Data

Connolly, S. J. (Sean J.)
Divided kingdom : Ireland, 1630–1800 / S.J. Connolly.
p. cm.—(Oxford history of early modern Europe)
Includes bibliographical references and index.
This volume is a continuation of the study previously published as
Contested island in 2007.
ISBN-13: 978–0–19–954347–2
1. Ireland—History—17th century. 2. Ireland—History—18th
century. 3. Ireland—Politics and government—17th century. 4.
Ireland—Politics and government—18th century. 5. British—Ireland—
History—17th century. 6. British—Ireland—History—18th century.
I. Connolly, S. J. (Sean J.) Contested island. II. Title.
DA940.C736 2008
941.506—dc22

2008009312

Typeset by Laserwords Private Limited, Chennai, India
Printed in Great Britain
on acid-free paper by
CPI Antony Rowe Ltd, Chippenham, Wiltshire

ISBN 978–0–19–954347–2

1 3 5 7 9 10 8 6 4 2

For Helen

Preface

Divided Kingdom is the second part of a study of the early modern origins of Irish society. As with the first volume, *Contested Island*, its main concern is with the changing relationships and patterns of interaction among the different sections of an ethnically, and by this time religiously, divided society, continuing the story from Ireland's part in the British civil wars of the mid-seventeenth century to the era of the American and French revolutions.

The chronology of this second volume brings me to the period in which my own research has been concentrated. But a broadly based survey of this kind has nevertheless made it necessary to rely in many respects on the work of other historians. As in the earlier volume, I have tried to avoid encumbering the main text with details of historiographical debates. However the footnotes should indicate where I am following the arguments of others, where I am taking sides on points of controversy, and where I am offering an opinion of my own.

The main part of the text was completed, along with the whole of the preceding volume, during a period of research leave supported by Queen's University and by the Arts and Humanities Research Board. For advice on a variety of points I am grateful to Dr Liam Chambers, Dr Neal Garnham, Mr Gordon Rees, and Mr James Wilson. I have learned much from a range of conversations, short and long, with my head of department, Professor David Hayton, himself a leading authority on one part of the period covered here. I must also thank Dr Micheál Ó Siochrú for a detailed critique, far above the call of duty, of the whole of Chapters 2 and 3. Professor Robert Evans has been a patient and unobtrusive editor. Mavis Bracegirdle has, as always, combined generous moral support for the project with a frank curiosity as to when, if ever, it was likely to reach a conclusion.

S. J. C.

Belfast
September 2007

Contents

List of Maps

List of Tables

Abbreviations

BL	British Library
Connolly, *Contested Island*	S. J. Connolly, *Contested Island: Ireland 1460–1630* (Oxford, 2007)
Connolly, *Religion, Law and Power*	S. J. Connolly, *Religion, Law and Power: The Making of Protestant Ireland 1660–1760* (Oxford, 1992)
CSPD	*Calendar of State Papers, Domestic Series 1547–1580* (London, 1856–)
CSPI	*Calendar of the State Papers Relating to Ireland 1509–1670* (London, 1860–1912)
DNB	*Oxford Dictionary of National Biography* (Oxford, 2004)
ECI	*Eighteenth-Century Ireland*
HMC	Historical Manuscripts Commission
IESH	*Irish Economic and Social History*
IHS	*Irish Historical Studies*
NAI	National Archives of Ireland, Dublin
NHI	*A New History of Ireland*: Vol. 2, *Medieval Ireland 1169–1534*, ed. Art Cosgrove (Oxford, 1987); Vol. 3: *Early Modern Ireland 1534–1691*, ed. T. W. Moody, F. X. Martin, and F. J. Byrne (Oxford, 1976); Vol. 4: *Eighteenth-Century Ireland 1691–1800*, ed. T. W. Moody and W. E. Vaughan (Oxford, 1986)
NLI	National Library of Ireland, Dublin
PRIA	*Proceedings of the Royal Irish Academy*
PRO	The National Archives, London, the Public Record Office
PRONI	Public Record Office of Northern Ireland, Belfast
TCD	Trinity College, Dublin

1

Lowestoft, Suffolk, 1665

On 3 June 1665 the fleets of England and of the Dutch republic, each amounting to around 100 ships, joined in battle off Lowestoft, on the Suffolk coast. The outcome was a decisive English victory in an otherwise inglorious war. But it was victory at a cost. As the commander of the English fleet, James, duke of York, brother of King Charles II, observed events from his flagship *The Royal Charles*, a Dutch chain shot killed three of his companions standing nearby. One of the dead was Cormac or Charles MacCarthy, Viscount Muskerry, son and heir to the earl of Clancarty. Contemporary reports of the young nobleman's blood and brains besplattering the royal duke beside him need not necessarily be taken at face value. This was in fact a standard motif in narratives of naval heroism, conveniently establishing the physical courage of commanders whose rank debarred them from personally taking a place in combat. But the regard in which young Muskerry was held was nevertheless clear. What remained of him lies buried in the north transept of Westminster Abbey, alongside the earl of Marlborough and two others, identified in a single inscription as 'four . . . honourable persons [who] died in his Majesty's service against the Dutch'.[1]

The soldier and courtier who thus met his death at the side of the heir to the English, Scottish, and Irish thrones was a member of what had once been one of the major Gaelic dynasties of southern Ireland. Other branches of the family had been among the many victims of the steady extension during the sixteenth century of English state control. The MacCarthys of Muskerry, however, had a long history of cooperation with the English crown, to whose local representatives they had looked for protection against their potentially oppressive neighbours, the earls of Desmond. In the first half of the seventeenth century, in consequence, they retained their large estate in the fertile valley of the River Lee. Donough, Viscount Muskerry, married the sister of the earl of Ormond, the young head of Ireland's leading noble dynasty. Reluctantly drawn into the civil war that erupted

---

[1] *The Marriage, Baptismal and Burial Registers of the Collegiate Church or Abbey of St Peter, Westminster*, ed. J. L. Chester (London, 1876), 162. The history of the last earls of Clancarty can be traced through J. A. Murphy. *Justin MacCarthy: Lord Mountcashel* (Cork, 1959); Frances Harris, *A Passion for Government: The Life of Sarah, Duchess of Marlborough* (Oxford, 1991), 80, 325–6, 345–8; James Jay Carafano, 'Maccarthy, Donough' and 'Maccarthy, Robert' (*DNB*). For the motif of the commander splattered with his subordinate's blood see Timothy Jenks, *Naval Engagements: Patriotism, Cultural Politics and the Royal Navy 1793–1815* (Oxford, 2006), 207.

in 1641, he had remained close to Ormond, now head of the royalist forces in Ireland, and in the 1650s joined Charles II in exile on the continent. His loyalty was rewarded when he became earl of Clancarty in 1658, and then regained full possession of his Irish lands at the restoration of the monarchy two years later.

The first earl of Clancarty died two months after Lowestoft. The title passed to Muskerry's 12-year-old son, and then, on his death shortly after, to the first earl's second son Callaghan. To take up the title Callaghan abandoned his studies in France, where he had been preparing to enter the priesthood, and further secured his position by declaring himself a Protestant. His younger brother Justin, on the other hand, remained a Catholic. Initially this meant that the military employment he found under royal patronage was outside the British Isles, in France and then in Sweden. But in 1685, in a changing political climate, he took command of a regiment in Ireland. He also married well, to a daughter of Charles I's strongman, and one-time lord deputy of Ireland, Thomas Wentworth, earl of Strafford. When the former duke of York, now James II, was driven from the throne in 1688 both Callaghan's heir Donough, fourth earl of Clancarty, and his uncle Colonel Justin McCarthy held commands in the army that unsuccessfully upheld his cause in Ireland. By 1694 both men were in exile in France, their lands forfeited to the victorious regime of William III.

An already complicated family saga did not, however, end here. At the very end of 1684, when it seemed clear that the future lay with the Catholic James II, the earl of Sunderland, the most unscrupulously ambitious of the king's English ministers, had arranged a politic marriage between his 14-year-old daughter and young Clancarty. In 1697 the exiled earl travelled secretly to England in an audacious bid to consummate his thirteen-year-old marriage and so establish a renewed foothold in aristocratic society. Dragged from the marital bed by his outraged father-in-law, who had already accommodated himself to the new regime and had no intention of jeopardizing his restored fortunes, Clancarty was briefly imprisoned. In the end, however, the couple were dispatched abroad with a generous royal pension of £ 2,500 between them. Later their son Robert, born in Hamburg around 1700, returned to England, where his relative the duchess of Marlborough, widow of Queen Anne's great general, deployed her still considerable influence on his behalf. With this support he gained a commission in the royal navy, and between 1733 and 1735 served as governor of Newfoundland. Following his father's death in 1734 he petitioned the government for the restoration of the estate forfeited by his father. The attempt failed, but the prospect of an unpicking of the confiscations of Catholic land that had followed the defeat of James II's forces in 1691 caused a brief panic among Irish Protestants. Clancarty resumed his service in the royal navy, but in 1744 expectations of an imminent invasion and a possible change of regime encouraged him to defect to the exiled Stuart court in France. He did not in the end take part in Prince Charles Edward's disastrous military adventure in Scotland during 1745–6. Instead a pension from Louis XV allowed him to live out his remaining twenty-five years in comfortable and sociable retirement among the dwindling remnants of the Jacobite diaspora.

The story of the MacCarthys of Muskerry was by no means a typical one. They were rare survivors in an age which saw the great majority of Catholic landed families, and an even higher proportion of those of Gaelic origin, stripped of their estates and status and wholly excluded from the ranks of the ruling elite. It remains of interest partly as a reminder of the human complexities that are likely to lie concealed behind any such bald summary of large-scale social and political changes. But it is also appropriate in another way. The same tangled Irish history that made the descendant of Gaelic chieftains governor of a British colony in North America produced other transformations and redefinitions, affecting much larger numbers. The half-century between the battle of Lowestoft and the exile of the fourth earl saw the disappearance of a whole nation, the descendants of the medieval colonists, who for centuries had seen themselves, and been accepted, as the upholders of the English interest in Ireland, but were now submerged in a Catholic population excluded from status and power. Meanwhile the New English settlers who had displaced these older colonists had, like the MacCarthys and others, to find their way through the political upheavals, first of the mid-century civil wars, then of the Revolution of 1688. The situation was further complicated by the presence in Ireland of not one new settler population but two; as late as 1705 there was anxious speculation about how what were still thought of as the Scots of Ireland would respond if England and Scotland went to war.

By the time the would-be fifth earl of Clancarty died in his comfortable French exile, on the other hand, the very success of these English and Scots in establishing themselves as what one of their number called 'the whole people of Ireland' had forced them to begin wrestling with new questions of identity and allegiance. Meanwhile the longer-established population, whether old colonist or old native, were also moving away from traditional loyalties, some towards new ideologies of opposition with their roots in America and France, others towards an accommodation with a Hanoverian state that was radically reassessing its own priorities in Ireland. There was nothing predetermined about these outcomes. On the contrary the short but vicious civil war that was to end the eighteenth century saw all the different groups that made up the island's population divided across as well as along lines of class, religion, and ethnic origin. It is this sense of the fluid and contingent, of identities made and remade against an uncertain and sometimes dangerous background, that the pages that follow seek to recapture, and to which the story of the Macarthys of Muskerry is as good an introduction as any.

2

The Crisis of Composite Monarchy

History, to return to a phrase that helped introduce the predecessor to this book, has been described as a pack of tricks that historians play on the dead. If so, one significant card among those they conceal up their sleeves is the setting of chronological boundaries. Most accounts of Ireland in the later part of the early modern period start either in 1603 or in 1641. The first places the reader at the end of the last and most brutal of the wars by which, over the preceding seven decades, the English state had extended its power across the whole island. It also leads on immediately to that war's slightly belated aftermath, the planting in the northern province of Ulster of a colony of English and Scottish settlers, at the expense of the Gaelic Irish inhabitants. The second date skips forward to the next great episode of violence, the Ulster rising of October 1641, and to the long and bloody civil war that followed.

In contrast to both of these choices, a narrative that begins in the 1630s has a different starting point, in an Ireland seen both by contemporaries and by later generations as having entered a new age of stability and peace. In 1633 James Ware, one of the earliest in a long line of scholars of English Protestant descent who were to distinguish themselves by their interest in the indigenous culture and language of their adopted country, produced the first printed version of the celebrated *View of the State of Ireland* written four decades earlier by the Munster settler and poet Edmund Spenser. In doing so, however, he edited the text to remove some of Spenser's more extreme attacks on the character of the native inhabitants. He also added a preface making clear that the poet's brutal prescription of unrelenting military repression as the only means of reducing an irredeemably barbarous nation to civility was a historical curiosity, rendered irrelevant by 'the good effects which the last 30 years peace have produced in this land'.[1]

The harmony, or more properly equilibrium, to which Ware referred was between three main groups, defined by a combination of ethnic and religious terms. The Gaelic Irish were the aboriginal inhabitants. They were heirs to an ancient culture whose distinctive feature was a reflection in part of the island's

---

[1] *A View of the State of Ireland*, in *The Historie of Ireland, Collected by Three Learned Authors*, ed. Sir James Ware (Dublin, 1633), preface. For a fuller discussion of the general background sketched out in the opening section of this chapter, see Connolly, *Contested Island*, esp. chs. 7–9.

peripheral location, in part of its not having shared in the general western European experience of formal incorporation into the Roman empire. After 1541 what had formerly been the 'wild' Irish became legal subjects of the crown, and their lords were encouraged to accept English titles of nobility and landownership. From an early stage, however, a strategy of reform and assimilation proceeded side by side with one of military conquest. The first plantation of English settlers, on land confiscated from the midland lordships of O'More and O'Connor Faly, commenced in 1549. A revolt in 1595 by the Gaelic lords of Ulster, initially aimed at defending their regional autonomy, expanded into a protracted nation-wide war. Its defeat, and the subsequent settlement across Ulster of thousands of English and Scottish settlers, marked the final extension to the island as a whole of the authority of the British state. There was still a Gaelic Irish landed gentry, some of them with noble titles, owning perhaps a third of Irish land. But most families had lost something over the preceding decades, and many prominent lineages had been almost wholly dispossessed.

The second group, generally referred to by this time as the Old English, were descendants of the first colony, established in the late twelfth century. In the early seventeenth century they remained concentrated in the lowland areas of the east and south that had formed the heartland of the medieval lordship. Old English proprietors held over half the profitable land in the counties of Dublin, Kildare, Louth, Meath, and Westmeath, the area still known as the Pale, as well as in Kilkenny and Wexford.[2] They were also well established in the counties of Galway and Mayo, partly through the land speculation of Old English merchants from the city of Galway and partly through the survival there of the Burkes, renegade English in the middle ages but now rehabilitated and headed by the influential earl of Clanricard, a prominent member of King Charles I's court. Old English merchants also dominated the trade of the other important coastal towns, Drogheda on the east coast, Wexford, Waterford, and Cork on the south, and Limerick on the west. Some of the Old English, particularly in outlying areas, had from an early stage adopted aspects of Gaelic language, dress, and culture. Others, however, especially in the Pale and in urban centres, continued to hold themselves self-consciously apart from the 'wild Irish'. Even those who had wholly or partly taken up Gaelic language and custom, moreover, could still exhibit a clear sense of their English identity and allegiance.

To these two long-established populations there had been added, by the early seventeenth century, what were generally referred to as the New English. During the sixteenth century the extension of government control over a steadily

---

[2] For the Old English share of profitable land by county see Aidan Clarke, *The Old English in Ireland 1625–42* (London, 1966), 25, 236. Clarke puts their total share of profitable land in 1641 at 'very nearly one-third' (p. 25). Taken together with J. G. Simm's estimate that the total Catholic share of profitable land in 1641 was 59%, this would suggest that the holdings of the Old English and Gaelic Irish were roughly equal in size. All such calculations, however, have a wide margin of error. See below, Ch. 4 n. 27.

expanding area, and the recurrent military conflicts it entailed, had created opportunities for soldiers, merchants, administrators, and land speculators. As in the more distant English possessions in North America, the risks were high but the rewards, for the fortunate and bold, potentially enormous. Richard Boyle, younger son of an obscure Kent family, arrived in 1588 to take up a minor administrative post. Forty years later, thanks to shrewd, and not always legal, dealings in the chaotic Irish land system, he was the earl of Cork, lord justice of Ireland, and possibly the kingdom's richest inhabitant. Arthur Chichester, from equally modest origins in Devon, came to Ireland as a soldier after earlier service in the West Indies and on the European mainland. By the time of his death in 1625 he was one of Ulster's greatest landowners, with an extensive estate taking in the north-east port of Carrickfergus and the nondescript settlement of Belfast, as well as the Inishowen peninsula further west.

Alongside this new elite of successful land speculators and self-enriching office holders there were more humble migrants. Between 1603 and 1641 an estimated 70,000 English and 30,000 Scots migrated to Ireland, whether as part of formal plantation schemes or as independent migrants attracted by the opportunities offered in a neighbouring island now pacified and opened up to new forms of commercial development. In Munster, where an English colony had been created on confiscated land in the 1580s and rebuilt following the war of 1595–1603, there were an estimated 22,000 English settlers by 1641. Lesser plantation schemes undertaken in the 1620s had created small concentrations elsewhere, notably in Wexford and Queen's County. Even outside the areas of organized plantation schemes, meanwhile, improving landlords, Catholic as well as Protestant, had sought to promote the economic development of their estates by bringing in English tenants and craftsmen. Most important of all, there was the settler population of Ulster, amounting by 1641 to perhaps 40,000 individuals. Two-thirds or more of these Ulster settlers, however, were Scots rather than English, adding a further element to an already complex mix of cultures and political allegiances.[3]

The labels Gaelic Irish, Old English, and New English highlighted ethnic identity. By the seventeenth century, however, language and culture were becoming less significant as markers of identity. The surviving Gaelic gentry increasingly adopted the lifestyle of their Old and New English counterparts—one reason why so many found themselves increasingly burdened with debt. The Gaelic peasantry remained distinctive in speech and appearance. But even there the spread of modest consumer goods, a move towards something closer to English

---

[3] For a detailed study of the distribution of New English settlers see Nicholas Canny, *Making Ireland British 1580–1650* (Oxford, 2001), ch. 6. For the total of 100,000 British migrants see idem, 'English Migration into and across the Atlantic during the Seventeenth and Eighteenth Centuries', in idem (ed.), *Europeans on the Move: Studies on European Migration 1500–1800* (Oxford, 1994), 62–4. For the figure of 40,000 settlers in Ulster, see Connolly, *Contested Island*, 301–2, and also Michael Perceval-Maxwell, *The Outbreak of the Irish Rebellion of 1641* (Montreal, 1994), 31.

styles of dress, and the growth of bilingualism modified what had earlier been stark differences. Instead the real line of division within Irish society, by the first half of the seventeenth century, was not ethnic origin or language but religion. The Reformation, dominant in England from the 1550s, had made little headway in Ireland, given a religiously conservative population and a government too preoccupied with the task of establishing political order to support a consistent strategy of promoting religious change. It was the New English settlers who became the main supporters of the Protestant Church of Ireland, while both Old English and Gaelic Irish remained loyal to a Catholicism reorganized, from the 1590s onwards, as a formidable ecclesiastical system along Counter-Reformation lines. The primacy of religion over ethnicity was evident in the careers of individuals like James Butler, who succeeded to the earldom of Ormond in 1633 after having been brought up as a Protestant in England, or James Ussher, son of a Dublin merchant, who became Church of Ireland archbishop of Armagh in 1625. Both belonged to English families long established in Ireland. But neither, despite their ancestry, was considered to be Old English.

This replacement of ethnic by religious markers of identity and allegiance had particularly serious consequences for the Old English. Their leaders continued to insist on their traditional role as the defenders of English civility, and of the rights of the English crown. All but a handful had remained loyal throughout the war of 1595–1603, despite the attempts of the Ulster lords to present the conflict as a Catholic revolt against a heretic queen. But following the end of the war, and the collapse of the last serious challenge from an unsubdued Gaeldom, their political cooperation suddenly became of less consequence, and their Englishness a less satisfactory compensation for their continued refusal to conform to the state religion. By this time too the growing population of New English provided the crown with an alternative body of local servants and administrators, trustworthy on religious as well as political grounds. By the 1630s the Old English, despite their continued appeals to their English blood and historic loyalty, were largely excluded from the more influential and lucrative offices of central and local government, and Catholic religious services were subject to sporadic repression.

Early seventeenth-century Ireland was thus heir to potentially serious divisions. In a Europe still torn by wars of religion, it was a society in which a clear majority of the population, including a substantial proportion of the propertied elite, rejected the state church, and suffered exclusion from power at the hands of a dominant and assertive minority. To this was added a legacy of recent conquest and dispossession. Later surveys suggest that by 1641 the New English controlled just under 40 per cent of the island's profitable land. Some of their gains had been at the expense of the Old English, particularly the break-up of the huge estate controlled by the Fitzgerald earls of Desmond in the south-west following a revolt there in 1579–83. The main losers, however, had been the Gaelic Irish, partly through confiscation, partly through the legal trickery in which some New

English planters excelled, and partly through their own inability to cope with the demands of a more commercialized social order. Members of these dispossessed or financially encumbered families survived as locally influential figures, and as a focus for continued discontent. Others had found a more distant, but potentially more dangerous, refuge as soldiers in the armies of England's continental rivals France and Spain.

With hindsight these religious and social conflicts can be seen as the basis of the explosion of violence that commenced in October 1641. A decade earlier, however, none of this could have been foreseen—any more than anyone could have predicted that the divisions troubling England, between a new king and his parliament and between factions within the Protestant state church, would eventually plunge that kingdom into civil war. And indeed it was only after the slide into chaos had begun in England that the social order of early Stuart Ireland was to begin to unravel. Until then the overlapping tensions between dispossessed native and propertied newcomer, Catholic and Protestant, were visible but contained. The Ireland of King Charles I was no model of harmonious communal living. The criminal law in particular retained an arbitrary and ruthless character that set it quite clearly apart from normal English practice. But many were to look back, through the blood and smoke of the 1640s and after, to what seemed in retrospect a lost age of peace.

'THOROUGH'

In the summer of 1631 it became known, after much uncertainty, that Ireland had a new lord deputy. Sir Thomas Wentworth, a prominent Yorkshire landowner, had opposed the court in the early years of Charles I. Since 1628, however, he had served as president of the council in the north, a body whose combination of administrative and legal authority allowed him firmly to control the region in the interests of the king. In this capacity he became an important part of the system of personal rule, without the cooperation of parliament, that Charles I initiated in England from 1629. In time, indeed, Wentworth was to become the hated embodiment of the regime. When he set out for Ireland, on the other hand, his relations with the crown were by no means straightforward. The objectives he was to pursue there, the establishment of royal authority on the basis of sound finances, combined with the imposition of religious uniformity, were the same as those that underlay Charles's personal rule in England. The king, however, seems never really to have liked him, and his support for his deputy was not to be taken for granted. Instead Wentworth's correspondence reveals a constant concern to present his proceedings in Ireland in a favourable light, sometimes to the point of mendacity. He had few friends at court and in 1636, in the interval of uncertainty between the death of one chief minister and the confirmation of another, felt it necessary to go in person to England to defend himself against critics. He was able to do this, however, because he had made the freedom to return at any time a condition of accepting the deputyship. He had also successfully insisted that his authority was not to be overridden by grants made, or decisions reversed, in England. Such hard-headed bargaining is perhaps the best clue to the symbiotic but arm's length relationship between the two men: a king determined to assert his authority free of constitutional shackles, and a deputy whose authoritarian temperament and rigid belief in order ensured that he would on his own initiative pursue that goal with relentless determination.[4]

Suggestions that the personal rule of Charles I grew out of a straightforward opposition between rival ideologies of 'absolute' and 'constitutional' government are now discounted. Instead, it seems clear, all parties to mainstream political debate in early Stuart England were agreed in accepting two principles: that the king's authority commanded the obedience of his subjects, and that law and custom provided a framework within which that authority was to be exercised. Where conflict arose was in those areas where the two propositions had to be reconciled. Where Ireland was concerned, the 1630s were even less clearly a decade of constitutional innovation. Already in the years after 1603 the judicial proceedings of Sir John Davies and others had openly subordinated legal principle to reasons of state, where necessary supplementing the resources of common law and statute with judicial resolutions and with the alternative principles of the continental civil law tradition.[5] Where Wentworth's proceedings were to differ from those of his predecessors was less in their underlying principles than in the concentrated energy that he brought to the exercise of power. The term most frequently used in his private correspondence was 'thorough', employed variously as a preposition (to go 'thorough' or through obstacles), as an adjective, and as a noun, denoting the radical reform of procedures and institutions in the interest of better upholding royal authority. His arrival presented a grave threat to the Old English, who over the previous two decades had already found the government willing to take advantage for its own profit of the flaws in land title that had accrued over centuries of political instability and fluctuating borders. But his commitment to asserting the rights of the crown over all rival interests was also to mean that the New English, after several decades in which they had been able to make the state their instrument, now found that they too became the victims of its capacity for the arbitrary exercise of power.

Wentworth's long-term aim was to increase the crown's scope for independent action. But he had first to deal with an immediate financial problem. In 1628

[4] There are detailed account of Wentworth's governorship in H. F. Kearney, *Strafford in Ireland 1633–41: A Study in Absolutism* (Manchester, 1959); Clarke, *The Old English in Ireland*, chs. 4–6. See also Clarke's broader account in *NHI*, iii. 243–69. For more recent analyses see the relevant chapters in J. F. Merritt (ed.), *The Political World of Thomas Wentworth, Earl of Strafford* (Cambridge, 1996).

[5] Connolly, *Contested Island*, 310–11.

the king had agreed a series of concessions, 'the Graces', most of them relating to Catholic grievances, in exchange for three annual subsidies or grants of taxation.[6] The last of these was due to be collected in autumn 1632. The war whose demands had led to the negotiations of 1628 was over. However the crown's usual Irish income, at £40,000, still fell short of expenditure by around £20,000 per year. There was also an accumulated debt of some £80,000. The dominant faction in the Irish council, headed by the earl of Cork, argued that the gap could be bridged by the aggressive collection of recusancy fines—a solution greatly preferable, in their eyes, to trading religious toleration for a subsidy that would be paid by Protestant and Catholic alike. Wentworth's plan, on the other hand, foreshadowed the detached pragmatism that was to be characteristic of his handling of all sections of Irish society. Given the weakness of the army, he suggested, it was less dangerous to impose a subsidy on the Protestants than to levy fines on the numerically superior Catholics. Accordingly he obtained a letter from the king, in April 1632, directing the Irish council to make preparations for the collection of recusancy fines, in the event that another subsidy was not voluntarily offered. The council, however, suppressed the king's letter, with its clear instruction to seek a renewed bargain with the Catholics, and instead proceeded directly to the levying of fines. Its self-interested obstruction forced Wentworth to turn instead to the Old English. During the summer he secured their support for a further subsidy of £20,000. By the end of the year Cork, having first been humiliated by the publication of the suppressed April letter, had been ordered to suspend recusancy fines and begin the collection of the subsidy. When a group of prominent Ulster settlers sought to obstruct the levy Wentworth promptly had some arrested and committed to Dublin Castle, while others were dismissed from commands in the army.

Wentworth himself arrived in Ireland in July 1633. His early actions provided a clear indication of what was to follow. He began by ostentatiously paying courtesy visits to the lords justices, 'being as then but a private person', a gesture designed to emphasize the respect that would be due to himself, once he had been sworn in as chief governor. When the privy council at its first two meetings failed to respond to his request for advice on how the army was to be paid, he moved quickly to threats, though also, in his own case, to some unconscious prophecy: 'there was no necessity which induced me to take them to counsel in this business, for rather than fail in so necessary a duty to my master, I would undertake upon the peril of my head to make the king's army able to subsist and to provide for itself amongst them without their help'.[7] In the event the council agreed to a further subsidy of £20,000, to run up to December 1634, though only on the understanding that a meeting of parliament would follow within that time.

    [6] Connolly, *Contested Island*, 367–9.
    [7] *The Earl of Strafford's Letters and Dispatches*, ed. William Knowler, 3 vols. (Dublin, 1740), i. 97–9.

Wentworth had achieved these initial successes by skilfully exploiting the hostility and distrust of Old English and New English interests. In the process, however, he had found it necessary to commit himself, in more explicit terms than he might have wished, on the subject of Catholic demands. If the Old English agreed to another subsidy, he wrote in October 1632, he undertook to be 'a means that the benefit offered them by his majesty's graces shall be honourably and justly complied with'.[8] So explicit an undertaking helps to explain why the Old English now accepted Wentworth's stipulation that the forthcoming meeting of the Irish parliament, unavoidable if any further subsidies were to be obtained, should consist of two sessions: the first, limited to twenty-one days, to deal with the king's business, the second to consider the redress of subjects' grievances. Elections in July produced a House of Commons comprising 142 Protestants and 112 Catholics. Around 50 of the Protestant members were office holders, providing the basis of what Wentworth saw as a government party, capable of holding the balance of power between the two religious groups. In the event the Commons voted unanimously to grant six subsidies payable over four years. This would normally have amounted to a grant of around £120,000, collected by means of assessments of the liability of property holders in each county made by locally appointed commissioners. However Wentworth went on to use the threat of replacing these with centrally appointed officials to bully the Commons into fixing the value at £40,000 for the first four subsidies and £45,000 thereafter, with a further £9,000 each time from the clergy and nobility. This gave him a total of £300,000 while also, as he reported triumphantly to London, setting a new standard of £54,000 for future subsidies.

As the bills made their way through both houses Wentworth allowed Catholic members to lay the groundwork for legislation based on the Graces. When parliament assembled for its second session on 4 November, with the subsidy bills safely through, he continued for a time to prevaricate, while Old English members showed their first signs of restlessness. On 27 November he at last revealed his true intentions. Ten of the Graces, of which the most important were two articles confirming the titles of the Ulster undertakers, were to be confirmed by statute. Others, including the right of Catholics to practise law without taking the oath of supremacy, were to be continued, but only at the king's pleasure. By this time, however, the main concern of the Old English was with two promised concessions: the confirmation of a general surrender and regranting of lands in Connacht negotiated and paid for in 1615 but never formally completed, and a statute placing a limit of sixty years on the revival of dormant royal titles. Wentworth rejected both as unacceptable intrusions on the king's interests. Outraged at his betrayal, the Old English members managed for some days to obstruct government business in the Commons. But Wentworth was quickly able to rally the Protestant majority to regain control of the house,

[8] Clarke, *Old English*, 69–70.

and subsequently to face down continued Old English opposition in a third session during January to April 1635.

The consequences of the refusal of what Wentworth privately referred to as the 'two darling articles' soon became apparent.[9] In the summer of 1635 he travelled in person to the west to preside over a series of inquisitions intended to provide the basis for a general plantation of Connacht. The case for royal title rested on precisely the sort of revival of long-buried claims that had provided the basis for earlier plantations and that the Graces had undertaken to abandon, looking back to a grant originally made in the thirteenth century to the earls of Ulster, whose estates had later passed by inheritance to King Edward IV. It dismissed claims based on a later agreement with the crown, the Compositions of Connacht of 1577 and 1585, pointing out, correctly, that these were concerned, not with ownership, but with the conversion of cess and other charges into a rent payment. It also dismissed appeals to the surrenders of 1615, claiming not only that those involved had had no valid title to surrender, but—what was clearly untrue—that the large sums they had paid on that occasion represented satisfaction for the illegitimate profits they had derived from the lands concerned, rather than the price of now acquiring secure titles.[10] On this basis Wentworth made clear his intention of asserting crown title not just to Roscommon, Sligo, and Mayo, the target of previous plantation schemes, but also to County Galway, home of the powerful earl of Clanricard and, for that reason, prudently omitted from earlier projects. His plan, following earlier precedents, was to establish crown title to the whole, retain one quarter to be disposed of profitably to planters, and grant the remainder to existing proprietors at increased rents and charges.

Wentworth's proceedings in the west revealed a style of government anxious to preserve legal forms without being bound by them. In Roscommon, his first stop, the deputy, by his own account, called for a jury composed of men of the best estates in the county, in order to give their findings credibility, and also because such individuals would be vulnerable to the heavy fines that could be imposed in the event of what the government considered a perverse verdict. In fact the jury was disproportionately composed of New English, and its foreman was Sir Lucas Dillon, a member of an Old English family but a Protestant and one of those involved in an earlier plantation scheme for the region. Wentworth's speech at the close of proceedings combined paternalist rhetoric and blatant menace. The king's purpose was 'to effect them a civil and rich people', not by taking anything that was justly theirs, 'but in truth to bestow amongst them a good part of that which was his own'. His title was so clear that it could be asserted by a simple action for possession. The jury's verdict was thus of no consequence, except

---

[9] Clarke, *Old English*, 90.
[10] *Letters and Dispatches*, i. 454–8. For the Composition see *Contested Island*, 217–18, and for its irrelevance to the matter of title Bernadette Cunningham, 'The Composition of Connacht in the Lordships of Clanricard and Thomond, 1577–1641', *IHS* 24 (1984), 11–12.

in giving those concerned an opportunity 'to weave themselves into the royal thoughts and care of his majesty through a cheerful and ready acknowledgement' of his title.[11] Responding to this clear warning to minimize their losses, the jury duly found for the king, as did its counterparts in Sligo and Mayo. Galway was a different matter. In addition to the expectation of Clanricard's political support, local landowners had had time to assemble the sort of documentary evidence of title not available at earlier hearings. The sheriff ignored a list of jurors drawn up by Wentworth, instead empanelling a jury of his own choice. After three days' deliberation, this offered to find crown title for certain specific lands attached to the earldom of Ulster, but not for the county as a whole.

The Galway proprietors apparently believed that this legal defeat would put an end to Wentworth's plans. They were quickly disillusioned. His response to the verdict was to have the sheriff imprisoned and fined for allegedly packing the jury, to make preparations to prosecute the jury itself, if possible for conspiracy, and also to initiate proceedings against a witness who had collected evidence of title. The landowners next sent agents to present their case at court, but suffered a substantial setback when the earl of Clanricard, whom they could have counted on to secure a hearing, died in mid-November. In early 1636 the agents were ordered back to Ireland where they were committed to jail. In May the members of the jury were fined £4,000 each and imprisoned. They were initially encouraged to continue their defiance by reports that Wentworth's political stock was falling in England. By the autumn, however, they were seeking a way of submitting without wholly losing face, something Wentworth contemptuously refused to facilitate. In December they offered their unconditional submission. Meanwhile the new earl of Clanricard, burdened by debts, was in no position to continue the struggle. In April 1637 Wentworth was able to organize a fresh inquisition which 'very readily' found the king's title to the county and town of Galway. Readiness, however, did not save the Galway proprietors from a punitive resumption to the crown of half rather than the usual quarter of their estates.

As his victory in Connacht became complete, Wentworth proceeded to other, lesser plantation projects. In August 1637 he arrived in County Clare with the intention of conducting an inquisition, only to find local landowners rushing to offer their acknowledgement of the king's title in advance of the formal proceedings. In Tipperary and Kilkenny, meanwhile, he had formed a profitable alliance with the young James Butler, who had succeeded in 1633 to the reunited but financially depleted estates of the earldom of Ormond.[12] In 1635 Ormond colluded in proceedings establishing the king's title to the territory of Idough in north Kilkenny. The king then regranted the lands to Ormond and a partner. They in turn sold them to Wentworth's cousin Sir Christopher Wandesford,

---

[11] *Letters and Dispatches*, i. 442–3.
[12] For the earlier troubles of the house of Ormond, see Connolly, *Contested Island*, 365.

who as master of the rolls had presided over the inquisition finding the king's title. Ormond subsequently directed a military policing action against those of the occupiers, mainly the O'Brennans, who resisted their dispossession. In 1637 the earl again assisted in claiming the Tipperary baronies of Upper and Lower Ormond for the crown. His reward in this case was a regrant to himself of some of the lands concerned. In addition, in a transaction designed to conceal from the king the scale of his profit, he sold to the crown a small property in Queen's County, Leix Abbey, yielding £85 per year in rents, for the hugely inflated sum of £10,500.[13] Wentworth's longer-term plans for plantation, if he had remained in office, were never clearly spelt out, but it is likely that they would have included a large-scale assault on at least the Gaelic proprietors of Munster.

From an early stage, however, it was clear that Wentworth's relentless pursuit of what he saw as the king's interests was to affect not only the native Irish and Old English, but also, directly and extensively, the settler population. At the time of his appointment the New English political elite remained divided between the earl of Cork's faction and a rival group headed by the vice treasurer, Francis Annesley, Viscount Mountnorris. Wentworth, coming on the scene at a time when Mountnorris was just extricating himself from serious corruption charges levelled by his opponents, initially allied with his party, using the viscount as his main go-between in negotiations with the Old English. Cork's faction did not dare to oppose the deputy openly, but attempted various forms of covert obstruction, including encouraging the Old English, in the first session of parliament, to raise awkward questions about the Graces. By 1635 Wentworth had become concerned at the extent of Mountnorris's power, which in addition to the financial resources of the vice treasurership included membership of the Court of Castle Chamber and, of most importance to Wentworth, a share in the lucrative arrangement whereby a consortium of private interests had taken over collection of customs duties in exchange for a fixed payment to the crown. When Mountnorris refused to withdraw, Wentworth attacked. Mountnorris, who held a captain's commission in the army, had made a joking remark over dinner about a kinsman who had accidentally injured the deputy's gouty foot. A court martial duly sentenced him to death for calumny and incitement to mutiny.[14] The sentence was remitted, once Mountnorris had surrendered his offices and the customs farm. But the extent of the deputy's determination to crush all forms of obstruction had been put beyond doubt.

[13] David Edwards, *The Ormond Lordship in County Kilkenny 1515–1642* (Dublin, 2003), 297–302; idem, 'The Poisoned Chalice: The Ormond Inheritance, Sectarian Division and the Emergence of James Butler, 1614–42', in Toby Barnard and Jane Fenlon (eds.), *The Dukes of Ormonde 1610–1745* (Woodbridge, 2000), 74–5.

[14] Mountnorris's relative, a gentleman usher, had injured Wentworth's foot while moving a stool. Mountnorris's calumny was to suggest that Wentworth had earlier insulted his kinsman, by reproving him for misbehaviour during a cavalry exercise; the alleged incitement was his added comment that he had another relative, also an army officer, who would take a different revenge. See *Letters and Dispatches*, i. 499–501.

Mountnorris's fall did nothing to dilute Wentworth's hostility to his rival Cork. In addition to launching punitive investigations into the earl's complex land acquisitions over the previous four decades, Wentworth in 1635 had the elaborate tomb he had erected for his wife moved from the east end of St Patrick's cathedral to a less conspicuous position. The reason was ostensibly liturgical: that the tomb blocked the proper site, in the more ritualistic liturgy currently being promoted in all three of Charles I's kingdoms, of the communion table. In reality, as Wentworth made clear privately, the attack was on Cork's social pretensions. The king's deputy, he wrote, should not appear to kneel to the earl and his lady, or to his son, 'the veriest shark in the realm, as they say'.[15]

Wentworth's harsh treatment of Cork, Mountnorris, and others went beyond personal animosity. A central part of his plans to strengthen royal authority was to use the breathing space provided by the subsidies granted in 1634 permanently to secure the crown's financial independence. This would require a frontal assault on all significant forms of wealth within the kingdom, in whatever hands they lay. The customs farm, wrenched from the grasp of the fallen Mountnorris and his associates, was one major resource. A contract in 1632 had increased the rent from the farm from £6,000 to £15,000 per year, with an entry fine of £8,000. A new arrangement instituted in 1636, on the other hand, gave the king, in addition to his rent, a five-eighths share in the profits, which in 1636–7 was worth £13,500. (Another quarter share, worth £5,400, went to Wentworth himself, as the principal farmer.) Over the next three years efficient management, in particular a tightening of control over the Ulster ports, pushed the overall yield from £40,000 to over £50,000, with a proportionate increase in profits. In addition Wentworth set out substantially to increase the crown's gains from the casino that, in recent decades, had been the Irish land market. At the beginning of his deputyship he had indicated that he hoped to raise £5,000 per year from the plantation of Ormond and Connacht, and a further £3,000 per year from the discovery of concealed crown lands.[16] The means of securing the second of these gains was a new Commission for Defective Titles, established by patent and act of parliament in 1634. A return of cases dealt with by May 1636 showed that the Commission had already increased a total rental of £738 to £1,293, comprising £417 in increased charges and £138 in new rents. The landlords thus pressurized into accepting more onerous terms as a condition of greater security included not only the Old English and Gaelic Irish, but also more recent settlers. Only a quarter of the cases included in the 1636 return, in fact, concerned Catholic landowners.[17]

The other main device for extracting a revenue from landed property, of which Wentworth had great hopes, was the Court of Wards, which administered

---

[15] Nicholas Canny, *The Upstart Earl: A Study of the Social and Mental World of Richard Boyle, First Earl of Cork 1566–1643* (Cambridge, 1982), 12.
[16] *Letters and Dispatches*, i. 191.   [17] Kearney, *Strafford in Ireland*, 83, 164–8.

estates held by those forms of feudal tenure that gave the king control during the minority of an heir. The parliament of 1634–5 had enacted an Irish version of the English Statute of Uses of 1535, eliminating the legal device of bequeathing lands for use rather than in absolute ownership, and thus evading the feudal obligations associated with inheritance. Revenue from the Court did not in fact rise significantly during Wentworth's period in Ireland, remaining at an average of around £7,000 per annum. In the longer term it would have done so: he estimated that the Statute of Uses alone would boost takings by some £4,000 a year. Further long-term gains were to be expected from a second initiative, the use of the Commission for Defective Titles to change the tenure of grantees in the Ulster plantation from common socage, where the only requirement was the payment of rent, to tenancy *in capite*, which would subject them to other obligations, and in particular bring them within the jurisdiction of the Court of Wards. Grants to both existing and new proprietors in the Connacht and other plantations were likewise to be *in capite*. In this case too the crown's gain was to be at the expense of New English as well as older interests.

One further intrusion on the New English interest was not Wentworth's initiative. In 1630 the crown had commenced proceedings in Star Chamber against the Irish Society, the consortium of London companies that had taken responsibility for the plantation of County Londonderry. The charges were numerous: fraud in the negotiation of the patent, failure to provide glebe lands for the church, the unauthorized commercial exploitation of woodlands, neglect of building and other obligations in the towns of Coleraine and Derry, and the continued presence of native tenants on lands that should have been reserved for British settlers. Allegations that the Society had made excessive profits were grossly unfair. By 1635 individual companies had spent some £22,000 on the management of their proportions, against gross receipts of £37,500. This modest profit, however, had to be set against the initial capital investment of £62,000 that had been required from the City, from which it had received just £6,000 in dividends.[18] The Society had indeed been guilty of sharp practice in trying to claim, contrary to what had been clearly understood, that the general articles of plantation relating to the removal of natives and the planting of British tenants did not apply to its holdings. Yet its failure in this area was no greater than that of other grantees. The Star Chamber's judgement, delivered in February 1635, was, however, unforgiving. The Society was fined £70,000 (eventually reduced to £12,000) and deprived of its patent. The king rejected several bids, including one from Wentworth, to manage the county for a fixed rent. Instead he appointed commissioners to negotiate hard bargains with the former tenants

---

[18] T. W. Moody, *The Londonderry Plantation 1609–41: The City of London and the Plantation in Ulster* (Belfast, 1939), 270–4, 335–9. For the episode in general see Jane Ohlmeyer, 'Strafford, the "Londonderry Business" and the "New British History"', in Merritt (ed.), *Political World of Thomas Wentworth*, 209–29.

of the Irish Society, the proceeds to be remitted directly to the English treasury. Wentworth had warned of the risks of weakening the plantation in the interests of profit, and had in fact initially urged the king to allow the Society to keep their patent on payment of a larger fine. But he nevertheless incurred the enmity of powerful interests. The City of London incorrectly blamed him for its misfortune. In addition he had obstructed two rival bids to take over the Londonderry project, one jointly by the earl of Antrim and the king's Scottish favourite the duke of Hamilton, the other by a well-connected Ulster landowner, Sir John Clotworthy.

Wentworth's other major task as lord deputy was to extend to Ireland the reshaping of the established church sought by Charles I and his archbishop of Canterbury, William Laud. Laud's aim was to restore Anglicanism to its proper status as a middle way between the errors of Rome and the excesses of continental Calvinism, a Protestantism purged of the corruptions of popery yet retaining a due respect for tradition. In practice this meant a new emphasis on the authority of bishops, on the special status of the ordained minister, and on the need for an outward show of reverence for the sacred. Wentworth's own religious sentiments were more conventionally Protestant than those of Laud. But his commitment to the assertion of royal authority was as unwavering in this as in other spheres, and the archbishop was in fact, throughout the 1630s, his closest ally at court. Laud, for his part, became during the same period the main arbiter of ecclesiastical patronage in Ireland. His most important correspondent was John Bramhall, a Yorkshire clergyman whom Wentworth had brought to Ireland as his chaplain and then recommended, in 1634, to the vacant bishopric of Derry.[19]

Many English Protestants found Laud's religious policies distasteful enough. That much became clear after 1640, when the collapse of royal authority led to widespread attacks on railed altars and other liturgical innovations. In Ireland the new stress on episcopal authority and on 'the beauty of holiness' was an even more jarring innovation. The articles of religion adopted by the Church of Ireland in 1613–15 were more rigorously predestinarian, more stridently anti-Catholic, and more unfriendly to ritual than their English equivalents. Moreover there was no requirement that ministers formally subscribe even to these articles. Concern at this divergence in ecclesiastical codes was not entirely new: already in 1622 the commission of inquiry into Irish affairs had noted with concern that some clergy did not use the liturgy prescribed in the Book of Common Prayer. A further spur to action was that opposition groups in England had cited the Irish canons as

[19] For ecclesiastical affairs see Kearney, *Strafford in Ireland*, ch. 10; John McCafferty, '"God Bless your Free Church of Ireland": Wentworth, Laud, Bramhall and the Irish Convocation of 1634', in Merritt (ed.), *Political World of Thomas Wentworth*, 187–208; idem, 'John Bramhall and the Church of Ireland in the 1630s', in Alan Ford, J. I. McGuire, and K. Milne (eds.), *As by Law Established: The Church of Ireland since the Reformation* (Dublin, 1995), 100–11; Linda M. Ross, 'The Legacy of John Bramhall as Laud's Alter-Ego', in Gerard O'Brien (ed.), *Derry and Londonderry: History and Society* (Dublin, 1999), 279–301.

evidence that a less ceremonial variety of Protestantism was already accepted as legitimate within the Stuart dominions.[20] Against this background Wentworth, in consultation with Laud, set out to give the Irish church an enforceable code of discipline compatible with that of its English counterpart. His aim was to replace the articles of 1613–15 with two documents: the 39 Articles adopted by the Church of England in 1571, representing the Elizabethan compromise between Rome and Geneva, and the canons introduced in 1604 as a specific rejection of Puritan demands that the English church move further away from its Catholic past. Subscription to both documents was to become compulsory for all clergy, permitting the same weeding out of dissenters that had already taken place in England.

The existing Irish canons had been drawn up by Convocation, the representative body comprising the bishops and delegates from the lower clergy sitting in upper and lower houses. This had been established in England since the middle ages but in the case of Ireland had met for the first time simultaneously with the parliament of 1613–15. Another Convocation was duly summoned alongside the parliament of 1634–5. The clergy in the lower house initially tried to assert their right to adopt the English 39 Articles of faith selectively, while simultaneously making subscription to the 1615 articles compulsory. After a dressing down from Wentworth, who told them their proceedings resembled 'all the fraternities and conventicles of Amsterdam', they accepted the English articles verbatim.[21] In the case of the canons, however, Wentworth and Laud were forced to accept a number of compromises. Bramhall, who took primary responsibility for the drafting, succeeded in introducing a provision for auricular confession, the shifting of communion tables from the chancel of church buildings to the east end, and the use of a silver cup at communion, as well as a requirement to use the ornaments and ceremonies of the Book of Common Prayer. However the Irish canons pointedly omitted more specific English provisions relating to kneeling and standing during ceremonies, and to bowing at the name of Jesus: 'they have no more joints in their knees for that', Wentworth complained to Laud, 'than an elephant.'[22]

The tussle over canons and articles was a matter principally of doctrine and liturgy. But it also raised difficult questions regarding the status of the Church of Ireland. Some of its members, and in particular the primate, James Ussher, archbishop of Armagh, had already shown interest in giving Irish Protestantism

---

[20] Conrad Russell, *The Fall of the British Monarchies 1637–42* (Oxford, 1991), 36–7, sees this challenge as first convincing Charles I of the need to impose uniformity throughout his kingdoms.

[21] *Letters and Dispatches*, i. 342.

[22] Kearney, *Strafford in Ireland*, 116. McCafferty (' "God Bless your Free Church of Ireland" ', 196–203) also notes the omission from the canon on ordination of several references to the practice of the primitive church, reflecting a radical Protestant belief that religion had to be purged of all non-scriptural accretions, as opposed to a Laudian commitment to balancing the rejection of popish superstition and corruption with a revived sense of tradition and continuity.

a separate history, with its roots in the pure Christianity, only later corrupted by the errors of popery, introduced to Ireland by St Patrick.[23] The demand for the wholesale adoption of the English canons and articles, by contrast, carried the clear implication that the Irish church was a subordinate offshoot of the English original. Ussher's objection to accepting the English canons verbatim, Wentworth reported, 'is merely point of honour . . . lest Ireland might become subject to the Church of England, as the province of York is to that of Canterbury'. Laud, for his part, met the proceedings in congregation with a sarcastic gibe: 'God bless your free church of Ireland.'[24]

If the new Irish canons represented at best a qualified victory for Wentworth and Bramhall, their implementation by the majority of the clergy was unenthusiastic. When Wentworth visited Ussher at Drogheda in 1638 he noted that there was no communion table in his chapel. The archbishop had already made his attitude of minimum compliance with unwelcome directives clear three years earlier, when he had told a visitor that ministers were not obliged to publicize the Book of Sports, Charles I's deliberate challenge to the Puritan sabbath, but could leave the task to their clerk or churchwarden. (With the Scottish minister Robert Blair he had reportedly gone further still, confessing to him that 'all these things you except against might, yea, ought to be removed, but that cannot be done'.) In the south Ulster diocese of Kilmore the bishop, William Bedell, kept the communion table in the chancel of his church, rather than moving it to the east end, and made no move to add the rails or steps that would have made it more like an altar. His son-in-law also noted with approval that he preferred biblical psalms to those of the Book of Common Prayer, and firmly opposed such innovations as bowing at the name of Jesus.[25] Ussher and other bishops also fought a rearguard action against the theological uniformity imposed in Convocation by requiring clergy admitted to their dioceses to subscribe not just to the 39 Articles but also to the Irish articles of 1615.

To counter this sort of passive resistance Wentworth and Laud could exploit the crown's right of appointment to senior positions. After 1634 Bramhall, the deputy's first protégé, took effective charge of the management of the Irish church, while Ussher, from 1636 resident in Drogheda rather than Dublin, concentrated on his theological and historical researches and on the management of his own diocese. In Trinity College Laud, as chancellor, initially accepted Ussher's kinsman Robert as provost, but in 1629 replaced him with William Chappel, whom Ussher regarded as unsound on the question of predestination. In Christ Church cathedral the appointment between 1632 and 1635 of seven

---

[23] Connolly, *Contested Island*, 352–3.

[24] *Letters and Dispatches*, i. 381; McCafferty, ' "God Bless your Free Church of Ireland" ', 187.

[25] Sir William Brereton, *Travels in Holland, the United Provinces, England, Scotland and Ireland*, ed. Edward Hawkins (London, 1844), 139–40; *The Life of Mr Robert Blair*, ed. Thomas M'Crie (Edinburgh, 1848), 80; *Two Biographies of William Bedell, Bishop of Kilmore*, ed. E. S. Shuckburgh (Cambridge, 1902), 152–4.

new chapter members, four of them from England, cleared the way for a new style of worship, organized round a raised and railed-in communion table, and accompanied by what one outraged contemporary described as 'all manner of instrumental music, as organs, sackbutts, cornets, violls, etc, as if it had been at the dedication of Nebuchadnezar's golden image in the plain of Dura'.[26] John Atherton, who as sub-dean took a lead in these innovations, went on in 1635 to become bishop of Waterford and Lismore. In 1638 Chappell was promoted to the bishopric of Cork and Ross, while remaining provost of Trinity. Meanwhile George Webb, a former chaplain to Charles I, had become bishop of Limerick in 1634. The appointment of these newcomers ensured a growing level of support within the Irish episcopate for Wentworth's religious policy, but only at the price of ignoring the claims to advancement of existing New English churchmen less in tune with the demands of the new ecclesiastical order.

The task of the new bishops was not just to support that order, but also to suppress those whose opposition to it went beyond acceptable bounds. In 1635 the king created a new court of high commission to deal with ecclesiastical offences. Earlier such commissions had concerned themselves primarily with recusant laymen and with crypto-Catholics among the native clergy. That of 1635, however, was to concentrate more on Protestant dissent. Open defiance was most notable in east Ulster, where Scottish settlers had brought with them their own traditions of worship and ecclesiastical discipline. A visitation of Down and Connor in 1634 identified twenty-four ministers as failing to use the full liturgy of the church, and found that not one in three parishes even possessed the Book of Common Prayer. Communion, likewise, was not taken kneeling but instead, as Bramhall complained, at 'a table ten yards long, where they sit and receive the sacrament like good fellows'.[27]

Action against such blatant nonconformity had in fact begun before the new canons and articles were adopted. In 1631 the complaints of Dean Leslie, a Scottish client of Laud, had forced a reluctant Bishop Echlin of Down and Connor to suspend four clergymen, among them the two leading dissidents, Robert Blair and John Livingstone. An intervention by Ussher, a direct appeal to the crown, and the imminence of parliament, allowed the offenders to secure several reprieves. However Blair and another minister were finally deposed in 1634 and Livingstone in 1635. By this time Leslie had replaced Echlin as bishop, and he proceeded during 1636 to deprive a further five ministers for their refusal to subscribe to the new canons. The same year Blair, Livingstone, and two other ministers, with around 140 followers, sailed for New England on the ship *Eagle Wing*, but were driven back by bad weather. 'If ever the Lord spoke

---

[26] Kenneth Milne (ed.), *Christ Church Cathedral, Dublin: A History* (Dublin, 2000), 197–9; *Two Biographies of William Bedell*, 154.

[27] Quoted in Ross, 'The Legacy of John Bramhall', 287. For other aspects of the distinctive religious culture of the east Ulster Scots, see Connolly, *Contested Island*, 355–8.

by his winds and other dispensations', Livingstone recalled thirty years later, 'it was made evident to us that it was not his will that we should go to New England.'[28] Both men travelled instead to Scotland, where they were to take a prominent part in the revolt against Laud's religious policies that commenced the following year.

The campaign to reshape the Church of Ireland was not concerned solely with rooting out dissidents. There was also a determined attempt to restore the church's finances. Wentworth's approach to what he saw as another example of New English corruption was characteristically combative. 'It was in my mind', he told Laud in December 1633, 'to trounce a bishop or two in the Castle Chamber.'[29] Soon afterwards the privy council duly pursued the case of Lewis Jones, the newly appointed bishop of Killaloe, who as part of a private arrangement had leased church lands worth £500 a year to Sir Daniel O'Brien for a rent of only £26. New legislation in 1634 reduced the scope for future such alienations and made it easier to recover church property. Over the next few years Bramhall and others engaged in a concerted campaign to increase incomes and recover lost lands and revenues, pushing up rents, buying out tithe farmers and impropriators, and using the court of high commission to recover assets covertly or illegally transferred into lay hands.[30]

Here, as in other areas, a particular victim of Wentworth's reforming zeal was the earl of Cork. In 1634 the Court of Castle Chamber took up the case of Cork's tenure of the lands and impropriate rectories attached to the collegiate church of Youghal. A year later Wentworth secured the appointment of John Atherton as bishop of Waterford and Lismore, where Cork, a cousin of Atherton's predecessor, was not only in possession of extensive diocesan lands but had made his residence in the bishop's palace. Atherton had proved himself useful to Wentworth both in Christ Church cathedral and during the recent controversies in Convocation. But he had also been in difficulties over an attempt illegally to sell his English benefice, as well as for allegedly fathering a child with his wife's sister. To Wentworth, however, he appeared the man to make Cork think 'the devil is let loose upon him forth of his chain'. In a little over a year Atherton had forced Cork to submit to arbitration leading to the surrender of some of the lands he held, along with a payment of £500 for the building of a new episcopal palace, only to then initiate legal action to recover the remainder of the disputed

---

[28] 'The Life of Mr John Livingstone, Minister of the Gospel, Written by Himself', in W. K. Tweedie (ed.), *Select Biographies* (Edinburgh, 1845), 154. See also Alan Ford, 'The Origins of Irish Dissent', in Kevin Herlihy (ed.), *The Religion of Irish Dissent 1650–1800* (Dublin, 1996), 9–30, and the accounts cited in n. 19 above.

[29] Quoted in McCafferty, 'John Bramhall and the Church of Ireland', 106, who also discusses the Killaloe case.

[30] Impropriations were parishes whose tithes and other revenues had become the property of laymen, most commonly during the vast seizure of church property that had taken place at the Reformation. Tithe farmers had acquired the right to collect tithes in a particular locality in return for paying a fixed rent to the clergyman concerned.

holdings. In the case of Youghal Cork's English political connections allowed him to escape the ruinous penalties Wentworth had hoped to impose on him. But he was nevertheless required to pay a fine of £15,000 to retain the lands, while losing the impropriate rectories.[31]

The campaign to recover the church's lost endowments achieved undoubted results. Increased revenues from land leased at economic rents provided funds to buy back alienated resources, and the threat of punitive legal action encouraged tithe farmers and impropriators to settle on terms favourable to the church. By 1640 Bramhall reported that revenues in the province of Armagh had risen by £14,500. In Waterford and Lismore Atherton claimed to have increased income from a mere £50 to £1,000. The income of the archbishop of Dublin seems to have grown over the same period from £450 to £1,000, and that of the bishop of the Connacht diocese of Elphin from £300 to £1,340. Some of these estimates, it has been pointed out, related to increases in projected rather than actual income.[32] The most widespread improvement in incomes, moreover, came in Ulster, where clerical and episcopal incomes were already higher than elsewhere, thanks to the re-endowment that had accompanied the plantation. But it remains the case that Wentworth and his clerical allies had initiated a policy which promised, over time, to remedy what had been from the start one of the chronic weaknesses impeding the progress of the Irish Reformation. The problem was that, in doing so, they had once again cut across powerful vested interests, Catholic and Protestant, New and Old English.

To the resentment among Irish Protestants caused by Laudian religious innovations and the aggressive defence of the church's financial interests must be added disquiet at the deputy's apparent toleration of Catholicism. Wentworth, in fact, shared the view that Ireland could never be wholly secure until Catholicism was eliminated. He was also perfectly willing to use the language of anti-popery, denouncing Old English opposition in parliament as due to the influence of 'friars and Jesuits'.[33] Until the incorporation of the whole population into a revived state church became a realistic proposition, however, he considered unnecessary interference with Catholic worship or ecclesiastical structures to be pointless, if not dangerously provocative, 'as a man going to warfare without munition or arms'.[34] Catholic bishops or clergy who, through bad luck or indiscretion, became the focus of attention, could still expect to face the consequences. In 1637, for example, the archbishop of Armagh was jailed for six months, possibly on the information of a discontented subordinate, just after he had presided over a provincial synod. In general, however, Wentworth forbade the church courts to

---

[31] Kearney, *Strafford in Ireland*, 119–29. For Atherton see Aidan Clarke, 'A Woeful Sinner: John Atherton', in Vincent Carey and Ute Lotz-Heumann (eds.), *Taking Sides? Colonial and Confessional Mentalities in Early Modern Ireland* (Dublin, 2003), 143–4.
[32] This point is emphasized in particular by McCafferty, 'John Bramhall and the Church of Ireland', 108.
[33] Kearney, *Strafford in Ireland*, 60.   [34] *Letters and Dispatches*, i. 187.

harass the Catholic laity, and made no serious attempt to obstruct the continued extension across the kingdom of a Counter-Reformation structure of dioceses and parishes.

At the same time that he campaigned relentlessly against the predatory activities of the New English, Wentworth did not by any means neglect his own financial interests. His most profitable venture, bringing him a total of some £35,000, was his share of the customs farm. In 1637 he took over what would probably, given time, have been a highly profitable monopoly of tobacco imports. In addition he acquired, by a combination of royal grants and purchase, more than 57,000 acres in Counties Wicklow and Kildare. By 1639 his income from Irish sources was £13,000 per year, as compared to £6,000 from his Yorkshire estates. None of this was necessarily unacceptable by the standards of the time. Crown servants were expected to reward themselves from the advantages conferred by office. Against his spectacular gains Wentworth could cite his investment in iron manufacturing and the production of linen cloth, ventures promoting general economic improvement on which he had lost substantially. The customs farm, enriching both king and farmer, even more clearly illustrated the interdependence of public good and private profit.[35] But then his New English opponents, convinced both of their civilizing mission in the face of Irish barbarity and, in some cases at least, of their status as God's elect, could view their own gains in a similar light. Cork, for example, repeatedly insisted that his huge acquisitions were justified by the service he had done 'to the affairs of the crown, and to the good of this commonwealth'. In the case of the college of Youghal his conviction of his own innocence was so strong that he was only with difficulty persuaded to accept the relatively lenient settlement eventually agreed.[36] To men of this outlook Wentworth's self-righteous assault on their interests, combined with his successful pursuit of his own, could only appear hypocritical as well as unjust.

In January 1638, after nearly five years in Ireland, Wentworth complained that he lacked companionship, having made no friends there. His isolation was in part self-imposed. From his arrival, he had insisted on the dignity appropriate for the king's representative. He restricted access to rooms of state, required the nobility to attend him to church, and demanded ceremonial deference at meetings of the Irish council. He also commissioned the construction near Naas of Jigginstown, a three-storey mansion with a frontage that would have made it one of the largest in King Charles's dominions, to serve as a royal palace and residence for chief governors. The real issue, however, was not Wentworth's sense of his own status, but his political tactics. With the exception

---

[35] Compare the assessments of Kearney (*Strafford in Ireland*, 183), who sees Wentworth as 'close in spirit' to the New English profiteers he denounced, and Aidan Clarke (*NHI*, iii. 261–2), who emphasizes the identification of public and private interests.
[36] Canny, *Upstart Earl*, 22, 26.

of the young earl of Ormond, whose catastrophic financial position made him reliably dependent on the deputy's goodwill, he had built up no significant local alliances. With some of the New English elite, such as Cork, he had been in conflict from the start. Others, like Mountnorris and Viscount Loftus of Ely, whom he removed as lord chancellor after a quarrel in 1638, had been used then cast aside. Instead Wentworth's confidants were, like himself, newcomers: his cousin Sir Christopher Wandesford, master of the rolls from 1633, his former secretary on the council of the north, Sir George Radcliffe, and his brother Sir George Wentworth. It was a high-risk strategy. Wentworth's own summary of his approach, delivered in advance of the 1634 parliament, was that he would 'bow and govern the native by the planter and the planter by the native'.[37] The simplistic antithesis of planter and native, discounting the claims of the Old English, was typical of his brutally reductionist approach to Ireland's intricate pattern of cultural and political allegiance. And it was a definition which in any case applied only to the early stages of his administration. Before long it had become inescapably clear that his policy was less to divide and rule than to attack every interest group simultaneously. His real problems were to begin when the external political structure on which he depended for his ability to despise equally all the different segments of Irish society began to fall apart.

PARLIAMENTARY OPPOSITION 1640–1641

On the day after Christmas 1629 the archbishop and mayor of Dublin, along with the city sheriffs, forced their way into the Franciscan friary in the city's Cook Street. There they damaged or destroyed some religious pictures, the pulpit, and a statue, seized a chalice and five suits of vestments, and arrested two of the friars. As they left the building, they came under attack. Catholic sources, possibly concerned at the vulnerability to legal reprisals of the more respectable, emphasized the low status of those involved: 'the devout women which were in the oratory' and some 'young men that came to the cry', along with children, servants, and some 'country folk' who had come to the city to visit a holy well dedicated to Stephen, the saint whose day this was.[38] But the menace of stones and clubs was sufficient to force the archbishop, the mayor, and their party to take refuge in a nearby house until rescued. Order, however, was quickly restored. The government imprisoned a number of Catholic aldermen and others for failing to come to the mayor's assistance, and initiated a drive to force the

---

[37] Kearney, *Strafford in Ireland*, 43–4. For Wentworth's complaint of social isolation see Canny, *Upstart Earl*, 11.

[38] *Wadding Papers 1614–38*, ed. Brendan Jennings (Dublin, 1953), 330, 333. See also F. X. Martin, *Friar Nugent: A Study of Francis Lavalin Nugent (1569–1635), Agent of the Counter Reformation* (London, 1962), 269–72.

closure of Catholic religious houses and places of worship that continued for most of the next two years.

This brief show of Catholic defiance, and the sharp retaliation it invited, can be contrasted with the events that took place eight and a half years later at the high church of St Giles in Edinburgh. On 23 July 1637 members of the Scottish council went to St Giles to hear the first use of the new Scottish Prayer Book compiled by order of Charles I. The book included a few concessions to Scottish feeling, notably the use of the term 'presbyter' instead of 'priest'. Overall, however, the new order of service, with its requirement that communicants should receive kneeling, its ban on extempore prayer, and its emphasis on the sacraments, represented a determined effort to replace the distinctive features of Scottish Protestantism with the Laudian Anglicanism that most regarded as little short of popery. The councillors were driven out of the church by a barrage of stools, clasp bibles, and other missiles. As in Dublin, women, less liable to reprisals, consciously took the lead. In this case, however, the immediate flurry of protest had a political aftermath. Noblemen, lairds, urban property owners, and ministers joined in a strongly worded 'supplication' addressed to the king, then organized the nationwide election of commissioners to receive his answer. When this proved unsatisfactory they proceeded in 1638 to adopt the National Covenant, proclaiming their absolute commitment to true religion, as well as a loyalty to the king conditional on his upholding their rights and liberties.

The contrast between the two episodes and their aftermaths is at first sight surprising. Of the three Stuart kingdoms, it was after all Ireland that had relatively recently been the scene of a bloody war of conquest, where native occupiers of land had been replaced by incoming settlers, and where a majority of the population retained a confessional allegiance directly opposed to the state church. But appearances were deceptive. The native Irish had lost heavily in recent decades. But the dispossessed among them had in many cases left the kingdom, either voluntarily or under duress; the most influential figures among those that remained possessed a stake of some kind, however unsatisfactory, in the reconstituted social order. The Old English remained divided from their Gaelic fellow Catholics by long-standing political and cultural animosities, and were inhibited in their capacity for protest by a continued sense of their role as the loyal upholders of the English interest in Ireland. The New English, formerly accustomed to make the state their instrument, had found Wentworth's government damaging to their material interests and offensive to their religious sensibilities. But their status as a newly arrived minority whose political dominance depended wholly on government support left them in no position to protest effectively. Instead it was in Scotland that a separate religious tradition deeply inimical to Laudian innovation combined with a contractual theory of monarchy to produce effective revolt. From there the crisis spread to England, where the king's sudden need for financial and military backing provided his subjects with the opportunity to press for redress of the many grievances arising out of eleven years of extra-parliamentary taxation and unpopular religious policies. It was only as control thus weakened both at the centre and at the other periphery that different groups within Ireland made their first attempts to assert themselves.[39]

Once the breakdown of political order had begun, however, the affairs of all three kingdoms became intimately linked. This was not simply a matter of events in adjacent territories influencing one another. The Stuart dominions were one example of a form of political organization common in early modern Europe, the multiple or composite monarchy. To rule over a conglomerate of territories, each with its separate laws and institutions, was demanding, but not impossible. Here Charles I, by failing to accept, in any of his three kingdoms, the need for a degree of partnership with local elites, contributed to his own downfall. Religion was a less tractable problem. Taxation regimes could differ from place to place; it was less easy to see how beliefs or practices that were permitted in one kingdom could be punished in another. In this respect the Scottish revolt takes its place beside two other notable crises of composite monarchy, the revolt of the Netherlands against Spanish rule, and of Bohemia against the Austrian Habsburgs. Nor was multiplicity a problem for the king alone. Once the crisis had begun, both his English and his Scottish opponents had to consider religious and constitutional arrangements in the neighbouring kingdom as well as in their own—partly out of conviction, but also because no victory achieved in one territory could be secure while conditions in the other provided the basis for a possible counter-attack by the forces of monarchy or episcopacy. For the same reason both Scots and English were forced to take a greater interest in the internal affairs of Ireland. This in turn led different groups in Ireland itself to ask new questions about Ireland's place within the Stuart multiple monarchy, both in its present form and as it might emerge from the crisis that now engulfed it.[40]

In 1637, however, all this was far in the future. Wentworth, having only recently overseen the suppression of Protestant nonconformity in Ulster, was initially scornful of the Scottish revolt. During 1638, however, it became clear that the example of the Covenanting movement had begun to undo what he had achieved. In Down and Connor Bishop Leslie reported that 1,000 people who the year before had taken communion on their knees had this year stayed away. In Derry Bishop Bramhall recorded the even more alarming appearance of 'anabaptistical prophetesses . . . gadding up and down'. In addition substantial numbers were reported to have travelled to Scotland to subscribe to the

[39] The fullest account of the political crisis of 1640–1 is Perceval-Maxwell, *Outbreak of the Irish Rebellion of 1641*. See also Kearney, *Strafford in Ireland*, chs. 13–14; Clarke, *Old English in Ireland*, ch. 8; and Clarke, in *NHI*, iii. 270–89.

[40] The concept of multiple monarchy has influenced much recent writing on the crisis of the 1640s. See in particular Russell, *Fall of the British Monarchies*, ch. 2.

Covenant. In April 1639, as the king prepared to march against the Covenanters, Wentworth stage-managed a petition by supposed representatives of the Ulster Scots population requesting an opportunity to profess their loyalty. This provided the basis for what became known to its opponents as 'the black oath', a declaration of obedience to the king, and an abjuration of all contrary oaths and covenants, to be administered throughout Ulster, by designated commissioners, to all persons over 16. Most initially complied, but resistance subsequently developed, especially after the king had backed down from an armed confrontation with the Covenanters, instead signing the Treaty of Berwick on 18 June. There was also a substantial outflow of dissidents from Ulster into Scotland, adding the problems of uncollected harvests and a shortage of labour in an economy already badly affected by the disruption of trade caused by the phoney war.

Wentworth, however, remained determined to make Ireland a stronghold for the crown. He had already quartered an extra 1,500 soldiers in Ulster, sent a further 500 to support the king in Carlisle, and ordered fresh supplies of weapons from the Netherlands. In September 1639 the Court of Castle Chamber imposed exemplary fines on five of those who had refused the black oath. Five months later, in a more dramatic demonstration of the narrow limits of permitted dissent, the court of high commission sentenced Archibald Adair, bishop of Killala, to be deprived of his diocese, fined £2,000, and imprisoned during the king's pleasure, for having allegedly expressed sympathy with the National Covenant. Wentworth himself had been in England since the previous September, where he became the king's leading adviser on English and Scottish as well as Irish affairs. In January 1640 Charles created him earl of Strafford and promoted him from deputy to lord lieutenant of Ireland. In March the new earl returned briefly to Ireland for a short session of parliament where members duly denounced the Covenanters and unanimously voted four subsidies, each at the new rate of £45,000. This was to be used to raise a new Irish army, amounting to 1,000 horse and 8,000 foot. Having thus crowned his successful stewardship of the kingdom, Strafford left Ireland for the last time in April.

When the Irish parliament assembled again, on 1 June, presided over by Wandesford, whom Strafford had appointed as his deputy, all had changed. In a session of just over two weeks, members attacked the administration for collecting the first of the new subsidies without authorization, then rejected the system of county quotas by which Strafford had sought to ensure that each subsidy would yield the projected £45,000. They also voted to restore the right to return members to seven boroughs whose charters Strafford had earlier declared invalid. The committee appointed to consider a government bill to confirm the plantations in Connacht, Clare, and Ormond quickly signalled its attitude by appointing as advisers two of the lawyers earlier victimized by Strafford for their defence of the Galway proprietors. There was also one notable act of vengeance. Along with a number of complaints relating to clerical fees and the proceedings of the court of high commission, the Commons took up a petition accusing

Bishop Atherton of Waterford and Lismore, Strafford's 'devil', of a variety of sexual offences, including sodomy, which the parliament of 1634 had made a capital offence. In addition to his role in the Convocation of 1634, and his relentless campaign to restore the church's lands at the expense of lay proprietors, Atherton had recently taken part in the deprivation of Bishop Adair. Whether his undoubted sexual voracity included a bisexual element is impossible to say. There are some grounds for suggesting that his opponents exploited a genuine proclivity—one that he may have shared, presumably by mere coincidence, with Strafford's other ecclesiastical manager, John Bramhall. In any case the bishop was committed to Dublin Castle, to be tried five months later and then hanged at Oxmantown Green on 5 December 1640. His body was buried in a churchyard, but at night and in a corner normally used as a rubbish dump.[41]

The sudden rebelliousness of a previously compliant Irish parliament was a hastily improvised response to events in England, where the 'Short Parliament', meeting between 13 April and 5 May, had refused to fund a new Scottish campaign, weakening the position not only of the king but also of Strafford, on whose recommendation it had been summoned. By the time the third session of the Irish assembly opened in Dublin on 1 October, the opposition was more purposeful and better organized. Members approved a new rating system calculated to reduce the yield of the proposed subsidies to around £12,000 each, demanded to know why the lord chancellor had failed to issue writs for the seven restored boroughs, and raised again the question of abuses in the church. On 7 November, ignoring threats from the increasingly desperate Wandesford, the Commons approved a 'Humble and Just Remonstrance' outlining the arbitrary and illegal proceedings of Strafford's administration: the determination of cases by the council rather than the courts of law, the imposition of monopolies, the activities of the court of high commission, the treatment of British planters in Londonderry, the disenfranchisement of ancient boroughs. Four days later, just before Wandesford suspended the sitting, the Commons appointed a committee of thirteen to travel to London to present this statement of grievances to the king.

In mounting this widening attack, the leaders of the Irish opposition were working in cooperation with the crown's leading critics on the other side of the Irish Sea. A key figure in coordinating opposition in the two kingdoms was Sir John Clotworthy. Born into a godly Devon family settled in County Antrim, he had been a noted patron of the dissident Scottish clergy, and his wife had been one of those summoned before the court of high commission to be questioned on her religious views. He was also the son-in-law of Roger Jones, Viscount Ranelagh, a prominent ally of the earl of Cork, and the brother-in-law of the English parliamentary agitator John Pym. Clotworthy had visited Scotland in June 1638 and had subsequently corresponded with Covenanting leaders. His

---

[41] Clarke, 'A Woeful Sinner', 138–49. For the hint relating to Bramhall, see ibid. 149.

importance as an intermediary with the English opposition was confirmed when he was elected, in two separate boroughs, to a seat in the new English parliament that the king had been forced to summon for November 1640. On 7 November, the same day that the Remonstrance had been introduced in Dublin, Clotworthy gave the Commons a detailed account of Strafford's administration in Ireland, stressing in particular the proceedings of the court of high commission and the imposition in Ulster of the black oath. He also drew attention to the new Irish army that had been raised, on Strafford's orders, during the summer. The nucleus of the new force consisted of 1,000 men transferred from the Protestant regular army. The remainder, however, raised by county levies over the summer, were predominantly Catholic. The senior officers were almost all New English, but a number of Catholics, mostly Old English, also held commissions. Clotworthy was thus able to hold out to his fellow parliamentarians the spectacle of a large popish force 'ready to march where I know not'.[42]

Events now moved quickly. The crown's English opponents had by this stage gone so far, particularly in their collusion with the Scots, that any successful recovery of the king's authority could be expected to result in their trial and execution for treason. The most likely agent of such a recovery was Strafford. On 11 November a Commons committee that included Clotworthy proposed his trial for treason. Among the early pieces of evidence assembled in preparation for the indictment was a petition from Scots claiming to have been driven out of Ulster by religious persecution. The delegation of thirteen MPs from the Irish parliament, arriving in London in mid-December, also contributed to the marshalling of evidence. When formal articles of impeachment were presented on 30 January, sixteen of the twenty-eight articles, some of them derived from the 'Humble and Just Remonstrance', related to his administration in Ireland. The witnesses against him included Cork, Ranelagh, Mountnorris, Loftus, and Clotworthy, as well as seven of the Irish parliamentary committee of thirteen. Their testimony offered English parliamentarians much of which to disapprove: open tolerance of Catholicism side by side with harassment of godly Protestants, the replacement of normal legislative and judicial processes by executive fiat, the imposition of burdensome monopolies. It was less clear that any of this constituted the capital offence of treason, while the potentially damning allegation that Strafford had been heard to urge the king to use the Irish army to restore his power in England could not be substantiated. In the end the Commons abandoned the judicial procedure of impeachment for an act of parliament declaring Strafford's guilt in having sought to impose an arbitrary and tyrannical government, thus permitting his execution by beheading on 12 May 1641.

Meanwhile the Irish parliament had continued to play its part in the campaign to reverse the tendencies of the previous eleven years. Wandesford died on

---

[42] Perceval-Maxwell, *Outbreak of the Irish Rebellion of 1641*, 96.

3 December 1640, apparently of shock on learning of his patron's arrest and impeachment. The committee in London successfully blocked proposals to appoint Ormond and another of Strafford's allies, Lord Robert Dillon, as lords justices. Instead the king appointed Sir William Parsons, an office holder but by this time hostile to the lord lieutenant, and Sir John Borlase, master of the ordnance. When the parliament reassembled on 26 January its members continued their denunciation of the abuses of Strafford's administration. In particular they attacked the tobacco monopoly, which was to provide one of the articles in the lord lieutenant's impeachment, and expelled the two MPs who had managed the concern for him. On 27 February the Commons initiated their own impeachments for treason, against Strafford's former secretary Sir George Radcliffe, who had already been imprisoned in England for alleged complicity in his master's plans for a coup, the lord chancellor Sir Richard Bolton, Sir Gerard Lowther, who was chief justice of the common pleas, and Bishop Bramhall. In addition both houses joined in a necessary revision of their own recent history. The subsidy bill passed in their compliant first session had included a preamble praising Strafford's government. Lords and Commons now entered formal protests alleging that this had been added without their knowledge. As in England, though to the much lesser extent dictated by religious demography, the parliamentary offensive went on side by side with extra-parliamentary agitation against what was seen as the betrayal of Protestant values by the Laudian church. In March and April Protestant crowds in Antrim and Down, with women once again prominent, attacked ministers whose services conformed to the official liturgy. Meanwhile Clotworthy was busy promoting two petitions from the British inhabitants of Ulster calling for the abolition of episcopacy, thus offering Irish support for the Root and Branch petition presented to the English Commons the previous December.

Even more striking than the close coordination between opponents of the crown in the two parliaments was the cooperation evident, in the Irish case, between representatives of what had been assumed to be the implacably opposed interests of the Old and New English. In 1634–5 there had been 112 Catholic MPs in a Commons of 254. In 1640 the elimination of eight Old English-controlled boroughs, combined with what it was claimed was aggressive management of the elections by Radcliffe, reduced this representation to 74 in a house of 235.[43] In the first session it was this depleted Catholic contingent that were reportedly the crown's most enthusiastic supporters in a wholly compliant assembly. In the context of a choice between a king who had once promised the Graces, and a fiercely anti-papist Scotland, this was hardly surprising. Subsequent sessions, on

---

[43] These are the figures offered in Bríd McGrath, 'Parliament Men and the Confederate Association', in Micheál Ó Siochrú (ed.), *Kingdoms in Crisis: Ireland in the 1640s* (Dublin, 2001), 92. Perceval-Maxwell, *Outbreak of the Irish Rebellion of 1641*, 70, suggests 76 Catholic MPs in a house of 238.

the other hand, saw Catholic and Protestant members become equally active in the mounting attack on the government's recent record. The opposition, not surprisingly, concentrated on issues of relevance to both groups, such as the increase in customs duties and the bypassing of normal judicial processes. But Protestant members nevertheless took a leading part in defending what was primarily a Catholic interest when they helped to kill off the bill to confirm the Connacht and other plantations. The relevant committee in fact comprised six Catholic members and ten Protestants. In addition the Remonstrance of 7 November included a complaint that 'the subject is in all the material parts thereof denied the benefit of the princely graces', and went on to instance the refusal of the statute of limitations on crown claims against defective titles promised 'for great considerations' in 1628.[44]

The willingness of a large part of the Protestant membership of the Commons to join the Catholics in obstructing the policy of plantation and demanding the Graces can in part be seen as purely tactical. Sir William Parsons, a member of Cork's circle with his own grudges against Strafford, was willing to play his part in the troublemaking of the second and third sessions. But by 1641, by now himself installed as one of the lords justices, he had begun to complain of the undue influence in both houses of a papist faction. Other Protestant MPs, however, continued to cooperate with their Catholic fellow members on a range of issues during the two further sessions held between January and August 1641. What was involved here seems to have been, not just factional advantage, but a real commitment to the assertion of constitutional principles. At this stage, of course, none of those involved saw themselves as choosing sides in the apocalyptic clash of religious and political allegiances that within a year was to engulf all three of the Stuart kingdoms. Instead, in seizing an unexpected opportunity to strike back against a regime that had given widespread cause for resentment, they were continuing a course of pragmatic accommodation between coexisting religious and ethnic groups that had been established over the preceding two or three decades. It is probably no accident, for example, that one of the Protestant members most prominently involved was Audley Mervyn, MP for County Tyrone, grandson of a servitor in the Ulster plantation, but also brother-in-law of the Gaelic peer Lord Maguire.

QUERIES AND ARGUMENTS

In developing this increasingly assertive attack on an authoritarian executive, parliamentarians relied heavily on the claim that they were entitled to the same rights and liberties as the people of England. The November Remonstrance began

---

[44] *The Humble and Just Remonstrance of the Knights, Citizens, and Burgesses, in Parliament Assembled in Ireland* (n. p., 1641), 4–5.

with the assertion that the 'loyal and dutiful people of this land of Ireland, being now for the most part derived from the British ancestor, should be governed according to the municipal and fundamental laws of England'. It went on to assert that Magna Carta, 'the great charter for the liberties of England', along with other 'laudable laws and statutes', had been adopted also by the Irish parliament.[45] In February 1641 the Commons drew up a set of twenty-one queries for submission to the judges. These related mainly to specific acts of the recent administration, such as the punishment of jurors for verdicts of which government disapproved, the use of martial law in time of peace, and the obstruction of appeals to England. The first, however, was more general: 'Whether the subjects of this kingdom be a free people, and to be governed only by the common laws of England and statutes of force in this kingdom.' The judges' answer was not offered until 25 May and even then only under pressure from the House of Lords. On most of the specific queries their response was to agree on the point of law, while declining to commit themselves on the scope of the king's prerogative. On the more general point of constitutional principle, they accepted that the claim implicit in the first query was 'for the general' correct, but nevertheless pointed to differences arising from judicial interpretation of obsolete statutes, proceedings in the courts of equity, or generally accepted custom.[46] This was not the bland evasion sometimes asserted. Military and political exigencies had dictated that the executive had long had a freer hand, and parliament a more limited role, in Ireland than in England. For that very reason, however, it was crucial for parliamentary spokesmen to establish that English law and precedent were now valid in Ireland as in England.

The task of doing so fell to Patrick Darcy, the Old English lawyer who had first achieved prominence through his legal rearguard action against the Galway plantation in 1634–6, and had subsequently been one of the two lawyers appointed to advise the Commons committee on the plantation bill. His recruitment to the Commons in May 1641 was a further example of Old and New English cooperation: he was returned in a by-election for County Tyrone with the assistance of Audley Mervyn. (Earlier, in an interesting prefiguring of the same broad alliance of Old and New English, he had acted as counsel for the earl of Cork in his legal battles with Strafford.) Between 7 and 9 June, addressing a joint meeting of the Lords and Commons in the Great Dining Room of Dublin Castle, Darcy delivered a comprehensive rebuttal of the judges' response to the queries. He began by reiterating that Ireland was governed by the common law of England, by generally accepted (as opposed to purely local) custom, and by those English statutes enacted into law by the Irish parliament. As for the courts of

---

[45] *The Humble and Just Remonstrance of the Knights*, 1.
[46] The queries, and the judges' response, are printed in C. E. J. Caldicott (ed.), 'Patrick Darcy: An Argument', *Camden Miscellany*, 31 (London, 1992). For query 1 see p. 232, and for the judges' response pp. 242–4. For a general discussion see Aidan Clarke, 'Patrick Darcy and the Relationship between Ireland and Britain', in Jane Ohlmeyer (ed.), *Political Thought in Seventeenth-Century Ireland* (Cambridge, 2000), 40.

equity and other agencies cited by the judges as authorizing differences in practice between the two kingdoms, their proceedings were 'bounded and controlled by the rules of the common law', like rivers within their banks. On this basis Darcy then employed a battery of English texts and precedents, most notably the acknowledgement of the limits of the prerogative that his English opponents had extracted from Charles I in the Petition of Right of 1628, to denounce what he called 'the late introduction of an arbitrary government in many cases by some ministers of state'.[47]

At this stage the main concern of Darcy and others, like that of their counterparts in England, was with the need to reaffirm the legal restraints on the use of executive authority. But the new political circumstances had also brought to the surface questions relating to the constitutional status of Ireland as a subordinate but separate kingdom. During its early sessions the Commons had reasserted its right, denied by Wentworth in 1634–5, to debate and frame draft legislation, despite the restrictions of the late fifteenth-century statute known as Poynings's Law.[48] In its fourth session it called for an explanatory bill confirming the legitimacy of this procedure and requiring the executive to transmit all such draft bills submitted to it to England for consideration. However neither the king nor his council in England were willing to see an informal procedure converted into a statutory right. The king likewise rejected the parliament's impeachment of Bramhall and the other three accused, on the grounds that there was no precedent for such proceedings. In this he was no doubt concerned mainly to protect his servants. But there was also an important point of principle: a right of impeachment would imply that Irish office holders, appointed from England, would not only have to work through an Irish parliament, but would become accountable to it for their actions. In response Audley Mervyn argued that precedents were not needed because the rights of the Irish parliament were identical with those of its English equivalent.[49]

Mervyn's claim for the equal status of the Irish parliament was once again a challenge to a declining executive. But it also implicitly raised questions that were shortly to begin complicating the relationship between Irish parliamentarians and their allies on the other side of the Irish Sea. Darcy had readily accepted that Ireland was bound by English common law. English statute law, on the other hand, applied to Ireland only if 'received and enacted in parliament in this kingdom'.[50] This was a long-established principle, based on the argument that

---

[47] Caldicott (ed.), 'Patrick Darcy: An Argument', 271, 254, and 253–309 *passim*.

[48] Poynings's Law, enacted in the parliament of 1494–5, laid down that no bill could be presented to the Irish parliament until it had been formally approved, under seal, by the English privy council. What the Irish parliament did in 1613–15, and again in 1640–1, was to produce draft bills which it then asked the Irish executive to transmit to London for approval.

[49] The debate on impeachment is summarized in Peerceval-Maxwell, *The Outbreak of the Irish Rebellion of 1641*, 166–72.

[50] Caldicott (ed.), 'Patrick Darcy: An Argument', 270.

Ireland's connection, first as a lordship and, since 1541, as a kingdom, was with the crown not the parliament of England. When English MPs had attempted in 1621 to impose restrictions on the Irish cattle trade the leading legal authorities of the day, supported by the king, had rejected their claims, on the grounds that Ireland was 'a member of the crown of England' and thus not subject to their enactments.[51] All this, however, was in the context of a monarch firmly in control of all three of the kingdoms united under his rule, taking advice as he saw fit from the parliament of each. By 1641, as the English parliament in particular began to assert its authority, the position became less clear. The impeachment and attainder of Strafford involved it in passing judgement on transactions which in most cases had directly affected only the people of Ireland. A more direct clash arose in July 1641, when the English House of Lords summoned the entire Irish privy council before them to answer the complaint of Henry Stewart, a Scot who had been imprisoned for refusing to take the black oath, provoking an indignant refusal from the Irish Lords. The issue in both cases lay in a grey area, involving the judicial rather than the legislative functions of the English parliament. In taking up the Stewart case, equally, the English Lords had been motivated, not by legal imperialism, but by a desire not to offend the Scots on whose continued support the English opposition depended.[52] But the potential for conflict was nevertheless becoming clear. Thus when the Irish Commons, on 26 July, adopted resolutions positively affirming the principles implicit in the queries, these included a more explicit statement than had previously been thought necessary of the exclusive right of the Irish parliament to make laws for the kingdom.[53] For its part the English council decided in October that both Poynings's Law and the queries should be referred for discussion to the English parliament.

At the same time that novel constitutional disputes began to threaten the unity of the king's Irish and English opponents, the earlier solidarity across religious lines of at least some on the Irish side also came under strain. The committee dispatched to England at the end of 1640 had been equally balanced, with seven Catholics and six Protestants. As negotiations progressed, however, a division of interests appeared. While Protestant members concentrated on the case against Strafford, some of the Catholics became involved in private discussions with the king. All this was at a time, March 1641, when initially promising negotiations between Charles and the English parliamentary leaders had collapsed, and when the king was contemplating a resort to armed action to rescue Strafford, a visit to Scotland for the purpose of building up support there, and possibly the use at some stage of Strafford's new Irish army to restore his authority. Against this

[51] Clarke, 'Patrick Darcy and the Relationship between Ireland and Britain', 40.

[52] Russell, *Fall of the British Monarchies*, 392.

[53] The case for a new sensitivity to constitutional issues on the Irish side is particularly emphasized by Clarke, 'Patrick Darcy and the Relationship between Ireland and Britain', 44.

background a settlement with the Irish Catholics made sense.[54] Accordingly he ordered the lords justices, in a letter of 3 April, to prepare bills to implement the Graces, including the confirmation of the Connacht surrenders and the statute of limitations on claims of crown title.

If the Old English had now come within sight of achieving their two main long-term goals, the lords justices and the Irish council responded as the voice of the New English settler interest. Their initial reply emphasized the value of plantations as the only way short of a full conquest of reducing the kingdom to obedience to English law. But they also shrewdly drew attention to the catastrophic decline that had taken place in the revenue from customs, wardship, and other sources following the collapse of 'thorough', which the new concessions would exacerbate while bringing no compensatory gains. Meanwhile the king's plans to use the Irish army had been overtaken by events, removing the single most important reason for purchasing Catholic support. His response was to revise his terms, demanding that concessions should be paid for by two new subsidies and legislation permanently improving the crown's customs revenue. A further round of negotiations with the Irish committee, during late July and early August, produced an agreement. But by then the Irish parliament had been prorogued. It was due to meet again on 9 November, but the king's English advisers, urged on by the Irish council, argued strongly that this should be postponed. The decision in October to refer the queries and Poynings's Law to the English parliament may have been at least in part a further element in these tactics of delay.

ULSTER'S VESPERS

An incidental but telling feature of the Remonstrance drawn up by the Irish parliament in November 1640 was its assertion that the inhabitants of Ireland, whose entitlement to the liberties enshrined in English law it sought to substantiate, were 'now for the most part derived from the British ancestor'. The claim, transparently false[55], was presumably intended to appeal to the English audience to which the Remonstrance was ultimately addressed. But it is also a reminder of how effortlessly the Old English elite, accounting as they did for all but nine of the Catholic MPs elected in 1640, monopolized the public representation of Catholic interests. A petition received by the House of Commons in February

[54] The fullest account of this episode, bringing out clearly the wider British background to the king's temporary surrender to Catholic demands, is Russell, *Fall of the British Monarchies*, 388–92.

[55] For estimates of recent settler numbers, see above, p. 6. The number of persons descended from medieval English settlers is impossible even to estimate, but clearly accounted for a distinct minority within the population, and its significance had in any case been eroded by the absorption of so many into the majority Gaelic culture.

1641 is thus of particular significance as a rare formal statement of the outlook and grievances specifically of the Gaelic elite. The petition was in the name of the Irish gentry of the planted areas of Leinster. Their complaint, however, did not concern the loss of lands that had been brought about by those plantations. Instead what they appealed against were the clauses in the grants made to the new proprietors that forbade them to lease or sell their land to native Irishmen. Such clauses, the petitioners argued, discouraged industry among the natives by giving them 'no hopes to gain further or great estates'. They also represented the denial to one section of the king's 'freeborn subjects' of the rights enjoyed by others.[56]

This petition of the Leinster natives, modestly assimilationist in its aims and decorously loyal in its language, must be set against a second transaction, one that became public only later and in the form of a confession. In June 1642 Conor, Lord Maguire of Enniskillen, a prisoner in the Tower of London, described how in February of the previous year he had been approached in Dublin, where he was attending the meetings of parliament, by Rory O'More. Both men belonged to that part of Gaelic society that had best survived the upheavals of the preceding forty years. Maguire had inherited almost 6,000 acres in County Fermanagh; O'More—significantly referred to in the statement by his Anglicized title of 'Mr Roger Moore'—held over 1,000 acres in County Kildare and another 7,000 in County Armagh. Yet their good fortune remained strictly relative. Maguire was the grandson of a man who had been bullied or swindled into exchanging title to the whole of County Fermanagh for the grant of a single barony.[57] Moreover he seems to have been one of those who had not adapted easily to the demands of a new economic environment, and by 1641 was heavily in debt. O'More was in a stronger financial position, apparently purchasing rather than mortgaging land in the years before 1641, and laying out some £4,000 in dowries for his daughters. But he appears nevertheless to have resented the loss of the midland territories once ruled by his family and of the regional pre-eminence that had gone with them. In his discussions with Maguire he began by speaking generally of 'the many afflictions and sufferings of the natives of this kingdom', especially under Strafford. He then 'began to particularise the sufferings of them that were the more ancient natives, as were the Irish; how that on several plantations they were all put out of their ancestors' estates'. Subsequently he turned to Maguire's own situation: 'the case that I was in there, overwhelmed in debt, the smallness of my now estate, the greatness of the estate my ancestors had, and how I should be sure to get it again, or at least a good part thereof'.[58]

---

[56] Perceval-Maxwell, *Outbreak of the Irish Rebellion of 1641*, 120–1. For the figure of nine MPs of Gaelic origin see ibid. 70.

[57] Connolly, *Contested Island*, 297–8.

[58] 'The Relation of the Lord Maguire . . .', printed in Mary Hickson (ed.), *Ireland in the Seventeenth Century* (London, 1884), ii. 341–2. Maguire's account was supposedly written in the Tower of London in June 1642. At his trial he denied having written the document, and it has

These two documents, taken together, make clear the uncertain state of allegiances among the Gaelic Irish. The Leinster petition reflected a pragmatic acceptance of the existing political and social order, within which its authors demanded only the right to compete on equal terms. Maguire's confession, by contrast, made clear the existence of a clear sense of collective grievance, even in the case of two of the more substantial of the surviving proprietors, at the loss of land and status experienced by their families and others over the preceding century. In the settled conditions of the previous three decades or so it had been pragmatism that had prevailed. But now, in the context of threatened political upheaval throughout the Stuart dominions, the deep wells of resentment created by the multiple inequalities of a society reshaped by conquest and confiscation were suddenly to overflow.

The decision of O'More and Maguire to respond to events in Great Britain with plans for an armed conspiracy was in part a matter of simple opportunity. If the gentry wanted to regain their ancestors' estates, O'More pointed out, 'they could never desire a more convenient time . . . the distempers of Scotland being then on foot'. But the political crisis of the other two Stuart kingdoms also had a more specific relevance. The challenge to arbitrary government was something with which Irish Catholics, following their experience under Strafford, could easily associate themselves. But English and Scottish opposition was also informed, from the start, by a deep anti-Catholicism. Popery, to most of Charles I's subjects, was a malevolent and powerful menace; the pope himself was seen by many as the Antichrist of the bible. Abroad, Spain continued to menace the Netherlands, the Habsburgs crushed Protestant Bohemia, and French Protestants faced intensifying persecution. At home a people brought up on memories of the martyrdom endured by Protestants under Mary, and of the treasonable conspiracy of the Gunpowder Plot, were forced to accept a French queen who openly maintained a Catholic household, and an archbishop of Canterbury who sought to move what many already considered an unsatisfactory religious establishment still closer to the practices and doctrines of the popish past. For the moment the Long Parliament concentrated on matters within its own jurisdiction, demanding the exclusion of Catholic peers from the English House

---

been argued that the plot it describes was in fact a fabrication, designed to legitimize the actions of the Dublin administration in the intervening period. (See, most recently, Brendan Fitzpatrick, *Seventeenth-Century Ireland: The War of Religions* (Dublin, 1988), ch. 6.) Perceval-Maxwell, pointing to limited but significant corroborative evidence, takes the account as broadly reliable (*Outbreak of the Irish Rebellion of 1641*, 204), and this view is shared by most other recent writers. (It is also worth noting that the existence of the Dublin plot was likewise confirmed, or at least not denied, in the near contemporary account of the Franciscan friar Tarlach Ó Mealláin. See Charles Dillon (ed.), 'Cín Lae Uí Mhealláin: Friar O Meallan Journal', in idem and H. A. Jefferies (eds.), *Tyrone: History and Society* (Dublin, 2000), 336.) However it remains unclear why Maguire should have composed a detailed confession, or what pressures he might have been under when he did so. That he did not come to trial until November 1644, and was then executed, suggests that some sort of negotiation may have taken place in the intervening period.

of Lords, the dispersal of the queen's personal servants, and a strict execution of the recusancy laws. But there was no reason to believe that this committed anti-popery, informed by the conviction that to tolerate Romanist idolatry was not merely politically dangerous but contrary to the law of God, would confine itself to any one part of the Stuart dominions. A failure to take proper measures against popery had been one of the accusations against Strafford, while his new Irish army had been the target of virulent anti-Catholic rhetoric. It was against this background that Rory O'More used what turned out to be, for the initially hesitant Maguire, the clinching argument: 'For, said he, it is to be feared . . . the [English] parliament intends the utter subversion of our religion, by which persuasion he obtained my consent.'

A second part of the background to the outbreak of rebellion is that Maguire and O'More were not the only, or indeed the first, group to consider taking up arms in response to developments in the three kingdoms. At the beginning of 1639 the king had authorized Randal MacDonnell, earl of Antrim, to mobilize his kinsmen and dependants in east Ulster for an invasion of western Scotland, where he would join up with the Scottish branch of his extended family and attack the Covenanters from the rear.[59] Antrim, who had never abandoned the hope of regaining his family's lost Scottish lands, responded eagerly, making plans to raise 5,000 men in Ulster and expecting another 4,000 to rally to him once he had landed in Scotland. Wentworth, determined as ever to retain sole control of Irish affairs, ensured that the venture came to nothing. But this sabotage of a potential rival was only a preliminary to the deputy's own preparations for a possible military solution, the new Irish army of 8,000 foot and 1,000 horse recruited during the summer of 1640. As commander in chief in his own absence Strafford nominated his political henchman, the young earl of Ormond. Day-to-day command, however, was consigned to the president of Munster, Sir William St Leger, a veteran of the Dutch wars, who assembled the new force at Carrickfergus in mid-July to begin their training and by late August declared them fit for service. By this time the Scots had already swept into northern England. In November, with money desperately short as parliament reneged on the subsidies, the new army had to be dispersed to winter quarters throughout Ulster. But it remained the most substantial military force at the disposal of an increasingly embattled king.

What remains unclear is how far Charles was prepared to go in making use of this tempting but dangerous asset. Some idea of incorporating Irish Catholic support into wider plans for a coup helps to make sense of his sudden willingness, in April 1641, to authorize the legalization of the Graces. By May the English

---

[59] The MacDonnells or Clan Donald had expanded from their original base in western Scotland, where their position was in decline, into north-east Ulster. Initially treated as alien interlopers, they had eventually been accepted as subjects of the crown and given the title earls of Antrim. See J. Michael Hill, *Fire and Sword: Sorley Boy MacDonnell and the Rise of Clan Ian Mor 1538–90* (London, 1993).

half of this strategy, if that is what it was, had rebounded disastrously, with the discovery of the ill-conceived plan to rescue Strafford from the Tower. Meanwhile it had become clear that the downward revision of the Irish subsidies made it impossible to go on supporting the 9,000 troops in Ireland. On 8 May the king ordered Ormond to disband the force, and soon afterwards licensed eight colonels to transport the troops abroad, to find employment in the Spanish army. The earl of Antrim, however, was later to claim that this order was bogus. According to his account the king sent secret instructions to Ormond and himself to keep the army together to be 'employed against the parliament'. When Antrim reported, in mid-August, that the army had already disbanded, Charles ordered him to bring the men together again and to make preparations to secure Dublin Castle and raise the kingdom for his service, 'if occasion should be for so doing'. Antrim communicated the plan to Lord Gormanstown, Lord Slane, and other leaders from among the Old English of the Pale, as well as to unspecified persons in Ulster. The plan he described was for a decisive assertion of authority rather than a military strike; there was even the hope that the lords justices would agree to support the action. However the Ulstermen, whom Antrim described as 'the fools', 'fell upon it without us, and sooner, and otherwise than we should have done . . . and so spoiled it'.[60]

Antrim's account presents serious problems. It was offered in 1650, at a time when the earl, having already deserted the royal cause for that of the more militant Irish Catholics, was coming to terms with a parliamentary regime anxious to legitimize the recent execution of the king. It clashes with other evidence indicating that after May Charles, having accepted the need to give up the Irish army, in fact made genuine efforts to have the disbanded troops shipped out of the kingdom.[61] It is also hard to see why, if Antrim had discussed his plans with the Ulster Irish, there is no mention of him in Lord Maguire's very detailed narrative of his conspiratorial activities. On the other hand the suggestion that the king tried to keep his options open is consistent with his general behaviour during the whole crisis of 1640–2, and also with other hints of plotting by soldiers and Palesmen in the tense spring and summer of 1641. Antrim, in other words, may well have exaggerated for the benefit of his new Cromwellian masters. But it is still possible that he and other associates of the court did in fact behave in ways that encouraged the belief that an armed intervention in defence of the royal prerogative would be both legitimate and welcome.

---

[60] Antrim's account is printed in Jane Ohlmeyer, 'The "Antrim Plot" of 1641: A Rejoinder', *Historical Journal*, 37 (1994), 434–7. Antrim does not specify when the king's original message arrived, and alternative chronological reconstructions are at the heart of the debate between Ohlmeyer and Perceval-Maxwell: Ohlmeyer, 'The "Antrim Plot" of 1641: A Myth?', *Historical Journal*, 35 (1992), 905–19; M. Perceval-Maxwell, 'The "Antrim Plot" of 1641: A Myth? A Rejoinder', *Historical Journal*, 37 (1994), 421–30.

[61] In addition to the exchange by Ohlmeyer and Perceval-Maxwell just cited, see Russell, *Fall of the British Monarchies*, 393–5; Perceval-Maxwell, *Outbreak of the Irish Rebellion of 1641*, ch. 8.

Even if Charles had abandoned the idea of using the Irish army to change the balance of political forces, moreover, others apparently had not. The first 1,000 disbanded men duly embarked in mid-June. At the end of July, however, the Irish parliament intervened to prevent further shipments. The reasons given were unexceptionable: that the loss of so many able-bodied men would create a labour shortage, and that it was dangerous to make Spain a gift of so many potential combatants. Parsons, however, noted suspiciously that it was Catholic members who were most active in opposing the departure. Maguire, likewise, later recalled that there had been discussions at this time among some MPs and some 'gentlemen of the Pale' about 'how they might make stay of the soldiers in the kingdom, and likewise to arm them in defence of the king . . . and to prevent any attempt against religion'. Parsons may have been scaremongering and Maguire, a prisoner, may well have been under pressure to confirm a tale of popish conspiracy. But other scraps of evidence suggest that certain among the Old English of the Pale were in fact involved, around this time, in discussions of some kind of military action. It has been speculatively suggested that they contemplated this desperate action on learning, in May, that Strafford's successor as chief governor was what was believed to be the militantly Protestant earl of Leicester. This hypothesis also helps to explain why whatever willingness there was in Old English circles to contemplate armed action does not seem to have lasted beyond August 1641, when the parliamentary committee returned bearing a satisfactory agreement on the Graces, while discussions with Leicester had shown him to be more accommodating than had initially been expected.[62]

A third strand of conspiracy has a name, being commonly referred to as 'the Colonels' Plot'. In other respects, however, it is as obscure as the first two. In late July or August 1641 a friar named John Barnewall, who had earlier kept Maguire and others informed of doings among the Old English, told them that some of the colonels licensed to transport the disbanded new Irish army to the continent were offering instead to stage a coup. The proposal was to use the men they had assembled to seize the Castle in Dublin and then use the arms stored there to equip their followers. It is possible that these plans by professional soldiers of Old English background had their origins in the king's hopes earlier in the year of forming a military alliance with loyal Irish Catholics against his insubordinate English subjects, so that the officers concerned now proceeded with an expectation of his approval, if not necessarily with his knowledge. Alternatively it may be that their plan was linked to the talk of military action that seems to have circulated in wider Old English circles during the summer. A third possibility is that the officers were responding to promptings from overseas. Owen Roe O'Neill, the senior commander among the Irish in Spanish Flanders, had been monitoring the developing crisis in Ireland. He had been in

---

[62] These are the suggestions of Perceval-Maxwell, *Outbreak of the Irish Rebellion of 1641*, 199–204.

communication, by cipher, with his cousin Sir Phelim O'Neill, and had recently sent his nephew Con O'Neill on a mission to England. Moreover one of the colonels involved in the plans for a coup in Ireland was Hugh Byrne, Gaelic Irish rather than Old English, who had formerly served in the earl of Tyrone's regiment of the Spanish army and who had visited Owen Roe in Flanders before receiving his licence to transport men overseas.

At this point we return to the conspiracy set in motion by O'More's approach to Maguire in February 1641. According to Maguire's own later account, O'More claimed already to have extensive support in Leinster and much of Connacht. This may well have been a fabrication: O'More did not subsequently bring forward any substantial body of supporters, and his unconvincing claims to Maguire that he also had the backing of an unidentified 'great man' cast doubt on his credibility. In any case he now looked to Maguire to help him recruit support among the Irish of Ulster, and it was there that subsequent activity was concentrated. The plan was basic. On a set day 'everyone in his own quarter should rise out' and seize what arms he could get in his county. This was to be done shortly before the beginning of winter, ensuring that no troops could be sent from England before spring 1642, by which time help would have arrived from the Irish on the continent, supported by either Spain or the pope. In August, following Barnewall's news of the Colonels' Plot, Maguire came to Dublin where he made contact with the ringleaders, Sir James Dillon, Colonel Richard Plunkett, and Hugh Byrne. Following their discussions what had formerly been separate plans, for a rising in the countryside and a Dublin-based coup, came together as two parts of a single strike that would secure Ireland for Catholicism and the king.

In September Maguire, back in Ulster, added a late recruit to the conspiracy, Owen Roe's secret correspondent Sir Phelim O'Neill. Sir Phelim was a grandson of the Sir Henry Óg O'Neill who had died, along with his son, Phelim's father, fighting for the crown against Sir Cahir O'Doherty's rebel forces in 1608.[63] He was, even more than Maguire and 'Roger Moore', a well-established figure in the new social and political order. Brought up as a ward of court, he had studied for a time at Lincoln's Inn in London, had inherited an estate of some 5,000 acres in County Tyrone, and was now both a justice of the peace and member of the House of Commons. He had even taken the oath of supremacy, although he had later reverted to Catholicism. Like Maguire he was deeply in debt, with mortgages of over £13,000 and a range of other liabilities. But this in itself hardly explains his decision to commit himself to armed rebellion. Later developments would suggest that he acted initially from the same concern felt by others that the survival of Irish Catholicism was in real danger from the threatened eclipse of the king's prerogative by a Puritan parliament and its equally anti-popish Scottish allies. There were also to be allegations that these concerns came together, at

---

[63] Connolly, *Contested Island*, 271, 298.

some stage if not from the start, with an ambition to claim the headship of the O'Neill dynasty, symbolized in the title of earl of Tyrone.[64]

Among those whom Maguire met during his visit to Sir Phelim was a Captain Brian O'Neill, recently arrived from Flanders to assure the Ulster Irish of Owen Roe's backing for a revolt. By this time too another of the exiled commander's agents, Heber MacMahon, the Catholic bishop of Clogher, had become involved in the conspiracy. When Maguire returned to Dublin for another meeting with the colonels, however, he found the majority of them suddenly anxious to back out of the whole business, on the grounds that the Palesmen they had previously been in touch with were no longer willing to act. Although Plunkett remained involved, the conspiracy now reverted to being primarily a native Irish venture. The conspirators, however, retained what had originally been the colonels' plan for an attack on Dublin Castle. O'More and Byrne, leading a detachment from Leinster, were to attack one gate of the fortress, while Maguire and O'Neill, commanding a body of Ulstermen, took another. Meanwhile Sir Phelim was to lead an attack on Londonderry and other centres in Ulster, after which he and his followers would march on Dublin. Both groups were agreed 'not to kill any but where of necessity they were forced to do so by opposition'.

The date set for the rising was Saturday, 23 October, a market day on which less notice would be taken of the movement of large groups of men. On the evening of the 22nd, however, a native Irish convert, Owen Connolly, appeared before Sir William Parsons to report that his foster brother, Hugh MacMahon, had revealed to him plans for a surprise attack on Dublin Castle, to coincide with a general massacre of Protestants throughout the kingdom.[65] In response the lords justices arrested Maguire, MacMahon, and others, mounted a guard, and closed the city gates. Even as they secured the capital, however, Sir Phelim O'Neill had mobilized in Ulster. On Friday, 22 October, a day earlier than planned, he presented himself, with a group of retainers, at Charlemont fort, standing at a strategic location on the River Blackwater. When the young proprietor, Lord Caulfield, politely invited him and his party to stay for dinner, O'Neill and his men seized control of house and fortress. Meanwhile other conspirators, similarly exploiting the assumptions of a society no longer as accustomed as it had once been to violence, gained entry to Dungannon Castle on the pretext of applying for a warrant against sheep stealers. By Saturday evening parties of rebels had seized a chain of positions extending across mid-Ulster from Newry in the south to Moneymore near the northern edge of Lough Neagh.

[64] See below, n. 69.
[65] Connolly was a servant of Sir John Clotworthy. This connection, along with his unconvincing account of how MacMahon came to betray the secret, have encouraged the suggestion that the whole story of a Dublin conspiracy was a fabrication. Aidan Clarke, however, suggests that it is more likely that the improbabilities in his account arose from his desire to conceal the extent to which he himself was implicated in the plot: *Old English in Ireland*, 161 n. 1.

Sir Phelim and his allies insisted from the start that they were not engaged in a rebellion. In a proclamation issued from Dungannon on the Sunday after his rising, he announced that he and his followers remained loyal to the king and intended no harm to either the English or the Scots, being concerned only to defend their liberties and those of other Irish natives. On 4 November Sir Phelim joined with Lord Maguire's brother Rory in a more explicit statement, claiming to have acted on the authority of a commission from the king himself, who called on his Catholic subjects to defend him from the English parliament and the militant Protestant party. Other Ulster leaders produced their own versions of the supposed commission: one, in Leitrim, used the seal on a patent for his lands to confer authenticity. The claim to be defending monarchy in its hour of desperate need was further reinforced by wild rumours circulated at popular level: that the king had already been deposed and replaced by his nephew, the exiled elector palatine, that the queen was being held prisoner, or that her confessor had been murdered in front of her. Sir Phelim's brother Turlough, who captured Armagh a few days later, was heard to declare that he would surrender the town if called on to do so in the name of the king, but not of parliament. In the same spirit the leader of the County Cavan insurgents, Mulmore O'Reilly, continued to employ the ceremonial of his office as sheriff of the county, laying his hand on the shoulder of the Protestant bishop, William Bedell, and telling him: 'I arrest you in the king's name; you are my prisoner.'[66]

How far these protestations of loyalty can be taken at face value remains unclear. Claims to be acting, not against the monarch, but against his evil subordinates were a standard feature of early modern revolt. They served both to legitimize the challenge to authority, and prudently to reduce the offence given. In the case of the Ulster Irish there was also the continuing aim of securing support from the Old English, as well as the hope of preventing or minimizing the resistance of the English and Scots. Some at least of the insurgent rank and file had from the start little interest in a rising in support of the just prerogatives of Charles I. In Armagh a Protestant prisoner heard Patrick MacCabe, a butcher in Tandragee, proclaim, 'If I had the king of England in the shambles . . . I would take off his head in half an hour.' Others stated in her hearing that when they had conquered Ireland they would make Sir Phelim king (though only, in a revealing display of localism, in the north).[67] Elsewhere too rebels talked openly of having their own ruler, identified variously as an O'Neill (either Sir Phelim or the exiled Owen Roe), a Maguire, or an O'Reilly.

Mutterings of this kind can in part be seen as evidence of the gulf between the native Irish elite who defined the rising's aims and a less politically sophisticated

---

[66] *Two Biographies of William Bedell*, 66.

[67] Deposition of Margaret Bromley, 26 Aug. 1642 (in Hickson (ed.), *Ireland in the Seventeenth Century*, i. 297).

rank and file. But by early 1642 the leadership also had begun to express more radical ambitions than it had initially admitted to, calling for a reversal of the plantations that had taken place since 1603. One suggestion is that they had no choice but to echo the expectations of their followers, if they were to build up support for what was now clearly going to be a prolonged conflict rather than a sudden coup.[68] But the Irish plot, as opposed to those of the Palesmen or the colonels, had begun, in Maguire's account, with the complaint that the ancient natives had been expelled from the lands of their ancestors. Hence it is also possible that what were now being expressed were underlying aspirations that initially had been prudently concealed. Robert Maxwell, a Protestant clergyman who claimed to have had several opportunities of discussing Sir Phelim's aims directly with him while his prisoner, reported that he initially spoke only of liberty of conscience, 'but afterwards as his power, so his demands were multiplied'.

They must have no lord deputy, great officers of state, privy councillors, judges, or justices of the peace, but of the Irish nation. No standing army in the kingdom. All tithes payable by papists to be paid to Popish priests. Church lands to be restored to their bishops. All plantations since [1603] to be disannulled, none made hereafter. . . . All strangers (meaning British) to be restrained from coming over. All acts of parliament against popery and papists, together with Poynings's Act, to be repealed.

Even then, Maxwell was told by others, the truth was that Sir Phelim would lay down his arms only if guaranteed the earldom of Tyrone and the ancestral lands of the O'Neills.[69] Another captive clergyman who spoke directly to O'Neill likewise reported his stated aims as moving beyond the simple defence of religious liberty, though without abandoning the claim to be engaged in a loyal, even royally sanctioned, rising. '. . . their intentions were only for the liberty of their religion, and for the recovery of their lands, which should appear by the laws of England to be unjustly held from them, and for the king's prerogative.'[70]

The gap between the political aspirations of the Ulster leadership and that of their followers was even more clearly revealed in the widespread violence dealt out to all sections of the settler population in the affected area. Friday, 22 October 1641 did not, as was subsequently claimed, mark the beginning of a coordinated attempt to wipe out the Protestant population of Ireland. But the ferocity of what took place is nevertheless undeniable. In the early stages of the rising the most common event was that the Irish descended on settler households, stripped

[68] Perceval-Maxwell, *Outbreak of the Irish Rebellion of 1641*, 236.

[69] Deposition of Robert Maxwell, 22 Aug. 1642 (in Hickson (ed.), *Ireland in the Seventeenth Century*, i. 330–1). These reports of Sir Phelim's ambitions come from hostile sources. But they are supported by his subsequent quarrel with Owen Roe O'Neill over his claim to the titular earldom of Tyrone, following the death of Hugh O'Neill's son John: Jerrold I. Casway, *Owen Roe O'Neill and the Struggle for Catholic Ireland* (Philadelphia, 1984), 60–3.

[70] Deposition of John Kerdiff, 28 Feb. 1642 (in Hickson (ed.), *Ireland in the Seventeenth Century*, i. 193).

the inhabitants of their possessions, including in many cases their clothes, and drove them away. The proceedings could be violent and frightening, especially if the victims were suspected of concealing money or goods. But killings, except in the case of resistance or where attackers seized the occasion to settle a private grudge, were at this stage relatively rare. Lethal violence was more likely to come later, as victims driven from their homes came up against natives who were not, like their initial assailants, neighbours or acquaintances. There is also the suggestion that assailants of this latter type were often those Irish living apart from the colonized areas, in forests or on marginal land, as opposed to those in regular contact with settler society.[71] There were also killings on a larger scale, such as the drowning of around 100 prisoners in the River Bann near Portadown in mid-November 1641. Some of these were in retaliation for the actions of British forces, by now beginning to fight back. The Portadown drownings, for example, may have been linked to the first serious defeats inflicted on the Irish when they failed to take Lisburn in three separate attacks during November. The killing near Charlemont in May 1642 of forty prisoners being evacuated from Armagh, likewise, followed the reported slaughter of civilian inhabitants by the Scottish army that had just retaken Newry. In other cases prisoners were killed, singly or in groups, when those to whom they had initially surrendered passed them into the hands of others, likely to see them less as a responsibility and more as a liability or a threat.[72]

How many died in these different types of incident will never be known with any precision. From the end of 1641 the government systematically collected sworn depositions from survivors of the revolt.[73] A modern computation based on the depositions from one county, Armagh, offers both a minimum figure, using only eyewitness accounts and taking the lowest numbers reported in cases of multiple homicides, and a maximum that also includes accounts based on

[71] Nicholas Canny, 'What Really Happened in 1641', in Jane Ohlmeyer (ed.), *Ireland from Independence to Occupation 1641–1660* (Cambridge, 1995), 36.

[72] This summary synthesizes the results of several recent analyses, notably Michael Perceval-Maxwell, 'The Ulster Rising of 1641 and the Depositions', *IHS* 21 (1978), 144–67; Raymond Gillespie, 'Destabilizing Ulster 1641–2' and Hilary Simms, 'Violence in County Armagh, 1641', both in Brian MacCuarta (ed.), *Ulster 1641: Aspects of the Rising* (Belfast, 1993); Canny, *Making Ireland British*, ch. 8; Perceval-Maxwell, *Outbreak of the Irish Rebellion of 1641*, ch. 10.

[73] For the complex origins of the thirty-three volumes of surviving depositions, collected across a decade, see Aidan Clarke, 'The 1641 Depositions', in Peter Fox (ed.), *Treasures of the Library: Trinity College Dublin* (Dublin, 1986), 111–22. For the subsequent use of highly selective extracts to support claims of an attempted general massacre of Protestants see below, Ch. 3. For a survey of the resulting controversy, continuing into the twentieth century, concerning the reliability of the depositions as evidence, see Toby Barnard, '1641: A Bibliographical Essay', in MacCuarta (ed.), *Ulster 1641*. Recent works, such as those cited in n. 72, have in general been willing to use those parts of the depositions drawing on direct personal observation. The extracts used here for illustrative purposes are taken from Hickson's *Ireland in the Seventeenth Century*, compiled with the polemical purpose of demonstrating the scale of what it described as 'the Irish massacres of 1641–2' but providing full and accurate transcriptions of the documents selected. The interpretation follows lines laid down by Perceval-Maxwell and Canny.

hearsay and selects the highest totals suggested for mass killings. The result is a total of somewhere between 527 and 1,259, out of perhaps 3,000 British inhabitants of the county.[74] This is not wildly out of line with the findings of the eighteenth-century clergyman and historian Fernando Warner, who worked through all thirty-three volumes of survivors' depositions to suggest that there was positive evidence of 2,109 killings, with a further 1,919 reported at second hand.[75] To those killed outright it is also necessary to add what may well have been a considerable number who died of exposure after being driven from their homes, frequently completely or nearly naked, and subsequently denied food or shelter as winter closed in.

Victims of robbery and assault presented the attacks they suffered as wholly unexpected, coming from a native population with whom they believed themselves to be living on terms of friendship. A former servant of Sir Phelim O'Neill, examined in 1652, maintained that the English in his district 'lived plentifully and peacefully, and were to this examinant's apprehension well beloved by their neighbours of the Irish'.[76] Specific accounts by settlers of how they were warned of impending dangers, or protected from attack, by acquaintances among the natives confirm that such claims were not simply a retrospective assumption of injured innocence. Moreover it appears that the well-born leaders of the revolt were likewise wholly unprepared for the uncontrolled violence, directed against the settler population, that they unleashed by their call to arms. On Sir Phelim O'Neill's own estate at Caledon in County Tyrone, around Christmas 1641, insurgents inflamed by drink killed at least twenty adults and twelve children from among his tenants and servants. The dead included a woman named Boswell, whom Sir Phelim had brought from England after she had nursed a child of his in London, along with her husband and a three-month-old child of her own, all three stabbed to death in their house. Sir Phelim, enraged, hanged eight or nine of the offenders. The following February he hanged or beheaded another six men for killing the young Lord Caulfield, his trusting dinner party host of the previous October.[77]

[74] Simms, 'Violence in County Armagh', 133. County Armagh contained 6% (747 out of a recorded total of 12,200) of the British males listed in the muster roll of 1630, and 8% (2,400 out of a recorded total of over 30,000) of the British and Irish inhabitants counted in a poll tax return of 1659 (Philip Robinson, *The Plantation of Ulster* (Belfast, 2000), 105, 223). This would suggest a British population in 1641 of 2,400 to 3,200.

[75] Warner's figures were reported in W. E. H. Lecky, *History of Ireland in the Eighteenth Century*, 6 vols. (London, 1892), i. 79. They gained wide currency, through their citation in the somewhat misleading form of a firm figure of 4,000 killed, with another 8,000 dying of hunger or exposure, in *NHI*, iii. 291–2.

[76] Hickson (ed.), *Ireland in the Seventeenth Century*, i. 203.

[77] For Caledon see Simms, 'Violence in County Armagh', 130–1, and Hickson (ed.), *Ireland in the Seventeenth Century*, i. 204–5. For the killers of Lord Caulfield see Dillon (ed.), 'O Meallan Journal', 338.

The reasons for the hostility that came so suddenly to the surface can in part be deduced from the details of what took place. The primary motive of those who first attacked the settlers was clearly to drive them from their houses and lands and to seize their money and possessions. In many cases attackers also sought out and destroyed both the leases giving settlers title to their lands and the bonds and other legal instruments recording debts owed to them by the native Irish. Some of this activity was no doubt opportunistic, motivated by material gain. But plunder was also legitimized by a range of grievances. The architects of the Ulster plantation had not set out systematically to confine the natives to the poorer and more marginal land. Over time, however, the superior economic resources of the settlers, along with the preference of landlords for improving tenants, had ensured that English and Scots came to dominate the most fertile areas, while the natives became their subtenants, labourers, or else occupiers of less profitable ground. Those Irish who were tenants faced the demand for cash rents and other tenurial obligations, not necessarily more onerous than those they had been subject to under their own lords, but nevertheless different. They were also subject to the supervision of a new legal system largely (though not exclusively) administered by the newcomers. To the inequalities directly attributable to the process of plantation, moreover, can be added the natural resentment directed by those disadvantaged for whatever reason towards conspicuously more prosperous newcomers. All of these economic tensions would have been exacerbated by a sharp economic downturn, particularly affecting Ulster, in the period immediately preceding the rising. The harvests in both 1640 and 1641 were poor, the Scottish crisis had severely disrupted trade, and the quartering in centres throughout Ulster of Strafford's new Irish army imposed a severe additional burden on an already impoverished population.

Direct economic motives, possibly combined with a more general resentment of inequality, seem also to have lain behind one of the most frequently noted outrages perpetrated on the settlers, the stripping completely naked of men, women, and children. The stripping, remarkably, seems almost never to have involved any form of sexual molestation. Nor was it intended to inflict shame. Although settlers clearly experienced forced nakedness as degradation, the Gaelic Irish themselves appear at this time to have had a distinctly matter of fact attitude to nudity. Instead it would seem that settlers were stripped to ensure that they concealed nothing, and because clothes were themselves valuable goods. In addition there may have been a desire to dramatize the upheaval taking place, as a formerly privileged group was turned out of doors, conspicuously bereft of all the things that had previously marked out their superior status. The same theme of a world turned upside down was visible in some of the other proceedings reported. In County Down the wife of a rebel leader looted the wardrobe of a local gentleman's wife, then ostentatiously took her place at the head of the table, attired in her new finery. Another female insurgent, the wife of Rory MacMahon, presided over the hanging of an English woman, walking before her with a white rod in her hand 'saying she would be sheriff for that turn'. Elsewhere those involved were reported to have told settlers that 'we have been your slaves all this time, now you shall be ours'.[78]

Other instances dramatized the hostility felt not just towards individual settlers but towards the new order they had brought with them. A number of reports spoke of the wholesale slaughter of English cattle and sheep. The captive Robert Maxwell claimed, though not necessarily from first-hand observation, that in some cases flesh was cut from the living animal, 'letting them there roar . . . so that sometimes a beast would live two or three days together in that torment'. Such unnecessary brutality, and the slaughter of whole herds at once, suggests a desire to erase an alien presence from the landscape, rather than a taste for fresh beef or mutton. In Monaghan a rebel commander, responding to decades of formal and informal proscription of Irish dress, hairstyles, and language, announced a fine to be levied—initially in the name of the king, but later in that of 'the earl of Tyrone'—on all those who spoke English.[79]

The second prominent motive for the violence directed at the settlers was religious hatred. Once again recent events contributed to the explosion. The openly anti-Catholic language both of the Covenanting movement and of the English opposition to Charles I had heightened awareness of religious divisions, and their military and political successes awakened widespread fears of a new wave of repression. The many attacks on Protestant clergy were probably in part fuelled by resentment of their economic exactions: the collection of tithes, the demand for fees as the price of allowing Catholics to resort to their own clergy for baptisms, marriages, and funerals, the well-documented extortions practised through the church courts. But there was also clear evidence of a visceral hatred of Protestantism itself. Protestants, a County Armagh man proclaimed, 'were all devils and served the devil'. When Richard Blayney, MP for County Monaghan, asked for a minister to attend him before he was hanged from a tree, Art MacBrian Savage MacMahon was heard to say: 'Truss him up. He goeth deep enough into hell, he needs no minister to plunge him deeper.' Before his death Blayney had refused an offer to save his life by accepting Catholicism, and similar attempts to persuade or force settlers to convert were reported elsewhere. In other cases violence was directed against the symbols of the settlers' religion, most commonly their bibles. One Fermanagh insurgent seized a clergyman's bible, 'and laying

---

[78] Canny, *Making Ireland British*, 487; Perceval-Maxwell, *Outbreak of the Irish Rebellion of 1641*, 232.

[79] Maxwell's Deposition in Hickson (ed.), *Ireland in the Seventeenth Century*, i. 335. See also, on slaughter of cattle, Perceval-Maxwell, *Outbreak of the Irish Rebellion of 1641*, 232–3. For Mayo see deposition of Thomas Johnson, in Hickson (ed.), *Ireland in the Seventeenth Century*, ii. 5, and for Monaghan Canny, *Making Ireland British*, 486.

the open side in a puddle of water, leaped and stamped on it, saying "A plague on this book, it has bred all this quarrel." '80

The deep religious passions that came to the surface in 1641–2 were also evident in the frequent claims, common to both sides, that what took place was accompanied by supernatural wonders. Among the insurgents the authority of the king's supposed commission was reinforced by that of ancient prophecies, attributed to St Patrick or to St Colmcille, foretelling the liberation of Ireland from its invaders. Rebel soldiers were also widely reported to go into battle carrying religious amulets, and to proclaim that if they died in combat their souls would go straight to heaven. Protestants, for their part, subsequently recalled the signs and wonders—a plague of rats and of a strange kind of worm, a blood-red sky or river—that had preceded the outbreak. Supernatural intervention continued after the event, with widely circulated tales of apparitions haunting the site of Irish atrocities. The most notable was at Portadown, where one account spoke of spirits singing psalms and brandishing swords. Another, more soberly, described a woman, with skin deathly pale, standing upright in the water while repeating the word 'revenge'.[81] Such manifestations are a reminder that the bloody events of 1641 and the years that followed can be understood only in the context of a world in which the supernatural was a constant and demanding presence.

Within the first few days of the rising Sir Phelim O'Neill and his associates, enjoying the advantage of almost complete surprise, were able to establish control of a substantial area, extending from the western side of Lough Erne to the shores of Lough Neagh, and south into the whole of County Monaghan. The composition and organization of the forces with which they achieved this initial success is not wholly clear. The recurrence of familiar names among those directing operations—MacMahons in Monaghan, O'Reillys in Cavan, Maguires in Fermanagh—suggests that members of leading Gaelic families drew on their continuing prestige and authority to mobilize tenants and other followers. This dependence on hastily recruited irregulars would in turn explain the widespread resort to violence of a kind directly contrary to the initially limited political aims of the leadership. There is also the likelihood that O'Neill and his allies were able to acquire a nucleus of trained men by recruiting members of the new Irish army still awaiting transportation out of the kingdom. However settlers' testimonies suggest that these rootless and armed men were in fact particularly prominent in the plunder and indiscriminate violence they endured.

One reason for the early success of the insurgents was their ability to exploit the ethnic division within the settler population. The supposed royal commission

---

[80] Gillespie, 'Destabilizing Ulster', 117; deposition of Henry Steele, 10 Jan. 1642 (in Hickson (ed.), *Ireland in the Seventeenth Century*, i. 213); deposition of Edward Flack, 4 Jan. 1642 (ibid. i. 173).

[81] Gillespie, 'Destabilizing Ulster', 115–19; Raymond Gillespie, *Devoted People: Belief and Religion in Early Modern Ireland* (Manchester, 1997), 110–11.

published by Sir Phelim and Maguire on 4 November authorized the Irish to seize the goods and persons of 'English Protestants', but not of 'our loyal and loving subjects the Scots', and other accounts testified to the same initial insistence that the rising was directed against the English alone. The distinction had some credibility because the king was at this time in Scotland, seeking to rebuild his political base. (The forged commission was in fact dated from Edinburgh, and supposedly bore the great seal of Scotland.) Sir Phelim and his allies may have believed that the visit would in fact lead to some new configuration of forces which would make it impolitic to attack the Ulster Scots in the name of the king. Alternatively they were simply concerned—correctly as it turned out—by the risk of military intervention from a physically adjacent Scotland already mobilized for war and recently victorious against England. Lord Maguire subsequently confirmed that 'there was a fear conceived of the Scots . . . to avoid which danger it was resolved not to meddle with them . . . and to demean ourselves towards them as if they were of ourselves'. The strategy was initially successful. In the early weeks of the rising many Scots reportedly ignored calls to mobilize for defence, refused to assist or shelter English settlers, and even in some cases joined in attacking and plundering English victims. Once again, however, the insurgent leaders proved unable to restrict their followers to the course dictated by political prudence. By mid-November Scots as well as English were being robbed and sometimes killed, destroying any hope, on either side, that they could remain neutral.

The early spread of the insurrection was impressive and, for those settlers engulfed in it, terrifying. But it was also clearly tied to the traditional territorial power base of the Gaelic lords who were its leaders. After their initial successes Sir Phelim and Maguire were still able to mount a drive to the south-east, capturing Armagh on 28 October and Dundalk on the 31st. To the east and west, however, they were now confronted by armed resistance. In Antrim and Down two leading landowners, Viscount Chichester of Carrickfergus and Viscount Montgomery of the Ards, mustered English and Scots for their own defence. On 2 November an Irish attack on Lisburn, the first of three unsuccessful attempts, was defeated. Meanwhile Sir Audley Mervyn joined with the Scot Sir William Stewart to create an armed force which managed to retain a foothold in west Tyrone, and was to stage a counter-offensive during the first half of 1642. Most important of all, in strategic terms, the Irish of Donegal, though some turned out in arms, failed to seize a single important stronghold. Their poor showing, possibly attributable to the particularly weak position in which the chief local dynasty, the O'Donnells, had been left following the plantation, meant that Londonderry too remained in British hands. Over the next few months the English and Scots of the north-west were to organize themselves into what became a formidable fighting force. None of this might have mattered if the Ulster rising had coincided, as planned, with a capture of Dublin. As it was the scene was set for several years of bloody and destructive warfare between settler and native.

THE HILL OF CROFTY

That this outbreak of ethnic and religious hostility in the last weeks of 1641 should have begun in Ulster, where the most Gaelic of Ireland's four provinces had been the scene of the most extensive plantation of British colonists, was hardly surprising. What is striking, however, is the speed with which the Catholic lower classes of other areas responded to news of the northern revolt. Two other counties, Leitrim and Longford, rose at almost the same time as Ulster. In the north Leinster counties of Louth, Meath, and Westmeath there were sporadic attacks on Protestant houses during the last week of October, as well as reports of jubilant celebration at reports from Ulster. By the first days of November there were also widespread disturbances in Wicklow, Wexford, and Carlow. The speed of response this far south has been seen as indicating some degree of coordination with the Ulster and Dublin conspirators; alternatively it may have testified to the continued presence in the mountainous region south of Dublin of cohesive networks of Byrnes, O'Tooles, and Kavanaghs, still unreconciled to the loss of their lands, by plantation and other forms of legal chicanery, over the past two decades.[82] In Connacht two counties, Mayo and Sligo, rose in arms during November. In Mayo, unusually, it was the Catholic bishop, Malachy O'Queely, who summoned his followers to arms, telling them that they were about to be massacred. These counties were also the scenes of probably the two most serious cases of large-scale killing outside Ulster. These were the slaughter on 13 January 1642 of around thirty-eight Protestants who had been consigned, for their supposed protection, to Sligo jail, followed a month later by the massacre of a party of fifty-five Protestant refugees at Shrule on the Mayo–Galway border. In Kilkenny, and in the Munster counties of Tipperary, Waterford, Limerick, and Clare, there were occasional attacks during November. There, however, the real breakdown of authority did not take place until December, by which time the political context had changed, so that what occurred was a gentry-led insurrection rather than a popular revolt.

The character that the revolt assumed as it spread beyond Ulster varied from place to place. Leitrim and Longford had both been planted in the 1620s, and the risings in each case followed the same pattern as in Ulster, with members of the formerly dominant Irish families, O'Rourke and O'Farrell, appearing as leaders while settlers were pillaged and assaulted. In Kilkenny an early target was Castlecomer, where Wandesford had established a substantial English settlement on the lands so dubiously acquired with Wentworth and Ormond's connivance. Elsewhere other grievances came to the fore. A Franciscan friar in County Sligo,

---

[82] Compare Perceval-Maxwell, *Outbreak of the Irish Rebellion of 1641*, 254, and Canny, *Making Ireland British*, 507.

recalling the authoritarian rule of the Elizabethan president of the region, spoke of 'the blood that the Binghams had formerly spilt in the province of Connacht'. In County Mayo insurgents combined the destruction of English breeds of cattle, the symbol of an intrusively improving agriculture, with a grim parody of what were clearly seen as the arbitrary procedures employed in the courts of criminal law. The animals were formally arraigned before a jury, then presented with a book with the words 'legit aut non'. When they did not reply, thus failing the test of literacy that allowed a first offender in certain capital cases to escape hanging by pleading benefit of clergy, they were formally sentenced to death. In King's County women were reported to have exchanged their English cloaks and gowns for 'kerfchiefs, mantles, trousses and all Irish habit'.[83]

In most of the south and south-east, where neither large-scale British settlement nor the forcible imposition of English institutions was an issue to the same extent, popular violence was directed mainly against Protestantism. There were killings, sometimes brutal in character, but apparently not on the same scale as in Ulster. The plundering and stripping of Protestants, on the other hand, was common practice. So too was the destruction or degradation of Protestant religious texts. One witness in Kilkenny town saw bibles and prayer books 'torn in pieces and used as waste paper to wrap up soap, starch, candles, and such wares'. There were also attempts to cajole or terrorize victims into converting to Catholicism. Robert Wadding, a gentleman in County Carlow, was forcibly brought before the priest of his parish, to find him giving absolution to a succession of 'poor English Protestant inhabitants'. The oath he heard administered to each new convert indicates that here, as in Ulster, aspirations to regain local dominance retained the shield of a loyal rebellion:

that they should continue true and faithful subjects to the king of England, and should honour and obey him in all matters temporal, and that they should acknowledge the Holy Church of Rome to be the true church, and the pope of Rome to be supreme head of the church of Ireland, and should honour and obey him in all causes spiritual whatsoever.

Wadding himself was told that if he converted he would recover his lost goods, but 'if not there would be no living in this country for [him], for no Protestants must abide there'.[84]

This last remark should be taken literally. There are clear parallels between some of what was reported in Ireland in 1641 and what took place during similar outbreaks of anti-Protestant violence in sixteenth-century France. In each case what was involved was not mere popular fury, but a ritualized purification of the community by the eradication or expulsion of alien elements. Priests, who

[83] Canny, *Making Ireland British*, 497, 523. For Mayo, see deposition of Thomas Johnson, 14 Jan. 1643 (in Hickson (ed.), *Ireland in the Seventeenth Century*, ii. 5).

[84] Deposition of James Benn, 3 July 1643 (in Hickson (ed.), *Ireland in the Seventeenth Century*, ii. 75); deposition of Robert Wadding, 17 Mar. 1642 (ibid. ii. 50).

in general seem to have sought to prevent the killing of Protestant civilians, actively encouraged the onslaught on both Protestant objects and Protestant souls. The prominent involvement of women alongside men in the most clearly anti-Protestant actions further supports the notion of a community cleansing itself of corruption. The same theme emerges in some of the steps taken to reclaim places of worship. In Ulster the construction of new Protestant churches had been part of the wider building project associated with the plantation. In Munster and Leinster, on the other hand, existing churches had been converted to Protestant worship at the Reformation. When these were now recovered and reconsecrated for Catholic worship, the purification process in some cases extended to the exhumation of Protestant corpses buried in the grounds. At Harristown, in King's County, corpses interred for seven years or more were dug up 'and their bodies and bones thrown into ditches and other base places'. In one case, in Waterford, disinterred bodies may subsequently have been boiled to produce saltpetre for the manufacture of gunpowder.[85]

In both England and Ireland, the emergency created by the Ulster rising quickly widened existing divisions and created new ones. Already on 23 October a proclamation by the lords justices, attributing the attempt on Dublin Castle to 'some ill affected Irish papists', had provoked immediate protest from Catholic spokesmen. A second proclamation on the 29th explained that the term 'Irish Papists' had been intended to refer only to 'the old mere Irish of the province of Ulster' and not to 'the Old English of the Pale'.[86] Yet when leading Palesmen had come forward a few days earlier to request weapons to defend their houses and lands, the lords justices prevaricated, unconvincingly pleading a lack of supplies, despite holding in Dublin Castle the weapons taken up from Strafford's disbanded army. (Later, in mid-November, arms sufficient for 1,700 men were handed out to the gentry of five counties, but 1,000 of these were repossessed less than a fortnight later.) The lords justices also tried unsuccessfully to resist demands that the Irish parliament meet, as scheduled, on 9 November. When it did so, sitting for just two days a week apart, Old English members joined in a declaration condemning the Ulster revolt, but refused to allow those involved to be described as rebels. The ostensible reason was a concern not to jeopardize any peace negotiations by intemperate language, and also, on the part of residents of the Pale, a reluctance to antagonize unduly a force at whose mercy they might shortly find themselves. But Protestant members, and the lords justices, were understandably outraged.

[85] Deposition of Nicholas Walsh of Harristown, 6 Jan. 1642 (in Hickson (ed.), *Ireland in the Seventeenth Century*, ii. 69). For Waterford see Canny, *Making Ireland British*, 515, and for the wider point regarding ritual purification, ibid. 546–50. The same theme is developed in W. J. Smyth, *Map-Making, Landscapes and Memory: A Geography of Colonial and Early Modern Ireland* (Cork, 2006), 126–41.

[86] Both proclamations are printed in John T. Gilbert (ed.), *History of the Irish Confederation and the War in Ireland 1641–1643* (Dublin: privately printed, 1882), i. 226, 228.

On the other side of the Irish Sea a similar atmosphere of mistrust prevailed, as the king's opponents in parliament baulked at giving him control of an armed force on the scale that would be needed for an expedition to Ireland. At the same time dislike of Covenanter extremism led many, in both Lords and Commons, to obstruct the only feasible alternative, an expedition from Scotland. One thousand nine hundred English troops eventually reached Dublin in late February, and a larger body of Scottish troops landed in Ulster by April 1642. Thereafter, however, the more pressing claims of what became the English and Scottish civil wars ensured that Ireland's conflicts would be fought out, for several years, by mainly indigenous forces.

Spokesmen for the Old English were later to claim that the anti-Catholic language of the Dublin administration, and its failure either to protect the Pale or to supply its landowners with the means of self-defence, were part of a deliberate attempt to drive the Old English into rebellion and so create a pretext for the future confiscation of their estates.[87] Any such strategy, however, would have required both a remarkable degree of forward thinking, and an even more remarkable detachment in the face of imminent peril. The initial failure to defend the Pale was not necessarily evidence of malice. In the first weeks of the revolt the lords justices were desperately seeking to bring together units of a regular army only 3,000 strong, from widely dispersed locations, to protect the capital from possible attack. Protestants as well as Catholics complained bitterly of their unwillingness to distribute weapons to outlying areas.[88] Where the initial characterization of the revolt as a papist rebellion is concerned, it is important to remember that what the lords justices were responding to was the information of Owen Connolly. This had concerned, not a rising in defence of the king's prerogative, but a general massacre: 'the Irish had prepared men in all parts of the kingdom to destroy all the English inhabitants there tomorrow morning by 10 of the clock, and that in all the seaports and other towns in the kingdom all the Protestants should be killed this night.'[89] The willingness of the Dublin administration to accept and stick to this interpretation must also be set in the context of contemporary assumptions. Most Protestants, on both sides of the Irish Sea, took it for granted that Catholicism was a malign and powerful force bent on their destruction, and these fears had been energetically

[87] Most recently by Micheál Ó Siochrú, *Confederate Ireland 1642–1649: A Constitutional and Political Analysis* (Dublin, 1999), 24. See also *NHI*, iii. 292. Clarke, *Old English in Ireland*, 230–3, sees it as unlikely that the lords justices would have wanted to make an already dangerous situation worse by driving the Old English into revolt in November 1641, but sees their 'calculated avarice' as an important reason for their refusal to accept surrenders once the military situation had improved.

[88] Robert Armstrong, *Protestant War: The 'British' of Ireland and the Wars of the Three Kingdoms* (Manchester, 2005), 29.

[89] Examination of Owen Connolly, 22 Oct. 1641 (in Hickson (ed.), *Ireland in the Seventeenth Century*, ii. 367–8).

exploited by opponents of Laud and the king during the political crisis of the past three years.

Against this background the attitude of the lords justices to the Old English appears to have been cautious rather than positively hostile. As late as 26 November they wrote to the lord lieutenant that, once they had built up their armed forces, 'many of the old English here may be fit to be put into pay and will doubtless fight well with us . . . however, till we be so strengthened, we cannot judge whom we may trust'. Nor were these suspicions wholly unfounded. Already by the time of this letter the lords justices had received reports that the gentry of County Louth, and the younger sons of the gentry in north County Meath, had begun to cooperate with the rebels.[90] Depositions later taken from Protestant refugees confirm these allegations, indicating that already by mid-November some of the minor gentry of the Pale had begun to support the plundering of Protestant houses. More revealing still, an Irish Franciscan, based in Antwerp but presumably writing on the basis of information from home, observed in February 1642 that some 'greater lords' had initiated the revolt through 'their cousins or brothers, who have little to lose if the main enterprise should miscarry'.[91]

This is not to suggest that the Old English elite welcomed the revolt. The likelihood is that most, like their counterparts in England, were deeply reluctant to challenge the structure of authority under which they lived. But the pressures on them had become intense. Quite apart from the argument that something had to be done to prevent the destruction of the king's prerogative, which alone protected Irish Catholics from the ruthless repression demanded by his Covenanting and Puritan opponents, they now faced the threat both of being overrun by the Ulster insurgents and of being swept away by the increasingly uncontrolled violence of their own tenants and labourers. At the same time their professions of loyalty were already being spurned by a clearly hostile local administration. The turning point came on 29 November, when the lords justices at last sent troops north against the rebels. A force of 600 foot and 50 horse marched to relieve Drogheda, now under siege, only to be ambushed and defeated at Julianstown bridge. Over the next few days the Old English of Louth and Meath held talks with Rory O'More, who reiterated that the rising was in defence of the king's prerogative. These prepared the way for a carefully staged piece of political theatre. At the beginning of December Lord Gormanstown, as governor of County Meath, summoned the nobility and gentry of the county to a meeting on the hill of Crofty (Knockcrofty in Anglicized Irish), where O'More and others appeared at the head of a guard of musketeers, carrying

---

[90] Lords Justices and Council to Leicester, 22, 25, 26 Nov. 1641 (HMC *Ormonde MSS*, NS, ii. 20, 23, 27).

[91] Quoted in Perceval-Maxwell, *Outbreak of the Irish Rebellion of 1641*, 242. For deposition evidence on the start of the Pale disturbances see ibid. 223–5.

weapons captured at Julianstown. Gormanstown demanded to know 'wherefore they came armed into the Pale', allowing O'More to make a pre-prepared speech insisting that they rose to 'vindicate [the king's] rights and prerogatives from the unjust encroachment made upon them by the malignant party of the parliament of England'. Gormanstown reportedly replied that 'Since such and no other are your intentions, we will likewise join with you', leading those present to respond 'with many acclamations and mutual congratulations'. Over the next few weeks he and his fellow magnates set about organizing recruits and supplies to support the army besieging Drogheda. At the same time they also drew up a long petition to the king, dispatched on 19 December, insisting on their continued loyalty.

The Knockcrofty meeting had involved only the landowners of the Pale. But even before it took place the Old English of other regions had begun to place themselves at the head of the rapidly spreading revolt. In Kilkenny Viscount Mountgarret, the leading figure in the earl of Ormond's network of mainly Catholic Butler relatives, had initially raised an armed company to maintain order. At the end of November, however, he took command of the insurgents in the county, joined forces with Butlers and others up in arms in Tipperary, and dispatched men into Counties Limerick and Waterford. In February he marched into Cork, forcing the Munster president, St Leger, to retreat. Soon after the leading Catholic landowner in that county, Sir Donough MacCarthy, Viscount Muskerry, who had earlier denounced the rising, also declared his support.

In making these choices Mountgarret, Muskerry, and others were in part concerned, like their counterparts in the Pale, to restore social order by taking command of a popular movement that otherwise threatened anarchy. Richard Bellings, Mountgarret's son-in-law, later wrote that he acted from 'the apprehensions he had of the height to which the meaner sort of people might grow up against the nobility and gentry'.[92] In addition they had come to believe, like their counterparts in the Pale, that a loyal revolt was indeed the only way to protect themselves and their church from imminent destruction. They were also in part driven to action by the increasingly ruthless actions of crown forces. This had been an issue from the start. The decision of the Palesmen at the beginning of December to turn to the Ulster Irish had been influenced, not just by the defeat at Julianstown, but by a brutal punitive raid into Wicklow by Sir Charles Coote, who had summarily hanged a number of non-combatants under martial law. Soon after a second raid on Santry, just outside the capital, seems to have led directly to a decision by the gentry of north County Dublin, assembled at Swords on 7 December, to take up arms for their own defence. It was in the south, however, that the tactics of crown forces played a possibly decisive role in convincing some. The main culprit was St Leger, who by mid-November was seeking to terrorize Kilkenny and Tipperary into submission by the widespread

---

[92] Quoted Clarke, *Old English in Ireland*, 196.

use of summary execution under martial law. When a group of nobility and gentry protested, he reportedly responded that they were all rebels and that the best of them should be hung. St Leger seems genuinely to have believed that his actions were the best means of preventing the threatened revolt. Later, as the war developed, he was in fact to come under attack from fellow Protestants because 'he sides so much with the Irish'. But the effect of his actions was the opposite of what he intended. Viscount Muskerry, six months later, explained to a Protestant friend that he had joined in the revolt having seen 'such burning and killing of men and women and children, without regard to age or quality, that I expected no safety for myself, having observed as innocent men and well deservers as myself so used'.[93]

There was one further moment at which the drift of the Old English into open revolt could possibly have been prevented. On 20 February 1642 copies arrived of a proclamation from the king himself denouncing all those in arms as rebels and traitors. Meanwhile the siege of Drogheda was proving unsuccessful, and in early March the Irish army retreated as government troops, now reinforced from England, began to push north from Dublin, laying waste the landscape as they went. The Pale, one observer wrote, was 'now all in fire and smoke like the city of Sodom and Gomorrah, as if God did rain down vengeance upon them'.[94] Denied their claim to act as loyal subjects, and deserted by their new allies, some of the Old English began desperately to seek a way out. The lords justices, however, made no attempt to encourage their submission. Instead they treated the small number who, in obedience to the king's proclamation, came forward to offer their submissions as captured prisoners, and subjected one of them, Patrick Barnewall, to torture. When the earl of Castlehaven, an English-born Catholic, brought a message from the Old English leaders seeking to open negotiations, they reprimanded him for associating with rebels. Two months later he was arrested and indicted for treason. A second person unwise enough to act as an intermediary—a Colonel John Read who had come to Ireland to assist in Antrim's proposed invasion of Scotland and then taken a commission in Strafford's army—was likewise imprisoned and tortured.

At this stage the responsibility of the lords justices for pushing the Old English irreversibly into revolt is beyond question. They wrote to the lord lieutenant on 19 March explicitly arguing that the government should not allow those guilty of rebellion to escape the consequences by a timely surrender. To do so would only encourage further such revolts in future, and would prevent the rebuilding of the English and Protestant interest in the kingdom, forcing 'the few British yet left undestroyed' to quit the kingdom. The most extreme interpretation of

---

[93] Quoted in Perceval-Maxwell, *Outbreak of the Irish Rebellion of 1641*, 258. For Mountgarret see also Edwards, *The Ormond Lordship*, 309 ff., and for St Leger David Dickson, *Old World Colony: Cork and South Munster 1630–1830* (Cork, 2005), 31–2, 35.
[94] Quoted in Clarke, *Old English in Ireland*, 206.

their motives, that the rhetoric of 'a full settlement and reformation of this kingdom' concealed a greedy anticipation of the personal gains that might be made from a new round of forfeitures by Catholic proprietors, remains improbably reductionist. Instead, it seems clear, their central concern was that popery, having yet again demonstrated its treasonable and destructive character, should be crushed once and for all, rather than being allowed to fight another day. It was an argument that looked back to the influential work of Sir John Davies, who thirty years earlier had attributed Ireland's long history as a drain on English blood and treasure to the willingness of its governors to accept token submissions rather than reduce the island to real obedience. It also looked forward to the very similar debates that were to follow another Catholic surrender, in 1691.[95]

Although the Old English and their Irish coreligionists were now committed beyond the point where their opponents would allow them to retreat, their alliance had as yet no formal structure. Even after they had joined in the siege of Drogheda, in fact, the Palesmen attempted to keep themselves separate from their new allies, naming Gormanstown as their commander in chief rather than placing themselves under the direction of Sir Phelim O'Neill. But the potentially disastrous consequences of a collapse of government authority could not be ignored for long. In February 1642 the earl of Clanricard opened discussions with the Pale leaders that included proposals for a provisional system of government. Clanricard, a Catholic but one whose future loyalty was to be firmly to the crown rather than his coreligionists, proceeded cautiously, using his chaplain to forward papers attributed to unnamed gentlemen from his region. But his willingness to associate himself in any way with what could be construed as setting up an alternative to the king's government is evidence of the level of alarm that the collapse of social order had created in the Catholic propertied classes. On 22 March a synod of the Catholic clergy of the ecclesiastical province of Armagh, held at Kells in County Meath, issued a declaration warning that the country was moving 'towards anarchy', and calling for a council of ecclesiastics and laymen to maintain law and order. A national meeting of clergy, held at Kilkenny between 11 and 13 May, reaffirmed that Catholics were engaged in a just war to defend the rights of the crown, the liberties of Ireland, and their own lives and fortunes 'against unlawful usurpers, oppressors, and their enemies, chiefly puritans', and called on the nobility and gentry to join them for discussions.[96] A body calling itself 'the lords and gentry of the Confederate Catholics' met at Kilkenny on 7 June, and appointed a supreme council comprising one bishop and ten laymen, which over the next months made arrangements to raise money for the maintenance of the army and ordered the creation of a system of local

---

[95] Lords Justices to Leicester, 19 March 1642 (HMC, *Ormonde MSS*, NS, ii. 95–7). For Davies see Connolly, *Contested Island*, 308–11, and for the debate surrounding the Treaty of Limerick, below, Ch. 5.

[96] Gilbert (ed.), *Irish Confederation*, ii. 34–5.

courts. On 24 October the first of what was to be a series of elected general assemblies met at Kilkenny. By this time the king was openly at war with his English parliament, leaving Irish Catholics to face both the opportunities and the dangers of defining their allegiances in a world about to be turned upside down.

3

A War of Many Parts

RELIGION, KING, OR NATION?

In the early 1670s the Old English lawyer Richard Bellings, former secretary to the Confederate Catholics of Ireland and thus a leading figure in the politics of the 1640s, began work on a history of the period. What he set out to describe was, in his own words,

a war of many parts, carried on under the notion of so many interests, perplexed with such diversity of rents and divisions, among those who seemed to be of a side, as will transmit to posterity observations perhaps as useful, although not so memorable and full, as a war managed with more noise, greater power, and between princes whose very names may bespeak attention for their actions.[1]

This acknowledgement of the extreme complexity of the events of 1641–52 is one that has probably been repeated, either privately or in public, by every historian who has tried to follow Bellings in recounting them. (His other concern, that what took place in so peripheral a location, among persons of limited consequence, might not in fact be worth reconstructing, has, for whatever reason, troubled his modern counterparts much less.) The period saw a bewildering succession of conflicts and alliances between competing parties. Much of what happened can be explained in terms of patterns of behaviour dictated by religious denomination, ethnic origin, or material interest. Some, however, can not. The story of the 1640s is also one of individuals and groups confronted with the inescapable necessity of choice, in a context where past experience provided little guidance, where deeply held notions of religious and political obligation could pull in opposite directions, and where the consequences of miscalculation could be terrifyingly final.

The most coherent and, for the greater part of the period, the most powerful of the different interests active during the 1640s was the body that referred to itself as 'the confederate Catholics of Ireland' but which historians, from the nineteenth century onwards, were to call the Confederation of Kilkenny.[2] The assembly of

---

[1] John T. Gilbert (ed.), *History of the Irish Confederation and the War in Ireland 1641–1643* (Dublin, 1882–91), i .2.

[2] For the origins and implications of the term see the pioneering article by J. C. Beckett, who argues that it misrepresents the intentions of those involved, since they saw themselves as

clergy and laity that met in Kilkenny in October and November 1642 was the first of nine such gatherings held between 1642 and January 1649, meeting for periods of between four and eighteen weeks at a time. Its members comprised the traditional three estates of church, nobility, and commoners. Representation of the clergy followed the practice of the post-Reformation parliament, in including all bishops but not heads of religious houses or orders. The lower clergy, again following parliamentary practice, met simultaneously in a separate assembly, Convocation. The commoners, probably numbering between 200 and 250[3], were either elected, on the existing franchise, by Catholic voters in the counties and parliamentary boroughs, or, in the case of areas outside Confederate control, nominated by the supreme council to represent the relevant constituencies. Meetings generally took place in a house belonging to the wealthy Kilkenny merchant Richard Shee. Members sat as a single chamber, arrayed on three tiers of benches arranged in the great hall, but with peers and bishops grouped at one end and enjoying precedence when they chose to speak.

The representatives thus assembled reflected the wealth and prestige still enjoyed, despite four decades of attrition at the hands of the Stuart monarchy, by the Catholic elite.[4] Of the twenty-eight Catholic holders of Irish peerages, nineteen attended at least one session of the assembly. The non-titled members held between them the equivalent of 7,000 acres of land per person.[5] Around one-fifth of the members of each assembly had previously sat in the Irish parliament.

creating an association of individuals bound by oath to pursue common objectives, rather than a federation of groups or territorial units ('The Confederation of Kilkenny Revisited', in J. C. Beckett, *Confrontations: Studies in Irish History* (London, 1972), 48–52). The most important modern accounts of the politics of the Confederate Catholics are Micheál Ó Siochrú, *Confederate Ireland 1642–1649: A Constitutional and Political Analysis* (Dublin, 1999), and Tadhg Ó hAnnracháin, *Catholic Reformation in Ireland: The Mission of Rinuccini 1645–1649* (Cambridge, 2002). The fullest accounts of the British, Protestant, and royalist forces are Robert Armstrong, *Protestant War: The 'British' of Ireland and the Wars of the Three Kingdoms* (Manchester, 2005); David Stevenson, *Scottish Covenanters and Irish Confederates* (Belfast, 1981); Patrick Little, *Lord Broghill and the Cromwellian Union with Ireland and Scotland* (Woodbridge, 2004), ch. 2. There are also two useful collections of essays: Micheál Ó Siochrú (ed.), *Kingdoms in Crisis: Ireland in the 1640s* (Dublin, 2001); Jane Ohlmeyer (ed.), *Ireland from Independence to Occupation 1641–60* (Cambridge, 1995). The military history of the war is covered in Pádraig Lenihan, *Confederate Catholics at War 1641–49* (Cork, 2001) and Martyn Bennett, *The Civil Wars in Britain and Ireland 1638–1651* (Oxford, 1997).

   [3] Since surviving lists seem to include observers as well as members, there is no clear indication of the number of elected representatives in any assembly. (See Ó Siochrú, *Confederate Ireland*, 210.) If the supreme council arranged for the nomination of representatives for all parliamentary constituencies outside its control, there would have been around 250 commoners, but it is possible that they did not in fact do so in all cases.

   [4] Information on the composition of general assemblies is taken from Ó Siochrú, *Confederate Ireland*, 208–17, supplemented in the case of former members of the Irish parliament by Bríd McGrath, 'Parliament Men and the Confederate Association', in Ó Siochrú (ed.), *Kingdoms in Crisis*, 90–105.

   [5] Ó hAnnracháin, *Catholic Reformation in Ireland*, 25, quoting unpublished research by D. F. Cregan.

Merchant wealth was also represented, rather better in fact than it had been in parliament, with members of leading families from Old English strongholds such as Galway, Limerick, Waterford, and of course Kilkenny, all regularly listed as participating. Around a fifth of all members had spent time at one of the English inns of court. Most would have done so, not as a professional qualification, but as part of their preparation for the life of a gentleman and landowner. However the small group of practising lawyers in the assembly exercised a disproportionate influence over its proceedings. This was particularly so when legal expertise was combined with experience in parliament. Such was the case with Patrick Darcy, who had initially condemned the Ulster rising, but had subsequently joined in creating a provisional Catholic administration in his native town of Galway, before joining the assembly, where he fulfilled the functions first of lord chancellor and then of judge. A second prominent lawyer was Nicholas Plunkett, who had sat as MP for County Meath in 1634 and 1640–1, and had served on the delegation of thirteen that went to lay the grievances of parliament in general, and of Catholics in particular, before Charles I in late 1640.

The domination of successive assemblies by landowners, merchants, and lawyers was clearly reflected in their geographical and ethnic composition. Membership was overwhelmingly drawn from the Old English strongholds of the south and east, with almost half of those who can be identified as having sat in one or more general assemblies coming from Leinster and just below one-third from Munster.[6] Connacht's low share of representation was the same as in the parliament of 1640–1, reflecting the province's meagre allocation of parliamentary boroughs. Ulster's poor showing, with only one-tenth of assembly members as compared to over a quarter of parliamentary seats in 1641, cannot be attributed to the occupation of the greater part of the province by Protestant forces, since the supreme council nominated representatives for constituencies in these and other occupied areas, and large numbers of Ulstermen were based in Confederate territory. Instead it seems clear that the Leinster and Munster elite consolidated their dominance by filling these seats with natives of their own provinces. Their preferences also affected the ethnic balance of the assembly. Surname evidence suggests that just over one-fifth of members of the assembly were of Gaelic Irish descent, a better showing than their representation in the parliament of 1640–1, but still reflecting the balance of property rather than numbers within the Catholic population as a whole.

Having assembled at Kilkenny in October 1642, the first general assembly quickly produced a framework for the interim government of the country. Catholics throughout the kingdom were to be required, on pain of excommunication, to take an oath of association, solemnly administered at churches after the taking of confession and communion. By this they swore to defend the 'just prerogatives,

---

[6] The exact figures are: Leinster 47%, Munster 32%, Connacht 11%, Ulster 10%: Ó Siochrú, *Confederate Ireland*, 210.

estates and rights' of the king and his successors, the rights of the Irish parliament, the fundamental laws of the kingdom, and the free exercise of the Catholic faith, while at the same time pledging obedience to the supreme council.[7] As a national executive the first assembly elected a supreme council of twenty-four, comprising six members from each province, entrusted with control of both military and civil affairs. Thereafter each assembly elected a new council, whose mandate ran until the next assembly convened. To finance this administrative system, along with four provincial armies, the Confederates appropriated the rents due from crown lands, as well as from the estates of those they categorized as enemies, and also levied their own taxes. In 1642, despite objections to so obvious an encroachment on the royal prerogative, they minted and distributed some £4,000 worth of coin. They also appropriated another traditional monopoly of government by operating printing presses at Waterford and Kilkenny. Between 1642 and 1649 these produced a total of sixty-eight items, including books and pamphlets as well as proclamations and orders issued on the authority of the assembly or supreme council.[8]

The main impetus towards the creation of a formal association had been the fears aroused, among the Catholic clergy and the propertied classes, by the widespread collapse of order. An early enactment of the first general assembly required that all lands seized since 1 October 1641 should be returned to their owners or—in the case of property owned by neutrals or enemies—handed over to the Supreme Council. Another stated clearly that the law to be observed was the common law of England, along with those statutes in force in the kingdom that were not prejudicial to the Catholic religion or the liberties of its natives. The provisions for local government also laid a heavy emphasis on law and order. County councils, comprising one or two members chosen from each barony, were among other things to discharge the functions formerly entrusted to the justices of the peace. Provincial councils, with two representatives from each county, were to meet a minimum of four times a year to review the proceedings of the county bodies, and were also to take over the criminal business normally handled at assizes. Each county was likewise to have a sheriff, coroner, constables, and jailers. Most revealing of all, the high sheriff of each county was to have the powers of a provost marshal, entitling him summarily to execute 'a layman not worth five pounds, and none other'.[9]

The structures created by the Confederate Catholics thus represented an ambitious attempt to duplicate many of the functions of both central and local

---

[7] For different versions of the oath, see Ó Siochrú, *Confederate Ireland*, 90 n. 16. The text quoted here is that given in *NHI*, iii. 298, from the memoirs of the earl of Clanricard.

[8] Jane Ohlmeyer, 'Introduction: For God, King or Country?', in Ohlmeyer (ed.), *Political Thought in Seventeenth-Century Ireland* (Cambridge, 2000). Ohlmeyer also counts in her total twenty-four publications issued from Cork during the period of Inchiquin's return to the royalist side (1648–50).

[9] Gilbert (ed.), *Irish Confederation*, ii. 78.

government. One hostile contemporary, indeed, believed that the Confederacy encumbered itself with an excessive level of bureaucracy, supporting a 'world of clerks and attorneys, a set number of commissioners in every county, receivers and applotters'.[10] The subsequent destruction of what appear at one time to have been detailed administrative records makes it impossible to reconstruct in any detail how Confederate government worked in practice. However fragmentary evidence from Wexford and other Leinster counties indicates that there at least the Confederates did in fact succeed in creating an effective machinery of local government, from county councils down to parish constables, and in collecting excise duties and a poll tax levied on the authority of the supreme council. In Connacht, on the other hand, only one county, Roscommon, recorded any tax revenues. The failure of Confederate administrative structures to take root elsewhere in the province can in part be explained by the refusal of the regional magnate, the earl of Clanricard, to join the Confederacy, and by the reluctance of the Confederates to force the issue by encroaching on what he regarded as his territory. But lesser Connacht landowners also seem to have taken a more independent path than their counterparts elsewhere. In 1644 Miles Bourke, Viscount Mayo, grandson of the legendary Grace O'Malley, resentful at not having been given command of the provincial army, broke with the Kilkenny assembly and took possession of castles in County Mayo on his own account, until put under arrest by Confederate forces. Tadhg O'Connor Sligo, excluded from participation in Confederate affairs because of his part in the massacre of Protestants in Sligo jail in 1642, may have given covert assistance to Protestant forces. The ability of such figures to steer a variety of independent courses reflects the still limited reach of government of any kind in those areas furthest from its control.

The Confederate Catholics were aware of the contradiction between their profession of loyalty to the crown and their actions in taking over so many of the functions of government. The decision to have the general assembly meet as a single body, rather than in separate houses of clergy, nobility, and commoners, was a deliberate attempt to head off the charge of setting themselves up as a parliament. (Significantly their concern was not at the potential offence to parliament itself, but at seeming to meet as such without the king's warrant.[11]) For the same reason the 'prolocutor' who acted as chairman at the assembly's proceedings was addressed consistently by his name, rather than as 'speaker' or by any other formal title. But such gestures could do little to blur the reality of an assembly claiming the legitimacy normally attached to a parliament, and taking over much of the traditional role of the king's

---

[10] Quoted in Bennett, *Civil Wars*, 197–8. For regional variations in the effectiveness of local government structures see W. J. Smyth, *Map-Making, Landscapes and Memory: A Geography of Colonial and Early Modern Ireland* (Cork, 2006), 147–8.

[11] See the comments of Belling in Gilbert (ed.), *Irish Confederation*, i. 111–12.

government. In their own defence, the Confederate Catholics pleaded necessity: because their enemies, 'the malignant party', controlled the seat of government at Dublin, the general assembly proclaimed in October 1642, they were forced to deviate in some respects from the English law they were committed to upholding, while nevertheless retaining as much as possible of its essence. But this was to acknowledge the central contradiction in their stance as conservative revolutionaries: the more they sought to replicate the familiar forms of law and government, the further they went in taking over functions that were clearly the preserve of the crown and its officers.

The area where the claim to loyalty and the necessities of self-preservation came most clearly into conflict was in the mobilization of military force. Accounts of armed encounters in the first months after 1641 indicate that the insurgents remained in many cases a loosely organized throng, armed with whatever weapons they had been able to seize or improvise. When Sir Phelim O'Neill, in April 1642, organized an 'army' to defend Tyrone and Londonderry, this was not a standing force, but a quota of armed men to be called out if attack threatened. By the end of the year, however, the general assembly had made provision for four provincial armies. That for Connacht, again due to Clanricard's stance, was never organized on a permanent basis. But the Ulster, Leinster, and Munster armies rose to a peak strength, in summer 1646, of around 25,000 men. In creating these forces the Confederates were able to call on the expertise of returning members of the Irish military diaspora. Two senior commanders from the Irish regiments in Spanish service, Thomas Preston and Owen Roe O'Neill, took command of the Leinster and Ulster armies respectively. The first commander of the Munster army, likewise, was Garret Barry, retired from the Spanish service and author of a handbook on military discipline published in 1634. In all some 1,000 veterans released from Irish regiments in the Spanish and French armies made their way back to Ireland to join the Confederate cause. This injection of professional expertise made it possible quickly to transform the much larger number of local recruits into a disciplined army, trained in the conventional battlefield tactics of the day: squares of pikemen moving forward in formation, while ranks of musketeers performed the complex manoeuvre known as the countermarch to deliver their volleys in succession.

The military achievements of the Confederate forces should not be overstated. The creation of four provincial armies rather than a single force was a capitulation to the continued primacy of local over national loyalties. Lack of resources meant that pikes continued to equal or outnumber guns in most Confederate regiments, at a time when the approved ratio was moving towards two firearms for every pike. Assessment of the pikes themselves vary: the small, light pike head issued to Confederate troops was said to have more penetrative power than the broader blade used by other forces, but it lacked the protective metal socket that prevented the whole metal fixture being lopped off from the shaft during combat. Most important of all, perhaps, Confederate forces were seriously deficient in cavalry, and the battlefield experience of their leading commanders, gained in a Flanders theatre dominated by infantry, left them ill prepared to make effective use of what horsemen they had.[12]

These deficiencies help to explain why the Confederates lost five of the six major battles in which they took part between 1642 and 1647. But it is nevertheless the case that in the sixth, at Benburb, O'Neill's northern army was able decisively to cancel out the memory of Kinsale, by defeating a force of Scottish veterans in a conventional battlefield confrontation.[13] Over time Confederate armies, particularly in Leinster, acquired a variety of pieces of artillery, mainly captured (though there were also some experiments with casting their own cannon). They also built up a formidable force at sea. As well as some vessels that had accompanied Owen Roe and other returning veterans, and a flotilla of six ships owned by the earl of Antrim, the Confederates offered credentials ('letters of marque') to a variety of privateers, both Irish and foreign. In all this created a fleet of forty to fifty ships, becoming in effect the navy of Catholic Ireland.[14]

In addition to acquiring an army and navy, Confederate Ireland also conducted its own diplomatic affairs. Agents, mainly continentally trained members of religious orders, represented their cause at European courts, reinforced by specialized missions headed by Catholic grandees like the earl of Antrim and expert negotiators like Nicholas Plunkett. The route to recognition was not an easy one. Even Spain, in the past the sponsor of Irish revolt against English rule, baulked at according full ambassadorial status to the agents of a regime set up in opposition to a legitimate monarch. By the same token the representatives that France and Spain eventually sent to Kilkenny were residents or envoys rather than ambassadors. Despite these handicaps Confederate diplomats were able to engage the attention of both France and Spain, whose rivalry forced both powers to take seriously the possibility that the other would gain a foothold to the west of an England itself open to foreign intervention at a time of civil war. Since all of the powers concerned were already overstretched in other theatres of conflict, however, the practical gains of successful diplomacy were relatively meagre: a

---

[12] Padraig Lenihan, '"Celtic" Warfare in the 1640s', in John Young (ed.), *Celtic Dimensions of the British Civil Wars* (Edinburgh, 1997), 134–5.

[13] The other five battles were Kilrush (15 Apr. 1642), Ballinvegga or Old Ross (18 Mar. 1643), Liscarroll, County Cork (25 Aug. 1642), Dungan's Hill (8 Aug. 1647), Knocknanuss (13 Nov. 1647). For Kinsale, representing the failure of an earlier attempt to introduce modern military methods to Ireland, see Connolly, *Contested Island*, 250–2.

[14] The main source for Confederate military operations is Lenihan, *Confederate Catholics at War*. For the more positive account of the Irish pike see G. A. Hayes-McCoy, *Irish Battles* (Belfast, 1990), 194. See also Rolf Loeber and Geoffrey Parker, 'The Military Revolution in Seventeenth-Century Ireland', in Ohlmeyer (ed.), *Ireland from Independence to Occupation*, 66–88, which among other things discusses privateering (pp. 86–7). Lenihan (p. 177) makes two important qualifications to the idea of a Confederate navy: the ships involved, frigates rather than men of war, were of limited use in real naval operations, and the captains were in any case more interested in plunder than in forming part of a regular fighting force.

total of around £70,000 in financial assistance, of which over three-quarters came from the papacy, along with access to arms, ammunition, and shipping. Both supplies and money, moreover, had to be paid for, in the cheapest currency of the 1640s, human lives. Between 1644 and 1649 the Confederates, in exchange, raised and exported no less than 7,000 men for the French army, and a further 4,000 for Spain.[15]

The motto of the Confederate Catholics was 'Hiberni Unanimes pro Deo Rege et Patria' ['Irishmen of one mind for God, King and Country']. The words appeared on the seal used by the Kilkenny assembly, surrounding a harp and crown arranged on either side of a cross.[16] Their insistence on a continuing loyalty to the Stuart monarchy became if anything more insistent as they moved further down the path of taking the government of a large part of the island into their own hands. By 1647 copies had arrived in Ireland of a book *Disputatio apologetica*, published two years before by Conor O'Mahony, an Irish Jesuit resident in Portugal. In a reading of Irish history radically different from that of Geoffrey Keating, he argued that the twelfth-century English conquest of Ireland had been an illegitimate intrusion, and that the native population had continuously contested English claims to sovereignty. Citing contemporary theologians on the right of a people to depose a heretical ruler, he called on the Irish to chose a new monarch from among themselves. (He also, in a bizarre endorsement of some of the wildest claims of recent Protestant propaganda, congratulated them on having already killed 150,000 heretics, and urged them to complete the task of extermination.[17]) O'Mahony's book was thus a classic expression of the militant ideology of faith and fatherland that had taken shape among the expatriate Irish over the previous half-century. The supreme council, however, accorded it the standard treatment for works of heresy or treason, by having the official executioner publicly burn the book in Kilkenny, and ordering all those in possession of copies to surrender them. In doing so it continued the stance of loyal subjects armed in self-defence earlier adopted, first by Sir Phelim O'Neill and his confederates, and then by the lords of the Pale.

Adherence to the king was to be combined with the defence of the Catholic church. Nearly two decades earlier, when Catholic representatives had sought to negotiate the Graces, the object of the proposed bargain had been toleration, or more exactly connivance. The decrees issued at the opening of the first general assembly, on the other hand, began with a ringing declaration that 'the Roman

---

[15] Jane Ohlmeyer, 'Ireland Independent: Confederate Foreign Policy and International Relations during the Mid-Seventeenth Century', in Ohlmeyer (ed.), *Ireland from Independence to Occupation*, 107.

[16] The seal and motto are discussed in a letter to *History Ireland* (Autumn 1994), 9.

[17] O'Mahony's text is analysed in Tadhg Ó hAnnracháin, ' "Though Hereticks and Politicians Should Misinterpret their Goode Zeal": Political Ideology and Catholicism in Early Modern Ireland', in Jane Ohlmeyer (ed.), *Political Thought in Seventeenth-Century Ireland* (Cambridge, 2000), 159–67.

Catholic church in Ireland' was to enjoy all the privileges granted by charter to the churches of England and Ireland in the reign of Henry III (1216–72). Theoretically this meant a repudiation of all that had been done in the course of the Protestant Reformation, and indeed of earlier measures, such as the mid-fourteenth-century statutes of praemunire, by which the rulers of medieval England had sought to restrict the power of the papacy within their dominions. What the assembly had given, however, it went on largely to take away. A later decree approved the transfer into Catholic hands of the church buildings and other property currently occupied by the Church of Ireland. But it also laid down that the administration of two-thirds of the revenue from such assets was to be taken over by laymen, and devoted to the upkeep of the Confederate armies. Equally important, tithe revenues and former church lands now in the hands of Catholic laymen were to be retained by them pending a settlement in parliament at some future date. The assembly thus asserted a principle of lay control of ecclesiastical assets of which Henry VIII would have been proud. Its members also showed themselves to be no more ready than Queen Mary's loyally Catholic parliament had been to reverse the huge transfer of ecclesiastical property into lay hands that had taken place at the Reformation.[18]

The issue of church lands was subsequently to create divisions between clerical and lay members of the Confederacy. More immediately, the commitment to restoring the rights and privileges of the Catholic church enormously complicated the efforts of the Confederates to present themselves as loyal subjects of the crown. Charles I had been willing, under duress, to suspend the more irksome penal statutes affecting his Catholic subjects. He was not prepared to see Catholicism take over the status of the established church in Ireland. To have done so would have been repugnant to his personal principles, and probably fatal to his chances of reasserting his authority in England and Scotland. Throughout the 1640s his unwillingness or inability to yield on this point was repeatedly to frustrate what would otherwise have been the obvious strategy of a Confederate–royalist alliance against their common enemies, the parliamentarians and Scots.

The decision of the Confederate Catholics to pitch their demands for their church at what proved to be an unattainable level has traditionally been attributed to the influence of the papal nuncio, Archbishop Giovanni Battista Rinuccini, who arrived in Ireland in November 1645. Rinuccini, a highly effective pastoral reformer in his Italian diocese of Fermo, was indeed a representative of the revived and assertive Catholicism of the Counter-Reformation. Recent work, however, makes clear that his contribution to Confederate politics was primarily to give leadership to an episcopate already committed to the same ambitious goals. All of the bishops serving in Ireland during the 1640s had been educated at seminaries in Catholic Europe. There they had absorbed, not just a political theory unfavourable to anything less than unrestricted ecclesiastical jurisdiction,

18 Connolly, *Contested Island*, 186.

but a new set of pastoral aspirations. In both respects they had found the realities of life in Charles I's Ireland deeply frustrating. Wentworth had quietly ignored routine Catholic worship. But he had not been prepared to tolerate anything suggesting the existence of an ecclesiastical jurisdiction independent of the king or rivalling that of the established church. Nor was he prepared to permit any exercise within Ireland of an authority derived from the pope. Hence bishops who organized diocesan or provincial synods, penalized unsatisfactory clerical subordinates, imposed sentences of excommunication on offenders of any kind, or even ordained priests, risked provoking arrest and imprisonment. Meanwhile shortage of money and other resources made it impossible to meet central Counter-Reformation goals such as the provision of schools, and the encouragement of popular devotion by a suitably impressive level of display in public worship. It was against this background that the majority of Irish bishops joined with the nuncio in demanding a formal recognition by the state of its jurisdiction over clergy and laity alike. They must have power, as they told a horrified earl of Ormond in 1644, to 'instruct, correct, and govern with impunity'.[19]

The third element in the motto of the Confederate Catholics, their commitment to 'patria', also played a part in negotiations with the king. Concern at the possibility that a hostile English parliament might claim the right to interfere in domestic Irish affairs, and in particular in religious policy, had been an important influence pushing Catholics down the road that led to their assembly at Kilkenny. In March 1642 the fear became a reality when the English parliament passed what came to be known as the Adventurers' act, inviting supporters to subscribe towards the cost of the war in Ireland in exchange for future grants of land there. The obvious risk, for investors, was that the war might end on terms that ruled out the large-scale confiscations of rebel estates from which these grants were to be made; some may have remembered the restoration of Tyrone in 1603. Accordingly the act reserved to parliament the right to decide when the rebellion was held to have ended, and also declared invalid any pardons granted by the crown without its consent.

If the Catholic landowning classes had already been alarmed at the possibility of the English parliament assuming control of Irish affairs, this particular assertion of legislative authority made resistance to its claims a matter of survival. One immediate result was the appearance in 1643 of a published version, printed in Waterford, of Darcy's *Argument* of two years earlier, reaffirming Ireland's claim to be a kingdom governed by its own laws.[20] In negotiations with the king the

---

[19] Quoted by Tadhg Ó hAnnracháin, 'Rebels and Confederates: The Stance of the Irish Clergy in the 1640s', in Young (ed.), *Celtic Dimensions of the British Civil Wars*, 105. For the wider reappraisal of Rinuccini's role, and of the formative influence on the Irish bishops and clergy of their pre-1641 experience, see Ó hAnnracháin, *Catholic Reformation in Ireland*, ch. 2.

[20] A second document from this period, a manuscript 'Declaration' making a more explicit case for Irish legislative independence, has likewise been attributed to Darcy, but has now been

Confederates consistently pressed for a repudiation of the Adventurers' act, as well as for a promise that he would give his assent to a formal declaration by the Irish parliament of its exclusive right to legislate for Ireland. They also raised the question of Poynings's Law.[21] Here too the concern with constitutional issues had a practical basis: a comprehensive settlement of Catholic demands, involving issues of property and ecclesiastical jurisdiction, would have to be implemented through one or more acts of parliament, and there were fears that the roundabout legislative procedure required by the statute could be used to obstruct or amend the bills concerned. Confederate negotiators initially demanded a review of the act itself. When Charles proved reluctant, they settled for a demand, again repeatedly rejected by the royalist side, that the specific legislation confirming any treaty should be exempted from its provisions.

The menace arising from the unprecedented challenge to the king's position in his Scottish and English kingdoms thus required the Catholic elite to think in a new way about the formal constitutional status of Ireland. But what wider concept of 'patria' or 'country' informed the mobilization of 1642 and after? At the heart of the Confederacy was an alliance of the Old English and Gaelic Irish. Bellings, writing thirty years later, presented the meeting on the Hill of Crofty as a historic turning point: '. . . distrust, aversion, force, and fear united the two parties which since the conquest had at all times been most opposite.'[22] The decrees of the first Kilkenny assembly included an injunction that no distinction was to be made, on pain of 'the highest punishment', 'betwixt old Irish, and old and new English, or betwixt septs or families, or betwixt citizens and townsmen and countrymen'. However this affirmation of a shared Irishness must be read side by side with the article immediately preceding. This provided that—'for the avoiding of national distinctions between the subjects of his Majesty's dominions, which this assembly doth utterly detest and abhor'—any English, Welsh, or Scottish Catholic who chose to settle in Ireland was to enjoy the same rights and protection as a native, and to be exempted from one-third of the taxes levied for the maintenance of 'this holy war'. Another clause laid down that members of the Confederacy were not to characterize their opponents as English or even Protestant. Instead they were to call them 'by the names of puritanical or malignant party'. If the Confederate Catholics can be seen as articulating a new ideal of an inclusive Irishness, based on birth rather than ancestry, in other words, they asserted it within the context of a wider commitment to the concept of a multiplicity of nations united under a single crown.[23]

---

convincingly ascribed to the royalist lord chancellor Sir Richard Bolton. See Patrick Kelly, 'Sir Richard Bolton and the Authorship of "A Declaration Setting Forth . . ."', *IHS* 35 (2006), 1–16.

[21] See above, Ch. 2 n. 48.   [22] Gilbert (ed.), *Irish Confederation*, i. 36–8.

[23] Ibid., ii. 79–80, 84. For the argument that the Confederates articulated a new sense of Irishness see in particular Ó Siochrú, who suggests that out of the Kilkenny assembly there emerged 'the genesis of modern Irish nationalism' (*Confederate Ireland*, 11, 238–41).

The high-flown rhetoric with which Bellings celebrated the coming together of the Pale and Ulster leaders was an exaggeration. The two groups were already well connected by marriage and other ties. Rory O'More, for example, was married to a daughter of the leading Pale spokesman Patrick Barnewall, while his co-conspirator Lord Maguire was married to one of the Flemings of County Meath. In the same way Donough MacCarthy, Viscount Muskerry, the leading Gaelic magnate in the south-west, was well integrated into both Old and New English society. Through his marriage to Eleanor Butler, sister of the earl of Ormond, he had connections with the extensive and still predominantly Catholic Butler network. He received word of the outbreak of the insurrection while at a dinner party that included the New English earl of Cork and his son Lord Broghill, and the Old English but Protestant earl of Barrymore. Lower down the social scale, on the other hand, long-standing ethnic animosities had by no means disappeared. A son of Bishop Bedell, held prisoner by the Ulster rebels, claimed to have heard them repeatedly express their dislike of the Palesmen fighting alongside them, the 'churls with the great britches' whose throats they would cheerfully cut once they had got rid of 'the other English . . . for you are all of one race with them'.[24] In later years, when the Ulster army was quartered mainly in the south, its presence provoked repeated, sometimes violent, demonstrations that made clear that this animosity was fully reciprocated.

A further threat to Confederate unity came from the return to Ireland of leading figures from the continental diaspora. Of the two senior commanders who returned from the Spanish service, Thomas Preston, younger brother of Viscount Gormanstown, one of the leading noblemen of the Pale, had always insisted on his continued loyalty to the English crown. Owen Roe O'Neill, on the other hand, had actively plotted for a Spanish invasion of Ireland. In the transformed circumstances of three Stuart kingdoms plunged into civil war, he and others accepted in principle that the best means of furthering the interests of Gaelic and Catholic Ireland was no longer through foreign intervention to separate Ireland from England, but rather through the Confederate strategy of an alliance, on favourable terms, with a beleaguered king. But their commitment to that alliance remained pragmatic and contingent. There was also a clear potential for conflict between men like Preston, whose families retained a substantial stake, even if now under threat, in the existing social order, and those whose only hope of improving their position lay in a radical revision of the land settlements of the past six decades. In many cases, as here, the division between those with and without a position to defend was also one between Old English and Gaelic Ireland. But ethnic divisions did not necessarily play a part. One of those most discomfited by Owen Roe's return, in fact, was his cousin Sir Phelim, who had his own ambitions to head the O'Neill dynasty. Their contest for primacy led

---

[24] Deposition of Ambrose Bedell, 26 Oct. 1642 (Mary Hickson (ed.), *Ireland in the Seventeenth Century* (London, 1884), i. 220).

Sir Phelim to seek an alliance with Preston, whose daughter he married, and also put the two cousins on opposite sides in the brief civil war that divided the Confederate Catholics in 1648.

The chief opponent faced by the Confederate Catholics, in the early stages of the war, was the Scottish army in the north-east. The use of troops from Scotland to crush a rebellion initially centred on Ulster made sense in geographical terms. It was in any case the only feasible response from the other side of the Irish Sea, given the deadlock between a king unwilling to part with his military prerogatives and an English parliament determined not to trust him with an army. Negotiations began in January 1642, and a treaty signed on 7 July provided for the dispatch to Ireland of 6,000 musketeers and 4,000 pikemen, to be paid by the English parliament. An advance party of 2,896 men landed at Carrickfergus on 15 April. By early August the force had grown to 1,119 officers and 10,042 men. Preference had been given in recruitment to men with experience of the recent successful invasion of northern England. The commander in the field was Robert Monro, who had served with a Scottish regiment in the Swedish army between 1626 and 1633. Superior training and discipline allowed his men quickly to establish themselves. They captured Newry at the beginning of May, and by June had established control of Counties Antrim and Down. By the autumn, working in tandem with English and Scottish forces in the west, they had driven Confederate forces out of most of Ulster. Thereafter, however, this large and professionally led force, stiffened by a veteran element, never realized its potential. One reason was the repeated failure of the English parliament to provide more than a small proportion of the money promised for its support. The main constraint, however, was the outbreak in August 1642 of civil war between king and parliament in England. The Covenanting leadership in Edinburgh, though initially neutral, now became reluctant either to risk such a potentially valuable military resource in ambitious expeditions within Ireland, or to allow it to move to locations in which it might be difficult to recall for service at home. In July 1644 Monro, responding to a threatened build-up of Confederate troops, led an expedition as far south as County Meath, where he burned the towns of Kells and Navan. Otherwise, however, he confined himself to maintaining his control of east and central Ulster.

The second major political and military force confronting the Confederate Catholics was the indigenous British and Protestant interest. On the east coast the retreat of the Irish army besieging Drogheda left the regular army, reinforced by 3,000 English troops landed in March 1642, in control of an area roughly corresponding to the old Pale, extending from south of Dublin to County Louth. In Antrim and Down, the forces raised among local settlers by Chichester and Montgomery cooperated with Monro's Scots, but regarded themselves as a separate body answering to the Dublin administration. In the north-west, meanwhile, settler forces from Tyrone, Donegal, and Londonderry had come together as what came to be known as the Laggan army, initially under the command of two brothers, Sir William and Sir Robert Stewart, both veterans of Swedish service in the Thirty Years War.[25] Here, as in Antrim and Down, Scots and English settlers joined forces against the common enemy, the short-lived attempt to divide them forgotten. Contemporaries, in a significant change in ethnic terminology, referred to the 'British' forces in Ulster. In Munster royal forces led by Sir William St Leger held Cork, Youghal, and an area of surrounding territory. After St Leger's death in July 1642 command passed to Murrough O'Brien, Baron Inchiquin. Inchiquin, born into a cadet branch of one of the great dynasties of Gaelic Munster, was, like Ormond, a product of the recent strategy of conversion by wardships. Inheriting at the age of about 10 he had been brought up under the guardianship of St Leger, whose daughter he later married, and had been educated as a Protestant. He was now to prove a formidable military commander, coming to be known among the Irish as Murchadh na dTóiteán, 'Murrough of the Burnings', for his ruthlessness in wasting disputed countryside.

Overall control of these government forces lay with the earl of Ormond, whom the lords justices, Sir William Parsons and Sir John Borlase, had reappointed as commander of the army following the outbreak of rebellion. In September 1642 the king gave Ormond a new commission, making him directly responsible to himself rather than to the Dublin administration. By this time Charles was openly at war with his opponents in England. In October the English parliament sent two commissioners to Dublin to solicit support. They received open encouragement from Parsons, who sponsored their admission to meetings of the Irish privy council. However Ormond, by now promoted to the rank of marquis and increasingly the king's most trusted Irish servant, organized a declaration of loyalty to the king from the officers under his command. In March the king appointed a royalist, Sir Henry Tichbourn, to replace Parsons as lord justice. In August he ordered his arrest, along with that of Sir John Temple, the master of the rolls, and two other privy counsellors openly sympathetic to the parliamentary cause. In November Charles completed the transfer of power by making Ormond his lord lieutenant.

With this promotion the former pliant instrument of the earl of Strafford emerged as a significant figure in his own right. For the next decade he was to be the acknowledged head of the royalist interest in Ireland. As such he was to take a leading part in the lengthy negotiations that sought to convert the proclaimed royalism of the Confederate Catholics into active support for the king's cause. He was in one respect ideally suited to the task. Although he never wavered from the Protestantism in which he had been brought up following the death of

---

[25] For Protestant mobilization in the north-west see Kevin McKenny, *The Laggan Army in Ireland 1640–1685* (Dublin, 2005). The Laggan, which also gave its name to one of the territorial divisions of Ulster Presbyterianism, was the fertile region immediately to the south of the Inishowen peninsula. It is not to be confused with the Lagan Valley, in east Ulster, at the mouth of which Belfast stands.

his Catholic parents, his status as head of the extended Butler kinship network gave him substantial influence among the Old English gentry and aristocracy of Leinster and Munster. His actual performance, however, remains the subject of debate. Historians for long took at face value his claims to have discharged a difficult mission with unswerving loyalty to his king. More recent studies, by contrast, suggest that his determination to maintain Protestant supremacy in Ireland led him to undermine attempts to create a Catholic–royalist alliance by repeatedly setting unnecessarily tough terms. The allegation of bad faith, a reaction to the idealized portrait offered by Ormond's first biographers, is perhaps overstated. Apart from his own religious convictions, Ormond, precariously in command of a restive conglomeration of Protestant forces, would have been acutely aware of how concessions to Irish Catholics threatened yet further to erode support, in all three kingdoms, for the royalist cause. But it is undoubtedly the case that the terms on which he insisted were less generous than those that the king from time to time offered through other intermediaries.[26]

Ormond's initial success in heading off an attempt to import English civil war divisions into Ireland was not surprising. The evidence is that the great majority of Charles I's subjects, in all three of his kingdoms, were reluctant to choose sides in an unpredictable and disruptive conflict. Geography, combined with local circumstances, gave his Irish subjects an excuse to avoid doing so for longer than most. In any case Irish Protestants, with their own war to fight against a common Catholic enemy, had no desire to weaken themselves further by taking sides in an English political quarrel. Over time, however, their pragmatic neutrality came under increasing strain. In April 1643 the king instructed Ormond to open negotiations with the Confederates for a one-year cessation of hostilities. In September, with the way smoothed by the removal of Parsons, Temple, and other hardliners, the two sides duly concluded a truce. For Charles the peace was a means to the end of diverting royal troops from the Irish theatre to fight instead against his enemies in England, and possibly of securing military support from the Confederate Catholics themselves. To many Irish Protestants, however, a compromise of any kind with the forces of militant Catholicism was deeply disturbing.

The second development undermining Irish Protestant neutrality concerned the Scottish army in Ulster. Its anomalous position—raised by treaty with an English parliament now at war with the king, but recruited from a still neutral Scotland and cooperating with royalist forces in Ireland—was emblematic of the confusion of allegiances that prevailed in the early 1640s. In September 1643,

---

[26] The image of Ormond as the noblest of the cavaliers was first established with the biography published in 1735–6 by the Jacobite Thomas Carte, and had its most recent expression in J. C. Beckett, *The Cavalier Duke* (Belfast, 1990). The predictable reaction against such hagiography colours the pages of T. C. Barnard and Jane Fenlon (eds.), *The Dukes of Ormonde 1610–1745* (Woodbridge, 2000), as well as the relevant sections of David Edwards, *The Ormond Lordship in County Kilkenny 1515–1642* (Dublin, 2003).

however, Scottish political leaders, alarmed at the potential consequences of a royalist victory, joined with the English parliament in a Solemn League and Covenant, committing both nations to defend the rights of their parliaments, extirpate popery, and establish a Presbyterian system of church government in Scotland, England, and Ireland alike. Monro's army and Ormond's Dublin administration were now on opposite sides, with the British inhabitants of Ulster caught in the middle. It was against this background that Ormond, in 1644 and again in 1646, agreed to give limited support to Confederate offensives against the Scots, by moving his forces north as a diversion. At the same time he refused all demands to join in the attack, telling a correspondent that if he did so his fellow Protestants would 'rise like one man against me, and adhere to the Scots'.[27]

Monro, for his part, began in April 1644 to administer the Solemn League and Covenant to his Ulster allies. Many among the settler population, English as well as Scots, subscribed willingly, either from enthusiasm for the principles of the Covenant or because of the promise of much-needed supplies from Scotland and the English parliament. Sir Audley Mervyn, an opposition spokesman in the parliament of 1640–1 but now an officer with the Laggan army, reported to Ormond that he had been forced to subscribe to the Covenant or lose all control over his soldiers. Others, however, resisted pressure to offer their allegiance to the king's declared enemies. In Belfast Arthur Chichester began to fortify the town in order to resist Monro, only to find himself betrayed by his own men, who on 14 May opened the gates to the Scots. At Lisburn, where the garrison under Sir Theophilus Jones remained defiant, Monro initially retreated rather than initiate a divisive conflict, but subsequently used the threat of cutting off supplies to force Jones's men to join his expedition into Leinster. At Dundalk and Newry garrison commanders loyal to Ormond refused the Scots army entry as it marched back towards its base in Carrickfergus.

By 1644, then, Irish Protestants were under growing pressure to choose sides in a civil war that now extended to all three Stuart kingdoms. Some, like Chichester and Jones, remained loyal to Ormond and the king. For many, however, the demand that they should swallow an accommodation with Catholicism was simply too much. In April 1644 a delegation approved by the now exclusively Protestant parliament still sitting in Dublin visited the king at Oxford to demand a commitment to the re-establishment of strictly enforced penal laws, along with a renewal of a policy of plantation, but were coldly received. In August one of their number, Sir Charles Coote the younger, who had taken over as the main Protestant commander in Connacht following the death of his father in 1642, declared his support for parliament. So, around the same time, did Inchiquin. He had initially accepted the cessation, and had even incurred an indictment for treason by the English parliament for having obediently sent five regiments to join the king's army. Having done so, he was bitterly disappointed not to be

---

[27] Quoted in Stevenson, *Scottish Covenanters and Irish Confederates*, 193.

rewarded with the presidency of Munster, then vacant. However his defection to parliament also reflected pressure from his Protestant followers, as well as fears that the Confederates, despite the cessation, were preparing a surprise attack on Munster.

The defection of Coote, Inchiquin, and others meant that four parties now competed for control in Ireland: Confederate Catholics, Scots, royalists, and supporters of the English parliament. Although the royalists were predominantly Protestant, they did include a number of Irish Catholics who put loyalty to the crown ahead of the claims of religious solidarity. John Barry, formerly an officer in the French service, was one of the colonels licensed to transport men from Strafford's army out of the kingdom in 1641. After war broke out, he continued to serve Ormond, as both an experienced military adviser and a trusted negotiator, until his death in combat in 1649. Theobald, Viscount Taaffe, heir to an estate in County Sligo and another of the 1641 officers, fought for the king in England in 1640–3. He accepted command of the Confederate army in Connacht, but only after Ormond and the Confederates had made peace, and he did not take the Confederate oath until after the royalist party in Ireland had collapsed with Ormond's withdrawal from the kingdom in 1647. Most important of all the earl (from 1645 marquis) of Clanricard, with the possible exception of the earl of Antrim Ireland's most important Catholic nobleman, willingly used his influence with both sides in repeated attempts to promote an accommodation between royalists and Catholics, but steadfastly refused to join the Confederacy. He fully committed himself only in 1648, when the Confederates had formally joined forces with the crown, and even then it remains unclear whether he took the oath of association.

If the careers of Barry, Taaffe, and Clanricard represent the primacy of political principle over religious allegiance, the career of a further important figure, the earl (later marquis) of Antrim, presents a more equivocal picture. In the early years of the war he followed the same course as Taaffe and Clanricard, maintaining close contact with the Confederates but doing so in the capacity of a crown servant seeking support for the royal cause. His particular interest, however, was in securing both royal and Confederate support for a private project: a revival of his plan of 1640 to mobilize his kinsmen on the western seaboard of Scotland, supported by an invasion from Ulster, so as to attack the king's Scottish enemies from the rear, and at the same time open the way to a recovery of the long lost MacDonald lands in the western Highlands and islands. By 1647, with the king's cause in decline, Antrim was to shift his allegiance to the militant party within the Confederate assembly, which rejected a compromise with the crown in favour of the demand for the full restoration of Catholic church lands and jurisdiction. During 1648, spurning the recent truce agreed by the Confederate moderates, he joined with Owen Roe O'Neill in military action against royal forces under Ormond. By 1649, on the other hand, he had begun to collaborate with the parliamentary army that now controlled a large part of Ireland, using his influence to discourage continued resistance and also, in 1650, offering his damning circumstantial account of Charles I's plans to use an Irish Catholic army against parliament in 1641. It was a political record more convoluted than most, and one that was to place him in serious peril when monarchy returned in 1660. But its twists and turns were no more than the trail of a born survivor picking his way through circumstances which few indeed were to negotiate without compromise.[28]

WAR AND PEACES

In normal circumstances the military conflict initiated by the rising of October 1641 would have been relatively short-lived. The arrival of 3,000 English reinforcements and 10,000 Scots in the spring of 1642 allowed crown forces to go on the offensive, with results that demonstrated once again the superiority of trained over untrained soldiers. At Kilrush, County Kildare, on 15 April 1642, troops under Ormond scattered a rebel army twice as large, which broke and fled almost on the first encounter. At Kilwarlin Wood outside Lisburn, two weeks later, Monro was able to force his way through an estimated 2,500 opponents occupying the classic ambush territory that normally favoured Irish irregulars. Inchiquin won a decisive victory over the Munster rebels at Liscarroll, County Cork, on 25 August. As early as July 1642 the leaders of the Ulster Irish, meeting at Glaslough in County Monaghan, gloomily concluded that their rising had failed and that the time had come to disband their forces and seek refuge abroad.

The collapse of the insurgent offensive was due, not just to their military deficiencies, but to the capacity of Irish Protestants to mobilize for their own defence. In some cases they were equipped to do so by prior military experience. Large numbers of Scots, in particular, had served during the 1630s in the armies of northern Europe, and it is probably this background that accounts for the success of the Laggan army, first in securing their base in the north-west and then in denying the Confederates control of central Ulster. Elsewhere too a military training could be part of the approved education of a gentleman, as in the case of the young earl of Inchiquin, who had spent two years in the Spanish army—not in the Irish Catholic Flanders contingents, but in Italy. Military expertise, however, could be less important than fighting spirit. This was most clearly evident in the case of those women who, as at other moments of crisis, were pushed by circumstances into taking over roles normally confined to men. In King's County, for example, Lady Forbes took command of her British tenants and withstood a nine-month siege of her castle until starvation forced her to surrender on terms. In County Limerick Lady Elizabeth Dowdall hired an

---

[28] Jane Ohlmeyer, *Civil War and Restoration in the Three Stuart Kingdoms: The Career of Randal MacDonnell, Marquis of Antrim 1609–1683* (Cambridge, 1993).

experienced soldier to train 80 men with whom she defended her castle against a large force, claiming to have killed 200 of the attackers.[29]

The return to Ireland in July 1642 of Owen Roe O'Neill, followed in September by Thomas Preston, accompanied by military supplies and a small but useful detachment of veterans from the Flanders theatre, played some part in arresting the insurgent military collapse. More important, however, was the beginning in August of open war between king and parliament in England, cutting off all prospect of further supplies or reinforcements for the Irish administration. There were some further isolated victories. In March 1643 Ormond, returning from an unsuccessful attack on New Ross, defeated a larger force commanded by Preston at Ballinvegga. In June the Laggan army scattered Owen Roe O'Neill's still untrained troops at Clones in Monaghan. For the most part, however, crown forces in Munster and Leinster were reduced to defending their existing enclaves, while Monro's Scots became even more reluctant to place themselves beyond reach of a speedy recall to their homeland by moving any distance from their base in the north-east.

The conclusion of a one-year truce with Ormond in September 1643 meant that the Confederates were now at war only in Ulster: initially against Monro's Scots, but also, from spring 1644, with those Ulster Protestants who accepted the Covenant and rejected the cessation. During 1644 they embarked on an ambitious two-pronged offensive. The Ulster army, reinforced by 4,300 additional men and under the command of the earl of Castlehaven, marched north to expel or subdue the Scots and their local allies. Meanwhile the earl of Antrim revived his pet project of an invasion of western Scotland, with the dual purpose of supporting the royalist cause in Great Britain and relieving the pressure on Ulster. Some 2,000 men under Antrim's kinsman Alasdair MacColla of Colonsay in the Hebrides landed in June and joined forces with the charismatic Scottish royalist James Graham, earl of Montrose. Their modest combined force, skilfully led and single-mindedly ferocious, achieved a series of impressive victories against superior forces, before finally encountering defeat at Philiphaugh in September 1645. Their successes forced the Scottish government to recall 2,400 soldiers from Ulster, and helped to ensure that the remainder remained inactive. This, however, was well short of the level of withdrawal the Confederates had hoped for. Meanwhile the much better supplied Ulster offensive had faded away, as Castlehaven confronted Monro in a seven-week stand-off near Charlemont but withdrew south without giving battle. By this time the defection of Coote and Inchiquin meant that the Confederates were again at war in the south and west. During 1645 they mounted a successful offensive in Munster, but lacked the artillery to dislodge Inchiquin from Youghal and other walled strongholds. In Connacht, on the other hand, Coote made advances, capturing Sligo town on 8 July.

---

[29] Mary O'Dowd, 'Women and War in Ireland in the 1640s', in Margaret MacCurtain and Mary O'Dowd (eds.), *Women in Early Modern Ireland* (Edinburgh, 1991), 92–3.

Meanwhile the Confederate supreme council had continued to negotiate with Ormond over the terms on which their truce could become a positive royalist–catholic alliance. The position of the two sides became clear in preliminary negotiations during 1642–3, and was confirmed when a Confederate delegation visited the king at his Oxford headquarters in March 1644. The Confederates demanded the repeal of all penal laws disadvantaging Catholics. The king was willing to offer only the same promise of a lenient application of existing laws earlier held out in the Graces. In September Ormond, commissioned to negotiate on the king's behalf, opened fresh talks with Confederate representatives in Dublin. At this point two further issues became important. The Catholic bishops and clergy, initially willing to take second place to the laity in the affairs of the Confederacy, had by this time become more assertive, leading negotiators to demand the repeal of pre-Reformation statutes limiting the exercise of papal and episcopal authority. Meanwhile Ormond demanded an explicit agreement that places of worship and other property seized from the Church of Ireland since October 1641 would be restored.

At this point the gulf between the two sides seemed unbridgeable. What broke the deadlock was the continued decline of the royalist position in England. On 13 May 1645 Charles authorized Ormond to offer the Confederates the repeal of anti-Catholic penal laws in exchange for their support. The following month the clergy, under pressure from the general assembly's negotiators, agreed that the commitment to uphold the rights of the Catholic church in the Confederate oath of association did not bind them to insist that a treaty explicitly guarantee the retention of all places of worship currently in Catholic hands. This concession opened the way to a possible settlement, based on a tacit understanding that the churches would eventually be repossessed, with the passive acquiescence rather than the active consent of the Catholic laity. Ormond, however, continued to demand an explicit commitment to the return of all former Church of Ireland possessions. And this, the Catholic clergy insisted, would represent a sinful breach of the Confederate oath.[30]

Ormond's obduracy on this point, combined with his failure to act on the king's revised instructions of 13 May, is central to the doubts as to where precisely his much-vaunted loyalty actually lay. Charles himself, indeed, had by this time concluded that he needed a more flexible representative, and had commissioned a trusted intimate, the Welsh Catholic earl of Glamorgan, to negotiate separately with the Confederates. On 25 August 1645, two weeks after arriving in Kilkenny, Glamorgan signed an agreement guaranteeing Catholics the public exercise of their religion, freedom from the ecclesiastical jurisdiction of the

---

[30] For these complex transactions, involving what looks like conscious sleight of hand on the part of some at least among the Confederate negotiators, see Tadhg Ó hAnnracháin, 'Conflicting Loyalties, Conflicted Rebels: Political and Religious Allegiance among the Confederate Catholics of Ireland', *English Historical Review*, 119 (2004), 863–6.

Church of Ireland, and possession of all church buildings acquired since October 1641. In exchange the Confederates were to raise 10,000 men to join the royalist forces in England. Confederate leaders now had the prospect of concluding a public deal with Ormond on terms acceptable to him, and not damaging to the royalist cause outside Catholic Ireland, while securing their religious objectives by the secret Glamorgan treaty. How far Ormond was also aware of this new two-strand approach remained unclear. When details of Glamorgan's agreement became public in late December—a copy was found on the body of Malachy O'Queely, the Catholic archbishop of Tuam, killed in a skirmish with British forces in County Sligo—he had the earl arrested, but released him a few weeks later.[31]

What happened over the next few months was subsequently to become the subject of intensely partisan debate. But the position was initially straightforward. The sixth general assembly of the Confederate Catholics, meeting in February 1646, endorsed the two-strand approach: there were to be separate negotiations for a political settlement with Ormond and for a religious treaty with the king, and neither agreement was to be concluded or published without the other. The key figure in the religious negotiations was now the papal nuncio, Rinuccini, who had arrived in Ireland the previous November. He had initially negotiated with Glamorgan, extracting a number of further concessions, notably a guarantee that the next lord lieutenant would be a Catholic and that Catholic bishops would have seats in the Irish House of Lords. By February, however, he was also aware of a separate agreement, even more favourable to Catholic interests, concluded in Rome between the pope and Sir Kenelm Digby, an English Catholic agent of the queen. While Rinuccini awaited the arrival of a public version of this document, the supreme council pushed ahead with its negotiations with Ormond. On 28 March the two sides signed a treaty. The Confederates agreed to supply the promised 10,000 men. In exchange, there was to be a general pardon for all offences committed since October 1641. All forfeitures that had taken place since the coming to Ireland of Strafford were annulled, thus securing the interests of the Old English victims of the Connacht plantation but doing little for the mainly Gaelic Irish losers by earlier confiscations. Catholics were to be admitted to office on taking the oath of allegiance alone. As regards religion itself, however, the articles offered only a general reference to the king's favour and to future concessions.

[31] Once again the historical tide currently runs against acknowledging Ormond's good faith in any transaction. Yet the suggestion that he was in fact a willing party to Glamorgan's negotiations sits rather oddly with complaints elsewhere (n. 26 above) that he deliberately placed obstacles in the way of a settlement between the king and his Catholic subjects. Ó hAnnracháin, *Catholic Reformation in Ireland*, 79 n. 239, suggests that Ormond's continued insistence on the restitution of churches in Catholic hands indicates genuine ignorance of Glamorgan's actions. Armstrong (*Protestant War*, 151–2) suggests that Ormond possibly took a different attitude to an agreement that did not involve him personally, and that, as a confidential transaction, would not undermine the royalist cause.

How far the supreme council's agents, by concluding but not publishing a formal agreement with Ormond, were in breach of their instructions remains a matter of interpretation.[32] Rinuccini certainly believed that they had acted deceitfully, and his sense of betrayal contributed to a hardening of his attitude to the advocates of peace. Over the next few months the supreme council pressed Ormond to agree to the publication of the Glamorgan treaty, which would have provided the explicit guarantees on religious matters missing from their own agreement. On the other hand they had signed their document just a fortnight after news had reached Ireland that the king had publicly disowned Glamorgan's negotiations. Their willingness to nevertheless agree terms, even if in secret, must cast doubt on whether their continued invocation of his treaty was more than window dressing, or at best a pious hope. Certainly the view, firmly held by Rinuccini and his supporters, that a king with Charles I's record could not be trusted to honour anything other than the most watertight formal agreement, was by far the more realistic stance.

At the same time that the Confederates negotiated, under truce, with Ormond, the war against supporters of the English parliament had continued. In June an offensive by Preston's Leinster army regained territory in Connacht, including the town of Roscommon. In July Confederate forces, joined for a time by the nuncio himself, captured the fortress at Bunratty near Limerick, where troops newly arrived from England had established a menacing Munster bridgehead in April. Most important of all, Owen Roe O'Neill won a major victory over the Scots at Benburb in County Tyrone. O'Neill had come to Ireland with a reputation as one of Europe's great generals. But his finest hour in continental warfare had come, significantly, when he held the town of Arras against an overwhelming French assault in 1640. His first years in Ireland had seen him adopt a similarly defensive role, repeatedly preferring a strategic withdrawal to risking his army in uncertain combat. In May 1646, however, he marched north to intercept Monro, who was planning a rendezvous in County Armagh with his nephew George Monro, moving south from Coleraine. On 4 June Owen Roe established his army of 5,000 foot and 500 horse on the north bank of the Blackwater, at Benburb, positioning himself between the two Monros. Next day he dispatched his cavalry and some foot north to deal with the Coleraine contingent, while his main force awaited the 5,500 or so foot and 800 horse approaching from the south. These reached Benburb by early evening, after a full day's march. Monro, overconfident due to earlier victories, nevertheless chose to attack. In a face-to-face confrontation of pike and musket Owen Roe's men repulsed a Scottish assault, then drove their opponents backwards, turning their

---

[32] Participants subsequently gave conflicting accounts of the precise powers given to the committee of treaty appointed to negotiate with Ormond, and also on how far a version of the agreement with Ormond presented to the Confederate Assembly in February 1646 corresponded with the treaty signed the following month: see Ó Siochrú, *Confederate Ireland*, 101–2.

line so that they were trapped with their backs to the river. Many drowned seeking to escape. Others were cut down in a pursuit reported to have continued to Caledon and Armagh, six or seven miles away. In all Monro lost between 2,000 and 3,000 men, representing a third to a half of his force, along with a baggage train that included six strategically important field guns.

O'Neill's victory was significant in itself, particularly given reports—contested but possible—that Monro's further destination had been a rendezvous with the Laggan army, for a strike at the Confederate capital of Kilkenny itself.[33] But it also helped to change Rinuccini's view of the strategic possibilities. His experiences in Ireland had led him to believe that the Catholic nobles, lawyers, and gentry who dominated the Confederate executive could not be trusted to uphold the interests of the church in any settlement they negotiated. But he had initially been prepared to accept that he might have to settle for an unsatisfactory peace. O'Neill's triumph, however, along with successes elsewhere, strengthened a view that he had already expressed as early as March 1646: that the defeat of the king in Great Britain would not necessarily be a disaster, and might indeed be of advantage in uniting Irish Catholics. Instead of seeking to prop up a failing royalist cause, the nuncio believed, Confederate strategy should be to build up a military position sufficiently strong to allow them to assert themselves against any future holders of power in England.[34]

By summer 1646, then, what were now clearly rival peace and clerical parties within the Confederate body were divided by mutual mistrust and conflicting priorities. What provoked the final breakdown of unity, however, was outside intervention. The French government, increasingly concerned that a royalist defeat in England would leave it facing a hostile Protestant republic, intervened to urge an immediate Confederate–royalist alliance in Ireland, offering both financial support and a guarantee that it would protect Catholic interests. In response Ormond, on 30 July, published the treaty he had concluded with the supreme council four months earlier. On 3 August the supreme council itself did likewise, and announced its intention of handing over power to Ormond as soon as he reached Kilkenny. However the Catholic bishops and clergy, then meeting in national synod under Rinuccini's chairmanship at Waterford, immediately denounced the treaty as a breach of the oath of association. Bellings, as secretary of the supreme council, replied by challenging the existence of any ecclesiastical authority separate from the supreme council and general assembly. His aggressive letter provoked the clergy, who on 17 August responded with an interdict suspending all religious services in towns that permitted the peace to be proclaimed. They also forbade the faithful to pay taxes to the apostate

---

[33] For conflicting views see Stevenson, *Scottish Covenanters and Irish Confederates*, 225–7; Lenihan, *Confederate Catholics at War*, 90–3.

[34] This is the interpretation offered by Ó hAnnracháin, *Catholic Reformation in Ireland*, 126–31, 134–9.

Confederate authorities. Nine days later they excommunicated Confederate tax collectors, and declared that these could legitimately be resisted with violence. On 1 September, following the arrival of Ormond in Kilkenny, Rinuccini and others pronounced a general excommunication against all those supporting the peace. These successive blows against the supreme council's authority had the desired effect. In Waterford, Limerick, and other towns, attempts by local oligarchies to arrange the ceremonial announcement of the peace were obstructed by hostile crowds. In Queen's County and elsewhere a wave of looting, along with renewed attacks on surviving Protestants, raised the spectre of a general collapse of social order.

From spiritual sanctions the nuncio turned to military force. Owen Roe O'Neill willingly obeyed a summons to march south with the Ulster army. Preston, who had initially had the peace proclaimed in the camp of the Leinster army, was more hesitant, but by 6 September he too had declared his support for the nuncio. On 13 September Ormond withdrew from Kilkenny and returned to Dublin. By now O'Neill's notoriously disorderly troops were camped just outside Kilkenny, causing near panic among the local inhabitants. On 18 September he escorted Rinuccini in triumph back into the city. Soon afterwards nuncio and general joined in arresting and imprisoning the main supporters of the Ormond peace and announced a new supreme council, with Rinuccini as president.

The nature of the split that thus opened up in the ranks of the Confederate Catholics has been much debated. Traditionally it was seen as a clash between Old English and Gaelic Irish, marking the collapse of the precarious alliance established, under pressure of circumstances, in late 1641. Recent research has questioned the idea of a division along primarily ethnic lines. Instead it has suggested that the real conflict was between those who had and had not lost property and status during the upheavals of the past sixty years. Surviving Catholic proprietors were reluctant to allow the religious demands of the clergy to jeopardize a settlement that might allow them to emerge from the crisis with their estates and social position intact. Nor, as they had already made clear, were they interested in an outcome that would see the church recover monastic or other lands that had passed into lay ownership. Circumstances dictated that this conservative possessor class were for the most part Old English. But the smaller number of Gaelic proprietors were equally aware of their stake in the established order. Prominent among the supporters of the Ormond peace now languishing in prison was Donough MacCarthy, Viscount Muskerry, and other landowners such as the head of the Fitzpatricks of Upper Ossory were likewise among its supporters.[35] By contrast it was the dispossessed, notably the Ulster Irish under the leadership of the returned exile Owen Roe, who sought to overturn a settlement that would do nothing to recover their lost estates, and had no

[35] For the earlier history of the Fitzpatricks, whose apparently Norman surname was in fact a translation of the Gaelic MacGiollaPadraig see Connolly, *Contested Island*, 125 n. 2, 151–2.

reason to challenge the clergy's demand that the church should regain its lost endowments.[36]

An apparent ethnic division, then, was in many cases based on what was in fact a straightforward conflict of vested interests. At the same time there are grounds for suggesting that long-standing loyalties and animosities were also at work. The anxiety of a section of the Old English to restore their relationship with the king, going well beyond tactical considerations to a desire for peace at almost any price, can best be explained in terms of a continuing sense that it was their role as the upholders of royal authority and English civility that legitimized their position in Ireland. At a more practical level, they may have feared that a repudiation of the king's authority could call into question the royal grants on which present ownership of estates long ago seized from the Irish depended.[37] Richard Bellings praised the Confederate assembly's early ruling that every man was to retain the property he had held on 1 October 1641 as a very necessary step, 'especially in that kingdom, where some are found, who believe no grant, no sale of their ancestors ought to put an end to their pretensions, or avoid the right which, in their opinion, remains perpetually in the family'.[38] The vehemence of his tone, thirty years after the event, conveys an uneasy awareness of potential native claims, extending beyond the injustice of particular confiscations to the whole process by which their share of Irish land had been whittled down over the decades. It also suggests a real sense of confronting an alien and, in his eyes, unreasonable notion of what ownership entailed.

If the promptings of vested interest were often reinforced by long-standing cultural and historical divisions, moreover, they could also be either strengthened or overridden by a sense of religious obligation. One member of the supreme council, Sir Richard Talbot, was alleged to have sworn 'a great oath that he would neither contest with his prince, or lose himself a foot of his estate for all the mitres in Ireland', and that he was indifferent whether mass was celebrated 'with solemnity in Christ [Church cathedral] or St Patrick's Church, or privately at his bedside'.[39] Others, however, were less confident of their priorities. Thomas Preston, general of the Leinster army, was genuinely torn between his conservative political loyalties and his dread of the church's sentence

[36] The first challenge to the prevailing emphasis on ethnic divisions within the Confederation came in the work of Donal Cregan. Much of this remains unpublished, but see D. F. Cregan, 'The Confederate Catholics in Ireland: The Personnel of the Confederation 1642–9', *IHS* 29 (1995), 490–509. The argument has been elaborated in Ó Siochrú, *Confederate Ireland*, 15–20. The alternative emphasis on divisions between those who had and had not retained a stake in the new social order established after 1603, along with the influence of differing degrees of susceptibility to religious scruple, is most fully developed in Ó hAnnracháin, 'Conflicting Loyalties'; idem, *Catholic Reformation in Ireland*.

[37] For the argument that the attachment of some to the Ormond peace was irrational, see Ó hAnnracháin, 'Conflicting Loyalties', 859–62. For evidence of continuing distrust of the native Irish see idem, *Catholic Reformation in Ireland*, 27–33.

[38] Gilbert (ed.), *Irish Confederation*, i. 113.

[39] Quoted in Aidan Clarke, *The Old English in Ireland 1625–42* (London, 1966), 216.

of excommunication—although these spiritual terrors were reinforced by the recognition that his soldiers would not in any case follow him in the face of such a sanction, and that his army was smaller than O'Neill's. More striking still was the way in which the same threat of excommunication led Patrick Darcy and Nicholas Plunkett, the two pillars of conservative Old English constitutionalism, to transfer their allegiance to Rinuccini as the crisis developed. Where the clergy were concerned, meanwhile, the nuncio seems at this stage to have had the support of all of the Irish bishops, both Old English and Gaelic Irish.

Having secured Kilkenny Rinuccini and the new supreme council ordered Preston and O'Neill to besiege Ormond in Dublin. The decision was to gain retrospective credibility when Ormond later began negotiations to hand the city over to parliamentary forces. At this point, however, he was prepared to resume talks with the Confederate Catholics. Instead the attack reflected Rinuccini's desire to remove what he saw as Ormond's corrupting influence, and to secure further papal support by a dramatic triumph.[40] It had the disadvantage of diverting resources from Munster, where Inchiquin was able to regain much of what he had lost the previous year. Meanwhile the Dublin offensive itself failed miserably. Continued internal divisions had required the use of both the Ulster and Leinster armies. O'Neill could not be sent alone, because the undisciplined rapacity of his troops made them deeply unpopular in Leinster. On the other hand Preston was not fully trusted, and did in fact engage in secret negotiations with Ormond, through Clanricard, during the campaign. By the time the two armies arrived Ormond had destroyed the harvest in the surrounding countryside, and the large combined force was unable to keep itself fed. Once the weather deteriorated, the siege had to be lifted. As with the earlier victory at Benburb, military failure had political consequences. Nicholas French, bishop of Ferns, now emerging as the most politically astute of the Catholic bishops, joined with Nicholas Plunkett in persuading Rinuccini of the need to rebuild Confederate unity by releasing Muskerry and the other imprisoned parties to the Ormond peace.[41] A new assembly in January 1647 rejected the treaty itself, but exonerated its signatories from any charge of having acted improperly. An amendment to the Confederate oath added an explicit commitment to securing the rights and property of the church, but added a rider authorizing the general assembly to decide at what point the full attainment of these objectives could be set aside in the interest of securing an agreement.

Despite this attempt at compromise, Confederate military affairs during 1647 were plagued by mistrust and conflicts of interest. A central problem was the

---

[40] See the discussion in Ó hAnnracháin, *Catholic Reformation in Ireland*, 160.

[41] Ó Siochrú, *Confederate Ireland*, 124–5, and Ó hAnnracháin, *Catholic Reformation in Ireland*, 172–3, agree on the part played by French and Plunkett in securing this change of course, but Ó hAnnracháin questions Ó Siochrú's identification of the two as central figures in a distinct 'moderate' party, occupying the centre ground between 'peace' and 'war' parties.

Ulster army. Protestant domination of the north, by the Scots in the east and the Laggan army in the west, meant that O'Neill's men, unlike the other three provincial forces, had no natural base from which to support themselves. In fact the fighting force was accompanied by a displaced civilian population of cattle-driving herdsmen known as *creaghts*. One estimate puts the number of these refugees at between 30,000 and 50,000.[42] The invasion of the southern provinces by this great train of hungry human and animal mouths was inevitably unpopular. On one occasion, in July 1646, local people massacred some 500 Ulster camp followers near Roscommon. A degree of antagonism towards outsiders was probably inevitable in what was still a very localized society, particularly when Gaelic Ulstermen encountered the more Anglicized sections of the southern population. But the Ulster army had also earned an unsavoury reputation for plundering friend and foe alike. O'Neill himself had complained shortly after his arrival that his soldiers 'behave nothing better than animals', and Rinuccini too was shocked at accounts of their depredations.[43] An incident in April 1647, when women claiming to have suffered abuse at the hands of the Ulstermen gathered outside the nuncio's window to perform the 'keen', the ritualized wails of lament normally uttered for the dead, helped to dramatize the issue. The solution was to send O'Neill's forces to campaign in Sligo and the north-west, rationalized by the hope that they would liberate from Protestant control the famous pilgrimage site of Lough Derg. In June a mutiny in the Munster army allowed its former commander, the strongly pro-peace Muskerry, to seize command from his successor, Glamorgan. Throughout the summer there were suspicions that both Muskerry and Preston were contemplating using their armies to overthrow the supreme council, or alternatively that they intended to take their men abroad and sell their services to the French.

While the Confederate war effort faltered amid these uncertainties, a parliamentary army 2,000 strong landed near Dublin on 7 June. Their commander was Michael Jones, son of the Church of Ireland bishop of Killaloe, who like his brother Sir Theophilus had initially served under Ormond, but had defected to the parliamentary army in England in 1644. Ormond himself had never negotiated solely with the Confederate Catholics. Indeed he had concluded the peace of March 1646 only after other negotiations, aimed at an alliance with the English parliament and the Ulster Scots, had collapsed under the strain of a developing conflict between these two potential partners. New talks in the autumn of 1646, following Rinuccini's coup at Kilkenny and the resumption of war with the Confederates, progressed as far as an agreement in principle to surrender Dublin, but then faltered, ostensibly because parliament would not

---

[42] Lenihan, *Confederate Catholics at War*, 120–5. For the Roscommon massacre see ibid. 124.

[43] Jerrold I. Casway, *Owen Roe O'Neill and the Struggle for Catholic Ireland* (Philadelphia, 1984), 65. For Rinuccini's sense of embarrassment at the depredations of the Ulster army, increased by their insistence on styling themselves the army of the pope, see Ó hAnnracháin, *Catholic Reformation in Ireland*, 154–5, 181.

allow Ormond to seek the king's consent to an agreement. By spring 1647, the king had given Ormond a freer hand, and the military options remained severely limited. Against this background he agreed to surrender Dublin to Jones on terms that included protection for those Catholics in the city that had been obedient to his government, as well as compensation for his personal financial losses.

In taking this decisive step Ormond was influenced, not just by events in Ireland, but by political developments on the other side of the Irish Sea. The negotiations of late 1646 had failed largely because the dominant group within the parliamentary camp at that time were the Independents. These were so called because of their support for a religious establishment of largely self-governing congregations. But they were also for the most part advocates of a radical political settlement in which the monarchy would be a powerless symbol, if indeed it survived at all. By spring 1647, on the other hand, power had shifted to the Presbyterians, advocates of a centralized national church with powers of coercive discipline over the whole population, and also more favourable towards a compromise settlement with the king. Ormond's often quoted justification of his action, that he preferred to hand the city over to Protestant rather than Catholic rebels, thus cloaked a much more complex set of calculations. These put him at some remove from the simple royalist of later legend; they do not in themselves undermine his claim to have served the crown as well as circumstances permitted.[44]

The passing of Dublin into parliamentary hands was only the first of a series of blows to the Confederate cause. In early August, once he had secured his new base, Jones made a first expedition into the surrounding countryside. Preston, sent against him with the Leinster army, was initially content to shadow and harass the English force, but then saw an opportunity to strike suddenly at the lightly defended capital. On 8 August, however, Jones overtook him at Dungan's Hill and scattered his army with heavy losses. In Munster Viscount Taaffe, who had succeeded Muskerry, pursued a similar evasive strategy, allowing Inchiquin to raid widely, until ordered by the supreme council to give battle. At Knocknanuss near Mallow, County Cork, on 13 November, Inchiquin's smaller force inflicted a decisive defeat. Confederate losses in both cases reportedly ran into thousands, effectively wiping out both the Munster and Leinster armies.[45]

As the Confederates lost ground in Ireland further developments in English politics prepared the way for a new realignment of forces. In August 1647 the army, dominated by religious and political radicals, occupied London and restored the Independent faction to dominance. By the end of the year former opponents of the crown in Scotland, alarmed by this lurch towards political and

---

[44] This follows the careful analysis in Patrick Little, 'The Marquess of Ormond and the English Parliament 1645–1647', in Barnard and Fenlon (eds.), *The Dukes of Ormonde*, 83–99.

[45] For contemporary reports of up to 3,000 dead at Dungan's Hill, and 4,000 at Knockanuss, see Scott Wheeler, 'Four Armies in Ireland', in Ohlmeyer (ed.), *Ireland from Independence to Occupation*, 56, 59.

religious radicalism, had reached an agreement ('the Engagement') with Charles I. Their support encouraged the king, in April 1648, to launch the second civil war. For Ireland the immediate consequence was that urgent needs closer to home once again cut off the reinforcements and supplies that had made possible the Protestant advances of the previous year. In addition Inchiquin, in May 1648, abandoned parliament, signing a truce with the Confederate Catholics and returning to the royalist cause. His motives were complex. He had been badly treated by the English Independents, whose leaders had openly attacked him as both a native Irishman and an alleged crypto-Catholic. Instead they had given their support to his main regional rivals, the Boyle family, headed by the earl of Cork's younger son Roger, Lord Broghill. He had also been left desperately short of food and supplies. But principles were also involved. Inchiquin had abandoned Ormond and the king because he could not accept the cessation with the Confederate Catholics. But he was, like the Scottish Engagers, alarmed by the radical turn English politics had taken since the summer of 1647. In future years he was to follow the king's son into exile, and return only after the restoration of the monarchy. In religion, on the other hand, there was to be one further twist in a complex journey, when he converted, in 1657, to the Catholicism of his ancestors. It was a decision that brought no worldly advantage, either before or after 1660, and that led to the permanent estrangement of Inchiquin from his wife, Elizabeth St Leger, pursued to the point of their being buried in separate places. As such it serves as another reminder that this was a period, not just of expedient transitions in the interest of self-preservation, but of anguished personal crises over religious and political allegiance.

The Inchiquin truce was a turning point in the politics of the Confederate Catholics. Rinuccini, supported by fourteen of the bishops, immediately denounced the truce as unacceptable. On 9 May, fearing that he was in danger of imprisonment or even assassination by supporters of a renewed royalist alliance, the nuncio fled from Kilkenny to Owen Roe O'Neill's camp at Maryborough. Eleven days later, acting on the erroneous belief that Preston was marching against the Ulster army, he publicly excommunicated all those who adhered to the truce. This time, however, the appeal to spiritual sanctions was less successful. His authority was no longer backed by the generous funds that had been at his disposal earlier in his mission. The disasters of Knockanuss and Dungan's Hill had weakened the case for an uncompromising strategy. Most important of all, the sentence of excommunication did not, as in 1646, have unanimous support among the Irish bishops. When a new general assembly met in September eight bishops, later joined by three others, defied the nuncio's orders by attending.[46] Once again the division was along largely, but not exclusively, ethnic lines. All

---

[46] The eleven bishops are listed in Ó Siochrú, *Confederate Ireland*, 186 n. 37. P. J. Corish, *The Origins of Catholic Nationalism* (Dublin, 1968), 52 n. 23, lists a total of ten, omitting Oliver Darcy, bishop of Dromore.

but one of the thirteen Irish bishops supported Rinuccini in rejecting the treaty. However Edmund O'Dwyer, bishop of Limerick, from a wealthy and Anglicized Gaelic family, supported the peace. Of the fourteen Old English bishops two gave the nuncio wholehearted support and three others provided lukewarm compliance, while the remaining nine openly opposed him.[47]

Against this background the supreme council stood firm, lodging an appeal to Rome against the censure of excommunication, and commissioning an Old English Franciscan, Peter Walsh, to publish a set of *Queries* challenging the nuncio's action. Meanwhile Owen Roe manoeuvred in the midlands, defying the Munster and Leinster armies, along with Connacht forces under Clanricard, but avoiding combat. At one point he camped briefly outside Kilkenny, but withdrew on the approach of Preston and Inchiquin. In October the marquis of Antrim, who had by now wholly abandoned the crown in favour of an alliance with the Gaelic Irish and the nuncio, sent 2,000 troops, including Ulstermen and Scottish survivors of MacColla's expedition, to County Wexford to rendezvous with the pro-nuncio O'Byrnes and Kavanaghs. They were ambushed and slaughtered by a section of the Leinster army, joined by forces loyal to Ormond. However this was the only episode of serious bloodshed arising from what was theoretically a Confederate civil war.

Rinuccini had opposed the Inchiquin truce so vehemently because he believed it was a mere preliminary to a renewed agreement with Ormond. In this he was largely correct. In March 1648 Viscount Muskerry and the Old English lawyer Geoffrey Brown, dispatched to France to negotiate with Charles I's exiled queen, Henrietta Maria, had taken the opportunity to open secret talks with Ormond (Muskerry's brother-in-law) about a new Catholic–royalist alliance. Meanwhile Ormond was also negotiating with Inchiquin through his agent Colonel John Barry. All this, moreover, took place against the wider background of the king's plans to mobilize the more conservative section of the Scottish elite through the Engagement, and also to gain support among English opponents, including former parliamentarians, of the Independents. In the event the timing worked against Ireland's effective participation in a pan-British royalist coalition. Ormond, delayed in France as he tried to raise money, did not return to Ireland until 30 September. By this time the hoped-for English rising had failed to take place on a sufficient scale, and an invading Scottish army had been defeated at Preston on 17 August and Winwick two days later.

Even after Ormond's return the construction of a new alliance was no easy matter. The presence at Kilkenny of a group of bishops who had been won over from the nuncio's side, but whose loyalty had now to be retained, imposed

---

[47] Calculated from the table in Ó hAnnracháin, *Catholic Reformation in Ireland*, 268–9, and the discussion ibid. 234–6. To this total of ten opponents of the nuncio must be added Patrick Comer-ford of Waterford and Lismore, categorized by Ó hAnnracháin as weakly pro-nucio, but one of the three bishops who joined the new General Assembly after its first meeting.

its own constraints on Confederate peacemaking. Ormond, on the other hand, confronted with threats of a mutiny in Inchiquin's army, had been forced to declare his determination to defend the Protestant religion. Negotiations quickly became bogged down on the familiar issues of the exercise of Catholic ecclesiastical jurisdiction, and the retention of places of worship in Catholic hands. The first impetus towards a settlement came with the return from Rome of two emissaries, Nicholas Plunkett and Bishop French. Both men had by now decided that a royalist alliance represented the only way forward. Their carefully loaded report, presented to the general assembly on 25 November, played down the level of papal support for Rinuccini's sentence of excommunication, and emphasized that Rome had set no specific limits on the terms that could be agreed for the Catholic church. They also made it clear that there was no prospect of the pope sending further financial or military aid to sustain Irish Catholics in standing alone. Next, at the end of December, Confederates learned, through news-sheets circulated in Kilkenny by Inchiquin, that the king was about to be put on trial in London for crimes against the people of England.

At this point the assembly voted to accept Ormond's most recent terms. These provided that Catholics were to remain undisturbed in their possession of church property, and the exercise of existing ecclesiastical jurisdiction, until the king declared his pleasure following debate in a free parliament. It was a clear advance on Ormond's earlier refusal to consider anything more than the toleration of private worship. But it contained no definite promise; the most that could be hoped for was that Catholics would emerge from the conflict ahead in a strong bargaining position. A further clause promised those affected by forfeitures and attainders since 1603 the right to petition a future parliament for redress. Once again this was an advance on Ormond's earlier willingness to discuss only plantations initiated since 1634, and as such offered some basis for a reconciliation with Owen Roe and the other Ulster Irish. But the final decision on such petitions would lie with the king. And a realist would in any case have to ask if even a parliament dominated by existing Catholic property holders would support anything as disruptive as a reversal of the Ulster plantation.

Against this background even the bishops who had defied the nuncio hesitated. They seem to have been won over partly by an address from French, who cited the recent Treaty of Westphalia, which had brought an end to thirty years of war in central Europe at the cost of a religious compromise opposed by the papal representative. Rinuccini, seizing the opportunity to escape from his failed mission, sailed back to Italy on 23 February 1649. Owen Roe O'Neill, ignoring the vague hopes held out to the Ulster dispossessed, also rejected the second Ormond peace. He had opened negotiations with Ormond on the lord lieutenant's return, protesting his continuing loyalty to the king. By this time, however, he had already begun to deal with the commanders of those forces still loyal to parliament, Colonel Jones in Dublin, George Monck at Dundalk, Sir Charles Coote in Connacht, agreeing an exchange of livestock from the herds of the Ulster *creaghts* for gunpowder from parliamentary arsenals. In May 1649 the two sides agreed a formal cessation of hostilities, with a guarantee of military assistance if either were attacked by the royalists.

This bizarre understanding, cutting across all lines of religious and political allegiance, was in part the result of desperate local circumstances. O'Neill was critically short of food and supplies. Writing to Rinuccini he explained his action in terms of 'pressure of necessity', forcing him to choose between two equally obnoxious forces, the parliamentarians and the Protestant Ormond: 'we view both, God knows, with the same hatred and horror.'[48] But there was also a wider background. The marquis of Antrim, by aligning himself with O'Neill and the nuncio, had destroyed his credit with both the crown and the Confederate Catholics. His characteristic response was to market his services elsewhere, by offering the support of the nuncio's party in Ireland, including O'Neill's still formidable Ulster army, to the English Independents, still at this stage struggling to achieve control in England itself. The vision was thus of English radicals and Irish traditionalists allied against a royalist centre. It made superficial sense in that, where Presbyterians demanded a centralized and authoritarian church establishment, Independents were theoretically advocates of religious toleration. But the argument that this might make them more willing to reach an accommodation with Irish Catholicism failed to take account of the firm belief of most English Independents that popery and religious intolerance were two names for the same thing, and that any connivance at Catholic idolatry went beyond toleration to become a breach of God's law. Nevertheless Antrim, during 1648, negotiated both with the Independent party in London and with Jones in Dublin. His agent was Patrick Crelly, Cistercian abbot of Newry. One early gesture of rapprochement was in August 1648, when Owen Roe released Jones's brother Sir Theophilus, whom he had been holding prisoner. Sir Theophilus was escorted to safety by Edmund O'Reilly, the former Catholic vicar general of Dublin, now suspended by his archbishop because of his activities as an intermediary between Owen Roe and the parliamentarians.[49]

For other groups too within Ireland, the twists and turns of English politics during 1648–9 made necessary a reassessment of alignments. The relationship between Monro's depleted Scottish army and its English paymasters had deteriorated along with Anglo-Scottish relations in general. In March 1647 the Scots defied an order from London that they disband without receiving the substantial arrears of pay due to them. When the Engagement was published at the end of the year two regiments, one belonging to the earl of Argyll, the leading opponent of the Engagement within Scotland itself, refused to accept it. Their defection,

[48] Casway, *Owen Roe O'Neill*, 246.

[49] Ohlmeyer, *Civil War and Restoration*, 208–9, 212, 217–18; Tomás Ó Fiaich, 'Edmund O'Reilly, Archbishop of Armagh 1657–1669', in 'The Franciscan Fathers' (eds.), *Father Luke Wadding Commemorative Volume* (Dublin, 1957).

along with the transfer of 1,900 men under George Monro to support the king in Scotland, further weakened Monro's military position. In September this weakness, along with internal divisions, allowed George Monck, parliament's newly appointed commander in eastern Ulster, to execute a bloodless coup. Aided by officers and men from the dissident regiments, he seized control of the garrisons at Carrickfergus, Belfast, and Coleraine, imprisoning Monro and other commanders.[50]

Monck's triumph was short-lived. Scots, in Ulster as in Scotland itself, were outraged by the execution on 30 January of Charles I. The presbytery of Ulster, representing the Presbyterian congregations that had multiplied since 1641, denounced 'the insolencies of the sectarian party in England', who in violation of the Solemn League and Covenant had abandoned Presbyterianism for a toleration of religious variety, and had executed the king 'against the interest and protestation of the kingdom of Scotland . . . an act so horrible as no history, divine or human, hath laid a precedent of the like'. A reply by John Milton, secretary to the English council of state, combined a robust defence of parliament's action with a demonstration of how quickly political disputes within the three kingdoms descended into crude ethnic abuse: the ecclesiastical authority appropriated by the presbytery made them 'the pontifical see of Belfast', described as 'a barbarous nook of Ireland', and its members were 'a generation of Highland thieves and redshanks', permitted 'by the courtesy of England to hold possessions in our province [i.e. Ireland], a country better than their own'.[51] By this time protest in Ulster had given way to open revolt. In the east Lord Montgomery of Ards, grandson of the pioneer of Scottish settlement in County Down, seized Belfast from Monck's forces and appointed Colonel James Wallace, an officer from Monro's army, as its governor. By April Monck had been forced to withdraw to Dundalk. In the west, the greater part of the Laggan army declared their support for the king and besieged Coote in Londonderry. It was against this background that Monck and Coote entered into their treaty with Owen Roe O'Neill in May. In July Owen Roe's forces appeared to scatter the contingents of the Laggan army besieging Derry, leading to a bizarre scene in which he and Coote toasted their joint victory. (When O'Neill died four months later there were to be reports that Coote had taken this opportunity to poison him.)

Although news of the second Ormond peace may well have encouraged the Ulster Scots in their decision to assert themselves, their revolt was initially an independent initiative. In May 1649, however, George Monro, another adept survivor in shifting political circumstances, reappeared in Ulster. After Preston,

---

[50] Monck had commanded the first English expedition to Ireland after the outbreak of revolt in 1641. He had subsequently fought on the royalist side in England, spent a period in prison, then joined the parliamentary army. He was later to play a decisive part in the restoration of Charles II.

[51] [John Milton], *Articles of Peace Made and Concluded with the Irish Rebels and Papists . . . and a Representation of the Scotch Presbytery at Belfast in Ireland, Upon all Which are Added Observations* (London, 1649), 42–3, 60, 64–5.

he had fled from Scotland to the exiled Charles II, and he now returned to Ireland, where Ormond sent him north at the head of a mainly Irish Catholic force, with some admixture of Scots and English. By this time tensions were already apparent between many of the rank and file among the Ulster Scots, whose commitment was to the National Covenant, and the conditional loyalty it promised to a monarch who upheld true religion, and leaders such as Montgomery or Colonel Audley Mervyn, the reluctant signatory five years earlier of the Solemn League and Covenant, whose allegiance was more directly royalist.[52] The new alliance with Irish Catholicism contributed further to the disintegration of what had been from the start a fragile anti-parliamentary coalition. The parallel defection from Monck's forces of soldiers unable to accept his understanding with Owen Roe, forcing him to abandon Dundalk to royalists under Inchiquin, offered only limited compensation.

BLOOD AND RUIN

Following the second Ormond peace the Confederate organization dissolved itself, handing over power to twelve 'commissioners of trust' who were to administer Catholic areas under the government of Ormond as lord lieutenant to Charles II, king of England, Scotland, and Ireland. With Inchiquin's capture of Drogheda and Dundalk in July, this royalist–Confederate alliance controlled all of Ireland except Dublin and Londonderry. But it was living on borrowed time. The defeat of the Engagers and the execution of the king meant that the reduction of Ireland was now the parliamentary government's sole major concern. In March it appointed its leading general, Oliver Cromwell, to command an expeditionary force made up of 12,000 veterans of the New Model Army that had now emerged victorious in two civil wars. The first troops began landing at Dublin in May and June. Ormond sought to prevent further landings by bringing an army to either capture or blockade the city. On 2 August, however, Jones launched a surprise attack on Ormond's camp at Rathmines, two miles outside Dublin, scattering his forces in disarray. (The anti-nuncio and pro-Ormond Franciscan Peter Walsh was later to allege that Edmund O'Reilly, the former envoy for Owen Roe and the earl of Antrim, who was still in Dublin under Jones's protection, assisted the parliamentarians with intelligence relating to Ormond's position.[53]) Jones's victory allowed Cromwell to land unmolested with the remainder of his army on 15 August. By 2 September he had marched north to besiege the nearest major enemy garrison, Drogheda, held by the English royalist Sir Arthur Aston. After a short siege his troops overran the town on 11 September.

---

[52] In the interval Mervyn had fought in the parliamentary army in Ireland, but had been imprisoned as a person of suspect loyalty during the second civil war.

[53] Ó Fiaich, 'Edmund O'Reilly', 181.

The details of what happened next are impossible to reconstruct exactly, given the contradictory nature of surviving accounts. Cromwell himself reported that he forbade his men 'to spare any that were in arms in the town', and that 'we put to the sword the whole number of the defendants'. The dead included nearly 1,000 who took refuge in the town's main church. Others who continued to fire from the steeple were disposed of by setting the structure on fire. Cromwell dispassionately recorded the screams of one victim: 'God damn me, God confound me, I burn, I burn.' He initially estimated the survivors from the slaughter at no more than 30, although other sources suggest between 200 and 400 prisoners out of a garrison of 3,000. These were sent for transportation to the West Indies. Cromwell also admitted freely that all those identified as Catholic clergy were killed on the spot. A more contentious claim is that Aston and around 200 men, holding out in a place of some strength, surrendered on a promise of quarter but were then killed. One account was that Aston was beaten to death with his own wooden leg. The real issue, however, is whether the killing extended to civilians as well as those 'in arms'. One modern analysis, citing a report by Cromwell's chaplain that the enemy death toll was over 3,500, along with an estimate of up to 400 survivors from a garrison of 3,000, concludes that there must have been some 1,000 civilian deaths. But then Cromwell also reported that some put the garrison at 'near 4,000'. In a public reply to the Catholic bishops written in January 1650 he denied, apparently in the expectation of being believed, that he had been responsible for the killing, anywhere in Ireland, of persons not in arms. A list of those killed at Drogheda that concludes with the potentially damning phrase 'and many inhabitants' appears to suggest otherwise. But there is the suggestion that this was tacked on by the printer to the dispatch by Cromwell with which it is published.[54]

The slaughter at Drogheda remains controversial to the present day. Contemporary military conventions sanctioned the denial of quarter to defenders who protracted the bloodshed by fighting on once defeat had become inevitable. Such severity could be justified, not just as revenge, but as a dreadful example that would prevent future unnecessary loss of life. Following the surrender of Colchester during the second English civil war, the victorious parliamentarians executed several of the commanders, forced rank and file prisoners to pass through the ordeal of decimation, the execution of a randomly selected one in ten, and sent the survivors for transportation to the West Indies. When George Monck, now commander of English forces in Scotland, captured Dundee in 1651, similarly, he ordered his men to give no quarter until they had reached the

---

[54] The key sources are Cromwell's letters of 16 and 17 Sept. (*The Writings and Speeches of Oliver Cromwell*, ed. W. C. Abbott (Oxford, 1939), ii. 124–9). The fullest recent analysis is James Burke, 'The New Model Army and the Problems of Siege Warfare 1648–51', *IHS* 27 (1990), 1–29, who suggests the figure of 1,000 civilian dead (p. 14). See also James Scott Wheeler, *Cromwell in Ireland* (Dublin 1999), 86–8. For the problematic phrase 'and many inhabitants' see *Writings and Speeches*, ed. Abbott, ii. 131.

very centre of the town, and then licensed twenty-four hours of indiscriminate plunder. The massacre of the Drogheda garrison was a bloodier version of the same response, and Cromwell himself pointed to the hope of preventing 'the effusion of blood for the future' as justifying that 'which otherwise cannot but work remorse and regret'. What is less clear is why he should also have invoked the memory of the events of 1641, arguing that the bloodshed represented 'a righteous judgement of God' on 'barbarous wretches' who had shed so much innocent blood. This was blatant mendacity. The town of Drogheda had in fact resisted a lengthy siege by the Catholic insurgents during 1641–2. The slaughtered garrison, meanwhile, consisted of soldiers from the Munster army left there by Inchiquin, many of whom were, like their commander, English rather than Irish. Of ten officers named as killed in an early skirmish, just four were Irish, comprising two Gaelic and two Old English.[55] The conclusion can only be that Cromwell felt the need to justify himself, by any means possible, for having either encouraged or permitted killing on a scale that, even by the harsh standards of the day, went beyond what the circumstances warranted.

From Drogheda Cromwell moved quickly south. By 2 October he had reached Wexford. What followed was, even more than Drogheda, a lesson in the ambiguity of the rules of war. As negotiations between the commanders continued, a subordinate officer commanding a castle that made up part of the town's defences chose to make terms for himself, allowing the attackers to storm the town. Cromwell had been preparing to make an offer of quarter to all defenders. However he also believed that the royalist commander had been spinning out negotiations in the hope of being reinforced. Accordingly, having taken the town without negotiation, he permitted the killing of the entire garrison, along with some townsmen who had taken up arms. There was no massacre of unarmed civilians, although the 300 or so drowned as they tried to escape by boat may have included women and children, and Catholic priests were once again killed out of hand. This second exercise in exemplary terror had its effect. A week later the royalist garrison at New Ross surrendered on terms after a short bombardment. Some 500 English troops among the defenders subsequently volunteered to join Cromwell's army. In Munster Cromwell had the assistance of Inchiquin's regional rival Broghill, who after some ambiguous negotiations with the royalists had committed himself firmly to the parliamentary side.[56] Through his influence the Protestant garrisons of Youghal and other towns defected to the Commonwealth. When Cromwell proceeded to the last major southern town in enemy hands, however, he encountered a defector who had moved in the opposite direction. Edward Wogan, a Protestant of Old English descent who

---

[55] Burke, 'The New Model Army and the Problems of Siege Warfare', 11.

[56] Broghill had strong personal ties to individuals on the royalist side, particularly through his brother, the second earl of Cork. But Little (*Broghill*, 51–3, 59) dismisses as a convenient post-Restoration fiction the claim that he had in fact made up his mind to join the royal court in exile, and was dissuaded only by the personal intervention of Cromwell.

had served in the New Model Army but was now a royalist, ignored the lessons of Drogheda and Wexford, holding Waterford and the fort at Duncannon until bad weather forced the besiegers to retire to winter quarters at the beginning of December.

Cromwell's offensive forced his opponents to reconsider their internal divisions. On 20 October Owen Roe O'Neill and Ormond reached an agreement, sweetened by the promise of an earldom for the Ulster general. But O'Neill was already ill and he died on 6 November. In December the Catholic bishops, including both supporters and opponents of the second Ormond peace, met at the ancient monastic site of Clonmacnoise in King's County, where they issued a declaration calling on the faithful to unite in support of church and king, and warning them to expect nothing from Cromwell, who had declared his intention of extirpating the Catholic religion. In response Cromwell issued a long declaration disavowing any intention of persecuting for belief alone. However he had already made clear, in the negotiations preceding the surrender of New Ross, that his promise not to interfere with 'what thoughts they have in matters of religion in their own breasts', while perfectly sincere and true to his Independent principles, did not imply any promise of toleration for institutional Catholicism: 'I meddle not with any man's conscience. But if by liberty of conscience you mean a liberty to exercise the mass, I judge it best to use plain dealing, and to let you know, where the parliament of England have power that will not be allowed of.'[57] The declaration referred in passing to the guilt associated with the murder of Protestants in 1641, but denied any intention of inflicting collective punishment. In addition Cromwell flatly denied that he had killed any not in arms (presumably discounting those whose crime had been to be in Catholic orders). All those who submitted, 'except only the leading persons and principal contrivers of this rebellion', would receive mercy. But the alternative was stark. If the Irish nobility, gentry, and common people persisted in following their clergy and other leaders, 'I hope to be free from the misery and desolation, blood and ruin that shall befall them, and shall rejoice to exercise utmost severity against them'.[58]

Bishop Nicholas French wrote, years later, that Cromwell 'like a lightning passed through the land'.[59] His success was due, not just to his own military expertise, and to the experience and commitment of his New Model Army veterans, but to superior logistics. He had taken particular care to ensure that he came to Ireland with adequate supplies, including carts and wagons for transport, and that he was regularly resupplied thereafter. None of this was enough to protect his men from the wasting effects of exposure, hunger, and disease. As early as 17 September he reported that 'the country sickness overtakes

---

[57] Cromwell to Lucas Taaffe, governor of New Ross, 19 Oct. 1649 (*Writings and Speeches*, ed. Abbott, ii. 146).

[58] *Writings and Speeches*, ed. Abbott, ii. 196–205.   [59] Quoted in *NHI*, iii.336.

many'.[60] By December 1649 his regiments contained on average between 300 and 500 men out of the original 1,000 in each. By the end of January, however, reinforcements from England had brought the average back to 900. In addition huge shipments of oats landed at Munster ports, combined with passable roads following an unusually dry winter, permitted his army to resume campaigning without the usual wait for the first spring grass on which its horses could feed. He took Fethard in County Tipperary on 3 February 1650, and Cahir-on-Suir on 24 February. At Kilkenny Ormond's brother Sir William Butler put up a stiff fight before surrendering on favourable terms on 27 March. At Clonmel, which surrendered in May, Cromwell honoured the protection guaranteed to the townspeople, even when he discovered to his fury that the defending force under Hugh Dubh O'Neill, Owen Roe's nephew, had slipped away. Two weeks later Cromwell returned to England, leaving his son-in-law Henry Ireton in command. Meanwhile Broghill had defeated the last significant royalist–Confederate force in Munster at Macroom on 10 April. Its commander, Boethius MacEgan, Catholic bishop of Cork, was hanged next day.

At the same time that Cromwell was subduing the south, his subordinates were regaining control of Ulster. After the siege of Drogheda he had sent Colonel Robert Venables north to support Coote. In November they took Carrickfergus, having first defeated George Monro's army at Lisnestrain in County Down. Monro was by this time marching alongside an unlikely ally, Sir Phelim O'Neill. In March 1650, however, the Ulster Confederate army chose as its general, to succeed Owen Roe O'Neill, Heber MacMahon, Catholic bishop of Clogher. At this point even George Monro's tolerance of an expedient alliance with popery reached its limit, and soon after he surrendered Enniskillen and other garrisons to Coote. In June Coote defeated MacMahon's Ulster army at Scarrifhollis near Letterkenny in County Donegal, killing some 3,000 Confederate troops. Among the captured officers summarily executed was Owen Roe O'Neill's son Henry. Coote brushed aside an appeal to their former alliance with the remark that O'Neill senior had been well paid at the time for the assistance he had given. Bishop MacMahon, captured later, was also hanged. In August Sir Phelim O'Neill surrendered Charlemont fort, in Catholic hands throughout all the vicissitudes of the past nine years, and now their last stronghold in Ulster.

By this time the two remaining garrisons in the south-east had also fallen, Carlow in late July and Waterford, along with Duncannon fort, in early August. Unsubdued armed bands continued to harass parliamentary forces across much of the country. But the Commonwealth now had overall control of the whole island, except for Limerick city, Athlone, and the counties west of the Shannon. Defections like those of Monro and the Munster Protestants had reduced the Confederate–royalist coalition in effect to a Catholic army supporting a Protestant lord lieutenant. And by this time that last conjunction

---

[60] Cromwell to Lenthall, 17 Sept. 1649 (*Writings and Speeches*, ed. Abbott, ii. 128).

too was breaking down. Limerick and Galway had refused to admit troops under Ormond's command, while the bishops and other leading Catholics criticized him for allegedly preferring Protestant over Catholic officers. In August 1650 the bishops published a repudiation of his leadership, citing his neglect of Catholic interests and his ineffective management of the war. In September they pronounced a sentence of excommunication against all those who supported his government. Meanwhile Ormond discovered that Charles II, desperate to secure Presbyterian support for a new royalist offensive from Scotland, had repudiated his treaty with what the king called 'Irish rebels'. In December Ormond, at last accepting defeat, sailed for France, appointing Clanricard as lord deputy in his place.

In early 1651, following this final collapse in their relationship with the Stuarts, the Catholic leaders explored the possibility of finding an alternative symbol of legitimacy by offering Charles, formerly duke of Lorraine and now, since his deposition there, a well-connected mercenary, the position of 'royal protector'. But time had run out. Once the new campaigning season began, Ireton began slowly but methodically to tighten the net round the remaining Confederate territory. Athlone surrendered in June and Limerick in October. Meanwhile Cromwell had defeated Charles II's Scottish army at Worcester on 3 September. A miserable November campaign in the County Clare countryside cost Ireton his life. But by this time only Galway held out against the Commonwealth forces, and it surrendered in April 1652, its excellent defences allowing the inhabitants to secure a guarantee of freedom from plunder and even protection for the city's Catholic clergy.

The overlapping military conflicts that took place between 1641 and 1653 were brutal as well as prolonged. Cromwell's massacres at Drogheda and Wexford have entered popular legend. But they were not unique. Similar wholesale slaughter of defending troops had taken place when Sir Charles Coote captured Sligo in 1645, and when Inchiquin took Cashel two years later. Indeed it has been argued that the most savage period of warfare was in fact the early years of the conflict, before combatants on both sides came to realize that the practice of killing prisoners out of hand might eventually rebound fatally on themselves.[61] Certainly Owen Roe O'Neill, despite four decades of military experience, was shaken by what he encountered when he landed in Ulster in the summer of 1642: 'Unless I saw it I would not believe it; for on both sides there is nothing but burning, robbing in cold blood, and cruelties such as are not usual even among the Moors and Arabs.'[62] Much of the viciousness displayed by the warring groups, like the ferocity of the attacks made on Protestants in late 1641 and early 1642, can be attributed to the lethal intermixing of political, ethnic, and religious conflicts. Yet brutality was not confined wholly to those occasions when Catholic fought Protestant. During the Ulster campaign of 1649–50, essentially a civil

---

[61] Lenihan, *Confederate Catholics at War*, 169–79.   [62] Casway, *Owen Roe O'Neill*, 64.

war between royalists and parliamentarians among the settler population, Coote's forces massacred an entire garrison at Coleraine, and shocked Protestant opinion elsewhere by their summary executions of all found in arms against parliament.[63]

Where English troops, like those deployed at Drogheda, were concerned, brutality reflected long-standing perceptions of the Irish as an alien people, culturally inferior yet threatening, as well as a visceral anti-popery now inflamed by propagandist accounts of the slaughter of Protestants in 1641 and after. In October 1644, after the cessation with the Confederates had released royalist troops for service in England, the London parliament gave official sanction to the classification of the Irish as something less than legitimate combatants, by ordering that all Irishmen taken in arms in England or Wales were to be put to death. In February 1646 a London diarist recorded matter of factly that the royalist town of Chester had surrendered 'upon terms very reasonable for the governor and persons of condition', who had been allowed to march away, but that 'the native Irish were left prisoners and shall be executed'. Nor was it only those taken in arms that suffered. After the New Model Army had shattered the king's forces at Naseby on 14 June 1645, its soldiers killed at least a hundred women from the royalist camp, while slashing the faces and slitting the noses of the rest, to mark them as women of ill fame. They did so in the belief that the women were Irish, although some may in fact have been Welsh. The Scots troops who defeated Montrose's mixed force of Highlanders and Ulster Irish at Philiphaugh on 13 September were equally brutal, massacring 300 accompanying women, along with their children.[64]

To the killing of prisoners and sometimes non-combatants was added the use by both sides of man-made famine as a weapon of war. Monro's Scots, frustrated, as Elizabeth's commanders had been half a century before, by the refusal of an elusive enemy to engage in decisive combat, resorted to the same expedients, burning crops, slaughtering livestock, and frequently killing or banishing the peasantry on whose labour their enemies' food supply depended. During the siege of Dublin in 1646 the Confederate supreme council called on Preston to destroy all stocks of food in the densely populated stretch of territory extending from the Liffey to Drogheda. Preston, a Palesman, declined, but Owen Roe, given the same orders following his rival's defeat at Dungan's Hill, had no such scruples. Observers watching from the spire of St Audeon's church in November 1647 counted 200 fires in a surrounding countryside about to begin a long winter. O'Neill, it was reported, 'spareth none of what religion soever; all are alike to him'.[65]

63 McKenny, *Laggan Army*, 104–5, 157.
64 Austin Woolrych, *Britain in Revolution 1625–1660* (Oxford, 2002), 318, 324. For Chester see *The Journal of Thomas Juxon 1644–1647*, ed. Keith Lindley and David Scott (Cambridge, 1999), 100, and for other examples ibid. 56, 110.
65 Stevenson, *Scottish Covenanters and Irish Confederates*, 106, 110, 112, 115; Lenihan, *Confederate Catholics at War*, 98–100, 100–2.

   The ambitions of princes, prelates, and parliamentarians, and the antagonism of settler and native, were thus pursued at a frightful human price. Physical destruction, considering the duration of the conflict, could be surprisingly localized. One study points to the contrast that existed within the single county of Wexford. In the north, a frontier zone for much of the war, a survey in the 1650s found 17 out of 21 castles and 22 out of 26 mills in ruins. In the south, a battleground only in the final stages, the corresponding figures were 11 out of 68 and 3 out of 27.[66] Deaths in combat, likewise, though running into many thousands, were, as always in early modern warfare, a mere fraction of the total loss of life. Disease, encouraged by exposure, poor nutrition, and the inevitable tendency of large bodies of men crowded into a limited space to foul their own environment, swallowed up many times more. Meanwhile the repeated devastation of crops, or their seizure at sword point by bands of soldiers, left the civilian population facing hunger at best, and possible famine. The supreme council justified the Inchiquin truce by pointing to 'so great a dearth of corn that Ireland had not seen in our memory, and so cruel a famine, which hath already killed thousands of the poorer sort'.[67] Outbreaks of typhus and dysentery were followed by the appearance in 1649 of bubonic plague. In Galway, where it first appeared, one estimate put the number of deaths at 20,000. Overall, it has been suggested, wartime losses cut the Irish population by between 15 and 20 per cent, from 1.5 million or above in 1641 to 1.3 million eleven years later.[68]
   All this was the consequence of a multi-sided conflict. As it unfolded Irish Protestants, initially united against the Confederates, split into conflicting parliamentarian and royalist factions. The Scottish army in Ulster, at first allied to Ormond's royalist administration, became after the Solemn League and Covenant its enemy, in theory at least. Later some of these Scots were to join longer-established British settlers, and their former Confederate enemies, in a royalist coalition under Ormond's leadership. The Laggan army, in fact, lost more men in its short war against Coote's parliamentarians in 1649–50 than it did in encounters with the Confederate Catholics.[69] Within the Confederation provincial armies pledging allegiance to one side or other in the dispute between the papal nuncio and his opponents menaced, and occasionally fought, one another. These internal divisions reached their logical, if bizarre, conclusion in

---

   [66] Raymond Gillespie, 'The Irish Economy at War 1641–1652', in Ohlmeyer (ed.), *Ireland from Independence to Occupation*, 161. Other information in this paragraph comes from the same article, as well as Padraig Lenihan, 'War and Population, 1649–52', *IESH* 24 (1997), 1–21.
   [67] Quoted in Lenihan, *Confederate Catholics at War*, 108.
   [68] Lenihan, 'War and Population', 18–21. Smyth, *Map-Making, Landscapes and Memory*, 161 suggests that population loss between 1641 and 1652 was as much as one-third. But this would suggest a population of 1.8 to 2 million in 1641, representing an improbable doubling of numbers, even taking account of an immigration of 100,000 British settlers, since 1603.
   [69] McKenny, *Laggan Army*, 157.

the brief alliance, given a superficial political credibility by Antrim's misreading of the Independent party's concept of religious toleration, between the Ulster Gaels and the defenders of the Protestant commonwealth.

Against this background it is possible to observe individuals, such as Inchiquin and Audley Mervyn (and to a lesser extent Broghill) on one side, Thomas Preston on the other, struggle with the demands of opposing claims on their allegiance. But there were many others, less well documented, whose behaviour falls outside the neat boxes that can be constructed from the different possible permutations of religion, political principle, and ethnicity. There were accounts from all parts of the country of members of the settler population appearing in the ranks of the Catholic insurgents. Some of these were already Catholics by 1641, having succumbed to the pressures of a predominantly Catholic environment. This was the case, for example, with some of the Brownes of Kerry, descendants of one of the chief architects of the Munster plantation, and some of the Cosbys who had been pioneers of the midlands plantation in Queen's County. Others were Protestants who now chose to join what had become the winning cause. In Waterford city, for example, the cathedral organist defected to the rebels while the teacher in the Protestant free school was seen on guard duty armed with a halberd.[70]

On the other side too there are indirect but telling indications that not all of those in arms were British Protestants. Monro, after seizing control of Belfast in August 1644, thought it necessary to disarm two companies from Chichester's regiment, said to include many Irish soldiers. In 1649 the Cromwellian force besieging Carrick-on-Suir was able to send forward a party of Irish speakers to trick a sentry into opening one of the gates. Some of these Catholics may have been part of the pre-1641 regular army which formed the initial core of Ormond's royalist force—even though this was in theory exclusively Protestant—and then found themselves transferred into the parliamentary army as local commanders like Coote and Inchiquin subsequently changed sides. However a refugee from County Antrim reported in June 1644 that the 'Scottish regiment now in Ulster take as many Irish papists daily as come to them'.[71] If so, then it is more than possible that even the New Model Army, forced continually to replenish ranks thinned by disease, desertion, and deaths in combat, was less than rigorous in applying a religious test to local recruits. Both royalist and Confederate Catholic commanders repeatedly condemned what they clearly regarded as a significant number of Catholics who collaborated with, or served in, the parliamentary army. Among the problems raised by the commissioners charged with implementing the post-war land settlement, likewise, was to be the

[70] Nicholas Canny, *Making Ireland British 1580–1650* (Oxford, 2001), 372–3, 285, 287, 493, 512–13, 529.
[71] Quoted in Smyth, *Map-Making, Landscapes and Memory*, 488 n. 68.

treatment of Catholics who had exposed themselves to penalties by serving in the Confederate forces, but had subsequently joined the parliamentary army.[72]

One minor incident provides a glimpse of the intricacies created as a national conflict was translated into alliances and oppositions at local level. In 1647 Sir Charles Coote, parliamentary commander in Connacht, reported on 'divers considerable services' rendered to parliament by Thomas and Dudley Costello of County Mayo, both papists, 'by prosecuting the rebels vigorously, and in time of our greatest distress continuing very faithful unto us'. The Costellos were Catholics, of wholly Gaelic background though reputedly descended from medieval English colonists. However they were also at odds with Coote's main opponent in the struggle for control of Mayo, Viscount Dillon, a former royalist who in December 1646 had announced his conversion to Catholicism and aligned himself with Rinuccini. The Costellos' hostility may in part have reflected that of Owen Roe O'Neill, who distrusted Dillon's motives and was refusing orders from Kilkenny to allow him to reoccupy the town of Athlone. But it is also likely that the feud had deeper roots, going back to the dubious transactions by which the Viscount's grandfather, Theobald Dillon, had acquired the lands of the Costellos of Mayo. Indeed one of the services to which Coote referred was the surrender to him by the Costellos of another Theobald, the current viscount's brother.[73]

In contrast to this comparatively well-documented case, nothing is known of another combatant: a 'stout blackamoor' whose apparent invulnerability under fire convinced the defenders of a Confederate stronghold in County Kildare that he was protected by witchcraft, inspiring them to shoot him dead using bullets marked with a cross.[74] But the very anomaly of his presence makes him too a fitting representative of the 'war of many parts'.

'TRANSPORT, TRANSPLANT, IS MY UNDERSTANDING OF ENGLISH'

In modern Irish legend Cromwell is remembered for the bloody capture of Drogheda and Wexford. Yet this image of a singularly brutal military commander

---

[72] Stevenson, *Scottish Covenanters and Irish Confederates*, 198; J. G. Simms, 'Cromwell's Siege of Waterford, 1649', in idem, *War and Politics in Ireland 1649–1730* (London, 1986), 15; J. P. Prendergast, *The Cromwellian Settlement of Ireland* (London, 1865), 46. For royalist and Confederate complaints see Micheál Ó Siochrú, 'English Military Intelligence in Ireland during the Wars of the Three Kingdoms', in Eunan O'Halpin, Robert Armstrong, and J. H. Ohlmeyer (eds.), *Intelligence, Statecraft and International Power* (Dublin, 2006), 54–6.

[73] Coote to Committee for Irish Affairs, 11 June 1647 (HMC, *Report 13, Appendix, Part 1, Portland MSS*, vol. i (1891), 427); Coote to Sir Philip Percival, 4 June 1647 (HMC, *Egmont MSS*, vol. i, part 2 (1905), 413). For Dillon's acquisition of the Costello lands see Connolly, *Contested Island*, 223.

[74] Lenihan, *Confederate Catholics at War*, 202.

appears to have taken shape only in nineteenth-century historical writing.[75] In contemporary and near contemporary Gaelic literature, by contrast, he appears, not primarily as a soldier, but as the architect of a social revolution: poets of the second half of the seventeenth century bewailed their subordination to a new breed of upstart, identified variously as 'Cromwellian dogs', 'Cromwellian scum of England', or 'Cromwell's raging, gluttonous mob'. Such rhetoric overstated the change that had taken place in the composition of the Irish ruling elite.[76] But the underlying perception was more accurate than that enshrined in the English-language texts of Victorian nationalism. Cromwell's military campaign in Ireland lasted for just ten months, and he was only one of many commanders willing to act ruthlessly when occasion seemed to require. But his victories prepared the way for a series of changes, implemented during a period in which he himself became ruler of both England and Ireland, that were to determine the overall shape of the Irish social order for the best part of two centuries.

When Cromwell returned to England in May 1650 it was as the most important military figure in a state still ruled by the parliament that, following a purge of conservative members in December 1648, had authorized the execution of the king. Responsibility for the government of Ireland passed to four parliamentary commissioners. By April 1653 Cromwell had lost patience with the failure of the Purged Parliament to devise an acceptable religious and constitutional settlement and dissolved the assembly. In December he became Lord Protector of England, Scotland, and Ireland. In August 1654 he appointed a lord deputy for Ireland, Charles Fleetwood, a New Model Army veteran who had come to Ireland two years earlier as commander in chief and a parliamentary commissioner. As the second husband of Ireton's widow Bridget Cromwell, he was also the Protector's son-in-law. After September 1655 day-to-day responsibility for the government of Ireland passed to Cromwell's son Henry but Fleetwood, back in England, retained his title and a degree of influence, a messy compromise that continued until Henry formally succeeded him as lord deputy in November 1657.[77]

The immediate task facing the first of these authorities, the parliamentary commissioners, was the consolidation of military control. The surrender of

---

[75] T. C. Barnard, 'Irish Images of Cromwell', in R. C. Richardson (ed.), *Images of Cromwell* (Manchester, 1993), 180–206.

[76] *The Poems of David Ó Bruadair*, ed. J. C. McErlean (London, 1910–16), iii. 97; Richard Bagwell, *Ireland under the Stuarts* (London, 1909–16), iii. 53–4; Michelle O'Riordan, *The Gaelic Mind and the Collapse of the Gaelic World* (Cork, 1990), 273. For the extent to which post-1660 Ireland was in fact dominated by Protestant families established before 1641, rather than men of low birth raised to power in the Cromwellian revolution, see below, pp. 138–9.

[77] The destruction of so many relevant records means that two older works, Prendergast, *Cromwellian Settlement*, and R. T. Dunlop, *Ireland under the Commonwealth* (Manchester, 1913), both of which reprint large amounts of documentary material, remain essential to the study of Cromwellian Ireland. The outstanding modern study is T. C. Barnard, *Cromwellian Ireland: English Government and Reform in Ireland 1649–1660* (Oxford, 1975). See also T. C. Barnard, 'Planters and Policies in Cromwellian Ireland', *Past & Present*, 61 (1973), 31–69. *NHI*, iii. 353–86 provides an admirable overview. Little, *Broghill*, is a more recent study of a key figure.

Galway in April 1652, and the capitulation soon after of both the Leinster army and Clanricard's forces, marked the end of full-scale warfare. However the last Confederate stronghold, at Cloughoughter, in County Cavan, did not surrender until 27 April 1653. Even after this date, moreover, the new regime continued to be harassed by outlaw bands, to which it referred as 'tories'. The term 'tory' (from Irish *toraidhe*, a raider) had originally applied to groups of bandits thrown up by the disorders of the war years. An excommunication issued by the Catholic clergy in December 1649 had distinguished between Confederate forces and 'tories and such plunderers not in colours'. It is likely that some of those who continued to plague the Cromwellian authorities were likewise primarily bandits, whether driven to desperation by, or opportunistically profiting from, the collapse of social order. Others, however, continued a religious and political war against a victorious enemy. The Leinster tory Dorogh O'Derrike referred to himself as 'general of His Majesty's small forces', and counted among his victims seven of the government surveyors engaged in preparatory work for a new round of confiscation and plantation. Gaelic poets, no friends of autonomous plebeian action, likewise celebrated the exploits of men like Sean Ó Duibhir an Gleanna (John O'Dwyer of the Glen), presenting them as dispossessed lords striking back at a new, usurping order.[78]

In response to this guerrilla warfare, as well as to the threat of a renewed royalist offensive from the continent, Ireland remained an armed camp. The army of occupation initially stood at some 35,000 men. By 1657 this had fallen to around 9,000, still three times the level of the pre-war military establishment. Continuing tory attacks provoked collective punishments. When raiders from County Waterford struck into neighbouring County Cork in late 1655, for example, the military governor instituted mass arrests, condemning two men to be hanged, six to be transported to the West Indies, 'and five whole villages to transplant'.[79] The men transported joined a broad stream of similar deportees. Once the war was over the Cromwellian authorities had encouraged the departure of disbanded soldiers from Confederate armies, allowing an estimated 34,000 to enter the armies of France and Spain, at war throughout the 1650s and desperate for recruits. But they also rounded up large numbers of others to be sent as involuntary migrants, some to Virginia but most to Barbados and other British possessions in the Caribbean, where they would be assigned to masters either as convict labour or as indentured servants bound to work for a stated term. Those transported were in some cases beggars, vagrants, and other social undesirables, many of them wives and children widowed, orphaned, or abandoned in the chaos of the preceding decade. Others were transported as criminals, or as an

---

[78] Éamonn Ó Ciardha, 'Tories and Moss Troopers in Scotland and Ireland in the Interregnum: A Political Dimension', in Young (ed.), *Celtic Dimensions of the British Civil Wars*, 141–6.
[79] Council to Colonel Robert Phaire, 10 Dec. 1655 (Dunlop, *Ireland under the Commonwealth*, ii. 556–7).

alleged danger to the state. A report in the late 1660s noted about 8,000 Irish in Barbados, 'derided by the negroes and branded with the epithet of white slaves', and 12,000 in the West Indies as a whole.[80]

At the same time that they sought to impose military control, the commissioners laid the foundations for the restructuring of Irish society. An act for the settling of Ireland, passed by the English parliament on 12 August 1652, began by repeating Cromwell's assurance that there was no intention to extirpate the entire nation.[81] 'Husbandmen, ploughmen, labourers, artificers, and others of the inferior sort' were to receive 'mercy and pardon' provided they lived peaceably under the laws. Among those 'of higher rank and quality', on the other hand, certain categories were wholly excluded from pardon: those who had been guilty of rebellion, murder, or massacre prior to the first general assembly at Kilkenny, along with those who had killed persons not in arms on behalf of the English against the Irish, or who at the time of the killing had not themselves been part of the regular Irish forces. By January 1653 a specially constituted high court of justice was reported to be engaged in 'diligent prosecution' of those held to be guilty of murders. However the sparse details given—16 condemned at Kilkenny, 6 at Clonmel, and 32 at Cork—suggest a policy of selective rather than wholesale retribution.[82] The most prominent victim of the court was Sir Phelim O'Neill, who excluded himself from any chance of saving his life by refusing to repeat his earlier claims that his rising had been commissioned by Charles I.

The distinction drawn between those who had and had not been part of the Irish regular forces acknowledged the combatant status of the Confederate Catholics. But the terms imposed on those who had served that cause were nevertheless harsh. Officers above the rank of colonel, commanders of garrisons, and administrators at national or provincial level were all to be banished. Their estates were to be forfeited, although their wives and children were to receive one-third of the value. Others who had borne arms against the Commonwealth of England were likewise to forfeit their estates, but were to be allowed the equivalent of one-third of its value. Catholics who were not in these categories but who 'have not manifested their constant good affection to the interest of the Commonwealth of England' also forfeited, but were to receive a two-thirds equivalent. These one-third and two-third allocations were to be provided 'in such place in Ireland as the parliament, for the more effectual settlement of the peace of that nation, shall think fit to appoint for that purpose'. What this was to mean in practice became clear only on 2 July 1653, when the English council

---

[80] *NHI*, iii. 364. For transportation as collective punishment see Ó Ciardha, 'Tories and Moss Troopers', 153.

[81] *Acts and Ordinances of the Interregnum 1642–1660,* ed. C H. Firth and R. S. Rait (London, 1911), ii. 598–602. For the penalties imposed on Protestant royalists see below, pp. 120–1.

[82] Commissioners for Ireland to Council of State, 15 Jan. 1653 (Dunlop, *Ireland under the Commonwealth,* ii. 310–11).

of state ordered that all those who had a right to favour or mercy under the act of 1652 were to remove themselves west of the Shannon, to the province of Connacht and County Clare. Their instructions were confirmed and amplified by an act of the Protectorate parliament on 26 September. Heads of families were to report by 30 January 1654 to commissioners at Loughrea, County Galway, who would assign them lands in the prescribed areas. Their families were to follow by 1 May. Within these western counties, no Catholic proprietor was to be given land within four miles of the coast, or of the River Shannon, or in any garrison or port town. What had initially been a punitive system of partial confiscation had now become a programme of internal exile, designed to contain its victims within a limited territory bounded by strong natural frontiers.[83]

How far this strategy had been envisaged from the start, and how far it represented the evolution of policy over time, remains unclear. An element of improvisation is strongly suggested by the uncertainty, continuing for some time, as to who exactly was required to transplant themselves to the western reservation. Did the reference to all those having a right to favour or mercy under the act of 1652 refer only to landowners, who were now being told where the one-third or two-thirds of their former estates to which they were entitled was to be located? Or did it also extend to the 'inferior sort', to whom the act had, after all, granted mercy, if not favour? That the government itself had not at this stage decided seems clear from one of the questions referred to a standing committee set up by the parliamentary commissioners on 1 August 1653:

whether it be advisable that all Irish papists be removed except those that dwell in those counties and places into which the said removal is to be made, or only out of some counties, as Kerry, Wexford, Waterford etc, and only the landed and popular men from other places.

By May 1654 the parliamentary commissioners appear to have accepted that there were Irish in County Cork who were not to be transplanted, since they ordered that these should be required to live in easily policed villages of at least thirty families. In March 1655 there was discussion of which parts of a five-county block comprising Dublin, Wicklow, Wexford, Carlow, and Kildare should be wholly cleared of Irish and papists, and which parts could be tenanted by 'such Irish as not being proprietors, nor men that have been in arms, shall be thought fit to be dispensed with from transplantation'.[84] On the other hand a petition submitted in the same month by officers in several Leinster counties claimed that the order of July 1653, later confirmed by act of parliament, had required the transfer to Connacht of the Irish in general, except for boys of up to 14 and girls of up to 12.[85]

[83] *Acts and Ordinances of the Interregnum*, ii. 750.
[84] Dunlop, *Ireland under the Commonwealth*, ii. 370, 425, 486.
[85] Prendergast, *Cromwellian Settlement*, 61. For the date of the petition see S. R. Gardiner, 'The Transplantation to Connaught', *English Historical Review*, 14 (1899), 723–6. Gardiner's article,

Differences in how the plantation policy was understood came into the open in an exchange of pamphlets between January and May 1655. Vincent Gookin, the son of an early seventeenth-century settler in County Cork, argued that the Irish Catholics, now rendered powerless by defeat, were best dealt with, not by banishment, but by exposing them to the influence of Protestantism and English civility, as a means towards their cultural and religious assimilation. In response Colonel Richard Lawrence, former master general of Cromwell's horse and military governor of Waterford, restated the case for settling English colonists on lands wholly cleared of the corrupting and potentially dangerous presence of the natives. Their exchange revealed a predictable contrast between the army radical who saw a conquered Ireland to be reshaped by uncontaminated English settlement, and the second-generation settler, accustomed to the pragmatic compromises of colonial society, and aware also of the dependence of the New English elite on the labour and rents of native workers and tenants.

In the end the debate was resolved in favour of the transportation of landowners only. There is no record of a formal decision. The transfer of immediate power from Fleetwood to the more conservative Henry Cromwell may have marked the turning point.[86] But it is also possible that the outcome was essentially settled by default, as the difficulties involved in transplanting even the Catholic elite became increasingly clear. The orders of July 1653, publicized in a declaration by the parliamentary commissioners in October, required transplanters to present to the commissioners at Loughrea a certificate issued by the authorities in their own locality. By July 1654 the commissioners had received 1,623 certificates covering more than 44,000 individuals. The disparity between the two figures reflected the number of transplanters arriving with a train of tenants and dependants. James Butler, Baron Dunboyne, from County Tipperary, came with twenty-one followers; two members of the Hore family, father and son, from County Waterford, came with 129 others, variously described as servants, freeholders, and tenants. But the government had also to deal with a flood of petitions from those pleading for exemption or contesting the order to leave. Some of these at least proved impossible to ignore completely. Members of the Leinster army who argued that their articles of surrender exempted them from transplantation obtained permission to remain until 1 May 1655, although in the end the commissioners ruled that the act of 1652 overruled all treaty terms. Meanwhile the deadline of 1 May 1654 for the departure of wives and children was extended by two months, to permit the harvesting of crops and the fattening of cattle prior to their journey, and local committees were authorized to consider requests for further delays.

again drawing on materials now lost, remains the most detailed analysis of the evolution of the transplantation project.

[86] For these changes, see below, pp. 115, 121.

Despite these concessions, the commissioners attempted to enforce the requirement to transplant with at least sporadic coercion. As early as July 1654 a man condemned to death for failing to remove himself to Connacht had his sentence reduced to transportation to Barbados. An order of 30 November set a new deadline, requiring all those obliged to leave to have done so by 1 March 1655. Once again the deadline had to be extended for wives and children after heavy rain made the roads impassable. But on 19 March Fleetwood and his council ordered a general search for transplantable persons still east of the Shannon, and set up courts martial for their trial. Edward Hetherington of Kilnemanagh, County Tipperary, was publicly hanged on 3 April 1655, wearing placards on his front and back with the words 'for not transplanting'. At least two others were similarly condemned, though no records survive of what sentences were carried out. By this time or soon after the heads of leading Pale families like the Bellews and the Barnewalls had prudently taken up residence in the western suburbs of Athlone, and were required to obtain special passes before they could cross the bridge into the main town for purposes of business. In July of the following year the Irish council noted that 'divers Irish papists' were being held in county jails throughout Leinster and Munster for not having transplanted as required, and ordered that one group imprisoned at Kinsale should be immediately loaded onto a vessel lying conveniently at hand and bound for the Caribbean.[87]

The design and implementation of this huge and not wholly coherent scheme of collective punishment rested on a combination, typical of the Cromwellian regime as a whole, of moral conviction and commercial interest. On the one hand there was the belief, confirmed and elaborated over the preceding decade, that Irish Catholics as a body had been guilty of bloody massacre on a scale that made any indulgence shown to them an offence against God himself. The extensive depositions collected from refugees fleeing the slaughter and pillage of late 1641 and early 1642 had proved valuable in the campaign to secure both charity for refugees in England and military support for the war in Ireland. In 1642 one of the committee appointed to collect the depositions, Henry Jones, dean of Kilmore, printed the first set of extracts, selected to demonstrate that there had been a conspiracy to wipe out the Protestant population of Ireland. In 1646, at a time when supporters of the newly appointed lord lieutenant, Viscount Lisle, were seeking support in England for an aggressive policy of conquest, Sir John Temple, the Irish master of the rolls, published his *The Irish Rebellion*, in which he put the number of Protestant dead at a statistically impossible 300,000. The extent to which this attribution of blood guilt had taken root in English minds was evident in Cromwell's justification of the massacre at Drogheda.[88] But the most effective use of the depositions was perhaps in 1652. In April Jones, by now

---

[87] For these details see Prendergast, *Cromwellian Settlement*, 33–5, 41–3, 50–4; Dunlop, *Ireland under the Commonwealth*, i, p. cxliii, ii. 613.

[88] Above, p. 93.

an active servant of the new regime, presented his abstract to the commissioners responsible for the government of Ireland, as they met with senior army officers at Kilkenny to consider the treatment of the defeated Catholics. The effect was electrifying. Reading his account of 'the blood guiltiness of this people in a time of peace' the commissioners became convinced, by their own account, that 'several visitations' they had recently suffered, including probably the appearance of plague, were God's punishment for the leniency they had shown to persons 'whom he is pursuing with his great displeasure'. Struck with remorse, they forwarded Jones's abstract to England, lest others at greater distance from the scene 'might be moved to the lenity we have found no small temptation in ourselves'.[89] The abstract duly circulated in the English parliament just as the 1652 act for the settlement of Ireland was taking shape.

Alongside this conviction of Irish Catholic blood guilt, however, there was also the need to address pressing financial obligations. The Adventurers' act of March 1642 had invited private subscriptions towards the cost of suppressing the Irish rebellion, the investment to be repaid in confiscated Irish lands. Citing a total investment of £356,874, these Adventurers now staked their claim to 1.6 million acres of Irish land. Arrears of pay to the 35,000 soldiers in Ireland, along with debts owed by the army, were estimated at a further £1.75 million. There was also the hope of recouping some at least of the £2.5–3 million estimated to have been already expended on the reconquest of Ireland. The act of 1653 reserved a block of ten counties, extending on a north-east/south-west axis from Antrim to Limerick and Waterford, to satisfy the claims of the Adventurers and soldiers. Four further counties, Dublin, Carlow, Kildare, and part of Cork, were reserved to provide a permanent revenue to the state (see Map 3). Forfeited lands in the remaining counties outside Connacht and Clare were to be available to settle other debts. To facilitate this massive redistribution the government initially had only what was called the 'gross survey', a crude reckoning of acreages within large blocks of land, completed for the ten designated counties by the end of 1653 then extended to other regions. Between 1654 and 1656 the civil survey, relying on inquisitions before juries of local inhabitants, offered a more detailed enumeration of land and property. But it was not until 1654 that Sir William Petty, an Oxford polymath who had come to Ireland as physician general to Cromwell's army, was commissioned to produce a full survey by measurement and mapping, and it was not until 1659 that this Down survey was actually completed.[90]

---

[89] Commissioners to parliament, 5 May 1652 (Dunlop, *Ireland under the Commonwealth*, ii. 178–9). It would, of course, be possible to dismiss these pious references to God's will as mere rationalizations of the politically necessary. But that would be to ignore a central reality of mid-seventeenth-century English political life. For Jones's convoluted progress from royalist bishop to Cromwellian administrator and back see below, p. 140.

[90] The key works on the land settlement are Karl Bottigheimer, *English Money and Irish Land: The 'Adventurers' in the Cromwellian Settlement of Ireland* (Oxford, 1971), and R. C. Simington

Against this background of hasty improvisation, the redistribution of land was inevitably a rough and ready business. Those who fared best were the Adventurers. On 24 January 1654, at Grocers' Hall in London, their representatives and those of the soldiers drew lots to determine which baronies in the ten counties were to be allocated to each set of claimants. The Adventurers were then permitted to take possession of the land allocated to them, and to agree their own division by lot and measurement. One thousand and forty-three Adventurers, comprising 664 survivors from the original 1,533 investors and 379 who had subsequently bought into the scheme, thus took possession of 1.1 million acres. Around one-fifth of the grantees had invested £50 or less and their allocations were correspondingly small, often well under 100 acres. Holdings of this size, in a ravaged and precariously pacified countryside, offered little temptation to migrate, and it seems clear that most disposed of their new Irish properties for the best price they could get—if indeed they ever managed to establish an interest strong enough to be marketable. Nearly 200 Adventurers, on the other hand, became owners of substantial estates of over 1,600 statute (1,000 Irish) acres.

Soldiers in general fared less well. They initially received debentures, setting out the sum of money owed to them. They were then to draw lots for their allocation of land as their regiments were disbanded. The scheme related only to arrears of pay since the arrival of the New Model Army in June 1649, and the ratio of acres to pounds was revised downwards as the amount of land available proved to be inadequate. Soldiers could thus expect to receive only modest holdings in a land where few wished to remain. Instead most sold their debentures, generally to their officers, and at prices that declined as the rush to sell grew. A memorandum written around 1659 argued that soldiers currently stationed in Ulster would have no objection to being transferred to Scotland, as 'not one in fifty of them have a foot of land in Ireland', the rest having sold out to their officers.[91] This was an exaggeration. Of 33,419 debentures issued, 11,804 were subsequently exchanged for certificates of possession, and there were still some 7,500 soldiers in possession of their lands in 1670. But the vision of an Ireland thoroughly colonized by a veteran yeomanry was not realized.

The other half of the process, the distribution of the designated western lands to partially forfeiting Catholic proprietors, was more arbitrary still. The initial assignments made by the commissioners at Loughrea were provisional allocations, based on the certificates issued before the transplanters set out for Connacht. They were to be replaced by a 'final settlement' to be made by a court of claims and qualifications, sitting at Athlone, which would determine each transplanter's entitlement. This would be assessed on the basis of their former property, as detailed in the civil survey, as well as their degree of guilt, as determined from

(ed.), *The Transplantation to Connacht 1654–58* (Dublin, 1970). Note that acreages taken from Simington's account have been converted into statute acres (1 Irish acre = 1.62 statute acres).

[91] *CSPI 1660–2*, 166.

copies of the depositions, and from the records of the Kilkenny assembly. By the time this court began sitting, in December 1654, it was becoming clear that the claims of the soldiers went far beyond what was available—even though their allocation had already been expanded from the ten counties they were originally to share with the undertakers to confiscated lands in other counties, with the exception of four (Dublin, Kildare, Carlow, and Cork) that were reserved for the government. Accordingly the counties of Sligo and Leitrim, along with one barony in County Mayo, originally designated for transplanted Catholics, were instead set aside for soldiers. Before 1641 Catholics had held 59 per cent of Ireland's profitable land. Now the same proprietors, or their heirs, were to receive the equivalent of one-third or two-thirds of their former holdings in not quite four counties.

A scheme in February 1656, setting out the parts of the remaining Connacht counties to which transplantees from each region should be allocated, illustrated the sheer impossibility of the task. County Galway alone was to receive transplanters from no less than nineteen other counties. Even with the trimming of the reserved area along the coast and River Shannon from four miles to one, the shortfall remained a huge one. By the time the Loughrea commissioners ended their work, in September 1657, they had issued around 1,900 decrees. Of these 1,124, covering a total of 454,000 statute acres, went to proprietors who had already held lands west of the Shannon but were now displaced to reduced holdings in a new location. Another 770 decrees, for some 680,000 acres, were to transplanters from other regions. Most new grants, not surprisingly, were small. One estate of 1,069 acres in County Roscommon was divided between nine transplanters, who received between 45 and 194 acres each.

If most Catholic proprietors fared poorly in the distribution of lands in the west, however, a number of individuals, such as Sir Richard Barnewall of the prominent Pale family, received conspicuously larger grants, amounting to 4,000 acres or more. One, the earl of Westmeath, received over 18,000 acres. What is striking is not only the size of these allocations, compared to what others received, but also that the grantees were in some cases among those excepted by name, in the act of 1652, from pardon for either life or estate. The favour shown to them demonstrates the extent to which the vengeful passions behind the act had given way to a more realistic perception that stable government—particularly in an outlying region like Connacht—could only be achieved by gaining the cooperation of men of standing and influence. The same recognition led the Cromwellian regime to show considerable indulgence towards the earl of Antrim, still a powerful figure in the north-east, and to a variety of other delinquents in what had been the three kingdoms of the Stuarts.[92] Precisely what form the collaboration of the Connacht grantees took—whether, for example, it included their acquiescence in the removal of more than two counties from the original

[92] Ohlmeyer, *Civil War and Restoration*, 282–8.

territory set aside for Catholic proprietors—remains a matter for speculation.[93]
What is clear is that by this time the Protectorate government was anxious to end
the chaos it had created. An act of July 1657 retrospectively legitimized the rough
justice dealt out over the past five years by proclaiming that all those liable to
transplantation had in any case been guilty of high treason. It then declared the
work of the Athlone and Loughrea commissioners complete. Anyone covered by
the different articles of the 1652 act who had not transplanted by 24 September
lost all claim to be allocated lands, and any such person who had not transplanted
within six months was liable, on apprehension, to be transported to America. This
last clause, even now, was no empty threat: in October 1658 the council made
arrangements for the shipment from Galway to Barbados of persons convicted at
that year's assizes of not having transplanted.[94]

At the same time that they sought to implement a radical land settlement,
the representatives of the Commonwealth and Protectorate had also to create
a new religious establishment. They did so in the novel situation of rivalry,
not just between Catholic and Protestant, but between competing varieties of
Protestantism. Differences over doctrine and practice had existed before 1641:
between the Scots of Ulster and the episcopalian establishment, between advocates
of the beauty of holiness and those committed to a Protestantism purged of every
suggestion of the corrupt popish past. But these had been contained within a
single establishment. After 1641, on the other hand, the Ulster Scots, both newly
arrived and longer established, quickly built up their own ecclesiastical system.
The parliamentary army, from 1649 onwards, brought with it supporters of
the different groups into which English Protestantism had fragmented: Baptists,
Independents, and the somewhat different English variety of Presbyterian. With
the coming of peace the first Quakers also appeared in Ireland. Meanwhile the
clergy of the disbanded episcopal church showed varying degrees of willingness
to be incorporated into an alternative ecclesiastical structure.[95]

The first religious group to arouse concern was the Scottish Presbyterians.
Shortly after their arrival in Ulster, chaplains and elders from some of Monro's
regiments organized themselves into a presbytery, which held its first meeting on
10 June 1642. Their example encouraged local Scottish-dominated congregations
to elect their own elders and apply to Scotland for ministers. By 1653 there were
twenty-four Presbyterian ministers and the following year the original presbytery
divided into three 'meetings', Antrim, Down, and Route. By this time many,
though not all, of the Ulster Scots had risen in support of the crown during

---

[93] As suggested by Simington, *Transplantation*, p. xxiv.
[94] Dunlop, *Ireland under the Commonwealth*, ii. 686–7.
[95] For Cromwellian religious policy see Barnard, *Cromwellian Ireland*, ch. 5–6; R. L. Greaves,
*God's Other Children: Protestant Nonconformists and the Emergence of Denominational Churches
in Ireland 1660–1700* (Stanford, Calif., 1997), 1–35; Stevenson, *Scottish Covenanters and Irish
Confederates*, 285–91; Phil Kilroy, 'Radical Religion in Ireland', in Ohlmeyer (ed.), *Ireland from
Independence to Occupation*, 201–17; *NHI*, iii. 375–85.

1648–9, and Scotland itself had gone to war against England, in the name of Charles II, during 1650–1. In 1653 renewed reports of royalist plotting led the Dublin government to order the transportation of leading Scots from Down and Antrim to counties Kilkenny, Waterford, or Tipperary. There they could help keep the Irish in subjection, while being well removed from their compatriots in Scotland. New orders in 1656 proposed a more sweeping banishment, extending to all Scots who had settled since 1650, as well as those who had fought against the English parliament, and also forbidding future Scottish settlement in Ulster. Neither plan, however, was implemented. By this time Presbyterians in Ulster, as in Scotland, had divided between a Resolutioner majority, still committed to both crown and Covenant, and a Remonstrant minority which disowned Charles II as religiously unsound. From 1654 some of these Remonstrant ministers, despite their rejection of the Protectorate's religious policy, accepted state salaries, while the political passivity of the theoretically royalist Resolutioners allowed them to be left largely undisturbed.[96] The truce with government permitted further organizational growth. By 1659 there were nearly eighty ministers serving in Ulster, and the appearance of two further 'meetings', for Tyrone and for the Laggan district, testified to the continued growth of Presbyterianism in central and west Ulster.

The other Protestant denominations that took shape around the same time were distinguished from one another primarily by their concept of the church. English Presbyterians did not necessarily share the vision of a nation in direct covenant with God that had inspired their Scottish counterparts. But having rejected episcopacy they nevertheless believed in a national church, in which behaviour and doctrine would be supervised by rising tiers of collective authority: the elders and minister of the local kirk, the presbytery, the synod, and the general assembly. The emphasis on discipline, and on a hierarchy of authority if not of persons, made this a vision that appealed to many former clergy of the Church of Ireland. In particular Edward Worth, formerly dean of Cork, became the leader of a group of Munster clergy that joined with English Presbyterians to work towards a national church on broadly these lines. The main alternative came from the Independents. Where Presbyterians demanded a centralized national church to which all would be required to belong, the Independent vision was of a network of gathered congregations, each determining its own doctrine and worship within broad limits set by the state, and each composed of committed believers. For example John Rogers, who became minister at the former Christ Church cathedral in Dublin in 1650, required members of his congregation to testify to the means, whether dreams, inner experience, or attendance at sermons,

---

[96] Barnard, *Cromwellian Ireland*, 122–4, and Greaves, *God's Other Children*, 18–19, emphasize the government's alliance with the Remonstrants. Stevenson, *Scottish Covenanters and Irish Confederates*, 290–1, suggests a more even-handed policy of expedient toleration towards two groups neither of whom could be wholly trusted, one because of its royalism, the other because of its refusal to accept any ecclesiastical settlement other than its own.

that had led them to a conviction of their election to eternal life. By 1651 there
were at least five Independent congregations in Dublin. Their main spokesman
was Samuel Winter, who was minister of St Nicholas's, the church attended by
aldermen of Dublin corporation, as well as provost of Trinity College. There were
also Independent congregations at Waterford, Youghal, Drogheda, and other
provincial centres, ministering mainly to recently arrived soldiers and officials.

A third group, the Baptists, took rejection of a national church in favour of 'a
company of saints in a congregational way' to a further extreme, symbolized in
their signature insistence that baptism was for the informed adult, not for infants.
It was a doctrine that lent itself to scepticism of social as well as religious hierarchy.
A letter sent by Irish Baptists to their English and Welsh counterparts in June
1653 proclaimed that God had stretched forth his hand 'to set his poor despised
ones on high from the kings of the earth'.[97] The aggressive egalitarianism, and
the emphasis on a self-selected elite, were both particularly attractive to soldiers,
and it was in the army that Baptists in Ireland found their main support. By
1653 there were congregations based on the garrisons of most of the main towns.

The other new group, the Quakers or Society of Friends, appeared in 1653.
William Edmundson, a former soldier who had settled in Ulster as a cabinet
maker before being converted during a visit to London, established meetings
at Lurgan in County Armagh. The first missionaries from England arrived the
following year. In contrast to both the Independents and the Baptists, the Friends
spread without the benefit of links with either the civilian or the military wing of
the Cromwellian establishment. Instead their principled rejection of social and
religious convention marked them out as unacceptable to the leaders of both.
They scorned prescribed religious forms in favour of the inner light, disrupted
more orthodox services with loud challenges to their validity, refused to take
oaths, and denied social superiors the conventional deference of a doffed hat and
the vocative 'you' rather than 'thou'. They also allowed women as well as men
to preach. Their initial successes, particularly among soldiers in the Munster
garrisons, provoked the government to harsh action, but repression slackened as
it became clear that they had no revolutionary intent. Seventy-seven Friends were
recorded as in prison during 1655, but only three in 1658 and one the following
year. Meanwhile the movement spread, mainly among tradesmen, shopkeepers,
and farmers. Their main successes were in Munster and, despite Edmundson's
complaints that he found there 'a thick dull sottish people', in Ulster.[98] By 1660
there were a total of thirty established meeting places for Friends in Ireland.

Faced with this proliferation of sects, successive Dublin governments made
halting efforts to define the shape of a new national church. The parliamentary
forces that occupied Dublin in 1647 had suppressed the Book of Common

---

[97] Kevin Herlihy, ' "A Gay and Flattering World": Irish Baptist Piety and Perspective
1650–1780', in idem (ed.), *The Religion of Irish Dissent 1650–1800* (Dublin, 1996), 48, 50.
[98] Edmundson, quoted in Greaves, *God's Other Children*, 34.

Prayer. A scheme drawn up by the English parliament the following year proposed a Presbyterian church structure for both England and Ireland. Already by this time, however, the English Presbyterians were losing ground to the Independents, who had the crucial backing of the army, and the scheme was never implemented. In England Cromwell, ignoring the more authoritarian impulses of the two parliaments summoned during his Protectorate, instituted a state church organized on congregational lines and tolerant of variations within a broadly based, non-episcopal Protestantism. Irish policy initially followed the same direction. There was no formal legislation to establish a new ecclesiastical system. But the instructions issued to the parliamentary commissioners in 1650 authorized them to employ and pay qualified ministers. Of these a small body, paid substantial annual salaries of £200 or more, acted as leaders of the new church. They represented a mainly imported and strongly committed elite: of the twenty-one ministers in this category, only three had connections with Ireland before 1649, and only four conformed to the restored episcopal church after 1660. The rank and file of the new clergy, by contrast, included a higher proportion with an Irish background (though there was still a heavy dependence on recruits from England), and a wider range of theological views. Of the whole group of 276 salaried ministers, at least 65 were former ministers of the Church of Ireland, and 67 Presbyterians.[99]

Behind this general toleration of diversity, however, important changes took place over time in the orientation of the state church, and there was also a perceptible organizational trend in the direction of tighter discipline. Fleetwood was himself an Independent, but his commitment to liberty of conscience, for the godly at least, made him reluctant to impede the Baptists as they consolidated their influence within both the army and the ministry. It was concern at their rising power that led Cromwell to send his son Henry to Ireland in 1655, and by the following year he had successfully displaced or marginalized the most active among them. His opposition rested in part on well-grounded fears that some Irish Baptists were associating with political radicals opposed to the Protectorate. But he was also concerned to establish closer relations with the leaders of the pre-1641 Protestant population, most of whom feared and disliked the disruptive and undisciplined religious enthusiasm that Fleetwood had indulged. In his struggle with the Baptists Henry Cromwell had the support of the Independents. However the alliance did not last. Winter and his colleagues, in Cromwell's words, 'thought they should ride when they had thrown the Anabaptist out of the saddle', and they turned against him when he refused to allow them to control the state church.[100] Instead he turned to two groups more acceptable to the older Protestant interest: the Munster-based party of former episcopalians headed by

[99] For these details see Barnard, *Cromwellian Ireland*, 136–7, 141, 143; *NHI*, iii. 377–8.

[100] Quoted in Aidan Clarke, *Prelude to Restoration in Ireland: The End of the Commonwealth 1659–1660* (Cambridge, 1999), 43.

Edward Worth, and the more amenable sections of the Ulster Presbyterians. In April 1658 Henry Cromwell summoned a convention of ministers in Dublin. Its discussions, overtaken by political events over the next two years, pointed clearly towards a conservative church settlement, with provision for regular ordination of ministers and enforcement of some level of theological and liturgical orthodoxy. One immediate decision, strongly opposed by the Independent minority, was that ministers should once again be supported by tithes collected from their parishioners, a clear step in the direction of compulsory membership of a national church.

Standing wholly outside all projects for an agreed religious settlement were the nine-tenths or so of the population who were Catholics.[101] Cromwell's declaration that he meddled with no man's conscience but could not permit the mass was not the double-think sometimes alleged. The mass, to most Protestants, was idolatry, the toleration of which would be sinful and might even, like leniency to bearers of the blood guilt of 1641, invite God's punishment. Bishops and priests, likewise, were servants of spiritual corruption, if not indeed of the Antichrist. On 6 January 1653, as the war wound down, the parliamentary commissioners issued an order banishing all persons in popish orders, and making those who failed to leave liable to the penalty of death by hanging, drawing, and quartering provided in an English penal law of 1585. The Irish Catholic church was later to identify seventy clergy killed between 1649 and 1655 and eligible for the status of martyrs. The full number was clearly much greater: the Dominicans alone counted twenty-five members killed in the three years to 1653, while the Franciscans reported over forty members executed between 1641 and 1659.[102] Meanwhile a much larger number of clergy, perhaps 1,000, fled Ireland for continental Europe. From 1655 executions gave way to transportation to Barbados, though in practice many arrested priests, unattractive commodities in the market for transported bondsmen, remained in prison, some in specially constructed camps on the western islands of Aran and Inisbofin. In 1657 the English parliament revived the idea of a general transplantation to Connacht for all those unwilling to take a new oath of abjuration which renounced the authority of the pope and certain Catholic religious doctrines. Henry Cromwell, however, vigorously opposed the idea of a new round of disruptive coercion, and the act was never enforced. Instead active repression seems to have eased somewhat from around this time, reflecting the generally conservative thrust of the lord deputy's religious policy.

Even at the height of the repression, exceptions were made for some individuals. The Cistercian Patrick Crelly, Antrim's agent, spent the 1650s in London, where

---

[101] As always, this figure is largely guesswork, but setting the influx after 1649 of 35,000 soldiers and their associates, and the renewal with the coming of peace of immigration from Scotland and England, against population loss from flight, war, and disease over the preceding decade, a Protestant population of 100,000–150,000 in a population of 1.3 million seems a reasonable guess.

[102] *NHI*, iii. 383; Benignus Millett, *Survival and Reorganization 1650–95* (Dublin, 1968), 6–7.

he enjoyed access to Cromwell's secretary of state, John Thurloe, whom he supplied with information on royalist conspiracy. Antrim himself was allowed to return to Ulster and to derive some income from his lands. Edmund O'Reilly, vicar general of Dublin, was convicted in 1653 of complicity in the massacre of Protestant prisoners in Wicklow, but was deported rather than executed—possibly a last acknowledgement of his services to Michael Jones. Another Catholic reported to have given Jones information of royalist dispositions immediately before the engagement at Rathmines, Robert Ussher, remained in Dublin during the interregnum, still in possession of his lands. Oliver Fitzwilliam, later Viscount Merrion, married to the sister of the English parliamentarian Denzil Holles, likewise retained his lands, held in trust for his wife, and travelled freely between England and Ireland. On one voyage he told an astonished Edmund Ludlow, a parliamentary commissioner and later commander in chief of the Irish army, that he could if necessary put in a good word for him with Cromwell.[103] Even at the early modern high point, in both Ireland and Great Britain, of the politics of conviction, personal and family connection could sometimes cut across religious, political, and ethnic lines of division.

Cromwellian policy towards the Catholic masses was not wholly negative. There were some limited attempts to provide for missionary work, including a recognition of the issue of language. There was regular preaching in Irish in one Dublin church, St Bride's. In 1657 Henry Cromwell provided money for the training in Trinity College of a native clergy, 'in order to the propagating civility as well as religion among the Irish hereafter'.[104] Godfrey Daniel, possibly a relative of the former archbishop of Tuam, published an Irish translation of *The Christian Doctrine* by the English Puritan William Perkins. For the most part, however, the regime seemed to work on the assumption that its main task was to destroy the institutions that kept the Catholic masses in thrall to popery. Their short-term success was considerable. By the late 1650s, only one bishop, too old and infirm to travel, remained in the country. Priests and regular clergy continued to operate where they could, but the parochial system built up in the three decades before 1641 had been largely obliterated. Repression, even in the absence of extensive evangelization, could produce results. In Counties Dublin and Wicklow alone priests were later to claim that they had reclaimed 4,000 souls who had converted to Protestantism during the 1650s. But the onslaught was short-lived. In 1657, at the first signs of greater moderation, Rome appointed a new archbishop of Armagh (the recently exiled O'Reilly) and a bishop of Meath, as well as thirteen vicars apostolic to administer other dioceses, and before long priests were said to be trickling back into the country.

---

[103] L. J. Arnold, *The Restoration Land Settlement in County Dublin 1660–1688* (Dublin, 1993), 30–3.
[104] Quoted in Barnard, *Cromwellian Ireland*, 175.

The trauma inflicted on the greater part of the population in the years after 1649 is undeniable. Policies of confiscation and transplantation affected only the Old English and Gaelic elite, and possibly their immediate dependants. But the population as a whole experienced military conquest and occupation, ruthless collective punishment in response to the continued activities of the tories, and a sustained campaign of religious repression. A County Cork poet summed up in verse what he called 'mo mheabhair ar Bhéarla'—'my understanding of Irish'. His words, with their mixture of two languages, have an unvarnished directness far removed from the allusive abstractions of the bardic poetry of earlier generations.

> Transport, transplant mo mheabhair ar Bhéarla
> Shoot him, kill him, strip him, tear him.
> A tory, hack him, hang him, rebel
> A rogue, a thief, a priest, a papist.

At the same time these bitter lines, savouring of the immediacy of real experience, must be set against indications of a different set of relationships. As early as May 1651 Ireton complained that 'divers officers and soldiers of the army do daily intermarry with the women of this nation who are papists'. Those who did so were to be dismissed, unless their brides could convince a tribunal of fit persons that they had experienced a conversion 'from a real work of God upon their hearts'. The order was renewed in 1652, 1653, and again in 1659.[105] The Cromwellian regime's management of Ireland had a clarity of purpose, and an edge of violence, that was not to be seen again until the 1790s. But even under its rule interaction took more than one form, and worked to change the conquerors as well as the conquered.

---

[105] Prendergast, *Cromwellian Settlement*, 106–7; Dunlop, *Ireland under the Commonwealth*, i. 121; ii. 363, 711–12.

4

Through the Looking Glass: Restoration Ireland

Three months after Charles II returned to claim his throne, one of the newly restored bishops of the Church of Ireland, John Lesley of Raphoe, petitioned for confirmation of a pre-war grant giving him possession of 'all islands yet undiscovered' lying within a hundred leagues (around 400 miles) off the north-west coast of Ireland. His interest in this long-dormant asset had apparently been reawakened by news that such islands had actually been seen by ships entering the harbour of Killybegs.[1] Leslie's application, and the king's subsequent promise to honour his father's gift of any such island that should be discovered, illustrates the extent to which Ireland in 1660 was still seen as lying on the edge of the known world. Thirty years later, it was still very much on the periphery. King William III, forced to campaign there in 1690, lamented that he would be 'as it were out of the knowledge of the world'.[2] But by then three decades of expanding trade and rising population had begun to reshape both lives and landscape. Dublin, in the 1630s a provincial centre to be measured against several others, had become unequivocally the second city in the Stuart kingdoms. Meanwhile the working out in Ireland of the terms of the Restoration had encouraged the emergence of a more cohesive ruling elite, bringing together those already established before 1641 and beneficiaries of the Cromwellian settlement. Their ascendancy was not untroubled. There were threats, on the one hand, from those not reconciled to the return of monarchy and episcopacy, on the other from the Catholics whom the Restoration settlement had cruelly disappointed. But the new social order, despite its origins in civil war and conquest, was to display a remarkable resilience. When it did come to be seriously challenged, at the end of the 1680s, the crisis, even more than had been the case in 1641, had its origins outside Ireland. The resulting period of conflict and uncertainty, likewise, was much shorter-lived.

[1] *CSPI 1660–2*, 29.
[2] Quoted in J. G. Simms, *Jacobite Ireland 1685–91* (London, 1969), 135.

THE BIRTH OF THE PROTESTANT NATION

The events of 1640–1 had forced Irish Protestants to begin thinking in new ways about the constitutional status of their adopted kingdom. Their initial concern had been with the abuse of executive authority they had endured under Wentworth. But, as the English parliament began to assert itself, questions also arose about its right to interfere in Irish affairs. The slide into civil war from the autumn of 1641 pushed such concerns into the background. But the underlying issue did not go away. The parliamentary opponents of Charles I initially showed no particular ambition to assert, as a matter of principle, their control of Ireland. On the contrary they continued, even after they had gone to war against the king, to appeal back to an instrument of March 1642 whereby he had delegated the management of Irish affairs to a parliamentary commission. In practice, however, the establishment of effective military control over Ireland brought with it the assumption of political authority. One of the first acts of the parliamentary forces that occupied Dublin in 1647 was to announce the abolition of episcopacy and to forbid the use of the Book of Common Prayer. Cromwell, in a muddle neatly illustrating the lack of coherent constitutional thinking, came to Ireland with the title of lord lieutenant, making him representative of a king that he and his associates had in fact just beheaded. He continued to hold the title until 1652. From 1650, however, the day-to-day government of Ireland was in the hands of four parliamentary commissioners.[3] In March 1653 the London parliament formally acknowledged its assumption of power by voting that in future Ireland was to be represented by thirty seats in the assembly.[4]

The experience of rule by these parliamentary commissioners was, for most Irish Protestants, an unsettling one. The most vulnerable were those, like the second earl of Cork or Viscount Mongomery in east Ulster, who had remained loyal to the crown. The act of 1652, in addition to categorizing the Catholic population by varying levels of guilt and penalty, provided that all Protestants who had not been 'in actual service for the parliament', and had not otherwise demonstrated 'good affections' towards it, were to forfeit one-fifth of their estates. Meanwhile even those who had supported the winning side, like Cork's brother Broghill, now found themselves shouldered aside as officers of the parliamentary army and their civilian supporters took over both central and local administration. The lack of sympathy between the new military establishment and even those

---

[3] Patrick Little, 'The English Parliament and the Irish Constitution 1641–9', in Micheál Ó Siochrú (ed.), *Kingdoms in Crisis: Ireland in the 1640s* (Dublin, 2001), 110–12.

[4] For government under the Commonwealth and Protectorate see T. C. Barnard, *Cromwellian Ireland: English Government and Reform in Ireland 1649–1660* (Oxford, 1975); idem, 'Planters and Policies in Cromwellian Ireland', *Past & Present*, 61 (1973), 31–69. For political and constitutional developments see Patrick Little, *Lord Broghill and the Cromwellian Union with Ireland and Scotland* (Woodbridge, 2004).

Irish Protestants who had been their allies was evident in the controversy between Gookin and Lawrence, where Gookin's humanitarian and practical arguments against wholesale transplantation led his opponent to attack him as an enemy of the army and a dupe or secret supporter of the Catholic interest. There were also religious tensions. The new administration, particularly under Fleetwood, gave free rein to Baptists and Independents, whose radicalism grated on the majority of the established Protestant population. In addition the huge military establishment had to be paid for. Between 1633 and 1638 Wentworth had raised the ordinary revenue of the Irish government from £40,000 to £80,000, while securing subsidies from parliament intended to yield £300,000. Between 1649 and 1656, on the other hand, Ireland contributed £1.9 million, of which £1.3 million came from a tax on property, the assessment.[5] These exactions added to the considerable burden of debt, through lost rents, the disruption of trade, and the cost of military operations, that already affected most landowners at the end of a decade of war.

Tensions between what before long came to be referred to as the Old and the New Protestants—those established in Ireland before 1641 and those whose involvement there had begun during or since the civil wars—eased significantly from 1655. The instrument of change was Henry Cromwell. By temperament and age (he had been born in 1628), he was more concerned with orderly government than with continuing the ideological conflicts of the 1640s. His initial mission was to curb Fleetwood's indulgence of religious and political radicals potentially hostile to his father's Protectorate, and the resulting purge of Baptists and others from positions of power in itself did much to reconcile Old Protestants to the regime. His appointment also seems to have brought the final abandonment of schemes for a general transplantation, which had threatened to bring disaster to a still fragile Irish economy. In 1656 major towns, up to then controlled by military governors, regained their charters, allowing a return to rule by mayors and corporations drawn from the urban elite. From 1655 commissions of the peace were likewise revived, permitting a transfer of law enforcement from military commanders to local gentlemen acting as justices of the peace. Pragmatic conciliation also extended to former royalists. Already in 1654 an ordinance had permitted those liable to forfeit one-fifth of their estates to pay a substantial fine instead. Under Henry Cromwell the attempt to collect these fines was quietly dropped.

The success of these attempts to win over the Old Protestant elite was evident in the support which some of its representatives duly gave to the Cromwellian Protectorate. The Long Parliament, which had sat since 1641, had been forcibly dispersed in April 1653. However the Instrument of Government, by which Cromwell became Lord Protector, confirmed Ireland's allocation of thirty seats in future assemblies. When the first Protectorate parliament met the following

[5] Barnard, *Cromwellian Ireland*, 28.

year Fleetwood, showing his awareness of the deep unpopularity of the military regime, argued unsuccessfully that his administration should nominate the Irish members. The elections confirmed his misgivings, returning sixteen Old Protestants and three others representing Old Protestant interests, as against only five that could be clearly identified with the army. By this time Broghill had emerged as the dominant figure in Old Protestant circles, while also retaining access to Oliver Cromwell and exercising increasing influence over Henry. Under his leadership the Irish members consistently supported measures aimed at increasing Cromwell's power as Protector. They also brought forward a bill for a formal union of England and Ireland, lost when Cromwell abruptly ended the parliament in January 1655.

Both strands of this political strategy made sense: a strong Protector, and a union defining Ireland's constitutional status, were at this stage the best protection against arbitrary military rule. The proposed union would also have allowed Ireland to trade with England without customs duties, and would have fixed its tax burden at a reasonable level. Hence Broghill and his allies came to the second Protectorate parliament, in 1656, with another union bill. An even more attractive possibility, however, was the transformation of the Protectorate into a hereditary monarchy. This would have the immediate benefit of ensuring that Cromwell was not succeeded by an army radical. A strong monarchy would also make Ireland less dependent on shifts in the balance of power in a British parliament in which it had only limited representation. How far Broghill was involved in the initial Remonstrance, presented on 23 February 1657, that invited Cromwell to assume the crown remains unclear. But he took a leading part in the drafting of the Humble Petition and Advice in which the proposal took firm shape, and Cromwell's rejection came as a heavy personal as well as political blow.[6]

Against this background the Old Protestants could only react with dismay to the events that followed the death of Oliver Cromwell on 3 September 1658. The succession of his son Richard as Lord Protector held out a brief promise of continuity. But in May 1659 dissatisfied army leaders forced Richard, first to recall the remnant of the Long Parliament that his father had dissolved in 1653, then to resign. Henry Cromwell, having cautiously explored the possibilities of raising forces in Ireland to support his brother, accepted his recall as deputy. In his place the new English council of state appointed five commissioners, three of whom had been Henry Cromwell's main opponents on the Irish council. These immediately remodelled the army, removing a quarter of those officers in senior command positions. Later Edmund Ludlow, the newly appointed commander in chief, extended the purge to junior officer level, allegedly dismissing 200 men. Of five new colonels appointed, four were Baptists whom Henry Cromwell had

    [6] Little, *Broghill*, 76–88, 124–60. See also Patrick Little, 'The First Unionists? Irish Protestant Attitudes to Union with England 1653–9', *IHS* 32 (2000), 44–58.

earlier dismissed. Meanwhile local proprietors suspected of having had too close links with the Protectorate were removed from their positions as sheriffs and justices of the peace, in some cases once again being replaced by Baptists and other religious radicals.

The fall of the Protectorate thus threatened to deprive the Old Protestants of everything they had gained under Henry Cromwell's conciliatory regime. Their opportunity to strike back came when the English army leaders, in October, dismissed the parliament that they had called back into existence five months earlier. In doing so, they precipitated a political crisis. By December some of the expelled MPs had set up a rival camp at Portsmouth, whose garrison had declared in their favour. In London apprentices rioted in their support, and a plot by some officers to seize the Tower of London was narrowly foiled. Most important of all George Monck, commander of the army in Scotland, came out in support of the expelled members. Monck had served twice in Ireland, first as a royalist and then as a parliamentarian, and he now established contact with old comrades such as Sir Theophilus Jones and Sir Charles Coote. On 13 December Jones and others organized a bloodless coup in Dublin, seizing control of the Castle and other strategic centres and arresting the parliamentary commissioners. Similar action followed, either by prior arrangement or in imitation, in towns and garrisons throughout the provinces. In Munster those involved were in many cases associates of Lord Broghill. In Connacht Coote personally led the operation, first surprising the garrison at Galway, then leading a large force of horse and foot to take control of Athlone. By the end of the month a council of officers, along with Coote and Broghill, had established what was in effect a provisional government.[7]

The declared aim of the Irish coup was to join with Monck and the Portsmouth garrison in demanding the restoration of the English parliament. Some of those involved were committed republicans, for whom the suppression of parliament had represented a betrayal of the cause in which they had fought the king. But for most Old Protestants, both civilians and soldiers, the issue was rather different. The purges that had driven them out of the army and from local administration, and the return to power of the detested religious radicals, had begun, not when the Long Parliament was closed down in October, but when it had reopened the previous May. The true basis of their revolt became evident when Ludlow sailed for Ireland to reassert his authority as commander in chief, arriving off Dublin on 31 December. A week earlier the English army leaders, their authority crumbling, had allowed the parliament to resume its sittings, and Ludlow came with its authority. Nevertheless his supposed subordinates firmly refused him permission to land. When he disembarked instead at Duncannon fort, still commanded by a Baptist protégé of his own, other Munster commanders united to keep him

---

[7] Aidan Clarke, *Prelude to Restoration in Ireland: The End of the Commonwealth 1659–1660* (Cambridge, 1999).

confined there. The council of officers and their civilian associates avoided direct confrontation with the restored parliament. They justified their action by sending lengthy articles of impeachment against Ludlow and the deposed commissioners, and later in January they abandoned their plans to set up what could have been seen as a rival authority by summoning an elected convention. But their determination to retain effective control of their own affairs was evident.

The extent to which those who had joined in the action of December 1659 out of republican principle had miscalculated became evident over the next few weeks. It was still not possible to discuss openly the possibility of a return to monarchy. Instead debate centred on the status of the parliament restored in May, and again in December. This consisted solely of the minority that had remained following the purge in December 1648 which cleared the way for the execution of Charles I. Its limited legitimacy was reflected in the nickname, gaining currency about this time, of 'the Rump'. But it was also widely recognized that either of the main alternatives, the readmission of the members excluded at that time, or the election of a new assembly, would produce a majority for some form of restoration. The excluded members would return, a Dublin-based pamphleteer warned, 'and then comes in ding dong bells, King, Lords and Commons.'[8] Sir Hardress Waller, a Kentish man who had settled in Ireland on marrying a County Limerick heiress in 1629, was one of those who had particular reason to be alert on this point. He had endorsed the December coup and had become head of the council of officers. But he was also one of the regicides who had signed King Charles's death warrant. On 15 February he tried to force the issue by demanding that his fellow officers subscribe to a declaration against the readmission of the purged members, and allegedly plotting the arrest of those who refused. When his opponents mobilized in arms he took refuge in Dublin Castle, only to have his own soldiers hand him over as a prisoner, following a two-day siege.

By declaring in support of the excluded members, the Irish leaders had again moved ahead of events in England. They strengthened their hand by reviving their plans for a convention. One hundred and thirty-eight members, comprising two from each county, from Dublin city, and from Trinity College, Dublin, along with one representative from each of the remaining constituencies, met at the Tholsel in Dublin on 27 February. Of these at least 98, and possibly 100, were from families present in Ireland before 1641. They included some men of modest origins, whose gains under the Commonwealth had turned them into landed proprietors. But the majority, 68 of the total, were from families that had been represented in at least one of the three pre-war parliaments. These details confirm the extent to which the December coup had placed power in the hands of the Old Protestant establishment. At the same time the division between Old and New Protestant was now of diminishing importance. As the return of

8 Quoted ibid. 129.

the monarchy became steadily more likely, past squabbles over the shape of a Commonwealth or Protectorate ceased to have relevance. By this time too some of the more recent arrivals had begun to make themselves a part of their new society. Many of those returned to the convention, particularly outside Leinster, had established ties of marriage, friendship, or clientship with longer-established families.

Most important of all, past conflicts were overshadowed by a powerful shared interest. Old Protestants as well as new had benefited from the huge redistribution of land that had taken place over the previous eight years. Some had themselves received grants, in recognition of services to the Commonwealth and Protectorate, or as settlement of arrears of pay for military service. Others had bought up some of the land available at low prices, as Adventurers and soldiers not inclined to settle hurried to cash in their Irish assets. The key question now was whether a restored monarchy would uphold the massive confiscations on which these grants and purchases rested. Even Old Protestants who did not stand to lose directly from a reversal of the Cromwellian land transfers, moreover, would have recognized the implications of stepping back from a society in which the Catholic landed interest had been all but wiped out to one in which a propertied elite could once again challenge the Protestant monopoly of power. Thus one of the first issues raised in the convention, in a declaration drawn up early in its proceedings, was the need to confirm the titles of holders of forfeited lands.

Where Old Protestant domination of the assembly did make a difference was in religious policy. The convention quickly turned its back, not just on the Baptists and other sects, but on the Independency that had been favoured during the Protectorate. Instead its declaration, while avoiding the contentious question of church government, prescribed an established church, with firm disciplinary structures and uniform worship and doctrine, to which all would be required to belong. It went on to set up a committee of advisers to decide which ministers should be permitted to preach, and to order that those so approved should be supported by tithes and other parochial revenues. Initially it was assumed that these decisions pointed towards some form of Presbyterian establishment. Of an initial list of 160 ministers approved by the advisers, 60 were members of the Presbytery of Ulster. But this was at a point when episcopacy was still proscribed by law, and it was widely known that Charles II had subscribed to the Solemn League and Covenant in 1650. Before long, the supporters of the traditional ecclesiastical order had begun to assert themselves. The first step was when the advisers, under pressure from a separate committee set up to organize the maintenance of licensed ministers, agreed to approve certain candidates who had conformed to the Commonwealth church but whom they nevertheless had initially objected to as 'prelatical'. Soon after the commissioners to whom the English council of state had now committed the management of Irish affairs intervened directly to order the reinstatement in their former parishes of some episcopalian ministers who had refused to join the Cromwellian establishment.

By 15 April five of the eight surviving bishops from the pre-1647 establishment had begun receiving salaries.

The drift to a religious as well as a political restoration did not go wholly uncontested. Of the four commissioners appointed by the English council of state, Coote, Broghill, Sir William Bury, and Sir John Clotworthy, Bury and Clotworthy were both strong Presbyterians, and there are indications of a behind-the-scenes struggle as they sought to counter Coote's increasingly open support for episcopacy. Meanwhile the Ulster Presbyterian leader Patrick Adair appealed directly to the convention to acknowledge the Solemn League and Covenant, as the English parliament had recently done, following the admission of the excluded members. However the chairman, Sir James Barry, effectively killed the proposal by declaring, to the applause of the majority, that he would leave the chair if the issue was even discussed. The hardening of attitudes may in part have been a response to better information as to the preferences of the court in waiting. In the case of Scotland, however, Charles II was initially willing to compromise with the preferences of his subjects, until bounced into a heavy-handed reimposition of episcopacy by his first local strongman, the earl of Middleton. If he showed no such hesitation in Ireland, it was presumably because the balance of forces there indicated no need to do so. The Old Protestants who dominated the convention had already made clear their preference for a return to the pre-war world of hierarchy and order, while the Ulster Scots, still disadvantaged by the open adherence of both Presbyterian factions to the Stuarts, were represented by only two members, neither a figure of much consequence.[9]

Where the political settlement is concerned it remains difficult, in relation to a time when thoughts were kept secret and options open, to speak with confidence of the preferences or aspirations of individuals or groups. However, the decisive rejection of Waller's attempted coup suggests that the leaders of Protestant Ireland had come to accept a restoration of the monarchy as the most likely, and probably as the most desirable, outcome. Irish Protestants had supported the king, or at least stayed passively loyal, in the early stages of the civil war, turning to parliament only when it seemed that no other power could rescue them from Catholic domination. Subsequently they had formed a solid block in support of a strong Protectorate, or even a Cromwellian monarchy. One main reason, in each case, was that strong central government in England itself was essential to the defence of English and Protestant interests in Ireland. A second, becoming clearer over time, was that a direct relationship with a single ruler, such as had existed up to 1641, was preferable to being subject to the shifts of

---

[9] In addition to the account in Clarke (ibid. 278–85), see J. I. McGuire, 'The Dublin Convention, the Protestant Community and the Emergence of an Ecclesiastical Settlement in 1660', in Art Cosgrove and J. I. McGuire (eds.), *Parliament and Community* (Belfast, 1983), 121–46. For Scotland see Claire Jackson, *Restoration Scotland 1660–1690: Royalist Politics, Religion and Ideas* (Woodbridge, 2003), 105–10.

mood and factional power that might take place within an English parliament. Beyond these local considerations lay the natural tendency of men of property everywhere to see the return of monarchy as the best guarantee that two decades of dangerous instability could at last be brought to an end.

The individual who came closest to decisive action was Sir Charles Coote. Despite his long service as parliamentary commander in Connacht, his commitment to the Commonwealth had remained suspect. In August 1659, during the English royalist rising led by Sir George Booth, the parliamentary commissioners had forbidden him to leave Dublin. However it was not until 10 February 1660 that he sent Sir Arthur Forbes, a Scottish Presbyterian with a history of royalist conspiracy, to carry a message to Charles II at Brussels. In response the king sent two blank commissions, which Coote could use, if necessary, to take power in his name, either alone or with others. In fact Coote chose not to force the issue, but to move forward gradually, in step with developments in England. However there was reportedly one brief period in which, alarmed at Monck's continued insistence that he intended to uphold the Commonwealth, Coote considered unilateral action. By contrast Broghill, despite ample potential channels of communication, through his royalist brother the earl of Cork and a range of other relatives and associates, was much slower to offer Charles his support. He accepted the likelihood of a restoration, but appears to have hoped for some time that it would be possible to impose binding terms on the returning king.

In the end both Coote's impatience and Broghill's belief in negotiating from a position of strength proved to be irrelevant. The excluded members had rejoined the Long Parliament on 21 February. On 16 March it dissolved, in preparation for a newly elected assembly. As soon as it did so, Monck at last received the king's emissary and declared his support for a restoration. On 4 April Charles II issued a crucial declaration from Breda, the Dutch town to which he had sensibly transferred himself from his earlier base in Spanish (and Catholic) territory. By promising a general pardon, liberty for tender consciences, and the payment of army arrears, while leaving all the difficult details to be resolved in a future parliament, he removed the main arguments for seeking to impose conditions for his restoration. On 1 May the English parliament (strictly speaking a convention, since the writs of summons were not issued by the monarch) declared Charles II king. The Irish convention, meeting the same day on the eve of a seven-week adjournment, knew only that the election results had made a restoration virtually certain. So they contented themselves with a strongly worded declaration condemning the execution of Charles I as 'the foulest murder and highest assassination that sacred or profane story hath recorded'. The proposer was Henry Whalley, a cousin of Oliver Cromwell's who held land as an Adventurer and whose own brother was a regicide.[10] When news of the English vote arrived two days later, Griffith Williams, bishop of Ossory,

---

[10] Quoted in Clarke, *Prelude to Restoration*, 290.

who had travelled on the packet boat, went straight to St Bride's church and seized the glory of being the first man in the kingdom to offer public prayers for the king.

The public proclamation of the restored monarch in Dublin on 14 May provided the occasion for wider participation in an episode otherwise dominated by the manoeuvrings of grandees and military commanders. In an elaborate piece of street theatre, a hearse bedecked with candles and the arms of state carried an effigy of the Rump, 'a seeming carcass of a man st[uffed] with hay, but without a head', followed by mourners with blackened faces. 'The people, with their naked swords and staves hacked at and battered the rump all along well favourably as it passed.' Eventually the procession stopped outside the residence of the lord mayor, who distributed funerary cakes and ale before the effigy was partly burned and 'part trod to dust and mortar by the rout'. The Anglican merchant who described the scene for the benefit of an English clergyman friend did so 'to show you the genius of this place, now the heretics and sectaries are deservedly laid aside'. Ten days earlier, in a more direct demonstration of popular antipathies, a crowd had attacked the Baptist church near Thomas Street, breaking up seats and tearing down the pulpit.[11]

The restoration of the monarchy was not effected in Ireland. The role of Irish Protestants was to fall in line with decisions made on the larger island, and they did so without receiving the guarantees, in relation to their holdings of forfeited lands, for which they had hoped. But the proceedings of the convention of 1660 nevertheless constituted a significant episode in their history, as pre-1641 settlers and new arrivals set aside past antagonisms to concentrate on the defence of their common interests. At the same time it has to be recognized that the alliances that made the assembly work were pragmatic in character. Nor was it clear exactly how the basis of that new cohesion was to be defined. One recent analysis suggests two contrasting versions. Some, such as Broghill, had by now become committed to the idea of a Protestant interest, uniting royalist and Cromwellian but strongly anti-Catholic. Others, such as Ormond, thought in terms of an English interest, which could still at some level include politically compliant Old English.[12] There was also the question of how any concept of a Protestant interest could accommodate the differences between Protestant dissenters and an episcopalian establishment. In Ulster this became in addition the question of how settlers still recognizably Scottish in origin fitted into what was still thought of as an English colony. The events of 1659–60, in other words, were a stage in the emergence of a new sense of group identity. But whether that identity was to

[11] Toby Bonnel to John Johnson, 16 May 1660 (Cambridge University Library, Strype Correspondence, vol. 1, fo. 2); R. L. Greaves, *God's Other Children: Protestant Nonconformists and the Emergence of Denominational Churches in Ireland 1660–1700* (Stanford, Calif. 1997), 260.

[12] For this argument see T. C. Barnard, 'The Protestant Interest', in Jane Ohlmeyer (ed.), *Ireland from Independence to Occupation 1641–1660* (Cambridge, 1995), 219–20, 240. For Broghill as champion of the Protestant interest see Little, *Broghill*.

be British, English, or Protestant remained a subject of contention for another half-century or more.

If ideas of identity remained fluid and imprecise, what was clearer was the conviction that collective interests were best defended through the maintenance of a set of distinctively Irish political structures. Once again the thinking was primarily pragmatic. During 1654–7 most Irish Protestants seem to have been willing to follow Broghill's lead in seeking a union in which their right to representation and equitable treatment would be protected by formal articles. When opponents of Richard Cromwell, in the last Protectorate parliament of early 1659, sought to eliminate some of his most reliable supporters by objecting to the presence in the house of MPs from Scotland and Ireland, the Irish members concerned reacted by emphasizing their British credentials. They were 'the English of Ireland', with no 'Irish teague' among them.[13] In the changed conditions following the collapse of the Protectorate, on the other hand, Protestant spokesmen turned to arguments similar to those that had already been put forward, by New and Old English alike, during 1640–1. As with earlier relations with the newly restored English parliament, there was no appetite for unnecessary confrontation. Members of the convention emphasized in their opening declaration that they had met before receiving news that the excluded members had taken their seats on 21 February, and proclaimed their attachment to the parliament of England. At the same time they noted pointedly that after what could now be condemned as the illegal purge of December 1648 'they who invaded the rights of the parliament of England invaded also the rights of the parliament of Ireland, by imposing taxes and assessments upon them'.[14] When on 7 April the English council of state sent an explicit order for the Irish convention to cease meeting, it failed to comply, and remained in session until 29 May.

The new interest in the defence of Ireland's status as a kingdom in its own right is also reflected in the survival of a manuscript 'disquisition', written some time during the summer of 1660, by the newly appointed attorney general, Sir William Domville. Whether Domville acted on his own initiative, or was asked to formulate an opinion, perhaps by the convention, remains unclear. But what he produced was a firm restatement of the case for Ireland's right to be bound solely by the laws made in its own parliament. His discussion drew in part on the arguments and precedents already assembled by Darcy and others in the early 1640s. Earlier writers, however, had based their claims for the historical status of Ireland as a separate kingdom on the case of John, son of Henry II,

---

[13] One Irish member, Arthur Annesley, son of Wentworth's old adversary Lord Mountnorris, took a different line, calling for the return of a separate Irish parliament on the grounds that Ireland was as entitled as England to its 'ancient constitution'. But this appears to have been part of a crypto-royalist strategy, intended to bring about the collapse of the Protectorate. See Little, 'First Unionists', 55.

[14] Quoted in Clarke, *Prelude to Restoration*, 249.

who had become lord there at a time when it was not foreseen that he would succeed to the crown of England. Domville added a second, less legalistic point: the assertion that Ireland had not in fact been conquered by Henry II. Instead he had become king by the voluntary submission of its lords and chieftains, who had in turn gained the right to live under laws made in their own parliament. It was a further twist in what was emerging as a coherent, if still finely spun, thread of Irish constitutional thinking.

One possible reason for the writing of Domville's disquisition was as a briefing paper for the commissioners, appointed by the Convention, who appeared at court on 18 June to present to the king the case of preserving the Cromwellian land settlement. When they did so, however, they faced a potentially difficult challenge. The Catholic lawyer and former Confederate Nicholas Plunkett put it to them that the settlement depended on an act of the English parliament, the Adventurers' act, which by their own constitutional principles could have no legal force in Ireland. The commissioners declined to debate the general issue of legislative independence. But neither did they take the easy route of defending the right of the English parliament to make laws disposing of Irish land. Instead they presented the settlement as resting on the right of the king to seize and dispose of the estates of rebels; the act of the English parliament had served only to validate those parts of his decision that had to be implemented in England. It was a transparently self-interested piece of sophistry. But the convoluted reasoning was itself testimony to an unwillingness to sacrifice the principle of legislative independence, even when it might have been expedient, in the short term, to do so.[15]

DECREES OF INNOCENCE

Charles II's initial arrangements for the government of his newly acquired second kingdom displayed the same pragmatism as his Declaration of Breda. Coote and Broghill were rewarded for their services by becoming, respectively, earl of Mountrath and earl of Orrery. Their fellow commissioner Clotworthy became Viscount Massareene. In England Annesley, who as president of the council of state in the period following the admission of the excluded members had played a vital part in the smooth management of the Restoration, became earl of Anglesey. Ormond, returning with the exiled court, was raised to the rank of Ireland's only duke, as well as receiving an English earldom. However, he remained for the

[15] The significance of the debate on the Adventurers' act is highlighted in Aidan Clarke, 'Colonial Constitutional Attitudes in Ireland 1640–60', *PRIA*, C, 90 (1990), 373. For the evidence linking Domville's disquisition to the commissioners see Aidan Clarke, 'Patrick Darcy and the Constitutional Relationship between Ireland and Britain', in Jane Ohlmeyer (ed.), *Political Thought in Seventeenth-Century Ireland* (Cambridge, 2000), 53 n. 44.

moment in England, as steward of the royal household. Instead Monck, now earl of Albemarle, became a wholly absentee lord lieutenant. The king experimented briefly with making an English parliamentarian, Baron Robartes of Truro, his deputy. When he proved difficult to work with Charles replaced him with three lords justices: the new earls of Mountrath and Orrery and, governing jointly with them, Sir Maurice Eustace, who had been speaker of the Irish Commons in 1640–1 and had remained in Ireland, enduring harassment due to his steadfast royalism, during the bleak years of the 1650s. In February 1662, as part of a wider series of changes in the arrangements for governing the three Stuart kingdoms, Ormond resumed his old post as lord lieutenant. Mountrath died of smallpox just after the appointment was announced.[16] However Orrery, the other Cromwellian strongman to whom Charles was indebted, was allowed to retain office as president of Munster.

The main issue facing the king and his Irish servants, in the years immediately following the Restoration, was the fate of the Cromwellian land settlement. The Protestant commissioners sent to the king in June 1660 proposed, as they could hardly have avoided doing, that Ormond and two or three other leading royalists should regain their estates; otherwise, they argued, existing proprietors should be confirmed in what they held. Behind the scenes, however, both Coote and Eustace argued for a more selective approach to the claims of those who had profited from the overthrow of the monarchy. Catholics, meanwhile, looked for the complete restoration of what they had lost. Their case was that they acted in the 1640s, not as rebels, but as loyal subjects of the crown. They could also point, in a more straightforward manner, to the services they had rendered to the house of Stuart during its eleven-year exile. Richard Bellings had proved himself, in the words of one courtier, a 'jewel' by his efforts to raise money from sympathetic princely courts during the king's impoverished sojourn at Cologne in 1654. Theobald, Viscount Taaffe, who had consistently ensured that his service to the Confederate Catholics never compromised his loyalty to Charles I, had gone on to become a stalwart of the court in exile, making himself the protector of Charles II's discarded mistress Lucy Walter and even adopting a daughter believed to be the king's. When Charles in 1656 agreed to raise troops from among his followers for the Spanish crown, as the price of diplomatic support, Viscount Muskerry provided him with the core of the required force by defecting from the French army, where he had taken a commission, with several hundred followers. In all, four of the six regiments raised for Spain were Irish. One of these was commanded by Charles's brother James, duke of York, who chose as his lieutenant colonel an ambitious member of his household, Richard Talbot, youngest son of a County Kildare gentleman and reputedly one of the few survivors of Cromwell's storming of Drogheda. Back in England in the summer of 1660, Talbot and others made

[16] For the important point that the decision to appoint Ormond preceded Mountrath's death, see Ronald Hutton, *Charles II: King of England, Scotland and Ireland* (Oxford, 1989), 189.

no secret of their expectations that these and similar services would now be rewarded by the overthrow of the Cromwellian settlement. They did, however, propose that restored proprietors should surrender one-third of their incomes, for a period of five years, to compensate the displaced Adventurers and soldiers. In Ireland itself there was a flurry of incidents as former proprietors attempted to anticipate a legal settlement by forcibly taking possession of their estates.[17]

The first attempt to resolve these conflicting claims was a declaration issued in the king's name on 30 November 1660. Its overall thrust was to make clear that none of the contending parties had a claim to anything more than royal favour. The gains of the Adventurers went far beyond what had been authorized by the acts of king and parliament on which they depended, and 'rather seem to be a structure upon their subsequent assent', while those of the soldiers depended on grants made 'by former pretended orders and powers'. At the same time agreements with the Irish Catholics, in the cessation of 1643 and the treaties of 1646 and 1648, had been forced on Charles II and his father by dire necessity.

The conclusions drawn from these denials of inherent merit were, however, very different. In the case of the Adventurers and soldiers, 'our natural inclination to mercy' on the one hand, and undertakings regarding the army given to Monck on the other, led the king to confirm them in possession of the lands they held on 7 May 1659. Where Catholics were concerned, those who had been dispossessed 'merely for being papists' were to be immediately restored to their former estates. This, however, applied only to those 'who never acted against our royal father or ourself since 22 October 1641'. In a different category were those involved in what the declaration still defined as 'the unnatural insurrection begun in the year 1641'. It acknowledged the obligation to honour the terms of the second Ormond peace, but only 'to those who had honestly and faithfully performed what they had promised us'. Those who had opposed the peace had forfeited all claim to favour. Those who had subsequently submitted to the Cromwellian regime by accepting new lands as transplanters in Connacht and Clare, equally, were to be held to that bargain 'and not to be relieved against their own act'. The only group to be promised favour, in fact, were those who had 'continued with us, or served faithfully under our ensigns beyond the seas'. These, what soon came to be known as 'ensign men', were to be restored to their estates, though only after alternative provision had been made for those currently holding the lands concerned under Cromwellian grants. The declaration, in other words, clearly envisaged some revision of the existing settlement. But it accorded only a strictly limited degree of legitimacy to the claims of the Confederate Catholics to have acted as loyal subjects, and latterly direct servants, of the crown.[18]

---

[17] For rival proposals, see L. J. Arnold, *The Restoration Land Settlement in County Dublin 1660–1688* (Dublin, 1993), 40. This case study is the fullest account of the overall process. See in addition the contrasting analyses of Hutton and Bottigheimer (below, n. 25).

[18] *His Majestie's Gracious Declaration for the Settlement of his Kingdom of Ireland* (London, 1660).

The declaration frankly presented itself as a pragmatic balancing of irreconcilable claims. To require transplanters to accept the consequences of their
bargain, it conceded, might seem hard, but no more so than the failure to
compensate royalists in both kingdoms for their financial losses 'in the evil
times'. To those who argued that to make the ensign men wait until the holders
of their lands had been compensated 'may eclipse much of our grace', equally,
it replied 'that the laying of the foundations is not now before us, when we
might design the model of the structure answerable to our own thoughts'.[19] This
eminently reasonable self-justification, however, must be set against a recognition
that what was proposed was still wildly unrealistic. The declaration not only
envisaged finding sufficient land to compensate Cromwellian grantees displaced
by the reinstatement of Catholics able to prove their innocence of rebellion, of
returning 'ensign men', and also of thirty-six individuals named as entitled to
immediate recovery of their estates. It also undertook to meet any outstanding
commitments to soldiers and Adventurers who had not yet had their legitimate
allocation. In addition it set aside land in four counties to fund payment of the
arrears due to officers who had served in the royal army before 1649.

What was available to meet these multiple commitments was primarily the
lands of the relatively small number excluded, as regicides directly implicated
in the execution of Charles I, from the indemnity guaranteed to most former
servants of the Commonwealth and Protectorate. Yet the king, both before and
after the declaration, insisted on disposing of much of this land in grants to
individuals of his own choosing. Ormond's early eighteenth-century biographer
Thomas Carte was to blame Orrery and Clotworthy, both anxious to protect
recent Protestant gains, for exaggerating the amount of land at the crown's
disposal. But Charles's record in other matters suggests that he would have
needed little encouragement to commit himself beyond his means. Ormond
himself commented that, if the declaration was to be implemented, 'there must
be discoveries made of a new Ireland, for the old will not serve to satisfy these
engagements'.[20]

The terms of the November declaration left the hopes of Catholics focused
mainly on the promise of immediate restoration for those who could prove that
they had been innocent of rebellion. In February 1661, however, the privy council
produced detailed instructions to govern the award of decrees of innocence. Their
terms were anything but favourable. They excluded not only those who had
supported the nuncio against the king, but also all those who had been 'of the
rebels' party', or had even lived in the territory under their control, before the first
Ormond peace of 15 September 1643, as well as those who had 'entered into the
Roman Catholic confederacy', sat in its assemblies, or acted on its orders, at any
time prior to the second Ormond peace. The king initially intended that claims

---

[19] Ibid. 27–8.
[20] Quoted in Richard Bagwell, *Ireland under the Stuarts* (London, 1909–16), iii. 22–3.

should be heard before thirty-six specially appointed commissioners. However the courts refused to accept the decisions of such a tribunal as having legal force. Instead hearings had to be postponed until an act of settlement, embodying the principles of the November declaration, had been drawn up for presentation to the Irish parliament.

At this point Charles, displaying the other side of his apparently divided sympathies, invited spokesmen for the Catholics, headed by Sir Nicholas Plunkett, to put their case. When Plunkett appeared before the committee on Irish affairs in March 1662, however, Orrery produced the instructions he had received for a mission to Rome in 1648, authorizing him to offer the protectorship of Ireland to either the pope or the king of France. An outraged Charles promptly banished Plunkett from court. Already before this date Ormond, who adopted the convenient stance of a sympathetic but helpless observer, had suggested that the Catholics had damaged their own case by seeking to justify themselves, 'instructing the king and his council in what is good for them', rather than offering 'a modest extenuation of their crimes' and submitting humbly to his mercy.[21] The consequence of this latest disastrous setback was that the king and council approved the act of settlement largely unchanged, though only after the Irish parliament had passed a series of measures substantially increasing the king's revenues.

The act provided that petitions for restoration to confiscated estates would be heard before a specially constituted court of claims. The hearings, before seven English commissioners chosen as having no connection with Ireland, began on 13 January 1663. The narrow definition of innocence embodied in their instructions should seriously have limited their scope for action. In fact the court, in the eight months during which it sat, granted decrees of innocence to 566 Catholic individuals or groups and to 141 Protestants, while finding 113 Catholics guilty of rebellion. One reason for this outcome was undoubtedly political interference on a massive scale. Well-placed courtiers, Catholic and Protestant, intervened to protect their own interests, to assist relatives, friends, or dependants, or in exchange for hard cash. The earl of St Albans, a favourite of the queen mother, accepted bonds of £1,000 each from four Catholic proprietors, payable on the restoration of their estates. A son of Viscount Taaffe, now earl of Carlingford, accepted a more modest £300 to have his father support another claimant. Two other supplicants promised the attorney general, Sir William

---

[21] Ormond to Eustace, 3 Sept. 1661 (Thomas Carte, *History of the Life of James, First Duke of Ormond* (2nd edn., Oxford, 1851), iv. 66). Ormond's acquiescence in a settlement that favoured Cromwellian partisans and collaborators over those who insisted that they had been loyal to the crown was much criticized by contemporary Catholic polemicists. This literature in turn forms part of the underpinning of the markedly more critical account of his record offered by recent historians. See Éamon Ó Ciardha, ' "The Unkind Deserter" and "The Bright Duke": Contrasting Views of the Dukes of Ormonde in the Irish Royalist Tradition', in T. C. Barnard and Jane Fenlon (eds.), *The Dukes of Ormonde 1610–1745* (Woodbridge, 2000), 177–94.

Domville, half of their recovered estates. Lower down the chain of influence William Montgomery of County Down secured his claim to certain lands purchased by his father by having the head of the vendor's family declared innocent. On the other hand he was outraged when Richard Talbot, riding high as a favourite of the king's brother, helped an Alen from County Kildare to regain lands in which Talbot himself had acquired an interest, but which were also claimed by Montgomery's patron the earl of Mountalexander. Mountalexander himself quoted the words of his counsel: 'Sirs, if you judge this man innocent we must believe the English cut one another's throats and that there was no Irish rebellion or rebels.' Talbot, meanwhile, complained piously of Mountalexander's 'horrid practices' of suborning witnesses.[22]

The high rate of acquittals in the court of claims may thus in part be one more reflection of the general profligacy of the Restoration court. How far did it also reflect the ability of large numbers of Catholics to show that they had not taken part in the killing of Protestants or in armed action against the king's government? To answer this it would be necessary to know a lot more about how the commissioners set about interpreting the definition of innocence laid down in the act of settlement. In assessing what would in many cases have been highly partisan evidence, relating to events up to two decades in the past, they must have enjoyed substantial personal discretion. Contemporaries identified four as showing a marked tendency to favour claimants and the other three as generally ruling against them. How far this pattern reflected the weight of the evidence, how far the personal preferences or prejudices of those concerned, and how far what some among them may have understood to be the private wishes of the court, is impossible to say.

The issue of so many decrees of innocence, entitling their holders to reclaim confiscated lands while leaving current occupiers to await compensation from clearly inadequate resources, provoked understandable alarm. Nor was it only newcomers who suffered. The granting of decrees to the former owners of lands now held by Old Protestants like Lord Chancellor Eustace and Sir Theophilus Jones confirmed the sense of a single Protestant interest whose survival depended on the defence of the Cromwellian settlement. In February the Commons denounced the proceedings of the court of claims. The speaker, Audley Mervyn, referred to the sense, 'hot throughout the Protestant plantations', that Hannibal was at the gates.[23] The following month, however, Ormond revealed a plot to seize Dublin Castle. Those incriminated were small fry, mainly former Cromwellian soldiers now working as tradesmen. But the Commons, reproached for having encouraged sedition, retracted their attacks on the land settlement. In May

---

[22] *The Montgomery MSS 1603–1706*, ed. Revd George Hill (Belfast, 1869), 232–5; Mountalexander to—, 7 Feb. 1663 (*CSPI 1663–5*, 19). For the background to this case, and for the other examples given above, see Arnold, *Restoration Land Settlement*, 73–8.

[23] *CSPI 1663–5*, 23.

Ormond announced the discovery of a second plot, for a seizure of Dublin Castle accompanied by risings in Louth, Meath, Ulster, and Munster. The ringleaders appear to have been Thomas Blood, a former Cromwellian soldier with land in County Meath, and his brother-in-law William Leckey, a Presbyterian minister. But those involved also included no less than ten members of the Irish House of Commons. Eight of these so accused were subsequently expelled from the Commons while one, Alexander Jephson, MP for County Meath, was hanged along with two other conspirators. Despite this second challenge, the court of claims continued with its work. But when the commission under which it operated expired on 21 August there was no attempt to renew it and the proceedings lapsed, even though the court had heard only an estimated one in seven of the cases pending before it.

Exactly how these different events were connected remains almost wholly unclear. The obvious inference is that Blood's plot, demonstrating a dangerous level of disaffection at the highest levels of Protestant society, frightened the king and his ministers into abandoning what had originally been an attempt to give Catholic claims some sort of hearing. But was the plot in fact so formidable? The published government account suggested an elaborate scheme to seize Dublin Castle, using a ruse connected with a supposed delivery of bread. But the presence in the state papers for 1663 of a document detailing just such a plan, but dating from the time of the coup of December 1659, must cast doubt on this official version.[24] It is unlikely that the crown could have hanged an MP, and expelled several others, on the basis of a wholly manufactured conspiracy. But the suspicion remains that Ormond and others may have built on whatever actual threat existed with a view to once again incriminating or wrongfooting critics of the government, as Ormond had already been able to do in March. This does not rule out the possibility that alarm over Protestant unrest led the king and his advisers prematurely to terminate the proceedings of the court of claims. But it could also be that they had concluded for themselves that the number of decrees of innocence that would follow from any such extension would require the restoration of former proprietors on an unworkable, and quite possibly undesirable, scale.[25]

Even with the abrupt conclusion of the court of claims, the completion of the settlement posed formidable problems. Land had to be found for the

[24] For the official account see *The Horrid Conspiracies of Such Impenitent Traitors as Intended a New Rebellion in the Kingdom of Ireland* (London, 1663), 3–4. Compare the document from 1659 in *CSPI 1669–70*, 454–6. The fullest account of the 1663 plot, though taking the official version wholly at face value, is Richard L. Greaves, *Deliver us from Evil: The Radical Underground in Britain 1660–1663* (New York, 1986), ch. 5.

[25] For the argument that Protestant reaction forced the king to retreat from an initial attempt to satisfy Catholic claims, see Karl Bottigheimer, 'The Restoration Land Settlement in Ireland in Ireland: A Structural View', *IHS* 18 (1972), 1–21. For the argument that Charles, while prepared to take steps on behalf of those who had a direct claim on his gratitude, had no desire to see a general Catholic restoration, see Hutton, *Charles II*, 196–7, 200–1, 207–10, 236–40.

Cromwellian grantees displaced by the 700 'innocents', as well as by others named for immediate restoration in the act of settlement. In addition there was the commitment to restore the ensign men, to pay the arrears of the pre-1649 officers, and, in theory at least, to meet any unsatisfied claims by Adventurers or Cromwellian soldiers. During 1663–4 a variety of hands, with Anglesey and Orrery playing a prominent part, painfully worked out a compromise solution. The resulting bill of explanation contained detail so complex that neither Ormond nor Charles's chief English minister, Clarendon, could understand it. But the basic principle was clear enough: proprietors of estates acquired from the Commonwealth and Protectorate—apart from some favoured individuals—were to surrender one-third of the land concerned, which would be used to meet the claims of those displaced by decrees of innocence, as well as other commitments. There were also to be some further restorations, but this time through a direct act of royal favour, rather than through any attempt at a judicial process. In addition to those nominated for restoration of their full estates, fifty-four others were to receive their principal residence and 2,000 acres. The bill had its final, difficult reading in the Irish House of Commons in December 1665. Sir Winston Churchill, who had been one of the judges of the court of claims, reported that members confronted one another 'with swords half drawn . . . some being heard to say that the lands they had gotten with the hazard of their lives should not now be lost with ayes and noes'. At one point, according to another account, opponents of the bill tried to force an adjournment by snuffing out the candles brought to light the winter dusk, so that the two sides 'wanted very little of going to cuffs in the dark'. Churchill attributed the eventual passage of the bill to Ormond's eloquence. Orrery, on the other hand, claimed the credit for himself, saying that he had secured the votes of all but one of the Munster members, comprising a quarter of the house.[26]

Detailed implementation of the act of explanation required a second court of claims. With the completion of its sessions, in January 1669, the Restoration land settlement assumed its final shape. In 1641 Catholics had owned 59 per cent of the profitable land in Ireland. The Cromwellian authorities had issued decrees for a total of around 700,000 Irish acres, just over 6 per cent of total profitable land, to Catholics transplanting to Connacht. By 1688, when the next set of figures becomes available, the Catholic share of profitable land had risen again to 22 per cent.[27] Not all of this improvement was necessarily a result of the acts of settlement and explanation. The depressed prices resulting from

[26] Churchill to Arlington, 27 Dec. 1665 (*CSPI 1663–5*, 699).

[27] For the figure of 700,000 acres see Robert C. Simington, *The Transplantation to Connacht 1654–58* (Shannon, 1970), p. xv. Other figures are those calculated by J. G. Simms from the Books of Survey and Distribution (J. G. Simms, *The Williamite Confiscation in Ireland 1690–1703* (London, 1956), 195). Preliminary reports from a more recent reworking of the data suggest a Catholic share of profitable land falling from 66% in 1641 to 29% by the late 1660s, but these new figures have yet to be tested. See Kevin McKenny, *The Laggan Army in Ireland 1640–1685*

uncertainty over land titles created opportunities for the bold, or those confident of their political connections, to exploit, and a number of well-placed Catholics, including Richard Talbot, seized the opportunity to acquire substantial estates. However the one detailed study so far available, for County Dublin, suggests that these gains by purchase were made mainly from less fortunate coreligionists, and involved no significant loss of Protestant land.[28]

The Restoration land settlement was both massively unjust in its overall outcome, and a crude lottery in individual cases. Recent work on the Catholic politics of the 1640s, highlighting the conditional nature of the loyalty they were willing to offer the crown, has done something to modify the image of suffering innocence. But it remains the case that those who had contributed directly to the downfall of Charles I fared much better under his son than those who, at worst, had sought to use his difficulties to improve their own position. The king made real efforts to ensure that individuals who had a direct personal claim on his gratitude were taken care of. Beyond this limited group, however, gains and losses depended heavily on the ability either to claim or to purchase political favour. Sir William Petty, writing in 1672, would say no more than that the Protestants, having played 'this game or match upon so great odds', had 'a gamester's right at least to their estates'. The earl of Essex, who became lord lieutenant in the same year, compared the whole process to 'flinging the reward upon the death of a deer among a pack of hounds, where every one pulls and tears what he can for himself'. The Gaelic poet David Ó Bruadair, in a variation of the same metaphor, saw the dispossessed Gaelic landowners as left 'to gaze at their lands like a dog at a lump of beef'.[29]

What Catholics lost, Protestants gained. Some went to Cromwellian newcomers. In all the settlement saw some 500 Adventurers and around 7,500 former Cromwellian soldiers confirmed in possession of their lands. It was these whom Ó Bruadair had in mind when he wrote of 'roughs formed by the dregs of each base trade' now occupying the houses of chiefs and gentlemen. Much, however, had gone to Old Protestants, either by purchase from Cromwellian grantees unwilling to settle or by grants from the Protectorate, the restored monarchy, or both. The relative proportion of New and Old Protestants in the propertied elite that dominated post-Restoration Ireland is suggested by the membership of the parliament of 1661–6. Of 254 MPs, 16 were Adventurers and fewer than 50 were soldiers with no pre-war connection with Ireland.[30] What emerged from the Commonwealth, the Protectorate, and the Restoration

---

(Dublin, 2005), 160–1, and review by S. J. Connolly, *Irish Economic & Social History*, 33 (2006), 135–6.

[28] Arnold, *Restoration Land Settlement*, 139.

[29] William Petty, *The Political Anatomy of Ireland* (London, 1691), 24; Essex, quoted in Kathleen Lynch, *Roger Boyle, First Earl of Orrery* (Knoxville, Tenn., 1965), 213; *The Poems of David Ó Bruadair*, ed. J. C. McErlean (London, 1910–16), iii. 17, 23.

[30] Bottigheimer, 'The Restoration Land Settlement', 7.

was thus a Protestant propertied class in which a minority of newcomers shared wealth and power with a longer-established group. Over the next three decades they were to reveal themselves as united in their determination to defend a common Protestant interest against Catholic attempts at counter-revolution. And the success with which they pursued that end ensured that their descendants were to dominate Irish society for the greater part of the next two centuries.

DISSENTERS AND REMONSTRANTS

That the restoration of the monarchy would be accompanied by the return of the full hierarchical structure of the pre-war Church of Ireland was not initially taken as inevitable. During the weeks before the king's return, feeling in the Irish convention clearly favoured some form of episcopacy. But there were also discussions, as there were in England at the same period, about a watered-down version that might allow the established church to accommodate at least the more moderate varieties of Independent and Presbyterian. The agents sent to the king in June 1660 had no instructions in the matter of church government. Their submission, probably reflecting a behind-the-scenes compromise, called for a restoration of the church, in doctrine, discipline, and worship, as it had been in the reign of Charles I, but also for 'liberty to tender consciences'. A further request, for 'godly, learned, orthodox, and ordained preaching ministers of the gospel', deftly combined acceptance of a sacerdotal ministry with the pastoral priorities of the godly. In the event it appears that the court had already begun to discuss the reconstitution of the Irish hierarchy. By the end of the month twelve names had been selected for vacant sees, and in January 1661 all twelve, along with a slightly later addition, were consecrated in an elaborate ceremony at St Patrick's cathedral, Dublin. One of the new bishops was Edward Worth, leader of the Munster network of former episcopalians who had worked towards a Presbyterian settlement under Henry Cromwell's patronage. The new archbishop of Armagh, on the other hand, was Wentworth's former ecclesiastical agent John Bramhall, who had endured twenty years of impoverished continental exile. Of the newly appointed bishops, equally, no less than five had begun their careers as chaplains to either Wentworth or Ormond. What was restored was not just episcopacy, but episcopacy strongly coloured by the values and principles of the Laudian era.[31]

---

[31] For the restoration of episcopacy see the rather different accounts in McGuire, 'The Dublin Convention'; Clarke, *Prelude to Restoration*, 310–16. For the evidence that the court had already made up its mind, see Greaves, *God's Other Children*, 45. The Laudian bias of the restored hierarchy is demonstrated in J. I. McGuire, 'Policy and Patronage: The Appointment of Bishops 1660–1661', in Alan Ford, J. I. McGuire, and Kenneth Milne (eds.), *As by Law Established: The Church of Ireland since the Reformation* (Dublin, 1995), 112–16.

Of the eight existing bishops (including Bramhall) who now resumed their position, the most complex career belonged to Henry Jones. His work in collecting depositions from Protestant survivors of 1641 had brought him early to the attention of the English parliament. However he had remained loyal to the king, being rewarded in 1645 with the bishopric of Clogher. It was only after Ormond's withdrawal in 1647 that he came to terms with the parliamentary regime, conveniently represented at that point by his brother Colonel Michael Jones. Over the next few years he was to serve as scoutmaster general, in effect chief of intelligence, to Cromwell's army, and then as a member of the civilian administration. But he had notably declined to take a position within the non-episcopal church created by the Commonwealth, and indeed had clung stubbornly to his title as bishop of Clogher until ordered to drop it in 1651. Despite this, his active collaboration earned him the snub of being excluded from full participation in the mass consecration of January 1661. By the following year, however, he had been promoted, with Bramhall's support, to the valuable diocese of Meath.[32]

Jones's combination of political flexibility and resolute loyalty to the church whose service he had entered permitted his rapid rehabilitation. For others, however, the return to an uncompromisingly episcopalian regime was unacceptable. How far a more broadly based settlement would have commanded wider support among Protestants remains open to question. That Baptists and Quakers would reject any structure likely to be acceptable to the majority was a foregone conclusion. Winter and the Independents had already demonstrated, under Henry Cromwell, their unwillingness to support any establishment they did not control. Samuel Mather, son of the founder of Massachusetts Congregationalism and Winter's fellow minister at St Nicholas's, was equally uncompromising, denouncing prelacy in September 1660 as 'the image of that beast the papacy'.[33] Ejected from St Nicholas's, he and Winter established an alternative congregation at New Row. By contrast the 'English' Presbyterians who had earlier cooperated with Worth's crypto-Anglicans might perhaps have been coaxed into a looser episcopal structure. As it was, several serving ministers, including Samuel Coxe, who had preached at the opening of the Convention only a year earlier, were likewise forced out of their livings. Where the Scottish Presbyterians of Ulster were concerned, Bramhall insisted that ministers wishing to continue in the re-established church should accept episcopal ordination and use the Book of Common Prayer, but did not require them to repudiate an earlier Presbyterian ordination or ministry. This was, by his standards, a conciliatory approach. However it was not sufficient. Sixty-one out of seventy serving ministers refused to conform to the restored episcopal order and were expelled from their livings.

---

[32] I owe this assessment to an unpublished paper, "Keeping up with Henry Jones', delivered as the J. C. Beckett memorial lecture in Queen's University Belfast by Professor Aidan Clarke in April 2005. See also Clarke, *Prelude to Restoration*, 38–9.

[33] Quoted Greaves, *God's Other Children*, 55.

Statistics on the different dissenting groups that thus emerged are necessarily imprecise. In the case of Dublin the exclusion of Independents, Presbyterians, and others created a significant body of Protestants outside the established church, some of them figures of substance. Baptismal figures suggest that the New Row congregation alone, at its peak in the mid-1680s, may have had up to 1,000 members. Between 1660 and 1687 the city's twenty-five-strong board of aldermen, all sitting for life, included five dissenters. There were also strong pockets of dissent elsewhere, particularly in the larger towns. An account of 1702 noted that the English Presbyterian meeting house in Cork had places for 400 people. At national level, however, the membership of these new Protestant denominations remained insignificant. What seems to be a complete list of signatures of heads of Quaker households from 1680 indicates a total of 798 families, which allowing for higher than average levels of fertility among Friends suggests a population of 5,500 to 6,500 in the country as a whole. References to Baptist meetings indicate a scattering of mainly small groups. By the 1670s congregations at Cork and Clonmel had become too small to support a pastor; in other places itinerant ministers seem to have preached in private houses. In the case of the Independents and English Presbyterians there was frequent interchange of both ministers and worshippers, with the Independents losing members over time to the more centrally organized Presbyterians. By 1695 there were only six distinctively Independent congregations. English Presbyterian numbers at the end of the seventeenth century have been estimated at 4,500, including Independents attending joint services.[34]

Across most of Ireland, then, the rich mix of doctrine and practice introduced by the military and civil agents of the English Commonwealth and Protectorate survived as a visible but numerically limited dissenting presence. In Ulster, by contrast, dissent was the result of the unwillingness or inability of the established church to continue the accommodation with the separate religious traditions of the Scottish immigrant population that it had maintained, however precariously, up to 1641. That population had suffered heavily from war, famine, and enforced flight during the 1640s. Of the surnames listed in muster rolls from the 1630s less than half, and in some cases as few as one-fifth, can be found in similar listings from the 1660s. However immigration had resumed from the mid-1650s, and once again Scots had predominated. By the late 1660s they made up an estimated 60 per cent of the British inhabitants of Ulster, and 20 per cent of the population as a whole.[35] What this meant in practice was that members of the Church of Ireland now constituted a minority even within the Protestant population. In

[34] Greaves, *God's Other Children*, 161–2, 260, 263, 266, 270; Phil Kilroy, *Protestant Dissent and Controversy in Ireland 1660–1714* (Cork, 1994), 42, 68, 90.

[35] William Macafee, 'The Population of Ulster 1630–1841: Evidence from Mid-Ulster' (D.Phil. thesis, University of Ulster, 1987), 85–7; idem and Valerie Morgan, 'Population in Ulster 1660–1750', in Peter Roebuck (ed.), *Plantation to Partition: Essays in Ulster History* (Belfast, 1981), 47.

the town of Antrim, by the late 1660s, not one in forty men attended the parish church. In nearby Templepatrick only the minister and parish clerk regularly attended services. This, of course, was in the heartland of Scottish settlement. But even in County Armagh the Catholic archbishop reported in 1679 that 'one could travel twenty-five miles . . . without finding half a dozen Catholic or Protestant families, but all are Presbyterians i.e. strict Calvinists'.[36]

For the Irish government this fragmentation of Protestantism represented a political as well as a religious problem. The crisis of 1659–60 had seen the Protestant propertied class unite behind a pragmatic acceptance of the return of monarchy. But there remained an acute awareness of the potential threat from what were commonly referred to as 'fanatics': Baptists and others whose radical religious principles were assumed to go hand in hand with a continuing commitment to the republicanism of the Commonwealth and Protectorate. There was also concern, of a different kind, about the loyalties of the Ulster Presbyterians. They had rallied to the crown in 1649–50, and had suffered for their royalism under the Cromwellian regime. But their loyalty at that time had been to a covenanted king who had now, by restoring episcopacy, failed to uphold his commitments. The close links between Ulster and Scotland, where the challenge to the Stuart monarchy had begun, and where Covenanting sentiment remained strong, added to the sense of potential danger. That these fears of the subversive potential of dissent were not wholly imaginary was confirmed by the conspiracy of May 1663. Those accused of direct involvement included not just Leckey but two other Scottish Presbyterian and two Congregationalist ministers, while there were claims that others, including possibly Samuel Coxe, had at least some knowledge of the plot. The declaration allegedly prepared by the conspirators, equally, had called for a settlement of religion according to the Solemn League and Covenant.

Despite these concerns, and despite the strident demands of the newly restored bishops for action to uphold their religious privileges, the secular authorities initially proceeded with caution. What seems to have been majority support for a return to the traditional forms, combined with a prudent accommodation to the wishes of the court, had led the Convention to support the restoration of episcopacy. But prominent figures like Orrery and Massareene retained a personal sympathy for dissenting principles. There were also practical political considerations. An assault on those unable to accept the new dispensation might disrupt the consensus that had permitted a bloodless restoration; magistrates, constables, or soldiers might refuse to cooperate; and divisions among Protestants might present dangerous opportunities to the Catholic majority. A proclamation in January 1661 banned assemblies of both Catholics and nonconformists. Quakers, widely seen as rejecting the essential decencies of religion, once again

---

[36] Greaves, *God's Other Children*, 98; *The Letters of Saint Oliver Plunkett 1625–1681*, ed. John Hanly (Dublin, 1979), 530.

became a particular target. The number imprisoned, down to only three or fewer in 1658–9, rose to 124 in 1660, and 135 in 1661. In May 1661 the House of Lords ordered the public burning of the Solemn League and Covenant, and a search of Dublin bookshops to hunt out and confiscate all available copies. Behind the scenes, however, Orrery discussed with Presbyterian representatives the possibility of toleration for discreet religious practice, provided there was no flaunting of a separate ecclesiastical jurisdiction. In February 1662 the lords justices temporarily suspended the penalties for both Catholics and dissenters failing to attend services in the established church. In April 1662, on the other hand, a new proclamation complained that both recusants and dissenters 'have grown worse by clemency', and warned of a stricter enforcement of the laws.[37]

By this time Ormond was about to resume power as lord lieutenant. Yet he too, despite his reputation as a royalist and Anglican stalwart, was initially moderate, allowing Massareene to arrange a meeting with Presbyterian representatives. His public stance remained that the liberty for 'tender consciences' promised in the Declaration of Breda extended only to private devotion, not public worship. But in practice the Presbyterian delegates seem to have understood, correctly, that there would be no serious interference with an unostentatious parochial ministry. The uncovering of the conspiracies of March and May 1663 temporarily moved the government to more decisive action. In Limerick Orrery organized the expulsion from the city of over 1,000 dissenters and Catholics. At least forty ministers, including Independents, Baptists, and Presbyterians, were arrested, forced into hiding, or fled the country. Even at this stage, however, Ormond and his council acknowledged the need to distinguish between those whose dissent was confined to religion, and those whose principles made them a threat to the state. Surveillance intensified again during 1665–6, as war with Holland inspired stirrings in the radical underground in Munster, and there were eventually a few arrests. A Presbyterian rebellion in south-west Scotland in November 1666 reawakened concerns about the security of Ulster. For the most part, however, harassment, whether by the civil or ecclesiastical authorities, was sporadic and inconsistent. A list of 102 excommunicants in the diocese of Derry in 1667 includes 37 condemned for nonconformity, defined as including 'not only absence from the church but baptising children by unlicensed ministers'. The 14 others guilty of fornication or adultery may likewise have included dissenters whose marriages before their own clergy the church courts refused to recognize as valid. But neither figure bears any relation to the numbers now conducting their devotional life wholly outside the established church.[38]

---

[37] The account in this and the next paragraph mainly follows Greaves, *God's Other Children*, ch. 1. J. I. McGuire, 'Ormond and Presbyterian Nonconformity 1660–63', in Kevin Herlihy (ed.), *The Politics of Irish Dissent 1650–1800* (Dublin, 1997), 40–51, presents Ormond's treatment of dissent in a somewhat harsher light.

[38] PRONI Dio 4/5/3/10.

In keeping with its primary emphasis on security, the government's proceedings against dissenters relied primarily on the general laws against riot and unlawful assembly. There was no attempt systematically to enforce the fines for non-attendance at church prescribed by the 1560 act of uniformity. A second act of uniformity, introduced in 1666, provided some additional sanctions. All clergy were required to give public assent to the Book of Common Prayer. Ministers who officiated without having been episcopally ordained faced fines of £100. Schoolmasters had to obtain a licence from the bishop. These stipulations retrospectively legitimized the expulsions that had taken place at the Restoration. On the other hand there was no Irish equivalent to the English conventicles act, forbidding assemblies for religious purposes other than the ceremonies of the established church. Indeed Ormond, in the early 1680s, was to express concern at the legality of any action against dissenters, on the grounds that the laws on religion (in which, rather oddly, he included the act of uniformity) had been enacted only with Catholics in mind, while large assemblies could be suppressed only if there was evidence of illegal intent.[39]

At the same time that it struggled to formulate a policy towards Protestant dissent the government had to deal with the numerically much greater problem of Catholicism. The rebuilding of the ecclesiastical structures shattered by the Cromwellian conquest had begun as early as 1657 with the appointment of two bishops and thirteen vicars apostolic. Figures available from a selection of dioceses suggest that the number of priests more than doubled during the 1660s. The religious orders also began to rebuild their numbers. Already by 1665, according to one account, there were 400 Franciscans and 200 Dominicans, as well as 25 Jesuits and small numbers from other orders. Provincial synods at Tuam in 1658 and 1660, Armagh in 1660, and Cashel in 1661 resumed the task of imposing a uniform code of discipline and pastoral services, built round the principles of the Council of Trent. Once again the statutes published laid down the minimum requirements for catechetical instruction and attendance at mass and the sacraments, and condemned unorthodox practices at holy wells and wakes for the dead. They also prescribed regulations for a new problem, the marriage of a Catholic with a Protestant, requiring guarantees that the faith of the Catholic partner would be respected and passed on to all children of the union.[40]

The task of responding to this rapid and visible revival was complicated, even more than in the case of dissent, by uncertainties as to the law. Old English recalcitrance had blocked the new anti-Catholic statutes planned for the parliament of 1613–15. Wentworth, in the 1630s, had abandoned, as premature,

---

[39] For Ormond's comments see Greaves, *God's Other Children*, 128–9; Kilroy, *Protestant Dissent and Controversy*, 239, neither of whom comment on this somewhat puzzling characterization of the act of uniformity.
[40] P. J. Corish, *The Catholic Community in the Seventeenth and Eighteenth Centuries* (Dublin, 1981), 49–59; Canice Mooney, *Survival and Reorganisation 1650–1695* (Dublin, 1968), 12–17.

systematic interference with Catholic worship. The Cromwellian regime, by contrast, attempted its complete suppression. The Convention assumed that these latter measures were still in force: in March 1660 it ordered that transplanted Catholics were to remain confined to Connacht, and that meetings of priests, Jesuits, and friars were to be prevented. The restoration of the monarchy, however, undid the de facto union which had provided the context for the policies of the preceding decade, leaving the representatives of a restored monarchy uncertain of their power. Mountrath and Bury, writing in December 1660, justified the arrest of priests who 'appear here boldly and in large numbers' on the grounds that 'these men have always been incendiaries', while admitting that their behaviour would have been 'more penal in England than in Ireland'. At the end of 1661 reports of a Catholic conspiracy provided a more clear-cut basis for a round-up of priests and friars. However, those arrested were released the following March. This was shortly after the lords justices, acting in response to a petition from Catholics indicted under the 1560 act of uniformity, had announced the suspension of its penalties until the king's pleasure was known. A new proclamation in November, warning of a return to strict enforcement of the laws, this time issued on Ormond's authority, presented Catholicism as a challenge to the king's authority rather than as religious deviance: 'a papal jurisdiction is attempted to be introduced, and heavy charges are laid upon the king's subjects.'[41]

Uncertainty also attached to the status of the Catholic laity. The king gave clear orders in May 1661 restoring to Catholics the entitlement, granted by his father in 1628, to practise law on taking an oath of allegiance. He also ordered that they should be readmitted to the cities and corporate towns from which they had been expelled by the Cromwellian regime. Initially this was taken as implying that they should also be readmitted to civic office. But in August the English privy council, responding to widespread Protestant alarm, confirmed that the king had intended only that Catholics should be free to live and trade in urban centres. The acts of settlement and explanation further whittled down the concession, by forbidding those who had not taken the oath of supremacy to acquire urban property, and providing that Catholics claiming the restitution of land or houses in corporate towns should instead be compensated with an equivalent in some other place. Outside the towns, on the other hand, Catholics were readmitted to lesser local offices. A survey in 1666 showed that about nine out of ten sheriffs, sub-sheriffs, bailiffs, and constables were Catholic, and that there were around 100 Catholic justices of the peace.[42]

Concern over the Protestant monopoly of urban corporations was due in part to the local power exercised by these bodies. An even more important

---

[41] Mountrath and Bury to Nicholas, 12 Dec. 1660 (*CSPI 1660–2*, 129); Proclamation of Lord Lieutenant and Council, 12 Nov. 1662 (ibid. 615).
[42] *CSPI 1666–9*, 261.

consideration, however, was that it was these that returned two-thirds of the members of the Irish parliament. Despite anxious discussion in the months preceding the meeting of parliament, focusing in particular on the threat to the smooth passage of the act of settlement, the English privy council had refused to sanction an explicit exclusion of Catholics from its sittings. Instead the government and its supporters had to rely on ad hoc methods. In Cashel, for example, the mayor and corporation responded to news of an intended Catholic candidate by creating 100 Protestant freeholders. The one Catholic returned, for Tuam, had his election declared invalid. The resulting all-Protestant House of Commons proceeded to produce two bills that would have resolved some at least of these legal anomalies, by extending to Ireland the English laws against Catholic clergy and by specifying what categories of people were to be required to take the oath of supremacy. However Ormond intervened to block both measures, acting on the direct orders of the king, though assuring his master that he had taken care to 'give myself the displeasure of those that shall be unsatisfied with it'.[43]

The instructions which inspired Ormond's carefully advertised act of political self-sacrifice raise the question of the king's own preferences. Some of the principles guiding Charles II's policy are clear enough. He was utterly unforgiving of religious tenets, Catholic or Protestant, that in any way challenged his own authority: hence the contrast between his easy acceptance of former servants of the Protectorate in both England and Ireland, and the bloody revenge that he took in Scotland on those who in 1650 had coerced him into declaring himself a covenanted king. He was also determined to reward and protect individual Catholics who had served him in adversity, or who subsequently won his favour or that of his intimates. Beyond this it is difficult to be sure. In the secret Treaty of Dover, concluded with Louis XIV in May 1670, Charles undertook, on a promise of French military and financial support, to declare himself a Catholic. On the evening before he died, in February 1685, he was received into the Catholic church. Taken at face value, these two episodes support the image of a king torn between political prudence and a secret sympathy for Catholicism. But it has also been argued that the 1670 promise was a ploy to win more generous terms from the French, and the deathbed conversion a good-natured gesture towards his pious brother James. On this reading the king's opposition to new religious statutes, and his occasional attempts to suspend those already in force, reflected his unwillingness to accept restrictions on his freedom to deal as he pleased with all individuals and groups within his kingdoms, and his lack of regard for the theological and liturgical distinctions that meant so much to his contemporaries. But, in either case, the opacity of the king's religious preferences added further to the fog of uncertainty hanging over policy towards both Catholics and Protestant dissenters in the 1660s and after.

[43] Ormond to King, 16 May 1663 (*CSPI 1663–5*, 91–2).

There was one serious attempt, early in the reign, to clarify the relationship between Irish Catholics and the restored monarchy. In December 1661, with the land settlement still under discussion, Bellings and others drew up a Remonstrance or 'loyal formulary' acknowledging Charles II as their lawful king and explicitly denying that any claims by the papacy could override their allegiance. As their agent in presenting the declaration they chose Peter Walsh, the Franciscan who had led the challenge to Rinuccini's condemnation of the second Ormond peace. As an Old English and royalist member of a predominantly Gaelic order, Walsh had found himself dangerously exposed, suffering imprisonment in a Franciscan house in Ireland and later in Spain before taking refuge for most of the 1650s in England. After 1660, by contrast, he enjoyed Ormond's patronage at court, and in January 1661 Archbishop O'Reilly and others had commissioned him to act as their representative there. His sponsorship of the Remonstrance, however, reopened old divisions. At a meeting of the Irish clergy then in London twenty-four out of thirty, including one bishop, agreed to sign the document. Ninety-eight leading laymen signed another copy. But when Walsh went to Ireland to seek further signatures he encountered rapidly mounting resistance. The other bishops and the heads of the main religious orders denounced the Remonstrance as unacceptable, as did the papal nuncio in Brussels and the theological faculty at the university of Louvain.

Ormond's response to these divisions was to adopt the Remonstrance as a touchstone of Catholic loyalty, extending toleration and protection to its supporters while harassing and imprisoning those known to oppose it. In June 1666 Walsh persuaded him to permit a synod of 100 clergy to meet in Dublin, and even to give a safe-conduct to O'Reilly, in exile since 1661. After fifteen days of deliberation the synod rejected the Remonstrance. Instead they accepted three propositions drawn up by the theological faculty of the Sorbonne in 1663. At first sight these seemed unequivocal. They declared that kings had no superior, in earthly affairs, other than God. Subjects were thus bound in conscience to obey them in all temporal matters, and no power could dispense them from that allegiance. Ormond, however, rejected the propositions as an inadequate alternative to the Remonstrance and dissolved the assembly. In correspondence with London he spoke of the possibility of using the original Remonstrance as a test of which Catholic clergy should be tolerated, while driving those unwilling to accept it out of the kingdom. But in practice he seems to have settled for the same sporadic harassment that had gone on since the early 1660s.

Ormond explained his insistence on the Remonstrance by presenting it as a means of distinguishing between loyal and disloyal Catholics. The involvement of Peter Walsh on one side, and of Owen Roe O'Neill's former agent Edmund O'Reilly on the other, may well have encouraged him to see the dispute as a re-emergence of the conflict of allegiances precipitated by Rinuccini. On this occasion, however, opposition to the Remonstrance was close to unanimous. Walsh himself was to admit that he had been able to gain the support of only

70 out of about 2,000 clergy active in Ireland, along with 124 laity. Its critics, moreover, included not just Gaelic Irish clerics like O'Reilly but Old English ecclesiastics of otherwise impeccable loyalty to the crown, such as Oliver Plunkett, archbishop of Armagh from 1669, and Peter Talbot, brother of Richard Talbot, the duke of York's favourite, who became archbishop of Dublin in the same year. This in turn must call into question Ormond's real motives. Although his upbringing in the Calvinist household of Archbishop Abbott had left him with a firm Protestant faith, his extensive Old English family connections ensured that he did not share the crude anti-Catholic prejudices common among the English and New English. When his brother-in-law, the earl of Clancarty, the former Viscount Muskerry, died at his house in 1665, the duke saw to it, as 'the part of a good Christian', that he was attended by a priest. At the same time his inflexibility in 1666 suggests that he had no real interest in finding a way for the Catholic clergy to demonstrate their loyalty to the crown. In private correspondence to fellow courtiers he more than once suggested that his real motive in pursuing the matter of the Remonstrance was to weaken the Catholic party by promoting internal disputes over the document. Peter Walsh seems likewise eventually to have concluded that he was an instrument in what was essentially a strategy of divide and rule.[44]

If Ormond's handling of the Remonstrance dispute was opportunistic, however, it is important to recognize that the problem of conflicting loyalties on which he focused was not entirely his invention. The Dublin synod had accepted three propositions from the Sorbonne but had rejected others, further limiting the pope's power, on the grounds that these were not appropriate to a kingdom where the monarch was not a Catholic. Yet when Archbishop O'Reilly returned to the continent, having endured some months of imprisonment and a threat of being tried for high treason, he found himself under attack from the church authorities for having accepted even the first three propositions. Irish Catholics, in other words, faced real difficulties in reconciling the claims of their church and the claims of their monarch in a manner acceptable to both. The search for an appropriate formula, in fact, was to continue for more than a century after 1666, and even then the issue was to be resolved only with some difficulty.

The continued sporadic harassment experienced by the Irish Catholic clergy and their congregations contrasts with the privileged position enjoyed by certain individuals linked to the royal court and household. Some quietly occupied positions of profit or influence. For example Sir Richard Bellings, son of the secretary to the Confederate supreme council, became secretary and master of requests in the household of the queen. Others, notably the Talbot brothers Peter and Richard, were active in factional politics. In their case hostility to Ormond

---

[44] The fullest account of the Remonstrance affair is now Margaret Anne Creighton, 'The Catholic Interest in Irish Politics in the Reign of Charles II' (Ph.D. thesis, Queen's University Belfast, 2000). Pending its publication, see Dr Creighton's biography of Peter Walsh in *DNB*.

led them into a bizarre alliance with the more strongly anti-Catholic Orrery. A contemporary poet recalled Richard Talbot's early military career in terms that testified to the suspicion and alarm which the spectacle of these well-placed Catholics aroused among English Protestants.

> His sword is all his argument, and his book.
> Although no scholar, yet can act the cook;
> And will cut throats again if he be paid;
> In the Irish shambles, he first learned the trade.[45]

In 1664, Sir George Rawdon and other Protestant grandees in east Ulster found themselves extending their hospitality to 'Father Patrick': the queen's chaplain, Patrick Maginn, who had gone there to take advantage of a grant permitting him to bestow the collection of the excise on beer and ale in County Down on his friends and relatives. Five years later, Oliver Plunkett, as an archbishop of Armagh newly arrived from Rome, had to be more circumspect. On his journey to Ireland he spent three months in London, during which he had two audiences with the queen. Once in Ireland, on the other hand, he initially disguised himself with wig, sword, and pistols and travelled under the pseudonym of 'Captain Browne'.[46] Both episodes were characteristic of the looking glass world of the Restoration, where former Puritan regicides, royalists, and Catholics rubbed shoulders within a court dominated by a king whose ultimate religious allegiances and aspirations remained mysterious, and within a political framework that seemed permanently established, yet had only recently been reassembled following its complete collapse.

By the time Plunkett arrived, however, the king had already initiated what was to be his most dramatic shift in religious policy. In February 1669 Charles had announced his intention of removing Ormond. The duke's fall came partly through factional politics. The impeachment and exile in 1666 of his ally, the earl of Clarendon, up to then the king's chief minister, had left him vulnerable. Orrery, in alliance with the duke of Buckingham, mounted a damaging attack during 1668–9, concentrating on what seem to have been genuine deficiencies in the management of the Irish public revenue, and Ormond had weakened his position by leaving Ireland without permission to confront his accusers at court. However there was also a wider context. Just two months earlier, Charles had taken the first steps towards the treaty with France that was to be concluded in May 1670. The removal of the staunchly Anglican Ormond cleared the way for a more flexible religious policy linked to the new diplomatic initiative. His immediate successor was John Robartes, a Presbyterian sympathizer who had been involved in an earlier attempt, in 1663, to suspend the English act of

---

[45] 'Advice to a Painter to Draw the Duke', attributed to Marvell but apparently by Henry Saville. See *The Poems and Letters of Andrew Marvell*, i: *Poems*, ed. H. M. Margoliouth (Oxford, 1971), 216, 420–1.
[46] Connolly, *Religion, Law and Power*, 19.

uniformity. When Robartes proved as uncongenial a colleague as he had been in his first short-lived Irish deputyship, in 1660, Charles replaced him with Lord Berkeley of Stratton, married to a Catholic and himself suspected of a politic conversion while a royalist exile in the 1650s.

Berkeley's arrival, in April 1670, initiated a period in which the Irish Catholic church enjoyed something close to official favour. The lord lieutenant, Archbishop Plunkett reported to Rome, 'is aware of his Majesty's good will towards his Catholic subjects', so that 'the clergy live here in freedom and are not disturbed in any way, although they are publicly known'. Plunkett himself had been invited to visit his Protestant counterpart, James Margetson, who 'gave me precedence in his own house, as well as those titles which belong to me'. Margetson also agreed to the Jesuits opening a school in Drogheda. When the governor of Dungannon objected to Plunkett performing confirmations in the town, the earl of Charlemont 'delivered a vigorous rebuke' and invited the archbishop to use the courtyard of his own residence for confirmation and even mass. The earl of Drogheda, meanwhile, allowed Catholics not only to have a church on his estate, but to equip it with bells.[47] Conditions were initially very different in Munster, where Orrery, as provincial president, continued to demolish churches and prevent public masses. When he ignored warnings of the king's anger, Charles responded by ordering the abolition of the presidency in summer 1672. A proclamation in March of the same year lifted the ban on Catholics purchasing property in corporate towns, and ordered that they should enjoy the same civic privileges as in the reign of Charles I. New rules for municipal government introduced in September required office holders and corporation members to take the oath of supremacy, but gave the lord lieutenant or deputy power to dispense with the obligation. Meanwhile the king had allowed Richard Talbot to present a petition from the Catholic nobility and gentry complaining of the injustice of the land settlement, and had set up a commission of enquiry into the acts of settlement and explanation. The sheriff of County Kerry complained in August 1672 that people were resisting the collection of quit rents on the expectation 'of having their estates suddenly restored to them'.[48]

By this time Charles II's wider design was in operation. France and England had jointly declared war on the Dutch republic on 17 March. Two days earlier Charles had issued a declaration of indulgence, suspending the laws against both Catholics and dissenters. The plan was apparently that victory over England's main commercial rival would reconcile his Protestant subjects to religious toleration. In fact the war went badly, and when the English parliament met in February 1673 the anti-Catholic outcry forced the king into a rapid retreat.

[47] Plunkett, *Letters*, 104, 93, 152, 166.

[48] *CSPD 1672*, 565. Quit rent was a new tax imposed by the acts of settlement and explanation on the lands of soldiers, Adventurers, and restored innocents. An account from 1682 seems to confirm that it was levied, as implied here, on the immediate occupiers rather than the proprietors: T. J. Kiernan, *History of the Financial Administration of Ireland to 1817* (London, 1930), 246–7.

In England he abandoned the declaration of indulgence and accepted a test act requiring holders of government office to have taken communion in the Church of England. In the months that followed he also wound up the inquiry into the Irish land settlement and banished Richard Talbot from court. In Ireland the earl of Essex, who had replaced Berkeley as lord lieutenant in August 1672, continued for some time with the policy of open toleration. As late as September 1673 Plunkett, while admitting that the clergy had of late avoided holding synods or other gatherings that might cause offence, paid tribute to 'our wise and prudent viceroy, who does not readily disturb whoever is content to live quietly'.[49] On 27 October, however, Essex, on orders from England, published a proclamation ordering all bishops and others exercising ecclesiastical jurisdiction, and all members of religious orders, to leave the kingdom by the end of the year. The persecution that followed was not particularly rigorous. Plunkett reported to Rome that Essex had carried out his orders very moderately, and that soldiers and constables had made little effort to enforce the edict. But religious services had once again retreated into cautious obscurity, and no more was heard of plans to admit selected Catholics to municipal corporations or other local offices.

At the same time that he kept up the necessary show of anti-Catholic measures, Essex had to work out a policy towards dissent. Soon after his arrival there was a crisis in Derry, where Presbyterians had built a large meeting house close to the bishop's residence and had begun to assemble in groups of up to 2,000, too many to be dispersed without risk of violence. He negotiated a compromise whereby the meetings moved outside the city walls. Meanwhile Sir Arthur Forbes, a Presbyterian sympathizer in good standing with the court ever since he had acted as Coote's emissary in 1660, had persuaded the king to make a grant of £1,200 (reduced to £600 when the funds available proved inadequate) for the support of Presbyterian ministers. The grant, known as the *regium donum*, was in practice to be paid only irregularly. But it represented a pragmatic acceptance of the advantages of attaching moderate dissenters to the crown, rather than driving them into the arms of extremists. At the same time military precautions were also necessary. Essex rejected the idea of raising a militia in Ulster, on the grounds that the Scots there could not be trusted in the event of a rising in Scotland itself. Instead he relied on the regular army, deploying extra troops there in 1674 and again in 1676, in each case in response to concern at the activities of disaffected Covenanters in Scotland.

As lord lieutenant Essex had inherited an arrangement whereby a consortium headed by Richard Jones, viscount and later earl of Ranelagh, a nephew of Orrery, took complete charge of the kingdom's finances, undertaking to clear the crown's debt and remit a surplus to the king. When Essex, alarmed at Ranelagh's failure to pay the army, began to challenge the scheme, thus threatening the steady flow of income it provided to a hard-pressed English treasury, the time had come for his

---

[49] Plunkett, *Letters*, 379.

removal. The choice of a successor illustrated once again the close interaction that now prevailed between English factional politics and the government of Ireland. Charles's initial plan was to make his illegitimate son, the duke of Monmouth, titular lord lieutenant, with one of Ranelagh's allies, Edward, Viscount Conway, as his deputy. However the duke of York, Monmouth's rival for the succession to the king, blocked the plan. Instead Ormond, more compliant in matters of finance than of faith, returned for a third period as lord lieutenant in 1677.

It was thus under Ormond's experienced and pragmatic leadership that the administration faced a second disruptive intrusion of external concerns on Irish religious policy. Titus Oates's revelations in September 1678 of a Catholic plot to murder the king and massacre his English Protestant subjects inspired both a popular panic and a political crisis. Over the next three years eighteen priests and a number of prominent Catholic laymen suffered execution on the basis of often bizarrely improbable allegations of conspiracy. Meanwhile a Whig party emerged, in both parliament and the country, demanding the exclusion from the succession of the duke of York, now known, since the test act of 1673 had forced him to resign his position as lord admiral, to be a Catholic. In Ireland Ormond took sensible precautions. A proclamation on 16 October 1678 ordered bishops, vicars general, and regular clergy to leave the kingdom. Another on 2 November required Catholics to surrender any firearms in their possession. On 20 November Catholics were banned from Dublin Castle and all except permanent residents were excluded from seven named garrison towns. Later, in April 1679, Ormond ordered the suspension of Catholic public worship in towns and cities. Searches and arrests continued into early 1681, with some of the regulars captured being deported. Peter Talbot, archbishop of Dublin, arrested at the very beginning of the crisis, died still a prisoner in Dublin Castle in November 1680. These, however, were the traditional targets: bishops or their equivalent who could be accused of exercising the jurisdiction of the pope within the king's dominions, and regulars acting under the direct control of foreign religious superiors. Ordinary priests, at least outside major towns, appear to have been left mainly alone. John Brenan, archbishop of Cashel, reported to Rome in 1681 that 'the government here is far more moderate and—not having given credence to the calumnies—has not oppressed us at all so much as in England'.[50] Indeed Brenan himself, though forced to go into hiding, continued to administer his diocese. There were also attempts, in Waterford and Limerick, to indict prominent Catholic gentlemen. But in contrast to the show trials that claimed the lives of several English Catholics, grand juries, encouraged by the judges, threw out the charges.

Assessment of the impact of the Popish Plot on Ireland is complicated by one exceptional episode: the trial and execution for treason of Oliver Plunkett,

[50] Patrick Power (ed.), *A Bishop of the Penal Times, Being Letters and Reports of John Brennan* (Cork, 1932), 70–1.

archbishop of Armagh, beatified as a Catholic martyr in 1920 and canonized in 1975. Allegations that Plunkett had conspired with France first appeared in October 1679. Ormond promptly had him arrested and imprisoned, but did nothing more. The following year William Hetherington, a former bounty hunter employed against tories, escaped from jail in Dublin, where he was imprisoned for debt. Making his way to London, he presented himself before the Whig leader, the earl of Shaftesbury, claiming to have information of an Irish Catholic plot. Shaftesbury, whose campaign to exploit Oates's original revelations was running out of steam, seized eagerly on the new opportunity, and had Hetherington sent back to Ireland to collect evidence. There he was able to take advantage of the enemies Plunkett had made as a Palesman, perceived as unsympathetic to both regulars and the Gaelic Irish, who had attempted to impose a strict Tridentine discipline on a province in which both were numerous. The two most prominent witnesses against the archbishop were Edmund Murphy, a suspended parish priest from Armagh, and John Moyer, a Franciscan also under suspension. Both men also had links to Henry Jones, now bishop of Meath and one-time custodian and publicist of the 1641 depositions, who along with Orrery was an open critic of Ormond's refusal to take the spectre of Catholic conspiracy as seriously as they wished. Even at this stage, however, the first attempt to secure a prosecution, at Dundalk in July 1680, collapsed when witnesses failed to appear. Instead Plunkett was transferred to London where he was convicted in June 1681 and executed a month later. His downfall casts light on the internal divisions, ethnic and otherwise, within the Irish Catholic church. But his martyr's death was the result of a wholly English episode of anti-Catholic hysteria.

Already by the time Plunkett died English opinion, alarmed by the prospect of a return to civil war, had begun to move against the Whig challenge to the principle of hereditary monarchy. The discovery in June 1683 of a republican conspiracy, the Rye House Plot, gave the court the excuse to mount a ruthless counter-attack. Those involved in the plot had only slender links with Ireland. But it nevertheless inspired Ormond to abandon the tacit toleration that he and others had permitted for most of the preceding two decades by ordering a general closure of dissenting meeting houses. The governor of County Londonderry reported in August 1683 that not a single 'conventicle house' had opened in the county on the previous Sunday. Early in the following year the authorities in County Tyrone even began to levy the fine of one shilling prescribed by the act of uniformity on those who failed to attend Anglican worship. It seems unlikely that many believed such tactics could at this stage coerce the whole dissenting population into returning to the established church. More probably those involved were seizing the chance to act on long-standing antagonisms. Presbyterian leaders, for their part, offered no resistance, but discussed among themselves the best time to begin petitioning for some relaxation of the ban on meetings. Meanwhile the Church of Ireland archbishop of Dublin reported that Catholic clergy had complied with instructions to keep their churches closed, in

order to avoid invidious comparisons between the treatment of different kinds
of religious dissident. Others who showed less discretion, such as the friars who
attempted to re-establish regular communities in County Galway and Kilkenny
city, were quickly slapped down. By the beginning of 1685 Ireland was thus in
the state which Ormond, and probably Charles II himself, had always wanted,
with dissenters and Catholics alike aware of their complete dependence on royal
indulgence. Within two months, however, Charles was dead and the crown had
passed to a monarch whose ambitions were very different.[51]

KING CHARLES'S IRELAND

In the years after 1641 the effects of wartime disruption, plague, and famine temporarily cancelled out the economic gains of the preceding decades. Population
fell by up to one-fifth. Large areas of land lay waste. Internal and foreign trade
stagnated. Landowners and others sank deeply into debt. In the early 1650s it
was necessary to import large quantities of both cattle and grain. Already by the
end of the decade, however, there were signs of recovery. Livestock numbers had
risen and trade had revived. In 1659–60 it was Ireland that exported grain to an
England hit by bad harvests. By 1665 Irish exports of beef and cattle were more
than a third higher than they had been in 1641. Expansion continued, with
interruptions, through the 1670s and 1680s. By the death of Charles II in 1685
Ireland was a very different country from the one he had recovered twenty-five
years earlier, much less the one his grandfather had inherited in 1603.[52]

Apart from the return of peace and stability, the dramatic economic growth
of the years after 1660 depended on two main developments. The first was the
opening up of new markets. In part, continuing a pattern that was to last into the
twentieth century, Ireland found its opportunities in those areas where it could
serve a growing English economy. It exported raw wool and sheep to supply
the expansion of the wool trade, and cattle, beef, and butter to supplement the
produce of domestic agriculture, particularly in feeding an increasingly hungry
London. But the proportion of Irish exports going to England actually fell during
this period, from 74 per cent in 1665 to only 30 per cent by 1683. One new
market was France, which by 1683 took 72 per cent of Irish butter, as well as a

---

[51] For Dublin see HMC, *Ormonde MSS*, ns vii (1912), 315. Otherwise see Connolly, *Religion,
Law and Power*, 23, 27; Greaves, *God's Other Children*, 123–32.

[52] The social and economic changes in the late seventeenth century are covered in a series
of excellent surveys: *NHI*, iii, ch. 15 (L. M. Cullen, 'Economic Trends 1660–91') and 18
(J. H. Andrews, 'Land and People *c*.1685'); L. M. Cullen, *Anglo-Irish Trade 1660–1800* (Manch-
ester, 1968), ch. 2; idem, *An Economic History of Ireland since 1660* (London, 1972), ch. 1;
David Dickson, *New Foundations: Ireland 1660–1800* (2nd edn., Dublin, 2000), ch. 4; idem, *Old
World Colony: Cork and South Munster 1630–1830* (Cork, 2005), ch. 2; Raymond Gillespie, *The
Transformation of the Irish Economy 1550–1700* (Dundalk, 1991). The export statistics cited below
are mainly from Cullen, *NHI*, iii. 392–6.

proportion of its export of hides. Another was the transatlantic trade, as Ireland began to supply beef, pork, and butter to the English and French colonies in the Caribbean and to the English colonies in North America. Irish merchants had long maintained a presence in continental European ports. But when the Blakes, Galway merchants ruined by the Cromwellian confiscation, set out to restore the family fortunes in 1668, they did so by sending two sons to the West Indies, while the eldest continued to trade from Galway. Henry Blake, the more successful of the two, acquired a plantation on Montserrat, from which he shipped indigo and tobacco to Ireland By 1676 he was able to return and buy an estate in County Mayo, leaving his somewhat less dynamic brother in possession of the Montserrat plantation.

The second major stimulus to late seventeenth-century growth was immigration. In part this was a product of the Cromwellian settlement. The thinning out that had taken place in the ranks of the Adventurers meant that those who actually took up their Irish holdings were likely to have made a positive decision to invest their energies and resources in recouping their investment. Ex-soldiers, equally, were not necessarily the ideal colonists, but a similar informal selection process in which the majority disposed of their debentures would have favoured those most likely to make an economic contribution. An account of County Longford in 1682 maintained that 'all such soldiers as had lots in this county have all improved on their proportions so that the county is much better than ever it was'.[53] Alongside this wave of government-sponsored settlement, meanwhile, there was also a revival from the 1650s of unofficial migration, largely but not exclusively into Ulster. Once peace had been restored an understocked but fertile landscape and a largely intact infrastructure had obvious attractions for the adventurous and far-sighted. The Quaker Anthony Sharp, for example, moved from Gloucestershire to Dublin in 1669, at the age of 26, to take advantage of the new opportunities opening up in the woollen trade. By 1680 his cloth manufactory employed 500 hands, and he was also involved in the regular export of raw wool. The growth of Belfast, similarly, owed much to an influx during the 1650s and 1660s of Scottish merchants and entrepreneurs, bringing with them capital, skills, and the commercial contacts needed to revive and expand trade. The scale of population movement is impossible to quantify, but one estimate suggests that by the late 1660s the British population of Ulster stood at around 120,000, compared to around 40,000 in 1630.[54]

The scale of economic expansion is most evident in the growth of Irish exports. Between 1665 and 1683 the value of total exports rose by just over 40 per cent.

[53] N. Dowdall, 'Account of County Longford, *c*.1682' (TCD MS 883/2, p. 267). Dowdall's account is one of a series of descriptions of Irish counties, several of which will be quoted here, collected by William Molyneux for publication in a proposed atlas: see *NHI*, iii. 447.

[54] R. L. Greaves, *Dublin's Merchant Quaker: Anthony Sharp and the Community of Friends 1643–1707* (Stanford, Calif., 1998); Jean Agnew, *Belfast Merchant Families in the Seventeenth Century* (Dublin, 1996); Macafee, 'The Population of Ulster 1630–1840', 74–5, 85–7.

This global figure, however, concealed important discontinuities. After 1667 exports of cattle and sheep were prohibited by an act of the English parliament. Their loss was compensated for, and overall growth ensured, primarily by a rise in exports of wool and butter, which between them accounted for 40 per cent of exports by 1683. Exports of salt beef, mainly across the Atlantic, already twice as large in 1665 as in 1641, more than doubled again by 1683. Fish and timber, two natural resources important to trade earlier in the century, were by this time insignificant, due in one case to the migration, and in the other to the exhaustion, of the natural resource. Depletion of timber stocks had also ended the hopes once vested in an Irish iron industry. What production continued was small in scale and poor in quality. The other main prospect for the development of manufacturing, textiles, grew impressively during the period, though as yet accounting for only a small part of overall economic activity. By 1683 exports of woollen cloth of all kinds were more than one-and-a-half times what they had been in 1665, and more than two-and-a-half times what they had been in 1641. But even at this later date they accounted for less than 9 per cent of total exports. Exports of linen yarn were only slightly higher in 1683 than they had been in 1665, and a modest 25 per cent higher than in 1641, while cloth production had actually fallen back since the 1660s. The next few years, however, saw a sudden surge in exports, almost certainly linked to the arrival in east Ulster, particularly along the Lagan Valley, of a new wave of English and Scottish settlers in the late 1670s and early 1680s.[55]

The revival of trade was reflected in the rapid growth of towns and cities. Urban expansion, as in the first decades of the century, was most dramatic in the case of Dublin. From 20,000 or somewhere above in 1641, its population rose to 45,000 by 1685. It was at this point that the city definitively burst its medieval boundaries: by 1685 more of Dublin lay outside the walls than within them (see Map 4). To the south of Dublin Castle a well-placed speculator, Francis Aungier, vice treasurer of Ireland and later master of the ordnance and earl of Longford, developed an exclusive residential district on former monastic land acquired by his family early in the century. Further east the corporation in 1663 laid out what had been a marshy common as an elegant park, St Stephen's Green, surrounded on all four sides by plots for housing. By 1694 there were more than fifty houses, varying from mansions to smaller properties. On the north bank of the river, another property developer, Sir Humphrey Jervis, developed a new quay and market, both named after Ormond, as well as a neat grid of residential streets the most important of which he named, with equal diplomacy, after the Capel earls of Essex. The growing importance of the north bank was reflected in the construction of four new bridges to supplement the single structure

[55] The official figures put exports of linen cloth in 1686 at 131,568 yards, compared to 51,100 in 1669, and only 23,136 in 1683 (Cullen, *Economic History*, 24). How far such an expansion in only three years can be taken at face value remains unclear.

that had formerly permitted access to Oxmantown Green. There was also new public building. In 1681 the city erected a two-storey Tholsel as a civic centre and financial exchange, replacing the much-restored early fourteenth-century building in which the convention had met in 1660. To the west the grounds of the former monastery at Kilmainham became the site of a new hospital for army veterans, accommodating up to 300 inmates in an elegant three-storeyed structure surrounding a spacious arcaded courtyard. Other lands of the monastery, south of the river, became the 1,700-acre Phoenix Park, designed as a royal deer park and enclosed to protect its stocks of game, but from the start freely used as a public amenity.

Along with streets, bridges, and public buildings went the facilities required to support the new style of cultivated sociability that was by this time growing up alongside an older pattern centred on the royal court and aristocratic houses. In 1637 John Ogilby, a Scottish dancing master brought to Dublin by Wentworth to polish the manners of his viceregal court, had opened a theatre in Werburgh Street, which had continued until the outbreak of war in 1641. After the Restoration Ogilby revived his patent and in 1662 opened a large, purpose-built theatre, with seating for some 2,000 patrons, at Smock Alley, an otherwise unprepossessing street in the heart of the old city. Surviving records suggest that Dublin audiences were conservative in their taste, preferring well-established texts to newer works. But the Smock Alley Company was considered sufficiently accomplished to make successful visits to Oxford and Edinburgh.[56] Other new urban amusements included a tennis court near Christ Church, open by 1663, and an elaborate bowling green at Oxmantown. During the same period the Curragh, twenty-five miles to the west in County Kildare, developed as a fashionable racecourse. On a smaller scale there was a proliferation of taverns and coffee houses, providing venues for formal and informal gatherings. William Molyneux, himself at the heart of the city's lively new intellectual life, wrote in 1684 to assure an absent brother that 'we are come to fine things here in Dublin, and you would wonder how our city increases sensibly in fair buildings, great trade, and splendour in all things—in furniture, coaches, civility [and] housekeeping'.[57]

As in the first half of the seventeenth century, Dublin's size and vitality gave it a unique position within Ireland. An account from the 1680s, comparing it with London, made the point neatly: 'men live alike in these two cities, though very different in the rest of the kingdom.'[58] Where trade was concerned, the imbalance was equally marked. In the years 1664–9 Dublin accounted for 40 per cent of the total customs revenue of the kingdom. Yet despite this continued

[56] W. S. Clark, *The Early Irish Stage: The Beginnings to 1720* (Oxford, 1955), 43–88.

[57] Quoted in J. G. Simms, *William Molyneux of Dublin: A Life of the Seventeenth-Century Political Writer and Scientist* (Dublin, 1982), 17.

[58] Quoted in *NHI*, iii. 476.

dominance by a single metropolis, there were also signs of the emergence of a more complex urban hierarchy. By the early eighteenth century the population of Cork, which from the 1660s displaced Galway as the main centre of transatlantic commerce, had grown to over 17,000, compared to around 6,000 four decades earlier. Limerick and Waterford retained their place as the other main centres of a steadily expanding trade, though their population in the 1680s was much smaller, around 5,000 in each case. Belfast, written off in the 1640s as a mere market town, also grew rapidly as the chief port for a hinterland transformed by English and Scottish settlement. Its population, less than 1,000 before 1641, rose to 3,200 by 1669 and was to reach 5,000 by the early eighteenth century, when it was reckoned the fourth most important port in Ireland.[59] A further development was the emergence of inland towns, serving as marketing centres for a surrounding area. Lisburn, in County Antrim, was to grow from a town of perhaps 700 in 1659 to around 4,000 by 1725. The basis of this expansion was laid in the period up to 1690, when it became both a centre of the emerging linen industry and a market for hides and butter destined for export through Belfast. On a smaller scale Ennis in County Clare 'derives a considerable trade in hides, tallow and butter, which are sent thence by boat to Limerick'. Around 1683 it had 500 or 600 inhabitants, living in 120 houses, of which around 20 were slated and the rest thatched.[60]

Change was equally evident, though unevenly, in the rural landscape. Even better land had not yet, for the most part, been subdivided by the permanent enclosures of walls, earthen banks or hedges. A Westmeath gentleman, in 1682, complained of the flimsy temporary fences that a local farmer had erected around his corn: 'if at any time he makes a fence likely to hold out a whole year, he triumphs, and with confidence pronounceth it a year's ditch, which among them passes for a very strong fence.' There were still large areas of underused land. Much of County Roscommon, in 1684, remained unprepossessing, 'for the greatest part waste and without culture, overspread in some plains and hills with heath, in other places with little black thorns, and other scrubs, to one standing on a hill yielding a prospect, in some parts, as of a black sort of a country'. Further evidence of an only half-tamed landscape came in the survival in many areas of the wolf, extinct in England since around 1500. In 1665, for example, wolves preyed on sheep on the Conway estate on the Antrim side of Lough Neagh. A report from Leitrim, in 1683, noted that they were now 'very few', thanks to a local system of bounties for those who killed them. In the south-west,

---

[59] Agnew, *Belfast Merchant Families*, 15. For Belfast in the 1640s see Connolly, *Contested Island*, 305. For other urban population figures see *NHI*, iii. 474; Dickson, 'The Place of Dublin in the Eighteenth-Century Irish Economy', in David Dickson and T. M. Devine (eds.), *Ireland and Scotland 1600–1850: Parallels and Contrasts in Economic and Social Development* (Edinburgh, 1983), 179; Dickson, *Old World Colony*, 662.

[60] Raymond Gillespie, 'George Rawdon's Lisburn', *Lisburn Historical Society*, 8 (1991); 'Account of County Clare', n.d. (TCD MS 883/1, p. 237).

on the other hand, the last bounties were paid as late as 1710. Some accounts, of questionable credibility, put the death of the last Irish wolf more than half a century later.[61]

Yet change was nevertheless taking place. The dominance of the export trade by cattle, sheep, and livestock products meant that large tracts were devoted to grazing. But there were also areas of more intensive agriculture. The Ards peninsula in County Down 'sends every winter great store of good wheat, beare, oats and barley to Dublin and elsewhere'. The whole of the barony of Forth, in County Wexford, 'at a distance, viewed in time of harvest, represents a well cultivated garden, with diversified plots'. Even in County Donegal 'they have great plenty of barley and oats with which they supply most neighbouring counties'. The barony of Onealand in County Armagh, it was claimed, served as 'the granary of Ulster. . . . The very roads are here so well planted with houses and other improvements, that they seem to be but as one continuous town.' An English soldier marching into Limerick in 1691 passed through 'lanes, cornfields and meadows on both sides, all enclosed as in England'.[62]

The emerging division between areas devoted to tillage and to pasture, and the frequent reference to the movement of produce from one to the other, testifies to a growing regional specialization, encouraged by the new commercial opportunities opened up by an expanding trade. Internal networks of exchange were still taking shape, and there remained a strong regional imbalance. Of the 500 or so markets for which patents were granted in the first half of the seventeenth century only just over 200 were still active. However others had taken their place: an almanac in 1684, in fact, listed a total of 503 fairs, although 43 per cent of these were in Leinster. Where Tudor and early Stuart maps had plotted the locations of towns and territories, those of the late seventeenth century showed roads linking the main centres. New bridges further facilitated travel. The road network, however, grew noticeably thinner as one moved from east to west. As late as 1704 the judges and lawyers travelling from Cork city to Tralee for the assizes had to pass over eight miles of mountain on horseback, with only a series of posts stuck in the ground to guide them through areas of bog. And travel everywhere remained an ordeal. An official returning in 1681 from an extended viceregal progress complained that 'in many places we met with ill

---

[61] Sir Henry Piers, *A Chorographical Description of the County of Westmeath, Written A.D. 1682* (Naas, 1982), 59–60; Account of Roscommon, 14 Mar. 1684 (TCD MS 883/1, p. 161); Sir George Rawdon to Viscount Conway, 3 Sept., 7 Oct. 1665 (*CSPI 1663–5*, 637, 649); 'Account of Leitrim', 24 Apr. 1683 (TCD MS 883/1, p. 138). For wolves see also J. S. Fairley, *An Irish Beast Book: A Natural History of Ireland's Furred Wildlife* (Belfast, 1975), 180–7.

[62] D. B. Quinn, 'William Montgomery and the Description of the Ards 1683', *Irish Booklore*, 2 (1972), 34; H. F. Hore (ed.), 'An Account of the Barony of Forth', *JRSAI* 7 (1862–3), 60; 'Account of County Donegal', 27 Apr. 1683 (TCD MS 883/1, p. 214); William Brooke, 'Account of Onealand', 26 Oct. 1682 (TCD MS 883/1, 223); *The Journal of John Stevens, Containing a Brief Account of the War in Ireland*, ed. R. H. Murray (Oxford, 1912), 163.

or no stabling and bad provision for the horses, so that we seldom or never go without loss of horses'.[63]

The other main change to the Irish landscape was the appearance of newly built country houses, ranging in size from Orrery's great mansion at Charleville, taxed in 1680 as having sixty-five hearths, to the more modest residences of the country gentry. These abandoned the defensive features, such as bawns and gun loops, that had still been included in their early seventeenth-century predecessors. Instead owners turned amateur architect, poring over drawings brought back from foreign travel, or over purchased pattern books, for models of the new classical style, emphasizing symmetry and balance. Equal attention was lavished on the surrounding gardens. In County Longford Sir John Edgeworth had built 'a fair house, planted orchards and gardens very sumptuous, and impaled a fair park for deer', as well as establishing nearby the 'very good country town' of Edgeworthstown. Near Newtownards Sir Robert Colvill had 'a large double roofed house' with 'spacious, well planted olitory [i.e. kitchen], fruit, and pleasure gardens, which have fish ponds, spring wells, long and broad sanded walks and a bowling green'.[64]

Along with economic expansion and agricultural improvement went a quickening of intellectual life. Ireland had, of course, long sustained a literary culture. In the mid-1580s Ludowick Bryskett, former clerk to the Irish privy council, composed his tract 'A Discourse of Civil Life', supposedly based on his conversations with a group of friends, including the young Edmund Spenser, who had walked out on successive days to visit him in the suburban cottage to which, in true Renaissance humanist fashion, he had retired from the bustle of Dublin administrative life. The same tradition of interchange within a closed circle of intimates continued into the seventeenth century. One consequence of the reliance on the private circulation of manuscripts, as opposed to the self-advertisement of print, was that women as well as men could take part. During her year in Ireland in 1662–3 Katherine Phillips, acclaimed as 'the matchless Orinda', established links with a group surrounding Ormond's viceregal court which included the duke's wife, his daughter Lady Mary Cavendish, and the wife and daughters of the earl of Cork. Yet the shift from a court to a public intellectual culture was under way. One of the early triumphs of the Smock Alley Theatre was its production of Phillips's rhymed translation of Corneille's *Pompey*.[65]

[63] Alan Brodrick to St John Brodrick, 7 Sept. [1704] (Surrey History Centre, Middleton MSS 1248/2, fo. 146); W. Ellis to Sir Cyril Wyche, 5 Nov. 1681 (NAI, Wyche Papers 1/1/35).

[64] Dowdall, Account of Longford, 1682 (TCD MS 883/2, p. 266); Quinn, 'William Montgomery and the Description of the Ards 1683', 40. For houses and gardens see also T. C. Barnard, *Making the Grand Figure: Lives and Possessions in Ireland 1641–1770* (London, 2004), ch. 2, 6.

[65] For Bryskett see Nicholas Canny, *Making Ireland British 1580–1650* (Oxford, 2001), 1–2. For women in literary circles, Mary O'Dowd, *A History of Women in Ireland 1500–1800* (Harlow, 2005), 225–6, and for *Pompey* Clark, *Early Irish Stage*, 62–5.

A very different intellectual coterie, this time exclusively male, appeared some time later, with the establishment in 1683 of the Dublin Philosophical Society. Once again the stimulus for Irish developments came largely from outside. The huge administrative undertakings of the Commonwealth government in the 1650s created employment for a number of individuals in the forefront of new movements in English intellectual life. The most prominent of these new arrivals was William Petty, who as a young man had been an associate of Samuel Hartlib, the Bohemian-born advocate of the new learning, stressing experimental science and useful knowledge. The reward for his services to the Commonwealth and Protectorate, a grant of some 18,000 acres in Kerry and elsewhere, ensured that his Irish contacts continued after 1660, and he became first president of the Dublin Philosophical Society. The main force behind its foundation, however, was a younger man, William Molyneux, descended from an Elizabethan settler transplanting from the English colony at Calais, who had begun to distinguish himself by his studies in optics and mathematics. Molyneux's model was the English Royal Society, established under Charles II's patronage in 1662. In the four years until its work was interrupted by political crisis the Dublin Society met regularly to pursue a variety of enquiries: studies of solar and lunar eclipses, a paper by Molyneux on the petrifying qualities of the water in Lough Neagh, a disastrous trial in Dublin harbour of the latest in a series of twin-hulled boats designed by Petty, and the dissection of a specimen of the fabled Connacht worm, a supposedly venomous creature with 'short feet, a large head, great goggle eyes and glaring', which turned out on inspection to be an elephant caterpillar.[66]

Alongside these exclusive literary and scientific clubs there was the beginning of a new culture of print. Late seventeenth-century Ireland had not yet reached the stage where a lack of basic literacy was an obstacle to the achievement of status and economic position. In Belturbet, County Cavan, in the 1680s half the members of the corporation were unable to sign their names. But the ability to read and write was nevertheless widespread. On the Herbert estate in County Kerry around the same time two-thirds of native Irish leaseholders, and 83 per cent of those with settler names, were able to sign their leases. These, of course, represented substantial occupiers holding directly from the landowner rather than the working peasantry, to whom they would have sublet. Women were in general less likely to be literate than men. But one-third of the female survivors who made depositions following the rising of 1641 nevertheless signed rather than making a mark.[67] By the late seventeenth century, a print trade serving

---

[66] Simms, *William Molyneux*, 42. See K. T. Hoppen, *The Common Scientist in the Seventeenth Century: A Study of the Dublin Philosophical Society 1683–1708* (London, 1970). For disagreement on the issue of how far the Society's origins should be traced to the 1650s, first raised in Barnard, *Cromwellian Ireland*, ch. 8, see the exchange between Barnard and Hoppen in *IHS* 19 (1974), 20 (1976).

[67] T. C. Barnard, 'Reading in Eighteenth-Century Ireland: Public and Private Pleasures', in Bernadette Cunningham and Máire Kennedy (eds.), *The Experience of Reading: Irish Historical*

this large and probably growing pool of readers had begun to develop. Printing itself continued to be inhibited by a series of patents, commencing in 1604, designating the holder king's printer and forbidding all others to print, bind, or sell books without his licence. In the 1680s, however, Joseph Ray successfully challenged the monopoly, producing fifty imprints between 1681 and 1689. Patents to king's printers continued to be issued until 1732, but their monopoly was now confined to official publications. By 1700 there were at least six printers at work in Dublin. The early ventures in provincial printing, at Waterford and Kilkenny, associated with the Confederate Catholics, did not continue beyond the 1640s. However a trickle of titles continued to appear in Cork, and a second provincial press began work in Belfast in 1694.

If printing was still on a small scale, the growth in bookselling was more dramatic. In the absence of significant local printing, their wares consisted mainly of imported works. Imports of bound and unbound books averaged around 10 tons per year, at an official valuation of around £1000 per annum. In 1670 the Guild of St Luke, composed of the odd combination of stationers, cutlers, and painter-stainers, received its royal charter of incorporation. It initially contained only five stationers, but by 1686 had around thirty. Booksellers also appeared from the 1660s in provincial centres such as Waterford, Limerick, and Belfast. The growth of specialization is evident in the scattered records of imports. Of twenty-eight individuals to whom books were shipped from Chester during 1681, only nine brought in other goods. Beyond the port towns, on the other hand, distribution was still mainly in the hands of general traders, to whom printers and booksellers dispatched their wares. The publisher of an almanac for 1697 listed twenty-two agents across the country, thirteen of them described as merchants. Lower down the scale itinerant pedlars carried chapbooks, small, cheaply bound texts, generally a single sheet of paper folded to give sixteen or thirty-two pages, along with their other wares. Print also circulated in more ephemeral forms, as single broadsheets containing news, or the texts of ballads.[68]

The appearance of chapbooks and broadsheets, joined from the 1690s by another staple, the supposed last speeches of executed criminals, marked the birth in Ireland of something wholly new, a popular printed literature. But the easier availability of print transformed attitudes and expectations even among the most educated. The change is evident in an embarrassed admission by Narcissus Marsh, the new provost of Trinity College. Twenty years earlier the college had acquired what was at the time regarded as the important library of Archbishop James Ussher of Armagh, acclaimed as one of the great European scholars of

---

Perspectives (Dublin, 1999), 61; Raymond Gillespie, 'The Circulation of Print in Seventeenth-Century Ireland', *Studia Hibernica*, 29 (1995–7), 31–58; Raymond Gillespie, *Reading Ireland: Print, Reading and Social Change in Early Modern Ireland* (Manchester, 2005), 39–45; O'Dowd, *History of Women in Ireland*, 210.

[68] Mary Pollard, *Dublin's Trade in Books 1550–1800* (Oxford, 1989); Gillespie, 'Circulation of Print'; R. J. Hunter, 'Chester and the Irish Book Trade, 1681', *IESH* 15 (1989), 89–93.

his day. By 1680, however, Marsh 'would not have it divulged that Primate Ussher's library (both manuscripts and printed books) comes very short of its owner's fame. It might have been thought a good library for another man but not for that learned primate.'[69]

The expansion of Irish trade, and the appearance of new modes of politeness and sociability among its leisured classes, were alike supported by the efforts of the labouring poor. Observers throughout the late seventeenth and eighteenth centuries were to lament the absence in most parts of rural Ireland of a yeoman class capable of renting and stocking a substantial holding with the aid of hired labour. Instead landlords leased land to chief tenants—what in the eighteenth century would come to be called middlemen—who in turn sublet to an occupying peasantry. Alternatively they let directly, with labouring tenants pooling their resources to hold a townland, typically a unit of between 200 and 400 acres, in partnership. An account from Westmeath in 1682 described what may have been a typical arrangement: up to ten or twelve ploughs at work in a single field, with each partner holding a share of perhaps three acres scattered about in six or more plots, while being permitted to graze cattle on common pasture in proportion to his allocation of tilled land.[70]

The living standards of this peasant population were, even by contemporary standards, low. Petty, writing around 1672, estimated that '6 out of 8 of all the Irish live in a brutish, nasty condition, in cabins, with neither chimney, door, stairs nor window'. The potato, nutritious, prolific, and easily cultivated even on poor land, was already prominent in the diet of most areas. Milk, reflecting the continued dominance of cattle in the rural economy, was also an important component, consumed sour and semi-solid as 'bonnyclabber' (from the Irish *bainne clabar*, thick milk), and also as butter, used as a staple food rather than an additive.[71] The main grains were oats and barley, eaten as cakes rather than bread. Yet conditions, though harsh, may well have been improving. Crop failures and loss of livestock could bring widespread misery. In particular the poor harvest of 1673, followed by a freezing new year that prevented spring sowing, had disastrous consequences. By June 1674 the Catholic archbishop of Armagh reported 'hundreds and hundreds of starved skeletons rather than men walking the roads'. By September 500 inhabitants of his diocese had died of hunger.[72] Yet this seems to have been the only serious subsistence crisis of the second half of the century. Instead the period saw a striking demographic recovery, with population rising from a low of 1.3 million in 1652 to almost 2 million by 1687. Growth on this scale, far above what could be accounted

---

[69] Quoted in Gillespie, *Reading Ireland*, 15.   [70] Piers, *Westmeath*, 115–18.
[71] Petty, *Political Anatomy*, 27, 81. For potatoes see also *Journal of John Stevens*, 138–40, and for a general discussion of diet L. M. Cullen, *The Emergence of Modern Ireland 1600–1900* (London, 1981), ch. 7; L. A. Clarkson and E. Margaret Crawford, *Feast and Famine: A History of Food and Nutrition in Ireland 1500–1920* (Oxford, 2001), ch. 4.
[72] Plunkett, *Letters*, 404–16, 428.

Table 1. Estimates of Population

	Ireland (millions)	Dublin	Cork
1600	1	10,000	
1641	1.5–1.6	20,000	
1660			6,000
1672	1.5		
1685		45,000	
1687	1.97		
1706	1.75–2.06	62,000	18,000
1712	1.98–2.32		
c.1719			27,000
1725	2.18–2.56	92,000	35,000
1732	2.16–2.53		
1744	1.91–2.23	112,000	37,500
1749	1.95–2.28		
1752			41,000
1753	2.20–2.57		
1760		140,000	44,600
1778		154,000	
1786			52,000
1791	4.42		
1793			54,000
1796			57,000
1800		182,000	
1821	6.8	224,000	71,500

Sources: Ireland: David Dickson, Cormac Ó Gráda, and Stuart Daultrey, 'Hearth Tax, Household Size and Irish Population Change 1672–1821', *PRIA* C (1982), 125–81; *Dublin*: David Dickson, 'The Place of Dublin in the Eighteenth-Century Irish Economy', in T. M. Devine and David Dickson (eds.), *Ireland and Scotland 1600–1850* (Edinburgh, 1983), 179; *Cork*: David Dickson, *Old World Colony: Cork and South Munster 1630–1830* (Cork, 2005), 662.

for by English and Scottish immigration, suggests that some part of the benefits of economic expansion reached even the labouring poor. The same point is suggested by the evidence of a modest but still significant degree of continuing commercialization. Imports of tobacco rose from 1.8 million pounds in 1665 to 2.8 million in 1683. Petty, eleven years earlier, varied what was otherwise a catalogue of material deprivation with the observation that 'tobacco, taken in short pipes seldom burnt, seems the pleasure of their lives'.[73]

A different insight into the lives of the Gaelic lower classes comes from an unexpected quarter. In the early 1660s an unknown author, possibly from Westmeath or nearby, composed a second version of the *Pairlement Chloinne*

[73] Cullen, *Anglo-Irish Trade*, 38; Petty, *Political Anatomy*, 81.

Tomáis. The satire on the pretensions of the boorish churls is as savage as in the early seventeenth-century original.[74] But it is given an additional twist by the bizarre suggestion that the peasantry meeting in comically solemn assembly have chosen as their hero Oliver Cromwell, who has liberated them from subjection to their lords and 'given the flail man his fill'. They proceed to draw up laws for their own future comfort and plenty, ignoring the warning of one of their number that 'until we give our lords coshering, feasts and necessary provision . . . we will have neither prosperity nor success'. Around the same time the priest and historian John Lynch, a member of the Old English civic elite of Galway but trained in the Gaelic literary tradition, complained from his continental exile of the 'insolence' now displayed by the common people.[75] Both comments may be particular to conditions in the 1650s, when widespread devastation and loss of population allowed the survivors to insist on modest rents as tenants and high wages as labourers. But they nevertheless raise the question of how far the native lower classes had in fact benefited, as their new English masters so proudly proclaimed, by their liberation from the multiple exactions of their traditional lords.

IRISH UNDERSTANDINGS

The social and economic changes of the years after 1660 unfolded against a background of continued political uncertainty. In the period immediately following the Restoration Ormond was particularly concerned about the loyalty of the army, still largely composed of veterans from the Commonwealth and Protectorate era. The problem, he wrote to London in 1663, was how to replace them, 'where good English are not to be had and Irish cannot be admitted without danger'.[76] His solution was to reduce the force he had inherited from 15,000 to less than 6,000, while at the same time creating a new regiment of 1,200 foot guards recruited entirely in England. Later, following the 1663 conspiracy, he systematically discharged more men from every company, again replacing them with new recruits from England. In the years that followed the government remained alert for possible republican and dissenting conspiracy, both among the Ulster Presbyterians and in surviving nonconformist circles in the south. In 1672 there were claims that Captain Thomas Walcott, an Independent later to be executed for his part in the Rye House Plot, was planning to seize Limerick and other places with the aim of bringing back the Long Parliament and abolishing episcopacy.[77]

[74] For this earlier text see Connolly, *Contested Island*, 386–7.
[75] *Pairlement Chloinne Tomáis*, ed. N. J. A. Williams (Dublin, 1981), 99, 109. Lynch, quoted in *NHI*, iii. 374.
[76] Ormond to Bennet, 20 June 1663 (*CSPI 1663–5*, 141). See J. C. Beckett, 'The Irish Armed Forces 1660–85', in John Bossy and Peter Jupp (eds.), *Essays Presented to Michael Roberts* (Belfast, 1976), 41–53.
[77] *CSPD 1672–3*, 120–1, 151–2, 336–8; HMC, *Ormonde MSS*, NS iii. 321.

Ormond's distrust of the New Protestant settlers of the Cromwellian era also led him to accede only reluctantly to the creation of a militia in 1666. And indeed even Orrery, the main advocate of arming Irish Protestants for their own defence, proposed that members of the new force should be required to take the oath of supremacy as well as of allegiance. The implicit endorsement of the established church would be unacceptable to 'fanatics' as well as Catholics, thus ensuring that the militia consisted only of 'old Protestants, who, I am convinced, are the only people who should serve in it'.[78] That such suspicions were not wholly groundless is suggested by the one surviving set of assizes records for the period, from County Tipperary, where a succession of clearly Protestant defendants appear charged with expressing seditious sentiments. One defendant had allegedly expressed his wish that the king 'were served as his father . . . was', another that 'Oliver Cromwell were alive again' and 'the king hanged'.[79]

The other threat, backed by much more formidable numbers, and incorporating the additional danger of foreign intervention, was of a Catholic rising. Memories of the events of 1641 were kept alive by the continued circulation of Sir John Temple's inflammatory history, reprinted in London at the time of the Popish Plot, as well as by a series of shorter published accounts. In addition 23 October, representing the providential deliverance of Dublin through the discovery of the conspiracy, but also the beginning of the Ulster massacres, had been made an official day of commemoration, marked by church services and a sermon.[80] The approach of war in 1665–6 led to a crop of reports purporting to reveal Catholic as well as 'fanatic' plots. In January 1667 claims that a party of Irish had assembled in County Cavan created alarm across a wide area. From Charlemont in County Tyrone to Lisburn in County Antrim, 'about Lurgan, Magheraline and all the way the English inhabitants were drawn together by 40 or 50 in a company, with pitchforks and such arms as they had, for their own defence'. An army officer alarmed at the open toleration being extended to Catholic ecclesiastics during Berkeley's viceroyalty commented grimly that 'we are courting the Irish to cut our throats, that have cut so many thousand before, and are as ready now to do it as ever'. A Cork gentleman explained in 1681 that he would not be sorry to have 'some small part of the inconvenient pieces of my estate' transferred to England: 'if trouble should come, I reckon a sum of money lodged in England is the best stake of security, next the having a small estate there'.[81]

---

[78] Orrery to Conway, 17 July 1666 (*CSPI 1666–9*, 157).

[79] Tim Harris, *Restoration: Charles II and his Kingdoms 1660–1685* (London, 2005), 97–8.

[80] Raymond Gillespie, 'Temple's Fate: Reading the *Irish Rebellion* in Late Seventeenth-Century Ireland', in Ciaran Brady and Jane Ohlmeyer (eds.), *British Interventions in Early Modern Ireland* (Cambridge, 2005), 315–33; T. C. Barnard, 'The Uses of 23 October 1641 and Irish Protestant Celebrations', *English Historical Review*, 106 (1991), 889–920.

[81] Rawdon to Conway, 11 Jan. 1667 (PRO, SP63/322/32); Major Joseph Stroud to Conway, 24 June 1671 (*CSPD 1671*, 340); Sir John Perceval to Sir Robert Southwell, 9 Aug. 1681 (HMC, *Egmont MSS*, ii. 105).

The foreign conspiracy, rebellion, and massacre that periodically seized the imagination of Protestant Ireland never materialized. But Catholic rejection of the new social order of post-Restoration Ireland nevertheless found some expression in the activities of the outlaw bands, now commonly referred to by their wartime name of 'tories', that remained active in many areas, robbing travellers, raiding houses, and occasionally mounting more formidable attacks on whole settlements. Already in the first half of the century, the authorities had routinely described such outlaws as 'rebels'.[82] In the period after 1660 the identification with the grievances of the Catholic dispossessed became explicit. The Catholic archbishop of Armagh explained to his superiors in Rome that the tories of Armagh and Tyrone were 'certain gentlemen of the leading families of the houses of O'Neill, MacDonnell, O'Hagan etc., up to twenty-four in number, together with their fellows', who had taken to assassination and robbery on the public highway after losing their estates.

It would be unrealistic to assume that all those referred to as 'tories' fell into this clearly defined class. One report of tories 'in the north' in 1668, in fact, noted that they included 'both Irish, English and Scots'. The revelation, at the height of the Popish Plot scare, that some Catholic gentlemen had licences to keep arms 'for the security of themselves and of their houses against the tories' confirms the overlap between toryism and simple banditry. Yet tory activity could also have a political edge. This was most clearly evident in the career of one of the most formidable outlaws of the period, Edward Nangle, killed leading 200 men in a raid on the town of Longford in 1666. A paper found on his body denounced the Restoration land settlement, in which the murderers of Charles I had secured their estates while innocent Catholics were dispossessed, and proclaimed allegiance to the pope as head of the church militant. One report testified to Nangle's status among the common people, 'insomuch that in some parts they fall down on their knees at sight of him'.[83]

The case of a second celebrated tory, Redmond O'Hanlon of County Armagh, killed by a confederate in 1681, is less clear cut. He was said to be 'a scholar and a man of parts', and the nickname 'Count O'Hanlon', noted in 1678, may indicate that he assumed the persona of a dispossessed aristocrat. But in fact his early career was as a servant and tax collector. A report that he 'kept two or three counties almost waste, making the peasants pay continual contributions' may indicate an exaction of the tributes that would once have been paid to the O'Hanlon lords of the region. But it could equally be taken as further evidence of the extent to which toryism covered, not just a rearguard action against the new social and political order, but also predatory banditry of the kind common throughout early modern Europe.

---

[82] See Connolly, *Contested Island*, 379.
[83] For a fuller discussion of toryism see Connolly, *Religion, Law and Power*, 203–9.

The activities of the tories, along with the visible presence of members of the dispossessed Catholic elite, gave credibility to warnings of Catholic disaffection and conspiracy. An appreciation of danger did not, however, mean a loss of perspective. The same observers who expressed concern at the possibility of a new Catholic rising repeatedly expressed their confidence at the outcome of any future conflict. Ormond, in 1666, had no doubt that the French would welcome disturbances in Ireland, 'and certainly all the old nuncio party, with those that have no estates, or who hope to recover their estates, will easily be persuaded into a rebellion'. But he also believed that any such rising, though causing great damage, 'will infallibly end in their own ruin'. Petty, six years later, pointed out that the Protestants, though heavily outnumbered, controlled the country's fortresses and towns, and had a higher proportion of men of military experience, while the poor diet and living conditions of the Catholic peasantry meant that 'their spirits are not disposed for war'.[84] The relatively restrained response in Ireland to the Popish Plot in part reflected Ormond's good fortune in not having to deal with an Irish parliament. But the contrast with England was nevertheless significant. In one case the imagined threat of an unseen popish enemy produced hysterical overreaction. In the other Protestants responded to the visible threat posed by a subjugated Catholic population with a controlled wariness based on a realistic assessment of the level of danger.

The perception of their own security prevalent among Irish Protestants must also be assessed against the background of a continued blurring of the cultural divide that had in the past set settler and native so clearly apart. The Gaelic Irish elite had suffered disproportionately in the sharp reduction in the overall Catholic share of land that had taken place since the death of Elizabeth. They had been the main victims of both the Ulster and the minor Jacobean plantations. They had also gained less from the Restoration, partly through lack of court contacts, and possibly also because of the order, moving outwards in widening circles from Dublin, in which the court of claims heard the cases submitted to it. The small number of proprietors who remained, however, were by this time fully absorbed into the ruling class. Some, like the O'Haras of County Mayo, had conformed to the established church. But the careers of Clancarty and his son Muskerry, the hero of Lowestoft, demonstrated the ability even of a Gaelic family still openly Catholic to obtain acceptance.

This level of cultural and political assimilation was, needless to say, for the few. But even in the case of the labouring poor cultural and religious divisions were being modified by closer contact. Already in the 1650s the integration of the Gaelic lower classes into the economic structures of English Ireland was sufficiently complete to make proposals for a segregation of settler and native, by means of the transplantation beyond the Shannon of the entire Catholic population, simply unworkable. In the same way Ormond, at the height of the

---

[84] Ormond to Arlington, 5 May 1666 (PRO SP63/321/8–9); Petty, *Political Anatomy*, 27.

Popish Plot scare, commented angrily on Protestant landlords who 'pretend they cannot sleep for fear of having their throats cut by the Papists, and asperse the government because there are so many of them, though they themselves are the men that brought them to inhabit their houses in towns and to plant and labour their lands'. By this time even proposals to expel all Catholics from the towns and cities, as had been done in the 1650s, were rejected as impractical.

With economic interaction went a partial but significant change in habits and appearance. Irish peasants were still distinctive in their footwear, the single-soled brogue dismissed by Petty as 'but $\frac{1}{4}$ so much worth as a pair of English shoes'.[85] But the other elements of a distinctive Gaelic dress, the hanging glib of hair, the mantle, and trews, had by this time been abandoned in favour of breeches, shirts, and long coats of coarse woollen frieze. The common people still spoke a different language from their rulers. But the same was true over much of Europe, and it is in any case likely that the bilingualism mocked early in the century in the first *Pairlement Chloinne Tomáis* had continued to spread. Sir Henry Piers, writing from Westmeath in 1682, observed that 'the inferior rank . . . seem very forward to accommodate themselves to the English modes, particularly in their habit, language and surnames'.[86] Such changes meant that the native lower classes were no longer as self-evidently alien as they had been to earlier settlers. The replacement of Gaelic lords by New English landlords, equally, meant that continuing differences in language and habits were no longer the attributes of an alternative social order, but rather the despised customs of a lower class. The landscape, too, was less threatening, as woods were cleared, roads built, and cultivation intensified. Against this background the lingering fear of another 1641 coexisted with the perception of a society in which the English, Protestant interest was at last secure, bringing with it rapid and tangible progress towards civility and prosperity.[87]

The decreasing sense of Gaelic Ireland as an alternative and menacing social order also had implications for the status of those who had defined themselves as the English of Ireland. Some contemporaries continued to recognize the distinction between Catholics of English and Gaelic descent. The attorney general, commenting on the land settlement in 1663, wrote of excluding Irish claimants to make way for 'such persons as are of honourable and ancient English extraction'. Richard Talbot too wrote of the need to preserve 'the old ancient English families of that kingdom'.[88] More recent settlers, whose first experience had been of the defeat or overthrow of the Confederate Catholics, would have been less sensitive to the distinction. The Cromwellian and Restoration land settlements further strengthened the perception of Old English and Gaelic Irish

---

[85] Petty, *Political Anatomy*, 76.   [86] Piers, *Westmeath*, 108.

[87] For a further discussion of variations in Protestant attitudes in this period see T. C. Barnard, 'Crises of Identity among Irish Protestants 1641–85', *Past & Present*, 127 (1990), 39–83.

[88] I owe both of these quotations to Dr Creighton's thesis (above, n. 44), 146, 151.

as drawn together by common grievances and ambitions. Petty, in 1672, argued that the real dividing line within Irish society was now between those 'vested and divested of the lands belonging to the Papists Ann. 1641', with those who had recovered estates at the Restoration seeming 'rather to take part with the divested'. As a result 'the differences between the Old Irish and Old English papists is asleep now, because they have a common enemy'.[89] Against this background the claims of the Old English to a distinct ethnic identity began to fade. The secretary to the earl of Clarendon, sent to Ireland in 1685 to implement the first stages of James II's new religious policy, consistently referred to Catholics as 'the Irish' and Protestants as 'the English'. At one point, discussing the drive to admit Catholics to municipal corporations, he even referred to the difficulty of finding suitably qualified men 'of that nation'.[90]

If economic growth helped to modify the way in which Irish Protestants thought about Ireland and those with whom they shared it, it also had implications for the relationship between Ireland and England. The expansion of Irish trade coincided with a new concern, commencing under the Protectorate and continuing under the restored monarchy, to maximize the benefits to England of a developing commerce, and in particular of the colonial trade, by policies of protection and exclusion. The first English navigation act, introduced in 1660, gave equal status to Irish and English shipping. An act of 1663, by contrast, restricted direct Irish exports to English colonies to three items, provisions, horses, and servants. The third navigation act, in 1671, cut off direct trade in the other direction, by requiring that imports of sugar, tobacco, and other colonial products should be landed in English ports. By this time there had also been two acts aimed at protecting English graziers from the competition offered by cheap Irish cattle. The first, in 1663, imposed a higher duty on Irish cattle imported after 1 June each year, a point at which Irish beasts had generally not yet recovered sufficiently from their poor winter feeding to be driven to distant markets. The second, in 1666, wholly prohibited imports of Irish livestock, pork, beef, and bacon.

The cattle acts did not in the event have the devastating effect on the Irish economy that might have been feared. Exports of barrelled beef had already been rising more quickly than those of live cattle, so that the effect of the new prohibition was to accelerate an existing trend away from livestock to finished or semi-finished products: preserved beef, pork and bacon, butter, and hides. Rising exports to France and the colonies more than compensated for the loss of English

---

[89] Petty, *Political Anatomy*, 42–3.

[90] Patrick Melvin (ed.), 'Sir Paul Rycaut's Memoranda and Letters from Ireland 1686–7', *Analecta Hibernica*, 27 (1972), 153. Elsewhere, in a revealing blunder, Rycaut identified the 'English' threatened by Catholic gains as 'they who have been the masters for above 400 years', a formulation which ignored the much more recent origins of most Irish Protestants and, more important, removed the Old English entirely from the historical record: ibid. 157; below, Ch. 5 n. 7.

markets. But the legislation was nevertheless contested, and the resulting debate raised once again the issues of Ireland's constitutional status that had earlier come to brief prominence in the crises of 1640–1 and 1659–60. The precise arguments varied. The earl of Anglesey, the former Arthur Annesley, based his case on ancestry: Irish Protestants were 'native Englishmen', and to exclude them from English markets invaded 'the common right and the subject's liberty'. A submission by Ormond and the Irish council, on the other hand, emphasized Ireland's constitutional status as 'united and belonging to his Majesty's imperial crown of England', so that his Irish subjects 'are by the laws of England and Ireland natural Englishmen'.

The English solicitor general, while opposing the bill, took a more nuanced view of Ireland's claims, seeing England as an elder brother who enjoyed a right of primogeniture but insisting that the king, as common father of his people, would not 'ruin the younger brother only to comply with the impatient unmindedness of the older'. Another passage neatly expressed the complexities of Ireland's position: 'Ireland is a conquered nation, but must not be so treated, for the conquerors inhabit there. The very government under the king is now in the hands of those who first made the conquest.' When the acts again came under discussion in 1679, on the other hand, an English MP brutally stated the opposite view: 'Ireland is but a colony of England. . . . Can any story give an account that colonies have been so indulged, as to prejudice the territory whence they came?' The debate also took on an edge of personal bitterness when the duke of Buckingham, who supported the bill as a means of weakening his rival Ormond, observed that anyone who opposed it 'was there led to it by an Irish interest or an Irish understanding'. Ossory, Ormond's son and a leading opponent of the measure, took the comment as a personal insult, and had to be prevented from forcing a duel.[91]

The significance of these clashes should not be overstated. Ossory's objection, after all, was precisely to being called Irish. But the conflict of interests highlighted by the navigation and cattle acts was one that was to continue. Buckingham's sneer, moreover, made clear how easily geographical separation could translate into condescension or hostility. Nor was the ill feeling, even at this early stage, entirely one-sided. Henry Bennet, later earl of Arlington, scheming to get his hands on the forfeited estate of Viscount Clanmalier, was warned in 1663 that 'the English that have been some time here hate as much that anything should come amongst them as the Creolians of Mexico and Peru do the natives of Spain that go every year to the Indies'.[92] Three centuries earlier the Statute of Kilkenny had condemned those who drew distinctions between the English by

[91] C. A. Edie, 'The Irish Cattle Bills: A Study in Restoration Politics', *Transactions of the American Philosophical Society*, 60/2 (1970), 14, 18–19, 47, 30. For Ormond's comment, and the question of conquest, see *CSPI 1666–9*, 185, 539.
[92] Sir Thomas Clarges to Bennet, 1 May 1663 (*CSPI 1663–5*, 73).

blood and the English by birth, 'by calling them *Englishobbe* or *Irishdog*'.[93] By the reign of Charles II the descendants of these medieval English colonists were increasingly being dismissed, along with their Gaelic coreligionists, simply as 'the Irish'. But even as that happened the New English who had supplanted them had begun their own journey towards another hybrid, and once again by no means straightforward, conception of their own identity.

[93] Connolly, *Contested Island*, 39.

5

Freedom, Religion, and Laws

THE CATHOLIC SUCCESSION

The fog of ambiguity that had from the start hung over the religious sympathies of Charles II persisted into the last months of his reign. In October 1684 he informed Ormond that he intended to replace him as lord lieutenant. The decision followed a campaign against Ormond's allegedly negligent management of the Irish army, in which Richard Talbot had taken a leading part. In January 1685 it became known that Talbot and Justin MacCarthy were each to be given command of a regiment. Would Charles have been content with the advancement of these two well-established courtiers, and perhaps a handful of others? Or was Ormond's removal intended, as in 1669, to clear the way for a more far-reaching attempt to modify or end the exclusion of Catholics from office? There is no certain way of knowing. Charles died on 6 February 1685, to be succeeded by his brother James. England, Scotland, and Ireland had, for the first time in two centuries, an openly Catholic monarch.[1]

The new king proceeded cautiously. When Ormond finally surrendered the sword of state, in March 1685, James appointed two impeccably Protestant lords justices: Michael Boyle, from a lesser branch of the great Munster dynasty, who combined the positions of archbishop of Armagh and lord chancellor, and Arthur Forbes, Coote's one-time emissary to the exiled Charles II, the cautious friend of the Ulster Presbyterians, and now earl of Granard and marshal of the army. The new lord lieutenant, sworn in at the beginning of 1686, was the second earl of Clarendon, brother of James's first wife, a firm Protestant and, for good measure, the son of one of the architects of the Restoration land settlement. Ormond, meanwhile, had retired to England. From there he watched with growing apprehension the unfolding of events in the kingdom he had governed

[1] The standard account of James II's reign is J. G. Simms, *Jacobite Ireland 1685–91* (London, 1969). For more recent assessments, see D. W. Hayton, *Ruling Ireland 1685–1742: Politics, Politicians and Parties* (Woodbridge, 2004), ch. 1, and Patrick Kelly, 'Ireland and the Glorious Revolution: From Kingdom to Colony', in Robert Beddard (ed.), *The Revolutions of 1688* (Oxford, 1991), 163–90. For the war of 1689–91 see W. A. Maguire (ed.), *Kings in Conflict: The Revolutionary War in Ireland and its Aftermath 1689–1750* (Belfast, 1990); John Childs, 'The Williamite War 1689–91', in Thomas Bartlett and Keith Jeffery (eds.), *A Military History of Ireland* (Cambridge, 1996), 188–210; Pádraig Lenihan, *1690: Battle of the Boyne* (Stroud, 2003).

for most of the past quarter-century. His death, on 21 July 1688, can be seen as having spared him the necessity of choosing between the two principles, Protestantism and monarchy, that had been the twin pillars of his long career. Alternatively it can be seen as depriving posterity of the opportunity at last to discover what really lay behind the mask of an unswerving Anglican royalism so carefully cultivated across the decades.

The main cause of Ormond's disquiet was the inexorable rise towards complete control of Irish affairs of his long-term factional rival Richard Talbot. Talbot was noted, even in the not particularly polished environment of the Restoration court, for his foul temper and violent language, as well as for his aggressive Catholicism. But he had been an intimate of James since their shared exile in the 1650s, and behind his blustering manner lay a shrewd political tactician. In June 1685 James created him earl of Tyrconnell, and instructed the lords justices to consult him on all matters relating to the army. The appointment of Clarendon as lord lieutenant was a setback, since Tyrconnell had lobbied hard for his own appointment. However he still had complete control of Irish military affairs. Already during 1685 risings in Scotland and the south-west of England in support of Charles II's illegitimate but Protestant son, the duke of Monmouth, had given him the excuse he needed to disband the militia established in 1666, and to confiscate arms held by Protestants. Next he began a systematic purge of the army, dismissing Protestant officers and men and recruiting Catholics to replace them. By September 1686 two-thirds of the rank and file and 40 per cent of the officers were Catholic.

Meanwhile James, urged on by Tyrconnell, had begun to make changes in central and local government. He added eleven Catholics, including Tyrconnell, to the Irish privy council, and ordered that Catholics be admitted to municipal corporations on taking a simple oath of allegiance. Early in 1686 he removed one of the three judges in each of the courts of King's Bench, Exchequer, and Common Pleas, in each case filling the vacancy with a Catholic. In addition Catholic bishops received permission to appear in public in ecclesiastical dress, and their clergy to conduct religious services without interference. By August 1686 the crown had begun paying salaries to the bishops. In all of this Clarendon, however reluctantly, complied with James II's orders. Tyrconnell, however, bombarded the king with complaints that the lord lieutenant was obstructing the admission of Catholics to office, while leaving Protestants of dangerous political principles in positions of power. In January 1687 James recalled Clarendon and appointed Tyrconnell as lord deputy. His appointment opened the way to further Catholic gains, including the installation of a second Catholic judge, and thus a Catholic majority vote, in each of the three main courts.

This pattern of steady Catholic gains did not take place uncontested. James's overall strategy was to ensure that at his death Catholics in his three kingdoms would be able to bargain from a position of strength with what it was assumed at this stage would be a Protestant successor. Tyrconnell's objective of an Ireland in which civil and military power was firmly in Catholic hands would clearly do much to advance that aim. At the same time English courtiers, from motives both of factional rivalry and genuine concern, warned of the dangers of alarming Protestant opinion in the larger kingdom. Tyrconnell's initial failure to secure the chief governorship, and his eventual appointment as lord deputy rather than lord lieutenant, were indications that James himself was unwilling to move too quickly. In August 1687, alarmed at reports of a decline in Irish revenues, he summoned Tyrconnell to meet him at Chester. But what began as a difficult encounter turned into a triumph, as Tyrconnell vigorously defended his policies, and returned to Ireland with his authority confirmed.[2]

By this time the central issue of contention in Ireland was no longer the admission of Catholics to civil or military office, but the fate of the Restoration land settlement. Clarendon had proposed a commission of grace which would confirm existing landowners in their titles. This would serve the dual purpose of calming Protestant nerves and securing the English interest in Ireland. At the same time the fees charged could be used to compensate deserving Catholics. In response to such proposals the Catholic lawyer Sir Richard Nagle, soon to be appointed attorney general, set out the opposite case: that a complete revision of the settlement was essential, not just to right past injustices, but to guarantee that current Catholic gains would be sustained. The offices that they currently held would end with the king's life. In consequence

nothing can support Catholic religion in that kingdom, but to make Catholics there considerable in their fortunes, as they are considerable in their number. For this must be the only inducement that can prevail upon a Protestant successor to allow them a toleration as to their religion, and a protection as to their estates.[3]

The successful outcome of the Chester meeting now allowed Tyrconnell to press ahead with plans for a revision of the settlement. By February 1688 his administration had prepared two proposals: to restore Catholic proprietors but to require them to compensate the displaced Cromwellian grantees with the equivalent of six years' rent, or alternatively to divide the estates concerned equally between old and new proprietors. Either measure, modifying existing legislation, would require a meeting of the Irish parliament. From late 1687 Tyrconnell engaged in a systematic campaign to ensure that this would have a Catholic majority. Assisted where necessary by now compliant courts, the government forced cities and corporate towns to surrender supposedly deficient charters, thus giving itself the opportunity to pack the corporations that would return the majority of MPs with reliable burgesses. The sheriffs who were to be charged with the supervision of county

---

[2] The complex chronology of Tyrconnell's progress is charted in John Miller, 'The Earl of Tyrconnell and James II's Irish Policy 1685–1688', *Historical Journal*, 20 (1977), 803–23.

[3] Nagle to Tyrconnell, 26 Oct. 1686 (HMC, *Ormonde MSS*, ns vii. 464–5). The document, known as the 'Coventry Letter' because written from there during a visit to England, was widely circulated and can be taken as a manifesto rather than a private communication.

elections were likewise reliable government supporters. The one Protestant chosen in 1687, it was alleged, had been confused with a Catholic of the same name.

Hostile observers made much of the lowly origins of the men thus brought forward to staff Tyrconnell's Catholicized establishment. The future Church of Ireland bishop William King, in what became the classic statement of Protestant grievances under James II, maintained that 'one that a few days before was no other than a cowherd to his Protestant landlord, perhaps, was set above him on the bench as a justice of the peace'. A ballad circulated at the time of Tyrconnell's appointment purported to be the complaint at his lack of a share in such preferment of Cormac O Rough, 'teacher in philosophy and argumentation':

> Dere ish Teague O Regan who did drive de plow
> At Enny Schilling not long ago,
> Ish now a fine offisher; why am not I
> That not only in fighting skill'd but poetry?

Caricature of this kind had an obvious propagandist purpose. Sir Teague O'Regan, for example, was indeed noted for his battered wig, wrinkled boots, and skewed cravat, and his knighthood was a late Jacobite creation. But he was no ploughboy: he had served in the French army during the reign of Charles II and was to conduct highly competent defences of Charlemont and later Sligo town in the war of 1689–91. At the same time even Clarendon's secretary Sir Paul Rycaut, who accepted unquestioningly the king's right to favour his coreligionists, complained of the difficulty of finding enough Catholics 'of sufficient parts, learning or estates' to hold the office of justice of the peace. Such comments highlight the extent to which a century and a half of punitive confiscation, licensed land piracy, and exclusion from office had already pushed Irish Catholics down the social scale. There was still a Catholic elite, whose vision of a restoration of their lost lands and status had the power to mobilize a large section of their social inferiors. But Tyrconnell's deputyship, and the military defeat that followed, should nevertheless be seen, not as a turning point in Irish history, but as a late and short-lived attempt to reverse a revolution that had already taken place.[4]

To Catholics at the time, however, the gains that followed James's accession were a cause for unqualified triumphalism. A Munster poet celebrated Tyrconnell's purge of the army in terms that reveal something of the rougher side of the interaction between settler and native across the preceding decades:

> Whither shall John turn? He has now no red coat on him,
> Nor 'Who's there' on his lips when standing beside the gate
> . . . .
> 'You Popish rogue' they won't dare to say to us,

---

[4] For Sir Teague see Andrew Carpenter (ed.), *Verse in English from Tudor and Stuart Ireland* (Cork, 2003), 495–6, and J. G. Simms, *War and Politics in Ireland 1649–1730* (London, 1986), 174. For other points in this paragraph, Connolly, *Religion, Law and Power*, 40.

> But 'Cromwellian dog' is the watchword we have for them,
> Or 'Cia súd thall' [Who's there?] said sternly and fearlessly,
> 'Mise Tadhg' [I am Tadhg], though galling the dialogue.[5]

In autumn 1686 Tadhg and his comrades made their presence felt when soldiers from the new Catholic army stationed in Dublin broke up the traditional Protestant celebrations of 23 October, the anniversary of the Dublin plot of 1641, and 5 November, scattering bonfires, smashing windows in the lord mayor's house, and killing 'one or two tradesmen'.[6] Already in July of the same year Rycaut had reported that 'the Irish talk of nothing now but recovering their lands and bringing the English under their subjection, which they who have been the masters for above 400 years know not how well to bear'.[7]

Irish Protestants were for the most part poorly equipped to respond to this imposition of an increasingly aggressive Catholic ascendancy. Contemporary political theory offered no basis for challenging the will of a legitimate monarch. The events of the 1640s and 1650s, moreover, had powerfully reinforced the sense that to oppose established authority was to risk a general collapse of the social order. When James II was first proclaimed king before a crowd of 1,000 at Downpatrick in February 1685, the governor of the neighbouring county of Antrim had no hesitation in hunting down the single dissident who had disrupted the proceedings. 'The beginning of our mischiefs', he wrote to Ormond, 'may be truly imputed to too great a liberty and freedom of speech against superiors.'[8] Religious principle was also involved. The Church of Ireland, like its English counterpart, had ever since 1660 committed itself wholeheartedly to the doctrine of unconditional obedience to a divinely ordained monarchy. In 1686 Edward Wetenhall, bishop of Cork, published a collection of his loyal sermons, dedicated to his Catholic monarch, and prefaced by an explicit undertaking:

We of the Church of England avow and protest we will be loyal, should we be put in never such circumstances; yea even in the worst circumstances, wherein any adversaries we could wish us. It is and ever has been our doctrine, it is and ever has been our practice, to be loyal absolutely and without exception.[9]

It would be naive to take such protestations wholly at face value. As a minority in a subordinate kingdom Irish Protestants had few options for independent action. Later, when the wider political context had changed, the imperatives of

---

[5] *The Poems of David Ó Bruadair*, ed. J. C. McErlean (London, 1910–16), iii. 97. The poem quoted is in fact the work of another Munster poet, Dermot MacCarthy.

[6] Patrick Melvin (ed.), 'Letters of Lord Longford and Others on Irish Affairs', *Analecta Hibernica*, 32 (1985), 40.

[7] Patrick Melvin (ed.), 'Sir Paul Rycaut's Memoranda and Letters from Ireland 1686–7', *Analecta Hibernica*, 27 (1972), 157.

[8] Colvill to Ormond, 16 Feb. 1685 (TCD MS 1178, No. 18).

[9] Edward Wetenhall, *Hexapla Jacobaea: A Specimen of Loyalty towards his Present Majesty James II in Six Pieces by an Irish Protestant Bishop* (Dublin, 1686), preface.

both political and religious doctrine were to become markedly more flexible. For the moment, however, principle and pragmatism combined to ensure that their main response to Tyrconnell's regime was one of flight, not fight. One estimate suggests that as many as 5 per cent left, some taking refuge in England, others setting out for a new life in the North American or West Indian colonies.[10]

The Protestant response to James's regime was further complicated by the continuing division between those within and outside the established church. Part of James II's strategy was to broaden support for his regime by extending toleration to dissenters as well as Catholics. Clarendon began cautiously, by allowing religious services in private houses; from March 1687 Tyrconnell, though personally hostile to dissenters, permitted them to resume the use of their meeting houses. In April 1687 James issued a declaration of indulgence, suspending the penal laws against Catholics and dissenters alike. In Derry, Belfast, and elsewhere, Presbyterians joined Catholics in municipal corporations from which they had formerly been excluded. The indulgence extended even to the Quakers, who were now invited to become magistrates and members of corporations. Meanwhile the knowledge that the Church of Ireland could no longer count on the wholehearted support of the government encouraged a spate of minor incidents in Ulster, in which members of the dissenting majority withheld tithes, took control of parish churches, and occasionally offered violence to ministers or their servants.[11]

By the second half of 1688 opposition in England to James's promotion of Catholic interests had reached dangerous levels. In particular the birth in June of a son to James's queen, Mary Beatrice of Modena, had transformed the temporary inconvenience of rule by a middle-aged Catholic king, whose heirs were two Protestant daughters, into the very different prospect of permanent subjection to a Catholic dynasty. In September Tyrconnell sent over three regiments of infantry and one of horse. For the second time in living memory, Catholic Irish troops were to protect a monarch against his English subjects. But the confrontation never came. When William, prince of Orange, husband of James's elder daughter Mary, landed in Devon on 5 November with an army of 5,000 men, support for James's regime melted away. Demoralized and fearing assassination, he fled to France on 23 December. On 13 February 1689 William and Mary took the throne as joint sovereigns. There remained the problem of Tyrconnell's soldiers. On the night of 11–12 December unfounded reports that they had begun to massacre and pillage caused a panic that spread across nineteen English counties. Their eventual fate, like that of so many of their predecessors in the 1640s, was to be treated as disposable cannon fodder. Two shiploads were transported to Hamburg to fight for the empire against the Turks, although 500 of these were

---

[10] Raymond Gillespie, 'The Irish Protestants and James II 1688–90', *IHS* 28 (1992), 124–33.
[11] R. L. Greaves, *God's Other Children: Protestant Nonconformists and the Emergence of Denominational Churches in Ireland 1660–1700* (Stanford, Calif., 1997), 134–47.

reported to have made their way instead to France, while some others may have succeeded in returning from England to Ireland.

Tyrconnell's initial response to William's seizure of power was to open negotiations, offering to surrender the government in exchange for promises that Catholics would be no worse off than they had been at the end of Charles's reign. Whether this was a delaying tactic, or whether he genuinely considered trying to negotiate favourable terms with England's new rulers, remains unclear. But by January he had openly committed himself to holding Ireland for James. At the end of the month he reported that he had raised no less than forty-six new regiments, amounting to a staggering 40,000 additional men under arms. The forthcoming conflict, however, was to be no mere Irish, or even British, conflict. Holland and France were by now on the point of war. William had intervened in England primarily to ensure that James did not commit England to joining France in an attack on his homeland. Louis XIV, for his part, prepared to make Ireland a battleground against his Dutch and English opponents. On 12 March James arrived at Kinsale, accompanied by a French ambassador, the comte d'Avaux, as well as some French army officers and a shipment of arms and ammunition.

At the same time that he further expanded his Catholic army, Tyrconnell sought to keep the Protestant population quiet. A potential early confrontation arose in Londonderry, when a new garrison composed of Catholics and Scottish Highlanders of Lord Antrim's regiment approached the town on 7 December. As the citizens dithered in panic, 'the younger sort, who are seldom so dilatory in their resolutions', shut the gates against the approaching soldiers.[12] In this case conflict was avoided by a compromise, whereby the citizens accepted an alternative garrison of Protestant troops under Colonel Robert Lundy. But elsewhere tensions increased over the weeks that followed, particularly due to the depredations of the much enlarged and inadequately provisioned army. Some of the resulting revolts were easily contained. In County Cork troops under Justin MacCarthy suppressed a rising by the townspeople of Bandon, long noted as a stronghold of Protestantism, who on 25 February had driven out the garrison, killing some of its members, and declared their allegiance to King William. In County Down Protestants led by the earl of Mountalexander mobilized in arms, but on 14 March were easily defeated at Dromore, the first battle of what was to become a civil war. In the north-west, on the other hand, the former battleground of the Laggan army, Protestant resistance was more effective. At Enniskillen Protestants had begun mobilizing in December. Their leader, Gustavus Hamilton, was a veteran of the Swedish army, a product of the

---

[12] This is the description of the Revd George Walker, who was to lead the city through the subsequent siege (*The Siege of Londonderry in 1689*, ed. P. Dwyer (London, 1893), 12). In later Protestant mythology the saviours of the city were transmuted into the somewhat tautological 'apprentice boys'.

same Scottish diaspora that had been a training ground for the warriors of the 1640s. In January Protestants in the area round Sligo, spurred to action, as in Derry, by reports that a Catholic garrison was about to take control of the town, likewise formed themselves into an armed association. Meanwhile the citizens of Londonderry had petitioned William for assistance, although they did not openly proclaim their new allegiance until 21 March, when a ship arrived carrying supplies and a new commission for Lundy in the name of King William III.

Such self-assertion, however, was possible only in parts of Ulster. Elsewhere Protestants had still to accommodate themselves to life under Tyrconnell's administration. When James reached Dublin on 25 March, he was greeted by a delegation of Church of Ireland clergy, headed by Anthony Dopping, bishop of Meath, who pledged their loyalty to him as king. The parliament which James summoned soon after his arrival in Dublin, returned mainly by the new corporations installed by Tyrconnell, was overwhelmingly Catholic. Among those taking their seats in the House of Lords, however, were five Protestant peers, including the earl of Granard, and four Protestant bishops, including both Dopping and Wetenhall. For Granard the turning point came when the parliament voted to overturn the Restoration land settlement. He retired to his family's house in King's County, withstood a subsequent siege by James's forces (as his mother, half a century earlier, had defended the same house against the Confederate Catholics), and then joined the advancing Williamite army. Dopping also opposed the repeal of the act of settlement. But he did so by calling on his fellow peers to concentrate on the defence of their king: 'Is it now a time for men to seek for vineyards and olive yards, when a civil war is raging in the nation and we are under apprehension of invasions from abroad?'[13] Yet almost exactly a year later, when William III entered Dublin after his victory at the Boyne, it was once again Dopping who led a delegation of Anglican clergy to welcome him as their king.

To critics the behaviour of churchmen like Dopping and Wetenhall, who likewise quickly transferred his allegiance to the victorious William, was evidence of simple opportunism. But their conduct was in fact quite compatible with traditional Anglican political theology. St Paul's celebrated injunction that 'the powers that be' were to be obeyed because they had been ordained by God was essentially a command to submit to de facto authority. On that basis conservatively minded individuals in all parts of the Stuart dominions rationalized their acceptance of William and Mary as submission to the will of God, whose providence had put them on the throne. For Irish Protestants, surrounded by a hostile Catholic majority, such ideas had a particular resonance. The events of 1641 and after had demonstrated all too clearly what could happen when the governing power there was divided or contested. Four decades later James II, however undesirable his religious principles, was, outside a few parts of Ulster, the

---

[13] Quoted Simms, *Jacobite Ireland*, 82.

only available guarantor of some sort of order. If the king should happen to die, one Protestant layman noted in April 1688, they could expect to be massacred by the Irish army. Dopping and Wetenhall, in this sense, were the heirs of Bishop Henry Jones, successively servant to a king, parliament, the Protectorate, and a restored monarchy.[14]

James II's Irish parliament sat between 7 May and 18 July 1689. If its proceedings confirmed the worst fears of Protestants, it also highlighted the limits of the accord between the king and his Catholic subjects. James agreed to the repeal of the act of settlement only reluctantly, and after the Commons had postponed the date for the collection of a promised subsidy. He was equally opposed to an act of attainder, which named 1,340 Protestants as already guilty of treason for their support of William, and required others who had fled the kingdom to return and make their submission, on pain of incurring the same penalty. James reportedly outraged the Commons by his remark: 'What gentlemen, are you for another [16]41?' But members had already made clear their distrust of the king's commitment to their cause when they included in the bill a clause, reminiscent of the Adventurers' act once forced on his father, that removed his right to grant pardons to those condemned. James also accepted only with reluctance an act denying the claim of the English parliament to pass laws binding on Ireland, and he refused to accept another repealing Poynings's Law. His stance in all these cases was in part due to his reluctance to do anything that might prejudice his chances of regaining support in England. But he was also clearly unwilling to contemplate any significant change in the relationship between England and Ireland. 'His heart', d'Avaux wrote, 'is too English for him to agree to anything that could displease the English. He still counts on being re-established soon in the kingdom of England, and . . . will do nothing to remove Ireland from its dependence on the English.'[15]

Even on the subject of religion, James quickly disappointed his Irish supporters. The bishops summoned to sit in the parliament were those of the established church, not their Catholic rivals. He refused to consider not only the disestablishment of the Church of Ireland, but even the repeal of the acts of supremacy and uniformity. Instead parliament passed an act for liberty of conscience, permitting all varieties of Christian to meet freely for public or private worship, and declaring invalid all statutory restrictions inconsistent with religious liberty. A second act provided that Catholics and Protestants should each pay tithes to their own clergy, but left the bishops of the Church of Ireland in possession of church lands. Meanwhile the Catholic church authorities discovered that even these limited gains came at a price, as James began to assert his right to nominate

---

[14] For a fuller discussion of these points see S. J. Connolly (ed.), *Political Ideas in Eighteenth-Century Ireland* (Dublin, 2000), 29–51.
[15] Quoted in John Miller, *James II: A Study in Kingship* (Hove, 1978), 224.

to ecclesiastical benefices, and to permit the lower clergy to take appeals against their superiors to him, rather than to Rome.[16]

'Is it now a time for men to seek for vineyards and olive yards?' Bishop Dopping had asked. At the same time that they squabbled with their king over the fruits of the new political order, Irish Jacobites were demonstrating the limits of their military capacity. In April Tyrconnell's army moved against the Protestants of Derry, who had taken up positions at crossing points along the Donegal side of the River Foyle. They scored an early success on 15 April, when they forced their way across at two points, Clady and Lifford, driving the Protestants back to the city. The same day two English regiments arrived in Derry. However Lundy sent them away, on the grounds that provisions were too short, and the city's defences too weak, to withstand a siege. By this time James had decided to assert his authority in the north-west in person. On 18 April he arrived outside Derry's walls, but was driven away by shots that killed several of his followers. A conservative group within the city sent emissaries to implore his pardon. But the majority were by now committed to resistance. Lundy, threatened by a hostile mob, fled the city in disguise.[17] The bishop, Ezekiel Hopkins, likewise withdrew rather than support resistance to the king. He was to die in June 1690, and so escaped having to decide whether, like Wetenhall and others, his conscience would allow him to accept a transfer of de facto power.

Derry was now under siege. As commander, in place of Lundy, the citizens chose George Walker, a Church of Ireland clergyman from County Tyrone who had fought at the Clady and Lifford engagements. He organized the city's male population into a defending force of 7,361 men. These in fact outnumbered the 4,000 strong Jacobite army, but would presumably have included a smaller proportion of younger and more able-bodied men. There were several bloody actions as the attackers tried to force a breach in the wall with which the London companies had enclosed the showpiece of their plantation. But low numbers on the attacking side, combined with a lack of heavy artillery, meant that they relied mainly on starving the defenders out. The city's population, normally around 2,000, was swollen by some 30,000 Protestant refugees from the surrounding countryside, and conditions quickly became desperate. Williamite accounts claimed that up to 15,000 people, mainly women and children, died of malnutrition and disease. The survivors were reportedly reduced to eating

---

[16] For details see Connolly, *Religion, Law and Power*, 35.

[17] How far Lundy's defeatism was based on a professional estimate of the military situation, and how far on an unwillingness to fight against James II, has never been resolved. On reaching England he was confined for a time in the Tower of London and forced to quit the army. Much later, however, from 1704, he was to serve again, commanding troops in the Portuguese service but on English pay. Protestants in modern Londonderry, faithful to history but untroubled by its uncertainties, continue to burn his effigy in December of every year.

rats, mice, and dogs fattened on human corpses. On 28 July, after 105 days, three merchant ships, escorted by naval vessels, managed to break the wooden boom that the Jacobites had placed across the river, and bring supplies to the city. This effectively ended the siege. Meanwhile Jacobite forces had been trying unsuccessfully to subdue the other main centre of resistance, at Enniskillen, where Protestants had found a charismatic leader in a local settler, Thomas Lloyd, admiringly referred to by his followers as their 'little Cromwell'. At Newtownbutler, County Fermanagh, three days after the relief of Derry, 2,200 of these Enniskillen men defeated a force of over 5,000 Jacobites, killing over 2,000 and taking their commander, Justin MacCarthy, prisoner. A fortnight later, on 13 August, an English expeditionary force under Marshal Herman von Schomberg arrived in Belfast Lough to begin the conquest of Ireland for William and Mary.

The poor showing of Jacobite troops at Newtownbutler, and their failure to capture Derry, were understandable. The four regiments that Tyrconnell had sent to England the previous September had represented one-third of the Irish army. The 40,000 he had since raised were hastily trained, inexperienced, and poorly equipped. Recruitment still bore traces of the traditional hostings, based on territory and lordship, of an earlier era. Of forty-three Jacobite regiments in 1689, all but seven were dominated by officers linked by kinship or location with their commander. Yet Ireland was no longer the militarized society it had been in the reign of Elizabeth or earlier. The French officers who arrived with James II, along with some later arrivals, provided a measure of professional expertise, as did Catholics like Justin MacCarthy and Patrick Sarsfield who during the reign of Charles II had been discreetly employed in English regiments in foreign service. But many of the commanders now committed to full-scale warfare had little or no military experience.

Recruitment at rank and file level was also on a communal basis. John Stevens, an English Catholic who came to Ireland to join the Jacobite army, reported that his fellow soldiers 'will follow none but their own leaders . . . The commissioned officer could not punish his sergeant or corporal, because he was his cousin or foster brother.' None of this was well suited to the requirements of late seventeenth-century warfare, with its emphasis on the sustained and concentrated firepower made possible by the coordinated movement of large formations on the battlefield. There was also a serious shortage of weapons. A French officer reported that many of the soldiers besieging Derry were armed only with pointed sticks, without even iron tips. One regiment had a total of seven muskets between them. Consignments of firearms that arrived from France in August 1689 and in March 1690 turned out to be obsolete and of poor quality. Of the troops that marched north to confront Schomberg in September 1689 most were armed with scythes, and Tyrconnell was later to claim that two-thirds of his soldiers had never fired a shot for want of powder. Even among the continental allies of the two sides, the regular French soldiers, armed with matchlocks, had little more than half the firepower of William's Dutch guards, who had the more modern flintlock.[18]

Schomberg's arrival in the north-east might have been expected to lead to a rapid offensive. Schomberg himself, of German and English parentage, was a veteran commander who had served under Louis XIV until forced out by the withdrawal of religious toleration from Protestants in France. He brought with him a force of over 20,000 men, comprising Dutch, French Protestant, and English troops. To these were added the Protestant forces from Derry and Enniskillen, now organized into regiments and numbering some 6,000 men. At the beginning of September Schomberg marched south to confront James's army at Dundalk, but failed to attack. Most accounts present Schomberg, at 74, as succumbing to an excess of professional caution. But it has also been argued that his expedition, though large, had not been properly funded, and that his fears concerning his lines of supply and the reliability of his soldiers were well grounded.[19] In any case he remained encamped at Dundalk until November, losing several thousand men to disease, then retreated to winter quarters at Lisburn, where cold, rain, and sickness carried off still more. Meanwhile Jacobite forces under Patrick Sarsfield, another veteran of the English regiments in French service, staged a successful counter-attack in the west, recapturing the town of Sligo from the Enniskillen men and securing control of north Connacht.

The failure of the 1689 expedition to make headway forced a deeply reluctant William III to come to Ireland in person. He landed at Carrickfergus on 14 June 1690. By this time he had reinforced Schomberg's depleted army with further English, Dutch, German, and Huguenot units, as well as a force of 6,000 infantry and 1,000 cavalry hired from the king of Denmark. The Jacobites had also received reinforcements, with the arrival in March of some 6,000 men, comprising three regiments of French troops, one of Walloons, and one of Germans. These, however, were in exchange for over 5,000 Irish troops dispatched to France under the command of Justin MacCarthy, who had managed to escape from Schomberg's custody. It was thus two international armies that confronted one another in Ireland, by now one theatre of many in a European conflict pitting Louis XIV's France against England, Holland, and the empire.

The location of the first confrontation was James II's choice. His army of 25,000 men was heavily outnumbered by William's 36,000. Moreover William had this time ensured that his forces were properly supplied. A fleet of 300 ships had brought large quantities of stores, as well as 550 wagons and 2,500 draught horses. James rejected suggestions that he defend the Moyry Pass, the hotly contested gateway to Ulster in Tyrone's rebellion and earlier conflicts, for fear of being encircled by a thrust along what by this time was probably the

---

[18] *The Journal of John Stevens, Containing a Brief Account of the War in Ireland*, ed. R. H. Murray (Oxford, 1912), 63–4. For other points, Lenihan, *Battle of the Boyne*, 23, 168–9.
[19] Lenihan, *Battle of the Boyne*, 72–5.

much improved route from Armagh to Dundalk. But he also rejected French suggestions that he fall back behind the line of the Shannon, as well as the other obvious option of retreating and fortifying Dublin. Instead he chose to make his stand at the River Boyne, a significant obstacle in William's path southwards but not, given the numerical superiority he enjoyed, a particularly formidable natural barrier. By 30 June the two armies were encamped on opposite banks at Oldbridge, a fordable spot three miles upstream from Drogheda.

What followed was a succession of strategic blunders. Early on the morning of 1 July William sent 8,000 men commanded by Meinhard Schomberg, the general's son, upriver towards the town of Slane, where there was, or had been, a bridge. His plan was apparently for simultaneous assaults there and at Oldbridge. But at Rossnaree, halfway to Slane, Schomberg came across a ford guarded by only 500 Jacobites, and forced a crossing before the main Williamite offensive was ready. William, fearing that a counter-attack by the main Jacobite army might wipe out Schomberg's detachment, sent a further 12,000 men upriver to reinforce him, thus depriving himself for the several hours of their progress of his entire advantage in numbers. But James II also overreacted. Obsessed with the risk of being encircled by William's larger force, he sent more than two-thirds of his force west to confront Schomberg. In the event the 40,000 or so men who thus massed at Rossnaree never engaged, because they turned out to be separated by the natural barrier of two deep ditches. But the 16,000 Williamites still at Oldbridge were now able to fight their way across the river, overwhelming the 7,000 Jacobites still there and leaving the remainder, outnumbered and now threatened on two sides, with no choice but to retreat.

James II had already suffered one paralysing breakdown in morale in England in November 1688. Defeat at the Boyne now precipitated a second collapse of nerve. Arriving in Dublin on the night of the battle, he allegedly declared to supporters that his Irish army had 'basely fled' and that he had accordingly decided 'to shift for myself, and so, gentlemen, must you'.[20] By the time Tyrconnell and the French commander the comte de Lauzun reached the city next day, James had already left for Kinsale, from where he sailed on 4 July to what was to be a permanent exile in France. Yet defeat at the Boyne, in purely military terms, had been far less conclusive than its subsequent fame was to suggest. The greater part of the Jacobite army had never engaged the enemy and had retreated largely intact, if in some disorder, having lost around 1,000 men to their opponents' 500. The Williamites entered Dublin unopposed on 5 July, and by the end of the month had occupied Leinster and had also taken Waterford, including Duncannon fort. The Jacobites, however, still controlled most of Munster, as well as Connacht, with their new headquarters at Limerick. Between 17 and 24 July a Williamite force numbering 10,000, but without siege equipment, failed to cross the Shannon at Athlone. William turned instead to a

---

[20] Quoted in Simms, *Jacobite Ireland*, 153.

direct assault on Limerick, commencing siege operations on 9 August. By this
time the return of troops to England, along with the need to leave garrisons
behind him, had reduced his army to a less formidable 25,000. It was also late
in the campaigning season, and the attack was further delayed when Sarsfield
led a daring night-time raid on the Williamite artillery convoy as it camped for
the night at Ballyneety, fourteen miles from Limerick. The surviving Williamite
guns were sufficient to breach the city wall but created only a narrow gap in
which the attackers lost over 2,000 men in vicious hand-to-hand fighting. Several
observers commented on the particular ferocity of the missile-throwing women
who appeared, with other civilians, to assist the defending troops. On 29 August
William lifted the siege, and six days later sailed for England, leaving a Dutch
general, Baron Ginkel, in command.

The successful defence of Limerick masked deep divisions within Jacobite
ranks. Lauzun and the other French officers had concluded, with professional
detachment, that Limerick could not be defended. They removed their men
to Galway, claiming to fear foul play from their outraged Irish allies, and in
mid-September abandoned Ireland altogether. Meanwhile the Irish too were
divided. Tyrconnell openly argued that the time had come to seek a negotiated
settlement with William, but was overruled by a group of army officers. The chief
spokesman for this war party was Sarsfield, the hero of Ballyneety, described by
James II's illegitimate son, the duke of Berwick, as 'a man of huge stature, without
sense, very good natured and very brave'. News that Tyrconnell had sent his wife
and daughters to France, along with 40,000 gold coins, further deepened hostility
towards him. After the lifting of the siege he himself sailed to France with Lauzun's
troops, leaving the 20-year-old Berwick in command. He returned in January
1691 with promises of renewed French support, as well as a patent creating
Sarsfield earl of Lucan. But the war party continued to distrust his leadership.

To some observers these disputes over strategy had an ethnic dimension. In
particular the County Galway gentleman Charles O'Kelly, in a thinly disguised
allegory, *The Destruction of Cyprus*, written around 1692, was to allege that the
Old English Tyrconnell had weakened the Jacobite cause by his hostility to
the Gaelic Irish. And indeed there had been indications, such as the overheard
conversation of two Old English noblemen in Tyrconnell's entourage on the need
to exclude the 'Os' and 'Macs' from the remodelled army, that earlier animosities
had not entirely disappeared. For the most part, however, intermarriage and
cultural assimilation had by this time largely deprived such distinctions of real
meaning. Justin MacCarthy and Richard Talbot were soldiers and courtiers of
almost identical background. Sarsfield, similarly, was born into a long-established
Old English family in County Kildare. But his mother was a daughter of the 1641
conspirator Rory O'More.[21] Where differences did exist was in relation to land.
Already during James's Dublin parliament the overthrow of the Restoration land

[21] For these points see in particular Hayton, *Ruling Ireland*, 16–17.

settlement had been forced through over the objections, not only of the king, but of a 'new interest', comprising those Irish Catholics like Tyrconnell who had acquired land since the Restoration and whose titles of ownership thus depended on the acts of settlement and explanation. As the war progressed, equally, it was natural that men whose families had lost all in the Cromwellian confiscation or earlier would be more inclined to fight to the end than those with estates that might be saved by a timely compromise. In both cases the Gaelic Irish were more likely to be on the side of the militants. But the real conflict of interest was one of property rather than ethnic origin.

In the winter of 1690–1 Ireland remained militarily divided. In September and October John Churchill, earl of Marlborough, had conducted a lightning three-week operation in Munster, capturing Cork and Kinsale, the two chief ports in Jacobite hands. However the Jacobites continued to control Kerry and most of County Limerick, as well as the counties west of the Shannon. During the winter Sarsfield, based in Athlone, repeatedly crossed the Shannon to raid the midlands. There was also sporadic skirmishing in Munster. In addition the Williamites had to cope with attacks by what were referred to as 'rapparees' (apparently from the Irish term *rapaire*, a short spear or half-pike), who raided camps and houses and stalked troops on the move. The rapparees recalled the tories of the last stages of the Cromwellian conquest, and had the same ambiguous character. Williamite accounts presented them as simple bandits, 'all those who have gone out for booty and plunder'. Yet the treaty that ended the war was to allow them the status of legitimate combatants, by extending the terms offered to the Jacobite army to 'those called rapparees or volunteers'.[22] The line between regular and irregular troops was further blurred by the appearance in July 1690 of an extraordinary freebooter, Hugh Balldearg ('red spot') O'Donnell, apparently a nephew of the Niall Garbh who had been rewarded for his assistance in Mountjoy's conquest of the north-west by ending his days in the Tower of London.[23] Balldearg had earlier served in the Spanish army, where he had been recognized as earl of Tyrconnell. Assisted by a prophecy stating that an O'Donnell with a red mark would liberate Ireland from English rule, he now assembled a force of several thousand in the north-west, but was kept at arm's length by Tyrconnell, who gave him a brigadier's commission, but no weapons. His disorderly following, recruited largely in Ulster and accompanied by women, children, and herds of cattle, recalled Owen Roe O'Neill's *creaghts* of forty years earlier, and they imposed a similar burden on the population of north Connacht, which became their main base of operations.

As the 1691 campaigning season approached, William sent Ginkel a new artillery train of thirty-six guns, along with other supplies. On 9 May, meanwhile,

---

[22] K. Danaher and J. G. Simms (eds.), *The Danish Force in Ireland* (Dublin, 1962), 88; Simms, *Jacobite Ireland*, 258.
[23] Connolly, *Contested Island*, 298.

a French convoy arrived at Limerick bringing arms, ammunition, and a new commander, the marquis de Saint-Ruth, appointed to end the continuing dissension between Tyrconnell and his critics in the army. On 30 June, after eleven days of fierce fighting, Ginkel's army forced their way across the Shannon at Athlone. Saint-Ruth, ignoring advice to retreat to Limerick and Galway, sought to erase this defeat by giving battle at Aughrim, sixteen miles to the south-west. He selected a strong defensive position on a hill behind a bog and stream, and the main Williamite force suffered heavily as they attempted a frontal attack. However a section of their cavalry pressed forward on the Irish left, where a narrow causeway led to Aughrim village. At the crucial moment Saint-Ruth was decapitated by a cannon ball, and the Irish defence collapsed. Having crossed the bog, the Williamites attacked the unprotected Jacobite flank, then scattered their opponents in a murderous pursuit that continued until nightfall. In all some 7,000 Jacobites died, along with about 2,000 Williamites, out of armies of around 20,000 on each side. It is a death toll that makes Aughrim probably the most bloody battle in modern Irish history.

One reason why the Jacobites fought on, despite the defeat and flight of their king, was that the terms of surrender on offer were deeply unattractive. On 7 July 1690, just after the battle of the Boyne, William had issued a declaration from his camp at Finglas outside Dublin, offering pardon to those common soldiers and working men who now submitted, but nothing to the leaders. In February 1691, with the Jacobites still in possession of the western third of the country, Ginkel published a somewhat more conciliatory declaration, disowning any intention of religious persecution, and referring vaguely to the possibility of reasonable terms for those who submitted. But William remained reluctant to close off the possibility of paying at least part of the cost of the war from the forfeited estates of those who opposed him. Others took the same view. When Ginkel, after the fall of Athlone, offered pardons to commanders who surrendered garrisons, or brought over substantial units of the Jacobite army, there were loud protests both from Irish Protestants and in England. By this time, however, Ginkel was anxious to ensure that the war did not drag on into a third year. A month of campaigning, he pointed out to one of the Irish lords justices, cost more than the whole of the potential forfeitures were worth. On 21 July he accepted the surrender of Galway, subject to articles guaranteeing the estates both of members of the garrison and of the inhabitants, and promising to permit the private exercise of Catholicism.

The surrender of Galway was the first of a series of defections. In August Balldearg O'Donnell, having been promised a military command in Flanders, joined with the Williamites in an attack on the Jacobite garrison in Sligo. His change of sides provoked a mutiny among his own men, and the Sligo Jacobites routed him and his new allies. But on 14 September the encircled garrison surrendered the town on terms that allowed them to march to Limerick. Within Limerick, the only significant Jacobite garrison remaining, Brigadier Henry

Luttrell, earlier a prominent member of the war party opposed to Tyrconnell, was discovered to be in secret correspondence with Ginkel.[24] Limerick itself seemed at this stage secure. Ginkel's forces laid siege from the east on 25 August, but Jacobite control of the west bank of the Shannon maintained communications between the city and its hinterland in County Clare. On the night of 15–16 September, however, the Williamites crossed the Shannon, using a bridge of boats. The Jacobite commander protecting the crossing, Robert Clifford, offered no serious opposition, giving rise once again to allegations of betrayal. Six days later the Williamites pushed forward from this bridgehead, this time against fierce resistance, to complete the city's encirclement. Tyrconnell had died suddenly of a stroke on 14 August, and Sarsfield, who took charge of the garrison, now made the decision to negotiate. The bargaining that followed was mainly with Ginkel. William's two lords justices, Thomas Coningsby and Sir Charles Porter, arrived at Limerick on 1 October, in time to give the approval of the civilian government to the treaty signed two days later.

The decision of Sarsfield, the former leader of the war party, to capitulate on terms caused some surprise. There was general agreement that Limerick, though encircled, could have held out until winter forced the Williamites to lift the siege. However his men were demoralized by repeated defeats; the French had failed to send further assistance; and the actions of Luttrell, Clifford, and O'Donnell made clear the dangers of fighting on. Sarsfield's aim, however, was not to surrender, but to withdraw his army intact and to continue the struggle elsewhere. In negotiation with Ginkel he made the best terms he could for those who would remain behind. Jacobites still in arms, and all those still in Jacobite-held territory, were to be guaranteed their estates, and liberty to follow their professions, on taking a simple oath of allegiance. Catholics in general were to have the same religious liberties they had enjoyed under Charles II—the same formula used by Tyrconnell in his first ambiguous negotiations with the new Williamite regime. But Sarsfield's main concern was with the military articles. These provided that those officers and men of the Irish army who wished to go to France would be transported there in British ships. About 70 per cent of the Jacobite force were to leave under these terms. However there was initially some resistance, in particular until it was agreed that soldiers could bring their dependants with them. In the event a number of families were torn apart as wives and children failed to find space on the last of the ships that sailed.

The redeployment of the tens of thousands who had fought the war of 1689–91 created two enduring military traditions. The 15,000 or so Jacobite soldiers who sailed to France, along with the 5,000 who had earlier left under Justin MacCarthy, became the basis of the Irish regiments that were to form

[24] Luttrell had earlier been entrusted with defending the crucial causeway across which the enemy had crossed at Aughrim, and his actions at Limerick led to retrospective allegations of treachery on that occasion too.

part of the French army up to the Revolution. Sarsfield, their most prominent commander, died in 1693 of wounds received fighting against William's Dutch and English forces at the battle of Landen in Flanders. Meanwhile three of the corps into which the Protestant irregulars of Enniskillen and elsewhere had been organized following Schomberg's landing survived the post-war reorganization to become permanent regiments within the British army. One of four regiments sent to England by Tyrconnell, the 18th foot, had been composed mainly of Protestants, and it too continued, remaining in being until 1922. They were joined, for a much shorter period, by 8,000 or so troops from the Jacobite army, brought over to the Williamite side by Henry Luttrell, in a private deal which gave him possession of the County Dublin estate properly belonging to his older brother Simon. These Catholic troops anomalously enlisted in the cause of the Protestant succession were disbanded in 1692, with the exception of 1,400, who were sent to join the army of William's ally the emperor. Once again the common soldier, especially those whom circumstances placed on the wrong side of the religious and ethnic divide, became a commodity to be traded.[25]

The war of 1691 was a hard-fought and destructive conflict. Yet its conduct nevertheless testified to the significant changes that had taken place, within a relatively short space of time, in relations between the kingdom's main religious and ethnic groups. There were numerous complaints during 1688–9 of the plunder of defenceless Protestants. Reports of cattle and sheep being killed and left to rot in the fields awaken echoes of 1641–2, although by this time the motive may have been less a symbolic destruction of one instrument of the new English order than a pragmatic desire to reverse the encroachment of large-scale stock rearing on the smallholdings of the rural poor. Yet there are no credible accounts, even in the most propagandist accounts of Protestant sufferings produced by contemporary or subsequent authors, of the sort of indiscriminate killing, torture, and mutilation that caused 1641 to be remembered with such horror. One reason was no doubt the restraint imposed by the Jacobite leadership who, unlike Sir Phelim O'Neill and his allies, had full control of a nationwide system of government. But it would also appear that, despite continuing and shared suspicion and hostility, the passions involved were less immediately murderous than they had once been. The effect of the more relaxed relationships that had prevailed for a time in the aftermath of the Restoration was also evident in the reciprocal civilities exchanged between local leaders. On 6 July 1691 Richard Cox, commanding Williamite forces in County Cork, wrote to a Jacobite counterpart, Sir James Cotter, 'upon the score of our former acquaintance', to assure him that if he surrendered he would be treated 'as a man of honour'.

---

[25] The number of troops going to France is variously given as 12,000, 15,000, and 19,000. Compare Simms, *Jacobite Ireland*, 260; Maguire (ed.), *Kings in Conflict*, 90; Bartlett and Jeffrey (eds.), *Military History of Ireland*, 209.

Cotter's refusal, though firm, was equally civil, concluding with 'my service to all old acquaintances'.[26]

This is not to deny that ugly incidents occurred. At Carrickfergus, taken by Schomberg in August 1689, there were allegations that women attached to the Jacobite garrison were made to run the gauntlet naked, and Schomberg himself had to intervene, pistol in hand, to stop local Protestants killing some of the prisoners. Later there was widespread agreement that the attempt of the Finglas declaration of July 1690 to drive a wedge between the Jacobite rank and file and the leaders was undermined by the indiscriminate violence of Williamite troops towards the civilian population both in Dublin and in the countryside. The growing prominence of the rapparees provided a further reason to lay aside the restraining conventions of regular warfare. Where Jacobite regulars were generally permitted to surrender, rapparees could be killed out of hand. One Danish officer reported seeing more than forty of their severed heads set up over the gate of Clonmel. The organization of a Protestant militia to counter the rapparee threat contributed further to the ethos of a sectarian civil war. Richard Cox, who had exchanged civilities with the Jacobite commander Cotter, reported that he had used the 'vagabond parties' of the enemy 'like nettles and squeezed them . . . so hard that they could seldom sting, having as I believe killed and hanged not less than 3,000 of them while I stayed in the county of Cork'.[27]

Yet if war was often brutal, it was not without limits; just as the period 1689–91 had no equivalent of the massacres at Portadown or Charlemont, so it produced nothing to equal the storming of Drogheda or Wexford. Nor, any more than in other conflicts, was the violence that did take place directed solely at religious and ethnic rivals. In preparation for William's march south in the early summer of 1690, the Jacobites systematically seized or destroyed crops, livestock, and foodstores north of the Boyne. A French official was horrified to see the peasantry reduced to 'eating grass like horses', so that 'every day we find their corpses on the side of the road'.[28]

SOLE RIGHT

Having withdrawn gratefully from Ireland in September 1690, William III appointed three of his English servants to govern the kingdom for the duration of the war and in the period that followed. Henry, Viscount Sidney, served briefly as lord justice, alongside Thomas Coningsby, until December, when he returned to England. In March 1692, he became lord lieutenant. In the interval Coningsby continued as lord justice, along with Sir Charles Porter, the lord

[26] Cox to Cotter, 6 July 1691, with reply, National Library of Ireland MS 711 (a nineteenth-century copy).
[27] Cox to—, 8 Oct. 1691 (TCD MS 1180, p. 158).   [28] Lenihan, *Battle of the Boyne*, 81.

chancellor. Sidney had secured his place in history by a clandestine mission in June 1688, when he had brought to William III the crucial invitation, signed by himself and six others, that legitimized his invasion of England five months later. Contemporaries, however, regarded him as an affable lightweight, whose prominence reflected the accident of a friendship with William established when he commanded troops in the Netherlands during 1678–85. Coningsby, who had come to Ireland in 1690 as joint paymaster of the army, had enjoyed an even more fortuitous moment of fame. On the eve of the battle of the Boyne, when a lucky shot from the Jacobite lines had grazed William's shoulder, he had been on hand to staunch the wound with his handkerchief. The third governor, Porter, had a very different history. Exiled in 1648 for royalist activities, he had prospered after the Restoration as solicitor to the then duke of York. In 1686 James made him lord chancellor of Ireland, but removed him the following year to make way for a Catholic. William III, on the other hand, rewarded his support for the Revolution by restoring him as chancellor, at the same time that he became lord justice, in December 1690.

Early in 1692, with the Jacobite army safely disbanded or overseas, ministers in Dublin and London began to plan an Irish parliament.[29] They were under no clear obligation to do so. The four parliaments that had met in the period between the death of Elizabeth and the Revolution (1613–15, 1634–5, 1640–1, 1661–6) had not been sufficient to establish the assembly as an indispensable part of the machinery of the government. Indeed there were now suggestions that the English parliament could handle the necessary legislative steps towards the post-war settlement of the kingdom, or even that the time had come for a formal union with England. As against this it could be argued that a new Irish parliament would be the most effective means of restoring a sense of normality—as well, perhaps, as the one most consistent with the principles of the recent Revolution.

There was also the crucial question of money. Charles II's parliament of 1661—6 had granted the crown three permanent taxes: a customs duty on imports and exports, an excise charged on imports and on beer and spirits (the inland excise), and a hearth tax, levied on houses in proportion to the number of fireplaces they contained. In addition quit rents, paid on estates held under the acts of settlement and explanation, served as the Irish equivalent of a land tax. With the dramatic growth in Irish commerce in the decades following the

---

[29] The long-term significance of William III's first Irish parliament was first highlighted by J. I. McGuire, 'The Irish Parliament of 1692', in Thomas Bartlett and D. W. Hayton (eds.), *Penal Era and Golden Age: Essays in Irish History 1690–1800* (Belfast, 1979), 1–31. For the 1690s as a whole, Wooter Troost, *William III and the Treaty of Limerick 1691–1697: A Study of his Irish Policy* (Leiden, 1983) presents a rather schematic picture of ideologically driven party alignments, to which Hayton, *Ruling Ireland*, ch. 2 offers a direct critique. C. I. McGrath, *The Making of the Eighteenth-Century Irish Constitution: Government, Parliament and the Revenue 1692–1714* (Dublin, 2000), is an exhaustive study of the connections between parliamentary politics and problems of public finance.

Restoration, these grants more than met the needs of the crown in Ireland. By the late 1670s, in fact, Ireland was supplying the free-spending Charles II with a valuable surplus of £97,000 a year. As the Williamite regime established control over the country, it was able to resume the collection of this hereditary revenue, but at a level much reduced by the after-effects of war. In 1692 the Irish treasury received £138,000, as compared to an average of £253,000 a year during 1683–7. Initially the government envisaged a first session in the autumn which would 'give so much satisfaction to the people in general' that a second session in spring 1693 would willingly vote additional taxes.[30] However Sidney, on arriving in Dublin in September, decided that the state of the finances, with revenue expected to fall short of expenditure by over £100,000, required immediate action. Accordingly the English privy council, following the procedures laid down by Poynings's Law, approved two finance bills, for an increase in the inland excise on beer and spirits, and for 'certain duties' on grain and house rents, both to run for one year.

What exactly the administration expected when parliament met on 5 October remains unclear. There were claims that Porter and Coningsby had sought to delay an assembly that might call them to account for their management of the kingdom over the preceding two years. Sidney, too, expressed some concern about 'the violence that will be against the Papists'. At the same time he claimed to have assurances from 'popular men' that the taxes requested would be readily granted. On 15 October, with the settling of disputed elections and other preliminary business concluded, the House of Commons did in fact agree in principle to grant up to £70,000. Three days later, however, it passed resolutions alleging embezzlement in the disposal of forfeited lands, and complaining of the failure to disarm the Catholic population and to exclude Catholics from the armed forces. A more pointed motion on 25 October complained of men in high office obstructing the course of justice by giving illegal certificates of protection to Jacobites. Meanwhile the Commons, on 21 and 24 October, had rejected a bill to confirm the acts of settlement and explanation, as well as another annulling the proceedings of the Jacobite parliament and ordering the destruction of its records. How far this rejection of what should have been two welcome bills arose from a general desire to wreck the administration's legislative programme, and how far from real fears that the measures concerned were intended somehow to obstruct the confiscation of Jacobite estates, remains unclear.[31] Two other parliamentary revolts were on more clear-cut grounds. On 31 October the Commons rejected a bill to create a Protestant militia, claiming that the number to be raised was unrealistic, and the power given to the

---

[30] Sidney to Portland, 26 July 1692 (Nottingham University Library, PwA 1344a).
[31] See McGuire, 'Irish Parliament of 1692', 16–19, who also suggests that an otherwise mysterious demand for the re-enactment of the English act of 1641 to abolish Star Chamber was a device to prevent the privy council adjudicating on claims to land ownership arising from the Articles of Limerick.

commissioners of array excessive. On 3 November they rejected a mutiny bill, seen as embodying the important principle that the crown could maintain a standing army only with the authorization of parliament, on the grounds that it was to run for three years rather than, as in England, requiring annual renewal.

Meanwhile the finance bills had also run into trouble. On 27 October the Commons objected to both, on the grounds that it was their house's 'sole right', not only to authorize taxation, but also to consider the ways and means by which money required for public purposes should be raised, and to frame the necessary legislation. They accepted the inland excise bill, on the grounds of urgent public necessity, but added a declaration stating that this did not constitute a precedent, and went on to reject the certain duties bill as not having had its rise in the Commons. In its place members resolved to draw up their own heads of a bill to raise the same sum by a poll tax. Before they could do so, however, Sidney, on 3 November, brought the parliament to a close, telling them that 'they had not answered the ends for which they were called together, but had behaved themselves undutifully and ungratefully in invading their Majesties' prerogative'.[32]

Several influences combined to bring about the collapse of the 1692 parliamentary session. Sidney identified three of the leading troublemakers, James Hamilton, James Sloane, and Sir Francis Brewster, as acting on behalf of the leaders of the parliamentary opposition in England. Three others, John Osborne, Robert Rochford, and Alan Brodrick, were lawyers possibly dissatisfied with the minor offices they held. Yet the success of these ringleaders in apparently uniting the greater part of the Commons in opposition to Sidney's administration made clear that more was involved than faction or frustrated ambition. One central grievance was resentment of the generous terms offered to the defeated Jacobites by the Treaty of Limerick. To Ginkel and William III these had seemed a reasonable price to pay for the early release of the military resources tied up in a peripheral conflict. To Irish Protestants, on the other hand, the treaty was a betrayal, leaving them open to renewed attack at any time from a Catholic elite still in possession of their estates and a population only superficially pacified. Resentment on this score explains the particular hostility directed towards Porter and Coningsby. Although the treaty had been negotiated primarily by Ginkel, Coningsby had been involved in earlier moves towards framing more favourable terms to be offered to the Jacobites, and both men had signed the final agreement. Since the end of the war, moreover, they had presided over the first restoration of estates to Jacobites claiming the protection of its articles. A second cause of resentment was the allegation, probably justified, of widespread corruption. Critics charged that members of the administration and their clients had bought up shares in the public debt on advantageous terms, that the management of confiscated Jacobites' estates had been farmed out to favoured individuals at low

[32] *An Account of the Sessions of Parliament in Ireland, 1692* (London, 1693), 25.

rates, and that there had been extensive misuse of public funds. Other complaints concerned the depredations of an unpaid army forced to live off the countryside, the levying of money without authorization, and the allegedly arbitrary behaviour of office holders.

Resentment of blatant profiteering and of the allegedly undue favour shown to Catholics merged with new constitutional aspirations of the kind shown in the claim to a sole right to frame financial legislation. Sidney had a vested interest in emphasizing this aspect of the opposition to his administration. Indeed there were suggestions that in coming ostentatiously to the defence of the king's prerogative, a full week after the offending Commons vote on the sole right, he was in fact concerned to forestall an imminent debate that might have seen Coningsby and others face serious charges of corruption. But his comments on 17 October, before his legislative programme had run into trouble, and before the first real attacks on his administration, suggest a genuine bewilderment:

They have begun like a company of madmen, for they don't know themselves what they would have. Whether they will come into better temper or no, I cannot tell, but at present they talk of freeing themselves from the yoke of England, of taking away Poynings's law, of making an address to have a habeas corpus bill, and twenty other extravagant discourses have been amongst them.[33]

The influence of heightened constitutional aspirations was confirmed, shortly before the parliament met, when Bishop Dopping of Meath published a medieval manual on parliamentary procedure, the *Modus tenendi parliamenta in Hibernia*, with an introduction arguing that it was an authentic record of the extension of English liberties to Ireland by Henry II. Dopping had acquired the manuscript from his uncle, the former attorney general William Domville, thus establishing a direct if tenuous link between the parliamentary revolt of 1692 and the earlier debates on Ireland's constitutional status provoked by the upheavals of 1659–60 and before that 1640–1.[34]

To these echoes of former debates was added the more immediate influence of the English Revolution. Some members of the Irish elite, like Alan Brodrick, had witnessed the dramatic events of 1688–9 at first hand, while living in England as refugees from Tyrconnell's government. And even those who had remained in Ireland would have known something of the sudden explosion of debate that had accompanied the Revolution: the critique of royal authority in terms of the fundamental law of the kingdom, the drafting of a declaration of rights, the heady talk in some quarters of a right of resistance to unjust rulers. Subsequent

---

[33] Sidney to Nottingham, 17 Oct. 1692 (*CSPD 1695*, 213).

[34] *Modus tenendi parliamenta et consilia in Hibernia, Published out of an Ancient Record by the Right Reverend Father in God, Anthony, Lord Bishop of Meath* (Dublin, 1692), preface. The *Modus* is first recorded in 1418, when a copy was found in the possession of Sir Christopher Preston, arrested in connection with a political feud. Most modern historians see it as an Irish copy of an English original dating to the early fourteenth century. See *A New History of Ireland*, ii: *Medieval Ireland 1169–1534* (Oxford, 1987), 550–1.

events were to show that to most of the members involved the specific demands made in 1692, including the sole right, were to some extent negotiable. But the initial call for the formal extension to Ireland of the law of habeas corpus, and of the same safeguards that were built into the English mutiny and militia acts, can nevertheless be seen as reflecting a general sense that Ireland, or at least Protestant Ireland, was entitled to share in the liberties secured by the overthrow of James II.

In June 1693, faced with continuing deadlock between the Irish administration and its critics, the English ministry replaced Sidney by three lords justices. Of these the most prominent was Sir Henry Capel, brother of the earl of Essex who had served as lord lieutenant during 1672–7 and had subsequently died in prison, a Whig martyr in the royalist reaction that had followed the Exclusion crisis. Capel had wanted the chief governorship for himself, and his ambition presumably explains why he now set about building connections with some of the leaders of the opposition to Sidney. By the end of 1694 he was able to present his terms to the English administration: a new parliament would grant additional taxation without insisting on the sole right, but only if Porter and others were dismissed, Capel's Irish allies were admitted to office, and he himself became chief governor. In the event the ministry refused to remove Porter. However two of the leading sole right men, Robert Rochford and Alan Brodrick, took office as, respectively, attorney and solicitor general, while several of their associates were appointed to lesser positions or to the Irish privy council. Capel himself became chief governor in May 1695, though his rivals in the ministry ensured that he had to be satisfied with the lesser title of lord deputy.

When parliament met on 27 August 1695, Capel laid before the Commons a bill imposing an additional inland excise for one year, thus formally reaffirming the crown's right to initiate financial legislation. Having done so, however, he invited the house to consider the ways and means of raising a further £163,000 in part settlement of the government's arrears. This carefully crafted compromise did not satisfy all. At the beginning of the parliament James Sloane attacked Brodrick and Rochfort as 'men quitting their country's interest by taking to be the king's servants'.[35] Later there were renewed attempts to introduce a habeas corpus bill and a bill of rights. Capel, however, had smoothed the way with two further bills, one to confiscate weapons and horses in Catholic hands, and the other to block what was seen as a dangerous channel of communication between Irish Catholics and their allies in mainland Europe by forbidding them to travel abroad for purposes of education. Thus reassured the Commons accepted the settlement put before them, passing the token inland excise bill, then drawing up their own heads of bills for an additional duty on tobacco and other imports, supplemented by a poll tax, to raise the further £163,000 requested.

[35] Capel to Shrewsbury, 25 Aug. 1695 (PRONI, T2807/5).

The inadequacies of the hereditary revenue that had led to the summoning of the first post-war parliament continued into the decades that followed. Income did not recover to pre-war levels until 1697. The huge costs of the war itself had been met primarily from England. But from January 1692 the Irish administration was required to pay for the expanded army required by the continuing European conflict, while at the same time coping with the arrears of official pay arising from the collapse of government finance over the preceding three years. When the European war finally ended in 1697, moreover, William III chose to sidestep strong opposition in England to the continuation of a large military establishment by creating an Irish standing army of 12,000 men, in effect imposing on Ireland a permanent contribution to imperial defence. Irish government expenditure between 1693 and 1697 averaged £215,000 a year. Between 1698 and the out-break of a new European war in 1702 the average was £404,000.[36]

It was against this background of a hereditary revenue that now fell invariably short of the needs of the executive that the outcome of the parliamentary sessions of 1692 and 1695 assumed a permanent significance. The Irish Commons had given way on the sole right to initiate financial legislation. But their proceedings during these two sessions had established what was in fact the more important principle that requests for supply were to be for fixed sums and specified purposes, and that the taxes granted would be for a limited period. Over the next two decades procedures were to be refined. In particular the Commons began, from 1703, to make the setting of the amount to be raised (known as the quantum) dependent on prior scrutiny of the government's financial statement, giving the committee of accounts a central importance. Grants of additional taxation, which in the 1690s had been for periods ranging from one year to more than four, moved thereafter towards a norm of two years. This in turn ensured more regular meetings of parliament. After sessions in 1697, 1698, and 1699, rising receipts from a restored tax base allowed the administration to avoid summoning parliament until 1703. Thereafter, however, there were meetings in 1705, 1707, 1709, 1710, 1711, and 1713. By the beginning of the eighteenth century the Irish parliament, like its English counterpart, had made the crucial transition from 'event' to 'institution'.[37]

PREVENTING THE FURTHER GROWTH OF POPERY

The 1690s and early 1700s saw the Irish parliament assume a new role as a regular part of the government of the kingdom. The same period saw, in a parallel and

[36] Calculated from the figures in McGrath, *Making of the Eighteenth-Century Irish Constitution*, 294–5.

[37] A phrase coined by Conrad Russell, and quoted in an Irish context by D. W. Hayton, 'Introduction: The Long Apprenticeship', in idem (ed.), *The Irish Parliament in the Eighteenth Century* (Edinburgh, 2001), 8.

sometimes closely connected process, the enactment of a series of laws imposing new and severe restrictions on Catholic religious practice, property rights, and political participation. The first step was the introduction, at the start of the parliament of 1695, of Capel's bills for disarming Catholics and preventing their travel to universities in Catholic Europe. An act of 1697 required all bishops, vicars general, and others exercising ecclesiastical jurisdiction, as well as members of religious orders, to leave the kingdom by 1 May 1698. Any remaining after that date were to be transported, and any returning from transportation were to be executed as traitors. A later act, in 1704, forbade ordained priests to enter the kingdom. Priests already there were to register with the authorities and to provide securities for their future good behaviour.

By this time parliament had also turned its attention to land. An act of 1697 provided that the estate of a Protestant heiress who married a Catholic was to pass instead to her nearest Protestant kin, while a Protestant proprietor marrying a Catholic woman thereby incurred all the restrictions attached to being a Catholic himself. In 1704 a major statute, the act 'to prevent the further growth of popery', forbade Catholics to inherit land from Protestants, or to acquire land of any kind by purchase, by lending money on mortgage, or by taking a lease for longer than thirty-one years. Existing Catholic estates were not to be transmitted by primogeniture, but divided equally among male heirs. An eldest son who conformed to the Church of Ireland would, however, inherit the whole; other heirs conforming would be guaranteed a reasonable maintenance. An act of 1709 provided for the effective enforcement of these prohibitions: any Protestant who became aware of a transaction violating the popery laws could file a bill of discovery, thereby becoming entitled to the Catholic party's share of the proceeds. Meanwhile an English act of 1691 had required members of the House of Lords and House of Commons in both kingdoms, as well as those practising law, and all those holding public offices, to subscribe to a declaration repudiating transubstantiation and other essential Catholic doctrines. An Irish act of 1698 repeated this stipulation for those practising law, and added the requirement that they must educate their children in the Protestant religion. Catholics were still permitted to vote, although from 1704 they could do so only if they were willing to take the oath of abjuration, denying the claim to the throne of the exiled descendants of James II. It was not until 1728 that an act formally excluded them from the parliamentary franchise.[38]

The statutes of 1695, 1697, 1704, and 1709, along with a variety of lesser measures, constitute what are today referred to as the penal laws, or even as the penal code. (Protestants, pointing to the example of states like France in which

[38] For general accounts of the penal laws see Maureen Wall, *The Penal Laws 1691–1760* (Dundalk, 1967); Thomas Bartlett, *The Fall and Rise of the Irish Nation* (Dublin, 1992), ch. 2; Simms, *War and Politics in Ireland*, chs. 17, 18, 20. The arguments in this section are developed in more detail in Connolly, *Religion, Law and Power*, ch. 7.

the law was genuinely penal, in the sense of imposing harsh punishments for the mere practice of a proscribed religion, rejected the term, referring instead to the popery laws.) Yet even the brief overview just given should indicate, in its confused chronology and absence of any clear set of priorities, that any suggestion of a coherent code is misleading. Instead the anti-Catholic legislation enacted under William III and Anne represented less the implementation of coherent policy than a by-product of new constitutional assumptions and of a new set of political relationships.

To see this it is only necessary to note how many of the prohibitions now embedded in statute law already existed. No Catholic commoner had sat in the parliament of 1661–6. Nor, since the Restoration, had Catholics been allowed to hold most offices in either municipal or central government, with the exception of a brief period in 1670–3. Catholic lawyers had once already been excluded from the courts, by the application of the oath of supremacy, from 1613, though they had been readmitted from 1628. Proclamations in 1673 and 1678 had anticipated the act of 1697 by ordering the banishment of bishops, vicars general, and regular clergy. The 1670s had also seen the closure of churches and schools, and in 1678 the confiscation of weapons in Catholic hands. If the revival of such prohibitions now took the form of acts of parliament, this was partly because Irish Protestants, deeply suspicious of the true loyalties of their recent governors, demanded an explicit commitment to the defence of their supremacy. In part, the reason lay in wider constitutional changes. The numerous shifts in religious policy that had taken place in the Restoration era, such as the banishment edicts of 1673 and 1678, or the short-lived admission of Catholics to office in 1670–3, had rested not on legislation but on the exercise of the royal prerogative. Even at the time the first duke of Ormond had expressed some anxiety about the limits of executive authority, at least in the case of action against Protestant dissenters.[39] After 1688, when James II's claim to suspend the statutory restrictions on Catholics and dissenters became one of the instances of arbitrary government held to justify his removal, reliance on prerogative authority became less satisfactory. Seen in this light much of the anti-Catholic legislation of 1695 and after was less a new departure than an acknowledgement that what had previously been done by executive fiat now required the explicit sanction of statute law.

Any attempt to understand the popery laws must also recognize the extent to which their scope and intent changed over time. The two measures enacted in 1695 were defensive in character. The confiscation of arms and horses addressed concerns about their physical safety that had been repeatedly expressed by Irish Protestants since the end of the war. The education act, equally, was intended to sever what was seen as a dangerous line of communication between James II's supporters at home and their allies in mainland Europe; the clause

[39] Above, p. 144.

forbidding Catholics to teach school within Ireland, misleadingly taken today as the main purpose of the act, was a secondary provision, restating a long-standing prohibition. The marriage act of 1697 was likewise defensive, seeking to ensure that the susceptibility of Protestant heiresses did not permit Catholics to regain in the boudoir what they had lost on the battlefield. The great popery act of 1704 and its 1709 sequel, on the other hand, quite clearly looked beyond self-defence to the erosion of the remaining Catholic landed interest, whether through the forced conformity of the remaining proprietors or, if they remained recalcitrant, the progressive subdivision of their estates.

The impetus behind this steady widening of the scope of anti-Catholic legislation came at least in part from the new bargaining power enjoyed by the Irish parliament once it had successfully asserted its monopoly of financial legislation. There was general agreement in the early 1690s that measures had to be taken against a Catholic counter-attack. The ban on Catholics owning horses worth more than £5, for example, had already been introduced in England in 1689.[40] Yet contemporaries were also clear that both the disarming and the education act of 1695 were part of the package by which Capel had secured the support of the former sole right men. A similar process of bargaining can be detected in late 1702, when the lords justices, having avoided meeting parliament for nearly four years, began negotiations for what was likely to be a difficult session by inviting some leading political figures to suggest 'what good could be done for Ireland', and duly took up one of the suggestions, a measure to prevent papists inheriting estates. At the end of 1704, with another session due, the lord lieutenant's secretary could write openly of the need 'to think of some brilliant to open the session withal that might have some relish with it for extraordinary good like our last Popery Act'. In the event government managers came up with a further tightening of the regulations on priests permitted to remain in the kingdom. When some MPs in 1709 objected that the English privy council had trespassed on their monopoly of financial legislation by making amendments to a money bill, the government was able to respond by warning that failure to pass the disputed bill would jeopardize the popery act also making its way through parliament.[41]

The enactment of this whole body of anti-Catholic legislation was complicated, initially at least, by the terms of the Treaty of Limerick. When the English privy council considered the heads of what became the disarming act, it felt obliged

[40] C. I. McGrath, 'Securing the Protestant Interest: The Origins and Purpose of the Penal Laws of 1695', *IHS* 30 (1996), 40–1. Dr McGrath challenges the argument (first developed in Connolly, *Religion, Law and Power*) that penal legislation can be seen in part as a by-product of the management of a newly assertive Irish parliament. His immediate point, that the acts of 1695 were consistent with other attempts, in both England and Ireland, to strengthen the Protestant interest against what was seen as a real Catholic threat, is fair enough. The sleight of hand comes in when these acts are christened 'the first penal laws', implying that what was true in 1695 must necessarily have been true of all subsequent legislation.

[41] For a fuller account of these transactions see Connolly, *Religion, Law and Power*, 264–78.

to insert a clause exempting nobles and gentlemen who claimed the benefit of the articles. Yet feeling against the agreement was so strong that they avoided mentioning the treaty by name, referring instead to those who had been in the Jacobite garrison, or had held commissions from James II. Since the treaty obliged William and Mary to use 'their utmost endeavours' to have its terms ratified in the Irish parliament, such evasion could not continue indefinitely. A ratification bill duly came before parliament in 1697. Ministers insisted, despite objections from the Irish council, on retaining a ban on lawsuits arising out of wartime events. In other respects, however, they made significant concessions to Irish Protestant feeling. The ratification bill omitted both the stipulation that Catholics were to be required to take no oath except a simple oath of allegiance, and the promise to allow them the same religious freedom as they had enjoyed under Charles II. It also omitted a further clause, extending the benefits of the treaty to non-combatants under the protection of the Jacobite forces, which had been accidentally left out of the original fair copy signed by both sides but which William had subsequently acknowledged by letters patent as part of the agreed terms.[42] In practice the government made no attempt to initiate the widespread forfeitures of property held by those not actually in arms in October 1691 that this last omission made possible. But Protestants were nevertheless reassured that the treaty was not to be allowed to deprive them of the fruits of victory. That reassurance in turn confirmed the new balance of power that had been established between crown and parliament.

To say this is not to suggest that the form in which the treaty was ratified reflected the unanimous wishes of the Protestant elite. In fact the bill passed through the Lords by only 23 votes to 20. Fourteen of those opposed, who included six bishops of the Church of Ireland, subsequently entered a formal protest against the bill, on the grounds that its omissions represented a breach of faith. In the same year the Lords rejected a draconian measure, proposed in the aftermath of an assassination attempt on William III, that would have allowed justices of the peace to require suspect persons, on pain of forfeiting all their possessions, to take an oath repudiating the power of the pope to depose heretical princes. Bishop King of Derry, who had also been a prominent critic of the ratification bill, objected that to subject individuals in this way to the discretionary will of two magistrates was a breach of Magna Carta, 'which is law in Ireland as well as in England'. More strikingly, he also argued that to require people to swear against an article of their faith—the deposing power of the pope—was 'a direct persecution', an objection that lends some credibility to the insistence of King and others that they did not see the other popery laws as 'penal'. In 1709 it was the turn of the Commons to challenge some of the harsher aspects of a popery bill, removing a clause banning Catholics from trading as merchants. MPs also rejected a proposal to exclude Catholics from voting, on

---

[42] Simms, 'The Treaty of Limerick', in *War and Politics in Ireland*, 203–24.

the grounds that 'it was unreasonable so great a body of people should be bound by laws which were not made by their representatives'. A more pressing reason, in this last instance, may have been a fear that disenfranchising Catholic voters would tilt the electoral balance too far in favour of dissenters.[43]

Anti-Catholic legislation was not only the product of a process of bargaining, explicit or understood, between the Irish executive and a newly assertive parliament. It was also the product of a complex legislative process, required by Poynings's Law, that allowed a variety of hands to contribute to the shape of an individual measure. The celebrated act to prevent the growth of popery provides an illustration. The initial proposal, offered by one of the judges in the consultations that preceded a meeting of parliament, was for 'laws against the Irish inheriting while they continued papists, and for admitting no priests into the kingdom'. The lords justices, clearly concerned at the reaction in London, hedged their bets. The bill they transmitted for approval by the English privy council was more limited, being intended only 'for preventing Protestants from turning papists, and for any estate of Protestants to descend or come to any Papist, and to prevent Papists from disinheriting Protestants'. But they also pointed out that the bill would be more acceptable if extended to preventing Catholics acquiring land 'by purchase or descent'.[44] The English privy council, on the other hand, saw even the existing draft bill as too harsh, and as possibly contravening the Treaty of Limerick. While it hesitated, members of the Commons, by now in session, drew up their own heads of a bill. These prohibited the acquisition of land from Protestants, not only by inheritance but by purchase or rental on long leases, and also required the division of Catholic estates among male heirs. When the heads were transmitted to London, several members explicitly warned that the fate of the money bill depended on their returning unaltered.

In the event the English council strengthened rather than weakened the bill, by extending the ban on purchase and long leases to cover, not just transfers of land from Protestants to Catholics, but the acquisition by Catholics of any land whatever. At the same time it engaged in some political horse-trading of its own, by adding a clause to impose the sacramental test. This was the requirement, in force in England since 1673, that anyone holding an office of trust or profit under the crown should qualify at regular intervals by producing certificates showing that they had taken communion in the Church of Ireland. The test made no difference to Catholics, already excluded by the declaration against transubstantiation. Instead a Tory English council took the opportunity to push an anti-dissenter measure through what it assumed might be

---

[43] Connolly, *Religion, Law and Power*, 271, 277.

[44] Lords Justices to Rochester, 30 Jan. 1703 (BL, Add. MS 9715, fo. 41ᵛ). For the preliminary consultations see Alan Brodrick to St John Brodrick, 29 Nov. 1702 (Surrey History Centre, Midleton MSS 1248/2, fos. 73–5). For a general account of the passage of the act see Simms, 'The Making of a Penal Law', in *War and Politics in Ireland*, 263–76.

an unreceptive Irish parliament, by making it the price of a satisfactorily forceful anti-Catholic bill.

A further complication affecting the enactment of anti-Catholic legislation was the intermittent intrusion of considerations of European diplomacy. In 1695 William III had blocked the first attempt to introduce legislation for the deportation of regular clergy and other Catholic ecclesiastics, partly at least in order to avoid damaging relations with the Holy Roman emperor, his main ally in the grand coalition against France. By 1697, on the other hand, the war was winding down, and differences over the peace settlement had led to a cooling in William's relations with the emperor. Hence he gave his assent to the bishops' banishment act, despite representations from the emperor's envoy. In the decades that followed British ministers continued regularly to show themselves to be unwilling to endorse harsh measures proposed in Ireland, partly to avoid causing difficulty with continental allies, and also because such legislation weakened their hand in pleading for more favourable treatment for Protestant minorities in Catholic states within the empire and elsewhere.

These different circumstances provide the essential background to any discussion of what the popery laws were intended to achieve. Measures adopted partly as an instrument of parliamentary management, through the mechanism of a complex drafting process, and against a background of internal debate, did not directly reflect the aims of any single individual or group. The general thrust of the civil legislation is clear enough. The laws enacted were intended to neutralize the military threat from a large Catholic population seen as having surrendered on terms rather than as having being decisively defeated, and to formalize and make complete their exclusion from political office at every level. The acts relating to landholding, equally, sought to complete what the generous terms of the Treaty of Limerick had prevented from occurring in 1691: the final elimination, as rivals for political power, of a Catholic aristocracy and gentry. The intent behind the religious legislation is less clear cut. The banishment act of 1697, looking back to the proclamations of 1673 and 1678, singled out the parts of the Catholic church establishment that most clearly presented a political threat. Bishops and vicar generals exercised an authority derived directly from the pope; friars and monks were members of disciplined religious orders whose headquarters were likewise located in Rome. The act of 1704 permitting one priest to register for each parish seemed to confirm that there was no intention of suppressing Catholic religious practice. The same act, however, forbade the entry into the kingdom of priests ordained abroad, opening up the possibility that there would be no successors to these registered clergy as they gradually died out. Some observers explicitly stated, both at the time and in retrospect, that this was what the law was intended to achieve. But the history of the next few years was to suggest strongly that for many the apparently rigid provisions of the 'penal code' were important more as a declaration of commitment to Protestant supremacy than as a detailed plan of action.

PREVENTING THE FURTHER GROWTH OF DISSENT

Sir Charles Porter viewed the 1695 settlement with predictable lack of enthusiasm. He deplored the removal from office of men 'who had always asserted the king's rights' to make way for 'those who had been the most active opposers'. As a lord justice, in 1692, he had opposed general searches for arms in Catholic hands as likely to provide an occasion for indiscriminate plunder. By 1695 he was willing to accept, and even approve, the acts to confiscate weapons and horses and to restrain foreign education. On the other hand he objected strongly to another aspect of the rhetoric of Capel and his supporters. This was their attempt to promote the notion of a 'British' interest in Ireland, uniting the English Protestant population with the Presbyterian Scots of Ulster. For Porter the Scots as well as the Irish were a potential threat to 'the English interest in this kingdom'. Indeed his main reservation about the disarming bill was that it required the chief governor to have the consent of the council before licensing Catholics to carry arms. This would make it more difficult, 'if any disturbance should arise from the Scots', to mobilize the Irish, who could otherwise be relied on to contain them, 'for though they do not love us, they hate the Scots more'.[45] These were attitudes more in tune with the pragmatic improvisations that had characterized the reign of Charles II than with the rhetoric of the Glorious Revolution. But they illustrate the continued problem created by the presence on the island of this third substantial population, neither English nor Irish, and combining their Protestantism with an aggressive rejection of the state church.

The uncertain position of dissenters within the new order established at the Restoration had been made clear during the reign of James II. Presbyterians and other nonconformists had initially accepted places on Tyrone's remodelled corporations, and some had seized the opportunity to defy or harass the Church of Ireland clergy. As the scale of Catholic ambitions became clear Protestants of all denominations had for the most part united against the common enemy. Presbyterians were prominent, possibly even dominant, among those taking the lead in organizing resistance at Enniskillen and Derry. Yet when George Walker, the Anglican clergyman who had acted as governor of Derry, published his *True Account of the Siege of Londonderry* in 1689, his blatant failure to acknowledge the Presbyterian contribution to the city's defence caused outrage, reflected in a heated pamphlet warfare that continued until Walker was killed at the Boyne in July of the following year.

Following the sporadic repression they had endured under Charles II, Presbyterians and other dissenters initially expected that the Revolution would bring a new era of toleration. One of William III's first acts, on arriving in Belfast in June

45 Porter to Sir William Trumbull, 9 July 1695 (HMC, *Downshire MSS*, i. 499–500).

1690, was to receive a deputation of Presbyterian ministers and promise them an increased *regium donum* of £1,200 a year. In 1692 and again in 1695 English ministers suggested the introduction of a toleration act similar to that passed in England in 1689, which would have recognized the right of dissenting Protestants to worship freely. In each case, however, they found the Irish parliament and privy council strongly opposed. Meanwhile the crown had appointed a new bishop of Derry, to replace the conveniently deceased Ezekiel Hopkins. William King, promoted in recognition of his services to the Revolution, quickly revealed himself as an uncompromising upholder of the rights of the established church, reasserting the authority of the church courts, and also seeking to prevent the election of a dissenter as the city's mayor. From 1698 the bishops in Ulster as a whole began a new campaign of harassment through the church courts. They prosecuted dissenting schoolmasters for not having the licence required by the act of uniformity, and ministers for marrying couples without authority. They also proceeded against the couples so married, using the threat of condemnation for fornication, and a judgement that any children were illegitimate, to force them to accept marriage by a minister of the established church.

The final blow to Presbyterian hopes for an early improvement in their legal position came from outside Ireland, when the English ministry, now in hands strongly hostile to dissent, used the act to prevent the growth of popery to extend to Ireland the sacramental test. The test did not prevent Presbyterians from voting or from taking seats in parliament. By this time, however, the number of Presbyterian landowners had been seriously thinned by the defection to the established church of those anxious to enjoy the full benefits of integration into the social elite, and their role in national politics was correspondingly weak. Already in 1703, before the introduction of the test, there had been only nine Presbyterian members in a Commons of 300. Even at the lower level of the commission of the peace, William King, now archbishop of Dublin, maintained that the test had excluded only twelve individuals in the whole of Ulster. Where the new act did have a definite impact was in municipal corporations. In Derry its introduction forced the immediate resignation of 9 out of 12 aldermen, and 14 out of 24 burgesses. In Belfast the new requirement was ignored until 1707, when legal challenges arising out of a disputed election forced the resignation of the five Presbyterian burgesses. Exclusion from these and other boroughs further diminished an already weak Presbyterian electoral interest. More important it excluded Presbyterians from participation in the local administration of urban communities in which they generally controlled the greater part of the commercial wealth.[46]

[46] For a detailed analysis of the electoral impact of the test, see Hayton, *Ruling Ireland*, ch. 6. For Church of Ireland claims that Presbyterians did not in any case have sufficient property to merit a share in political power, Connolly, *Religion, Law and Power*, 163. J. C. Beckett, *Protestant Dissent in Ireland 1687–1780* (London, 1948) remains the fullest general survey of the politics of the test.

One reason why defenders of the established church had intensified their attack on dissent was that the 1690s and early 1700s saw a new surge of Scottish immigration into Ulster, following a series of disastrous harvests between 1695 and 1698. Alarmist accounts spoke of 50,000 or 80,000 families, although the true figure was probably around 40,000 individuals.[47] Boosted by this influx of new members, the number of Presbyterian congregations increased by up to half between 1689 and 1707, and by another 30 per cent by 1716. In Antrim, Down and Londonderry dissenters by this time almost certainly outnumbered members of the Church of Ireland by more than two to one, and in the country as a whole their numbers, at their early eighteenth-century peak, may well have equalled or even exceeded those of the established church.[48]

This rapidly expanding Presbyterian population was a threat, not just because of its numerical strength, and its concentration in the province of Ulster, but because of its tight ecclesiastical organization. Restoration Presbyterianism had already had a formal territorial structure, with congregations grouped into presbyteries that supervised their affairs through regular visitations. By 1689 there were five such presbyteries, increased by 1697 to seven. By 1671 there was also a general meeting to coordinate the affairs of the different presbyteries, and from 1691 ministers and selected elders began to meet annually as the Synod of Ulster. Discipline within Presbyterian congregations was strict. Ministers and elders were expected to monitor individual behaviour, citing offenders to be dealt with either locally or, in the case of more serious charges, by the presbytery. The most common offences were adultery and fornication, but individuals were also cited for drunkenness, sabbath breaking, disputes with neighbours, slander, and failure to pay debts. Punishment generally took the form of a humiliating public confession, on one or more occasions, before the congregation, backed by the threat of excommunication for those who refused to submit. To upholders of the Church of Ireland the existence of this autonomous and highly organized ecclesiastical system was both unacceptable and alarming. Archbishop King, for example, justified his church's hard line on dissent by insisting that Ulster Presbyterians were wholly different from their English counterparts. 'They are a people embodied under their lay elders, presbyteries and synods . . . and will be just so far the king's subjects as their lay elders and presbyteries will allow them.'[49]

---

[47] Patrick Fitzgerald, ' "Black '97": Reconsidering Scottish Migration to Ireland in the Seventeenth Century and the Scotch-Irish in America', in William Kelly and J. R. Young (eds.), *Ulster and Scotland 1600–2000* (Dublin, 2004), 77–9. This is at best a speculative figure, based on the proportion of Scottish population loss during these years estimated to have been due to emigration rather than mortality, minus estimated emigration to America.

[48] The first reliable statistics on membership of the different churches become available only in 1834, when 11% of the population of Ireland as a whole were members of the Church of Ireland, and another 8% were Presbyterians. This was at the end of over a century of fairly heavy emigration that, for most of the period, had disproportionately affected Presbyterian Ulster.

[49] King to Wake, 24 Mar. 1716 (TCD MS 2533, 165). For a fuller discussion see Connolly, *Religion, Law and Power*, 159–71.

The unease created by the spectacle of Presbyterian discipline and solidarity also drew on memories of a time when religious commitment had been translated into a political programme. By the early eighteenth century most Presbyterians no longer believed that they were obliged to withhold recognition from a government that did not uphold the principles of the Solemn League and Covenant. The only opposition came from small groups of Covenanters or Reformed Presbyterians, initially sustained by itinerant ministers from Scotland, but from 1757 developing their own organization and ministry. Yet the allegation that Presbyterianism went hand in hand with the rejection of secular authority, and ultimately with republicanism, remained, given credence by the continued inclusion of the Covenant in Presbyterian catechisms, as well as by the determined rejection of hierarchy that characterized their ecclesiastical system.

To the theological and political principles of Ulster Presbyterians, finally, must be added their distinctive ethnic identity. The continued arrival of immigrants, extending into the early years of the eighteenth century, reinforced what were in any case strong cultural and institutional links with Scotland. Although the educated elite had by the end of the seventeenth century abandoned Lowland Scots for standard English, the dialect of the majority was still recognizably Scottish. Presbyterian ministers were almost invariably educated at Scottish universities, and there was regular consultation on ecclesiastical matters between the Synod of Ulster and the Church of Scotland. Well into the eighteenth century Ulster students attending Scottish universities registered themselves as 'Scotus Hiberniae'. During the period of Anglo-Scottish tension that preceded the negotiation of the union of 1707 there was anxious speculation about which side the Ulster Presbyterians would take if matters came to a military confrontation. The crisis passed, and the Anglo-Scottish union of 1707 put an end to such speculation for the future. But for a few anxious months it had been clear that Sir Charles Porter's vision of a possible ethnic conflict between Scots and English was not as far fetched as, in the long sweep of history, might appear.

6

Metropolitan Province

THE CASE OF IRELAND

The compromise of 1695 had resolved the original sole right debate to the satisfaction of most. But issues touching on the status of the Irish parliament had still to be handled delicately. In 1697 and again in 1698 the lords justices left the drafting of money bills entirely to the Commons (the second time incurring criticism from London, on the grounds that in a new as opposed to an adjourned parliament the king's rights should have been reaffirmed by a token bill). The government was also concerned to uphold the superior authority of the English parliament. When the Irish Commons in 1697 sent the English privy council heads of a bill copying an English act to protect the king's person and government, the council made minor amendments in order to rule out the implied suggestion that English acts needed to be formally adopted in order to have force in Ireland. By this time, however, such procedural concerns were about to be overshadowed by a much more politically charged debate about the place of the Irish kingdom in the post-Revolution order.

The issues that were to be at stake had their first airing in 1697, when the Irish House of Lords gave judgement in favour of Bishop William King of Derry. King had sued the Irish Society, the corporate proprietor of the Londonderry plantation, over lands and fishing rights which he claimed belonged properly to his diocese. The Irish Society appealed successfully to the English House of Lords. Patrick Darcy, in 1641, had accepted that the English parliament, though having no power to pass laws binding on Ireland, should constitute the final court of appeal in legal cases. By the 1690s, however, the Irish Lords were no longer willing to accept such a subordinate status. They reiterated their support for King, and ordered the arrest of those who sought to implement the English judgement. Eventually, under pressure from the Irish administration, King accepted his defeat. But a few years later, in 1704, the Irish Lords were to seize the opportunity presented by another lawsuit, involving the earl of Meath, to pass resolutions reaffirming their claim to be the final court of appeal for all Irish cases.

At the same time that the bishop of Derry's case was proceeding through the Irish courts, a campaign was developing in England for action to restrict the

Irish wool trade. Concern that Ireland should not interfere with England's most important export had existed as far back as Wentworth's deputyship.[1] In the 1690s, however, a rapid rise in Irish exports, including not just the traditional low-value friezes but the finer 'new draperies', coincided with a recession in the English trade. In January 1698 a bill to ban Irish exports appeared in the English Commons. Discriminatory action against Irish products was not new. Both the cattle acts and navigation acts of the 1660s, however, had been solely concerned with what could and could not be imported into England, shipped from English colonies, or carried on English ships. The proposed woollen act, by contrast, prohibited the export of Irish wool or woollen cloth to any destination whatever. It thus represented a direct assertion of English legislative supremacy: an act of the London parliament that would have to be enforced by officials operating in Irish ports.

The threat of the woollen act produced the first major political text from post-Revolution Ireland. *The Case of Ireland being Bound by English Acts of Parliament Stated*, published in April 1698 by William Molyneux, founder of the Dublin Philosophical Society and now MP for Trinity College, Dublin, was set out in the form of a case presented for the consideration of the English parliament. Its starting point was the proposition that Ireland was not a conquered country. Instead the Irish chiefs of the late twelfth century had accepted Henry II as their lord. In return Henry had granted them the same liberties, including the right to be governed by laws made in their own parliament, that were enjoyed by the people of England. From this Molyneux went on to provide an exhaustive account of the different occasions on which Ireland's right to legislate for itself had been acknowledged, emphasizing in particular the creation of a separate lordship of Ireland for Henry II's son John, the *Modus tenendi parliamenta* recently published by Dopping, and the 'Magna Carta' granted to Ireland by Henry III in 1216. He also offered convoluted explanations why a variety of English statutes that had undeniably been taken as binding in Ireland did not in fact imply a general legislative supremacy.[2] This part of Molyneux's argument, with its laborious citation of precedents and documents, was heavily indebted to the work of predecessors. In particular he drew on the 'Disquisition' that his father-in-law, Sir William Domville, had written for the Irish convention in 1660, as well as on the earlier declaration of the rights of

---

[1] Above, Ch. 2. For the 1698–9 debate see Patrick Kelly, 'The Irish Woollen Export Prohibition Act of 1699: Kearney Revisited', *IESH* 7 (1980), 22–44.

[2] For Molyneux's use of overlapping and mutually incompatible arguments, see S. J. Connolly (ed.), *Political Ideas in Eighteenth-Century Ireland* (Dublin, 2000), 135–7. For other assessments of *The Case* see in particular Jacqueline Hill, 'Ireland without Union: Molyneux and his Legacy', in John Robertson (ed.), *A Union for Empire: Political Thought and the British Union of 1707* (Cambridge, 1995), 271–94; Patrick Kelly, 'Recasting a Tradition: William Molyneux and the Sources of *The Case of Ireland . . . Stated*', in Jane Ohlmeyer (ed.), *Political Thought in Seventeenth-Century Ireland* (Cambridge, 2000), 83–106.

the Irish parliament, probably composed by Sir Richard Bolton, that had been circulated in 1644.[3]

The most striking feature of Molyneux's argument is, at first sight, his willingness to base the claims to political autonomy of the New English elite on rights granted five centuries earlier to the Gaelic lords whose descendants they had only recently finished dispossessing. At one level this was a dramatic acknowledgement of the dilemma of the colonist turned patriot. At another, it was no more than a rhetorical fiction. For Molyneux, having set out the case that Gaelic Ireland had not been conquered, went on to suggest a series of further lines of argument, each undermining the one that had gone before: that even if a conquest had taken place, it conferred no rights unless carried out in a just cause, that any rights it did confer could not affect those who had not positively resisted the conquest, and that any rights that did in fact affect the population as a whole could bind only those alive at the time of the conquest, not their posterity. The culmination of this series of rhetorical retreats was a final claim, that a conquest, however all embracing, would in any case have given Henry II power only over the Gaelic inhabitants.

Now 'tis manifest that the great body of the present people of Ireland are the progeny of the English and Britains, that from time to time have come over into this kingdom; and there remains but a mere handful of the ancient Irish at this day, I may say, not one in a thousand.[4]

This remarkable claim, like much else in Molyneux's text, was not new. The Remonstrance drawn up by the Irish parliament in November 1640 had already stated that the 'loyal and dutiful people of this land of Ireland, [are] now for the most part derived from the British ancestor'.[5] In neither case was any evidence presented for such a sweeping assertion, and it is open to question whether the authors, in either case, really believed it. Instead the passage highlights the legalistic and impersonal nature of Molyneux's remarks. What he offered was not a statement of faith or a declaration of identity, but the courtroom logic of an advocate free to advance a series of incompatible, even contradictory, arguments on the basis that if any one could be sustained his case was proved.

If the historical sections of Molyneux's *Case* had less significant implications than might at first appear, however, other parts of his argument went beyond the flat recitation of past cases and the pronouncements of legal authorities to appeal to broader principles, of more recent origin. Having argued at some length

---

[3] For Molyneux's sources see in particular Kelly, 'Recasting a Tradition'. For the 1644 declaration, see above Ch. 3 n. 20.

[4] William Molyneux, *The Case of Ireland Stated*, ed. J. G. Simms (Dublin, 1973), 35.

[5] *The Humble and Just Remonstrance of the Knights, Citizens, and Burgesses, in Parliament Assembled in Ireland* (London?, 1641), 1.

that there was no valid precedent for English legislation binding on Ireland, he signalled yet another sudden shift in the basis of his argument:

And I shall yet go a little further, and venture to assert, that the right of being subject only to such laws to which men give their own consent, is so inherent to all mankind, and founded on such immutable laws of nature and reason, that 'tis not to be aliened, or given up, by any body of men whatsoever. For the end of all government and laws being the public good of the commonwealth, in the peace, tranquillity and ease of every member therein, whatsoever act is contrary to this end, is in itself void, and of no effect.

Later he offered a close, though unacknowledged, paraphrase of a passage from Locke setting out the thesis that all government rested on an original compact, whereby men surrendered the freedom they enjoyed in the state of nature in order to enjoy the benefits of civil society. He also appealed, in his conclusion, to the notion of a 'Gothic constitution', an ancient heritage of liberty now extinguished in most parts of Europe through the rise of absolutism, but still surviving in a few corners, most notably Holland and the English dominions.[6] This was a more conservative idea than Locke's claim regarding an original compact, and the appearance of the two side by side is further evidence of Molyneux's ideological promiscuity. Yet both had figured prominently in the English debate over the removal of James II, and their citation is further evidence of the way in which the rhetoric of the Revolution of 1688 had expanded Irish political aspirations.

Molyneux's willingness to combine the detailed exposition of Ireland's constitutional rights with broader affirmations of political principle explains the enduring appeal of his work. His *Case* was to become a staple of Irish constitutional argument, repeatedly reprinted at times of further controversy. Yet this posthumous enthusiasm must be contrasted with the silence, quite possibly an embarrassed one, with which his Irish Protestant contemporaries greeted its initial publication. With action against the Irish woollen trade threatened but not yet enacted, the preferred response of most was to conciliate not to challenge. Sir Francis Brewster, one-time champion of the sole right, also published a pamphlet against the proposed English act. His argument, however, was based not on constitutional entitlements but on a claim that the destruction of the Irish woollen industry would not damage the Irish or Scots but only the English inhabitants, 'flesh of their flesh, and bone of their bone'. A second author likewise appealed to shared ancestry and interest. Irish Protestants were 'Englishmen sent over to conquer Ireland, your countrymen, your brothers, your sons, your relations'.[7] The Irish executive, meanwhile, encouraged proposals to promote

6 Molyneux, *The Case of Ireland Stated*, 93, 116–17, 132.

7 [Francis Brewster], *A Discourse Concerning Ireland and the Different Interests Thereof* (London, 1698), 50; *Some Thoughts on the Bill Depending before the Right Honourable the House of Lords for Prohibiting the Exportation of the Woollen Manufactures of Ireland* (London, 1698), 17–18. *Some Thoughts* is generally attributed to Sir Richard Cox, but Patrick Kelly has suggested that the author was in fact Francis Annesley. See Kelly, 'Irish Woollen Export Prohibition Act', 35 n. 47.

the spinning and weaving of linen, of limited significance in England, as an alternative to wool. But it was too late. The English parliamentary session ended with resolutions calling on the government to check both the growth of the Irish wool trade and the pretensions of the Irish parliament. The following year the ministry, under attack on a range of other fronts, reluctantly accepted a bill prohibiting the export from Ireland of either raw wool or woollen cloth to any destination other than England, where the finer Irish cloths were already subject to a prohibitive import duty.

A further reason for not seeing Molyneux's defence of Ireland's right to legislative independence as representing the aspirations of most Protestants is provided by the interest shown, at much the same time, in a very different solution to the problem of Ireland's constitutional status, the supersession of the Irish parliament by a legislative union with England. Indeed Molyneux himself observed at one point that an alternative means of allowing the Irish to live under laws of their own making would be by giving them representation in the parliament of England, something they would willingly accept, but a 'happiness' they could hardly hope for. Other pamphlets published during the 1690s and 1700s, many of them in response to the negotiation of the Anglo-Scottish union of 1707, argued the case in more detail. The best known, in 1704, by the County Down gentleman Henry Maxwell, took as its starting point the principles of classical republicanism. To hold Ireland as a conquered country would require a large standing army. The threat this would constitute to the liberties of England had already been seen under Charles I and James II. Deliberately to keep it poor would pose similar dangers. A union, on the other hand, would make Ireland 'into the nature of a county of England'. The result would be the equivalent of a happy marriage, 'where though the husband, as head, really governs, yet the wife does not seem to obey'.[8] Other authors, perhaps wisely, avoided dubious conjugal metaphors and concentrated instead on the tangible economic benefits that incorporation into a broader British state was expected to bring. Meanwhile the two houses of the Irish parliament, in 1703–4, in 1707, and again in 1709, passed resolutions declaring support for the principle of a union.

The apparent flowering of unionist sentiment in the Ireland of William III and Anne has attracted considerable attention. The most recent study, however, suggests that professions of enthusiasm for incorporation into a unitary British state should not be taken too literally.[9] Few of the authors showed much

---

[8] *An Essay upon an Union of Ireland and England* (Dublin, 1704), 11–12, 35. David Hayton, 'Ideas of Union in Anglo-Irish Political Discourse 1691–1720: Meaning and Use', in D. G. Boyce, Robert Eccleshall, and Vincent Geoghegan (eds.), *Political Discourse in Seventeenth and Eighteenth-Century Ireland* (Basingstoke, 2001), 151, questions Maxwell's authorship of the Essay, but has since established that this can in fact be documented. See idem, 'Henry Maxwell, MP, Author of *An Essay upon an Union of Ireland with England* (1703)', *ECI* 22 (2007), 28–63.

[9] Hayton, 'Ideas of Union'. For earlier discussion of the idea of union see in particular James Kelly, 'The Origins of the Act of Union: An Examination of Unionist Opinion in Britain and

appetite for getting to grips with the practicalities either of how Ireland would be represented in a united parliament or of how clashes of commercial or other interest would be resolved. Their failure to do so suggests that their purpose in raising the issue at all was primarily rhetorical: by expressing a longing for union, authors aimed either to highlight the evils of Ireland's current circumstances, or to counter charges that Irish Protestants were disloyal to England. (This is almost certainly the case, for example, with Molyneux's throwaway remark, although the relevant sentence was nevertheless quietly dropped when his work was reprinted as a text for the much more assertive patriotism of 1782.) The three parliamentary resolutions, in 1703–4, 1707, and 1709, seem likewise to have been tactical in character, the first offered as a theoretical alternative to the remedying of various constitutional grievances, the other two tied up with complex infighting relating to the repeal of the sacramental test. What is significant, however, is that expressions of support for a union, rhetorical or not, were uncontentious. The concern, as Molyneux's pamphlet made clear, was with ensuring that Irish Protestants had a say in the laws by which they were governed. Whether this was achieved within the framework of a genuinely autonomous Ireland, or a wider British union, seems at this stage to have made little difference. Later generations, on the other hand, were to see things very differently.

THE RAGE OF PARTY

The controversies of the 1690s, over the sole right and more particularly over the Treaty of Limerick, created deep divisions within the Irish parliament. These continued even after the compromise money bill of 1695, as Porter's opponents tried unsuccessfully to have him impeached, alleging corruption and a treasonable partiality towards Catholics. It was not yet a clear-cut party conflict. The leading figures on both sides were office holders, rather than constituting anything resembling a government and opposition. Contemporaries, in fact, reported events in terms suggesting a personalized conflict, referring to 'my Lord Capel's friends' on the one hand, and the lord chancellor's party on the other. And indeed the conflict did not survive the removal of the two principals, with the death of Capel in May 1696 and of Porter in December; by the time parliament met again in 1697, politics was no longer organized round two clearly defined rival interests. At the same time it would be wrong to see the divisions of 1692 and 1695 wholly in terms of a factional rivalry. When, a decade later, Irish politics did become a contest between rival parties, the allegiance of those MPs whose experience stretched back to the 1690s was to show a definite continuity.

Ireland, 1650–1800', *IHS* 25 (1986–7), 236–63; Jim Smyth, ' "No Remedy More Proper": Anglo-Irish Unionism before 1707', in Brendan Bradshaw and Peter Roberts (eds.), *British Consciousness and Identity: The Making of Britain 1533–1707* (Cambridge, 1998).

In seven cases out of every ten, those who had supported Porter's impeachment became Whigs, while those who had opposed it became Tories. In this sense the politics of the 1690s prefigured what was to be no mere competition for place and profit, but an intense ideological struggle.

The labels Whig and Tory went back to the crisis of 1678–82, when Whigs had sought the exclusion from the throne of James, duke of York, while Tories had upheld the principle of hereditary monarchy. The first steps towards their importation into Ireland came with the accession in March 1702 of James II's younger daughter Anne, and the appointment in accordance with her conservative and Anglican principles of a predominantly Tory ministry. As lord lieutenant of Ireland the ministry chose the second duke of Ormond, grandson of Charles II's most noted Irish servant. Ormond initially held back from reconstructing the Irish executive along partisan lines. In particular he retained Alan Brodrick, the Irish parliamentarian most closely identified with the English Whigs, as solicitor general and accepted his election as speaker of the Commons. Brodrick, however, did not reciprocate, but instead launched a sustained campaign of opposition to the new viceroy. Returning to the tactics of 1692, he first sought to persuade the Commons to vote taxes for one year rather than the two requested by Ormond. Having failed he then tried to sabotage the returned money bill by objecting to some minor amendments made by the English privy council. As soon as the parliament was over Ormond dismissed Brodrick and others identified with the Whig opposition in England, and replaced them with men identified as Tories. His successor, the earl of Pembroke, appointed in 1707 by a ministry that itself contained both Whigs and moderate Tories, made a last attempt at non-party government, by admitting some Irish Whigs to office beside men kept on from Ormond's administration. But it was too late. The new Whig office holders remained dissatisfied because they did not have complete control, while Tories resented the dismissals of some of their number to make way for the new appointments.[10]

The extension to Ireland of party politics was not always openly acknowledged by those most closely involved. Identification with a party still had implications of devotion to a faction rather than to the public interest. Whigs often referred to themselves as 'honest men'. Tories, in the period after Ormond's first lieutenancy, were 'his Grace's friends', on other occasions 'the church party'. Yet the primacy of party divisions was inescapable. There was no sign, in a society where political legitimacy rested on property not numbers, and where single patrons controlled whole boroughs, of the constituency organizations that were to develop in the era of mass politics.[11] But candidates, though coming forward on their own

---

[10] The fullest account of Whig and Tory politics in early eighteenth-century Ireland is D. W. Hayton, *Ruling Ireland 1685–1742: Politics, Politicians and Parties 1685–1742* (Woodbridge, 2004). See also Connolly, *Religion, Law and Power*, 74–84.

[11] For the workings of electoral politics, see below, Ch. 8.

initiative or through the outcome of local negotiations, were clearly identified as Whigs or Tories. Those of the electorate who enjoyed a degree of autonomy cast their votes according to party, and loyalties were in some cases strong enough to divide families or disrupt relations between patrons and clients. Parliamentary and government business, likewise, was now conducted on clear party lines. By the end of 1708, with the Whigs now dominant in the English ministry, the earl of Wharton, sent to replace Pembroke, had created an executive dominated by the Brodricks and their allies, so that the parliamentary session of 1709 saw a straightforward contest between a Whig party of government and a Tory opposition.

The extension to Ireland of the politics of Whig and Tory, like the political divisions of the 1690s, must be understood in terms of a combination of practical politics and ideology. The dependence of the Irish executive on the English ministry, on the one hand, and Ireland's potential as a source of patronage on the other, made it impossible for politicians in either kingdom to remain wholly indifferent to events on the other side of the Irish Sea. In addition, it has been suggested, the success of Alan and Thomas Brodrick in placing themselves at the head of a succession of agitations, combined with their flexibility when the prospect of office required a sacrifice of opposition principles, were of particular importance both in providing a centre round which an Irish Whig interest could form and, arguably, in provoking others to rally to its Tory rival.[12] Neither of these circumstances, however, can account for the depth and passion of the conflicts that tore Protestant Ireland almost apart in the first and second decades of the eighteenth century. For that it is also necessary to take account of two great political questions, each of which came for a time to seem to those involved central to their interests, and indeed to their very survival.

The first of these was religion. English Whigs emphasized the need for unity among Protestants of all denominations in the face of the threat from popery at home and abroad. Tories, by contrast, saw dissent as also presenting a serious threat to both religious and social order. The danger from Catholicism was greater and more immediate in Ireland, and the argument for Protestant unity correspondingly stronger. But the demographic balance within Protestantism was also wholly different: where dissenters made up less than 10 per cent of the population of England, the Presbyterians of Ulster accounted for half or more of the Protestant population of Ireland. Irish Whigs, in consequence, while strongly anti-Catholic, were noticeably less enthusiastic than their English counterparts about the admission of dissenters to full political rights. However, they were concerned to protect them from undue harassment, and in particular to oppose anything that might discourage or disable them from rallying to the defence of the kingdom in a new emergency. Irish Tories, on the other

---

[12] Hayton, *Ruling Ireland*, ch. 2. For a more sympathetic view of Alan Brodrick's attempts to reconcile principle and pragmatism see Connolly, *Religion, Law and Power*, 89–91.

hand, resolutely upheld the privileged position of the Church of Ireland and the exclusion of dissenters from office by the sacramental test. Tories were also less likely than Whigs to support the more extreme measures against Catholics proposed from time to time, or to give credence to wild tales of popish or Jacobite conspiracy. This in turn meant that they tended to receive the electoral support of those Catholics still able to vote, and that the handful of converts from Catholicism who sat in the parliaments of the period were Tories rather than Whigs. Irish Tories as a body were not pro-Catholic, any more than Irish Whigs were wholeheartedly pro-dissenter. But, in the increasingly fevered atmosphere of the years before 1714, Tory calls of 'the church in danger' competed with Whig charges that the Protestant interest was being dangerously—perhaps even deliberately—neglected.

The second issue that in the years after 1700 increasingly divided Irish Protestants into contending parties concerned divergent interpretations of the events of 1688–9. The detailed arguments were complex, and there were marked differences in emphasis on both sides of the party divide. But in broad terms Whigs saw the overthrow of James II as the legitimate assertion of the principle that kings ruled within the law and could in the last resort be removed, while Tories shrank from any such endorsement of a general right to challenge established authority. In the immediate aftermath of the Revolution these differences had been smoothed over in the interests of a united front against the deposed monarch and his French and Irish Catholic supporters. In the years before 1714, however, consensus rapidly broke down. Tory propagandists presented their Whig opponents as violent republicans, drinking toasts to the memory of Oliver Cromwell and teaching that the queen ruled only with the consent of her subjects. Whigs for their part charged that Tories were covertly scheming to bring about the return of the exiled Stuarts.

Both sets of allegations were wildly exaggerated. For Irish Protestants the overthrow of James II had meant liberation from the reality, rather than the mere prospect, of Catholic tyranny, and few went so far as to reject the occasion of their deliverance. Irish Toryism thus lacked the element of Jacobitism found within its English equivalent. Few Irish Whigs, heirs to a long tradition in which strong central government in England had been seen as central to the survival of the Protestant minority in Ireland, embraced radical theories regarding the contractual nature of monarchy or the subject's right of resistance. When a Dublin clergyman preaching at the annual commemoration in 1709 of the execution of Charles I seemed to suggest that the act had been a legitimate blow against tyranny, Whigs as well as Tories reacted with outrage. '. . . though they espouse the Revolution', the archbishop of Dublin explained, 'they heartily abhor [sixteen] forty-one.'[13] But there were nevertheless real points at issue. For

---

[13] S. J. Connolly, 'The Church of Ireland and the Royal Martyr: Regicide and Revolution in Anglican Political Thought *c.*1660–*c.*1745', *Journal of Ecclesiastical History*, 54 (2003), 492–5.

Tories the difficulty was that Whig talk of 'Revolution principles' seemed to open the door to a world in which any discontented group could claim the right to overthrow the government. A County Antrim clergyman, writing in 1714, insisted on his support for 'that happy Revolution', but strongly attacked 'these republican principles . . . foisted in under the cover of that single unavoidable act'.

When a man's house has been on fire, the people have pulled down the next neighbours, and have used irregular and uncommon methods to prevent a general destruction. But it does not from thence follow that my neighbour's house must be blown up every time the mob cries fire.

In the same way the Tory-dominated House of Lords, in 1711, attacked a Commons resolution referring to 'Revolution principles': 'it is the known nature of principles to be as well the rule and guide of future as of past actions.'[14] For Whigs the problem was that such objections raised the question of how far Tories could be trusted to uphold the Revolution in the future. They might plead their obedience to the de facto authority of William and Mary or Anne. But if they were not willing to acknowledge unambiguously that the overthrow of James II had been a legitimate defence of civil and religious liberties, what would happen the next time the claims of hereditary monarchy had to be weighed against the preservation of Protestantism? Nor was this a purely theoretical question. The death in 1700 of Princess Anne's only living child made it unavoidable that at the end of her reign the rights of the Catholic descendants of the exiled James would indeed have to be measured against those of an alternative Protestant claimant.

Party conflict reached its peak in the period after August 1710, when a Tory ministry once again came to power in England and the duke of Ormond returned to Dublin as lord lieutenant. Harassment of dissenting ministers and their congregations resumed. The new lord chancellor, Sir Constantine Phipps, embarked on a bitter struggle to impose a Tory lord mayor on the Whig corporation of Dublin. Whigs complained that the Protestant milita was being deliberately run down, and of the favour supposedly shown to crypto-Catholic converts. The government prosecuted several Whigs for allegedly seditious speeches, while failing to take action against the printer of an overtly Jacobite work. Elections for a new parliament in November 1713 were marked with violence, including a riot in Dublin in which troops shot dead a Tory protester. When parliament met the Whig majority voted taxes for a period of only three months. Attempts by the duke of Shrewsbury, who had replaced Ormond, to negotiate a compromise met with no success.

By this time it was clear that the queen would not live much longer, and that the long-awaited succession crisis was at hand. The leaders of the Tory ministry

---

[14] John Winder, *The Mischief of Schism and Faction to Church and State* (Dublin, 1714), 8, 13–14; *Journals of the House of Lords* (Dublin, 1780), ii. 414–15. For a fuller account see Connolly, *Political Ideas in Eighteenth-Century Ireland*, 27–56.

had abandoned their hopes of bringing in James Stuart, the son whose birth in 1688 had brought about his father's downfall, and were instead resigned to the accession of George, elector of Hanover, the nearest Protestant successor. Their proceedings in Ireland were part of a last-ditch strategy of entrenching Tory power at every level of government in the hope of ensuring their survival under the new king. Whigs, however, lived in dread of a Jacobite coup. Reports that agents of the Pretender were openly recruiting large numbers for the Irish regiments in France, with the inevitable allegations that the ministry was conniving at their efforts, added to the atmosphere of tension. Archbishop King of Dublin, who had already lived through one episode of Jacobite rule, reported from Dublin in June 1714 on an atmosphere of imminent crisis. 'Men's hearts melt for fear, and many are at their wit's end what course to take.'[15]

In the event the return to the dark days of Tyrconnell's ascendancy never came. When Queen Anne died on 1 August 1714 the new George I took her place unobstructed. By the time Jacobites in England and Scotland rose in arms the following year, a Whig administration was firmly in place to crush them. But those few fraught years nevertheless had a long-term impact. In 1736 the earl of Orrery, a man of self-consciously refined sensibilities and of at least some Jacobite leanings, complained of the 'bacchanalian loyalty' that prevailed in upper-class Protestant circles. 'The right jolly glorious memory Hibernian' was 'a yahoo that toasts the glorious and immortal memory of King William in a bumper without any other joy in the Revolution than that it has given him a pretence to drink so many more daily quarts of wine'.[16] The allegation of alcoholic self-indulgence no doubt had some justification. But an obsessive habit of challenging assembled company openly to affirm their commitment to the Revolution can also be seen as a legacy from a time when Irish Whigs had for a few years genuinely believed that their world was in danger of being overthrown, not by the conspiracies of the Catholics and their European allies, but through betrayal by their fellow Protestants.

A DEPENDENT KINGDOM

The death of Queen Anne marked the sudden end of the first age of party. In Ireland, as in England, the Tories, tarnished by their perceived unsoundness in defence of the Protestant succession, faced a ruthless onslaught from their triumphant Whig rivals. Already over the previous decade intensifying party conflict had led to a politicization of public office, with a widening circle of

[15] King to Samuel Molyneux, 17 June 1714 (TCD MS 750/4/1, 305). For a fuller account see D. W. Hayton, 'The Crisis in Ireland and the Disintegration of Queen Anne's Last Ministry', in *Ruling Ireland*, 159–85.
[16] *The Orrery Papers*, ed. Countess of Cork and Orrery (London, 1903), i. 157, ii. 39.

dismissals at each change of administration. But the purge of 1714–15 was unprecedented in its scope. The victorious Whigs, one observer reported, 'are resolved not one Tory shall be as much as a high constable'.[17] The new administration removed all but two of the ten judges, and at least seventy-two justices of the peace and governors or deputy governors of counties, as well as senior army commanders and a large number of other office holders great and small. Tory bishops could not be removed. However the creation of eleven new peers, along with appointments to three vacant sees, ensured an immediate Whig majority in the formerly Tory-dominated Lords, and future episcopal appointments and promotions were strictly reserved for Whig churchmen. In four former Tory strongholds, Kilkenny, Galway, Coleraine, and Youghal, parliament or the privy council imposed new Whig-dominated corporations. Meanwhile a series of prosecutions secured the imprisonment or exile of the proprietors of the main Tory newspapers.[18]

Faced with this onslaught the Irish Tory party crumbled. Although eighty-two men who had sat as Tories in one or more previous parliaments were returned in the general election of 1715, the active Tory grouping in the new Commons was reckoned in May 1716 to comprise only around thirty members. Within a few years rehabilitated former Tories were beginning to make their way back into office, although a party of some kind, opposed to successive ministries, continued to exist up to the late 1720s. This is in sharp contrast to England, where a significant Tory parliamentary grouping continued into the 1750s. One obvious explanation for the more rapid demise of the party in Ireland would be that any hint of ambivalence towards the exiled Stuarts was far more damaging there than in England. Irish Toryism was also badly hit by the defection of the second duke of Ormond. His direct electoral interest, except when he had the patronage attached to the lord lieutenancy, was modest, generally extending to half a dozen seats or less. But his family's prestige placed him at the head of an extensive following. His decision to escape possible impeachment by fleeing to the Pretender's court removed a leader and discredited his followers. Most important of all, perhaps, the strong hostility of most Irish Whigs to any major concessions to dissenters deprived Irish Tories of what was to remain the single most potent rallying cry of post-1714 English Toryism: the defence of the established church.

As party divisions lost their relevance the constitutional conflicts that had dominated the early and mid-1690s reappeared. 'Now the Tories are brought low', the English-born bishop of Kilmore wrote in 1717, 'I find the distinction

[17] *The Inchiquin Manuscripts*, ed. John Ainsworth (Dublin, 1961), 121.
[18] For general accounts of Irish politics after 1714 see R. E. Burns, *Irish Parliamentary Politics in the Eighteenth Century*, i: *1714–1730*, ii: *1730–60* (Washington, DC, 1989); Patrick McNally, *Parties, Patriots and Undertakers: Parliamentary Politics in Early Hanoverian Ireland* (Dublin, 1997); Hayton, *Ruling Ireland*, chs. 7–8.

between English and Irish grows more wide.'[19] The first major cause of dispute concerned what was essentially a re-emergence of the question of appellate jurisdiction raised twenty years earlier by the bishop of Derry's case. The former Tory MP Maurice Annesley had appealed to the English House of Lords against a judgement by the Irish house in favour of Mrs Hester Sherlock, with whom he was in dispute over his administration of her family's estate. The Irish Lords formally stated their claim to be the rightful court of last resort in appeals, and ordered the sheriff of County Kildare to put Mrs Sherlock in possession of the disputed lands. After the session had ended an Irish office holder, almost certainly acting on behalf of the administration, persuaded her to sell her interest. But this discreet attempt to defuse the dispute came too late. The three judges of the court of exchequer, acting on orders from England, fined the sheriff for not executing the judgement of the British Lords in favour of Annesley. When parliament met again in 1719 the Irish Lords responded by having the judges taken into custody for contempt, and drew up a representation asserting the equal status of the Irish and British parliaments.

Such a direct challenge was unlikely to go unanswered. At the beginning of 1720 the British House of Lords produced its response. What subsequently became known as the declaratory act, or (from the year of its enactment) as the Sixth of George I, was an uncompromising assertion of Irish constitutional subordination. An aggressive preamble, alleging that attempts had been made 'to shake off the subjection of Ireland' to the crown, was eventually dropped. But the act, given the royal assent in April, nevertheless declared explicitly that the kingdom of Ireland was 'subordinate and dependent upon the imperial crown of Great Britain'. It went on not only to confirm that the British Lords were the final court of appeal in Irish cases, but also to declare that the king, Lords, and Commons of Great Britain had full power, where they chose, to pass laws binding on the kingdom and people of Ireland. Short-term political calculations may have encouraged the ministry to allow this extension of the controversy, from the issue of appellate jurisdiction to the broader question of legislative supremacy. The call to squash Irish pretensions allowed them to rally support at Westminster at a time of internal divisions. In addition they may have anticipated using a British act to circumvent Irish resistance to the abolition there of the sacramental test, as a first step towards improving the condition of dissenters in both kingdoms. However, the link between the two issues had already been established at the time of the bishop of Derry's case, when the English attorney general had argued that the power of the English parliament to make laws for Ireland would be rendered meaningless if the final interpretation of those laws were left to an Irish court.[20] The publication in 1719 of a new edition of Molyneux's *Case* indicates that in Ireland too the two issues were seen as intimately connected.

[19] Timothy Godwin to—, 9 Oct. 1717 (PRO, SP 63/375/208).
[20] Burns, *Irish Parliamentary Politics*, i. 37.

The declaratory act caused outrage in Ireland. One English bishop wrote with bewilderment of the rage of 'our gentlemen (whose fathers or grandfathers were true-born English or Scotch)' against what he revealingly described as 'the independency bill'. Another maintained that 'all reasonings and common sense too on this head are really lost among them . . . All distinctions are laid aside but English and Irish.'[21] It was against this background that the man who was to become Molyneux's successor in the developing canon of patriot writing made his first appearance. Jonathan Swift, dean of St Patrick's cathedral in Dublin, was an unlikely champion of Irish national aspirations. In the last years of Queen Anne he had ridden high in England as a pamphleteer for the Tory ministry. In return he hoped for promotion to an English bishopric. The sharp change in the political wind after 1714 had banished him to the Dublin deanery that was all his patrons had been able to obtain for him before their fall from power. In 1729 he was still unreconciled to his exile, writing to one of his former patrons that he would 'die here in a rage, like a poisoned rat in a hole'.[22]

The same all-encompassing bitterness is evident in the anonymous pamphlet *A Proposal for the Universal Use of Irish Manufacture*, with which Swift now responded, in May 1720, to the declaratory act. Its account of Ireland's evils began with random gibes about the rapacity of landlords, and the interference in church affairs of the Whig-dominated Irish parliament. Its main purpose, however, was to call for a boycott of imported—in practice, English—fabrics in favour of locally manufactured goods. Nothing could please the king better, Swift mused, 'than to hear that his loyal subjects, of both sexes, in this kingdom, celebrated his birth-day (now approaching) universally clad in their own manufacture'. A few lines further on, however, sarcastic deference gave way to abuse, as Swift first quoted 'a pleasant observation' of the late archbishop of Tuam that a law should be passed to burn all things that came from England except her people and her coal, then added his own gloss: 'that, as to the former, I should not be sorry if they would stay at home, and, for the latter, I hope in a little time we shall have no occasion for them'.[23] When the government retaliated by prosecuting

---

[21] William Nicolson, bishop of Derry, to William Wake, archbishop of Canterbury, 3 Apr. 1720 (Dublin Municipal Library, Gilbert MSS, xxvii. 258); John Evans, bishop of Meath, to Wake, 23 Apr. 1720 (Christ Church Oxford, Wake MSS, xiii. 170). Evans was in fact Welsh, but consistently presented himself as spokesman for the English interest in Ireland.

[22] Swift to Bolingbroke, 21 Mar. 1729 (*Correspondence of Jonathan Swift*, ed. Harold Williams (Oxford, 1963–5), iii. 383). The literature on Swift is enormous. The standard biography is Irvin Ehrenpreis, *Swift: The Man, his Works and the Age* (London, 1962–83). The best general introduction to his political thought is James Downie, *Jonathan Swift: Political Writer* (London, 1984). For a sceptical view of his status as spokesman for Protestant Ireland as a whole, see S. J. Connolly, 'Swift and Protestant Ireland: Images and Reality', in Aileen Douglas, Patrick Kelly, and Ian Campbell Ross (eds.), *Locating Swift* (Dublin, 1998), 28–46.

[23] *A Proposal for the Universal Use of Irish Manufacture*, in Jonathan Swift, *Irish Tracts 1720–23 and Sermons*, ed. Louis Landa (Oxford, 1948), 16–17. The archbishop was presumably John Vesey, who had died in 1716. The hope of being able to do without the coal rested on plans to develop deposits in County Tyrone.

the printer of the pamphlet for seditious libel, a Dublin jury resisted sustained pressure from the judge to find him guilty, and the case was eventually dropped.

The controversy surrounding the declaratory act arose from a direct conflict of constitutional claims. A second dispute, commencing three years after the act became law, involved a more complex mixture of patriot sensitivities and practical economic concerns. There had been frequent complaints at the inconvenience, and the obstacles to commercial development, arising from the shortage of small-value coin. In 1722 George I approved a patent authorizing the issue of more than £100,000 in copper halfpennies and farthings for Ireland, which he granted to his mistress the duchess of Kendall. She cashed in her windfall by selling the patent to William Wood, a Staffordshire ironmaster who also had contracts to supply copper coins to both the Royal Mint and the American colonies. Wood's designs catered dutifully to Irish sensibilities: one side of his halfpenny bore the profile of George I, while on the other a slender female held a harp beside the legend 'Hibernia'. Modern research suggests that the metal content of the coin was well up to specification. However the idea quickly spread in Ireland that the kingdom was to be flooded with base coin, leading to a general collapse of trade. Faced with a mounting public outcry, and alienated by not having been consulted beforehand, the ministry's leading Irish allies withdrew their support. The revenue commissioners refused to accept the coin for official transactions, and were supported in their stand by the privy council. There were also demonstrations of popular hostility. A ship entering Cork harbour was surrounded by a flotilla of small craft and forced to sail away without landing a cargo of the coin, while crowds in Dublin burnt Wood in effigy.[24]

It was against this background that Swift consolidated his claim to be Ireland's leading patriot polemicist, with the publication during 1724–5 of six pamphlets written under the pseudonym of 'M.B.', supposedly an ordinary Dublin draper or dealer in cloth. The first three of the *Drapier's Letters* concentrated on the practical details of Wood's scheme. But the fourth in the series, published in October 1724, abandoned questions of metallurgy, and of Wood's supposed dishonesty, for a more wide-ranging polemic. Responding to what he claimed were accusations that opposition to the coin was a challenge to the royal prerogative, the work of papists and Jacobites, Swift offered an angry defence of the legitimacy of Irish resistance. He referred briefly to the case against England's legislative supremacy developed by 'the famous Mr Molineaux an English gentleman born here'. However he made no attempt to repeat or add to Molyneux's pedantic amassing of precedents and legal judgements. Instead his appeal was to natural rights. Government without the consent of the governed was 'the very definition of slavery'. Swift had to acknowledge that the recent

---

[24] The implications of the Wood's Halfpence affair for the management of Irish politics are considered in more detail below, pp. 230–3.

declaratory act had asserted that Ireland was a dependent kingdom. But this, a statute of the British parliament, had been an act of power, not right: '. . . eleven men well armed will certainly subdue one single man in his shirt.' In any case 'a depending kingdom is a modern term of art, unknown, as I have heard, to all ancient civilians and writers upon government'.

The letter *To the Whole People of Ireland* became the occasion for a second confrontation in the courts. Although Swift's responsibility for the letters was well known, the Irish privy council, under pressure from the lord lieutenant, went through the motions of offering a reward for the discovery of the author, and ordered the arrest of the printer, John Harding. Swift responded by publishing *Seasonable Advice to the Grand Jury*, warning that to find a true bill of indictment against Harding would in effect be to support Wood's patent. When the crown attempted to initiate a prosecution against the printer and author of this new piece, two successive grand juries refused to make the necessary presentment, despite heavy pressure from the judge. Their defiance, coming from bodies recognized as representing leading citizens, was an important blow to the government's prestige, and contributed to its decision to abandon the patent.

English ministers, and the more recent English arrivals in Ireland, reacted strongly to the constitutional disputes of the 1720s. John Evans, a Welshman translated to the bishopric of Meath in 1716, complained to the archbishop of Canterbury that 'words can't represent their rage and fury against every thing that is English'. He even went so far as to warn of the danger posed by the number of senior military commands held by what he offensively referred to as 'our dear joys'.[25] Sir Robert Walpole, echoing Viscount Sidney three decades earlier, observed bluntly that 'the Irish had a mind to be independent'.[26] In fact the behaviour of the Irish political elite does little to bear out such charges. The general response to the woollen act, despite the lead given by Molyneux's confrontational pamphlet, had been to seek a compromise. Opposition to Wood's patent, likewise, arose mainly from genuine if mistaken concerns about the economic implications. Swift's introduction of the broader issue of Ireland's constitutional status seemed to most an unnecessary provocation. In the case of the Church of Ireland there were undoubted tensions. The appointment of Evans to Meath, and of William Nicholson to Derry two years later, were resented as the bestowal on outsiders of two of the most attractive positions within the Irish ecclesiastical system. In addition these and other appointees of the English Whig ministry were willing to break ranks with their Irish-born colleagues and vote in favour of the legal rights of dissenters. For the most part, however, it seems to have been the newcomers themselves who extrapolated from these and other

[25] Evans to Wake, 18 Sept. 1719 (Wake MSS, xiii. 109).
[26] Sir Robert Walpole, quoted in D. W. Hayton, 'The Stanhope/Sunderland Ministry and the Repudiation of Irish Parliamentary Independence', *English Historical Review*, 113 (1998), 619.

specific disputes to infer an institutionalized opposition of 'Irish' and 'English' interests.[27]

The true priorities of the Irish elite were more clearly revealed in another political controversy of the period, the proposal to create a chartered bank similar to the Bank of England. In emphasizing the constitutional dangers of the scheme, opponents certainly noted Ireland's particular vulnerability as a dependent kingdom. The main arguments against the scheme, however, were the same as those used by critics of the financial revolution that King William's wars had brought to England: a belief that landed property, as the only sure source of social and political stability, should not be eclipsed by the rise of a moneyed interest based on paper fortunes, and that over-powerful central institutions could pave the way to absolutism. The debate, in other words, says more about the shared values of the Irish and English political elites than about national differences between them. It also illustrates the extent to which concern with the protection of specifically Irish interests overlapped with a broader commitment to the defence of civic virtue and the public interest against corruption and the abuse of power.[28]

Rather than reflecting the spontaneous birth among Irish Protestants of new aspirations to 'independence', the growing disharmony in relations between Ireland and England in the decades after the fall of James II can be understood as a by-product of the changes in the nature of government that followed the Revolution of 1688. The Confederate Catholics who had supported Charles I against his parliamentary enemies, and the Old Protestants who had sought to press the crown upon Oliver Cromwell, had both been aware that any major transfer of power from king to parliament within England could have damaging consequences for Ireland. After 1688 just such a transfer took place. One consequence became evident in the woollen act: the new centrality of parliament allowed an English pressure group, in this case the grazing and manufacturing interest of the south-west, to assert itself in ways with which an Irish rival could not hope to compete. The real change, however, was that after 1688 English control over Ireland no longer took the form of the subordination of both kingdoms to a shared monarch. Instead dependency came to mean, inescapably, subordination to whatever political grouping currently held power in London.

These implications of the events of 1688, however, become apparent only from the perspective of hindsight. The formal Revolution settlement had been a cautious business, playing down the intrusion on the principle of hereditary monarchy in the interests of maintaining national unity. Government was still, in theory, the king's government, and the ministers his servants. This made it possible for the more extreme defenders of Irish political autonomy to go on

---

[27] See in particular McNally, *Parties, Patriots and Undertakers*, 170–1.

[28] Michael Ryder, 'The Bank of Ireland, 1721: Land, Credit and Dependency', *Historical Journal*, 25 (1982), 557–82.

arguing the case that had been formulated by Molyneux in 1698: that Ireland's dependence was on the crown of Great Britain, and in no way subordinated it to that country's parliament. Swift, in the fourth *Drapier's Letter*, developed the point in a characteristic spirit of subversive mischief.

I M.B. Drapier . . . declare, next under God, I depend only on the king my sovereign, and on the laws of my own country. And I am so far from depending upon the people of England that, if they should ever rebel against my sovereign (which God forbid) I would be ready at the first command from his majesty to take arms against them, as some of my countrymen did against theirs at Preston. And if such a rebellion should prove so successful as to fix the Pretender on the throne of England, I would venture to transgress that statute so far, as to lose every drop of my blood to hinder him from being king of Ireland.[29]

The argument was both historically accurate and, even without the fantasy of the Irish making legitimate war on a rebellious England, politically satisfying. But it was nevertheless a political blind alley, depending as it did on a rigid distinction between crown and parliament that was already unrealistic in the 1720s, and was to become steadily more so in the decades that followed. The immediate consequences were limited. Few Irish Protestants shared Swift's taste for pushing an argument to its confrontational limit, and the two kingdoms were in any case unlikely to be wrenched apart by the power of ideas alone. But Irish self-delusion and English constitutional fiction had nevertheless combined to open up what was in the long term to prove a serious gap between constitutional rhetoric and reality.[30]

THE WHOLE PEOPLE OF IRELAND

In 1633, on the eve of the civil wars of mid-century, the priest Geoffrey Keating had produced a history of Ireland specifically intended to create a common past for Old English and Gaelic Irish Catholics, setting them apart from the Protestant New English whose intrusion menaced both groups. Half a century later, in the midst of a second revolution that was to complete the transformation of both Irish and British political systems and relationships, a member of that New English elite responded with a history of his own. Sir Richard Cox, born in County Cork in 1650 and the son of a Protestant royalist army officer, had moved to Bristol to escape Tyrconnell's Catholic regime. There, during

---

[29] Jonathan Swift, *The Draper's Letters and Other Works*, ed. Herbert Davis (Oxford, 1941), 62. For a detailed discussion of the Wood's Halfpence controversy, placing Swift's work in the context of other contemporary writings, see Sabine Baltes, *The Pamphlet Controversy about Wood's Halfpence (1722–25) and the Tradition of Irish Constitutional Nationalism* (Frankfurt, 2002). For the battle of Preston, see above, Ch. 3.

[30] Below, Ch. 10.

1689–90, he published the two volumes of *Hibernia Anglicana*, covering the period from the twelfth-century conquest to his own day. His approach was uncompromising. He dismissed Keating's exalted vision of the Gaelic past as 'an ill digested heap of very silly fictions'. In place of a traceable descent from the Mediterranean cradle of civilization, he suggested that the indigenous Irish had mainly come to the island via Britain, their language a jumble of elements from different tongues. The Irish rulers whose histories Keating had traced so carefully were not kings, but war chiefs comparable to those found among the Indians of Virginia. Cox admitted that Ireland had for a time been a centre of learning. But that had been through a temporary influx of refugees from Dark Age Europe. Once these were able to go back to their homelands, 'Ireland soon returned to its former ignorance'. It was rescued again from backwardness and anarchy only by the English intervention of the twelfth century. But that conquest had been incomplete, so that it was only in Cox's own day, with the extension of English authority over the whole country, that Ireland could be called truly civilized.

Cox's emphasis, as his title suggests, was on the opposition between Irish barbarity and English civility. Where the English colonists of the middle ages were concerned he followed earlier authors such as Spenser and Davies in noting their adoption of Irish manner and customs, 'so that this difference of nation was on the old English side designed to be buried in oblivion'. Later the Old English and native Irish had been drawn closer together by Catholicism, and by their shared interest in the recovery of estates confiscated as punishment for their repeated joint rebellions. Cox retained a lingering sense that their union was unnatural; if the Catholics should triumph the Irish would be sure to turn on their Old English allies 'upon the old indelible national antipathy'. But his overall conclusion was nevertheless stark:

that at this day we know no difference of nation but what is expressed by Papist and Protestant. If the most ancient natural Irishman be a Protestant, no man takes him for other than an English man. And if a cockney be a papist he is reckoned, in Ireland, as much an Irishman as if he was born on Slevelogher.

Sir Francis Brewster, writing in 1698, likewise explained that 'the Irish Papists . . . consist of Popish English families, as well as of the ancient natives of that kingdom, in which sense I desire to be understood all along, when I mention the Irish'.[31]

If the Catholic inhabitants of Ireland were 'the Irish', what were the Protestants? Their first instinct was to call themselves English (although for a time in the mid-1690s Whig spokesmen anxious to promote the idea of a Protestant solidarity including the Ulster Scots tried to popularize the term 'British').

---

[31] Richard Cox, *Hibernia Anglicana, or The History of Ireland, Part One* (London, 1689), 'Address to the Reader', not paginated; [Brewster], *Discourse Concerning Ireland*, 13.

However the need to be specific, and also the pressure towards different forms of collective political self-assertion, also imposed other usages. 'The people of Ireland', one critic of Porter's administration wrote in the early 1690s, 'think themselves treated like enemies, while the Irish with their spoils make themselves favourites to men of public employments.' A decade later, with a French invasion apparently imminent, the archbishop of Dublin reported in similar terms: 'the Irish according to their laudable custom are insolent and foolish', while 'the people of Ireland' demonstrated their zeal for the Revolution.[32] The indifference to what appears in retrospect a glaring lack of logic is revealing—all the more so because it looks forward to the better known contradiction embodied in the title of the Drapier's fourth and most celebrated letter. Swift addressed his text 'To the Whole People of Ireland'. Yet a central part of his argument was to reject official smears claiming that opposition to the new coins was the work of Catholics and Jacobites: '. . . it is the true English people of Ireland who refuse it, although we take it for granted that the Irish will do so too whenever they are asked.' In all three cases the assumption was the same. The people of Ireland, in the sense of those whose voices were entitled to be heard, were the Protestants of the kingdom, a minority, but possessed of the greater part of its commercial and landed wealth. 'The Irish', by contrast, were the Catholics, numerically strong but justly excluded from citizenship by their adherence to a religion dangerous to the state, as well as by their steadily diminishing share of the kingdom's real estate.

This unashamedly exclusive definition of 'the people of Ireland' is essential to an understanding of the nature of Irish Protestant patriotism as it developed in the first half of the eighteenth century. In an *ancien régime* Europe dominated by hierarchy and privilege, conflict characteristically arose from the defence of sectional and exclusive rights, rather than from notions of universal entitlement. Dutch 'patriots' sought to uphold the decentralized structures of the Dutch republic against the pretensions of the house of Orange. The *parlements* of provincial France defended tax exemptions and other local immunities against the intrusions of the central state. In the same way Molyneux, Swift, and others upheld the liberties of one particular community, Protestant Ireland, and its distinctive institutions. They saw no contradiction between this stance and their equal commitment to the complete exclusion from any share in those liberties of the Catholic majority.[33]

---

[32] Unsigned paper on the state of Ireland (PRONI T3222/1/10); King to bishop of Clogher, 20 Apr. 1708 (TCD MS 750/312, 205); King to Southwell, 13 Mar. 1708 (ibid. 194).

[33] The *ancien régime* context was first stressed in J. Th. Leersen, 'Anglo-Irish Patriotism in its European Context: Notes towards a Reassessment', *ECI* 3 (1988), 7–24. J. R. Hill has developed similar themes, summed up in the term 'corporatism': see her essay 'Corporatist Ideology and Practice in Ireland 1660–1800', in Connolly (ed.), *Political Ideas in Eighteenth-Century Ireland*, 64–82, and her major study of Dublin politics *From Patriots to Unionists: Dublin Civic Politics and Irish Protestant Patriotism 1660–1840* (Oxford, 1997).

Both Cox's *Hibernia Anglicana* and the Drapier's fourth letter can thus be read as classic creole texts. Both articulate the outlook of a dominant minority whose power was based on a process of conquest and colonization which they presented without apology as a liberation from barbarity and backwardness. Yet there is also, as with the writings of other colonial elites of the period, a distinct element of ambivalence.[34] The detailed nature of Cox's account, supported by extensive if often tendentious marshalling of documentary evidence, testifies to the felt need to provide the English of Ireland with a history of their homeland to which they could relate. The dismissal of Gaelic antiquity was balanced by clear indications of a pride of place. Ireland was 'reckoned among the principal islands in the world, and deserves to be esteemed so (whether you consider the situation of the country, the number and goodness of its harbours, the fruitfulness of the soil or the temperature of the climate)'. Nor did his strictures on native culture imply an inherent inferiority. On the contrary the Irish had in recent years managed their affairs with what Cox regarded as remarkable dexterity. Ten years later, arguing the case for a serious effort to convert the Irish natives to Protestantism, he paid tribute to their generosity, patience, and fidelity. 'And, in short, if it were not for the bad principles of their religion, they would be very good neighbours, good subjects and good men.'[35]

If Cox mixed the pride of the conqueror with clear signs of an identification with the conquered land, Swift gave expression to another classic creole attitude, a growing resentment at the failure of the metropolitan homeland to do justice to its colonial offspring, or even to acknowledge their common citizenship. The fourth *Drapier's Letter* combined its insistence on the English character of the Irish Protestants with complaints about the provincialism and ignorance of the people of England itself, who 'look upon us as a sort of savage Irish, whom our ancestors conquered several hundred years ago'. There was also a clear sense of injustice. 'The whole people of Ireland' had reduced the kingdom to obedience to England. For this service 'we have been rewarded with a worse climate, the privilege of being governed by laws to which we do not consent, a ruined trade, a house of peers without jurisdiction, almost an incapacity for all employments, and the dread of Wood's halfpence'. A similar awareness of English perceptions was evident in the comments a decade earlier of the New English Whig Alan Brodrick, who in 1712 explained why he had declined the offer of a seat in the

---

34 For a detailed comparison between Irish Protestant attitudes and those of the descendants of the conquistadors in Peru and Mexico see S. J. Connolly, 'Tupac Amaru and Captain Right: A Comparative Context for Eighteenth-Century Ireland', in David Dickson and Cormac Ó Gráda (eds.), *Refiguring Ireland* (Dublin, 2003), 94–111.

35 Cox, *Hibernia Anglicana*, 'Address to the Reader' (not paginated); [Cox], *An Essay for the Conversion of the Irish* (Dublin, 1698), 42. Cox's reputation as a cultural bigot depends partly on the often repeated claim that, as a judge, he jailed the Gaelic poet Hugh MacCurtin for having criticized *Hibernia Anglicana*. This charge, however, first appears in 1749, in the writings of Charles Lucas (see below), then engaged in a fierce political dispute with Cox's grandson, and is therefore best treated with some caution.

Westminster parliament: in a country where he was unknown, and a parliament with whose procedures he was not familiar, 'I shall be thought and perhaps find that I am (what of all things I would least choose to be) an Irishman'.[36] His words are a striking echo of the comments over a century earlier of the Pale nobleman Sir Christopher St Lawrence, who in 1598 had complained to the English privy council that 'when I am in England I should be esteemed an Irish man, and in Ireland an English man'.[37] In the early eighteenth century, just as the Old English completed their long decline into invisibility, the New English who had supplanted them were being forced to come to terms with the realization that they too were no longer who they had once thought they were.

GOOD WORDS, BURGUNDY, AND CLOSETING

The practical irrelevance after 1714 of Whig–Tory conflict raised new questions concerning the management of Irish politics. After a decade in which the task had devolved naturally on the leading figures in one of the two parties, it now became necessary to find other ways of identifying those who were to be entrusted with responsibility for steering government business through the biennial meetings of parliament. In practice the choice was between the two leading Irish Whigs. William Conolly was not, as legend later had it, the son of a County Donegal publican; both he and his father were men of sufficient substance to be included in a list of Protestant landowners attainted by James II's Irish parliament. But he was indeed a largely self-made man, who had converted a modest inheritance into what was reportedly the largest private fortune in the kingdom by skilful speculation in the turbulent post-revolutionary land market. By his death in 1729 he was reportedly worth an enormous £17,000 a year, and had confirmed the heights to which he had risen by the construction of what was to remain one of the most impressive of Ireland's great houses, Castletown in County Kildare. His ally, and later rival, Alan Brodrick, was from a wealthier background, in that his father had acquired substantial lands in Cork during the Cromwellian settlement. As a second son, however, he had largely to build his own fortune, from his earnings as a lawyer and, like Conolly, by seizing the opportunities offered by the post-war economic uncertainty and the market in forfeited lands. Both men had a substantial parliamentary following, Brodrick's being mainly in Munster and Conolly's in Ulster.

The immediate outcome of the Whig triumph of 1714 was what seemed at the time an appropriate division of the spoils. Brodrick, the leader of the Whig party in recent difficult times, became lord chancellor with the title of Baron

---

[36] Alan Brodrick to Thomas Brodrick, 1 Nov. 1712 (Surrey History Centre, Woking 1248/3, fo. 91).
[37] Connolly, *Contested Island*, 371–2.

Brodrick. Conolly, his most prominent associate, became speaker of the House of Commons and first commissioner of the revenue. But Brodrick proved to be a difficult partner in power. His dissatisfaction became clear as early as the parliamentary session of 1715, when his son St John joined with the Tories in a sustained attack on the public accounts. His recalcitrance was in part a matter of temperament, or even principle: earlier, in the 1690s under Sidney and again under Ormond, he had insisted that the fact of holding office did not compromise his independence, or bind him to a 'servile compliance' with the government of the day. But there was also a strong element of frustrated ambition. As his share of the fruits of victory, Brodrick had carried off the most prestigious prizes, a peerage and the lord chancellorship. But it was the speakership and control of the revenue, with its extensive patronage, that represented the real levers of power. His resentment at being eclipsed by Conolly as the government's chief manager was also sharpened by contempt for what he saw as his rival's lowly social origins.

In 1717 the appointment as lord lieutenant of the duke of Bolton, a distant relative by marriage, made Brodrick temporarily more cooperative. He was promoted in the peerage as Viscount Midleton, and for a time was assumed to be the government's chief manager. However Conolly prudently declined to be provoked into opposition, and Midleton was outraged when Bolton refused wholly to exclude him from favour. In particular he resented having to serve alongside the speaker as lord justice, on equal terms, during Bolton's absence. In 1719, possibly in retaliation, he refused, in his capacity as a member of the Westminster parliament, to support a peerage bill intended to consolidate the ministry's control of the British House of Lords. Soon after St John Brodrick, ostensibly against his father's wishes, played a leading part in blocking Bolton's attempt to repeal the Irish sacramental test. This failure, along with the quarrel over jurisdiction that provoked the declaratory act, led the ministry to consider a radical new departure: by reducing expenditure to the level of the hereditary revenue they would dispense, for a time at least, with the fractious Irish parliament. In addition they planned to remove Midleton.[38] In the end, however, ministers chose to avoid a confrontation of uncertain outcome. Midleton continued as lord chancellor, despite his renewed insistence that holding office brought with it no limitation on his freedom to speak and vote on issues of principle, and the duke of Grafton, who had replaced Bolton in June 1720, took up the familiar task of balancing his demands with those of Conolly.

It was in the end the furore over Wood's Halfpence that forced a resolution of the long-standing uncertainty over how Ireland was to be managed. As the depth of Irish opposition to the patent became clear, Sir Robert Walpole, by now the dominant figure in the English ministry, replaced Grafton, in April 1724, with

---

[38] Hayton, *Ruling Ireland*, 228–9. This, along with the same author's 'The Stanhope/Sunderland Ministry', is the fullest account of an exceptionally complex sequence of events.

John, Baron Carteret. The appointment was a political move, holding out the prospect either that Walpole's most able colleague would solve the Irish crisis or that his most threatening rival would damage himself by failing to do so. In the event Carteret did neither: he settled the issue by eventually persuading the king and the ministry that the patent had to be withdrawn, a decision finally confirmed in September 1725. Before then, however, the long stand-off between Conolly and Midleton had at last come to an end. Carteret's strategy had been to remain aloof from local factions. He had taken up residence in Ireland in September 1724, a full year before parliament was due to meet, in order to take personal charge of affairs, and had kept his distance from both men. Midleton, with whom Carteret had had links before his appointment, may have been more prone to perceive this studied neutrality as a rebuff. In addition, Carteret made clear that he considered the chancellor bound by his office to support the halfpence. Unwilling to do so, and probably believing that his dismissal was in any case only a matter of time, Midleton resigned in April 1725.

Midleton's resignation, and his subsequent move into opposition, ended a ten-year rivalry within the Whig establishment. At the same time it opened the way to a significant new departure in the management of Irish affairs. Thomas Lindsay, archbishop of Armagh, had died in July 1724. A highly partisan Tory in the reign of Anne, he had been politically marginalized since 1714. Instead the church's effective head had been William King, archbishop of Dublin. King, author of a celebrated defence of the Revolution of 1688, was untainted by Jacobitism. But his stand on the declaratory act and other issues had led ministers to regard him, in Grafton's phrase, as 'to a ridiculous extravagance national'.[39] Accordingly Lindsay's successor, announced in August 1724, had not been King but an Englishman, Hugh Boulter, bishop of Bristol. Now, in July 1725, the government chose as Midleton's successor an English lawyer, Richard West. When West died after only eighteen months in office, his replacement was another Englishman, Thomas Wyndham. There was not in fact to be another Irish-born chancellor until 1798, or an Irish-born archbishop of Armagh until 1822.

These two appointments were of particular importance because from this point on an English primate and an English lord chancellor were to make up two of the three lords justices who administered the kingdom during the substantial periods, generally extending to most of the interval between biennial meetings of parliament, during which the lord lieutenant was not resident. But Boulter, writing to a member of the English ministry shortly after his arrival, referred back to their earlier discussions of 'the necessity of filling the great posts here with English'. And indeed several other legal appointments around the same time

[39] Grafton to Walpole, 19 Dec. 1723 (W. Coxe, *Memoirs of the Life and Administration of Sir Robert Walpole, Earl of Orford* (London, 1798), ii. 357).

went likewise to candidates from England, as part of what was clearly a wider strategy of strengthening the English interest in Ireland.[40]

The new policy was accompanied by much aggressive language, on both sides of the Irish Sea, regarding the need to contain the supposed aspirations of the Irish. Boulter, early in 1727, warned in the most sweeping terms that no 'native of this country' could be considered for the archbishopric of Dublin: 'whatever his behaviour has been or his promises may be, when he is once in that station, he will put himself at the head of the Irish interest, in the church at least.'[41] But rhetoric had to be reconciled with political reality. Carteret learned this quickly, when he tried even after Midleton's resignation to keep Conolly at arm's length. The parliamentary session of autumn 1725 saw a self-styled country party headed by St John Brodrick join the Tories in a vigorous attack on irregularities in the government finances. By the end of the year Carteret had reached an accommodation with Conolly, and was openly acknowledging him as the Castle's chosen manager. London ministers, and Boulter, were slower to appreciate the need for compromise, and for some time continued on occasion to override Carteret and Conolly's recommendations regarding appointments in order to continue their strategy of strengthening 'the English interest'. Yet when Conolly himself died in October 1729, after suffering a stroke on the floor of the Commons, Boulter and Wyndham joined with Carteret in agreeing that 'it will be for his majesty's service that a native succeed him' as commissioner of the revenue.[42] In the event Sir Ralph Gore, the Donegal MP who had been Conolly's long-standing second in command, preferred to retain his existing lucrative position as chancellor of the exchequer. But in other respects he succeeded his patron as the acknowledged manager of government business. Control of the revenue, meanwhile, went to Marmaduke Coghill, another of Conolly's followers, who now became Gore's second in command.

Gore's death in 1733 introduced what was to be the last phase in the emergence of a durable, if never wholly trouble-free, system of parliamentary management. Midleton had died in 1728, and his son and political heir St John had predeceased him by six months. Leadership of their Munster-based grouping in the Commons had passed to Henry Boyle, from a lesser branch of the great dynasty established over a century earlier by the earl of Cork, and Boyle now emerged as the most credible of those willing to take over the role of parliamentary manager. He was duly elected speaker in October. The lord lieutenant, the duke of Dorset, who had succeeded Carteret in 1730, was initially distrustful, because of Boyle's recent history of opposition. Boyle himself was reluctant to shed his claims to political independence. He also refused to support Dorset's attempt during that

[40] Boulter to Newcastle, 3 June 1725 (*Letters Written by his Excellency Hugh Boulter . . . to Several Ministers of State* (Oxford, 1769–70), i. 31). For other appointments, and for policy in general, see Hayton, *Ruling Ireland*, 240–2.
[41] Boulter to Carteret, 9 Feb. 1727 (*Letters*, i. 133).
[42] Boulter to Newcastle, 30 Oct. 1729 (ibid. i. 334).

autumn to secure the repeal of the sacramental test. At a dinner in December, 'after the company had drank very hard', he defended his conduct, telling the chief secretary that 'he had no obligations to the court, for he set up on the foot of the country party, and the court when they found they could not hinder him, they concurred to make him Speaker'.[43] By the following year, however, lord lieutenant and speaker had established a working relationship, and Boyle had embarked on a career as the government's parliamentary manager that was to continue for over two decades.

The political arrangements that took shape in the aftermath of the Wood's Halfpence crisis thus had two complementary aspects. On the one hand there was an undoubted determination to provide for more reliable control of the kingdom's affairs by creating a substantial 'English interest' within the judiciary, church, and civil administration. On the other there was a recognition that smooth political management required the assistance of members of the local Protestant elite. The mid-1720s were at one stage seen as marking the origins of an 'undertaker system'. The term is doubly misleading. 'Undertaker' is a historian's term, avoided by those concerned because of its connotations of a discreditable bargain. Secondly, and more important, the need for local managers to organize parliamentary support for an externally appointed and partially absentee lord lieutenant had been clear long before Wood's patent became a subject of controversy. One MP in 1707 wrote that 'the managers or undertakers rather' had persuaded the lord lieutenant to smooth the passage of a finance bill by asking for one and three-quarters rather than two years' supply.[44] What was new in the rise to prominence of Conolly, Gore, and then Boyle was not the concept of undertakers, but the emergence of one individual as chief undertaker, and his acceptance as in effect a partner in the government of the kingdom.

The division of power and status inherent in the new system was evident in the choice of lords justices. If two of the three places were, from 1725, for an English primate and an English lord chancellor, the third, on every occasion between 1734 and 1753, was reserved for Boyle. The same balance was evident in the allocation of patronage. In this respect, indeed, the rhetoric of Boulter and others was misleading. In 1727 Boulter blocked the efforts of Carteret and Conolly to secure the archbishopric of Cashel for Theophilus Bolton, a protégé of Archbishop King and, in Boulter's eyes, his likely successor as leader of an 'Irish party' within the church. Two years later, on the other hand, Boulter himself recommended that the appointment of an Englishman, John Hoadley, to succeed King at Dublin should be balanced by the appointment of Bolton

---

[43] Marmaduke Coghill to Edward Southwell, 4 Dec. 1733 (*Letters of Marmaduke Coghill 1722–1738*, ed. D. W. Hayton (Dublin, 2005), 145).

[44] Robert Rochfort to Edward Southwell, 26 July 1707 (BL, Add. MS 9715, fo. 183). Long-standing misconceptions on this point were firmly cleared up in Hayton's pioneering article 'The Beginnings of the "Undertaker System"', first published in 1979 and now reprinted as *Ruling Ireland*, ch. 3.

to Cashel, vacant again after the short reign there of the former bishop of Derry, the English-born William Nicolson. In other cases too the drive to insert Englishmen into every available vacancy, initiated in the heat of the Wood's Halfpence contest, was not sustained. Of the judges appointed during the whole reign of George II, between 1727 and 1760, 14 were Irish and 9 English, as compared to 12 English and 11 Irish in the previous two reigns. The ethnic balance in the church, with 11 Irish and 11 English bishops, was the same in 1760 as it had been in 1727.[45]

This acknowledgement of the need for a reasonably equitable division of patronage was one important contributor to the more tranquil political weather that prevailed from the early 1730s. At the same time the concept of opposing English and Irish interests within the establishment was itself to become less relevant as time went on. English observers of the squabbles of the 1720s had been baffled by what they saw as the absurd adoption of an Irish identity by recent settlers from Great Britain. Henry Downes, bishop of Killala, writing during the agitation that led to the declaratory act, complained of hearing 'natives of one, two or more descents' condemn the intrusion of English 'foreigners'. Another bishop, William Nicolson of Derry, referred sarcastically to a 'quarantine' after which 'our posterity (of the very next generation) will be as true born Irishmen as if they had been brought out of Egypt in Scota's lap'.[46] Both men wildly exaggerated the extent to which Irish Protestants had adopted a new national identity. But the more mundane process of establishing connections in their new country of residence was to affect this generation of English-born appointees just as much as it had their predecessors. John Hoadley, the Englishman for whose appointment as archbishop of Dublin Boulter had campaigned so energetically, was subsequently to see his daughter marry a son of Henry Boyle. Robert Jocelyn, the Londoner who succeeded Wyndham as lord chancellor in 1739, took as his second wife the Dublin-born widow of an Irish peer, the earl of Rosse. Against this background the rhetoric of opposing national interests that had been so prominent, on the English side at least, in the 1720s lost much of its relevance in the decades that followed.

A balance between central and local interests may also be seen in the workings of the Irish parliament. By this time all but a few token bills, even in the case of government measures, were introduced directly into the Commons under the heads of bills procedure that had evolved as a means of circumventing the restrictions on parliament's legislative initiative imposed by Poynings's Law. The Irish executive and the British privy council could still alter or block any such proposed enactment, and recent work shows that both powers were used more

---

[45] F. G. James, *Ireland in the Empire 1688–1770* (Cambridge, Mass., 1973), 131. See also Burns, *Irish Parliamentary Politics*, i. 199–201.

[46] Henry Downes to Nicolson, 20 Feb. 1720 (J. Nichols (ed.), *Letters on Various Subjects . . . to and from William Nicolson* (London, 1809), ii. 509–10; Nicolson to Wake, 19 Mar. 1721 (Dublin Municipal Library, Gilbert MSS 27, 282).

freely than was at one time recognized. Of 207 heads of bills accepted by the two houses of parliament during 1761–8, 29 got no further than the Irish privy council, 16 were not returned by the British council, and 89 underwent some amendment before return. The less detailed statistics so far available suggest that a similar level of interference probably obtained in earlier decades.[47] Not all such amendments, however, necessarily represented serious meddling with the intentions of the Irish legislature: privy counsellors complained more than once of the frequency with which they had to correct sloppy drafting in the heads placed before them. Despite such interference, moreover, the heads of bills procedure allowed the Irish parliament to make a major contribution to the framing of laws. The proportion of heads that returned to the parliament to be voted into law rose from just over 60 per cent during 1711–30 to more than 70 per cent in the next two decades. More revealing still was the sparing use made of the right asserted in 1720 to pass British acts binding on Ireland. Ministers may have flirted during 1719–20 with the notion of dispensing, at least temporarily, with the Irish parliament. But in practice they continued to summon it every second year, and to treat its assent as essential both for changes in the law and for raising taxes. There was much frustration, for example, at Dorset's failure to secure the repeal of the sacramental test. But there seems to have been no suggestion of using a British act to bypass the uncooperative Irish assembly.

The task of the undertaker, then, was to act as intermediary between the lord lieutenant and the Irish parliament, securing the majorities required for the biennial grant of additional taxes and for other necessary legislation. In discharging that task he could deploy the votes of his own supporters. Boyle's personal following in the early 1750s was estimated at around 40 members. To these could be added a small group, somewhere between a dozen and 20, whose position as senior office holders required them to support the administration. In a parliament of 300 members the two together formed a significant Castle party, but by themselves fell well short of a reliable majority. The shortfall was made up partly by the distribution of patronage. But it also required other forms, more subtle and therefore more easily overlooked, of parliamentary management.

Patronage, in Ireland as in Great Britain, was an abiding concern at all levels of public life. The list of potential prizes was a long one. Bishoprics and other church livings in the gift of the crown, judgeships and other offices connected with the four courts of justice, the 650 to 700 officers' places on the military establishment, the 52 patentee offices, and 1,100 or so other posts connected with the revenue: all were allocated on the basis of political influence. The greater offices among them were to be prized, not just for the prestige and income they brought,

---

[47] For a detailed discussion see James Kelly, 'Monitoring the Constitution: The Operation of Poynings' Law in the 1760s', in D. W. Hayton (ed.), *The Irish Parliament in the Eighteenth Century: The Long Apprenticeship* (Edinburgh, 2001), 87–106, and Hayton's 'Introduction: The Long Apprenticeship', ibid. 8–12.

but because they provided the holder with his own opportunities to dispense favours and advance clients or dependants. Some were sinecures, carrying income without significant responsibility. In 1782 the MP for Portarlington received £300 a year as secretary to the Board of Stamps, leaving the duties to a clerk paid £40 a year. Around the same time John Foster, MP for County Louth and a rising figure within the administration, held the customership of Dublin port, worth an annual £1,000. A radical polemicist in 1832, at a time when the crusade against 'Old Corruption' was in full flow, commented scornfully on the bizarre system by which 'many noble lords and their sons, right honourable and honourable gentlemen, fill the offices of clerks, tide-waiters, harbour masters, searchers, gaugers, packers, craners, wharfingers, prothonotaries and other degrading situations'.[48] More blatant still, in terms of the use of public funds to provide rewards and favours, was the payment of pensions from the civil establishment. Peerages, and promotions within the peerage, though carrying no financial reward, were also coveted favours in the hands of government. There was no neat formula for the disposal of these various prizes. The recommendations of the chief undertaker, themselves a response to the solicitations of a variety of local interests, jostled alongside those of the lord lieutenant, of English office holders such as the primate and lord chancellor, and of well-placed British claimants. But a reasonable voice in the allocation of what was available was essential, as a reward for the undertaker's services, as a confirmation of his primacy within the domestic political system, and as part of the wherewithal that allowed him to discharge his side of the bargain by delivering the required parliamentary majorities.

The part played by patronage in the management of the Irish parliament is undeniable. Contemporaries, indeed, came to regard Irish politicians as exceptionally venal. 'But here everything is a job', one lord lieutenant complained in 1785, 'from the highest to the lowest; the whole people are an interested, selfish, savage race of harpies and plunderers.'[49] Such personalized criticism missed the point. The kingdom of Ireland, like that of Great Britain, had an executive required to work in harmony with parliament. But the Irish executive did not come into being, like the British, by establishing its command of a parliamentary majority; and there was no mechanism, as there was in Great Britain, for defeat in parliament to be followed by a change of administration. Instead majorities had to be constructed and sustained by a constant process of bargaining. These circumstances may well have created a political culture in which the pursuit of private advantage was particularly blatant. But the reason

---

[48] John Wade, *The Extraordinary Black Book* (1832), quoted in W. D. Rubinstein, 'The End of "Old Corruption" in Britain', *Past & Present*, 101 (1983), 67. For Portarlington see E. M. Johnston, *Great Britain and Ireland 1760–1800* (Edinburgh, 1963), 232, and for Foster, A. P. W. Malcomson, *John Foster: The Politics of the Anglo-Irish Ascendancy* (Oxford, 1978), 451. For a survey of the scale of official patronage, McNally, *Parties, Patriots and Undertakers*, 90–3.

[49] The duke of Rutland, quoted in Johnston, *Great Britain and Ireland*, 231–2.

lay, not in the deficiencies of the Irish character, but in the anomalies built into the kingdom's constitution.

If patronage was not evidence of a venality inherent in the Irish character, neither could it in itself be a guarantee of automatic parliamentary majorities. Patronage, in the first place, could not be applied indiscriminately. Contemporaries distinguished between the legitimate deployment of influence and an unsuitable appointment damaging to the public interest. The appointment in 1774 as provost of Trinity College of John Hely-Hutchinson, a politician with no academic credentials, was widely denounced as a 'job'. Nor was it legitimate to make the bestowal of favours dependent on total compliance. On the contrary leading landowners expected a reasonable level of attention to their requests, in recognition of their status and their role as the unpaid local representatives of government. Where routine patronage of this kind was in fact withdrawn as a consequence of political disobedience—for example, when the marquis of Downshire was dismissed from the governorship of County Down on account of his opposition to the act of union in 1800—this was widely seen as an extreme step.

Even where patronage could be applied for more narrowly political purposes, furthermore, its efficacy was much less than is commonly supposed. Favours, in the first place, could not always be revoked: a promotion to the peerage, or an office held for life, provided no guarantee that the beneficiary, or his patron, would remain a reliable supporter. Even in the case of those holding their positions during pleasure, rather than during good behaviour or for life, dismissals for political disobedience aroused adverse comment and were not undertaken lightly. Where issues arose on questions of principle or major public interest, such as the resistance to Wood's Halfpence or the attempt to repeal the sacramental test, it quickly became clear that office holders could not in fact be counted on to support the administration. Finally, and most important, the supply of patronage, for all its variety, was finite. To gratify one applicant for a particular position was frequently to disappoint several others. Perceived access to patronage, in this sense, could be as much a burden as an asset. When the appointment of a new archbishop of Dublin was under discussion in 1729, Boulter expressed concern at the damage that would follow if it appeared that his recommendation had been ignored, and appealed to the bishop of London 'to hinder such a disgrace from happening to me'. A lord lieutenant, in 1745, used exactly the same term: rival factions 'are considered by the public as supported or disgraced in proportion as the favours of the government are granted or refused to each'.[50]

---

[50] Boulter to Bishop of London, 28 Aug. 1729 (*Letters*, i. 322–3); Chesterfield to Hardwicke, 28 Nov. 1745 (*The Letters of Philip Dormer Stanhope, 4th Earl of Chesterfield*, ed. B. Dobree (London, 1932), iii. 706). The limitations of patronage are discussed in detail in Malcomson, *John Foster*, ch. 6; McNally, *Parties, Patriots and Undertakers*, ch. 5.

Even with the resources of patronage at their disposal, then, the lord lieutenant and his undertakers had to find other ways of ensuring the successful passage of business through parliament. Swift, in full flight against Wood's patent, offered a vivid account of the methods by which such a measure might normally have been expected to be eased through.

Depending persons would have been told, in plain terms, that it was a service expected from them, under the pain of the public business being put into more complying hands. Others would be allured by promises. To the country gentlemen, besides good words, burgundy and closeting, it might, perhaps, have been hinted how kindly it would be taken to comply with a royal patent, although it were not compulsory. That if any inconveniences ensued, it might be made up with other graces or favours hereafter: that gentlemen ought to consider whether it were prudent or safe to disgust England. They would be desired to think of some good bills for encouraging of trade, and setting the poor to work; some further acts against popery, and for uniting Protestants. . . . Perhaps a seasonable report of some invasion would have been spread . . . and we should have been told, that this was no time to create differences, when the kingdom was in danger.[51]

The account is hostile satire. But it is realistic in the sense of balancing the use of patronage, the pressure put on 'depending persons', and the promises of 'graces or favours', with other devices: hospitality, the trading of popular against unpopular measures, and the manipulation of public opinion. What it describes, in other words, is 'management' in the proper sense of the term: not the mechanical exchange of patronage for votes, but instead the complex arts of bargaining, persuasion, and the establishment of personal relationships. The dinners and drinking bouts that figure in contemporary political correspondence were no mere indulgence, but an important part of the conduct of politics. So too was argument. The successful transaction of government business, it was generally recognized, required not just tame votes but good speaking men whose arguments could gain or shore up support.

Against this background, too, it becomes possible to reassess the personality, or at least the persona, of the most successful of the undertakers, Henry Boyle. Marmaduke Coghill, right-hand man to the deceased chief undertaker Gore, noted condescendingly that Boyle was 'a country gentleman of great good nature and probity, well beloved but not of extraordinary abilities'. His first speech as speaker of the Commons 'was spoke, or rather read, with as much indifference and as little concern, as if it had been at a tavern amongst a few of his friends, and indeed he read it as a schoolboy does his lesson'. For Coghill this performance, along with Boyle's 'natural modesty, and his little application to the knowledge of parliamentary proceedings', demonstrated his unfitness for his new office. An alternative view would be that it was precisely this image of a straightforward, not unduly sophisticated country gentleman that fitted Boyle so ideally for the task

---

[51] Swift, *The Drapier's Letters*, 60.

of mediating between a parliament of provincial squires and the representatives of the metropolitan power.[52]

The relationship between lord lieutenant and local managers established in the late 1720s and early 1730s could not be expected to continue wholly unchanged through successive periods of office. However current assessments, in the absence of detailed studies of individual administrations, must remain provisional.[53] The duke of Devonshire, who took over from Dorset as lord lieutenant in 1737, has been presented as a somewhat ineffective figure, under whom power passed more clearly into the hands of Boyle and other local figures. His successor, Chesterfield, by contrast, has been credited with seeking to take a more active role in management, while keeping his distance from local factions. However he held office for only two years (1744–6) and spent only nine months in an Ireland preoccupied by the Jacobite threat, and in practice he seems to have paid due attention to most of Boyle's requests in matters of patronage. The earl of Harrington, lord lieutenant from 1746 until 1750, was politically weakened by the personal hostility towards him of the king. Archbishop Stone of Armagh was to claim some years later that in consequence he placed himself wholly in the hands of Boyle and his associates. However this was an assertion made at a time when Stone had his own political agenda, requiring him to present himself as the champion of the English interest and Boyle as its chief opponent.

Boyle's accession as chief undertaker did not mean an end to factional conflict within the Irish administration. His chief rival was Brabazon Ponsonby, Lord Duncannon. The Ponsonbys were Cromwellian grantees who had taken advantage of the break-up of the huge Ormond estate to convert a modest inheritance into a substantial landed property in Counties Tipperary and Kilkenny. By the 1730s Duncannon had emerged as leader of the former Conolly grouping in parliament. In 1739, in the first of two marriage alliances of central political significance, Duncannon's eldest surviving son William married Caroline Cavendish, eldest daughter of the lord lieutenant, and soon after became Devonshire's private secretary. In 1743 his second son John married Caroline's sister Elizabeth Cavendish. Duncannon, meanwhile, had risen in the peerage to become earl of Bessborough. He had also, in 1739, replaced Boyle as one of the revenue commissioners. How far this was a surrender forced on the speaker remains unclear: he had been slow to take on the burdensome duties associated

---

[52] Coghill to Southwell, 15 Mar., 20 Oct. 1733 (*Letters of Marmaduke Coghill*, ed. Hayton 122, 137). A very similar point has been made about a later figure who combined the roles of speaker and leading Castle servant: Malcomson, *John Foster*, 18–19, 344–5, 429–30.

[53] James, drawing on the pioneering work of J. L. McCracken, sees Chesterfield as more forceful than his predecessor or successor (*Ireland in the Empire*, 187). By contrast Burns, *Irish Parliamentary Politics*, ii. 50, 83–90, sees him as perpetuating a pattern of yielding power to local managers that he had inherited from Devonshire and that was to continue under Harrington. Eoin Magennis, *The Irish Political System 1740–1765* (Dublin, 2000), 30–1, agrees in rejecting the suggestion that Chesterfield's viceroyalty saw any significant change in the balance between lord lieutenant and undertakers.

with a revenue position, and may simply have wished to exchange them for the less demanding office of chancellor of the Irish exchequer, carrying with it a salary of £800 a year. But by the winter of 1739–40, whether for this or other reasons, there were reports of open friction between Boyle and Ponsonby factions within the administration.

PATRIOTS AND UNDERTAKERS

The succession of constitutional disputes that began with the disastrous parliament of 1692 and continued up to the confrontation over William Wood's patent can be seen, in retrospect, as marking a period of adjustment. In a political environment transformed by the removal of James II, members of the Irish political elite and British parliamentarians and ministers each sought to test the limits of their power. The emergence from the mid-1720s of a succession of acknowledged undertakers represented the achievement of an agreed balance of British and Irish interests, and brought a new stability to relations between the two kingdoms. Part of the accommodation, however, was an acceptance of the necessity to defer to what remained a lively sense of the need to uphold Irish interests. In 1737, for example, the English-born bishop of Derry demonstrated his support for local sensitivities when he sought to ensure that some black cloth he had ordered while in England arrived in time to be made into gowns before he left for Ireland. 'It will not be quite decent to carry it with me in its native form, but will seem to upbraid the country with being unable to supply me. It cannot indeed so well, but I will not tell them so.'[54] His caution was understandable. At times of economic difficulty, in 1731 and again in 1750, demonstrations by weavers and other artisans included real or threatened violence against those of their betters seen to be wearing imported cloth.[55]

At the other extreme from such plebeian street politics, the government remained wary of the potential of patriot issues to disrupt parliamentary business. Boulter, in 1732, complained of there being 'so many young giddy members in the house, under no direction and full of a false patriotism, who are too likely even to throw out a thing they liked, merely for its coming from England'. The chief secretary, two days earlier, pleaded with his masters in London not to meddle with a revenue bill, since 'you know, in that case, how ready the gentlemen here may be to take a handle for rejecting the whole'.[56] In 1737 there was substantial opposition to a proclamation fixing new values for the different

---

[54] *Letters of the Late Thomas Rundle* (Dublin, 1789), 233.
[55] *Dublin Intelligence*, 9, 14, 16 June 1731; *The Synge Letters: Bishop Edward Synge to his Daughter Alicia, Roscommon to Dublin 1746–1752*, ed. Marie-Louise Legg (Dublin, 1996), 184–5.
[56] Walter Cary to—, 2 Jan. *1732* (PRO, SP63/395/13); Boulter to Delafaye, 4 Jan. 1732 (PRO, SP63/395/18).

varieties of gold coin circulating in the kingdom. The aim was to reduce the valuation to a more realistic level, and so remedy a continuing shortage of silver, but the measure raised misleading echoes of the Wood's Halfpence controversy. In parliament the attack was led by Anthony Malone, a son-in-law of Ralph Gore, Richard Cox, grandson of the former lord chancellor, and Eaton Stannard, recorder of Dublin. When parliament met in the autumn Cox and Stannard continued the offensive with an attack on the damage done to the country's economy by government overspending. Members of the lord lieutenant's circle complained of Boyle's failure to restrain the troublemakers, but recognized that he was awkwardly caught between his fairly newly assumed duties to the Castle and the pressures of a popular cause.

Not all of this parliamentary activity can be taken at face value. An effective display of nuisance value on the floor of the Commons was a recognized route to office. And indeed in 1743 Malone accepted the position of prime serjeant. In 1749, however, the administration faced a different challenge, from a figure outside the political establishment, and in the name of a far more radical version of patriot values. Charles Lucas had been born in County Clare in 1713, the great-grandson of a Cromwellian army officer, but made his career as an apothecary in Dublin. In 1741 he was elected to represent his guild in the lower of the two houses of the Dublin corporation, and almost immediately began a campaign to reduce the power of the upper house, controlled by a narrow elite of wealthy merchants. His campaign suffered a setback when he and his main ally, the merchant and member of a leading banking family James Digges La Touche, lost their seats on the common council in 1744. But when the city's two MPs died in 1748 and 1749, Lucas and La Touche contested the resulting by-election on a reform platform. In a sequence of election addresses, Lucas broadened his campaign to include an aggressive assertion of Irish constitutional rights and an insistence on the primacy of representative institutions over monarchy and aristocracy. In October 1749 the Irish Commons introduced resolutions condemning Lucas's writings as seditious, declaring him an enemy of the kingdom, and ordering his imprisonment. Confinement for any length of time in an eighteenth-century jail involved real risks to health and indeed to life itself, and Lucas chose to flee, first to the Isle of Man, then to London and mainland Europe. His running mate, La Touche, was returned at the subsequent by-election; his success, against the concerted opposition of the city oligarchy, was clear evidence of the extent to which Lucas's campaign had attracted popular support. However the House of Commons subsequently declared his election invalid.[57]

---

[57] The fullest account of the Lucas affair is Hill, *From Patriots to Unionists*, 83–96. See also Sean Murphy, 'Charles Lucas and the Dublin Election of 1748–1749', *Parliamentary History*, 2 (1983), 93–111; Jim Smyth, 'Republicanism before the United Irishmen: The Case of Dr Charles Lucas', in D. George Boyce et al. (eds.), *Political Discourse in Seventeenth and Eighteenth-Century Ireland* (Basingstoke, 2001), 240–56.

Lucas's writings of the 1740s establish him as the most prolific Irish political thinker of the mid-eighteenth century. Their substance is more difficult to assess. Self-educated and obsessive, he pulled together ideas from a range of sources that he then laboriously summarized for his popular audience in a succession of didactic pamphlets. From radical Whig writers, whether directly from Locke or from followers such as Molesworth, he took the principle that the authority of government depended on an original compact between rulers and ruled. But he also drew on the older tradition, developed in antiquity and revived by the political thinkers of the Renaissance, that good government depended on a balance between the three principles of monarchy, aristocracy, and democracy, each kept by the other two from developing into its debased form of tyranny, oligarchy, or mob rule. Elsewhere again his appeal was to the notion of an ancient constitution, unique to the British dominions, in which rights and liberties had been established by centuries of usage. He also borrowed openly from Molyneux, repeating at length the argument that the terms on which the Gaelic lords of the twelfth century had accepted Henry II as their ruler had guaranteed Ireland's status as a free and independent kingdom, to be governed only by laws made in its own parliament.

Lucas's political thought, then, was derivative and not always consistent. But there were two respects in which he went beyond his predecessors, whether Whig or patriot. The first was in relation to parliament. Establishment Whiggery exalted the role of the Commons as the popular element in a balanced constitution. But it also jealously guarded the status of its members, as representatives not delegates even of the restricted electorate on whose votes their legitimacy depended. To print either the debates or the votes of members within the house constituted a legally punishable contempt. To Lucas, on the other hand, members of the Commons were 'but servants to their constituents', and 'a people zealous for preserving their natural rights and liberties must ever be watchful, if not look on these their delegates with a jealous eye'. In the last resort, in fact, MPs who succumbed to self-interest or corruption 'dissolve the original compact implied between the representative and the represented'.[58] It was a radically different vision, of popular not parliamentary sovereignty, and does much to explain the willingness of the Dublin parliament to consign its author to oblivion.

A second respect in which Lucas went beyond his predecessors was in his treatment of the Irish past. Molyneux had made much of the 'original compact' between Henry II and the Gaelic lords. But he had passed quietly over the process by which those Gaelic ruling families had subsequently been displaced by the New English property owners in whose name he himself wrote. Lucas took a different, and more realistic view. The native Irish had not only survived; the compact they had made with Henry II had been 'perfidiously broken'. The

---

[58] Charles Lucas, *A Nineteenth Address to the Free-Citizens and Freeholders of the City of Dublin* (Dublin, 1749), 10; idem, *The Complaints of Dublin, Humbly Offered to his Excellency, William Earl of Harrington* (n.p., 1747), 6.

rulers of medieval Ireland had made laws excluding Irish natives from English law and liberty, treating them 'like slaves and barbarous enemies to the crown'. Indeed 'this nation has not been better treated by some of the ancient English governors than the Peruvians or Mexicans by the Spaniards'.[59] Elsewhere, in a passage that provided part of the basis for the parliamentary proceedings against him, he suggested that when Irish Catholics had taken up arms in 1641 they had done so in self-defence. None of this led Lucas to question the system of religious inequality in the Ireland of his own day. He believed that Catholics were entitled to equal property rights and the free exercise of their religion, but that as long as they upheld the temporal authority of the pope there could be no question of admitting them to political power. Later in his career he was to be prominent in the campaign to continue the practice of demanding that Catholic merchants and traders pay quarterage fees to the guilds from which they were excluded by law. But his writings are a striking early indication of the way in which the logic of patriot argument could push its practitioners towards a reassessment of long-standing inequalities and exclusions.

Lucas's exile, and the disallowing of La Touche's election, demonstrated how far their challenge fell outside the bounds of acceptable political debate. In particular Lucas's appeal to popular opinion outraged the political elite. One hostile pamphlet dubbed him 'our modern Massienello', after the fisherman leader of the celebrated Naples revolt of 1647.[60] Among those who joined in rejecting his presumption were two prominent parliamentary patriots. Eaton Stannard, who as recorder of Dublin had a personal interest in the case, published a pamphlet denouncing Lucas as a vain opportunist.[61] Sir Richard Cox took a leading part in the parliamentary proceedings against him, and also published a series of pamphlets under the title *The Cork Surgeon's Antidote against the Dublin Apothecary's Poison*. These offered a comprehensive rebuttal both of Lucas's methods and of his arguments. In particular Cox dismissed Lucas's obsessive citations of historical texts, arguing instead for a sense of historical context: documents like Magna Carta were inescapably products of a particular time and place, and it was only with the Revolution of 1688 that Britain could be said to have a settled constitution. By the same token Molyneux's laborious collection of medieval precedents demonstrating Ireland's legislative autonomy had been rendered irrelevant by subsequent developments: the declaratory act had asserted the authority of the British parliament, 'and by the operation of their and our laws we are in fact become absolutely dependent for all we have'.[62]

---

[59] Lucas, *Nineteenth Address*, 18–19. See also Sean Murphy, 'Charles Lucas, Catholicism and Nationalism', *ECI* 8 (1993), 83–102.

[60] James Taylor, *Lucas Detected, or A Vindication of the Sheriffs and Commons of the City of Dublin* (Dublin, 1749), 12–13.

[61] Eaton Stannard, *The Honest Man's Speech* (Dublin, 1749).

[62] 'Anthony Litten', *The Cork Surgeon's Antidote against the Dublin Apothecary's Poison for the Citizens of Dublin, Numbers 1–7* (Dublin 1749), Letter 3, p. 4.

The involvement of Stannard and Cox in Lucas's expulsion from political life raises questions about the true character of their brand of patriotism. And indeed Cox himself, within a year of his attack on Lucas, was to be made collector of customs for County Cork. Yet his response, however well rewarded, had a depth and conviction that lifted it beyond mere political hackwork. In rejecting Lucas's obsession with 'ancient grants, moduses etc . . . musty old records scarcely legible', and calling instead for an acknowledgement that the events of 1688 had established a new political system, he accurately identified a central weakness in his opponent's case. He was equally correct in dismissing out of hand Lucas's attempt to perpetuate the distinction between allegiance to the crown of Great Britain and subordination to its parliament. Because the king could discharge his functions only with parliament's financial support, 'whoever hath been dependant upon the force of Britain for protection, must have been strictly and truly dependant upon the people of Britain, through its representatives in parliament'.

At the same time that he rejected Lucas's claim, Cox offered his own alternative definition of what patriotism consisted of:

Patriotism is to be always defined, from the circumstances of the country: and he, who makes the best of her condition, and creates most friends for her, is certainly her true lover. But the Don Quixote, who calls sheep, wolves; and rushes his countrymen into disputes with windmills, deserves to be pitied, but not to be followed.[63]

Nor was this empty rhetoric. Cox had a record as a highly active legislator, supporting a steady succession of measures promoting economic development. His estate at Dunmanway in County Cork, where he had built up an extensive linen works using both imported and local labour, was a showpiece of improving landlordism. Against this background his attack on Lucas can be seen as the expression of an alternative patriotism, pragmatic in its acceptance of political reality, and concerned with practical benefit rather than abstract constitutional issues. Such a stance was not incompatible with the acceptance of office on satisfactory terms. And indeed, when he accepted his reward for his part in the crushing of Lucas, if that is what it was, Cox drew an important distinction, insisting that the collectorship, a salaried post with actual duties, was compatible with his continued political credit in a way that a pension would not be.[64]

Already by the time of this apparently satisfactory resolution of the demands of moderate patriotism and political career, however, new developments were under way that were to upset the framework of consensus on which it rested. The central figure in the escalation of tension was George Stone, a Londoner brought to Ireland as chaplain by the duke of Dorset, lord lieutenant from 1730 to 1737,

---

[63] 'Anthony Litten', Letter 4, pp. 13–14. For dependence on the British parliament see Letter 3, p. 6.
[64] For information on Cox's activity as a legislator, and for the terms on which he accepted office, I am indebted to my research student Mr Gordon Rees.

who had launched his career in the Irish church by making him dean of Ferns. Succeeding Hoadly as archbishop of Armagh in 1747, Stone took over Boulter's political role, serving regularly as one of the three lords justices. However he showed none of his predecessor's willingness to combine this political charge with a genuine commitment to his pastoral duties. Instead he concentrated his efforts on establishing his own network of political connections, including an alliance with the rising Ponsonby family. His moment came in late 1750 when his old patron Dorset returned for a second term as lord lieutenant, joined as chief secretary by his son Lord George Sackville. Before long Stone and Sackville were working closely together to control the disposal of patronage and in what seems to have been a general drive for greater administrative efficiency. When parliament met in October 1751 Boyle was still the government's acknowledged manager, but his primacy was clearly under threat. His response was to steer the government's main business through as usual, but to give a small but effective demonstration of his power by encouraging a Commons attack on the surveyor general, Arthur Jones Nevill, a client of Stone's, for alleged corruption associated with the building and repair of military barracks.[65]

During 1752–3 the power struggle within the administration continued behind the scenes. Both sides appealed to London. Stone and Sackville argued that previous administrations had allowed power to slip disproportionately into the hands of an Irish interest, and that the only hope of preserving English government was for the Castle to reassert control. Boyle and his associates denied the allegation that they aimed at 'setting up for an independency', and instead attacked Stone and Sackville's mismanagement. British ministers differed in their assessment of the conflicting claims, but agreed in seeing the affair as a matter of personal rivalries rather than principle. When parliament met again in October 1753 the attack on Nevill resumed. On 23 November the Commons voted to censure his conduct and expel him from the house.

Meanwhile the usual money bills were making their way through the procedures prescribed by Poynings's Law. As in two previous years, 1749 and 1751, higher than expected tax receipts thanks to expanding trade had permitted a surplus of revenue over expenditure. The heads of the 1753 money bill, the usual grant of two further years' supply, were thus accompanied by another measure applying the balance left over from the previous grant to the reduction of the national debt. The English privy council amended the heads of this latter measure to include an explicit statement of the king's consent to this use of the money. A similar amendment had been made in 1751 but Boyle, not yet ready for open confrontation, had helped to damp down discussion of the issue. This time, however, the implied denial of parliament's right to determine the use of surplus funds, with its distant but clear echo of the sole right controversy

---

[65] The fullest account of the money bill dispute is now Magennis, *The Irish Political System*, chs. 3–4. See also Burns, *Irish Parliamentary Politics*, ii, chs. 4–5.

of sixty years earlier, became the ground on which he chose to fight. On the evening of 15 December, in a bizarre scene, Boyle and other office holders attended to hear Dorset read a letter from the English privy council instructing them to defend the king's prerogative, then walked out without having spoken. Two days later the Commons rejected the amended money bill by 123 votes to 118.

The claims of Stone and Boyle that national issues were at stake were, on both sides, transparently false. Stone had energetically formed connections with Irish interests such as the Ponsonbys; Boyle had for two decades managed the Irish parliament on behalf of a succession of English viceroys. But their factional conflict, once redefined in these terms, took on a momentum of its own. Chesterfield, observing events from London, noted accurately that 'the beginning of the whole affair was only the old question, who should govern the government', producing 'violent personal piques and acrimony'. Now, however, 'the affair is become national, and consequently very serious'.[66] His alarm was understandable. The developing conflict between actual and would-be political managers took place at a time of economic difficulty: the harvest of 1753 had been poor, prices for linen and livestock were depressed, and some banks had been in danger of collapse. Against this background Boyle's campaign, cast as a defence of Irish interests against English mismanagement, attracted widespread support. Following the rejection of the altered money bill a crowd of 1,000 escorted the speaker and his ally, the earl of Kildare, in triumph to their homes, while elsewhere celebratory bonfires blazed and known government adherents were jeered or attacked. Supporters in the provinces organized themselves into Patriot Clubs. Stone became the object of particular hostility. Historically minded critics compared him to earlier examples of ill-fated turbulent priests, from Henry II's Becket to Henry VIII's Wolsey and Charles I's Laud. Others referred, with varying degrees of explicitness, to his rumoured homosexuality. The common people, presumably with the same libel in mind, 'abuse him publicly by turning up their children's backsides and saying, "What a fine pair of buttocks they are" '.[67]

The government's immediate response to the rejection of the money bill was to dismiss several leading office holders, including Anthony Malone and the master of the rolls, Thomas Carter. In April 1754 it went on to remove Boyle from the chancellorship of the exchequer, and also dismissed Sir Richard Cox from his recently acquired collectorship. When Dorset left for England in the same month the lords justices appointed were Stone, the English-born lord chancellor Robert Jocelyn, and Stone's ally the earl of Bessborough. But English ministers

[66] Chesterfield to Solomon Dayrolles, 1 Jan. 1754 (*Letters*, ed. Dobree, v. 2070).

[67] Diary of Sir Dudley Ryder, 9 Jan. 1754 (PRONI T3228/1/61). Jacqueline Hill, ' "Allegories, Fictions and Feigned Representations: Decoding the Money Bill Dispute 1752–6', *ECI* 21 (2006), 79–82.

had moved against Boyle only reluctantly, and Dorset failed to allay their fears concerning his ability to control the next meeting of the Irish parliament in the face of the speaker's continued opposition. In March 1755 Lord Hartington replaced Dorset as lord lieutenant. As the eldest son of the duke of Devonshire, to whose title he succeeded in December, Hartington was brother-in-law to both John and William Ponsonby. But his aim was to negotiate a settlement with both sides. The key to a successful deal was the exclusion from power of Stone. In September 1755, under pressure from both London and Dublin, the primate reluctantly lodged a formal request to be excused from further service as a lord justice. When parliament met the following month Boyle, restored to his position as chancellor of the exchequer, once again helped to ease the customary addresses, and the money bills, smoothly through the Commons. By spring 1756 he had agreed to move to the House of Lords, with the title earl of Shannon and a pension for life of £2,000 a year. His allies Malone and Carter returned to office, as chancellor of the exchequer and keeper of the privy seal respectively, while John Ponsonby succeeded him as speaker.

The pensioning off of Boyle ended the political crisis that had begun with the rejection of the money bill. It did not secure a quiet parliament. When the duke of Bedford succeeded Devonshire at the beginning of 1757 he discovered four main political factions. Two of these were headed by Ponsonby and by the newly created earl of Shannon. The other two were led by the earl of Kildare, who had established a claim on the government's gratitude by his role in brokering the reconciliation with Boyle, and by Stone, still unreconciled to his enforced retreat from office. Bedford's strategy was to divide the government's favour between all four. But when parliament met in the autumn Ponsonby and Stone quickly showed their displeasure by colluding in the attacks on the administration of a patriot grouping headed by Edmund Sexton Pery and Robert French, both former followers of the primate. In November the Commons passed resolutions condemning the increased amount paid in pensions out of public funds, and in particular the granting of such pensions to non-residents. When Bedford refused to transmit these to the king, the Commons delayed consideration of the money bills until he gave way. After convoluted negotiations Bedford secured a new agreement, whereby Stone, Ponsonby, and their old rival Shannon would share power. Kildare had refused to consider an accommodation with the primate and Shannon's willingness to serve without him led to an estrangement. But an appointment as master general of the ordnance, with a substantial salary which he badly needed, proved enough to keep him quiet.

If the parliamentary aftermath of the political excitements of 1753–6 was not easily dealt with, the popular response was even less susceptible to control. Boyle's reconciliation with government should have been no surprise: he had taken up a patriot stand only slowly, under pressure from his allies, and there had been doubts from the start as to his commitment. But his defection, given the heightened excitement of the previous two years, was bitterly resented. On

17 March 1756 Dublin witnessed what one woman, the wife of a judge and MP, believed was 'the greatest mob ever was known here'.

They got a cart painted black, with the Speaker in his gown and large wig in it, a paper on his breast was wrote in large letters, 'He betrayed the city in 1749'. They followed the cart, saying he must die, was carrying him to the gallows . . . They was forced to have the army to disperse them, the lord mayor was in great danger.[68]

The choice of date, St Patrick's day, was significant. So too was the reference to parliament's condemnation of Lucas in 1749. As then, the political establishment had for the moment closed ranks. But it was beginning to find that the wider popular opinion some of its members had briefly exploited for their own purposes was becoming more difficult to exclude.

[68] Anne Ward to Michael Ward, 18 Mar. 1756 (PRONI D2092/1/8/53).

7

New Lights and Old Faiths

By the eighteenth century Irish religious affiliations, the product more of patterns of immigration over the previous 200 years than of internal shifts in spiritual allegiance, had assumed what was to remain their permanent shape—at least until the belated arrival, in the dying years of the twentieth century, of the forces of secularization. The most complete attempt at a religious census, carried out by the hearth tax collectors in 1732, indicated that 73 per cent of the houses on their lists were Catholic. Modern research suggests that the hearth tax returns of the period understated the true number of houses by between 14 and 34 per cent. Since the low-value and inaccessible houses that made up a large proportion of these omissions were predominantly Catholic, it seems safe to conclude that Catholics actually made up somewhere between three-quarters and four-fifths of the population.

This Catholic numerical superiority was evident everywhere outside Ulster, where the Jacobean plantation and subsequent immigration had created Protestant majorities in four or five counties. But its full significance was for a time concealed by the strong Protestant presence that had been established in the towns of Munster and Leinster, as a result partly of the forcible expulsion of Catholics during the 1650s, and partly of the arrival during the same period of a new wave of English settlers. In the 1670s and 1680s, according to the reports of Catholic ecclesiastics, Protestants made up three-quarters of the population of Dundalk, a clear majority in Drogheda, and up to half the inhabitants of Waterford.[1] During the first half of the eighteenth century this urban superiority was steadily eroded, as expanding towns drew in migrants from a predominantly Catholic countryside. By the 1730s Protestants accounted for just over a quarter of the population of Drogheda, and one-third of the population of Cork. In Dublin, on the other hand, they still made up around one-half of the inhabitants.[2]

---

[1] *The Letters of Saint Oliver Plunkett 1625–80*, ed. John Hanly (Dublin, 1979), 73; Patrick Power, *A Bishop of the Penal Times: Being Letters and Reports of John Brennan, Bishop of Waterford (1671–93) and Archbishop of Cashel (1677–93)* (Cork, 1932), 29, 91.

[2] *Abstract of the Number of Protestant and Popish Families in the Years 1732 and 1733* (Dublin, 1736). For urban population in the late seventeenth century see Connolly, *Religion, Law and Power*, 145–7, and for the 1730s David Dickson, '"Centres of Motion": Irish Cities and the Origins of Popular Politics', in L. M. Cullen and Louis Bergeron (eds.), *Culture et practiques politiques en France et en Irlande* (Paris, 1991), 106–7.

The gradual reshaping of attitudes to Catholicism that took place during the eighteenth century was a consequence of, among other things, a belated coming to terms with demographic reality.

DEFENDING ASCENDANCY

At the beginning of the eighteenth century the Irish Catholic church was still struggling with the impact of the flurry of hostile legislation imposed by the newly empowered parliaments of William III and Anne.[3] The immediate impact of the bishops' banishment act had been considerable. During the early months of 1698 the government transported 424 regular clergy to continental Europe, while as many as 300 more departed of their own accord, leaving an estimated 200 still in the country. Two of the eight Catholic bishops likewise left voluntarily; a third, arrested but found to be too ill to travel, was kept in prison. There were attempts in the years that followed to detect and arrest those who remained, and to prevent further priests entering the country. But action seems from the start to have been sporadic. A return by six judges of all cases involving either regular clergy or persons exercising ecclesiastical jurisdiction between 1698 and 1703 listed a total of only twenty-seven persons coming before them either at assizes or in the central courts. In 1709 a new act required registered priests to take the oath of abjuration, going beyond a de facto acceptance of the Revolution to deny that the exiled son of James II had any legitimate title to the crown. All but a handful refused, thereby forfeiting the legal status conferred by the act of 1704. The response was a flurry of searches and arrests, forcing many priests into hiding, and leading churches to close their doors. Harassment eased off when a new Tory ministry took office in 1710, but in 1712 a localized outbreak of agrarian protest led the government to order the arrest of priests in seven western counties. Later the same year revelations of what was seen as an unacceptable level of activity by regulars provoked a proclamation calling for a strict enforcement of the laws throughout the country.

Almost from the beginning, then, the laws against Catholic clergymen were enforced intermittently rather than with anything like consistency. This was in part because nothing else was practical. Early eighteenth-century Ireland had no regular machinery for law enforcement. Local men of property, acting in their

---

[3] The most comprehensive account of the impact of penal legislation on the Irish church remains Maureen Wall, *The Penal Laws 1691–1760* (Dundalk, 1967). More recent accounts are available in histories of individual dioceses: Liam Swords, *A Hidden Church: The Diocese of Achonry 1689–1818* (Dublin, 1997); Ignatius Murphy, *The Diocese of Killaloe in the Eighteenth Century* (Dublin, 1991); James Kelly, 'The Impact of the Penal Laws', in James Kelly and Dáire Keogh (eds.), *History of the Catholic Diocese of Dublin* (Dublin, 2000), 144–74. The interpretation offered here, differing somewhat in its emphasis from both the older and more recent of these works, is developed in more detail in Connolly, *Religion, Law and Power*, ch. 7.

capacity as magistrates, were expected to take the initiative, supported only by a loosely regulated network of constables (themselves predominantly Catholic) and, in emergencies, by whatever military force might be available. In the case of the popery laws they faced the determined resistance of a predominantly Catholic population. A report from County Galway in 1703 told how the bishop of Clonfert had been rescued from custody. 'A great multitude of persons near 300 in number, some whereof were mounted on good horses and well armed', had disarmed the four men guarding him and left two of them seriously injured. In Youghal in 1712 a priest taken by three constables and two others was rescued, somewhat less dramatically, by 'a great number of women'. To open resistance was added the risk of subsequent reprisal against over-zealous individuals. The portreeve of Wicklow, in 1702, called in soldiers to disperse Catholics who had erected a mass house in the town. Soon after one of his outhouses was burnt down, in an arson attack that eventually consumed eight buildings. Since then, it was reported, the Catholics 'have met every Sunday . . . in the very middle of the town'. Five years later a gentleman in County Cork who arrested a regular lost his entire house and goods in a fire.⁴ Against this background it is hardly surprising that many magistrates took action only when prodded by the central government, or when provoked by what was seen as a proper lack of discretion on the part of local Catholics.

At the same time it would be misleading to suggest that intimidation alone inhibited a vigorous enforcement of the laws. The mayor of Derry complained in 1703 that several gentry in County Donegal had appeared to lobby vigorously for the release of a priest imprisoned for performing marriages where one of the partners had been Protestant. In Belfast five years later Protestants came forward to offer bail for a priest imprisoned for refusing the oath of abjuration, citing his services in protecting their persons and property during the period of Jacobite domination. In Waterford the same year there were complaints that a nominally imprisoned priest was lodged in the house of a constable 'not a musket shot from his parish . . . and has been suffered to come abroad and officiate'. In County Clare in 1712 a magistrate objected that the sheriff could not be trusted to enforce the latest proclamation, since the only foreign-educated priest in the district had been acting as tutor to his son. In cases of this kind it seems clear that orders to enforce the penal laws were unwelcome to some, not only for the danger that might be involved, but because they cut across local relationships of clientship or mutual accommodation.⁵

Both prudence and local or personal understandings became less significant, naturally enough, at times of acute crisis. In the summer of 1714 the atmosphere

---

⁴ W. P. Burke, *The Irish Priests in the Penal Times (1660–1760)* (Waterford, 1914), 136, 377, 309, 213. Burke's volume, reprinting numerous official documents now lost, represents the fullest single source of information on the day-to-day enforcement of penal legislation.

⁵ Samuel Leeson, mayor of Derry, to King, 23 July 1703 (TCD MSS 1995–2008, No. 1035); Burke, *Irish Priests*, 281, 367, 399.

of panic created by the impending death of the queen inspired repressive action of a kind possibly not seen since the end of King William's war. Throughout the country sheriffs and magistrates summoned Catholics to testify under oath as to where they had last heard mass, then issued warrants against the unregistered or non-juring priests thus identified. The following year, however, when Jacobites rose in arms in Scotland and northern England, there was no new flurry of arrests and searches. Thereafter serious attempts at action against bishops, regulars, or unregistered clergy became rare. The retreat from more than a token enforcement of the law was confirmed in 1718 when John Garzia, a Spanish immigrant turned bounty hunter, provided information leading to the arrest of the Catholic archbishop of Dublin. When the case came to trial the authorities, faced with what they clearly regarded as the embarrassment of having acquired so prominent a prisoner, extricated themselves by not allowing Garzia, by then in protective custody, to testify, so that the archbishop was acquitted. Six others unlucky enough to have been arrested with him were sentenced to be deported as regulars or unregistered priests. Three of them, however, were subsequently recorded as officiating in Dublin parishes, indicating either that they returned from exile or that the sentence was never carried out.[6]

The failure of the Williamite statutes to achieve the intended aim of suppressing Catholicism provoked two contrasting responses among some Irish Protestants. One was to demand harsher penalties and stricter enforcement. In 1719, as complaints multiplied about the rising number of priests and friars active in the kingdom, the House of Commons approved heads of a bill providing that regulars and unregistered priests found in Ireland should be branded on the face. In 1723 they presented another draft bill under which forbidden categories of Catholic ecclesiastic would be liable to being hanged, drawn, and quartered, while those harbouring them, along with Catholic teachers, would be hanged. An alternative solution was to replace the existing unworkable laws with a more moderate set of prohibitions, which it would then be possible to enforce consistently. The Irish peer Robert Molesworth, author of a classic statement of Whig principles, argued in 1723 that to deny a numerous people the exercise of their religion was 'both tyrannical and impolitic'.[7] Instead he proposed that Catholic priests should be paid a salary from public funds, while the more dangerous religious orders would be rigorously excluded. In the parliamentary session of 1725–6 the House of Lords passed a resolution in favour of the principle of permitting a number of licensed priests. The leading figure in the new initiative was Henry Downes, bishop of Elphin, who went on to introduce more specific proposals to allow a maximum of 600 priests, with one bishop to ordain replacements.

[6] Kevin McGrath, 'John Garzia, a Noted Priest-Catcher and his Activities 1717–23', *Irish Ecclesiastical Record*, 72 (1949), 494–514.

[7] Robert Molesworth, *Some Considerations for the Promoting of Agriculture and Employing the Poor* (Dublin, 1723), 30.

Meanwhile Edward Synge, archbishop of Tuam, revived proposals he had earlier made for a new oath that could be taken by conscientious but loyal Catholics, who would then be allowed a limited toleration. Synge's son Edward, a rising young clergyman, used the unlikely occasion of a 23 October commemoration sermon to the Commons to urge a similar strategy of selective toleration.[8]

Faced with these rival strategies the Irish executive and the English government seem instead to have chosen a third, more pragmatic course. The Irish privy council duly transmitted to London the heads of bills of 1719 and 1723; in the first case, indeed, it amended the penalty of branding proposed by the Commons to castration. But it is hard to believe that its actions in either case were anything other than tactical: a device to transfer to the English privy council the opprobrium of having blocked a popular measure, as indeed the English council did in each case.[9] In the case of calls for a more moderate, and so enforceable, system of prohibition, neither London nor Dublin Castle showed any interest in such radical, and potentially contentious, projects. Instead their preference, probably shared by the silent majority among Irish Protestants as a whole, was to leave well enough alone. The sweeping prohibitions of the popery acts remained nominally in force, as a resource to be invoked in times of crisis, and as a symbol of the continued commitment to Protestant dominance. But there was no longer to be any attempt, in normal circumstances, to put them into effect.

Conflicting attitudes to the laws against Catholic ecclesiastics were once again evident in a flurry of activity in the early 1730s. In 1731 the House of Lords required sheriffs, magistrates, and Church of Ireland clergy throughout the kingdom to provide a comprehensive return of secular and regular clergy, and of Catholic schools, operating within their area. The following year collectors of hearth money were required to submit returns of the numbers of Catholic and Protestant families in the districts for which they were responsible. Although there is no direct evidence, it seems reasonable to assume that these demands for information were linked to the introduction in the parliamentary sessions of 1729–30 and 1731–2 of heads of new bills to register the secular clergy and expel regulars. The English privy council refused to approve either measure. But in January 1734 the lord lieutenant, prompted by the Commons, issued a new proclamation for the enforcement of the existing laws, leading to several months of disruption as churches closed and priests went into hiding. On closer examination, however, the impression of a new surge of persecuting zeal becomes less clear cut. The demand for a proclamation, according to the papal nuncio, was motivated primarily by pique at the success of Catholic agents, allegedly aided by bribery, in having the two bills killed off in London. Archbishop Boulter of Armagh, the government's leading adviser on Irish affairs, was clear that parliament's apparent enthusiasm for new repressive measures could not

---

[8] For a fuller account see Connolly, *Religion, Law and Power*, 285–7.
[9] The case for this view is argued in more detail ibid. 281–4.

be taken at face value. In January 1732 he warned against proposals to force through a repeal of the sacramental test by attaching the relevant clause to a popular anti-Catholic bill. The test had originally been introduced in that way; but 'then there was a very great spirit against Popery amongst the Commons, which I cannot say now'.[10]

The broad truth of Boulter's observation is borne out by the detailed returns supplied in response to the orders of the House of Lords in 1731. Tolerance could not be taken for granted. The bishop of Derry reported that Catholic schoolmasters occasionally set up in his diocese, 'but upon being threatened, as they constantly are, with a warrant, or a presentment by the churchwardens, they generally think proper to withdraw'. In another Ulster diocese, Clogher, the Catholic bishop lived under the assumed name of 'Ennis' and 'disappears since these enquiries'. Elsewhere too it was clear that anything smacking of presumption would not be tolerated. A vicar in County Kildare had had a mass house pulled down, 'it standing in the direct road to my church'.[11] In general, however, the returns made clear that sheriffs, magistrates, and clergy of the established church were perfectly aware of the identity of the Catholic bishops, priests, and schoolmasters operating in the districts for which they were responsible. The rector of Skibbereen complained that when he approached local magistrates about the open proceedings of the Catholic clergy 'their answer is that the same things are done under the nose of the government at Dublin, and why should they trouble themselves to put the laws in execution, while their governors and superiors are so remiss in the executing of them'.[12] A report by the mayor of Galway that the sheriffs had been unable to discover a certain Augustinian friary must be set against an entry in the account book of the house concerned: 'November 9th . . . a bottle of wine for the sheriffs . . . 1s 1d'. The Dominicans of the same town, more hospitable or more cautious, spent 2s. 2d. 'for claret to treat the sheriffs in their search'.[13]

The lapsing into disuse of the laws against Catholic ecclesiastics took place against the background of a long period of international peace. When the threat of invasion reappeared, following the outbreak of war with Spain in 1739 and with France the following year, the initial response was entirely traditional. Early in 1744, in response to news that a French fleet had sailed, the Irish privy council issued a proclamation calling for the enforcement of the laws against Catholic ecclesiastics. Once again, churches closed their doors and a handful of priests were arrested, while others went into hiding. When a Jacobite rising took place in Scotland and England the following year, on the other hand, there was no similar crackdown. The new lord lieutenant, the earl of Chesterfield, took the credit for the new departure, reporting that he had responded to assurances

---

[10] Boulter to Delafaye, 4 Jan. 1732 (NA, SP63/395/18).
[11] 'Report on the State of Popery', *Archivium Hibernicum*, 1 (1912), 17, 16; 4, (1914) 159.
[12] Ibid. 2 (1912), 144.   [13] Quoted Wall, *Penal Laws*, 51.

of loyalty from Catholic leaders by promising them that they would remain undisturbed if they behaved, while warning of the dreadful consequences that would follow any show of disloyalty. However it is possible that Irish Protestants themselves had realized in retrospect that the previous year's sudden revival of dormant laws had been an overreaction. A grim incident in February 1744, when a decrepit building in which Dublin Catholics had assembled for a clandestine mass collapsed, killing ten worshippers, may have helped to discredit the policy of indiscriminate suppression. In any case throughout 1745–6, as a Jacobite army overran Scotland and marched south into England, Catholic places of worship remained open as normal.

The events of 1744–6 can thus be seen as a turning point in the enforcement of the penal laws relating to the Catholic clergy. In subsequent periods of perceived danger, such as the threatened French invasion of 1758–9, the possibility of a general round-up of priests, or the closure of Catholic chapels, does not seem even to have been considered. Catholic clergy, and more particularly Catholic bishops, could not take their new security wholly for granted. In 1751 Nicholas Sweetman, bishop of Ferns, was arrested on the information of a delinquent priest he had suspended from duty. Five years later magistrates detained Archbishop Michael O'Reilly of Armagh, along with eighteen of his diocesan priests, as they met at Dundalk to transact diocesan business. In each case, however, the potential charges against the bishops were political, relating to the alleged raising of money for the Pretender rather than to their still technically illegal status. Both men, moreover, were quickly released after token questioning. In this sense the two incidents were evidence less of any return to former ways than of the extent to which attitudes and assumptions had changed since the beginning of the century.

In contrast to the patchy and diminishing enforcement of the laws against Catholic ecclesiastics, most of the laws relating to the Catholic laity were consistently and rigorously applied. The one area in which the Protestant establishment showed any real concern with their possible ineffectiveness was in relation to the practice of law, where there were repeated complaints of Catholics continuing to practise behind a screen of nominal conformity. An act of 1727 required converts to certify that they had been Protestants for at least two years, and to educate their children in the same religion. An act of 1733 debarred any lawyer marrying a papist. Otherwise, the exclusion of Catholics from parliament, from public office, from urban corporations, and from the grand juries that administered county government was taken for granted. The only exception was the lowly but necessary office, as much a burden as an entitlement, held by a high constable in each barony and the constable in each parish. Here demographic reality—the absence outside parts of Ulster of anything like the number of Protestants required—imposed its own restrictions. High constables and constables were not required to take the oath of abjuration, or subscribe to the declaration against transubstantiation and other doctrines. An act of 1715 requiring that all constables should be Protestants was quietly allowed to lapse three years later, and it appears that the majority of those constituting this bottom tier of the hierarchy of local government and law enforcement were in fact Catholics.[14]

The other major group of penal enactments related to land. The Treaty of Limerick had allowed Catholics to escape the full effects of military defeat. Proprietors who could establish that they had been in arms, or (under the controversial 'missing clause') had been living in Jacobite-controlled territory, at the time of the treaty were protected against attainder and forfeiture. Of 1,283 such claims heard before the Irish privy council, and subsequently before a special court of claims, all but 16 were accepted. The post-war confiscations were thus confined to those who had been killed or captured or who had surrendered before the end of the war, as well as those who had chosen the option of transportation to France. Even in these cases, moreover, relatives were sometimes able to save all or part of the estate by producing leases, deeds of mortgage, or family settlements establishing an interest separate from that of the forfeiting individual. Protestants complained, almost certainly with some justification, that the documents concerned were often forged or backdated. But the commissioners responsible for the administration of the forfeitures nevertheless restored some forty confiscated estates to the families that had formerly owned them, as well as ruling that fifteen more should revert on the death of a forfeiting proprietor possessed only of a life interest, and allowing a variety of lesser claims to jointures, marriage portions, or other entitlements.[15] Despite this determined rearguard action, however, the overall loss of Catholic land was significant. By 1703, their share had fallen to 14 per cent, compared to 22 per cent in the late 1680s.[16]

Following the popery act of 1704, and even more the introduction of the discovery procedure in 1709, the surviving Catholic proprietors faced a new series of obstacles. There was some scope for evasion. The requirement that estates be subdivided on the death of each proprietor could be circumvented by younger sons declining to assert their rights. Proprietors taking long leases or engaging in other transactions discoverable under the act of 1709 could protect their interest by having a trusted Protestant file a collusive bill of discovery. Such devices were rendered more effective by the willingness of the courts to regard the popery laws as penal, in the technical sense of requiring strict adherence to the letter of the law for prosecutions to succeed (as opposed to ameliorative legislation, where more attention would be paid to the intentions of the legislature). But there was still the risk of falling victim either to a discontented relative or a predatory outsider. There were also other burdens: exclusion from participation in both central and

---

[14] Neal Garnham, *The Courts, Crime, and the Criminal Law in Ireland 1692–1760* (Dublin, 1996), 28–9.

[15] J. G. Simms, *The Williamite Confiscations in Ireland 1690–1703* (London, 1956), ch. 12.

[16] These are the figures offered ibid. 195. For a more recent calculation, as yet untested, see above, Ch. 4 n. 27.

local politics, the inconvenience of being treated as a politically suspect person during episodes such as the invasion scares of 1744–5, even, at a time when suitable marriages were an essential part of any landed family's economic strategy, the limited pool of potential partners available to a Catholic suitor.

Against this background growing numbers of landowners and their heirs chose to conform to the Church of Ireland and assume their rightful place within the kingdom's ruling class. There was also a secondary shrinkage of the proportion of land in Catholic hands, as estates sold as a result of demographic or economic failure—especially during the depressed 1720s and 1730s—passed into what by law could only be Protestant hands. Precise statistics are not available: the often-quoted figure of a 5 per cent share of land in Catholic hands by the 1770s relies on a throwaway remark by the visiting agriculturalist Arthur Young.[17] But by the last quarter of the eighteenth century the Catholic landowning class had been reduced to a handful of survivors. Of these the most prominent were the earls of Kenmare, descendants of the Elizabethan adventurer Valentine Brown, the ancient Pale families of Plunkett and Preston, now earls of Fingal and Viscounts Gormanstown, and the Catholic branches of the great Butler dynasty in Tipperary and Kilkenny.[18]

At the level of landownership, then, the popery laws were the final blow to an already shrunken Catholic interest. Among other sections of rural society, their impact was much less. The stipulation that Catholics should not take leases for longer than thirty-one years, or at a rent less than two-thirds the value of the lands concerned, placed tenants at an undoubted disadvantage compared to their Protestant counterparts. The second restriction, however, seems rarely to have been enforced; the first, in what, from the 1740s onwards, was a period of rapidly rising prices, still left ample scope for profit. And in fact it was precisely the middle decades of the eighteenth century, when this part of the popery acts was in force, that saw the emergence from what had previously been a largely undifferentiated peasantry of a new farming class, distinguished by its ownership of livestock and other forms of capital. If the proportion of land owned outright by Catholics had fallen sharply, moreover, there remained a substantial body of middlemen, many of them members of former landowning families, who maintained a gentry lifestyle on the profits derived from renting and then subletting large tracts of land. Their extensive holdings on long leases entitle them to be included, alongside the small number of surviving proprietors, in any overall assessment of Catholic landed wealth.[19]

---

[17] 'Upon the whole nineteen twentieths of the kingdom changed hands from Catholic to Protestant': Arthur Young, *A Tour in Ireland 1776–1779*, ed. A. H. Hutton (London, 1892), ii. 59.

[18] List of the annual incomes of leading Irish Catholics, *c.*1780 (PRONI, D1514/1/5/40).

[19] For general surveys of the social effects of the penal laws see L. M. Cullen, 'Catholics under the Penal Laws', *ECI* 1 (1986), 23–36; T. P. Power and Kevin Whelan (eds.), *Endurance and Emergence: Catholics in Ireland in the Eighteenth Century* (Blackrock, 1990), essays by Cullen, Dickson, Power, and Harvey.

Where mercantile wealth is concerned, a similar picture emerges. Once again the real losses had taken place in the seventeenth century, particularly in the 1650s, when the formerly dominant Old English had for a time been expelled from the major towns, and had forfeited assets not subsequently recovered. The erosion of Catholic landed property, at a time when land remained the main source of capital for trade and manufacturing, was a further blow. In the eighteenth century Catholics continued to dominate the trade of Limerick and Galway; in Limerick, in fact, a local priest, in 1768, went so far as to complain that leading merchants were endangering this monopoly by their willingness to accept Protestant apprentices in return for large fees. But both ports were by this time in relative decline. In Cork, the great centre for the expanding Atlantic trade, Catholics in 1758 made up only one-fifth of merchants trading overseas. In Dublin in 1780 they made up three-eighths of all merchants.[20]

In comparison to these earlier losses, the new burdens imposed after 1691 on a reduced but still significant Catholic commercial interest were serious, but more manageable. Its members were less likely to be awarded government contracts, they could not take very long leases on urban property, and they were excluded from participation in municipal government or from full membership of the guilds that continued to regulate economic activity. On the other hand their wealth was to grow with the general expansion of Irish commerce across the century, and it was in fact from among these merchants and manufacturers that a new Catholic elite was to emerge and to commence the campaign for readmission to political rights.

For all the controversy that surrounded them, both during and after their operation, the impact of the penal laws is easily overestimated. The bishops' banishment act and other measures caused severe short-term disruption, but did not in the long term have any significant impact on the continued adherence to Catholicism of four-fifths of the population. Restrictions on landed and (to a much lesser extent) mercantile wealth served largely to confirm a massive transfer of resources that had already taken place by the 1690s. The resulting concentration of wealth in Protestant hands, equally, severely limited the significance of the restrictions on Catholic participation in a political system in which property not numbers was the key to power. Catholics, after all, were to regain the right to vote in 1793 and became eligible to sit in parliament from 1829. But it was not until the 1880s that the secret ballot, combined with new forms of mass-based political organization, finally ended the dominance of Irish electoral politics by a small and almost exclusively Protestant landlord class.

Yet if penal legislation did not radically change the structure of Irish society, its impact on the day-to-day lives of Irish Catholics should not be discounted.

---

[20] David Dickson, 'Catholics and Trade in Eighteenth-Century Ireland', in Power and Whelan (eds.), *Endurance and Emergence*, 90. For Limerick see John White, 'Annals of the City and Diocese of Limerick' (NLI MS 2714), 169–70.

The laws against Catholic clergy had fallen into disuse, but could be invoked at a whim. At Castle Lyons, County Cork, for example, a dispute in 1733 over a turnpike road led a Protestant magistrate to retaliate against his Catholic opponent by having the door of the local mass house nailed up. The Protestant monopoly of law enforcement, equally, provided constant opportunities for assertions of superiority of the kind that Daithi Ó Bruadair had earlier recalled with such distaste. At Youghal in 1743 a Protestant mob reacted to news of a British naval defeat by plundering the local Catholic church and creating a bonfire of the altar and seats. In 1746, during the crisis precipitated by the last great Jacobite rising in Great Britain, a militia troop in Mallow extorted contributions from local Catholics towards the cost of new uniforms by thinly veiled menaces. A few years later Stephen Roche, a member of Limerick's leading Catholic merchant family, was humiliatingly arrested as he showed a visitor, an Irish-born officer in the Austrian army, around the city's walls.[21] Indeed it was arguably these multiple petty tyrannies, rather than their declared aim of controlling access to the upper levels of the political system, that constituted the real impact of the penal laws on the social and political life of eighteenth-century Ireland.

DEFENDING ESTABLISHMENT

At the same time that they debated the policy to be adopted towards the Catholic church and its followers, the dominant Anglican minority had also to consider the position of their fellow Protestants among the Presbyterians and other nonconformist denominations. By the early eighteenth century policy towards dissenters had become, as in England, one of the main issues separating the two political parties, Whig and Tory. Harassment by the civil authorities and church courts abated under the Whig-dominated executive during 1704–7, then resumed with a new vigour under a strongly Tory administration between 1710 and 1714. In the summer of 1714 the *regium donum* was suspended, there was a rash of persecutions under the act of uniformity, and Anglican mobs attacked meeting houses.

The death of Queen Anne in August 1714, and the subsequent collapse of the Tory party in both kingdoms, put an end to this surge of Anglican aggression. Yet the gains to Irish dissenters from the triumph of their supposed Whig allies proved to be much less than might have been expected. This was partly because the church courts, largely outside the control of the government, continued for some years to act against Presbyterians marrying without the rites

---

[21] Burke, *Irish Priests*, 383; David Dickson, *Old World Colony: Cork and South Munster 1630–1830* (Cork, 2005), 249, 271; Nini Rodgers, *Ireland, Slavery and Anti-Slavery 1612–1865* (Basingstoke, 2007), 138.

of the established church. Prosecutions seem to have tailed off only in the early 1720s, and it was not until 1737 that an act confirmed that the marriage of two Presbyterians before their own minister was valid in law. More important, however, proceedings in the Irish parliament quickly demonstrated once again that the majority of Irish Whigs were not prepared to carry solidarity with their dissenting fellow Protestants to the point of allowing them to compete on equal terms for political power.

The first test of the state of political opinion was in 1716, when friends of the dissenters introduced heads of a bill to indemnify those who had accepted commissions in the militia during a recent invasion scare without having taken the sacramental test. Opponents, however, were quick to recognize the thin end of a wedge. An alternative resolution declaring anyone who prosecuted a dissenter in those circumstances an enemy of the Protestant interest addressed the specific concern while leaving the principle of the test untouched. Despite this symbolic but significant defeat, the dissenters, confident that they had the backing of the London government, continued to press the case. In 1719 the ministry ordered the lord lieutenant, the duke of Bolton, to proceed with a bill to abolish the test. He duly deputed the chancellor of the exchequer, Sir Ralph Gore, to introduce a bill to allow dissenters to be justices of the peace and to hold certain other civil and military offices. Before Gore could do so, however, opponents of the dissenters once again responded with their own pre-emptive measure: a toleration act that conferred nothing more than exemption from the largely defunct provisions of the acts of uniformity. Attempts during the passage of the bill to widen its provisions beyond this purely formal concession were voted down by majorities reportedly as high as 200 to 20, leading the chancellor to abandon his proposed bill. In the same year parliament introduced the first of a series of indemnity acts, extending the time allowed for holders of paid offices to take the test. The lack of debate, however, suggests that this was a device to protect Anglican officers from the consequences of oversight, rather than (as is sometimes suggested) a mysteriously uncontested liberalization of the law.

The scale of defeat in 1719 was sufficient to push the claims of the dissenters into the background for over a decade. In 1731–3 Sir Robert Walpole, concerned to ensure continued electoral support from English dissenters, initiated a new drive to secure the repeal of the Irish test. He initially proposed to attach the repeal clause to a bill to tighten the prohibition on Catholics owning weapons, but reluctantly retreated when Irish office holders assured him that any such measure had no chance of passing. Instead he ordered the lord lieutenant to proceed with a straightforward bill to abolish the test. When parliament met in October 1733 dissenters and Anglican clergy crowded into Dublin to lobby for and against repeal. Within parliament, the administration's best strategy was clearly to hold back until the normal grants of additional taxes were safely through, and possibly to attempt a surprise attack in a thin house. In December, however, a motion setting a deadline after which no legislation to repeal any part of the popery acts should be introduced passed the Commons without a division, 'for the nos did not exceed a dozen'.[22] A few days later the parliamentary friends of the dissenters informed them that they saw no hope of a repeal bill passing.

The debate on the failed repeal of the sacramental test in 1733 produced one powerful voice from an earlier time. An anonymous pamphlet by Jonathan Swift, *The Presbyterian's Plea of Merit*, took the debate back to the seventeenth century, emphasizing the involvement of Presbyterians as well as Independents in the murder of Charles I, and accusing them of having collaborated with James II until it had become clear that his was the losing side. A second pamphlet, published only later, was more provocative, taking the form of a supposed petition by Catholics pointing out that their historical record as defenders of monarchy entitled them to as much favour as dissenters, who 'were always republicans both in principle and practice'.[23] For the most part, however, the debate made clear how far the antagonisms and uncertainties of Queen Anne's reign had faded from immediate memory. Presbyterian strength was no longer being reinforced by an apparently endless stream of immigrants from Scotland. On the contrary, the commencement from around 1718 of large-scale emigration to the North American colonies seemed likely to erode their numerical superiority. Meanwhile the other great source of Presbyterian strength, their rigid discipline, had also been compromised, as internal theological disputes led to the emergence of separate New and Old Light wings of what had previously seemed a frighteningly single-minded and cohesive body.[24]

For all of these reasons the passions aroused by this last attempt, for two generations, to obtain the repeal of the sacramental test were less intense than those of the years immediately before and after 1714. Even among the clergy, Boulter predicted after the vote, 'the heat . . . will, I think, be soon over'.[25] The vote against any explicit proposal for repeal, he estimated, would have been three to two, again a less conclusive rejection than might have been seen two decades earlier. But the level of opposition was nevertheless enough to make clear that confessional exclusiveness, blended with ethnic and social antagonisms, was not solely a matter of Protestant discrimination against Catholics. The Irish Anglican elite, with the possible exception of some high Tories, were willing enough to let dissenters worship God in their own way. But most had clearly no desire to share power with so numerous and independent minded a body. In refusing to do so, moreover, they had the reassurance of knowing that any resentment that the dissenters might feel at their second-class status within Protestant Ireland

---

[22] *Letters of Marmaduke Coghill 1722–38*, ed. D. W. Hayton (Dublin, 2005), 147.

[23] Jonathan Swift, *The Presbyterians Plea of Merit in Order to Take off the Test Impartially Examined* (*Irish Tracts 1728–1733*, ed. Herbert Davis (Oxford, 1955), 263–79); *Reasons Humbly Offered to the Parliament of Ireland for Repealing the Sacramental Test*, ibid. 286.

[24] See below, p. 281.

[25] *Letters Written by his Excellency Hugh Boulter DD, Lord Primate of All Ireland* (Oxford, 1769–70), ii. 109–12.

would be heavily outweighed by the fear and hatred with which they regarded Catholicism. It was not until the last decades of the eighteenth century that this certainty began to waver. And when it did so it opened the way to a wholly different pattern of alliances and antagonisms.

THE CHURCH OF ROME

The banishment act of 1697, combined with subsequent restrictions, should in theory have left Ireland with a rudimentary ecclesiastical establishment restricted to a declining body of parish clergy. In practice the decades that followed saw a steady increase in numbers. A survey undertaken in 1697 in connection with the implementation of the bishops' banishment act returned 872 secular clergy and 495 regulars. A total of 1,089 priests registered under the act of 1704. The House of Lords committee in 1731 counted 1,445 secular clergy and 254 regulars. All of these figures are probably underestimates, more especially so in the case of regulars. Modern research suggests that there were in fact around 900 male members of religious orders in 1697. Of these more than 700 left or were deported following the banishment act, but by 1750 their numbers had recovered to around 800. How far the two-thirds increase in the number of secular clergy between 1697 and 1731 reflects the better information available in the more relaxed period of the later survey is unclear. However complaints by Protestants suggest that there was in fact a large influx of priests, particularly in the period after 1714.[26]

A figure of 1,445 parish priests and curates in 1731 suggests a ratio of one clergyman to every 1,245 Catholics. This was a level of staffing comparable with that achieved in Victorian Ireland, in the period of what has been called the 'devotional revolution'. Both Catholic and Protestant observers, in fact, believed that Ireland in the first half of the century had too many priests. By 1800, on the other hand, the population was twice what it had been in the 1730s, while the number of parish clergy had risen by only one-tenth, to about 1,614. Failure to expand was due partly to the limited number of places available in the European seminaries where Irish priests were trained. In part it reflected the inability of the rural poor who made up the greater part of the expanded population to contribute to the support of a greater number of clergy. The number of regulars, meanwhile, had fallen to around 400. Their decline was due, not to government repression, but to the old antagonism, founded partly on disputes over jurisdiction and

---

[26] The assessment of eighteenth-century Catholic life offered here is developed in greater detail in S. J. Connolly, *Priests and People in Pre-Famine Ireland 1780–1845* (Dublin, 1992), and in Connolly, *Religion, Law and Power*, ch. 5. For a short general survey see P. J. Corish, *The Catholic Community in the Seventeenth and Eighteenth Centuries* (Dublin, 1981). Oliver Rafferty, *Catholicism in Ulster 1603–1983* (Dublin, 1994), ch. 2, is a useful provincial survey.

partly on competition for limited resources, between seculars and regulars. In 1751 the Congregation of Propaganda, responding to complaints regarding the poor level of training provided, ordered Irish religious houses to cease taking in novices. This reduced recruitment to the minority who could afford to travel to a continental house for their training. Even with 150 of the surviving regulars drafted in to serve as parish priests and curates, there were now 2,676 Catholics for every parish clergyman, and the church was experiencing the beginnings of a manpower crisis that was to continue until the Famine of 1845–50.[27]

If the church was, initially at least, well staffed, it was less well provided with accommodation. In Dublin and other major towns affluent congregations were able to support substantial, well-maintained buildings, fitted out with pews and internal galleries, and with paintings and decorated altars providing a modest level of visual display. In most of the countryside, however, even the better churches were plain rectangular structures, with thatched roofs and walls of stone or mud. In the diocese of Cloyne, in 1731, the seventy 'mass houses' were 'generally mean thatched cabins, many or most of them open at one end'. Some congregations had no church, but heard mass in private houses or in the open air. This was particularly the case in Ulster, where Catholics were both poor and, in some parts, a minority. The Church of Ireland bishop of Derry, in 1731, reported only nine mass houses, 'mass being said in most places sub dio, or under some sort of shed, built up occasionally to shelter the priest from the weather'. But even the dioceses of Leighlin and Ferns, both areas where the Catholic population should have been relatively prosperous, had respectively three and eleven 'moveable altars in the fields'. In parts of Ulster and Connacht mass was still being said in the open air as late as the 1820s and 1830s.[28]

The great struggle of the seventeenth century had been to reorganize the Irish church along Tridentine lines. By the early eighteenth century the essential framework of parish and diocese was firmly established. But rigorous internal discipline remained difficult to maintain. The political uncertainties of the Restoration period had permitted only a partial restoration of episcopal government, and the fall of James II began a new period of disruption. In 1697 there were only eight bishops in the country, and by 1707 only two. The appointment of five new bishops in that year began the reconstruction of a Catholic hierarchy. However it was not until 1747 that the last long gap in the episcopal succession ended with the appointment of a bishop to Dromore, vacant since 1716. Even where bishops were in place, moreover, the continued sensitivity of the authorities to anything that could be construed as the exercise of a foreign jurisdiction made it necessary to tread carefully.

---

[27] For statistics on the number of Catholic priests see Connolly, *Priests and People*, 260–1. For the regular clergy see Hugh Fenning, *The Undoing of the Friars of Ireland: A Study of the Novitiate Question in the Eighteenth Century* (Louvain, 1972).

[28] 'Report on the State of Popery', *Archivium Hibernicum*, 2 (1913), 127, 1 (1912), 17, 4 (1914), 165, 170. See also Connolly, *Religion, Law and Power*, 151; Connolly, *Priests and People*, 107–9.

For the Roman authorities likewise Ireland's status as a missionary territory, governed by the distant figure of a papal nuncio based in Brussels, made effective supervision difficult. Throughout the first half of the eighteenth century, in fact, the nuncio and his superiors in the Congregation for the Propagation of the Faith had difficulty even ensuring that the bishops themselves resided in the dioceses for which they were responsible. Dominic O'Daly, bishop of Achonry, was alleged in 1734 to visit his diocese only once a year, to collect money from his clergy and to ordain, for a fee, any candidate who presented himself. The following year Ambrose O'Callaghan, bishop of what should have been the reasonably congenial diocese of Ferns in the south-east, was described by an exasperated papal nuncio as a prelate in perpetual motion, on account of his frequent visits to the continent. James O'Daly, bishop of Kilfenora 1726–49, was a double absentee, who not only remained in France after his appointment, but insisted on his right to live in Paris rather than at Tournai, where he held a benefice in the cathedral. As late as 1775 Propaganda was forced to suspend the archbishop of Armagh, Anthony Blake, on discovering that open feuds among the clergy of the diocese were to be blamed on Blake's insistence on performing his administrative duties from his brother's house in County Galway.[29]

The quality of the lower clergy also varied. By the mid-eighteenth century the great majority would have received some formal seminary training in one of the colleges now scattered throughout Catholic Europe, in Spain, Portugal, France, and the Spanish Netherlands. However, most would probably have been ordained before leaving Ireland, so that they could support themselves during their studies with the money earned through saying masses. Of the 1,089 registered under the act of 1704, only 255, mainly from the richer provinces of Munster and Leinster, had in fact been ordained abroad.[30] How many, once overseas, completed a full course of study, and whether there were any who still found their way into a parish without having ever left Ireland, remains unclear. Where discipline is concerned, there were occasional instances of serious delinquency. Patrick Scanlan, a parish priest in Limerick city, was suspended in 1755 after two women had apparently borne his children. However he remained in the parish, protected by a group of supporters, including some Protestants who could legally carry firearms and used them to drive off the bishop when he attempted to take possession of the church. In general, however, the complaints recorded in visitation records and similar documents relate to less spectacular instances of negligence and lack of decorum. Priests drank too much, and socialized too freely with their parishioners. They failed to preach regularly, or to catechize children. Their churches were dilapidated and their vestments torn

---

[29] Connolly, *Priests and People*, 82–3; Patrick Whelan, 'Anthony Blake, Archbishop of Armagh 1758–87', *Seanchas Árdmhacha*, 5 (1970), 289–323.

[30] Tomás Ó Fiaich, 'The Registration of the Clergy in 1704', *Seanchas Árdmhacha*, 6 (1971), 49–50.

or shabby. The bishop of Ferns, inspecting his diocese in 1753, found one priest not 'very zealous or diligent in his duty' and another 'neither very instructive or edifying to his flock', while a third 'minded dogs and hunting more than his flock'. The archbishop of Baltimore, writing in 1788 to his counterpart in Dublin about possible recruits for the American mission, felt it necessary to explain, somewhat apologetically, that any volunteers would have to realize that on his side of the Atlantic clergymen were expected to be sober 'to a great degree', so that what elsewhere might be acceptable would be regarded in his diocese 'as unbecoming excess'.[31]

The level of popular religious education and practice achieved against this unpropitious background was inevitably uneven. The 1731 inquiry noted a total of 549 popish schools. The true figure, given the dormant but still menacing provisions of the act of 1697, was probably higher. Teachers of elementary schools generally worked in cooperation with the Catholic clergy, often using the church as a schoolhouse, and were expected to provide regular religious instruction. Others provided the teaching in Latin that would be required for recruits to the priesthood. On both counts the maintenance of this educational counter-establishment was one important element in the resilience of Irish Catholicism in a period of political disadvantage. In poorer areas, unable to support significant numbers of schools, on the other hand, religious education would have depended on whatever arrangements the priest was able to make for the rote teaching of the catechism. Reports on the state of religion generally emphasized the piety of the people, and their commitment to the church. At the same time there were also complaints that large numbers failed to meet the minimum requirement of confessing and receiving communion at least once each year. Statistics from the 1830s indicated that at that time average attendance at Sunday mass in rural areas may have been as low as 40 per cent of the population. This may well have reflected a decline in attendance over the preceding half-century or more, as rising Catholic numbers outstripped the supply of both priests and places of worship, and as the proportion of the very poor within their ranks increased. At the same time a shortfall of this proportion would also suggest that the Tridentine ideal of universal attendance at Sunday mass had in fact never been fully realized in most parts of Ireland.[32]

In Ireland, as in other parts of Catholic Europe, popular religious culture was a blend of the orthodox and the folkloric. Many of its beliefs and practices

---

[31] White, 'Annals of Limerick' (NLI MS 2714), 144; W. H. Grattan-Flood, 'The Diocesan Manuscripts of Ferns during the Reign of Bishop Sweetman', *Archivium Hibernicum*, 2 (1913), 101–5; J. Carroll to John Thomas Troy, archbishop of Dublin, 11 Aug. 1788, in P. F. Moran (ed.), *Spicilegium Ossoriense: Being a Collection of Original Letters and Papers* (Dublin, 1874–84), iii. 505).

[32] For the 1830s evidence, D. W. Miller, 'Irish Catholicism and the Great Famine', *Journal of Social History*, 9 (1975), 81–98. For religious practice in general, Connolly, *Priests and People*, ch. 3. For a more optimistic assessment of both clergy and laity, Corish, *Catholic Community*, ch. 5; S. A. Meigs, *The Reformations in Ireland: Traditionalism and Confessionalism 1400–1690* (Dublin, 1997), ch. 8.

reflected the social and psychological needs of a population living close to subsistence, and at the mercy of unpredictable fluctuations in weather, crop yields, and disease. Charms, spells, and traditions relating to the activities of the fairies or the workings of the evil eye offered some explanation for an apparently arbitrary pattern of good and bad fortune, and at least the hope of influencing the outcome. Ceremonies such as the hanging of protective symbols in the house on 1 February, the ancient spring festival of Imbolc, or the lighting of bonfires at the midsummer solstice, marked out turning points in the agricultural year. The superficial redefinition of these festivals as, respectively, the feast of St Bridget and the eve of St John was characteristic of the blending of Christian and non-Christian elements. A similar mixture was evident in the widespread celebration of patterns, festivals held at what was believed to be a holy well on the feast day (*patrún* or patron day) of the saint to whom it was dedicated. Superficially a commemoration of a local saint, the pattern combined sometimes brutal physical penance, such as a circuit of the well on bare knees, protective rituals believed to have supernatural efficacy, and carnivalesque celebration. Funerals, meanwhile, provided the occasion for another distinctive popular custom: a festive wake, at which the passing of a friend or neighbour was marked by drinking and games, some of them with a strong sexual element.

A reaffirmation of the boundary between acceptable and unacceptable varieties of supernatural belief and practice was another prominent concern of the Counter-Reformation. From the early seventeenth century onwards, bishops expressed concern at the interaction of Christian and non-Christian traditions, and condemned the drinking and other excesses associated with wakes and patterns. The lower clergy, closer to their congregations in their upbringing and daily circumstances, were not always so critical. The bishop of Ferns in 1771 found it necessary to forbid his priests 'to act the fairy doctor in any shape', by reading prayers over 'the already too ignorant' or blessing water with which to sprinkle sick persons or cattle.[33] Elsewhere priests came forward to give their blessing to the lighting of midsummer bonfires, or to preside over the ceremonies at holy wells. By the end of the century, however, such collaboration in popular rituals, even by the lower clergy, was becoming less common. The change reflected a tightening of ecclesiastical discipline, improvements in clerical education, and the rising status of the Catholic priest as a figure in local society. The result was a division between official and popular Catholicism that was to become of increasing importance in the decades after 1800.[34]

One area in which the divergence between popular and official standards of behaviour was no longer the problem it had once been was attitudes to marriage. By the eighteenth century the toleration of irregular unions, and the acceptance

---

[33] W. H. Grattan-Flood, 'The Diocesan Manuscripts of Ferns during the Reign of Bishop Sweetman', *Archivium Hibernicum*, 3 (1914), 117.
[34] This developing clash of religious cultures is explored in detail in Connolly, *Priests and People*.

of possible impermanence, that had caused such concern a hundred years earlier appears to have wholly disappeared. The first Catholic parish registers, available from the 1750s, indicate that the proportion of births classified as illegitimate was around 5 per cent—almost twice the level that was to be seen in the late nineteenth and twentieth centuries, but still relatively low by international standards. The proportion of brides pregnant at the time of their marriage, possibly a more revealing statistic, was about one in ten, compared to one in three in rural England in the same period. How far this revolution in sexual conduct can be attributed to a more effective moral discipline imposed by the Catholic church remains unclear. But the evident ineffectiveness of repeated ordinances against other forms of delinquency, such as the festivities at wakes and patterns, would suggest that the influence of the church alone can hardly have been responsible for such a significant shift in attitudes and behaviour. An alternative explanation might be that falling extramarital fertility reflected the changes that rising population and the commercialization of agriculture had produced within rural society. In a world where the survival of families was tied to the management of small plots of land, and their orderly transmission from one generation to the next, there was a new and powerful incentive to regulate the sexual behaviour of the unmarried young.[35]

THE CHURCH AS BY LAW ESTABLISHED

Any comparison either with Catholicism or with Protestant dissent can, at first sight, work only to the disadvantage of the established church. Measured against the perseverance of these denominations under differing levels of political and social disadvantage, the Church of Ireland must appear as the unworthy beneficiary of privilege: complacent, hidebound, and lacking in zeal. On closer examination, however, a different picture emerges, of an institution that was insecure, divided within itself, and seriously at odds with the Protestant elite whose interests it supposedly shared. The church's pastoral failings, equally, were well advertised. William III's Queen Mary told her husband in 1690 that the Church of Ireland was the worst in Christendom. But here too the abuse of privilege, undeniable though it was, may not have been quite as widespread or grotesque as has generally been assumed. There was certainly a painful awareness, among churchmen themselves, of the extent to which the institution fell short of its mission as a national church, inspiring a variety of limited but nevertheless significant movements for internal reform.[36]

[35] S. J. Connolly, 'Illegitimacy and Pre-Nuptial Pregnancy in Ireland before 1864: The Evidence of Some Catholic Parish Registers', *IESH* 6 (1979), 5–23.
[36] The interpretation of the Church of Ireland offered here is once again developed in more detail in Connolly, *Religion, Law and Power*, ch. 5. For a general treatment of its history see the

The first of these came in the period immediately following the Revolution. The resolution of long-standing political and religious uncertainties created a sense that the time had come for a new beginning. There was also a widespread belief that the recent losses and mortal peril endured by Protestants had represented a taste of divine vengeance on their society for its moral failings and lack of religious zeal. The leaders of the reform party were William King and Nathaniel Foy, newly appointed to the sees of Derry and Waterford and Lismore, along with Anthony Dopping, the longer-serving bishop of Meath. Together these sought to promote higher standards of pastoral service within their own dioceses, and at the same time lobbied the government and parliament for reforms. In Dublin Archbishop Francis Marsh promoted the creation of voluntary societies of young men who assembled for prayer and religious discussion. Around the same time Anglican clergy and laity joined with dissenters in a short-lived but vigorous movement for the reform of public manners, having prostitutes arrested and whipped, prosecuting conspicuous breaches of the sabbath, and enforcing a new statute whereby swearing and blasphemy could be punished by a fine or the stocks. Another statute in 1696 strengthened the requirement that clergy should maintain a school in each parish, and there was also a drive to establish charity schools for the better religious and moral education of the poor.[37]

The swearing and education statutes of 1695 and 1696 indicated that the efforts of the reform movement had some wider support. Its leaders also scored one notable success, in 1694, when the king and queen appointed King and Dopping as royal commissioners charged with inspecting the notoriously disordered diocese of Down and Connor. Thomas Hackett, bishop since 1672, was a blatant absentee, whose frequent absences in London had earned him the nickname of 'bishop of Hammersmith'. The commission confirmed that he had consistently failed to carry out essential episcopal functions such as confirmations and the consecration of new churches, and had taken money for appointments to benefices and ecclesiastical offices. He had also provided certificates falsely testifying that candidates seeking appointments had taken the oaths prescribed by law, 'by which means one Moor a papist got into a great living'. More recently he had allowed control of diocesan affairs to pass largely into the hands of a Mrs Cole, whom he himself referred to as 'Bishop Cole'.[38]

relevant essays in A. Ford, J. McGuire, and K. Milne (eds.), *As by Law Established: The Church of Ireland since the Reformation* (Dublin, 1995).

[37] J. C. Beckett, 'The Government and the Church of Ireland under William III and Anne', *IHS* 2 (1941), 280–302; T. C. Barnard, 'Reforming Irish Manners: The Religious Societies in Dublin during the 1690s', *Historical Journal*, 35 (1992), 805–38; D. W. Hayton, 'Did Protestantism Fail in Early Eighteenth-Century Ireland? Charity Schools and the Enterprise of Religious and Social Reformation *c.*1690–1730', in Ford et al. (eds.), *As by Law Established*, 166–86.

[38] Abstract of the articles exhibited against the bishop of Down and Connor (PRONI T545/7); King to James Bonnell, 21 Mar. 1694 (TCD MS 1995–2008, No. 341).

Hackett was duly removed from office, along with several of his clergy, and his place taken by the reform-minded Samuel Foley. In other cases, however, the reformers came up against the forces of inertia in church and state. A bill to regulate the union and division of parishes that would have tightened the requirement on clergy to reside was lost in the House of Lords in late 1695. Meanwhile the government had filled a number of ecclesiastical vacancies in a manner that made clear that political patronage continued to count for more than considerations of pastoral merit. By the late 1690s campaigners for change had begun to look for an alternative path to reform, through a meeting of Convocation, the representative body of the clergy, sitting alongside the two houses of parliament, which had last met in the 1660s. A wider group of bishops and clergy, alarmed at the government's indulgence of dissent, joined in the campaign for Convocation to be summoned. In late 1703, faced with a threat that the clergy would assert their rights by meeting even without a summons, the government reluctantly complied.

In surrendering to the demand for an Irish Convocation, the government was also giving way to the high church movement which over the past few years had been gaining ground in England. To conservative churchmen the toleration act of 1689, granting freedom of worship to dissenters, represented a grave act of apostasy on the part of the new monarchy. In addition the new freedom of expression permitted by the lapsing of systematic censorship of publications had permitted what was perceived as an explosion of deism and a general collapse of morals. There was also a widespread sense that the events of 1688 had shaken the foundations of social order—a perception possibly heightened, in the minds of some Anglican traditionalists, by unease at the manner in which they themselves had been forced to retreat from the principle of unquestioning obedience to temporal authority that they had earlier presented as unshakeable religious truth. In response to these multiple ills high churchmen sought to reiterate the traditional Christian ideal of a society in which church and state would operate as mutually reinforcing parts of a single, organic whole. Accordingly they called on crown and parliament, not just to defend the church's remaining privileges, but to restore its lost coercive authority and to join with it in a campaign to impose religious orthodoxy and moral discipline.

The extension of the high church campaign to Ireland was undoubtedly facilitated by personal contacts. Several of those who were to emerge as its most prominent spokesmen, such as William Perceval, archdeacon of Cashel, and Thomas Lindsay, archbishop of Armagh, had been born or educated in England, and acted in close consultation with the leading high churchmen there. But the concerns that fuelled the English movement also had relevance on the other side of the Irish Sea. Conscientious Irish divines had had their own difficulties in coming to terms with the Revolution, and even when they had done so were alarmed by the rhetoric adopted by its more committed defenders. Dissent, in the form of an already large Presbyterian population now being further reinforced by immigration from Scotland, was an even more formidable threat than in England. The spectre of irreligion, or at least heterodoxy, had also made its appearance, with results that made clear the hostility of the majority towards any deviation from orthodoxy. In 1697 the Dublin grand jury referred to the committee of religion of the Irish House of Commons the book *Christianity not Mysterious*, published two years earlier by the Donegal-born John Toland, who had just reappeared in the kingdom seeking preferment. Toland, having early abandoned his family's Catholicism, had studied at Glasgow, Leiden, and Oxford, and was now a correspondent of Locke and other advanced thinkers of his day. His book, a robust attack on the needless mystification erected around what he presented as rational religious truth, was a controversial but respected text. In Ireland, on the other hand, the Commons committee ordered that it be burned by the public hangman, and Toland himself escaped arrest only by a hasty flight.[39] Six years later Thomas Emlyn, minister to the Presbyterian congregation at Wood Street, Dublin, became involved in a debate with other ministers over his rejection of the doctrine of the Trinity. By thus publicizing his views he brought on himself a prosecution in the Dublin episcopal court, which fined him £1,000 and sentenced him to two years in prison. He was spared the additional penalty of a spell in the pillory, on the grounds that 'by reason of the great abhorrence the people had to his doctrine, this would be equal to death'.[40]

In Ireland as in England, then, fear of deism and dissent, along with the loss of traditional political certainties, made the high church ideal of a campaign to restore the church's lost coercive authority an attractive one to many. Its influence was quickly seen once Convocation met at the end of 1703. Members made clear from the start their determination to present themselves as the ecclesiastical counterpart of the Lords and Commons, setting up committees of grievances, rights and privileges, and elections, and insisting that they and their servants enjoyed the same immunity from arrests and lawsuits as members of the other two houses. Such claims provoked strong hostility. The bishops, a disgruntled Whig chief secretary complained in 1707, were 'as high as Laud was', and the country 'is priest rid very near as much as the Portuguese and Spaniards are'. In fact, the majority of the laity were no more tolerant than he was of clerical pretensions to form a separate and equal estate. Already in 1705 the lower house of Convocation had seriously overreached itself when it formally objected to a proposal then before parliament to remove the tithe on flax and hemp as a means of encouraging the linen trade. Its claim to act as the body 'assembled to represent the said clergy, and . . . entrusted by them with the care of their rights as well civil as ecclesiastical' provoked the Commons into a ferocious

[39] John Toland, *Christianity not Mysterious*, ed. Philip McGuinness et al. (Dublin, 1997).

[40] Theophilus Harrison to Revd J. Strype, 30 June 1703 (Cambridge University Library, Strype Correspondence, III, fos. 118–19).

reaction before which the clerics had no choice but to make a humiliating retreat.[41]

Side by side with attempts to assert their status as an equal partner with parliament, the members of Convocation pressed ahead with attempts to ensure that religious and moral values were once again legally enforced. In a society where nine out of every ten were papists or dissenters, there was no point in harking back to the act of uniformity. Instead resolutions drawn up in February and March 1704 proposed action against the openly irreligious, by requiring the churchwardens in each parish to present for prosecution those who did not attend some place of worship at least once a month. There were calls for new laws against blasphemy and sabbath breaking, strict censorship of the theatre, and a revitalization of the church courts. None of these proposals was followed through. Instead Convocation became side-tracked by further political squabbles, particularly with the strongly Whig and openly anticlerical earl of Wharton, lord lieutenant between 1708 and 1710. A final session, summoned between 1711 and 1713 following the return to power of a Tory ministry, produced nothing more substantial than a few minor canons, and some new forms of prayer. A representation on the state of religion, drawn up in 1711, once again reflected the characteristic tunnel vision of the high church movement, emphasizing in particular the dangers of dissent and deism, and presenting even the resilience of popery in Ireland as a result of the scandal given by divisions within Protestantism.

The brief reign of the high church party cannot be seen in isolation from the partisan politics of the day. Its chief spokesmen were the ecclesiastical wing of the Tory party, and their ascendancy ended with the death of Queen Anne.[42] After 1714 Tory bishops who had supported the high flyers in the lower house, like Thomas Lindsay of Armagh, were marginalized. The change of leadership, however, did not mean that commitment to defending the claims of the church gave way to a supine acceptance of subordination. The new leaders of the church were men like William King, by now archbishop of Dublin, who served as lord justice in the period immediately after the change of dynasty and on several further occasions, and Edward Synge, translated in 1716 from the poor north-west diocese of Raphoe to the archbishopric of Tuam. These were reliable Whigs, who had kept their distance from the partisan excesses of the high churchmen in Convocation and elsewhere. But they were also strongly committed to defending the rights of their church. In doing so they were concerned, not just to contain the challenge of the numerically formidable Presbyterians, but to suppress what

---

[41] George Dodington to—, 28 Aug. 1707 (PRO, SP63/366/241); memorial of the deans, archdeacons, and proctors, n.d. (PRO, SP 63/365/145). For a fuller discussion of proceedings in Convocation see S. J. Connolly, 'Reformers and Highflyers: The Post-Revolution Church', in Ford et al. (eds.), *As by Law Established*, 152–65.

[42] The interaction of high church and Tory party politics is particularly emphasized in D. W. Hayton, *Ruling Ireland 1685–1742: Politics, Politicians and Parties* (Woodbridge, 2004), ch. 4.

they saw as false doctrine. Thus King argued consistently against the extension of toleration to the Quakers, despite their small numbers and political passivity, on the grounds that their rejection of such basic doctrines as the Trinity and the atonement put them in a different category from other nonconforming groups. In 1719 both he and Synge strongly opposed the toleration act, despite the clear intent of its sponsors to block off any real improvement in the condition of dissenters. The reason, King explained, was that the act contained no provision for an enquiry into the tenets of the sects it exempted from penalty, and because it removed all restraint from 'those that are resolved to trouble themselves with no religion'.[43]

If churchmen like King and Synge remained committed to the enforcement of orthodoxy, however, the English clergy that began to be appointed to Irish sees in the period following the Whig triumph of 1714 quickly diluted what had been a united front of confessional solidarity and theological conservatism. The new appointees were not necessarily lacking in religious commitment. But on the whole they brought with them a greater acceptance of diversity of theological opinion. In 1719, for example, King complained that all five of the bishops who supported the toleration bill were Englishmen recently appointed to Irish sees. Anger at this and similar betrayals from within added to the existing resentment at outsiders promoted to prime Irish benefices. More galling still to conservatives was the nomination of Thomas Rundle as bishop of Derry in 1735, a consolation prize agreed after the bishop of London had blocked his appointment to Gloucester on the grounds that he was a secret deist. Another English bishop, John Hoadley, appointed to Ferns in 1727 and archbishop of Dublin from 1730, was likewise suspected of heterodox views. The third and most spectacular deviation from orthodoxy, by contrast, involved a bishop of Irish birth. Robert Clayton, appointed to Killala in 1730 and subsequently bishop of Cork and Ross and then Clogher, was the son of a dean of Kildare and had been educated at Trinity College, Dublin. However he owed his appointment to his social connections in England. His *Essay on Spirit* (1750), denying the divinity of Christ, had been published anonymously. But in 1757, perhaps already heading for the mental breakdown that was soon to become evident, he openly proclaimed his Arianism in the third part of his *Vindication of the Histories of the Old and New Testament*, and called in the House of Lords for the removal from the liturgy of the traditional creeds. His death in February 1758 almost certainly saved him from being formally deprived of his bishopric on grounds of heresy.

The privileged position of the Church of Ireland might suggest an institution existing in comfortable symbiosis with the Protestant political elite. Yet the clergy themselves saw their relationship to the wider society of Protestant Ireland as anything but comfortable. The aristocracy and gentry who dominated the Irish parliament may have been willing to silence a Toland or an Emlyn, to legislate

[43] Connolly, *Religion, Law and Power*, 174–5.

vigorously against popery, and to keep dissenters in their place. But this did not mean that they were friends of the established church. The active support of so many clergy for the Tory party provoked open displays of anticlericalism from a predominantly Whig gentry. Alan Brodrick, in a private letter, referred revealingly to a relative as 'an honest man at all times, though a clergyman'.[44] At Cork Whigs celebrating the accession of George I in 1714 drank the toast 'confusion to the clergy'. To this political rift arising from the age of party was added an economic rivalry, as landlords and clergy each viewed the other as unworthy claimants of an excessive share of the limited surplus to be extracted from a poor rural population. The proposal in 1705 to encourage the textile industry by removing tithes from hemp and flax moved Archbishop King to bitter satire:

> I understand that steeping clothing in cow dung, milk or blood doth much contribute to whiten it, especially human blood. Pray take a care next time that a clause be not put in to oblige clergymen and their families to give a certain quantity of their blood every spring to this use, for they are fat and may spare it.[45]

In 1736 the House of Commons passed a resolution which, though not legally binding, was taken as effectively ending the collection of tithes on pasture land, thus securing for landlords the entire profit that could be extracted from their tenantry in the most profitable sector of Irish agriculture. The resolution, Archbishop Boulter reported, was accompanied by 'a rage stirred up against the clergy that they thought equalled anything they had seen against the Popish priests, in the most dangerous times they remembered'.[46] Clergy and laity may have been beneficiaries in a system of shared privilege. But the marriage of self-interest that bound them together was often a loveless one.

Lay encroachments on the clergy's finances reflected a clear economic self-interest. But they could also be legitimized by pointing to the self-evident failure of the church to fulfil its pastoral mission. Contemporary assessments painted a bleak picture. The supply of clergy was inadequate, with incumbents commonly holding several benefices in plurality. Even then many were absentees, leaving their parishes in the care of poorly paid and unsupervised curates. Bishops too were frequently non-resident, spending long periods in Dublin or, like Bishop Hackett, outside the kingdom altogether. For many the decay of the church found visible expression in the high proportion of church buildings lying in ruins. In Meath in 1697 only 43 were in repair out of a total of 197; in the Munster counties of Waterford, Cork, and Kerry around 1750 the proportion was 126 out of 340.

Detail of this kind has helped to create the widely accepted picture of the eighteenth-century Church of Ireland as a religiously moribund playground for

[44] Midleton to Thomas Brodrick, 14 June 1717 (Surrey History Centre, Midleton MSS 1248/4, fo. 35).
[45] King to St George Ashe, bishop of Clogher, 28 April 1705 (TCD MS 750/3/1, p. 151).
[46] Boulter to earl of Anglesey, 8 June 1736 (*Letters*, ii. 192).

politically appointed placemen. Yet both the specific criticisms and the general tone of contemporary comment need to be looked at more critically than has often been the case. The failure of the Church of Ireland to keep the majority of the places of worship that it had inherited from its pre-Reformation predecessor in even minimal order is indeed evidence of the hollowness of its pretensions to be a national church. When we turn to the equally valid, and quite separate, issue of the fitness of the church to deliver pastoral services to those who genuinely were its adherents, on the other hand, the picture is somewhat different. The 43 functioning churches in the diocese of Meath, and the 126 in the three Munster counties, may have represented a remnant of a decayed medieval inheritance. But they still provided a place of worship for every 300–50 Anglicans in the regions concerned. The 600 incumbents and 200 curates estimated to be serving in Irish parishes in 1728, equally, represented a perfectly respectable ratio of one minister for every 312 church members. Individual Protestants outside Ulster and the major cities may well have found themselves at a prohibitive distance from the nearest clergyman or Sunday service. But that was the unavoidable consequence of a small and thinly dispersed population, rather than of any institutional failing on the part of the church.

If the church's material resources were less self-evidently inadequate than they seemed at first sight, the incidence of indifference and neglect of duty has also possibly been exaggerated. The Hackett affair, like the absenteeism of the Catholic Archbishop Blake, or the defection to the Church of Ireland of another Catholic bishop, John Butler of Cork, in 1787, was exceptional, one of the great ecclesiastical scandals of the period.[47] Pluralism, the holding of several ecclesiastical benefices, may in some cases have represented greed divorced from any sense of pastoral responsibility. In other cases, however, it was the only possible response to the high proportion of parishes in which the tithes were wholly or partly diverted either to senior officers of the church or to laymen. In some Leinster dioceses, Archbishop King claimed in 1712, clergy held eight, nine, or ten parishes while enjoying an annual income of less than £40. Absenteeism, equally, could represent simple dereliction of duty. But it must also be seen in the context of the practical difficulties of residence. Only a minority of parishes had a purpose-built residence for a minister, or glebe lands attached to the living. Large parts of the countryside contained neither suitable houses available to rent, nor markets that could supply food and other necessaries. Even conscientious churchmen can be found retreating from rural dioceses and parishes as they became older and less well able to withstand the rigours of travel and sparse lodgings. Visitation records, where available, suggest that absenteeism, though

---

[47] John Butler, Catholic bishop of Cork from 1763, succeeded unexpectedly to the family estate, and the title Lord Dunboyne, on the death of the second of his two brothers. He resigned his see in 1787, conformed to the established church, and married, in the hope of providing an heir. He returned to Catholicism on his deathbed, and left a part of his fortune to the seminary at Maynooth, Co. Kildare.

undoubtedly a problem, should not be overemphasized. In Clogher in 1700 19 out of 22 incumbents were resident in the diocese. In the probably less congenial environment of Raphoe a year later the figure was still 18 out of, again, 22.[48]

If conditions were not as uniformly bad as has been claimed, neither were the undoubted problems of neglect and malpractice wholly ignored. After 1714 the church became more clearly subordinate to the state in matters of policy, while its patronage became more systematically part of the spoils system of English and Irish political life. If some of the political appointees of the long Whig supremacy were neglectful careerists, however, others were able to combine their political role with a conscientious discharge of their clerical duties. Hugh Boulter, for example, was appointed archbishop of Armagh in 1724, over the head of a resentful William King, specifically as a means of strengthening the English interest within the kingdom in the wake of the Wood's Halfpence crisis. But he was also a hard-working ecclesiastical administrator who at his death left most of his personal fortune for the augmentation of poor benefices and the purchase of glebe lands. In place of the sweeping pretensions of the high churchmen of the previous reign, he and others pursued pragmatic, piecemeal, but cumulative measures of reform, notably legislation in 1728 to facilitate clerical residence and improve the maintenance of curates. Later in the century the Irish-born Charles Agar, bishop of Cloyne from 1768 and archbishop of Cashel from 1779, was likewise a political prelate, a member of a leading Kilkenny political connection, an adviser to successive lords lieutenant, and a government spokesman in the House of Lords. But he was also, like Boulter, an efficient and conscientious diocesan administrator, scrupulously defending the church's material interests and working effectively to promote a resident and active parish clergy.[49]

The long-term effect of these efforts at improvement is difficult to assess precisely. An account that concentrates on the work of committed reformers would be as misleading as one that focused on the occasional spectacular scandal. However the general impression is that by the mid-eighteenth century prolonged absenteeism, and other forms of blatant neglect of duties, had come to seem less acceptable, so that most Protestant congregations received at least a competent level of pastoral service.[50] There were also clear improvements in the physical resources of the church. In the diocese of Dublin the number of churches fit for use rose from 27 at the beginning of William King's episcopate in 1703 to 69 by the time of his death in 1729. The number of clergy rose from between 87 and 100 under King's administration to between 115 and 120 by 1753, permitting a reduction in the number of livings held in plurality. In the province of Ulster the

[48] Connolly, *Religion, Law and Power*, 178–90.

[49] A. P. W. Malcomson, *Archbishop Charles Agar: Churchmanship and Politics in Ireland 1760–1810* (Dublin, 2002), esp. ch. 5.

[50] On this point T. C. Barnard, 'Improving Clergymen 1660–1760', in Ford et al. (eds.), *As by Law Established*, 138, seems to confirm the tentative suggestions of Connolly, *Religion, Law and Power*, 189–90.

number of churches rose from 90 in 1622 to nearly 130 by the mid-1680s. By 1740 there were six cathedrals, around 210 parish churches, and an additional 30 subsidiary chapels.[51]

How far this improvement in opportunities for piety was of real interest to the laity is another matter. Complaints abounded of indifference to religion, neglect of public worship, and declining public morals. On the other hand there was also, in the 1690s and early 1700s, a vigorous movement for the reformation of manners, involving both Anglicans and dissenters. Casual references suggest that formal prayer was a standard part of the routine of upper- and middle-class households. The practice, as contemporaries were fully aware, had its utilitarian as well as its spiritual advantages. Regular prayers, the future Bishop Dopping pointed out in the 1670s, made children dutiful and servants 'more faithful and diligent'. But there are also indications that the spirit of godly Protestantism evident in the seventeenth century had not entirely disappeared. Dudley Cosby of Queen's County, who died in 1729, was commemorated by his son for the way in which he 'held the keeping of the Christian sabbath, seldom or never missed public worship, and had most every night worship in his own family, reading the scriptures of the Old and New Testament, and on Sabbath days other good books, and singing of psalms and reading of prayers'. Elsewhere too private letters suggest that an unobtrusive, conventional, but genuine piety was at least as common as indifference. Statistics from the dioceses of Ossory and Derry in the early 1730s suggest that an average of one person per Church of Ireland household took Easter communion, amounting probably to between a third and a half of the adult population.[52]

One further potential criticism is that the church made no real effort to fulfil what should have been a primary duty by attempting the conversion of the Catholic majority among whom it existed. Once again judgement depends on what one chooses to emphasize. The issue of the conversion of the Irish never wholly vanished from sight; but neither was it at any stage effectively pursued. Part of the problem was that the popery laws provided a convenient alibi for inaction, allowing churchmen to claim, and possibly even to persuade themselves, that the dismantling of the Catholic church establishment, and the outlawing of Catholic schools, would in itself be sufficient to bring the masses, by default, into the established church. There was also the old question, serving to paralyse missionary effort at every stage from the reign of Elizabeth onwards, of whether the religious conversion of the natives should come before or after they had been induced to adopt English language, customs, and habits of industry. The genuine perplexity created by this issue of priorities is evident in the case of Anthony

[51] R. T. C. Kennedy, 'The Administration of the Diocese of Dublin and Glendalough in the Eighteenth Century' (unpublished M.Litt. thesis, University of Dublin, 1968), 45–51, 102, 156–7, 160–2, 172–3; W. J. Roulston, 'The Provision, Building and Architecture of Anglican Churches in the North of Ireland, 1600–1740', *IESH* 32 (2005), 85–6.

[52] Again, these points are documented in detail in Connolly, *Religion, Law and Power*, 190–7.

Dopping, bishop of Meath. In the 1680s Dopping initially supported Robert Boyle's plans to print bibles in Irish, but withdrew his backing on the grounds that it contradicted the policy of promoting the use of English. In the 1690s he again took up the idea of preaching and printing in Irish, but then dropped it once more, on the same grounds.

Boyle's printing venture involved the publication in 1681 of a second edition of William Daniel's Irish New Testament of 1603, followed in 1685 by an Old Testament based on the translation prepared before 1641 by Bishop William Bedell and his native assistants.[53] The transcriber employed to produce a fair copy of Bedell's text worked in premises provided by Narcissus Marsh, provost of Trinity College, Dublin, who about the same time had revived compulsory Irish classes for those students admitted under the original statutes as 'natives'. There proved to be little demand for the volumes, and most copies eventually found their way to the Gaelic-speaking Protestants of the Scottish Highlands. The teaching of Irish resumed at Trinity, after a lengthy interval, with the appointment of a convert, Charles Linegar, to provide classes. Archbishop King, in 1715, drew up a list of forty-five students, all intended for the ministry, to whom Linegar had taught the language. Meanwhile Convocation, in 1703–4 and again in 1709, had passed resolutions calling for preaching and the printing of basic religious texts in Irish. In 1711 a Cavan clergyman, John Richardson, who had purchased the font of Irish type used thirty years earlier for Boyle's New Testament, produced Irish versions of a catechism and a Book of Common Prayer. His venture attracted declarations of support from the lower house of Convocation, the House of Commons, the second duke of Ormond, in his capacity as lord lieutenant, and a range of other dignitaries. However no practical steps were taken to provide either the schools or the Irish-speaking ministers for which Richardson had called, and he himself was left heavily out of pocket by his expenditure on type and printing.[54]

Irish Protestants, then, recognized clearly that confronting the problem of the Irish language would be central to any realistic attempt at mass conversion. But they never succeeded in bringing together the resources that would have been required for so enormous an undertaking. Instead they eventually settled, assisted perhaps by a gradually developing sense that the triumph of civility over Gaelic barbarism was at last in sight, for the more manageable task of providing an improving Protestant education through English. The first wave of charity schools, established in the 1690s and early 1700s, had been primarily concerned

[53] See Connolly, *Contested Island*, 350–1.

[54] T. C. Barnard, 'Protestants and the Irish Language c.1675–1725', *Journal of Ecclesiastical History*, 44 (1993), 243–72; R. E. W. Maddison, 'Robert Boyle and the Irish Language', *Bulletin of the John Rylands Library*, 41 (1958), 81–101; N. J. A. Williams, *I bPrionta in Leabhar* (Dublin,1986); Raymond Gillespie (ed.), *Scholar Bishop: The Recollections and Diary of Narcissus Marsh 1638–1696* (Dublin, 2003), 58–67; M. H. Risk, 'Charles Lynegar, Professor of the Irish Language', *Hermathena*, 102 (1966), 16–25.

with the education and moral improvement of the Protestant poor. A minority, however, especially in the anxious years leading up to 1714, had also seen such establishments as a means of converting and socializing the Catholic masses. In 1730 Henry Maule, bishop of Cloyne, inaugurated a more ambitious venture by launching the Incorporated Society for Promoting English Protestant Schools.

As a bishop Maule was better placed than Richardson had been to promote his plans, and he was also a superior political tactician. In addition he had the support of the powerful Archbishop Boulter. The Incorporated Society received a royal charter in 1734, and by 1748 had thirty schools attended by 900 pupils. The principle behind the scheme was that the pupils selected were to be removed completely from the corrupting influence of a popish environment. Instead they were to lodge in schools at a distance from their homes, where they would be trained in habits of industry, useful skills, and the truths of the Protestant religion. Over time the scheme degenerated badly: enquiries in the early nineteenth century discovered that the inmates of charter schools were poorly fed and clothed, worked remorselessly, and provided with little in the way of education. In the first decades of their operation, however, the schools were widely seen as holding out the promise of both social and religious transformation. 'The wit of man', the staunchly Protestant antiquarian Walter Harris observed in 1744, 'could not suggest a more effectual or rational scheme for making this a Protestant nation.'[55]

The outcome of any assessment of the condition of the post-Revolution Church of Ireland must thus depend on the perspective from which one starts. The limited pastoral presence that it maintained across the greater part of the kingdom made nonsense of its claims to be a national church. And in the context of the privileged status it enjoyed, this is a valid criticism. At the same time the scale of those privileges should not be overstated. The revenues of Irish bishops in the early 1720s ranged from around £900 for the western diocese of Killala to £2,200 for Derry and Dublin, generally recognized as the two richest sees. This placed most bishops on roughly the same level of income as the more substantial gentry: in 1713, for example, the average income of the members of parliament representing Irish counties was estimated at £1,585.[56] On the other hand Archbishop King claimed that not more than 200 out of 600 beneficed clergy in the kingdom had annual incomes of more than £100. Overall the parochial and diocesan revenues of the Church of Ireland amounted to no more than a fraction of the total rental received by Irish landlords. In return the church offered what seems to have been in proportion to its actual adherents an adequate provision of clergy and places of worship. If levels of zeal varied, there

[55] Walter Harris and Charles Smith, *The Antient and Present State of the County of Down* (Dublin, 1744), 17–18. For a general account, Kenneth Milne, *The Irish Charter Schools 1730–1830* (Dublin, 1996).

[56] T. C. Barnard, *A New Anatomy of Ireland: The Irish Protestants 1649–1770* (London, 2003), 61.

were at every period advocates of reform and the raising of pastoral standards. Absenteeism and scandalous neglect of duty were probably less common than has been claimed. Among the laity, too, there is evidence of piety as well as indifference. If neither clergy nor laity ever really faced up to the challenge of converting the Catholic majority, likewise, the recognition that they ought to do so, and the belief that it might in fact be possible to create a wholly Protestant Ireland, never entirely vanished.

DISSENTING PROTESTANTS

Ulster Presbyterians, possibly the kingdom's second largest denomination, shared to a minor degree in the status of a group subjected to civil penalties for standing outside the established church. In contrast to the material poverty that circumscribed Catholic religious practice, however, they and their church enjoyed a modest prosperity. Scottish immigrants in the late seventeenth and early eighteenth centuries had established themselves as the dominant group in the most fertile parts of the province, displacing not only native Irish but also English competitors in areas such as Londonderry, Tyrone, and east Donegal. Their superior resources and commercial acumen had also given them control of the main commercial centres. In Belfast, for example, a visitor in 1752 found only 60 out of 400 families attending the Church of Ireland, 'and most of them of the lower rank', so that the Anglican church was 'a very mean fabric for such a considerable place'.[57] Presbyterian services took place in plain but solid meeting houses. Congregations were served by a clergy made up exclusively of university graduates. The prosperity of those they ministered to, along with the modest supplement of the *regium donum*, provided an income that placed these ministers on the fringes of gentility. In 1753 the Synod of Ulster fixed the minimum stipend at £40 a year, which contemporaries saw as just about the level required to be part of polite society. In 1770 the Synod increased the minimum stipend to £50, although in practice not all congregations managed quite to meet this commitment.[58]

Presbyterian religious culture retained the strong communal element that led their Anglican rivals to regard them as such a threat. At the core of their public worship, true to their seventeenth-century origins, was the sermon, an elaborate discourse closely based on a biblical text. A second main element, singing, likewise remained true to the reformed tradition: there was no music, the texts sung were metrical versions of the psalms and other scriptural texts, and the performance proceeded by a leader giving out each line, which the congregation then sang. But singing the word, in this form, gave worship an important participatory character,

---

[57] *Pococke's Tour in Ireland in 1752*, ed. G. T. Stokes (Dublin, 1891), 21.
[58] Barnard, *New Anatomy of Ireland*, 113.

and the practice carried over from the meeting house to family devotions, the workplace, and even social gatherings.[59]

The conspicuous assemblies for communion that had been such a prominent feature of Restoration Presbyterianism continued into the early eighteenth century, once again provoking Anglican hostility. From the 1690s, however, church leaders in both Ulster and Scotland sought to discourage overlarge gatherings by limiting the number of ministers participating to three or four. By the mid-eighteenth century communions were generally based on a single congregation. Nevertheless they retained their character as important expressions both of community and exclusivity. The service generally extended over three days, with a Saturday devoted to preparatory sermons, communion on Sunday, and a service of thanksgiving on Monday. During this time participants submitted to a personal examination as to their beliefs and spiritual state, and received a token or ticket permitting them to take communion. The sacrament itself was still taken seated at long tables, passing the bread and wine from hand to hand in a manner that emphasized common participation and equality rather than any lingering trace of a supposed transformation of the elements.[60] The link between worship and sociability was further confirmed by the general acceptance that services were appropriately followed by drinking. When a County Antrim land agent in 1720 alerted his employer to a scheme to move the meeting house from his town of Ballyclare to another location, his main point was the potential loss to two tenants keeping public houses at each end of the town, from where 'they have the whole change of the people'.[61]

In addition to the strong communal character of their worship, Presbyterians also retained the close supervision of moral conduct that had likewise alarmed outsiders. Ministers and elders meeting in session would scrutinize the behaviour of all members of the congregation, summoning those found deficient for public or private rebuke. A study of one County Antrim parish during the last three decades of the eighteenth century shows that in 96 per cent of cases where the date of baptism of a first child suggested a pre-marital conception the couple concerned were brought before the session to answer a charge of fornication. Exactly how effective this system of moral regulation was remains unclear. By the early nineteenth century illegitimacy rates among Ulster Presbyterians seem to have been high by Irish standards. One suggested explanation is that reliance

[59] Raymond Gillespie, '"A Good and Godly Exercise": Singing the Word in Irish Dissent, 1660–1701', in Kevin Herlihy (ed.), *Propagating the Word of Irish Dissent 1650–1800* (Dublin, 1998), 24–45.

[60] For general surveys of Presbyterian religious culture see R. L. Greaves, *God's Other Children: Protestant Nonconformists and the Emergence of Denominational Churches in Ireland 1660–1700* (Stanford, Calif., 1997), ch. 5; Marilyn J. Westerkamp, *Triumph of the Laity: Scots-Irish Piety and the Great Awakening 1625–1760* (New York, 1988), ch. 2; Andrew Holmes, *The Shaping of Ulster Presbyterian Belief and Practice 1770–1840* (Oxford, 2006).

[61] James Kirk to Agmondisham Vesey, 13 Aug. 1720 (NAI Sarsfield Vesey Correspondence, No. 131).

on the kirk session had the potential disadvantage that a delinquent, having submitted to a rebuke or performed a public penance, had to be treated as having given satisfaction for their offence. Hence neither illegitimacy nor unmarried motherhood carried the social stigma that came to prevail in other parts of rural Ireland, where pregnancy outside marriage doomed both woman and child to a lifetime of ostracism and contempt. However it is less clear how far these higher levels of extramarital fertility can be projected backward in time, or whether the real issue is the weakening of a previously strong communal discipline, presumably under the influence of rapid economic and social change, in the late eighteenth or early nineteenth century.[62]

By the early eighteenth century a growing conflict was evident, in Ulster as in Scotland, between the historical roots of Presbyterianism in the passionate certainties of the Reformation, and its more recent development as the creed of an affluent commercial elite. In 1705 a group of clergy of advanced views founded the Belfast Society, to promote theological debate. In 1719 one of their number, John Abernethy, minister for Antrim, preached a sermon calling for a clear distinction between essential and non-essential matters of faith, and for the light of the individual conscience to be accorded priority over man-made theological formulae. In doing so he implicitly challenged the requirement, introduced in 1705 in response to the embarrassment created by Emlyn's prosecution, that ministers subscribe to the Westminster Confession of Faith. The initial response of the Synod was conciliatory. A pacific act, introduced in 1720, permitted ministers, provided they had the consent of their presbytery, to modify the Confession so as to accommodate scruples on particular points of doctrine. However the debate on the principle of subscription continued, and in 1725 the Synod agreed to segregate the non-subscribers in the Presbytery of Antrim. The following year it excluded this presbytery from communion with other parts of the Presbyterian body. In practice the split proved to be less than total. Ministers from the two sides officiated on occasion in one another's meeting houses, and representatives of the Presbytery of Antrim continued to attend meetings of the Synod. Over time, moreover, the requirement for subscription began to lapse even within the main body. By 1783 the Synod formally accepted that it was for individual presbyteries to regulate the licensing of ministers. At the end of the century only four out of fourteen presbyteries demanded even nominal subscription to the Westminster Confession.

---

[62] Both the figure of 96% and the suggested weaker coercive power of public penance are derived from Andrew Blaikie and Paul Gray, 'Archives of Abuse and Discontent? Presbyterianism and Sexual Behaviour during the Eighteenth and Nineteenth Centuries', in R. J. Morris and Liam Kennedy (eds.), *Ireland and Scotland: Order and Disorder 1600–2000* (Edinburgh, 2005), 69–70. For high levels of illegitimacy among Presbyterians see Holmes, *Shaping of Ulster Presbyterian Belief and Practice*, 225–6. Note, however, that Blaikie and Gray's figures for Carnmoney between 1767 and 1805 indicate a pre-nuptial pregnancy rate of less than 15%—much closer to the 10% recorded in the Catholic south than the one in three in rural England—and an illegitimacy rate of below 2%.

The liberal theology of what soon came to be referred to as the New Light party offered an optimistic vision of an orderly universe, in which men and women were naturally inclined to virtue and religious truth and reason were in close harmony. These convictions linked them to the Moderate party who at the same period were coming to dominate Scottish Presbyterianism. The ideas of Abernethy, Francis Hutcheson, and others had been formed by their education at Glasgow university. Hutcheson, in turn, having presided for some years over a dissenting academy in Dublin, succeeded to the chair of moral philosophy at Glasgow, where his lecturing and writing influenced the work of both David Hume and Adam Smith, and established him as an important figure in the development of the Scottish Enlightenment.

Opponents of the New Light movement claimed that its resistance to sub-scription arose from unorthodox doctrinal views. In particular they suspected it of Arianism, a denial that Jesus was fully divine and an equal member of the Trinity. The non-subscribers themselves claimed that their objection was to giving man-made formulae a binding status that should be accorded only to the direct word of God. Yet the rise of the New Lights, even if those involved were for the most part sound on the question of the Trinity, did indeed represent a revolution in religious culture. After the young Francis Hutcheson, born in 1694, had preached to his father's Armagh congregation, an elder reportedly commiserated with the older Hutcheson on his 'mishap'.

Your silly loon, Frank, has fashed a' the congregation wi' his idle cackle; for he has been babbling this oor aboot a gude and benevolent God, and that the sauls of the heathens themsels will gang to Heeven, if they follow the licht o' their ain consciences. Not a word does the daft boy ken, speer, nor say about the gude auld comfortable doctrines o' election, reprobation, original faith and salvation. Hoot man, awa' wi' sic a fellow.[63]

This was a satirical anecdote, reflecting the New Light party's perception of the outmoded forms of thought they had left behind. But the truth was that an emphasis on reason carried some individuals at least a long way from the fundamentals of conventional Christian doctrine. In 1777 Martha McTier, wife of a Belfast merchant, confessed to her brother her fears that belief in an afterlife, 'of which there is so little of that evidence most satisfactory to such creatures as we are', might be no more than a comforting delusion. Her husband was more phlegmatic: 'he tells me he has done no ill to others, as much good as in his power, therefore *if* he exists after this life he shall be happy, if not he is contented, as he is sure that is for the best.'[64]

---

[63] Quoted in Michael Brown, *Francis Hutcheson in Dublin 1719–1730* (Dublin, 2002), 88–9. Hutcheson, it should be noted, avoided the label New Light, and had in fact subscribed to the Westminster Confession when he accepted his chair. However he was widely suspected of heterodoxy, and a student at one point tried to bring charges of heresy against him.

[64] Martha McTier to William Drennan, Dec. 1777 (*The Drennan–McTier Letters 1776–1793*, ed. Jean Agnew (Dublin, 1998–9), i. 30–1).

This new variety of Presbyterianism, with its emphasis on the connections between morality, politeness, and sociability, and its vision of religion as a rational instrument of social improvement, had a particular appeal to the more prosperous participants in the busy commercial society that had begun to develop in both Glasgow and Belfast and their respective hinterlands. Of eleven Ulster congregations paying their ministers salaries of over £100 a year, nine were New Light; of 150 paying less than £70, all but a handful were orthodox. From mid-century these overlapping social and religious distinctions led to further divisions within the Presbyterian body. From 1746 the Seceders, who in 1733 had broken away from the main Presbyterian body in Scotland following a dispute over lay patronage of congregations, began to organize in Ulster. Their spread clearly drew on popular unease at the prevalence, even within the supposedly orthodox wing of Presbyterianism, of New Light doctrines. It may also have been encouraged by resentment at the disproportionate influence within the Synod of Ulster of the wealthier congregations. On the other hand a subsequent split among the Scottish Seceders, into Burgher and anti-Burgher factions, arose from issues of municipal government that had no counterpart in Ulster; the extension of the division to Ulster is perhaps best explained by the particular appeal of the Secession church to recent immigrants from Scotland. Meanwhile a further breakaway group, the Reformed Presbyterians, had also begun to organize in Ulster, providing ministers to what had been scattered remnants of the old Covenanting tradition. A first presbytery, established in 1757, collapsed in 1763 due to a shortage of ministers. A successor appeared in 1792. By this time there were 185 ministers in Ulster attached either to the Synod of Ulster or the Presbytery of Antrim, 46 Seceders, and 6 Reformed Presbyterians.[65]

The other branches of Irish dissent were, compared to the Presbyterians, numerically insignificant. By the 1720s there were perhaps 1,500–2,000 Baptists, falling by 1800 to around 500, organized in five congregations. There was also a handful of Independent Congregationalist communities, although the high level of local autonomy meant that these tended to appear and then fade away more frequently than was the case with other denominations. The southern Presbyterians too had a relatively fluid organization. From 1695 some of their number, along with some Independents, were loosely linked in a union known as the Southern Association. But some southern congregations were also in communion with the Synod of Ulster. The Quakers, on the other hand, had developed a strong organizational structure. There was no professional ministry. Instead representatives of the whole body of Friends participated in six-weekly provincial and half-yearly national meetings. A further distinctive feature, again with important implications for denominational cohesion, was the institution at all levels of separate women's meetings. Eighteenth-century Irish Friends

[65] The most recent detailed survey of these developments is Ian McBride, *Scripture Politics: Ulster Presbyterians and Irish Radicalism in the Late Eighteenth Century* (Oxford, 1998), 41–83.

continued to be distinguished by their insistence on absolute plainness in dress, home furnishings, and speech (including the characteristic use of 'thou' and 'thee'). They also refused, at the cost of continued loss by fines and occasionally of imprisonment, to pay tithes or other dues to the established church, or to take oaths in the courts of law. These external signs of conscious difference masked what was in fact a successful transition from charismatic sect to institutionally based denomination.[66] But the numbers involved were once again small, around 5,000 to 6,000 in the mid-eighteenth century.

Statistics of denominational membership and organization, however, provide only a static picture of religious behaviour. The future Methodist leader George Whitfield, preaching at Limerick and Dublin in 1738, was impressed by the enthusiasm of the crowds that flocked to hear him. When the English itinerant preacher John Cennick came to Dublin in 1746, similarly, what he found was a fluid and lively Protestant culture, in which doctrines were passionately debated and believers moved from group to group in search of vital preaching and the company at prayer of other godly souls. He had come at the invitation of two young Baptists, and began preaching in a Baptist meeting house in Skinner's Alley, where he had the support of two other ministers from that denomination but was opposed by a third. A society of Anglican laymen, 'chiefly serious young men, about 200 in number', invited Cennick to preach to them, at which 'many wept and followed me to our own place afterwards'. On another occasion, however, a group of young gentlemen, presumably Anglicans, disrupted one of his meetings brandishing drawn swords. Other groups he encountered included a society organized by a Presbyterian tradesman, whose members met to discuss difficult passages in Scripture and to review the doctrines they had heard taught at different churches and meeting houses, 'which they either approved or condemned, as also all unsound experiences or principles'. There was also 'the remains of a strict set called Bradilonians', established some forty years earlier by a tradesman of that name.[67]

In addition to these small and often transient groups, two larger movements emerged during the eighteenth century. Cennick himself had made the journey from Methodism to the Moravians, a revivalist sect with central European origins, and by 1747 he had recruited over 500 members to a Dublin meeting. In 1746 he paid his first visit to Ulster, at the invitation of a Presbyterian shopkeeper in Ballymena, County Antrim, who was unhappy with his local minister 'because he suspected him to be of the Arian or New Light party'. Over the next decade Cennick was to establish over 200 further Moravian societies, mainly in County Antrim, although most of these faded away following his death in 1755. John

[66] For this point see in particular Greaves, *God's Other Children*, 2–3.
[67] John Cennick, 'An Account of the Most Remarkable Passages Relating to the Awakening in Dublin in Ireland' (Moravian Church House, London). I am grateful to Professor David Hempton for showing me a transcript of this document.

Wesley, who visited Ireland for the first of twenty-one visits in 1747, had a more lasting success. By his death in 1791 there were 15,000 Irish Methodists, as well as many others who regularly attended Methodist meetings.[68] Neither movement radically altered the religious demography of Ireland. But their emergence, and the lively and varied subculture of prayer groups and meeting houses out of which they arose, is nevertheless a warning against taking the decline or stagnation of the seventeenth-century sects as evidence of a moribund popular religious culture. Irish Protestantism in the eighteenth century no longer burned with the fires that had fuelled the Reformation. Nor was it any longer reinvigorated by continued immigration from England or Scotland. But it had not entirely lost its capacity for growth and innovation.

[68] D. N. Hempton, *The Religion of the People: Methodism and Popular Religion c.1750–1900* (London, 1996), ch. 2.

8

Rulers and Ruled

ALARMS AND EXCURSIONS

On 6 July 1726 Moses Nowland, described as a young man and apparently from County Carlow, was executed at St Stephen's Green, Dublin, for the crime of enlisting men to serve the exiled Stuart Pretender. A broadsheet printed by the celebrated Dublin publisher George Faulkner purported to be his last confession. Here Nowland admitted that he had recruited men for foreign service. But he also claimed that mention of the Pretender had been only 'a bait which the ignorant readily swallow, and by which they are easily deluded'. The real destination of the men enlisted had been the Spanish army, and the confession concluded with a lengthy repudiation by Nowland of his 'villainous and diabolical action' in furthering 'the designs of a foreign potentate, whose actions have always tended to the subversion of our growing commerce, and the flourishing estate of these kingdoms'. On the scaffold, the condemned man disowned the confession printed in his name, saying instead that 'he died for no crime' and that if he had known he was really to be executed he would have produced a longer declaration. He was then hanged, 'his bowels being burned, his head cut off etc', though whether these mutilations began before or after death remains unclear.[1]

The conflicting claims surrounding Moses Nowland's miserable end are at first sight a straightforward matter. He was only one of many who were involved during this period in raising recruits among Irish Catholics for the Irish regiments in French and Spanish service.[2] The apparently fabricated confession printed by Faulkner was presumably an attempt to discourage continued enlistment. The complication is that the words put into the unfortunate Nowland's mouth were true: the thousands who left Ireland to serve in foreign armies were in fact destined to spend their lives fighting, not for the Stuarts, but for the European powers whose service they entered. The invented confession was still propaganda, of a

[1] Nowland's declaration is printed in James Kelly, *Gallows Speeches from Eighteenth-Century Ireland* (Dublin, 2001), 208–11. For its repudiation see ibid. 32, 45; *Dublin Intelligence*, 2, 9 July 1726.

[2] For recruiting for foreign service see Connolly, *Religion, Law and Power*, 237–9, 243–4; Éamonn Ó Ciardha, *Ireland and the Jacobite Cause 1685–1766: A Fatal Attachment* (Dublin, 2002), 142–3, 196–9, 204–6, 256–7; David Dickson, *Old World Colony: Cork and South Munster 1630–1830* (Cork, 2005), 263–8. See also below, Ch. 9.

clumsy and unsubtle nature. But it can no longer be read as simple anti-Jacobite misinformation. Faulkner, moreover, was no anti-Catholic zealot; he supported a relaxation of the popery laws and was later to print an early statement of the Catholic case for toleration by Henry Brooke. He may well have believed that his fiction served, not only to protect the Hanoverian dynasty, but to save the poorer Catholic Irish from the consequences of their own delusions.

If the background to Faulkner's fabrication was more complex than appears at first sight, so too was the fate of Nowland himself. He was not the only recruiting agent to die on the gallows. In the uncertain summer of 1714, the raising of men for the French regiments had added to the panic surrounding the imminent death of Queen Anne, and three of those involved had been executed. More recently some highly visible enlistment for the Spanish army during 1720–2 had led parliament to rush through a bill making it a felony to enlist in, or recruit for, the service of any foreign power without licence, and between six and ten offenders had been hanged over the next few months. But these harsh examples did not necessarily reflect the settled view of the Protestant establishment as a whole. Even in the tense circumstances of 1714 the Tory lord chancellor Sir Richard Cox had been equivocal. He and his colleagues had issued a proclamation against recruitment, 'to show we don't countenance it'. His private view, however, was that the enlisting of footloose Irish Catholics for foreign service had always gone on, and that 'this country is the better to be rid of them and their brood'.[3] Against this background Nowland's apparent belief, a dozen years later, that his sentence of death would not actually be carried out becomes easier to understand.

Attitudes to recruitment were further complicated by shifts in Great Britain's relations with the other European powers. The Spain whose recruiting activities caused such concern in the early 1720s—and for whom Nowland had been recruiting a few years later—was an enemy state, which in 1719 had sponsored an attempted Jacobite invasion of the British Isles. France, in 1714, was likewise a hostile power, with whom Britain had only just concluded a controversial peace after two long wars, during 1688–97 and 1702–13. From 1716, on the other hand, Britain and France entered a period of good relations that continued into the late 1730s. Against this background the British government, in 1730, took a step beyond its existing policy of tacit toleration by formally licensing some French officers to visit Ireland and collect recruits. In the event a wave of protest in both England and Ireland forced the authorities hastily to cancel the arrangement. Feelings ran so high that the Irish lords justices were for a time unwilling to use their influence in other cases concerning recruitment. In particular they refused, despite French diplomatic intervention, to reprieve Martin Mooney, a Wexford man who had returned from France on the promise of a commission there if he brought back twenty recruits from Ireland. Mooney

---

[3] Cox to Southwell, 19 Feb. 1714 (BL, Add MS 38,157, fo. 69ᵛ).

may have brought his fate on himself: the charge against him was not just of enlisting men, but of kidnapping.[4] However it is also possible that, like Nowland, he was simply unlucky: a victim of the ambiguous waters of post-Revolution Ireland, in which genuine uncertainties regarding the threat to be anticipated from domestic and foreign enemies combined with discrepancies between official and private attitudes, and where the pragmatic outlook of the administrative and political elite contrasted with the more straightforward prejudices of a wider Protestant public opinion.

These transactions provide an appropriate introduction to the wider question of popular political loyalties, and the significance of political disaffection, in post-revolutionary Ireland. It is a topic that has only recently begun to receive serious attention. Catholic writers in the late eighteenth and early nineteenth centuries, working against the background of the campaign for Catholic emancipation, had good reason to play down the active disloyalty of their recent ancestors. Even later, when the last of the legal disabilities imposed by the Williamite and later popery laws had been removed, it remained convenient to pass over this particular phase in Ireland's political history, and instead to present the Catholics of what was dubbed the penal era as passive victims of Protestant prejudice and exploitation. It is only in recent years that the real history of Catholic politics in the early and mid-eighteenth century has begun to be written.[5] Yet the excitement of discovering a new subject can introduce its own oversimplifications. That the primary political allegiance of Catholics of all classes, for several decades after the conclusion of King William's war, was to the exiled Stuart dynasty was indeed one of the central political realities of early eighteenth-century Irish politics. But Irish Jacobitism was a complex, and in some respects contradictory, ideology. The response of the Protestant establishment to the threat it posed, equally, was more sophisticated and discriminating than has sometimes been acknowledged.

One useful starting point for a reassessment of Catholic political allegiances is provided by the agreement that had ended the war of 1689–91. In Catholic nationalist narratives of the nineteenth and twentieth centuries the Treaty of Limerick became a statement of the conditions, soon brutally discarded by the Protestant establishment, on which Catholics had agreed to live under William III and his successors. To contemporaries, on the other hand, the treaty represented no more than the terms of a local truce, to continue pending the outcome of the great European war that would determine the fate of the crowns of England and Ireland alike. Protestant observers commented repeatedly on the

---

[4] Mooney's case is documented in PRO SP63/395/337–43, SP63/396/1-5. See also Ó Ciardha, *Ireland and the Jacobite Cause*, 256–7, which somewhat plays down the role of the alleged kidnapping in aggravating his offence.

[5] The two main works in the recent rediscovery of Irish Jacobitism are Breandán Ó Buachalla, *Aisling Ghéar: Na Stíobhartaigh agus an t-Aos Léinn 1601–1788* (Dublin, 1996); Ó Ciardha, *Ireland and the Jacobite Cause*. See also, for a later period, Vincent Morley, *Irish Opinion and the American Revolution 1760–1783* (Cambridge, 2002).

close attention with which Catholics, over the next two decades, followed reports from distant battlefields, noting their 'dejection' following Marlborough's great victory at Blenheim in August 1704, and their 'insolent behaviour' when the French defeated England's Portuguese allies at Almanza three years later. The end of the war in 1713, and the long period of better relations with France that commenced soon after, damped down immediate hopes. But Catholics continued to look to some new conjunction in the affairs of Europe that would favour the Stuart cause. In 1716 they lamented the defeat of France's clients, the Turks, by England's ally Austria. In 1734, on the other hand, French successes against Austria once again made them 'more than ordinarily insolent'.[6]

The hopes thus vested in the exiled dynasty and its foreign backers derived much of their potency from the close links between Ireland and Catholic Europe. Catholic merchants trading with the continent, along with what were by now substantial communities of Irish merchants permanently resident in the major seaports of France and Spain, provided a network of messengers and contact points. The Irish colleges, as in the seventeenth century, offered a base for intellectual and literary activity of the kind not possible to sustain within Ireland itself, while the passage back and forth of students and newly ordained priests was a ready channel of communication between Ireland and Catholic Europe. Most important of all, as a visible symbol of the possibility of an eventual war of liberation, there were the Irish troops in foreign service. Those leaving came to be familiarly known as 'wild geese', a term that first appears, or at least was first noted by Protestant observers, in 1722.[7] Recruitment had a strong regional bias. Of 2,100 Irishmen admitted to the veterans' hospital, the Hôtel Royal des Invalides, between 1690 and 1769, 40 per cent had been born in Munster, 28 per cent in Leinster, 22 per cent in Ulster, and 10 per cent in Connacht.[8] As in the seventeenth century, this outflow must be seen in context. Ireland was one of several peripheral and economically underdeveloped societies that responded to the constant need for men to fill up the armies of the European powers by exporting surplus manpower; from the late eighteenth century, once legal prohibitions had been relaxed, recruits of very much the same type were to make up a growing proportion of the forces of the British crown. Yet contemporary accounts make clear that the promise of serving the Jacobite cause was also, as George Faulkner had warned, a significant aid to recruitment. One group enlisted in Dublin in 1714 had been assured that 'they were to serve King James the Third and that they should not fight a battle until they landed in England or Ireland'. Men recruited in Cork in 1726 were likewise told that 'although they were enlisted to go to Spain yet they were designed for the service of King James

---

6 For these and other examples see Connolly, *Religion, Law and Power*, 234–6.

7 It is mentioned, as a term requiring explanation, in *Dublin Intelligence*, 3 Apr. 1722, and almost three months later, again with an explanation, in William King to Samuel Molyneux, 23 June 1722 (TCD MS 750/7, 142–3).

8 Eoghan Ó hAnnracháin, 'Who were the "Wild Geese"', *Études irlandaises*, 25 (2000), 105–21.

the Third'.[9] Against this background, the predominance of Munster recruits can be seen as reflecting both the strength of the Jacobite tradition in the region and the close trading links between its ports and those of continental Europe. The relative insignificance of Connacht, equally, points both to a greater commercial and geographical isolation, at least beyond the immediate hinterland of Galway, and possibly to a less developed political awareness.

In addition to its base in the Irish diaspora, Jacobitism had the support of the Catholic church, both in Ireland and abroad. The pope continued up to 1766 to recognize the Stuarts as the rightful monarchs of Ireland, England, and Scotland, and to allow first James II and then his son, the supposed James III, to nominate candidates to vacant Irish bishoprics. When the Irish government, in 1709, tried to require priests to take the oath of abjuration, formally repudiating the Pretender's claim to the throne, all but 33 out of something over 1,000 refused, even though by doing so they forfeited the benefits of having registered under the popery act of five years earlier. This concerted refusal was not necessarily the positive repudiation of the Hanoverian state that is sometimes assumed. Many contemporaries, Protestant as well as Catholic, were prepared to fall back on the distinction between de facto and de jure authority, accepting the outcome of the Revolution but not necessarily the legitimacy of what had been done.[10] And indeed the requirement, at the time of the 1704 registration, that priests should take an oath of allegiance to Queen Anne does not seem to have given rise to any similar difficulty. At the same time it is clear that some Catholic churchmen at least were actively engaged in the cause of the house of Stuart. The Franciscan Sylvester Lloyd, bishop of Killaloe (1728–39) and then of Waterford and Lismore (1739–47), though born a Protestant and at one time a soldier in the Williamite army, was one particularly active Jacobite agent, transmitting wildly unrealistic accounts of the support that could be expected, from Protestant and Catholic alike, for a Stuart restoration.[11] And even the less politically committed found themselves required, by the need to transact ecclesiastical business or to seek preferment for themselves, to maintain contact with the Stuart court.

Jacobitism, or at least symbolic expressions of attachment to the exiled dynasty, was not entirely confined to the Catholic population. There were regular complaints of seditious sentiments among both staff and students at the

[9] Report by John Forster on a trial at Wexford Assizes, 19 July 1715 (PRO, SP63/373/34–5); information of Owen Sweane, printed in Breandán Ó Buachalla, 'Irish Jacobitism in Official Documents', *ECI* 8 (1993), 133–4.

[10] For an explicit defence of the taking of the oath of allegiance in these terms by a Dublin priest, see Cornelius Nary, *The Case of the Roman Catholics of Ireland, Humbly Represented*, printed in Hugh Reily, *The Impartial History of Ireland* (Limerick, n.d.), 122–43. Nary's pamphlet was reportedly published in 1724, in response to a threatened popery bill, but no copy has been found to confirm that it was in fact ever printed. See Patrick Fagan, *Dublin's Turbulent Priest: Cornelius Nary 1658–1738* (Dublin, 1991), 114–15.

[11] Patrick Fagan, *An Irish Bishop in Penal Times: The Chequered Career of Sylvester Lloyd OFM 1680–1747* (Dublin, 1993).

exclusively Protestant Trinity College. A student was expelled and deprived of his degree in 1708 for comparing William III's seizure of the crown to the behaviour of a common highwayman. Two years later three undergraduates were convicted of defacing the statue of the king on College Green. There were also complaints in 1714 of clergy who pointedly omitted to pray for the newly installed George I, or who suddenly felt impelled to preach sermons denouncing the theological errors of the Lutheran variety of Protestantism practised by his family. The crowds that during the 1720s assembled on St Stephen's Green on 10 June to celebrate the birthday of the Pretender, and on occasion to brawl with what was described as 'the Whig mob', were generally dismissed as a 'popish rabble'. But one report noted the slogan 'high church and Ormond', suggesting that they also included representatives of an Anglican Tory interest. Such glimpses of a Protestant anti-Whig culture are an important reminder that the party divisions of Anne's reign had arisen from real differences of interest and allegiance. At the same time there was general agreement that Irish Protestants, however much out of sympathy with Whig triumphalism, had too much to lose from a possible Stuart restoration to become active supporters of the Jacobite cause. The three apparent exceptions, the second duke of Ormond, hailed by the Stephen's Green rioters in 1726 and by then a refugee at the Stuart court, and the earls of Orrery and Barrymore, implicated in different Jacobite conspiracies, were all Irish landowners whose political careers and attachments lay mainly in England rather than in Ireland.[12]

For its Catholic supporters Jacobitism could have a variety of meanings, varying with both social status and cultural background. A set of papers compiled between 1702 and 1714 by an anonymous author, possibly a member of the Plunkett family of County Meath, reflected the outlook of the conservative Old English elite. A pamphlet addressed to the English argued that it was both prudent and moral to support the cause of the Stuarts, founded on divine justice and therefore destined eventually to be victorious. Other papers somewhat anachronistically made the case for a league of Catholic powers to restore the exiled dynasty. In addition, taking up issues that had come to the surface in the parliament of 1689, the unknown author argued that a future Ireland under Stuart rule would enjoy control of its own affairs.[13] For the Jacobite rank and file, by contrast, the glimpses available suggest that support for the exiled dynasty was tied up with vague but powerful aspirations for an escape, not only from

[12] Ormond fled to France in 1715, to escape prosecution for treason arising out of his role in winding down the war against France in 1712–13. The fourth earl of Orrery was implicated in the English Jacobite plot of 1723. His son, the fifth earl, was also for a time in correspondence with the Stuart court. Allegations that his cousin, the earl of Burlington, head of the Boyle family but based entirely in England, was an active Jacobite continue to be debated. See Dickson, *Old World Colony*, 251–2, 575–6. For Barrymore's involvement in Jacobite military plans during 1744–5 see ibid. 252–3.

[13] Patrick Kelly, ' "A Light to the Blind": The Voice of the Dispossessed Catholic Elite in the Generation after the Defeat at Limerick', *IHS* 24 (1985), 431–62.

religious inferiority, but from social subordination. William Lahey, enlisted in County Waterford in 1714, was told that he and his companions 'should all return for Ireland again in less than a year's time, with an army to destroy and root out the Protestants there'. William Headen, tried at Wexford the same year for enlisting in the Pretender's service, had allegedly declared that 'he would not stay to be a slave here, since he was to return again in the harvest'. A similar vision of an unjust order corrected excited a Dublin tanner named Cusack, who found himself in trouble for observing of the arrested recruits: 'Who would blame them for endeavouring to get estates if they could, for that fellows that came over in leathern breeches and wooden shoes now rides in their coaches?'[14]

The fullest expression of the continued attachment of Irish Catholics to the house of Stuart was in the Gaelic poetry of the period. The eighteenth century was the great age of the aisling, or vision poem, a poetic genre of ancient origin but now given a political twist. Typically the sleeping poet encountered a beautiful woman representing Ireland, who recounted her sorrows but looked forward to the return of a bridegroom or rescuer from overseas. In one of the most celebrated specimens of the genre, by Egan O'Rahilly (*c.*1670–1729) of County Kerry, Ireland was 'Gile na Gile' (Brightness of Brightness), held prisoner by 'a clumsy lubberly clown', but awaiting her rescue with 'the return of him to the place that is his by kingly descent'. In another poem, cast in the alternative genre of a prophecy supposedly uttered by Donn Firinne, a potentate in the Munster spirit world, O'Rahilly offered a more straightforward expression of his allegiance to the house of Stuart. 'The son of Charles, who was our king', was dead, and oaths were being imposed denying the hereditary title of his descendants. But their restoration was at hand, and with it sweeping changes:

> Erin will be joyful, and her strongholds will be merry;
> And the learned will cultivate Gaelic in their schools;
> The language of the black boors will be humbled and put beneath a cloud,
> And James in his bright court will lend his aid to the Gaels.

> Luther's bible and his false, dark teaching
> And this guilty tribe that yields not to the true clergy,
> Shall be transported across countries to a new land from Erin,
> And Louis and the Prince shall hold court and assembly.[15]

Another text, attributed to O'Rahilly but probably composed some years after his death, adopted the traditional vocabulary of *Gaeil* and *Gaill*, envisaging

---

[14] Examination of William Lahey, 26 Jan. 1714 (Surrey History Centre, Midleton Papers 1248/3, fo. 159); Forster's report (PRO, SP 63/373/34–5); John Brady, *Catholics and Catholicism in the Eighteenth-Century Press* (Maynooth, 1965), 311.

[15] *Dánta Aodhagáin Uí Rathaille* [The Poems of Egan O'Rahilly], ed. P. S. Dinneen and Tadhg O'Donoghue (2nd edn., London, 1911), 18–19, 166–7. 'To a new land' appears in the original as 'go Neuuland', suggesting either an incorrectly understood English term, or an attempt to indicate a generic foreign destination.

Frenchmen, Spaniards, and Gaels uniting 'until the expulsion of the foreigners [*Gaill*] out of Ireland'.[16]

Texts of this kind continued a long literary and political tradition. The glorification of the house of Stuart as Ireland's rightful rulers went back to the beginning of the seventeenth century, when the Gaelic literati had invented a Milesian pedigree for James VI and I.[17] O'Rahilly's vision of the changes that would accompany the return of James Edward Stuart echoed the terms in which Ó Bruadair, thirty years earlier, had acclaimed the accession of his father. The vision of an Ireland liberated from foreign conquerors was older still. Yet this very persistence of long-established genres and motifs must raise questions about how far the poetry concerned can be read as a straightforward political statement. Even in the late middle ages the rousing language of Gaedhil and Gall had been deployed with a pragmatic regard for the political realities of a society in which a poet's patrons could be of either race, and where alliance with the crown's Irish representatives was as valid a political strategy for an Irish chief as waging war against them. The incorporation of the same language into eighteenth-century Jacobite literature created a new set of contradictions. O'Rahilly envisaged the triumphant restoration of the Stuarts to the united crowns of England, Scotland, and Ireland. But he also saw their return to power as bringing with it the victory, not just of Catholic over Protestant, but of Irish over English. Such an identification of the Stuart cause with Gaelic civilization ignored the Old English, who had in fact taken the lead in Irish Catholic support for James II. It also ignored the wider framework of an Ireland that would still be a subordinate kingdom, attached to the crown of England, and the political constraints that would surround any realistic project for securing the acquiescence of all three kingdoms in a Stuart restoration. The Jacobite parliament of 1689, and before that the first Stuart restoration in 1660, had both already made clear just how little Catholic Ireland, much less its Gaelic component, could expect from a monarch intent on securing his position on the English throne.

Contradictions of this kind can in part be explained as reflecting the literary nature of the material. In deploying traditional motifs of Gael and foreigner, O'Rahilly and his contemporaries may well have engaged in the same sort of self-conscious literary artifice once mocked by the fourteenth-century poet Geoffrey Fionn O'Daly.[18] But in doing so they also highlighted the complex nature of Ireland's Jacobite tradition. There is little doubt that Jacobitism became the vehicle for protest against a variety of grievances specific to the Catholics

---

[16] *Dánta*, 142–3. The editors deduce from the poem's reference to a deliverance 1,711 years 'since Christ suffered the passion on the cross' that the poem was composed around 1711. But the crucifixion was, of course, around AD 33. For the medieval precedents of *Gaeil* and *Gaill* see Connolly, *Contested Island*, 48–9.

[17] Connolly, *Contested Island*, 388.

[18] 'In poems to the *Gaill* we promise the driving of the *Gaeil* from Éire; in those to the *Gaeil* we promise the driving of the *Gaill* east overseas.' See Connolly, *Contested Island*, 49–50.

of Ireland: religious inferiority, social subordination, the sense of being subject
to the rule of usurping intruders. At a later period these resentments provided
the basis for the development of a vigorous popular nationalism. In the early
and mid-eighteenth century, on the other hand, they found their outlet in a
movement that presupposed the continuing unity of Ireland and Great Britain.
At the battle of Fontenoy in 1745 the Irish Brigade reportedly charged into
battle to the cry: '*Cuimhnigi ar Luimneach agus Feall na Sasanach* [remember
Limerick and the treachery of the English]'. But these were troops who still wore
the red uniforms of men enlisted in the essentially British cause of restoring a
Scottish dynasty to the combined thrones of England, Scotland, and Ireland,
and whose flags bore the cross of St George.[19] Irish Jacobitism, like its Scottish
counterpart, can be considered as a prime example of what has been described
as 'proto-nationalism': a movement expressive of national consciousness that
nevertheless did not take the form of a demand for national independence.[20] But
any realistic analysis must also place it firmly within its contemporary context, as
a characteristic part of an *ancien régime* world of dynastic and religious loyalties.

In the period following the war of 1689–91, then, the Protestant establishment
ruled over a Catholic majority unreconciled to its recent defeat and committed
to the overthrow of the new political order. They responded with appropriate
security measures. In 1692 fears of a French invasion led to a general round-up
of former officers in the Jacobite army. During a further invasion scare in 1696
ex-officers in Dublin were allowed to give securities that they would remain in the
capital, but elsewhere some were again briefly detained. In 1708, during a minor
Jacobite rising in Scotland, the lords justices and local authorities summoned
leading Catholic gentry to take the oath of abjuration, and imprisoned those who
refused. In addition civic authorities temporarily expelled all Catholics from the
towns of Limerick and Galway. In 1715 a much larger Jacobite insurrection in
England and Scotland again led to leading Catholics being detained, although
on this occasion they were released on giving security to be of good behaviour,
and there were also searches for arms and horses.

Irish Protestants in the generation after the Boyne, then, did not take their
security for granted. But they also saw the threat in perspective. There had been
serious unease, in the immediate post-war period, at what was seen as the failure
of Porter and Coningsby to take the Catholic threat seriously enough. Later, in
1710–14, doubts as to the commitment of the English Tory ministry to the
defence of the Revolution settlement produced mounting alarm. But these were
fears of betrayal from within. On other occasions, as in 1708, 1715, and again in
1718–19, the general response to the threat of invasion or to reports of Jacobite

---

[19] Harman Murtagh, 'Irish Soldiers Abroad 1600–1800', in Thomas Bartlett and Keith Jeffery
(eds.), *A Military History of Ireland* (Cambridge, 1996), 298–9.
[20] Eric Hobsbawm, *Nations and Nationalism since 1780: Programme, Myth, Reality* (Cambridge,
1990), ch. 2.

conspiracy was one of wary caution, rather than anything approaching panic. By 1731, after four decades of undisturbed internal peace, a clergyman preaching before the House of Commons on 5 November, the potentially inflammatory anniversary of the English Catholic conspiracy against James I, could devote his sermon to the abject condition of the Catholics, still possibly malevolent but deprived of power to hurt, and invited his audience to say with the psalmist that God had subdued their enemies.[21]

This growing confidence was based on the same appreciation of social and political realities, combined with the assumptions of a pre-democratic society, that allowed Swift, during the same period, to address Protestants as 'the whole people of Ireland'. Catholics may have been numerically dominant. But they were leaderless, demoralized, and disarmed. Sir Richard Cox, whose own dedication to the defence of the Protestant interest had been put beyond doubt through his leadership of a bloody campaign of counter-insurgency in Munster during the later stages of the Jacobite war, wrote scathingly of the efforts of Whig critics of the Tory administration of Queen Anne's last years to talk up the Catholic threat.

Their first and main cunning is to represent the Irish as formidable though they really despise them, and know that their youth and gentry are destroyed in the rebellion, or gone to France; that those who are left are destitute of horses, arms, and money, capacity and courage; that five in six of the Irish are poor insignificant slaves, fit for nothing but to hew wood and draw water.

And indeed even the Whig Robert Molesworth, writing privately to his wife in 1705, regarded claims of a Catholic plot as 'a very silly business, and which ought not to have been regarded by any man of sense, who might easily see that the Irish are in no manner of condition to do the least mischief, much less to massacre'.[22]

There remained the risk of invasion by a large force of French regular troops. But in this context the common idea of Ireland as England's vulnerable western flank is seriously misleading. At times of European war, as in 1689–91, diversionary operations in Ireland could serve as a means of tying down large numbers of British troops. But for a sudden drive to overthrow the Hanoverian dynasty the only strategy that made sense was an invasion of the British mainland, and a rapid strike towards London. An invasion of Ireland might yield a quick local victory; but it would have to be followed by a second seaborne operation against a regime that had by then had time to assemble its naval and other forces for the defence of the British mainland, where the real outcome of any new challenge would be decided. It was for this reason that the British government

---

[21] Henry Jenney, *A Sermon Preached at St Andrew's, Dublin, . . . on Friday, the 5th of November 1731* (Dublin, 1731).

[22] Cox to Southwell, 24 Oct. 1706 (BL, Add. MS 38,154, fo. 86); Molesworth to Letitia Molesworth, n.d. (HMC, *Various Collections*, viii. 232–3). For a range of other comment see Connolly, *Religion, Law and Power*, 249–58.

responded to the Jacobite rising of 1715, and to a second, threatened invasion in 1719, by moving troops from Ireland to Scotland. The Irish administration, and Protestant public opinion, by acquiescing without protest in both cases, indicated clearly that they too appreciated the strategic realities.

The relative confidence displayed by the Protestant elite for most of the 1720s and 1730s also reflected a particular diplomatic background: the long détente between Great Britain and a France no longer driven by the ambitions of Louis XIV. From 1739, however, George II's dominions were at war with Spain, and from 1740 with France. By 1744–5 there was a real prospect of a French and Jacobite assault on some part of the British Isles. The threat inspired a sharp reversion to traditional defensive strategies. A proclamation in November 1739 ordered searches of Catholic houses for arms. In 1744 the privy council forced a reluctant lord lieutenant to order the closure of Catholic churches and the enforcement of the laws against regulars and those exercising Catholic ecclesiastical jurisdiction. Chesterfield, taking charge of the kingdom early the following year, mocked the prejudices of 'my good subjects', who 'are in general still at the year 1689, and have not shook off any religious or political prejudice that prevailed at that time'. His dismissive attitude caused grave offence. Yet his predecessor, the duke of Devonshire, had offered an equally sober assessment of the threat. Once the Protestants had been armed and mobilized through the militia, he reported in January 1744, they 'will be able to keep the papists quiet', making it possible, if need arose, to withdraw almost all regular troops from Ireland to defend other threatened areas.[23] And indeed local Protestants themselves, while irritated by Chesterfield's air of supercilious insouciance, nevertheless expressed confidence that, with proper security measures, they could deal effectively with anything short of a full-scale foreign invasion.

Confidence in the capacity of the Protestant minority to contain a more numerous but leaderless and unarmed Catholic population reiterated a long-standing assessment of the balance of risk. What was new in the crisis of 1744–5 was the first tentative suggestion, from some quarters, that Irish Catholics might not in fact flock to join the standard of the Pretender or his French supporters. The general closure of churches, and the attempted round-up of unregistered priests and regular clergy, on which the privy council had insisted in 1744 were not repeated during the much more serious crisis of the following year. Instead several bishops of the Church of Ireland responded to the emergency by calling on their clergy, not just to exhort their own congregations to mobilize for their own defence, but also to address their Catholic parishioners. They were to point out to them, not only the degree of practical toleration they enjoyed

---

[23] Devonshire to Newcastle, 31 Jan. 1744 (PRO, SP63/406/32–3). Ó Ciardha, *Ireland and the Jacobite Cause*, ch. 6, makes rather more of Protestant insecurity. For the assessment offered here see Connolly, *Religion, Law and Power*, 255–9.

under the current regime, but also the civil liberties that they shared equally with Protestants, but that would be swept away in the event of a French conquest.

How far was this perception that Catholics might be induced to give at least passive acquiescence to the political order justified? It is impossible to speak with confidence. The experience of other political crises, from 1641 to 1688, was that allegiances were most commonly translated into action only when circumstances made commitment impossible to avoid. In Ireland in 1745 that point was never reached. There was clear evidence of continuing enthusiasm for the Jacobite cause. The writings of Gaelic poets show a keen interest in the political possibilities opened up by the renewal of war from 1739. In County Down a Catholic farmer was arrested for drinking the Pretender's health and declaring 'that he would drink it over and over again in spite of all present, who might kiss his arse, for that if he was hanged for it 500 of them should hang along with him'.[24] Elsewhere there were reports of tenants withholding rents and other payments in the expectation of an invasion. On the other hand Patrick Wall, who arrived in Scotland early in 1746 with a message of support from Ireland, admitted that he did so without the backing of any of the surviving Catholic proprietors: 'they are known to be attached to the present ruling dynasty, and any upheaval would be dangerous for them.' The Catholic gentleman Charles O'Conor, in the privacy of his diary, described Charles Edward's Scottish campaign as 'the last flicker of a candle that has been going out for sixty years, unless God prevents it'.[25] Such comments would suggest that the public expressions of loyalty offered by the Catholic clergy and by leading Catholic gentry as the crisis unfolded were not merely prudential, but reflected a real weakening of commitment to the Stuarts.

The defeat of Charles Edward's expedition of 1745–6 marked the end of Jacobitism as a force in European politics. Thereafter neither France nor any other European power was willing to invest significant resources in a further attempt to restore the Stuart dynasty. When James III, the old Pretender, died in 1766, the pope declined to recognize his son Charles Edward as Charles III. Against this background the Catholic propertied classes became increasingly ready to distance themselves from their Jacobite past by public assurances of their allegiance to the Hanoverian dynasty. In 1759, when a series of military reverses revived the risk of a French invasion, Catholics in the major towns formed associations 'in support of his majesty, his crown and his dignity'.[26] An address to George III by the Catholic nobility and gentry of Meath and Westmeath in January 1761 lamented the death of 'our late good and merciful king', but claimed to see in his grandson 'all his shining virtues . . . as hereditary as his crown'. A companion address offered by the recently established Catholic committee, signed by 600

---

[24] Robert Ward to Michael Ward, 10 Feb. 1746 (PRONI D2092/1/7/40).
[25] M. de la Poer Beresford, 'Ireland in French Strategy' (unpublished M.Litt. thesis, Trinity College, Dublin, 1975), 175–7, 423; Morley, *Irish Opinion and the American Revolution*, 8.
[26] Faulkner to Derick, 18 Dec. 1759 (*Prince of Dublin Printers: The Letters of George Faulkner*, ed. R. E. Ward (Lexington, Ky., 1972), 57).

gentry and merchants, was equally careful to advertise its repudiation of the dynastic claims of the Stuarts, congratulating the new king on his accession 'to the throne of your ancestors'.²⁷ In all this, however, the Catholic elite could speak only for itself. In 1755 the Protestant archbishop of Tuam, discussing yet another invasion scare, reported that 'the popish gentlemen' themselves 'do not conceal from us their fears that the populace, of which 99 in 100 are Papists, would not be restrained from any violence on the landing of a foreign force'.²⁸

The fullest expression of post-1745 Jacobite thinking is once again the writings of the Gaelic poets. As in earlier periods, however, there are major problems of interpretation. By the eighteenth century the Gaelic literary tradition had adapted to changing circumstances. Its verse forms were simpler, and its language closer to the ordinary spoken tongue. But this does not mean that it can necessarily be taken as the representative voice of the Catholic poor. Poets were no longer the privileged specialists once produced by the bardic schools. But the high level of literacy and technical accomplishment still required to participate in their craft nevertheless ensured that they were drawn mainly from a rural middle class, from among schoolmasters, tenant farmers, or artisans, rather than the labouring poor. They also retained a strong sense of their own identity as the representatives of an ancient literary tradition. In consequence, it has been argued, their political poetry must be read in context.²⁹ A poem on the collapse of the Gaelic social order does not necessarily reflect the sentiments of the labouring farmer on the demise of the ruling class to whom his ancestors once paid tribute; rather it is the lament of a particular individual, the poet, for the disappearance of a social order in which he and his craft would have enjoyed both prestige and material reward. Conscious participation in a long-standing literary tradition also raises the question of genre. Even in the first years of the eighteenth century, when a foreign-backed Stuart assault on the dynasty's lost possessions was still a real possibility, there are elements in Jacobite poetry, such as O'Rahilly's vision of a return to Gaelic cultural hegemony, that seem to represent the working out of a traditional theme rather than a realistic political aspiration. After 1745, with Jacobitism no longer a credible political force, the case for reading references to a Stuart restoration primarily as literary flourishes becomes even stronger.

This is not to suggest that poetry in Irish had wholly lost touch with the real world of politics. In some respects, indeed, the continued attention paid to international affairs is impressive. Poems composed in the early 1780s showed

²⁷ Brady, *Catholics and Catholicism*, 99–101. Morley, *Irish Opinion and the American Revolution*, 45, sees the Meath address, drafted by the conservative Lord Trimleston, as reflecting a higher level of commitment to the Hanoverian regime, but the careful inclusion in both of the question of hereditary right suggests that any such differences are in tone rather than substance.
²⁸ John Ryder to Sir Dudley Ryder, 20 May 1755 (PRONI T3228/1/69).
²⁹ The classic exposition of this point is L. M. Cullen, 'The Hidden Ireland: Reassessment of a Concept', *Studia Hibernica*, 9 (1969), 7–48. For the context of his critique, and a fuller discussion, see the final section of this chapter.

a close familiarity with the American War, identifying battle sites and military commanders on both sides. One drinking song even included mention of a victory over British forces by Hyder Ali of Mysore, as well as the French capture of the Caribbean island of Tobago. More striking still are the occasional references to the upheavals simultaneously taking place in Irish domestic politics. One poet, in a striking blend of traditional and contemporary vocabulary, reported the departure to England of the patriot leader Henry Flood, and hoped that he would suffer injury from no foreign Whig ('Galla-Whig'). Yet if Irish-language poets paid close attention to events outside their own immediate environment, they also persistently interpreted them within a frame of reference largely divorced from contemporary political reality. The war in America became, in language straight from the Irish annals, 'cogadh an dá Ghall' ['the war of the two groups of foreigners']. If names like Washington were sometimes repeated, there was no awareness of the ideological issues that underlay the conflict in North America; instead poets saw the war there as primarily an extension of a European conflict in which they could hope to see Britain defeated by the traditional friends of Catholic Ireland, France and Spain.

Most revealing of all were the wild attempts to fit the Volunteers and their patriot allies into categories derived from the Jacobite tradition. Seán Ó Coileáin, a County Cork teacher, showed his familiarity with current patriot politics when he wrote of 'bands of strong men with shining weapons' demanding 'téarma is saoirse céirde' (a time limit—possibly a short money bill, or a limited rather than perpetual mutiny bill—and free trade). But when he went on to suggest that the next step would be for these bands to give their allegiance to Prince Charles Edward, identified for good measure as a Whiteboy or agrarian rebel, he moved from political commentary into pure fantasy. Another Munster author, even more wildly, linked celebration of the 'hostings of heroes' at the Volunteer provincial conventions at Dungannon and Ballinasloe to visions of a French and Spanish victory, and a return of 'King Charles like a valiant Caesar'. As with O'Rahilly, sixty years earlier, two interpretations are possible. One is that superficial references to personalities and events concealed the inability of the Gaelic literati, lost in their own self-referential world, truly to understand the political events taking place either in Ireland or abroad. The other, probably more accurate, is that their supposedly political poetry was, even more than in earlier decades, an exercise in literary artifice rather than an expression of real beliefs or aspirations.[30]

An alternative window on the outlook of plebeian Catholics, suggesting conclusions very different from the dubious evidence of the poetry, is provided

---

[30] The examples in this and the preceding paragraph are all taken from Morley, *Irish Opinion and the American Revolution*. They are used, however, to reach a conclusion very different from that argued for in Dr Morley's study. For a fuller discussion, and detailed references, see S. J. Connolly, 'Jacobites, Whiteboys and Republicans: Varieties of Disaffection in Eighteenth-Century Ireland', *ECI* 18 (2003), 63–79.

by a new development, occurring just as the Jacobite menace began to recede. This was the appearance of recurrent waves of organized agrarian protest. Conflict between competing economic interests within rural society, leading to violence and intimidation, was not a wholly new feature of the Irish countryside. During 1711–12 a group known as the Houghers sought to prevent the expansion of stock rearing at the expense of small-scale tillage farming in parts of the west just beginning to be touched by the forces of commercialization.[31] In a short but intense campaign, commencing in the territory known as Iar Connacht, west of Galway city, and spreading from there into the adjoining counties of Clare, Roscommon, Leitrim, Sligo, and Mayo, they destroyed thousands of cattle and sheep. Their activities anticipated much that was to be characteristic of later movements of agrarian protest, notably the invocation of a mythical leader, Ever Joyce, and the use both of threatening letters and of formal proclamations mimicking the tone and language of government.

The Houghers, however, were not a purely popular movement. They operated with the connivance of members of the local Catholic gentry, possibly influenced by political or religious considerations, but probably motivated also by their own concern at the threat to their way of life from a more competitive, market-oriented system of agriculture. Nor did they have any immediate successors. There are occasional reports across the next four decades of threatening letters, the maiming of cattle, the levelling of fences, and similar occurrences. But it was not until the 1760s that an organized movement of protest again appeared in the Irish countryside. The Whiteboy movement originated in County Tipperary in 1761, spreading over the next four years into the counties of Limerick, Waterford, Cork, and Kilkenny. A second wave of protest, again by what were known as Whiteboys, took place in 1769–75, this time concentrated further east and north, in the counties of Kilkenny, Tipperary, Queen's, Carlow, and Wexford. A third, in 1785–8, involving Rightboys or followers of a supposed 'Captain Right', began in County Cork and once again spread into Tipperary and Kilkenny, as well as into Waterford, Kerry, and Limerick.[32]

At first sight these successive waves of agrarian protest, pitting a mainly Catholic small farming and labouring class against the descendants of their New English conquerors, were further evidence of the religious, ethnic, and political divisions that had until recently found expression in popular Jacobitism. The Whiteboys and their successors, however, were not movements of political, or even social

---

[31] S. J. Connolly, 'The Houghers: Agrarian Protest in Early Eighteenth-Century Connacht', in C. H. E. Philpin (ed.), *Nationalism and Popular Protest in Ireland* (Cambridge, 1987), 139–62.

[32] The best general introduction to Irish agrarian disturbances is Samuel Clark and J. S. Donnelly (eds.), *Irish Peasants: Violence and Political Unrest 1780–1914* (Madison, 1983). For particular outbreaks see J. S. Donnelly, 'The Whiteboy Movement 1761–5', *IHS* 21 (1978), 20–54; idem, 'The Rightboy Movement 1785–8', *Studia Hibernica*, 17/18 (1977–8), 120–202; idem, 'Irish Agrarian Rebellion: The Whiteboys of 1769–76', *PRIA*, C, 83 (1983); Maurice Bric, 'Priests, Parsons and Politics: The Rightboy Protest in County Cork, 1785–1788', in Philpin (ed.), *Nationalism and Popular Protest*, 163–90.

revolution. Instead, like movements of protest elsewhere in early modern Europe, their aims were limited and primarily defensive. The first outbreak, in 1761–5, arose at a time when high wartime provision prices had encouraged a further expansion of pasture at the expense of small-scale tillage. Protest in 1769–75, on the other hand, occurred in south-eastern counties where the expansion of tillage in response to state bounties had led to increased competition for land. The response of those engaged in protest was to seek to preserve their position within the existing system: during 1761–5 by resisting increases in the cost of conacre and preventing large farmers and landlords from fencing in rougher grazing land formerly available as 'commonage'; in 1769–75 by seeking to hold down rents, resist evictions, and discourage interlopers from taking land over the heads of sitting tenants. Claims that some of those involved in the earlier movement advertised their disinclination to challenge the political order by linking the reigning monarch with a mythical Gaelic goddess in the slogan 'Long Live King George III and Queen Sive' may or may not be well founded.[33] But they are not inherently improbable, given the frequency with which those involved in movements of protest throughout the early modern world sought to make clear that their actions were directed not at the monarch but at his dishonest or malicious subordinates. Protest against tithes, important in all three southern outbreaks, unavoidably raised the issue of a Catholic peasantry being required to support an established church. Once again, however, the purpose of protest was not to challenge the tithe system, but to keep its demands within customary bounds. Tithe was an issue in 1769–75 because of the exemption of pasture forced through the Irish parliament sixty years earlier, which meant that the swing towards tillage now taking place made the church's financial demands expand beyond customary levels. The main grievance in 1785–8, when tithe became the single most important cause of agitation, was an increase in the practice of farming out the collection of tithes to proctors, who pursued their legal entitlements with an assiduity rarely matched where clergy collected on their own behalf.

If agrarian protest cannot be interpreted as political revolt, neither should it be seen as a straightforward conflict between settler and native, or between Catholic and Protestant. The Whiteboy movement of 1761–5 drew some support from small farmers, and also from urban craftsmen, many of whom regularly rented small plots of conacre land. But its members were for the most part smallholders and landless labourers. The grievances against which they rose, such as the enclosure of common land or the conversion of tillage gardens into pasture for cattle and sheep, were the work, not just of landlords, but of larger farmers and middlemen, Catholic as well as Protestants. The agitation of 1769–76, more concerned

---

[33] For doubts about the reliability of this claim see Vincent Morley, 'George III, Queen Sadhbh and the Historians', *ECI* 17 (2002), 112–20. For a response, see Connolly, 'Jacobites, Whiteboys and Republicans', 72–3.

with rents and evictions, had rather greater support from small farmers. Once again, however, better-off Catholics were more likely to be its victims than its supporters. In one celebrated case, in February 1775, Whiteboys attacked the house of Robert Butler of Ballyragget, brother of the Catholic archbishop of Cashel, who had earlier organized his tenants into an armed association for their suppression.

The anti-tithe agitation of 1785–8 was more broadly based, attracting support from all sections of Catholic society. But the Rightboys also had the backing, or at least connivance, of several members of the Protestant landed gentry, motivated partly by resentment at clerical support for the dominant Shannon interest in Cork politics, and partly by a dislike of tithes, seen either as a genuine social evil or, possibly, as an inconvenient alternative claim to the tenant farmer's surplus income. The Rightboys, moreover, did not confine their attentions to the Church of Ireland. They also protested forcefully against what they presented as a recent and unjustified increase in the fees demanded by their own clergy. They published tables setting out the maximum to be paid in future for baptisms, marriages, and other services, and in the annual dues expected from each family, backing up their demands with threats and violence. In one incident near Tralee in 1786 a priest who had accepted five shillings for a licence to marry without the calling of banns, 'contrary to Captain Right's rules', was accosted by men who fired three shots at him as he fled. In Cork the Catholics of several parishes demonstrated their resentment of clerical demands by abandoning their own chapels and instead attending Church of Ireland services. The bishops of the province of Munster were sufficiently shaken by such tactics to issue a conciliatory pastoral letter promising to enquire into any abuses, and calling on their clergy to refrain from unreasonable demands.[34]

Nor was it only Catholics who took the lead in agrarian protest. The Oakboys or Hearts of Oak appeared in Armagh, Tyrone, and Monaghan in 1763. Their initial grievance was the rising burden of cess for the upkeep of roads, blamed by protesters on abuse of the system by landlords for the benefit of their own estates, although the real underlying reason was the unprecedented demands made on the province's transport system by the continued growth of linen manufacturing. To this was added protest at certain fees demanded by the Church of Ireland clergy. The movement appears to have involved Catholics, Anglicans, and dissenters, but to have reflected in particular the grievances of Presbyterians. A second Ulster agitation, by the Hearts of Steel or Steelboys, began in 1770 in the solidly Presbyterian county of Antrim, spreading over the next two years to Down, Londonderry, and Armagh. The agitation originated in grievances arising from a general reletting of lands owned by the marquis of Donegall as existing leases fell in. A demand for high entry fines alarmed tenants, and frustrated the ambitions of those who had hoped to displace existing middlemen and hold directly from

[34] S. J. Connolly, *Priests and People in Pre-Famine Ireland, 1780–1845*, 2nd edn. (Dublin, 2000), 228–31.

the Donegalls. From there the agitation expanded into a general protest against rising rents at a time of poor harvests and a faltering cattle market. The Protestant Steelboys were as willing to defy the law as their southern Catholic counterparts. Their most spectacular exploit came on 23 December 1770, when a party of 500 to 600 marched into Belfast and liberated a prisoner from the town jail. The response of the authorities was also fairly ruthless. Despite the restraints imposed by the reluctance of juries to convict, at least seven offenders were hanged in County Antrim in 1772.[35]

This is not to deny the importance of agrarian protest as an insight into the divisions that existed within Irish society. The protests of the Whiteboys and their successors may have had parallels elsewhere in early modern Great Britain and beyond. But the recurrence of disturbances in successive decades suggests a deficiency either in channels of communication or in levels of mutual comprehension between rulers and ruled, reflected in a ready resort to open protest over grievances that elsewhere might have been more often dealt with through either formal or informal representations to social superiors. At the same time it is important not to exaggerate. The major outbreaks of protest remained discrete episodes, clearly limited in both space and time. Across a period of some forty years from 1760 just over half the counties of Ireland experienced disturbances on a significant scale. If they resorted more frequently to open protest than comparable groups elsewhere, moreover, the Irish rural poor remained sparing in their use of violence. Attacks on property—the burning of houses, the killing or mutilation of livestock, the levelling of fences, or the digging up of grassland so that it could be used only as arable—were the most common mode of action. Where individuals were attacked, it was often in a highly public and ritualized manner that placed the emphasis more on the community's rejection of one who had violated its ideas of right behaviour than on terror for its own sake. A common tactic of the Rightboys, for example, was to conduct offenders in solemn procession through a district, before burying them up to their necks in pits or, possibly in imitation of the rituals of the criminal law, cropping their ears. Lethal violence was relatively rare. The Whiteboys of 1761–5 did not kill anyone; during the Rightboy disturbances of 1785–8 there were six homicides, of which three appear to have been unpremeditated and one in pursuit of a private quarrel. One estimate puts the total number of killings attributable to agrarian protest across the whole period 1761–90 at no more than fifty.[36]

The campaigns of the Whiteboys and similar bodies to protect the interests of the rural labouring and small farming class had a counterpart in the food riots and

---

[35] J. S. Donnelly, 'Hearts of Oak, Hearts of Steel', *Studia Hibernica*, 21 (1981), 7–73; Eoin Magennis, 'A Presbyterian Insurrection? Reconsidering the Hearts of Oak Disturbances of July 1763', *IHS* 31 (1999), 31–62; W. A. Maguire, 'Lord Donegall and the Hearts of Steel', *IHS* 21 (1979), 351–76.

[36] Thomas Bartlett, 'An End to Moral Economy: The Irish Militia Disturbances of 1793', in Philpin (ed.), *Nationalism and Popular Protest*, 193.

other forms of popular protest that occurred across the century in Dublin and other urban centres. The expansion of manufacturing during the late seventeenth and early eighteenth centuries provided the basis for a growth of organization among skilled workers, provoking Ireland's first major anti-union legislation in 1729. These combinations sought to protect customary wage rates and conditions of work, and to prevent skilled workers being displaced by cheaper unskilled labour, sometimes by industrial action but often by violence and intimidation. Food rioters, as in contemporary England, sought to uphold a 'moral economy' which outlawed profiteering at the expense of the poor during times of scarcity, in some cases making their point by formally carrying corn or other goods seized from ships or warehouses to the marketplace to be sold off at the customary price.[37]

The contrast between a continued tradition of popular Jacobitism, sustained in song and story, and the limited and pragmatic aims of popular protest, both urban and rural, is not as surprising as it might appear at first sight. All over early modern Europe the poor and weak amused or consoled themselves with visions of a society transformed: images of the world turned upside down, legends of noble bandits who would befriend the poor while plundering and humiliating the rich and powerful. On occasion, as in the repeated popular risings in support of Pretenders claiming to be the real tsar that disrupted eighteenth-century Russia, such aspirations could be translated into action. More often they remained an escapist fantasy, coexisting with a pragmatic acceptance of the existing social hierarchy even at times when grievances became acute enough to warrant the risk of engaging in social protest. Within this context the behaviour of plebeian Irish Catholics, entertaining themselves with tales of deliverance from overseas, while confining their acts of open resistance to the calculated and realistic strategies of the Whiteboys, no longer seems particularly anomalous, or strikingly out of the range of the general European experience.

All this, however, is with the benefit of hindsight. Protestant contemporaries in the last decades of the eighteenth century had to make their own assessment of how far Catholic disaffection had ceased to be a threat. When a French invasion seemed imminent during 1758–9 the archbishop of Armagh expressed confidence that propertied Catholics would support the government, while the lord lieutenant clung to the more traditional view that the 'popish and disaffected counties' of the south-west would rise in support of an invader. Lord Chief Justice Richard Aston, presiding over a special commission set up to try Whiteboys in Limerick and Tipperary in 1762, concluded that the disturbances were purely economic in character, and threw out capital charges against a series of defendants. As he left Clonmel local Catholics reportedly lined the road to demonstrate their gratitude for his intervention. The gentry, by contrast, remained convinced that they faced a new popish insurrection. This was particularly the case in Tipperary, where the assertive behaviour during a recent by-election of a prominent convert

---

[37] Connolly, *Religion, Law and Power*, 219–20.

family, the Mathews, had already raised the spectre of a resurgence of Catholic political power. During 1762 the sheriff and local gentry reinvoked the long dormant laws against Catholic schools and unregistered priests. Two years later they brought charges of inciting a rebellion against Nicholas Sheehy, parish priest of Clogheen, a prominent critic of the tithe system. A trial in Dublin ended in acquittal, but Tipperary magistrates had Sheehy rearrested and transported back to Clonmel, where he was convicted on a clearly trumped-up charge of murder and hanged in March 1766. Meanwhile more than a dozen Catholic gentlemen and middlemen had been arrested on similar charges. Three went to the gallows two months after Sheehy, and the rest remained in prison until their eventual acquittal at the spring assizes of 1767.[38]

Later outbreaks of agrarian protest, in the 1770s and 1780s, produced no comparable action against priests or other prominent Catholics—partly, perhaps, because the outrageous proceedings in Tipperary temporarily discredited Protestant alarmism. But the Rightboy outbreak of 1785–8 produced new reports of foreign gold allegedly circulating in the disturbed areas. A coercion bill debated in 1787 included a clause authorizing the destruction of any Catholic church in or near which illegal oaths were found to have been administered. However the clause was abandoned in the face of strong opposition; the patriot spokesman Henry Grattan denounced it as sacrilegious.[39] When the Waterford loyalist Sir Richard Musgrave, in 1801, published his account of the rebellion of 1798, he began his narrative with the Whiteboys, presented as a Catholic movement, led by officers 'bound by oaths of allegiance to the French king, and prince Charles the pretender to the crown of England', and encouraged by their clergy, including the executed Sheehy.[40] The appearance of this work in print, and the enthusiastic welcome it received, reflected the hardening of attitudes that had taken place in the aftermath of the recent bloodshed. But Musgrave was probably doing no more than giving voice to what many provincial gentry had all along muttered into their cups. It was against this background of conflicting perspectives that the government, and some Irish politicians, began in the 1770s seriously to consider whether the time had come to readmit Catholics to at least a partial share in Irish public life.

RULING CIRCLES

In 1716 the Irish parliament abolished the last significant relic of the decentralized, feudal lordship that the Tudor dynasty had inherited more than two centuries

---

[38] T. P. Power, *Land, Politics and Society in Eighteenth-Century Tipperary* (Oxford, 1993), 257–65.

[39] Gerard O'Brien (ed.), 'An Account of a Debate in the Irish Parliament 1786', *Analecta Hibernica*, 33 (1986), 149–50.

[40] Sir Richard Musgrave, *Memoirs of the Different Rebellions in Ireland* (repr. Fort Wayne, Ind., 1995), 27–8.

earlier. The Fitzgeralds of Desmond and the Burkes of Clanricard were long gone. The inclusion in 1714 of Robert Fitzgerald, nineteenth earl of Kildare, as one of the three lords justices appointed by the new Whig ministry of George I marked the beginning of that ancient family's re-emergence from a long period of political eclipse. But the modest prominence of his heirs, the first and second dukes of Leinster, was to be as heads of an electoral interest. The Butlers of Ormond were in a different category. The twelfth earl, returning from exile as one of Charles II's closest associates, had been rewarded with the recovery of his family's vast estates in Tipperary, Kilkenny, and elsewhere. In addition a grateful crown restored the palatine liberty of Tipperary, suspended in 1621 during the assault on the Catholic earl Walter.[41] For the next half-century officials appointed by the first and second dukes maintained a system of courts which dealt with both civil cases and all but a few reserved criminal charges. In 1715, however, the second duke, facing impeachment for his part in what was now being presented as the previous Tory ministry's treasonable winding down of the war against France, fled to the Stuart court. The subsequent confiscation of his estates provided the opportunity at the same time to end the Tipperary palatinate.

The belated abolition of what by this time had become the anomalous relic of an earlier concept of government completed a long process of centralization. After 1716 Ireland had a single uniform system of law enforcement and of civil and criminal justice. There remained a few areas, in Connacht, south Ulster and the far south-west, in which these agencies had in practice only limited authority. But these too were being brought gradually under control. The rise to new prominence over the preceding two decades of the Irish parliament provided the basis both for a closer alignment of legislation to the needs of the society and for a more organized system of taxation and government spending. There was also by this time a denser network of local government, at the level of county and parish. At this point, however, it becomes possible to see the limitations as well as the achievements of the long-standing programme of creating in Ireland a replica of the institutions associated with the civility and good order of English society.[42]

At the centre of government, as in preceding centuries, was the viceroy, now always a lord lieutenant rather than a lord deputy. The office had changed radically since the days of Wentworth or the first duke of Ormond. Eighteenth-century lords lieutenant, still nominally the king's representative, were in practice senior members of the current British ministry. One consequence was that none, after

---

[41] For the campaign against Earl Walter see Connolly, *Contested Island*, 365.

[42] The best survey of the institutions of central and, more particularly, local government is T. C. Barnard, *The Kingdom of Ireland 1641–1760* (Basingstoke, 2004), chs. 3 and 5. R. B. McDowell, *The Irish Administration 1801–1914* (London, 1964), opens with an account of structures at the end of the eighteenth century. There are also useful chapters by J. L. McCracken and McDowell in *NHI*, iv. 57–83, 695–712.

the younger Ormond's second term of office in 1710–13, was Irish by birth or previous residence. Up to 1767 these English chief governors visited the kingdom only during the parliamentary session, entrusting administration at other times to lords justices. Thereafter, following the move from reliance on undertakers to direct political management from the Castle, they resided throughout their term of office. The other duty of the lord lieutenant was to maintain a viceregal court, intended to provide a centre for high society and to add a mixture of ceremonial and graciousness to the business of government. But such efforts were hampered by the lack of a suitably impressive venue. The abandonment long before of Wentworth's Jigginstown meant that lords lieutenant had no country mansion in which to hold court. A drawing of Dublin Castle in the late 1720s reveals an unimpressive combination of modest new construction—arcaded terraces erected around three sides of the Castle yard—and medieval ruin, in the form of a massive gateway linked on one side to a curtain wall, and the stump of a ruined tower in an opposite corner. Further building in the 1740s and 1750s created a reasonably elegant upper yard, and a graceful front gate, repositioned to permit a vista, and perhaps a processional route, to the main bridge across the river, as well as refurbished state apartments. But the new yard was less spacious than the forecourt of the duke of Leinster's town house, erected in the newly fashionable west quarter of the town in the mid-1740s, and the Castle never established itself as more than one of several fashionable venues for Dublin high society.[43]

In their role of chief governor, lords lieutenant had the support of a chief secretary, likewise appointed by and responsible to the British government. Originally the viceroy's personal assistant, the chief secretary was by now an important figure in his own right. His main concern, like that of his master the lord lieutenant, was with political management. He sat in the Irish parliament and acted as spokesman for government. But his office was also the central executive agency of government. In 1777, in response to the widening range and volume of official business, the chief secretary's office was divided into separate military and civil departments, each with an undersecretary. A post office came into existence in 1784 and a treasury, charged with more systematic management of public spending, in 1793. But even at the end of the century the machinery of central government remained striking mainly for its small scale. There had been a steady expansion in the revenue service, from 1,100 office holders in the 1720s to 1,600 by the late 1750s and nearly 3,000 by 1800. But this was exceptional, reflecting the rapid growth of the Irish economy. The total number employed in the twenty-two departments of Irish government by around 1800 was just over 4,700. Of the 1,700 or so not employed by the revenue service nearly half, 800,

---

[43] Edward McParland, *Public Architecture in Ireland 1680–1760* (New Haven, 2001), ch. 4; T. C. Barnard, *Making the Grand Figure: Lives and Possessions in Ireland 1641–1770* (New Haven, 2004), ch. 1.

were attached to the wagon train maintained by the army commissariat.[44] Nor could any part of this public sector be characterized at this stage as a bureaucracy. Recruitment was largely by patronage, and payment was in many cases by fees rather than a salary.

The most significant institution of central government was the Irish parliament. Following the disastrous short session of 1692 new parliaments were elected in 1695, in 1703 following the death of King William, and again in 1713. Thereafter, up to the Octennial Act of 1768, general elections took place only, as required by law, at the accession of a new monarch: in 1715, 1727, and 1760. The by-elections held as members died or were promoted to the peerage or judiciary ensured that between 1727 and 1760 the 300 seats in the House of Commons were occupied by a total of 669 individuals. But no fewer than 56 members held their seats undisturbed for the whole thirty-three years. If elections were infrequent, however, the principle of control of taxation so firmly asserted in the 1690s ensured that sittings of parliament, an occasional event in the seventeenth century, now took place with predictable regularity. Between 1715 and 1783 a session began in October of every second year, continuing generally until the following May. Thereafter parliament generally met in January of every year, normally for a session of four or five months. Between 1729 and 1731 the new status thus achieved as the senate of an increasingly self-conscious Protestant nation found physical expression in Edward Lovell Pearce's magnificent new parliament building. Its predecessor, Chichester House, had sat back from College Green, behind a courtyard and two gatehouses. By contrast the massive colonnaded forecourt of Pearce's new building, erected on the same site, was designed as a public statement, facing directly onto the square. The interior design, too, was a bold acknowledgement of political realities, giving unabashed primacy to an octagonal Commons chamber topped by a large dome.[45]

The pretensions expressed in Pearce's stone masterpiece were in some respects bogus. The Irish parliament continued to operate under the constraints imposed by Poynings's Law: heads of bills, the only way in which members could initiate legislation, could be suppressed or amended in either the Irish or the British privy council, and it is now apparent that this power was used more frequently than was once realized. At the same time the statistical record suggests a legislature growing both in ambition and in effectiveness. The proportion of all bills introduced in parliament that eventually reached the statute book rose from only 38 per cent in the 1690s to 47 per cent in the following decade, and to over 60 per cent

---

[44] McDowell, *The Irish Administration*, 3–4. For the numbers employed by the revenue in earlier periods see Eoin Magennis, *The Irish Political System 1740–1765* (Dublin, 2000), 47.

[45] McParland, *Public Architecture*. The Lords, in the 1780s, redressed the balance slightly by having James Gandon give them their own colonnaded entrance, masking the alterations with the curved wall that now forms the east side of the building.

thereafter. The number of heads introduced in each session fluctuated in the first half of the century, but rose consistently from the 1760s.[46]

The membership of this increasingly active legislative body was distinctly narrow. Catholics were excluded by an English act of 1691 from the parliaments of both kingdoms. Presbyterians fared little better. No general election between 1692 and 1727 returned more than nine dissenters to a House of Commons of 300 members, and their representation does not seem to have increased significantly thereafter. One obvious reason for such under-representation was the sacramental test, which between 1704 and 1780 excluded dissenters from the boroughs that returned the great majority of MPs. But their poor electoral showing before 1704 suggests that their real disadvantage was the absence of a significant dissenting landed interest. The central importance of landownership as the key to political power is borne out by other evidence. Of 669 members who sat between 1727 and 1760 at least half, and probably more, were themselves owners of land. The other two important occupational groups, the 128 lawyers and the 88 army officers, were also recruited largely from landed families. The world of business, by contrast, was scantily represented, with between 18 and a dozen merchants, and 17 or 18 bankers. The representation of lawyers seems to have declined in the second half of the century, with fewer than 50 in the parliaments of 1768–83. Non-landed wealth, however, remained a marginal presence, with no more than 30 MPs in any parliament in the second half of the century actively engaged in commerce or finance.[47]

The dominance of parliamentary representation by members of the small landowning class reflected the narrowness of the electoral system.[48] Of the 300 members sitting in the House of Commons, 64 represented the 32 counties, where the electorate were the forty-shilling freeholders, adult males who held property with an annual value of at least two pounds a year either as owners or on the

---

[46] D. W. Hayton, 'Introduction: The Long Apprenticeship', in idem (ed.), *The Irish Parliament in the Eighteenth Century: The Long Apprenticeship* (Edinburgh, 2001), 12. The pioneering work on the Irish parliament of J. L. McCracken is summarized in his *The Irish Parliament in the Eighteenth Century* (Dundalk, 1971), and his contribution to *NHI*, iv. 71–8. The other important early work is E. M. Johnston, *Great Britain and Ireland 1760–1800* (Edinburgh, 1963). For more recent thinking see the chapters in Hayton's volume just cited, and the work by A. P. W. Malcomson cited below. E. M. Johnston-Liik, *History of the Irish Parliament 1692–1800: Commons, Constituencies and Statutes*, 6 vols. (Belfast, 2002) is a heroic attempt by a single scholar at a comprehensive survey of members and constituencies.

[47] J. L. McCracken, 'Central and Local Administration in Ireland under George II' (Ph.D. thesis, Queen's University Belfast, 1948), 110–11; Johnston, *Great Britain and Ireland*, 246.

[48] There is a pioneering survey of the electoral system, still valuable, in J. L. McCracken's 'Irish Parliamentary Elections 1727–68', *IHS* 5 (1947), 209–29. The fullest account is now Johnston-Liik, *History of the Irish Parliament*, which provides (ii. 371–81) the figures on electorates cited below. A. P. W. Malcomson, ' "The Parliamentary Traffic of this Country" ', in Thomas Bartlett and D. W. Hayton (eds.), *Penal Era and Golden Age: Essays in Irish History 1690–1800* (Belfast, 1979), 137–61 and idem, *John Foster: The Politics of the Anglo-Irish Ascendancy* (Oxford, 1978), ch. 7, emphasize the need to look beyond economic coercion to the role of deference and personal relationships in electoral management.

indefinite tenure of a lease for lives. Two represented the university constituency of Trinity College, where they were elected by the Fellows and Scholars. The remaining 234 sat for the 117 boroughs. The franchise here varied, reflecting the piecemeal extension of parliamentary representation to new areas, and new centres of population, across a period of centuries. Fifty-seven constituencies were corporation boroughs, where members were returned by the 12 or 13 members of the corporation. In another 36 the electors were the corporation and those admitted as freemen of the borough. In 11 boroughs the franchise lay with the potwallopers or heads of household, while in 7 more the freeholders of a landed estate possessing the legal status of a manor had the right to send two members to parliament. Finally there were the 8 county boroughs, Dublin, Cork, Galway, Drogheda, Waterford, Kilkenny, Limerick, and Carrickfergus, taking in an urban centre and the area immediately surrounding, where the voters were the forty-shilling freeholders and freemen.

In the early eighteenth century many of these constituencies had been the scene of a lively popular politics. After 1714 the decline of party conflict, and the consolidation of major property interests against a background of rising prosperity, allowed control of the great majority of constituencies to pass into the hands of a small group of ruling interests, and often indeed into the hands of a single patron. The freeman borough of Fethard, County Tipperary, for example, was contested for much of the eighteenth century by a variety of local families. By 1787, however, two of these had agreed to split the representation between them, and went on to secure their control by cutting the number of freemen, and thus the electorate, from 900 to just 300. Elsewhere too judicious restriction of this civic honour ensured a small and docile electorate. Corporation boroughs were still more easily controlled, since these were self-perpetuating bodies, so that a patron having once gained control had only to ensure that those co-opted to vacancies were reliable allies or dependants. Potwalloping boroughs had a less restrictive franchise, but most were small centres with a handful of voters, all under the control of a single landlord. Rathcormack in 1783 had 7 electors and Baltimore 11. In Knocktopher, County Kilkenny, the Langrishe family reportedly avoided giving leases to Protestants within the borough, so that in 1783 there was just one qualified voter. The manor boroughs, all coterminous with a particular landlord estate, were even more clearly the property of the proprietor concerned.[49]

The outcome of this steady tightening of proprietorial control was that contemporaries, by the late eighteenth century, counted only ten Irish boroughs

---

[49] For the age of party see D. W. Hayton, 'Voters, Patrons and Parties: Parliamentary Elections in Ireland *c*.1691–1727', in Clyve Jones et al. (eds.), *Partisan Politics, Principle and Reform in Parliament and the Constituencies, 1689–1880* (Edinburgh, 2005), 45–70. For Fethard see Power, *Land, Politics and Society*, 226–7, and for Knocktopher idem, 'Parliamentary Representation in County Kilkenny in the Eighteenth Century', in William Nolan and Kevin Whelan (eds.), *Kilkenny, History and Society* (Dublin, 1990), 318–19.

as 'open', in the sense that the return of MPs depended on a contest of some kind. In the eight county boroughs the electorates ranged from 3,000–4,000 in Dublin to only 500 in Drogheda, but were in all cases too large and diverse in their composition to be reliably controlled by any one or two interests. The remaining two open constituencies were the potwalloping borough of Swords, in County Dublin, where ownership of the land concerned was divided between several proprietors, and the town of Derry, where the automatic grant of freeman status to all who had served an apprenticeship in the city created an unusually large voting body. Some of the remaining 107 boroughs, returning between them almost three-quarters of the members of the Irish Commons, were under the control of a single patron; in others two or at most three interests united in controlling successive elections. In many cases, indeed, control was sufficiently tight to permit the sale of borough seats, although such transactions became common only after 1761, when the eight-year limit on the duration of parliament made it possible to fix a realistic price. Less frequently a proprietor could offer a permanent transfer of control of a borough, in practice the resignation of an existing corporation and its replacement by nominees of the purchaser. In 1744 Robert Colvill sold control of the corporation borough of Newtownards to the Ponsonbys after Alexander Stewart, who had purchased the landed estate on which it stood, had refused to pay an extra £500 for the electoral patronage. A subsequent court case confirmed the legitimacy of a political interest thus divorced from the lordship of the soil.[50] Half a century later the government likewise acknowledged the fact of patronal control, when it smoothed the passage of the act of union by agreeing that proprietors of boroughs that were not to be represented in the united parliament should receive compensation for the loss of a valuable asset.

In the thirty-two county constituencies electorates, given the restriction of the franchise to Protestants, were inevitably largest in Ulster. County Down had 6,000 voters, Counties Antrim and Tyrone 3,500 each. There were also large electorates in Counties Cork (3,000) and Wexford (2,500). Elsewhere most county electorates outside Ulster were between 1,000 and 2,000 strong, although a thin Protestant population produced low county electorates of 700 or so in Galway, Longford, and Waterford, 550–650 in Carlow, and perhaps as few as 400 in Louth. None of the counties was closed in the sense that a single family had absolute control. A number, however, had one or two dominant interests. The Ponsonbys, for example, held one of the County Kilkenny seats almost continuously from the 1660s, as well as having complete or partial control of several boroughs. In County Louth two families, Foster and Fortescue, dominated the county representation from 1745. Even where this was not the case, landlord control of the tenant farmers who made up the great bulk of the

[50] A. P. W. Malcomson, 'The Newtown Act of 1748: Revision and Reconstruction', *IHS* 18 (1973), 313–43.

electorate was sufficiently strong to ensure that the results of a county contest could generally be predicted once the leading proprietors had declared their allegiance. In consequence only a minority of seats were formally contested.

A discussion of the basis on which this landed control of voters rested takes us to the heart of the difficulties involved in any attempt to define the true character of eighteenth-century Irish society. Coercion was clearly important. Owners of large estates were in a good position to ensure that tenants, casting their votes without a secret ballot, should follow their directions. Non-compliance could be punished by the strict enforcement of tenurial obligations, and by a demand for immediate payment of rents conventionally levied six months in arrears, as well as by the unpredictable but potentially disastrous consequences that could flow from forfeiting the favour of one's immediate social superior in a world dominated by relationships of clientship and patronage. Yet naked intimidation was rare. Instead it suited both sides to proceed with the appearance of consensus, as proprietors or their agents canvassed tenants for their votes and encouraged their compliance by pre-election dinners. Voters going to and from the poll could likewise expect to be entertained for their trouble. Such courtesies meant that two candidates in the County Antrim election of 1761 spent £2,502 between them. In Louth seven years later the Fosters, though the dominant interest in the county, spent over £1,400. For most of the eighteenth century, all of this careful management of vertical relationships for electoral purposes was confined to the minority of the population that qualified, as Protestants, for admission to the franchise. But the restoration to Catholics of the right to vote in 1793 had no significant impact on the ways in which the system operated. The main consequence was a sharp increase in what one later writer described as 'political agronomy', as proprietors rushed to confer leases on small tenants at will so as to create what they correctly assumed would be fresh squadrons of wholly compliant voters.[51]

Seen from this perspective, the typical election, with freemen and artisans enjoying music, food, and drink as they made their way to give testimony to their status as full citizens by the act of casting their vote, may well have been as much a festival of reciprocity as a ritual of social subordination. Such displays were less likely to occur in the boroughs, with their restrictive franchises and small electorates. But there too successful political management required attention to people as well as institutions. At the beginning of the eighteenth century the main branch of the Boyle family controlled or had a substantial interest in half a dozen boroughs in south Munster. But with the succession in 1704 of the fourth earl of Cork, a minor and then an absentee, the agents left to manage the family's Irish estates were unable to prevent the intrusion of rival political interests, or to curb stirrings of independence within the boroughs themselves. In Antrim during the 1770s and 1780s the earls of Massareene faced a strong

---

[51] The phrase is Edward Wakefield's. See Malcomson, *John Foster*, 298.

though ultimately unsuccessful challenge from the Thompson family. These put themselves forward as representing a popular challenge to aristocratic dominance. But there are also indications that they had built up an economic interest in the town, as property owners and possibly linen dealers, whereas the Massareenes, though lords of the soil, had let most of the land concerned in perpetuity. The earls of Abercorn lost control of Strabane in the 1730s, when a distant relative they had nominated to one of the seats allied with a local family to exclude them. Thirty years later the Abercorns regained control, but to do so they, like the Massareenes in Antrim, had to wear down their opponents by a series of expensive legal actions against the borough corporation.[52]

If the workings of electoral politics were more complex than a simple description of the franchise would suggest, the same was true of the behaviour of the members returned to parliament. At one level the record is a discreditable one. The Commons of the 1740s provided a theatre for the modest, and sometimes equivocal, patriotism of figures like Anthony Malone and the younger Sir Richard Cox, but its members dealt brutally with the challenge of Charles Lucas. Ostensible revolts on constitutional issues in the viceroyalties of Dorset and Townshend were in fact exercises in factional politics. Later MPs were to give strong support to the free trade agitation of 1778–9, but a majority were to ignore the subsequent campaign for legislative independence until a change of government in Great Britain made patriotism expedient. Soon after that members closed ranks, with an appropriate display of indignation, against proposals for electoral reform.

At another level, however, what is striking about Irish parliamentary politics is the extent to which—within the limits set by a system based on a frank acceptance of oligarchy—individuals observed certain conventions of good behaviour. If some patrons used control of a borough simply to enter parliament and then trade their vote for a string of government favours, others took seriously their role as local representatives, sponsoring legislation, presenting petitions, and soliciting funds for public works.[53] If some sold seats in a straight cash transaction, likewise, the majority returned relatives, friends, or political associates, producing more complex and varied relationships between patron and member. Most revealing of all, there was a general acceptance that legitimacy could not be measured solely in terms of the raw numbers generated by a flawed electoral system. The speeches, and on important issues the votes, of the sixty-four county MPs and

---

[52] T. C. Barnard, 'Considering the Inconsiderable: Electors, Patrons and Irish Elections 1659–1761', in Hayton (ed.), *The Irish Parliament*, 107–27; A. P. W. Malcomson, 'Election Politics in the Borough of Antrim 1750–1800', *IHS* 17 (1970), 32–56; idem, 'The Politics of "Natural Right": The Abercorn Family and Strabane Borough 1692–1800', in G. A. Hayes-McCoy (ed.), *Historical Studies*, x (Indreabhán, 1976), 43–90.

[53] See, for example, Malcomson's comments on the amount of time devoted by John Foster to the affairs both of County Louth and of Drogheda: *John Foster*, 348–9. For other points in this paragraph see idem, 'The Parliamentary Traffic of this Country'.

the representatives of the ten 'open' boroughs had a greater weight than those of their more numerous colleagues representing 'closed' constituencies. On an important issue like the Commercial Propositions of 1785 a narrow victory for the government, with the majority of county members voting against, was recognized as in reality a defeat.[54]

One reason why MPs involved themselves so freely in promoting economic improvement, both in their own localities and more generally, was that the new status that the Irish parliament achieved from the 1690s onwards involved not just complete control of the raising of taxation, but also a substantial voice in the way in which the money was spent. The award of just over £2,500 to the Linen Board in 1721–2 marked the beginning of what became an elaborate body of grants and bounties. The reason for the development of this system of parliamentary appropriation was in part political: by attaching revenue to particular purposes, the Commons ensured that lords lieutenant did not build up a surplus that might reduce their dependence on parliament. But parliament's eagerness to spend money also reflected the general enthusiasm for 'improvement' evident in mid- and late eighteenth-century Ireland. The promotion by the Linen Board of spinning and weaving, the financing of canals and harbours, the promotion of fisheries, the encouragement of tillage by bounties on the transport of grain all reflected standard prescriptions for the more effective exploitation of the country's resources. Not all of the money was wisely spent. The funds poured into collieries at Ballycastle on the Antrim coast and in County Tyrone did not uncover the expected rich reserves of coal. The Grand and Royal canals, extending west from Dublin through the same midlands region, reaching the Shannon at points less than fifty miles apart, were a grandiose folly. The ignominious collapse in 1786 of the cotton manufactory impractically sited at Prosperous in County Kildare was further evidence that indiscriminate enthusiasm was no basis for economic planning. But the involvement of parliament in the spending as well as the raising of public money gave its members a role as intermediaries between state and people that belied the arbitrary process by which most of them had achieved that status.[55]

The other major institution of government in Hanoverian Ireland, this time operating at county level, was the grand jury. Chosen by the high sheriff in advance of the twice-yearly assizes, grand juries, normally consisting of twenty-three members, scrutinized bills of indictment to decide which 'true bills' should proceed to trial. They could also act as prosecutors, by a presentment naming an individual for trial, and in some cases, notably the transportation of those presented as vagrants, could themselves dispense summary punishment. In addition they made presentments authorizing the construction or repair of roads, bridges, jails, court houses, and other public buildings, paid for by a county cess levied on the occupiers of land, as well as appointing and paying clerks, jailers, constables, and other local officials. The range of responsibilities, and the sums of money raised and spent, rose over time, particularly after 1765, when grand juries took over complete responsibility for the upkeep of roads.

In nominating grand jurors, with their considerable and expanding range of patronage and their extensive discretion in criminal cases, sheriffs were expected to select from among persons of suitable standing. However there was no fixed property qualification, and the number of jurors required, along with the administrative burden involved, ensured that membership was in fact quite widely distributed, including lesser landowners, clergy and other professional men, substantial leaseholders, and businessmen. The largest proprietors rarely sat in person, being more commonly represented by agents. A law of 1708 debarred Catholics, but only if suitable Protestants were available, and some apparent Catholics do in fact appear on grand jury lists, as do larger numbers of dissenters. By the second half of the eighteenth century there are signs that membership in most counties was becoming more narrowly concentrated in a group of leading families. This was probably due mainly to the expanding functions of the grand jury, and the larger sums of money at stake. But it may also reflect the appearance of a more stable social hierarchy in an increasingly prosperous and settled countryside. Even at this point, however, grand juries represented a broad cross-section of respectable society. As such they served as an important channel of communication between the centre and the localities. The charges delivered to them by the judges as they made the twice-yearly assizes circuit could be statements of government policy, while addresses by grand juries could reflect the concerns of propertied society on both local and national issues.[56]

The system of urban government, regulated, like the electoral system, by long-standing charters that bore increasingly little relation to the needs of a changing society, was more varied and considerably less effective. Dublin, as befitted a capital, had an elaborate structure of corporate self-government, with a City Commons elected every three years by the city's twenty-five guilds. The Commons in turn elected an upper house of aldermen, but these had to be chosen from the restricted group who had acted as sheriffs, and once elected served for life. In Drogheda and Cork, guilds in the first case and the city's freemen in the second had a limited role in choosing the members of the corporation. Elsewhere vacancies were filled by co-option. In Dublin and some other centres corporations were highly active, providing street lighting, refuse collection, and other local services, keeping streets clear of beggars and stray animals, regulating markets, and upholding building standards. Others, by contrast, existed only as instruments of a patron's political control, meeting solely to return members

---

[56] Neal Garnham, 'Local Elite Creation in Early Hanoverian Ireland: The Case of the County Grand Jury', *Historical Journal*, 42 (1999), 623–42.

to parliament at elections. In such cases alternative means had to be found to regulate urban life. In Ennis a grand jury of the fifteen to twenty-five principal inhabitants, including Catholics and Protestants, was allowed to manage local affairs, despite having no basis in the town's charter or any other legal provision.[57] In Belfast a police committee, elected by ratepayers, came to take responsibility for most of the routine functions of local government, though only after 1800. By this time even the more active corporations were proving increasingly incapable of dealing with the full range of demands thrown up by urban growth. By the end of the century Dublin had a separate paving board, and a ballast board to regulate shipping, as well as a police committee and a wide streets committee. Cork and Waterford also had wide streets commissioners, and Wexford and Drogheda harbour commissioners.

The workings of the other main unit of local government, the parish, represented an uneasy juncture between the principle of an established church and the reality of a religiously divided society. Parishes had a variety of civil functions. They were responsible, up to 1765, for road maintenance. They had a role in law enforcement, through the appointment of watchmen and constables, and churchwardens also had responsibility for proceeding against keepers of disorderly houses, those engaged in trade on Sundays, and other breaches of moral discipline. The parish was also central to what limited provision there was for poor relief. But it was also the unit of organization of a church whose adherents comprised only about one in eight of the population. Problems arose when Catholics or dissenters exercised their right to attend vestry meetings as parishioners, and then sought to obstruct proposals for spending on church purposes. An act of 1725 barred Catholics from vestry meetings concerned with church repairs. An act of 1774 similarly excluded dissenters, but was repealed the following year. However the oath for churchwardens was carefully constructed to present no doctrinal problems, and there is evidence that in some cases at least Catholics did in fact hold this position, as well as the less prestigious and more onerous office of constable.[58]

As the century progressed the central state made some efforts, mainly ineffective, to respond to new, or more keenly felt, social needs. Of these the most prominent was the relief of poverty. The first half of the century saw repeated subsistence crises. National prosperity increased rapidly from the late 1740s, but rising numbers and commercialization nevertheless swelled the ranks of the needy, both vagrant and sedentary. In England and in Scotland poor relief was primarily the responsibility of the parish. In the case of Ireland, Church of Ireland congregations in east Ulster, and in some urban centres elsewhere, operated a looser version of the same system, keeping lists of the deserving poor

[57] Brian Ó Dálaigh, *Ennis in the Eighteenth Century* (Dublin, 1995), 42–3.
[58] T. C. Barnard, 'The Eighteenth-Century Parish', in E. Fitzpatrick and R. Gillespie (eds.), *The Parish in Medieval and Early Modern Ireland* (Dublin, 2006).

who received relief from parochial funds, or in some cases were issued with badges entitling them to beg with impunity. However there was no statutory basis for such activities, and attempts in 1695 and 1697 to promote bills authorizing parishes to raise funds for poor relief failed to pass. The famines of 1726–9 and 1739–41 inspired uneven but in aggregate significant efforts to raise money by subscription for the purchase and distribution of food. Dublin acquired a work-house in 1706, and Belfast in 1757. But more general provision remained at the level of voluntary contribution. An act of 1772 authorized county corporations to provide badges for the deserving poor and to establish houses of industry, financed by voluntary subscription. By 1800 there were about ten such houses, including those in Belfast and Dublin. But progress towards a scheme that would entitle the destitute to relief, funded out of compulsory taxation, had to wait until the 1830s, when the direction of Irish social policy was no longer in the hands of a parliament of Irish landowners.[59]

The other main form of poor relief was the provision of medical services for those unable to pay for them. Here too progress was uneven, and depended mainly on voluntary support. By 1800 Dublin had eight hospitals, the earliest a Charitable Infirmary set up in 1718, and there were also medical institutions of different kinds in Belfast, Cork, Limerick, and Waterford. All depended for their main support on a mixture of endowments, subscriptions, donations, and charity sermons. In Dublin Dr Steevens's Hospital, opened in 1733, had its origins in a bequest by the former professor of medicine at Trinity College. St Patrick's Hospital, established in 1757, was the 'house for fools and mad' provided for in the will of Jonathan Swift. The Lying-In Hospital, opened in 1745, received income from the pleasure gardens laid out nearby by its entrepreneurial founder, Dr Bartholomew Mosse, and later from the concert hall attached to it. An act of 1765 provided for an annual parliamentary grant to three of the Dublin hospitals. It also authorized the establishment of county infirmaries, to be funded by a mixture of voluntary subscriptions, central government grants, and grand jury presentments. But the gains from this new initiative were questionable. Enquiries in the 1780s indicated that county infirmaries contained an average of eleven patients each, poorly fed and housed in dilapidated and filthy buildings.[60]

Where education was concerned, legislation dating back to the Henrician Reformation required each parish to maintain an elementary school. Late seventeenth-century visitations suggest that only a minority of the parish clergy complied, although the campaign for a general reform of morals and pastoral standards in the 1690s and afterwards appears to have produced a significant improvement, which may or may not have been sustained. Each diocese was

[59] David Dickson, 'In Search of the Old Irish Poor Law', in Rosalind Mitchison and Peter Roebuck (eds.), *Economy and Society in Scotland and Ireland 1500–1939* (Edinburgh, 1988), 149–59.
[60] Lawrence M. Geary, *Medicine and Charity in Ireland 1718–1851* (Dublin, 2004), chs. 1, 2.

likewise required to maintain a grammar school, but a survey in 1791 indicated that only 18 out of 34 actually did so, for a total of 324 pupils. These were supplemented from 1733 by the work of Bishop Maule's Incorporated Society, but the number of charter schools never rose above sixty or so.[61] In 1787–91 the chief secretary Thomas Orde drew up ambitious plans, further elaborated by a commission of inquiry in 1791, for a nationwide scheme of elementary and further education. But these came to nothing. The marked increase in the ability to read and write evident in the last decades of the eighteenth century was achieved entirely through an expanding network of pay schools, depending for their support on the small sums that a population still poor but suddenly aware of the advantages of basic literacy and numeracy was prepared to pay for its children to acquire those skills.[62]

FRONTIER JUSTICE

In May 1754 a party of soldiers surrounded a house at Eyeries near Bantry Bay, the home of Morty Óg O'Sullivan. O'Sullivan was a former officer in the French army. More recently, he had taken to sailing between France and this base in the remote south-west, bringing smuggled brandy in one direction and recruits for the Irish regiments in French service in the other. A few weeks earlier he had assassinated a revenue officer, John Puxley, and it was this act that brought the army, led by a nephew of Puxley's, to his door. O'Sullivan and others within the house initially held off the soldiers with gunfire, but were eventually forced out as the roof was set on fire. O'Sullivan was shot dead as he tried to break through the line of attackers, and his severed head was subsequently put on display outside Cork city jail.[63]

The gunfight at Eyeries was at first sight a late manifestation of a small-scale war of resistance that had been in progress since the 1660s, when armed tory bands had first appeared to prey on the beneficiaries of the mid-century revolution in landownership. For three decades or so after the capitulation of Limerick similar groups of 'tories' or 'rapparees' remained active in parts of Cork and Kerry, with the connivance both of the local peasantry and of surviving members of the Catholic elite. Sir Francis Brewster, writing from Killarney in 1704, complained of 'the daily rescues, the insolence of the old proprietors, this whole side of the country sheltering and siding with the tories at one time by whom they are protected at another'. Tories were also active in Catholic parts of Ulster, in Redmond O'Hanlon's old stamping ground of south Armagh, in the Sperrin Mountains, straddling Counties Londonderry and Tyrone, in parts of Donegal,

[61] Above, Ch. 7.   [62] For education and literacy, see the final section of this chapter.
[63] J. Featherstonhaugh, 'The True Story of the Two Chiefs of Dunboy', *Journal of the Royal Society of Antiquaries of Ireland*, ser. 5/4 (1894), 35–43, 139–49.

and on the Antrim plateau.[64] Morty Óg O'Sullivan, a member of one of the most prominent Gaelic clans of the south-west, a participant in the Jacobite-inspired military diaspora, the killer of an intrusive servant of the Hanoverian state, would seem to fit the same pattern of continued Catholic resistance to the political and religious order created by the Cromwellian confiscations and confirmed by the Williamite victory of 1689–91.

On closer examination, the picture becomes less clear. John Puxley had not always been a revenue officer. He and his brother—clearly, on the basis of their later careers, Protestants—had arrived in the Bantry area more than two decades earlier, from County Galway. There they had in fact involved themselves in the local smuggling economy. They first came to official notice following an incident in 1732, when an armed party had boarded a confiscated vessel and rescued the contraband on board, killing two of the men guarding the haul. The actual perpetrators were once again O'Sullivans, though a different branch of the family from Morty Óg's. But subsequent intelligence indicated that they had been encouraged, and supplied with arms, by the Puxley brothers. (Also apparently complicit was the local Church of Ireland clergyman, who reportedly volunteered to lure the leader of the revenue party involved and two subordinates away from the seized vessel by inviting them to his house.) Later the Puxleys were reported to have been responsible for the killing of one of their former O'Sullivan allies, allegedly with the assistance of three Flahertys they had brought from their native County Galway to serve as strongarm men as they established themselves in this new territory. However the case, like many others from the same remote region, was never pursued to an arrest or trial. Instead John Puxley survived, eventually exchanging the risky trade of smuggler for the safer employment of revenue official—safer, that is, until his activities brought him into conflict with Morty Óg.

Behind the apparently straightforward tale of a revenue officer killed by an Irish outlaw, who in turn then dies at the hands of the authorities, there thus lies a much more complex history. Nor was this case unique. Other accounts from the south-west, even in the immediate aftermath of the war of 1689–91, reveal a similar pattern of of alliances across as well as along the lines of ethnic and religious division, as gentry and half-gentry, Catholic as well as Protestant, joined with their social inferiors in resisting the intrusions of a distant central state. Complaints from Kerry in the 1690s spoke of Protestant proprietors 'courting and making friends with the Irish', and of magistrates who sold protections and safe conducts to tories. Official correspondence over the next four decades contains numerous complaints concerning the depredations of the MacCarthys, the O'Sullivans, and, in particular, the O'Donoghues, whose stronghold was in Glenflesk to the south-east of Killarney. But there were also other names: the

---

[64] For this and the succeeding paragraphs see the fuller account in Connolly, *Religion, Law and Power*, ch. 6.

brothers Francis and Timothy Eager, grandsons of an English army officer who had come to Ireland in the 1740s, the former married to a daughter of the O'Donoghue himself, and Francis Herbert, from a cadet branch of the Shropshire-based landed family, who in 1734 joined with followers of MacCarthy Mór in attacks on the main Herbert estate and other properties. Against this background the ability of a John Puxley to transform himself from smuggler to revenue officer becomes easier to understand. On the other hand the case for seeing Morty Óg O'Sullivan or the other turbulent figures active in more remote parts of the island in the early decades of the eighteenth century as soldiers in a continued campaign of ethnic and religious resistance becomes less convincing. Morty Óg had his French and Jacobite links. But his activities took place in the wider context of a south-western region in which all sections of society, like their counterparts in Calabria or the Scottish Highlands, were only slowly made amenable to any externally imposed rule of law.

Against this background the establishment of central government control across the whole island was a gradual process. In the immediate aftermath of the Williamite war outlaw bands of tories or rapparees remained a threat even in areas close to the eastern commercial heartland. In Tipperary as late as 1694 parties of up to thirty were reported to 'surround the fairs etc and set upon persons going to or coming from them, so that trade or commerce in this county is almost totally damped'. In the mountainous regions of Ulster a last wave of tory activity, possibly related to a deterioration in economic conditions, began around 1718 and continued for around ten years. In the south-west the campaign against banditry continued up to 1711, when a last major outbreak was brought under control. Its elimination was achieved partly by repression, in particular the stationing of small detachments of soldiers in redoubts or temporary forts located at strategic points, and partly by judicious leniency, whereby those who brought in the severed heads of confederates received pardons and rewards. Even after the last tory bands had been broken up or wiped out, however, the far south-west remained outside the normal processes of law enforcement. During the 1720s there were lurid accounts of the activities in County Kerry of Daniel Mahony. Mahony was a classic example of a descendant of old proprietors successfully adapting to a new status as middleman, paying a reputed £1,500 a year in rent to different landlords while still occupying his family's castle at Dunloe. He was also reported to have organized his subtenants into a clandestine army, the 'fairesses', who roamed the countryside with faces blackened, or disguised in women's clothing, making it unsafe to execute any legal process against himself or his dependants. The early career of the Puxley brothers, a decade later, made clear that not much had changed. Another district slow to submit to the discipline of the central state was Iar Connacht, lying immediately beyond Galway town, where as late as 1759 the inhabitants were 'the ancient Irish, who never yet have been made amenable to the laws. No sheriff dares go there to execute any process.'

Even outside these peripheral regions the hold of central government on law and order, in the first half of the century, was often far from secure. As late as 1738–40 the Kellymount gang, said to number thirty or more, terrorized Kilkenny and the surrounding counties, reportedly extorting supplies from the local gentry 'as soldiers do in an enemy's country'. Urban areas, with their densely packed populations and their relative anonymity, provided an even more attractive hunting ground for criminal gangs. They could also erupt into periodic revolt. Urban protest could at times be highly disciplined, as when crowds protesting at artificially high food prices at times of shortage broke open storehouses and forced the sale of supplies at their normal market price. But it could also be frighteningly violent. In August 1734 Paul Farrell, a Dublin constable apparently involved in serious crime, became the object of a brutal demonstration of mob fury when a crowd rescued him from custody on his way to prison, castrated him, and beat him to death. The mutilated body remained hanging from a tree in the city's western liberties for a night and most of a day, before the authorities could muster enough force to retrieve it.[65]

By the second half of the century such open challenges to the government and its code of law had become significantly less common. Urban riot remained a recurrent problem. But in the countryside the building or improvement of roads, the clearing of the last forests, and a greater density of population had at least partially tamed even the more remote areas. The mail coaches travelling in increasing numbers along major routes had armed guards to deter or fight off highwaymen. But large outlaw bands like the Kellymount gang, or the tories of the post-war decades, no longer operated. By the end of the century the Mourne Mountains of south Ulster, County Kerry, and Connemara in the former Iar Connacht had all, like the Scottish Highlands, made the transition from regions of lawless menace to tourist destinations where the traveller could admire the unspoiled majesty of nature.[66] Yet if Ireland had become more law abiding, it was still by British standards a fairly violent society. The only extended runs of crime figures are based on records of indictments in the counties of Armagh from 1736 to 1775 and Tyrone from 1742 to 1801. The number of indictments for homicide, taken in relation to population, was more than twice the level recorded at the same time in Kent, Surrey, and Sussex. The figures for the Ulster counties, in fact, were roughly comparable with those recorded in southern England in the late seventeenth century. These statistics, moreover, relate to numbers of prosecutions. If, as seems likely, the proportion of serious crime that resulted in prosecution was lower in Ireland than in England, then the gap in levels of lethal violence between the two societies must have been wider still.[67]

---

[65] Neal Garnham, 'The Short Career of Paul Farrell: A Brief Consideration of Law Enforcement in Eighteenth-Century Ireland', *ECI* 11 (1996), 46–52.

[66] Barnard, *Making the Grand Figure*, 343–4.

[67] The Armagh and Tyrone figures are analysed in Neal Garnham, *The Courts, Crime and the Criminal Law in Ireland 1692–1760* (Dublin, 1996), ch. 10. See also idem, 'How Violent was

The mechanisms available to control this disorderly and violent society derived from the extension to Ireland of the English tradition of the self-policing community. The key figures in this system were the magistrates or justices of the peace, men of property and standing appointed to serve as the unpaid agents of government in their local area. Magistrates acted as the lowest tier of the judicial system, meeting to dispense justice at courts of quarter session. But they were also expected to take an active role in law enforcement, intervening to curb disorder or apprehend offenders. In practice only a minority were fit or willing to take on such arduous duties. A survey of surviving assizes records suggests that fewer than 500 of the 2,000 or so individuals in the commission of the peace were actively engaged in any part of the criminal justice system.[68]

For those who were so engaged, the resources available to support them were distinctly limited. An act of 1715 empowered the quarter sessions to appoint a high constable for each barony, and a petty constable for each parish. In theory these high and petty constables would have been local householders of some standing taking their turn, unpaid, at a necessary communal obligation. In practice paid substitutes were permitted, and were probably common. The result was a thinly spread network of untrained, indifferently supervised, and often part-time officials. The demographic realities that prevailed in most parts of the country also required that the office of constable should be one of the few that did not require holders to take the oaths of supremacy and a declaration rejecting the doctrine of transubstantiation.

In urban areas the resources available to deal with crime and disorder were somewhat more substantial. By the eighteenth century most towns maintained a night watch, often armed with halberds or similar weapons. Belfast, for example, had twelve men and a captain in 1694, and the same number in 1759. Dublin had its own police system, governed by specific legislation, under which each parish appointed a body of paid watchmen, and elected constables from among its householders to supervise their work. There was also a strict requirement that watchmen and constables should be Protestants. By 1780 there were about 24 constables, and 400 watchmen. Yet this reliance on something closer to a professional police force created its own problems. In 1729 complaints of corruption among the Dublin constables became so serious as to require a parliamentary inquiry. The case five years later of 'Gallows Paul' makes clear that even after that date the line between thief-taker and thief was often a thin one.

Where significant physical force was required, magistrates and urban authorities could turn to the armed forces. An English act of 1699 fixed the size of

Eighteenth-Century Ireland?', *IHS* 30 (1997), 377–92. For an attempt to put these and other statistics in comparative perspective see S. J. Connolly, 'Unnatural Death in Four Kingdoms', in idem (ed.), *Kingdoms United? Great Britain and Ireland since 1500: Integration and Diversity* (Dublin, 1999), 200–14.

[68] Garnham, *The Courts, Crime and the Criminal Law*, 34–5.

the Irish military establishment at 12,000 men, although the use of Ireland as a barracks from which to defend the Hanoverian dominions as a whole meant that a third or so of these were normally stationed outside the kingdom. There was also a part-time force, the militia, revived sporadically from 1690 and given statutory recognition in 1716, in which all Protestant males aged between 16 and 60 were in theory liable to serve. In the early eighteenth century both soldiers and militia were routinely used to pursue tories and robbers. The militia, however, seems to have atrophied as an effective military force, possibly from as early as the 1720s. Regular troops, by contrast, continued to be frequently employed in policing duties. The fortified outposts or redoubts constructed to keep control of disturbed areas like south Armagh had largely been abandoned by 1720, allowing soldiers to be concentrated in more centrally located barracks. But they were still regularly summoned to suppress riots or other disturbances, to provide escorts for cash or prisoners, or to support officials engaged in unpopular duties, such as revenue officers pursuing smuggled goods. From the 1760s they were also called out in response to successive waves of agrarian disturbance. Yet their deployment in these different capacities was no simple matter. Central government, anxious not to allow local authorities to shirk their responsibilities, was often slow to accede to requests for military support. Where soldiers used lethal force against civilians, equally, both their officers and the civilian officials involved could face charges of murder. The army undoubtedly played a larger part in law enforcement in Ireland than it did in England. But in normal circumstances the maintenance of order remained the responsibility of local men of property, relying on the dubious backing of parish and baronial constables, as well as whatever informal assistance they were able to recruit among their friends, neighbours, or households.[69]

By the 1780s the deficiencies of this decentralized and largely amateur apparatus of law enforcement had become too obvious to ignore. The appearance of the Rightboys in Munster during 1785–8 brought yet another outbreak of agrarian protest, on a larger scale than previously, and with the alarming added element of a direct attack on the privileges of the established church. Meanwhile the rise of the Volunteers had demonstrated the perils of relying on the voluntary mobilization of the armed citizen. In addition the Volunteer and patriot campaigns for free trade and constitutional reform had given a new political edge to the street disorders of the kingdom's capital. A campaign for free trade had involved not just a boycott of dealers in imported goods, but the wrecking of shops and the tarring and feathering of offenders. There had also been large-scale riots, notably in November 1779. Another alarming development, dating back to the early 1770s, was a campaign of attacks on soldiers, whose attackers in many cases sought to cripple them permanently by hamstringing

---

[69] For a fuller discussion see S. J. Connolly, 'The Defence of Protestant Ireland', in Bartlett and Jeffery (eds.), *Military History of Ireland*, 231–46.

or houghing. The motives behind such viciousness remain unclear. It may have represented no more than an escalation of traditional hostilities between soldier and civilian, at a time when street demonstrations made clashes between them more frequent. But it also raised the possibility that the anti-English rhetoric of the patriots and their Volunteer allies was being translated into dangerous new forms of popular disaffection.[70]

In response to these growing problems the Irish administration introduced during the 1780s a series of measures that, taken together, pointed in the direction of a novel concept of law enforcement. The riot act of 1787 was primarily a belated extension to Ireland of the English act of 1714, giving magistrates the power to disperse any gathering they judged to be tumultuous, although its authors also took the opportunity to convert the administration of unlawful oaths and other offences characteristic of agrarian agitation into capital crimes. The first attempted reforms of rural policing were also cautious. An act of 1773 empowered county grand juries to appoint four subconstables to assist the head constable in each barony, and a second act of 1783 increased this number to eight. A new act in 1787 introduced a modest element of central control, by empowering the lord lieutenant to proclaim a district as disturbed, and then to appoint a chief constable for each barony, who would supervise a locally recruited force of sixteen subconstables. It also provided for the employment in each county of an assistant barrister, paid by the government, who would provide magistrates with legal advice. The real innovation, however, came in the Dublin police bill of 1786. In place of the existing parish-based system, three commissioners, appointed by the government from among the city's magistrates, were to supervise a single force of 40 constables and over 400 watchmen, uniformed and equipped with muskets and bayonets. In a striking departure from the general trend towards the relaxation of religious distinctions, both the Dublin and baronial forces were to be exclusively Protestant.

All of these innovations were at the initiative of central government. The Dublin and county police bills were principally the work of the chief secretary, Thomas Orde, and the attorney general, John Fitzgibbon. Patriot and radical spokesmen, not surprisingly, attacked them as instruments for the repression of popular liberties. But there was also much more widespread opposition to what were seen as illegitimate intrusions on matters of local concern. In the case of Dublin hostility to the new police was strong enough to force a retreat. An act of 1795 created a new, unarmed force, most of whose members would be appointed by the parishes, but with the mayor and aldermen exercising a greater degree of central control than had existed before 1786. When an act of 1792 reaffirmed the right of counties to appoint baronial constables, thirteen counties

---

[70] For innovations in policing during the 1780s see S. H. Palmer, *Police and Protest in England and Ireland 1780–1850* (Cambridge, 1988), chs. 3–4. For the wider political background see below, Ch. 10.

voted not to do so. This opposition to centralization, combined with the limited scope of the legislation itself, ensured that the county police act made only a minor contribution to law enforcement. The lord lieutenant initially extended its provisions to the four counties of Cork, Kerry, Kilkenny, and Tipperary, leading to the deployment of almost 500 men. In 1795 his successor, responding to the spread of Defenderism, deployed another 600 men in a block of seven counties extending from Meath to Sligo. The creation of these forces looked forward to the part Ireland was to play during the nineteenth century in leading the conversion of the British state to a system of professional policing under central government control. In the short term, however, the response of central government to the rising disorder of the 1790s was to develop new forms of military force. Regular soldiers were joined, from 1793, by the militia, and from 1796 by the yeomanry. It was at this point, against the background of the international revolutionary crisis precipitated by the fall of the French monarchy, that Ireland did indeed for a time become a society held down by armed force.

Early modern states typically sought to compensate for their failure to apprehend more than a proportion of criminals by imposing harsh punishments on those that did fall into their clutches. Irish criminal law, like its English model, had none of the refinements such as breaking on the wheel still used in continental Europe. The punishment for serious crime was hanging, although in Ireland the further penalty of drawing and quartering was added, not just in cases of treason, but also, up to 1791, in cases of premeditated murder. The main alternative was transportation, for periods of seven or fourteen years or for life, to penal servitude in the North American colonies. Lesser offences could be punished by short periods of imprisonment, the pillory, or whipping. By the late eighteenth century the last two of these penalties seem to have been significantly more common in Ireland than in England, once again giving judicial punishment there a harsher physical character. Where the more extreme penalties are concerned, on the other hand, the limited evidence available suggests that the Irish state was significantly less bloodthirsty than the English. County Cork between 1767 and 1806 saw an average of just over three executions a year. Surrey, with about two-thirds of the same population, saw an average of more than seven.[71] Where transportation is concerned, the average number sent from England stood at 620 a year. In Ireland, with around half the population, the average was probably well below 150.[72]

Relatively low levels of execution and transportation can be directly related to a second striking feature of the Irish criminal justice system, the small proportion of prosecutions that ended in convictions. Grand juries seem typically to have rejected around half of the bills of indictment laid before them, on the grounds

[71] For this and other comparative statistics see Connolly, 'Unnatural Death'.

[72] James Kelly, 'Transportation from Ireland to North America 1703–1789', in David Dickson and Cormac Ó Gráda (eds.), *Refiguring Ireland* (Dublin, 2003), 112–25. Note that Kelly's figures represent a significant reduction on the figure of over 200 a year suggested by A. R. Ekirch, *Bound for America: The Transportation of British Convicts to the Colonies 1718–1775* (Oxford, 1990).

either that there were legal flaws or that there was no case to answer. Petty juries, likewise, acquitted more than half of the cases brought before them, leaving a conviction rate of no more than about one-quarter, as compared to the 60 to 70 per cent that was common in eighteenth-century England. Contemporaries explained this low level of successful prosecutions in terms of a more general corruption and partiality. Witnesses were bribed or intimidated, and juries were reluctant to bring in verdicts against neighbours or acquaintances. In particular there were complaints that landlords and others frequently intervened to protect their dependants. Nor did these instances of clientship and personal connection, characteristic of a small-scale society resistant to the intrusions of outside authority, work for the benefit only of the dominant minority. A calculation on the basis of surname evidence suggests that the Armagh grand jury, in fact, found slightly more true bills (55 per cent as compared to 53) in cases where the prosecutor was a Catholic, and a higher proportion still, 59 per cent as opposed to 52, in cases where the defendant was a Protestant.[73]

The workings of the Irish system of criminal law should not be idealized. The penalties for those who fell foul of the system could be extreme: the hangman's rope, the lash, or a lifetime of forced labour in the harsh environment of the Carolinas (or later, from 1788, Australia). Grand jurors could use their discretion to acquit the guilty. But their arbitrary power could also work in the opposite direction: a number of cases can be discovered where grand jurors, disgruntled at the acquittal of a particular offender, used their own powers of summary justice to have the individual concerned presented as a vagrant and transported.[74] At the same time the statistics of convictions, executions, and transportations make clear that order in eighteenth-century Ireland, whatever else it depended on, was not sustained by a particularly effective system of judicial terror. Instead it seems clear that the workings of the criminal law, as in contemporary England, must be placed in the context of a society governed by complex relationships of clientship, patronage, and deference. The gallows clearly had its part to play. But the 'men of fortune' whom Arthur Young criticized in 1780 for their willingness to use their influence on behalf of 'all sorts of offenders' clearly knew that there were other and more effective ways of maintaining their authority.[75]

By the middle of the eighteenth century Ireland had thus acquired a complex system of central and local administration. Historians have concentrated on the workings of parliament and central government. But a much wider cross-section of the Protestant population owed their experience of public life to their involvement in local bodies, from the county grand jury or municipal corporation down to the parish vestry. The range of functions undertaken by these corporate bodies, and the amounts of money they disposed of, increased markedly across

---

[73] Garnham, *The Courts, Crime and the Criminal Law*, 235, 238.   [74] Ibid. 241.
[75] Arthur Young, *A Tour in Ireland 1776–1779* (London, 1892), ii. 154. For a fuller discussion see Connolly, *Religion, Law and Power*, 224–5.

the century. Yet even at this stage the governmental system revealed its origins as one imposed from above. Ireland, like England, had its assizes circuits, and its lower courts of quarter session. What it did not have was the lowest rung of the judicial system: the petty sessions, at which justices disposed of minor offences without a jury. More seriously, the parish in Ireland could and did take on a range of administrative functions. But it could never become the central institution of a self-governing community in the way that it could in more religiously homogeneous England. This is not to suggest that the structures of government in Ireland were doomed to inevitable collapse. The restraint with which the courts applied an apparently bloody criminal code, and the at least occasional participation of dissenters and Catholics in aspects of parish business, both testify to the potential for compromise and mutual accommodation. But there remained a hollowness at the centre, which the exceptional stresses of the 1790s were all too clearly to reveal.

HIDDEN IRELANDS

Daniel Corkery's classic study *The Hidden Ireland* first appeared in 1924. Today, not far off a century after its publication, it remains perhaps the single most influential book to have informed the prevailing image of eighteenth-century Ireland. Corkery was not a historian, but a schoolmaster, a former nationalist political activist, and above all a scholar of Gaelic literature. His book bore the subtitle 'a study of Gaelic Munster in the eighteenth century', and was based primarily on the poetry of the region and period. What he offered, however, was a compelling vision of eighteenth-century Irish society as a whole. Three decades earlier the Victorian scholar W. E. H. Lecky had produced a detailed, elegantly written 'history of Ireland in the eighteenth century'. But his primarily high political narrative, Corkery insisted, had not in fact been a history of Ireland. Its focus had been on the narrow, unrepresentative world of the Protestant ruling class, focused on Dublin Castle and on the Irish parliament, 'that noisy side show, so bizarre in its lineaments and so tragicomic in its fate'. Beyond this metropolitan world, and beyond the demesne walls and iron gates of the great country houses that studded the countryside, lay what Corkery saw as the real Ireland: the world of a Gaelic-speaking, Catholic peasantry, materially poor but possessed of a sophisticated literary culture, united in their unremitting hostility to the culture, religion, and political allegiances of an alien and oppressive ruling class.[76]

[76] Daniel Corkery, *The Hidden Ireland: A Study of Gaelic Munster in the Eighteenth Century* (Dublin, 1967). Corkery, it is important to emphasize, was no provincial polemicist, but a literary scholar with a European frame of reference. See Patrick Maume, *Life that is Exile: Daniel Corkery and the Search for Irish Ireland* (Belfast, 1993).

The response to Corkery's study has followed a familiar trajectory. In 1968, as one part of a much broader critique of what was then the received image of a uniformly impoverished and crisis-ridden eighteenth-century Ireland, L. M. Cullen offered a searching critique of the ways in which Corkery's poetic sources failed to reveal the reality of a complex social hierarchy and, from mid-century on, a dramatically expanding economy. More recent writing, however, has sought, implicitly or explicitly, to rehabilitate Corkery's work, by reaffirming the value of the Gaelic literary sources as a guide to the deep political and religious divisions that existed beneath the surface calm of Hanoverian Irish society.[77] One aspect of this revised model, the assumption of an exceptionally high level of popular disaffection, has already been discussed. But it is also important, in this renewed debate, not to lose sight of the related but separate question of the relationship between elite and popular culture. Corkery was ahead of his time in highlighting the need for historians to look beyond the cultural world of a narrow propertied elite to the thoughts, feelings, and aspirations of other sections of society. It is that which has given his work its enduring resonance. Where he was mistaken was in his simple model of two antagonistic cultures, Gaelic and English, conqueror and conquered. For the long-term legacy of Ireland's forced incorporation into the Tudor and then the Stuart state was not one hidden Ireland, but several. Nor was there any simple polarity between the cultures of rulers and ruled. Instead the picture, as elsewhere in *ancien régime* Europe, was of a deeply unequal society, but one in which there were complex relationships of exchange and interaction between different cultural groups and different social levels.

Table 2. Language and religion

| | % Speaking Irish[a] | | % Catholic |
| | Decade of birth | | |
	1771–81	1801–11	1861
Leinster			
Carlow	5	2	88
Dublin	7	4	75
Kildare	2	2	87
Kilkenny	57	45	95
King's County	4	2	89
Longford	22	8	90
Louth	57	42	92
Meath	41	28	94
Queen's County	6	1	88
Westmeath	17	7	92

[77] Cullen, 'The Hidden Ireland': see above n. 29. For the more recent rehabilitation of the concept see, in particular, Ó Ciardha, *Ireland and the Jacobite Cause*, 45–7.

Wexford	3	1	90
Wicklow	1	1	81
Total	17	11	86
Munster			
Clare	92	90	98
Cork	84	82	91
Kerry	93	93	97
Limerick	76	73	95
Tipperary	51	45	94
Waterford	86	81	95
Total	80	77	94
Connacht			
Galway	91	89	96
Leitrim	52	43	90
Mayo	95	94	97
Roscommon	74	65	96
Sligo	84	82	90
Total	84	80	95
Ulster			
Antrim	3	2	25
Armagh	18	15	49
Cavan	39	29	81
Donegal	56	53	75
Down	3	1	32
Fermanagh	16	9	57
Londonderry	10	7	45
Monaghan	33	28	73
Tyrone	19	14	56
Total	19	15	51
Ireland	45	41	78

[a] Percentages show the proportion of persons born in the decades specified that were recorded in later census returns as able to speak Irish.

Source: Garret Fitzgerald, 'Estimates for Baronies of Minimum Level of Irish Speaking', *PRIA*, C, 84 (1984), 117–55, reprinted in shorter form as 'The Decline of the Irish Language 1771–1871', in M. E. Daly and D. Dickson (eds.), *The Origins of Popular Literacy in Ireland* (Dublin, 1990); W. E. Vaughan and A. J. Fitzpatrick (eds.), *Irish Historical Statistics: Population 1821–1971* (Dublin, 1978), 51–3.

To appreciate the complexity of the real history of cultural change, in the eighteenth century and earlier, it is only necessary to look at the first available statistics on spoken language. These were collected only in 1861. However the published results were broken down by age group in a way that allows the results to be projected backwards so as to depict the experience of separate birth cohorts across most of the preceding century (Table 2). The results reveal a pattern of striking geographical contrasts. In the east and north these were closely related to patterns of settlement in the seventeenth century and earlier.

In Ulster Irish survived in the less densely settled counties of Donegal, Cavan, and Monaghan, and in some remote subdistricts elsewhere, such as the rugged Glens of Antrim and the mountainous and proverbially lawless southern part of Armagh. Elsewhere, however, English was now the language, not just of the descendants of English and Scottish settlers, but of the majority of those tracing their ancestry to what had once been the most strongly Gaelic region of Ireland. In Leinster, Irish remained remarkably strong in Louth and Meath. This was the heart of the old medieval lordship, but it was also an area where the early establishment of a pattern of intensive, commercial agriculture provided the basis for a greater degree of cultural continuity than existed elsewhere, while a denser population created fewer openings for New English incomers.[78] The Church of Ireland clergyman Anthony Raymond, writing in the 1720s, noted that two-thirds of his County Meath parishioners, 'though within 20 miles of the metropolis of the kingdom, are as great strangers to the English tongue as they are to the Coptic or Arabic'.[79] In Wicklow, King's County, and Queen's County, all former Gaelic strongholds planted in Tudor or early Stuart times, by contrast, English was now the language of the descendants of settler and native alike. In the same way more Irish was spoken in Kilkenny and Tipperary, former outposts of the medieval colony, than in Longford, which had up to the sixteenth century been the autonomous Gaelic lordship of the O'Ferralls. The same pattern of continuity in the areas of the oldest English settlement was seen in part of County Wexford, and in the district of Fingal north of Dublin, but there it took the form of the survival into the late eighteenth century of a distinctly archaic dialect of English. The language of the Wexford baronies of Forth and Bargy, one observer in the early 1740s maintained, was 'that of Geoffrey Chaucer, Robert of Gloucester, or the Monk of Lithgate, and as hard to be understood'.[80]

In Munster and Connacht the statistics derived by working backwards from nineteenth-century censuses reveal a very different pattern. Irish had retreated significantly in Leitrim, the scene of a plantation in the 1620s. On the other hand neither the colonizing efforts of the Binghams and others in late sixteenth-century Mayo and Sligo, nor the town of Galway's long history as a centre of self-consciously English culture, had made a perceptible impact on the language of the population as a whole. More striking still was the failure of either the late sixteenth-century and early seventeenth-century plantations, or the rapid commercialization of rural society that had taken place from the 1740s, to

[78] The significance of this stronger position of Irish in areas of pre-Tudor English settlement was first emphasized in L. M. Cullen, *The Emergence of Modern Ireland 1600–1900* (London, 1981), 88–9, 107, 204, 248–9.

[79] Quoted in Alan Harrison, 'More Hidden Irelands: Some Light on the Irish Eighteenth Century', *Études irlandaises*, 26 (2001), 58.

[80] W. R. Chetwood, *A Tour through Ireland in Several Entertaining Letters . . . by Two English Gentlemen* (Dublin, 1746), 169. For other observations to the same effect see Alan Bliss in *NHI*, iii. 547–9.

weaken the dominance of Irish in Cork, Kerry, and Waterford, or, to more than a minor degree, in Limerick. Once again it is clear that economic growth did not in itself entail large-scale language change. Instead, west of a line from Waterford to Sligo, there lay a solid block of territory in which children growing up in three-quarters or more of all households acquired a knowledge of Irish as they did so.

This surviving Irish-language tradition existed largely without the support of the printed word. There was no commercial imperative to cater for the linguistic peculiarities of a generally poor and geographically and socially marginal population. Meanwhile the only realistic potential patrons of Irish-language printing, the Catholic clergy, failed to build on the legacy of the Louvain Franciscans of the early seventeenth century. Catholic ecclesiastics did not wholly ignore the problem of language. Some of the Catholic colleges in continental Europe required their students to keep up the use of spoken Irish. In 1765 John O'Brien, bishop of Cloyne and Ross, appealed to Rome for financial assistance with the publication of an English–Irish dictionary for the use of priests, pointing out among other things that the survival of the language was crucial to the preservation of Catholicism: 'experience has taught us that it is only those ignorant of Irish, or those who become fluent in English, who abandon the Catholic religion and embrace that of the Protestants.' The work eventually appeared, from a Paris printer, in 1768.[81] Earlier, in 1738, Bishop James Gallagher of Raphoe had produced sixteen sermons in Irish for the use of preachers. But these were isolated exceptions. John Carpenter, archbishop of Dublin from 1770 to 1786, was a tailor's son who in his youth had mixed with the scholarly circle round the scribe Tadhg Ó Neachtain. But the religious publications he organized, such as the 1780 version of Butler's *Lives of the Saints*, were in English. In the same way Anthony Coyle, Gallagher's successor at Raphoe, preached and composed prayers in Irish. But his *Pious Miscellany*, published in Strabane in 1780 to raise money for church building, consists of poems and other pieces written in a conventional literary English.[82]

The lack of impetus towards sustained printing in Irish meant in turn that no progress was made towards the development of a standardized written form. Gallagher's sermons, for example, produced by a Dublin printer, had the telling subtitle 'in English characters; as being the more familiar to the generality of our Irish clergy'. Gallagher also felt it necessary to include a preface explaining his use of 'an easy and familiar style', including 'words borrowed from the English, which practice and daily conversation have intermixed with our language, choosing with St Augustine rather to be censured by the critics, than not to be understood

[81] F. M. Jones, 'The Congregation of Propaganda and the Publication of Dr O'Brien's Irish Dictionary 1768', *Irish Ecclesiastical Record*, 77 (1952), 29–37.

[82] J. J. Silke, 'Bishop Coyle's Pious Miscellany', *ECI* 9 (1994), 114–28. For Catholic printing in general see Thomas Wall, *The Sign of Dr Hay's Head* (Dublin, 1958).

by the poor and illiterate'. His comments, strikingly reminiscent of those of his Franciscan predecessors a century earlier, are testimony both to the changing character of popular speech and to the continued failure to bridge the gap between the literary and everyday languages.[83]

Despite this failure to join the world of print, Irish remained throughout the eighteenth century not just a peasant vernacular but the medium for a sophisticated literary culture. The final collapse of the Gaelic political and social order meant the disappearance of the bardic schools. But there continued to exist networks of poets and scholars, exchanging manuscripts and maintaining a body of traditional learning. There were also scribes, labouring to produce fresh manuscript copies of old and new texts. In the early eighteenth century many of these poets and scribes found employment as tutors in the homes of surviving men of property from among the native elite. By the second half of the century, as such patrons became less common, some found new opportunities as teachers in an expanding school system, or in catering for the growing interest in Gaelic antiquities among the descendants of the New English.[84] The poets and scribes continued to see themselves as an elite, set apart from the unlettered commonality. But in practice the adaptation of the learned tradition to altered circumstances permitted a new interchange between literary and popular culture. Versions of classical tales entered the folklore tradition. Individual poets, like the proverbially hard-drinking womanizer Eoghan Ruadh Ó Súilleabháin (1748–84), became figures in popular legend. Poetic texts found their way from manuscript form into a well-developed oral culture.[85] In Gaelic Ireland, as in other societies not dependent on the written word, moreover, this oral tradition was itself a powerful tool of cultural preservation. In one revealing case study the spoken version, collected in 1942, of a poem datable from internal evidence to between 1712 and 1726 has been found to remain impressively close to the only known written version, made in the 1750s and then lost to view for two centuries.[86]

This continuing tradition of Gaelic poetry and learning did not flourish only in the more remote parts of an underdeveloped countryside. One of the most active Gaelic scholars of the early eighteenth century, Tadhg Ó Neachtain, was at the centre of a group of literati based in Dublin. Another scribe, Dermot O'Connor, likewise worked in Dublin before moving to London, where he published in 1723 the first English translation of Keating's *Foras Feasa ar Eirinn*,

---

[83] James Gallagher, *Sixteen Irish Sermons, in an Easy and Familiar Stile, on Useful and Necessary Subjects* (Dublin, 1736), p. iv. For the apologies of early seventeenth-century writers of devotional texts for their use of the vernacular, see Connolly, *Contested Island*, 383–4.

[84] L. M. Cullen, 'Patrons, Teachers and Literacy in Irish 1750–1850: Presence and Absence', in M. E. Daly and David Dickson (eds.), *The Origins of Popular Literacy in Ireland: Language Change and Educational Development 1700–1920* (Dublin, 1990), 15–44.

[85] Dáithí Ó hOgáin, 'Folklore and Literature 1700–1850', in Daly and Dickson (eds.), *The Origins of Popular Literacy*, 1–13.

[86] P. A. Breathnach, 'Oral and Written Transmission of Poetry in the Eighteenth Century', *ECI* 2 (1987), 57–65.

as well as engaging in the lucrative business of providing pedigrees for émigré Irish families seeking to establish themselves in the status-conscious world of *ancien régime* Europe. Forty years later another Dublin-based literary figure, Muiris Ó Gormáin, likewise supported himself as a teacher and scribe. An agreement of 1762 committed him to teaching two youths 'writing, arithmetic and the English tongue'. But he also advertised himself in a Dublin newspaper, four years later, as willing to teach Irish, and in 1782 he styled himself 'Professor of the Gaelic language in Dublin and the last of the Irish bards'. The context for this last grandiose self-description was the presentation of the third of three odes, in Irish with English translation, that he produced in 1763, 1767, and 1782, to welcome newly arrived lords lieutenant. Whether any of those so honoured responded we do not know, although two of the three odes survive in the papers of the families concerned. What is clear is that Ó Gormáin's position within the rarefied world of Gaelic texts and manuscripts did not cut him off from either the commercial or the political realities of the capital city in which he lived and worked.[87]

Although Ó Gormáin was willing to appeal directly to the patronage of Dublin Castle, others among the Gaelic literati continued to give at least rhetorical support to the cause of the exiled Stuarts. The result, particularly in the second half of the century, as Jacobitism largely lost its moorings in political reality, was at times a strikingly parochial reinterpretation of European or North American conflicts in terms of the immediate concerns of Catholic Ireland. In other cases, however, contemporary Gaelic treatments of conflicts such as the so-called War of Jenkins's Ear, fought between England and Spain from 1739, or of the Seven Years War of 1756–63, reveal an impressive familiarity with the detailed course of events.[88] In domestic affairs likewise poets did not by any means confine themselves to rehearsing the glories of a long-vanished, and partly imagined, Gaelic world. A poem describing a fair, written at the very end of the century, possibly in County Mayo, reveals a capacity to deal in vivid and concrete detail with the contemporary reality of an increasingly commercialized provincial society. A County Cork text from the early nineteenth century borrows the form of *Pairlement Chloinne Tomáis* to comment on the behaviour and grievances of the handloom weavers, thus providing a commentary on recent developments in the local industrial economy.[89]

[87] Nessa Ní Shéaghdha, 'Irish Scholars and Scribes in Eighteenth-Century Dublin', *ECI* 4 (1989), 41–54; Diarmaid Ó Catháin, 'Dermot O'Connor: Translator of Keating', *ECI* 2 (1987), 67–87; R. Mahony, 'Muiris Ó Gormáin and the Lord Lieutenant of Ireland', *Éigse*, 22 (1987), 25–36.

[88] Cornelius Buttimer, 'An Irish Text on the "War of Jenkins Ear"'. *Celtica*, 21 (1990), 75–98; idem, 'Gaelic Literature and Contemporary Life in Cork 1700–1840', in Patrick Flanagan and C. G. Buttimer (eds.), *Cork: History and Society* (Dublin 1993), 588–96. For the other side of the picture, the distortion of foreign affairs to fit local concerns, see the depictions of the American War discussed earlier in this chapter.

[89] Cornelius Buttimer, 'Tuairisc Amhaill Uí Iartáin: An Eighteenth-Century Poem on a Fair', *ECI* 7 (1992), 75–94. See also Buttimer, 'Gaelic Literature and Contemporary Life', 620–3.

The Gaelic Irish literature of the eighteenth century, then, was a living culture, responding to and reflecting the changing world around it, as well as the long tradition, rooted in the institutions of a vanished social order, from which it derived. By the end of the century, however, the signs of contraction were evident. The proportion of children born in the first decade of the nineteenth century who grew up with a knowledge of Irish was only slightly lower than the level of three decades earlier (Table 2). But this apparent resilience is misleading. The rapid growth of population that began in the last decades of the eighteenth century was particularly concentrated in those regions and among those social groups most likely to be Irish speaking. Against this background of a natural demographic advantage, the apparently healthy overall proportion still acquiring the language in childhood is of less significance than the marked decline that was nevertheless evident in some counties, notably in Kilkenny, Longford, Louth, and Meath.

How is this decline to be explained? The statistics from the 1770s make clear that the survival of Irish was not necessarily incompatible with rising living standards and an increasingly commercial economy. By the last decades of the eighteenth century, however, there was also a growing demand for literacy, reflected in the rapid increase in the number of elementary schools. And it was here that the failure of Irish to adapt to the printed word became crucial. In Wales or in Brittany during the late eighteenth and nineteenth centuries, successive generations were able to master reading and writing through a reasonably abundant printed literature in their own language. Their Irish counterparts were able to do so only by working with texts in English. The collapse of Irish as a spoken language came only after the Famine of 1845–50. But already among those born during the 1830s the proportion that were later to claim a knowledge of Irish had fallen to 28 per cent. If more than two out of every five children born in the last decades of the eighteenth century seem to have grown up in households where Irish was commonly spoken, in other words, the same appears to have been true of only just over one in four of the households these children were themselves to create as adults.[90]

The division between speakers of Irish Gaelic and English was the most significant linguistic frontier in eighteenth-century Ireland. But it was not the only one. In parts of Ulster the Church of Ireland also found it necessary to make provision for immigrants from the Scottish Highlands, episcopalian in religion yet speaking only Gaelic. In the diocese of Down the labours of two such Irish-speaking ministers were credited not only with winning back those Protestant Highlanders who had temporarily defected to the Catholic church

---

[90] For the comparison with Wales and Brittany see Niall Ó Ciosáin, 'Printed Popular Literature in Irish 1750–1850', in Daly and Dickson (eds.), *The Origins of Popular Literacy*, 50–4. V. E. Durkacz, *The Decline of the Celtic Languages* (Edinburgh, 1983) likewise emphasizes the link between literacy and language.

in search of services in their own language, but also with converting significant numbers of natives.[91] In Rasharkin, County Antrim, a minister reported 'above a hundred souls (as I am since credibly informed) who understand not the English language, and all of them of our church'. In Clonmany on the Inishowen peninsula the number of Gaelic-speaking Protestant migrants was said in 1703 to be nearly 300. A visitation of the parish thirty years later noted that the curate 'preaches every Sunday, but every second Sunday in Irish for these thirteen years past, for the convenience of a good number of Highlanders who are of the parish and three converts of the native Irish'.[92]

If Gaelic-speaking Irish Protestants were a minor curiosity, Scottish settlement in Ulster had also left a more substantial linguistic legacy in the dominance across a large area of a distinctive form of spoken English. The status of this tongue, as language or dialect, fluctuated over time. The Elizabethan lord deputy Sir Henry Sidney noted without condescension that Lady Agnes Campbell, wife of Turlough O'Neill, was 'a grave, wise and well spoken lady, both in Scots-English and French'. Scottish landowners and aristocrats in the early seventeenth century continued to speak and write in their own distinctive manner, and even petitioned the Dublin administration for the appointment of a clerk who could understand 'the Scotch hand'.[93] Over the next few decades, however, this elite for the most part abandoned its Scots speech for standard English, just as most abandoned Presbyterianism for the established church. Scots became for a century a dialect, spoken by farmers, weavers, and labourers.[94] By the late eighteenth century, on the other hand, the example of Burns and others encouraged the emergence of a new genre of poetry in the Ulster Scots vernacular, as in the Antrim weaver James Orr's vivid description of an emigrant voyage to North America:

> Wi' frien's consent we prie't a gill
> An' monie a house did call at,
> Shook han's an' smil't, tho' ilk fareweel

---

[91] John Richardson, *A Short History of the Attempts that have been Made to Convert the Popish Natives of Ireland* (1713), 29–30.

[92] King to Samuel Foley, 9 May 1693 (TCD MSS 1995–2008, No. 274); John McLaine to King, 13 Aug. 1694 (ibid., No. 372); Patrick McLachline to King, 25 Nov. 1703 (ibid., No. 1051); Visitation of the diocese of Derry, *c*.1733 (Representative Church Body Library, Dublin, GS 2/7/3/34, p. 10). The Presbyterian General Synod of Ulster also gave serious attention in the early eighteenth century to the need to provide ministers capable of preaching in Irish. In this case, however, their concern, presumably reflecting the greater strength of episcopalianism in the Highlands, seems primarily to have been to provide for converts from among the native population. In 1710 the Presbytery of Dublin appealed to the Synod for help in providing for some Gaelic-speaking Highlanders, but it is likely that these were soldiers stationed in the city rather than permanent residents. See Terence McCaughey, 'General Synod of Ulster's Policy on the Use of the Irish Language in the Early Eighteenth Century: Questions about Implementation', in Kevin Herlihy (ed.), *Propagating the Word of Irish Dissent 1650–1800* (Dublin, 1998), 46–62.

[93] *A Viceroy's Vindication: Sir Henry Sidney's Memoir of his Service in Ireland 1556–78*, ed. Ciaran Brady (Dublin, 2002), 76; Connolly, *Contested Island*, 302.

[94] Philip Robinson, 'The Scots Language in Seventeenth-Century Ulster', *Ulster Folklife*, 35 (1989), 86–99.

Strak, like a weighty mallet,
Our hearts, that day.[95]

In addition to this linguistic distinctiveness, temporarily obscured then proudly rediscovered, there were other indications of a clear Scottish element in Ulster culture. Observers of early nineteenth-century County Antrim noted the preference for New Year over Christmas day as an occasion for festivity, and the presence of a stick and ball game identifiable as Scottish shinty rather than Irish hurling. One account even claimed to distinguish the border between predominantly Presbyterian and Anglican areas from the way in which the trees and gardens of an area of English settlement gave way to the bare functional farmsteads characteristic of the Scots.[96]

The roots of Ulster's Scottish culture in the seventeenth-century plantation are obvious. The origins of the equally important English element that existed in popular as well as elite culture are by contrast more diffuse. In custom as in spoken language County Wexford and north County Dublin stand out as areas of striking continuity. In both areas nineteenth-century sources testify to the popularity of the English custom of costumed mummers visiting houses around Christmas time to perform an elaborate play in rhyme and be rewarded with food, drink, or money.[97] In both areas, likewise, the first of May was marked not, as in most parts of Ireland, by celebrations round a decorated bush, but by the erection of a May pole. But May poles were also reported in Kilkenny city, and in towns and villages in Kildare, Queen's County, and Westmeath. In these cases it seems more likely that the custom had been introduced by English newcomers of the sixteenth or seventeenth century, than that it represented a survival of Old English culture. But if so it and other customs and pastimes had long spread beyond the new settler community to the population as a whole. William Farrell, born in Carlow town in 1772 and subsequently apprenticed to a saddler, recalled in old age a range of amusements most of which could have been found in any comparable English urban centre: 'hurling, football, cudgelling, tennis or handball, leaping, wrestling, vaulting, throwing the sledge or bar or grinding-stone'. There was also bull-baiting, cock-fighting, and above all 'the humours of a May day', when costumed players danced about May poles erected in different parts of the town.[98]

Dublin, with its metropolitan character and large, mobile population, had a particular place in the development of a hybrid Irish-English popular culture.

---

[95] Andrew Carpenter (ed.), *Verse in English from Eighteenth-Century Ireland* (Cork, 1998), 544, from a collection of Orr's poems published in 1804.

[96] For a fuller discussion see S. J. Connolly, 'Popular Culture in Pre-Famine Ireland', in C. J. Byrne (ed.), *Talamh an Eisc: Canadian and Irish Essays* (Halifax, NS, 1986), 14–15.

[97] Alan Gailey, *Christmas Rhymers and Mummers in Ireland* (Ibstock, 1968).

[98] Roger McHugh (ed.), *Carlow in '98: The Autobiography of William Farrell of Carlow* (Dublin, 1949), 14–23. For May poles elsewhere see William Wilde, *Irish Popular Superstitions* (Dublin, 1852), 36–67; Kevin Danaher, *The Year in Ireland* (Cork, 1972), 86–128.

Its civic rituals, such as the annual riding of the franchise by the mayor and members of the corporation, and the elaborate processions staged by the guilds into which the city's different trades were organized, closely mirrored English urban traditions. A newspaper reported in late August 1733 that the festival of St Bartholomew, marked by a celebrated fair at Smithfield in London, had also been observed in Dublin, with the usual fair and the roasting of a whole ox, but with less disorder than was normal on that day.[99] Another newspaper, eight years later, commented with disapproval on 'a new kind of merchandise' lately introduced into the town, where a butcher had 'sold' his wife to another man for a sum of 20 guineas. The paper speculated sarcastically on whether this new custom had been imported from China. In reality what had taken place was clearly the form of plebeian divorce by means of a ritual 'sale' that was widely reported in eighteenth-century England and was later to be somewhat inaccurately commemorated by Thomas Hardy.[100]

Another side of the distinctive popular culture of English-speaking Dublin can be glimpsed, if not necessarily quite at first hand, in the corpus of verse and prose recitations now preserved in a variety of printed texts and manuscripts dating from the later decades of the eighteenth century. How far these represented a transcription, and how far a mere imitation, of genuine popular compositions is now impossible to say. But the picture they present is a vivid one: a plebeian counter-culture, characterized by celebration of the deeds of underworld heroes, a defiant awareness of the gallows, and a vigorous rejection of authority. In the best known of these pieces, 'The night before Larry was stretched', the eponymous Larry's friends 'sweated dir duds' in the pawnshop to raise the money for a last drinking bout before he faced the hangman. Two other pieces commemorate Luke Caffrey, who likewise 'caper'd de Kilmainham Minit [minuet]'. A mention of the coins paid to the hangman who ended his life—'a few hump back'd Williamites, and a bloody queen Anne's tester'—converts the momentous dynastic conflict of a few decades earlier into the small change of the Dublin streets. In a fourth poem the narrator, transported for seven years for having carried away a bull belonging to Lord Altham to be baited by dogs, vows vengeance on his noble prosecutor: 'if ever I come back from his Majesty's tobacco manufactory, I'll butter my knife in his tripes and give him his guts for garters. All de world knows I've de blood of de Dempseys in me.'[101]

The exact status of these public texts remains unclear. But there was also, by the late eighteenth century, a rapidly expanding body of printed material that was unambiguously aimed at a popular audience. Statistics on literacy do not become available until the census of 1841. Like the language data, however, the

[99] *Dublin Intelligence*, 30 Aug. 1731.
[100] *Dublin Daily Post*, 10 Mar. 1739. For the English custom see E. P. Thompson, 'The Sale of Wives', in idem, *Customs in Common* (London, 1991); Thomas Hardy, *The Life and Death of the Mayor of Casterbridge* (1886), ch. 1.
[101] Carpenter, *Verse in English from Eighteenth-Century Ireland*, 430, 437–9, 445.

results are broken down by age cohort, so as to provide a measure of change over preceding decades. The results are impressive. Among men the proportion of persons listed in 1841 as unable to read and write falls from 63 per cent of those born in 1751–60 to 49 of those born in 1761–70; among women the decline is from 81 to 68 per cent. A more limited study of leases from landed estates in north-west Ulster presents a similar picture. Among tenants judged likely, on the basis of surnames, to have been Protestant, the proportion signing rather than making their mark rose from 69 per cent in leases dating from 1750–79 to 83 per cent in those issued between 1780 and 1799. Among Catholics change came later. But the proportion signing rose dramatically, from only 33 per cent in leases dating from 1780–99 to 64 per cent in 1800–19.[102]

Against this background, the trade in chapbooks, already developing in the late seventeenth century, now entered its golden age. The small, cheap volumes stocked by local shopkeepers, or carried by itinerant pedlars, included religious texts, histories, books of instruction in spelling or arithmetic, compendia of general knowledge, and tantalizing exoticisms such as Ovid's *Art of Love* and the *Works of Aristotle, the Famous Philosopher*. Few of these titles were specific to Ireland. One striking feature, in fact, was the continued popularity, there as elsewhere, of works like *Valentine and Orson*, first published in France in 1489, or the *Seven Champions of Christendom*, an English text from the 1590s—tales of knights and chivalry in a genre that had first emerged to entertain the aristocracy of medieval Europe and now circulated, often in abridged form, at a wholly different social level. What emerges, in other words, is a literate popular culture created for, rather than by, the readers concerned, from the largely random selection of texts available to printers. At the same time it must also be assumed that consumer choice played some part in determining what works were most often reprinted. Two popular books with a more local flavour were the autobiography of the County Kilkenny highwayman James Freney, first published in 1754, and James Cosgrave's *Genuine History of the Lives and Actions of the Most Notorious Highwaymen* (1776), later reprinted as *Irish Rogues and Rapparees*. But these too were in a genre, tales of bandits, smugglers, and highwaymen, familiar in England, France, and elsewhere.[103]

Corkery's idea of a 'hidden Ireland', then, is misleading in two important respects. His depiction of a culture of defeat, broodingly preserving the remains of a devastated social order, failed to do justice to the capacity of the Gaelic literary tradition to respond to a changing world, while his simple two-culture model ignored the variety of influences that had gone into the making of eighteenth-century Ireland's patchwork of popular custom and expression. A

---

[102] *Census of Ireland for 1841* (Parliamentary Papers 1843, vol. 24), pp. xxxv–xxxvi; Graeme Kirkham, 'Literacy in North-West Ulster 1680–1860', in Daly and Dickson (eds.), *The Origins of Popular Literacy*, 74–6.

[103] J. R. R. Adams, *The Printed Word and the Common Man: Popular Culture in Ulster 1700–1900* (Belfast, 1987); Niall Ó Ciosáin, *Print and Popular Culture in Ireland 1750–1850* (London, 1996).

third implication of his thesis was that this was a uniquely fractured society, in which an English Protestant gentry and a Gaelic Catholic peasantry remained wholly set apart, in language, custom, and forms of sociability. And it is indeed the case that in Ireland cultural divisions between elite and people were reinforced by differences in religion and political allegiance that did not exist in most other early modern societies. But that only makes it all the more striking that there should nevertheless have been so much interaction, between landlord and tenant, high culture and low, across these lines of division. In this respect too eighteenth-century Ireland begins to appear as far less clearly an exception to the norms that prevailed in *ancien régime* Europe than is generally supposed.[104]

A central element in Corkery's image of a society marked by an unparalleled cultural divide was the different languages spoken by rulers and ruled. Yet Ireland was not, in this respect, any different from Wales or Highland Scotland. Further afield there were parallels in Bohemia, Norway, and Finland, in each of which the language of polite society was, respectively, German, Danish, and Swedish, while what was in time to become the native language was the dialect of servants and peasants. Even in states with only one language, such as France and Italy, the speech of the lower classes was in many cases fragmented into a variety of dialects, not all of them mutually intelligible. As in other linguistically divided societies, moreover, landowners and other members of the social elite seem frequently to have had at least enough Irish to communicate as necessary with tenants, servants, and other social inferiors. In one celebrated instance during 1798 Thomas Judkin Fitzgerald, high sheriff of Tipperary and noted for the ferocity with which he stamped out the United Irish movement in his county, was reported to have harangued a crowd for three hours, speaking part of the time in Irish. Such functional bilingualism was facilitated in many cases by early exposure to the company of servants and nursemaids. A daughter of Lord Nugent, writing from Westmeath in 1744, reported that 'my little boy speaks nothing but Irish, which I fear will prevent him being a scholar so soon'.[105] At a different social level the Synod of Ulster in the early years of the eighteenth century seems to have had no difficulty in identifying ministers capable of speaking, and in some cases reading, Irish. Some of these were of Highland origin but others, including apparently the celebrated New Light minister John Abernethy, were Irish born and had acquired their knowledge of the language through growing up in the linguistically mixed environment of post-plantation Ulster.[106]

---

[104] The points that follow are discussed in greater detail in Connolly, *Religion, Law and Power*, ch. 4.4; idem, ' "Ag Déanamh Commanding": Elite Responses to Popular Culture 1660–1850', in J. S. Donnelly and K. A. Miller (eds.), *Irish Popular Culture 1650–1850* (Dublin, 1998), 1–29. For the wider European background, the classic introduction remains Peter Burke, *Popular Culture in Early Modern Europe* (London, 1978).

[105] Barbara Reilly to Andrew Savage, 21 Aug. 1744 (PRONI D552/A/2/7/11). For Fitzgerald see R. B. McDowell, *Ireland in the Age of Imperialism and Revolution* (Oxford, 1979), 580.

[106] McCaughey, 'General Synod of Ulster's Policy', 46–7, 56–7.

In other respects too, the relationship between high and low culture in eighteenth-century Ireland was much closer than has normally been recognized to the pattern common across most of early modern Europe. The political and social elite had their own exclusive culture: the balls, concerts, and stage plays of the capital and the larger towns, and the smaller-scale entertainments held in country houses; the higher learning of the grammar school, the university, and the pulpit; the polite British and French literature of the day. There were also cultural forms identified primarily with the common people: the celebration of wakes and patterns; observance of May Day, St John's eve, and other turning points in the yearly cycle; an oral tradition of songs and folktales, increasingly supplemented by cheap print in the form of chapbooks. But there was also interaction, in both directions, between these separate cultural levels. Poems circulating in the oral and manuscript Gaelic tradition contain material drawn from the contemporary newspaper press. The compositions of the harper Turlough O'Carolan, celebrated as the last of the Irish bards, reveal traces of the influence of Italian art music. The popular dance tradition was a hybrid one, applying native steps and measures to elite forms such as the cotillion and the minuet.[107] Elite culture, likewise, incorporated elements from the popular tradition. Piper and harpers playing in the native idiom found regular employment in the houses, not just of the surviving Catholic gentry, but of the new Protestant landowning class. Tunes by O'Carolan and others were printed, inserting them into the polite repertoire. At the Belfast theatre in 1770, audiences attending a performance of *The Merchant of Venice* were entertained between acts by 'an Irish jig by Logan and Mrs Logan and an Irish song called *Ellen a Roon* by Mrs Ryder'.[108]

At a different cultural level the Irish aristocracy and gentry, like their counterparts elsewhere in pre-industrial Europe, joined with their social inferiors in supporting a wide range of sports and entertainments. Prize fights and horse races regularly attracted both gentlemen and commoners.[109] William Farrell recalled that the different factions in the town of Carlow competed in their celebration of May Day: 'every gentleman they had influence on they went to him for a maypole, and were never refused'. Hurling, later to be promoted by the cultural nationalists of the late nineteenth century as part of an exclusively native sporting tradition, flourished in the eighteenth century as a team sport heavily dependent on patronage from the wealthy. In August 1746, for example, a match to be played in County Galway between two teams of twenty-one, married men and bachelors, for 'a belt of forty guineas', was transferred to a new venue 'for the better accommodation of the ladies and gentlemen, and the benefit of a good

---

[107] Breandán Breathnach, 'The Dancing Master', *Ceol*, 4 (1970), 116–17.

[108] J. C. Greene, *Theatre in Belfast 1736–1800* (London, 2000), 127.

[109] David A. Fleming, 'Diversions of the People: Sociability among the Orders in Early Eighteenth-Century Ireland', *ECI* 17 (2002), 99–111 offers a range of examples, but is perhaps unduly concerned to emphasize the obvious point that such shared entertainments did not mean that confessional and social distinctions became irrelevant.

road for carriages'. In 1792 the countess of Westmorland, wife of the lord lieutenant, attended a hurling match in Phoenix Park, along with 'several of the nobility and gentry, besides a vast concourse of spectators'. Nor did members of the elite confine themselves to the role of spectators. In County Kilkenny John Cuffe, a son of Baron Desart who died in 1767, was celebrated locally as 'Seán a' Chaipín', an enthusiastic hurler: a local song, revealingly mixing languages, described him, in his green jacket and red cap, *'ag déanamh* commanding *ar na hiomanaithe maithe'* [' "commanding" the fine hurlers']. Dudley Cosby, a landowner in Queen's County who died in 1729, was likewise remembered for his accomplishments in following hounds on foot, rope dancing, and tennis, and also as 'a most extraordinarily fine hurler'.[110]

In addition to joining with their social inferiors in shared appreciation of a variety of sports and entertainments, the rulers of eighteenth-century Ireland, like their counterparts elsewhere, sponsored other occasions of conviviality and celebration. When Dudley Cosby's son returned in 1724 from three years' study in the Netherlands, he was met at the county boundary 'by several gentlemen, friends and tenants, and garlands and long dancers, and my father invited them all home to dine with him, and gave drink and money to the common people and dancers'. In County Monaghan in 1773 Baron Dartry celebrated the fifteenth birthday of his son 'in a very hospitable and princely manner, 150 poor people to dinner and . . . very elegant fireworks'. Nor was it only members of the landed classes who organized events of this kind. A merchant in Mullingar, County Westmeath, celebrated the completion in 1736 of a new windmill by a dinner for the gentlemen and merchants of the town. But when this select company reached the stage of proposing and drinking toasts, 'two boxes or chests of lemons and oranges, with the just proportion of spirits etc. were thrown to the millstones . . . [and] immediately ground down to punch through a conduit prepared, which conveyed the liquor into a cistern without side for the use of the populace, who also drank the aforesaid healths with acclamations of joy'.[111]

Carefully staged displays of this kind did not imply any weakening of the distinction between rich and poor, rulers and ruled. On the contrary the proceedings were in many cases themselves a theatrical representation of social hierarchy. At young Dartry's birthday celebrations, for example, '160 workmen of several kinds made a solemn procession round the bonfire, with each the instruments of his employment on his shoulder'. Nor can the appearance of benevolence on the one hand, and of grateful deference on the other, be taken at face value. Chesterfield, writing some twenty years after his period as lord lieutenant, maintained that 'the poor people in Ireland are used worse than negroes by their lords and masters'. 'A landlord in Ireland', Arthur Young

---

[110] For these and other examples see Connolly, 'Ag Déanamh Commanding'.

[111] Once again the points in this and the succeeding paragraphs are discussed in greater detail in Connolly, *Religion, Law and Power*, 133–43.

reported, 'can scarcely invent an order which a servant, labourer or cottier dares to refuse to execute. Nothing satisfies him but an unlimited submission.'[112] Such comments by outsiders suggest that relations between different social levels, in a society marked by a past history of revolt and conquest, and by continuing sectarian divisions, had an edge of brutality not seen in contemporary England. But there are also indications that demonstrations of reciprocity of the kind organized by Dudley Cosby and Lord Dartry were not wholly without meaning. When Cosby's son Pole lost a legal action against a neighbouring gentleman in 1738, his rival's tenants tried to stage a celebratory procession in the town of Stradbally, 'with garland, piper and long dance', only to be driven away in a violent assault by Cosby's tenants. In County Longford in 1818, likewise, tenants celebrated a legal victory of a popular local landlord: 'the neighbourhood for miles around appeared studded with fires . . . the town being brilliantly illuminated, the numerous and respectable inhabitants paraded the streets, expressing their heartfelt joy on the occasion.'[113]

These were special occasions. The most frequent and intimate interactions across social boundaries were those between household servants and their employers. Here an unusually full set of household letters by Edward Synge, bishop of Elphin, covering the period 1746–52, provides an insight into the day-to-day reality that lay behind the rhetoric of the period. The correspondence shows the bishop fulfilling both the roles expected of him, as paternalist and disciplinarian. An old servant past being able to work was to have 'a small annual allowance', or else be sent from Dublin to Elphin, 'where she may be more easily supported, and perhaps have a better chance for something like health'. 'The son of a favourite labourer' was to get medical attention. A local artisan was to be consulted about the repair of a well, despite being 'not what he was . . . that the honest man, who has been so useful to me, may not feel the pain of being passed by'. An incompetent servant was to be sidelined but was to keep his title of butler, 'to save his credit that he may not appear degraded'. When he seemed to baulk at the arrangement, however, Synge quickly made clear that the alternative was for the man to leave his household, and there are several other references to the summary dismissal of drunken or otherwise unsatisfactory servants. Writing to his daughter, the bishop justified his 'strict and severe' management of servants: 'harshness . . . I find necessary to keep them in order.' Yet harshness did not mean that he was in fact served as he wished. Instead his letters contain endless complaints. One servant 'is a glum, conceited fool and plagues, I won't say frets, me every day of my life'. He was eventually replaced. But the housekeeper, a Mrs Heep, remained a trial. 'She lies a bed till eight or nine, then saunters

---

[112] Chesterfield to Bishop of Waterford, 1 Oct. 1764 (*The Letters of Philip Dormer Stanhope, 4th Earl of Chesterfield*, ed. Bonamy Dobree (London, 1932), vi. 2617); Young, *A Tour in Ireland*, ii. 54.
[113] Connolly, *Religion, Law and Power*, 139; W. S. Mason (ed.), *A Statistical Account or Parochial Survey of Ireland* (Dublin, 1814–19), iii. 366–7.

about as she pleases.' 'Her carelessness appears in every thing . . . when I speak to her she answers with sullenness, that she does all she can, and this with an air of turning me off.' If employers sought to maintain their superiority with a carefully calculated mixture of severity and benevolence, it seems clear, some at least among their subordinates responded with their own, equally calculated strategy of obstruction, petty cheating, and dumb insolence.[114]

The recipient of the bishop's letters, his daughter Alicia, 13 when the correspondence begins, remained in her father's Dublin home, located not in the newly fashionable eastern quarter but in Kevin Street, on the edge of the working-class Liberties area. Synge's prescriptions for managing relations with what he called 'your low neighbours . . . the rabble among whom you do and I must live' are again revealing. When, in 1750, local weavers took to the streets to demonstrate against imported cloth, he cautioned Alicia against appearing at the window in clothes that might give offence. However she was to leave his window curtains in place for 'I had rather have the windows broke than appear to yield to a rabble'. The following year one of the servants shot and killed a local butcher as he tried to rob the house. This in turn provoked an attack by a mob led by the dead man's father and brother. Synge praised the courage displayed by members of the household, and advised them to continue to appear 'stout and fearless'. But he also advised his daughter to consent to the release of the imprisoned father and brother. 'I had rather have you the object of love than of fear, among your low neighbours, and they seldom distinguish between justice and cruelty. Nothing conciliates them so much as compassion deserved or not.' Implicit negotiations of this kind across the boundary between rulers and ruled are less visible than other features of the society: the gallows, the convict transport, and the whipping post on one side, or on the other the Jacobitism of the early decades, the outbreaks of agrarian violence in the 1760s and after, above all the events of 1798. But they nevertheless have a place, as glimpses of a more complex and varied pattern of day-to-day relationships, across the century as a whole, than can be revealed by looking solely at its bloody and rancorous conclusion.

---

[114] *The Synge Letters: Bishop Edward Synge to his Daughter Alicia, Roscommon to Dublin 1746–1752*, ed. M.-L. Legg (Dublin, 1996), 69, 161, 184, 224, 227, 257, 289, 295, 383.

9

Atlantic Island

CATTLE AND LINEN

The Irish economy recovered rapidly from the effects of the civil war of 1689–91. The conflict itself had been both shorter and less indiscriminately destructive than that of 1641–53. Harvests in the 1690s were generally good, at a time of food shortages—and consequent high demand for Irish exports—elsewhere in western Europe. The last great surge of migration, particularly from Scotland to Ulster, brought a substantial inward flow of capital. The exchange rate against the Scottish and English pound was also favourable. The prohibition of exports of woollen cloth, effective from mid-1699, was a serious short-term blow. But the general economic downturn that had occurred by 1701, reflected in a one-third decline in exports generally compared to 1698, was mainly due to the passing of what had been a period of exceptionally favourable conditions. The War of the Spanish Succession, beginning in 1702, once again cut off foreign markets, forcing prices downwards. A poor harvest in 1709 brought hardship though not, apparently, famine.[1]

Conditions improved over the next decade, particularly when the war ended with the peace of Utrecht in 1713. In 1720–1, however, a combination of poor harvests and economic recession in England following the collapse of the South Sea Company brought mass unemployment and starvation. Recorded burials in the Church of Ireland parish of Donnybrook just outside Dublin almost doubled between 1719–20 and 1720–1. In Derry the Church of Ireland bishop witnessed a graphic display of the desperation of the local poor:

One of my coach horses, by accident, was killed in a field within view of my house. Before the skin could be taken off, my servants were surrounded with 50 or 60 of the neighbouring cottagers, who brought axes and cleavers, and immediately divided the carcass, every man carrying home his proper dividend for food to their respective families.

---

[1] L. M. Cullen in *NHI*, iv. 138. The best general account of economic development in eighteenth-century Ireland is David Dickson, *New Foundations: Ireland 1660–1800* (Dublin, 2000), ch. 4, now reinforced by his superb regional study *Old World Colony: Cork and South Munster 1630–1830* (Cork, 2005). See also Cullen's two chapters in *NHI*, iv; L. M. Cullen, *An Economic History of Ireland since 1660* (London, 1972), chs. 2–4; idem, *Anglo-Irish Trade 1660–1800* (Manchester, 1968); Thomas Truxes, *Irish-American Trade 1660–1783* (Cambridge, 1989).

Famine, accompanied by typhoid fever and dysentery, returned during 1728–9, following a series of poor harvests in 1726, 1727, and 1728. The effects of excess mortality, combined with a surge in emigration to the American colonies, were seen in a slight but definite fall in a population that had been rising steadily, if slowly, since the 1650s.[2]

Recurrent crises of subsistence, along with slow overall economic growth, help to explain the pervasive sense of malaise that colours economic writing and thinking from early eighteenth-century Ireland. Contemporaries dwelt obsessively on what they saw as the obstacles blocking any prospect of progress: restrictions on the export of wool and livestock and on trade with the colonies; the burden of taxation; excessive spending on foreign luxuries; the drain on the kingdom's economy from pensions paid out of Irish revenues to English courtiers and clients of the great, as well as from rents remitted to absentee landlords. The timing of the most notable texts closely followed the vicissitudes of a fragile economy. The famine of 1728–9 inspired Jonathan Swift's most notorious pamphlet. *A Modest Proposal for Preventing the Children of Poor People from being a Burthen to their Parents or Country* (1729) set out in elaborate and specific detail a scheme to have the poor breed and fatten their children as food for the rich.

As to our city of Dublin, shambles may be appointed for this purpose, in the most convenient parts of it, and butchers, we may be assured, will not be wanting; although I rather recommend buying the children alive, and dressing them hot from the knife, as we do roasting pigs.

How far Swift's savagery was directed at England, for its oppression of Ireland, how far at the Irish themselves, for the degraded condition to which they had let themselves be reduced, and how far at humanity as a whole, remains open to debate. Quite probably there were elements of all three, reflecting the ambivalence of a reluctant patriot towards the homeland he saw as a prison.[3] The same crisis produced a more conventional polemic, Thomas Prior's *A List of the Absentees of Ireland*, which put the total sum paid in rents and remittances to persons living outside the kingdom at more than £600,000 a year.[4] Later, between 1735 and 1737, George Berkeley, Church of Ireland bishop of Cloyne, published the three parts of his *Querist*, in which a succession of leading questions conducted readers to the conclusion that Ireland's only hope of escaping from poverty was to opt out of the international economic system. Instead it should become 'a society or nation of human creatures, clad in woollen cloths and stuffs, eating

[2] William Nicolson to Archbishop Wake, 2 June 1721 (Dublin Municipal Library, Gilbert MS 27, 287). For a general account see James Kelly, 'Harvest and Hardship: Famine and Scarcity in Ireland in the Late 1720s', *Studia Hibernica*, 26 (1991–2), 65–105, who also cites the data from Donnybrook (pp. 65–6).

[3] *A Modest Proposal for Preventing the Children of Poor People from being a Burthen to their Parents or Country* (Dublin, 1729), 8. For the basis of Swift's ambivalence towards Ireland, see Ch. 6 above.

[4] Thomas Prior, *A List of the Absentees of Ireland* (2nd edn., Dublin, 1729), 9–19.

good bread, beef and mutton, drinking ale, mead and cider . . . depending on no foreign imports either for food or rainment'.[5]

The economic miseries of post-Revolution Ireland reached a peak in the winter of 1740–1. At the beginning of 1740 cold of a severity outside living memory gripped the whole of western Europe. Lakes and rivers froze. At Portumna on the Shannon a party of gentry gathered on the ice to roast a whole sheep, and watch a hurling match between two gentlemen's teams. But festive enjoyment of novelty soon gave way to crisis. The immediate effects were at their worst in the towns, where frozen water wheels brought manufacturing to a standstill, and transport of food and fuel came to a halt. As the frost receded, however, it became clear that the real damage had been the devastation of a large part of the potato crop, the main food of the rural poor. Abnormally low rainfall throughout the spring and summer dealt a further blow. Stocks of cattle and sheep, already depleted by the winter freeze, suffered further, as beasts died for lack of fodder and survivors failed to produce calves and lambs. Meanwhile drought severely depleted the corn harvest. By the winter of 1740–1 the country was in the grip of famine. Malnutrition in turn created the conditions for epidemic disease: smallpox, dysentery, and what was probably typhus. By the time of the adequate though not exceptional harvest of autumn 1741 the kingdom had lost between 13 and 20 per cent of its population, an estimated 310,000–480,000 people, a death rate equal to that caused by the much more famous, and much more protracted, Great Famine of 1845–50.[6]

How is this sequence of disasters, and the miserable level of poverty that lay behind it, to be explained? For contemporaries one obvious answer lay in the restrictions imposed on Irish trade as a consequence of its political subordination to Great Britain. The cattle acts of 1663 and 1671 had closed the English market to Irish livestock. The navigation acts prohibited direct trade with Britain's colonies. The woollen act had choked off a flourishing export trade. Modern historians, by contrast, have emphasized the extent to which these successive restrictions redirected rather than stifled economic activity. The ban on live cattle exports to Great Britain diverted enterprise towards the more capital- and labour-intensive business of exporting beef, pork, and butter, laying the basis for a steadily expanding provisions trade. Although woollen cloth could no longer be exported, there was still an extensive manufacturing industry, concentrated in the towns of Munster and Leinster, that supplied the greater part of the domestic market. Meanwhile the rapid growth of an export-based linen manufacture provided an alternative outlet for capital and entrepreneurial initiative.[7] Commercial

---

[5] Joseph Johnston, *Bishop Berkeley's Querist in Historical Perspective* (Dundalk, 1970), 135, query 123.

[6] David Dickson, *Arctic Ireland: The Extraordinary Story of the Great Frost and Forgotten Famine of 1740–41* (Belfast, 1997).

[7] The case against seeing economic restrictions as an important cause of Irish underdevelopment is argued with particular force by Cullen: see above, n. 1. See also T. M. Devine, 'The English

restrictions imposed from London must also be balanced against the gains that flowed from the English connection: the free entry of linen into England itself, unrestricted exports of Irish provisions to the West Indies, the bounties that from 1743 gave Irish linen a competitive edge in the American market. Overall it could be argued that Ireland was a net beneficiary from its place within a tightly regulated British colonial system. These benefits, however, were to become apparent only from the mid-eighteenth century onwards. In the decades after 1688 it seems perverse to suggest that the cutting off of two of the most obvious sources of profit for hard-pressed Irish farmers and manufacturers, English demand for food and European demand for woollen cloth, did not have a negative effect.

A second popular explanation for Ireland's recurrent economic problems was the character of its landlord class. Contemporaries wrote critically of the rapacity with which Irish landowners extracted rents from their tenants, their absenteeism and neglect of their estates, and their ruinous indulgence in imported luxuries. Later writers, particularly in the aftermath of the bitter agrarian conflicts of the nineteenth century, willingly drew on such complaints to support the image of a parasitic proprietorial class, whose greed and oppression soaked up resources and destroyed incentives. Modern research makes clear that Irish landlords in the late seventeenth and eighteenth centuries were more economically active than was previously recognized. Throughout the country proprietors invested in roads, canals, and collieries, laid out model villages, encouraged the spread of spinning and weaving, and experimented with new farming methods. Such efforts cannot always be taken at face value: much-vaunted experiments with novel plants or the reshaping of landscape could turn out on inspection to have more to do with aesthetic enhancement, or a dilettantish curiosity, than with economic improvement.[8] But the hostile stereotype of the parasitic rentier, partly contemporary and partly of later manufacture, is no longer possible to maintain.

A more convincing analysis of the contribution of landlords to Ireland's economic weakness concentrates less on their entrepreneurial shortcomings than on their lack of effective power. The financial position of many left little scope for economic innovation. Fortunes made in the seventeenth century sometimes rested on shaky foundations. The debt-ridden history of the eighteenth-century earls of Donegall, descendants of Sir Arthur Chichester, provides a striking example of the long-term difficulties that arose when military and political service brought broad acres into hands unequipped with the capital to develop

---

Connection and Irish and Scottish Development in the Eighteenth Century', in T. M. Devine and David Dickson (eds.), *Ireland and Scotland 1600–1850* (Edinburgh, 1983), 12–29.

[8] For a general survey of Irish landlord performance, L. J. Proudfoot, 'Spatial Transformation and Social Agency: Property, Society and Improvement *c*.1700 to *c*.1900', in B. J. Graham and L. J. Proudfoot (eds.), *A Historical Geography of Ireland* (London, 1993), 219–57. For scepticism as to the real value of much of what passed for 'improvement' see T. C. Barnard, *Making the Grand Figure: Lives and Possessions in Ireland 1641–1770* (London, 2004), 222–5.

them.[9] Even those better placed to contemplate long-term strategies of economic development, moreover, were constrained by the absence in most parts of Ireland of an equivalent to the English tenant farmer: a yeoman class with the resources to rent, stock, and manage a substantial holding as a profitable commercial venture. Instead landlords unwilling to undertake the risky and uncongenial task of letting directly to an impoverished peasantry leased their estates in large blocks to middlemen who would then sublet at a profit to an occupying tenantry. In the first half of the eighteenth century, when substantial tenants were difficult to come by and hard economic times made it necessary to trade future rents for the immediate benefit of large entry fines, such leases frequently ran for fifty years or more. The middlemen who benefited from such circumstances, like the landlords themselves, do not wholly deserve their poor historical reputation. Standing above a subsistence-level peasantry, they could play an important role in providing capital (for example, by letting out milch cows in dairying areas) and coordinating economic activity.[10] Their long dominance did, however, mean that most Irish landlords were unable to take on the role of active managers of their lands, even if they had wished to do so.

Commercial restrictions and a weak landlord class can thus be seen as playing some part in the economic malaise of early and mid-eighteenth-century Ireland. But there are also other, weightier explanations. First, and most obviously, Ireland had begun the seventeenth century as a thinly populated and underdeveloped society on the western edge of Europe. Even in the absence of a political connection with Great Britain, this low starting point, combined with physical proximity, would probably have ensured that its development was dominated by its economically stronger neighbour, locking it into an inherently unequal pattern of trade in which it exchanged finished and half-finished products, such as beef, butter, and yarn, for manufactured goods. Lack of raw materials, once the abundant woodlands that had supported iron smelting had been exhausted, restricted the opportunities for manufacturing. The absence of a yeoman class, as well as causing problems for landlords, meant that agricultural production was small scale and undercapitalized. A further problem, specific to the early eighteenth century, was that Ireland was attempting to market its main source of wealth, agricultural produce, in a Europe where most societies were self-sufficient in food. England in the 1660s closed its markets to protect its own farmers—as it would presumably have done even more quickly if Ireland had not been another of its king's dominions. France, a major importer of Irish hides and butter in the 1680s, ceased thereafter to provide

      [9] Peter Roebuck, 'Landlord Indebtedness in Ulster in the Seventeenth and Eighteenth Centuries', in J. M. Goldstrom and L. A. Clarkson (eds.), *Irish Population, Economy and Society* (Oxford, 1981), 135–54.
      [10] David Dickson, 'Middlemen', in Thomas Bartlett and D. W. Hayton (eds.), *Penal Era and Golden Age: Essays in Irish History 1690–1800* (Belfast, 1979), 162–85. See also the detailed discussion of landlords and tenants in Dickson, *Old World Colony*, ch. 6.

a market for Irish livestock produce as its own farmers switched from grain to cattle.

The main reasons for Ireland's low level of economic development can thus be located in geography and market conditions rather than in its political circumstances or the behaviour of its ruling class. What is less clear is that a weak manufacturing sector and a poorly developed agriculture are themselves sufficient explanation for the levels of poverty that so appalled Swift, Berkeley, and others. Contemporaries in fact seem to have believed that the living standards of the Irish poor were desperate even by the standards of other peripheral and underdeveloped regions. William Nicolson, transferred from the bishopric of Carlisle to that of Derry in 1718, remarked that the 'dismal marks of hunger and want' he observed in the mountains of south Ulster on his first journey north exceeded anything he had seen in Picardy, Westphalia, or Scotland. George Whitefield, just returned from missionary work in America, was equally appalled by what he found in County Clare: 'If my parishioners at Georgia complain to me of hardships, I must tell them how the Irish live.'[11] The grim catalogue of famine, culminating in the loss of up to one-fifth of the population in 1740–1, bears out the image of a society in which a large section of the population clung to the barest subsistence.

At this point it becomes necessary to consider, not just the overall health of the Irish economy, but the internal distribution of wealth. For a poor society, Ireland was exceptionally commercialized. Already by 1700 its exports amounted to an estimated 6s. per head of population, compared to only 4s. in contemporary Scotland.[12] The 1720s and 1730s saw an expansion in the banking system, as well as a sharp increase in the circulation of paper money. The two main trading towns also expanded rapidly, with the population of Dublin rising from an estimated 62,000 in 1706 to 112,000 in 1744, and that of Cork from 17,600 to 37,500. Well-developed systems for extracting a high proportion of the country's output from its immediate producers and directing it towards external markets help to explain why the first half of the eighteenth century, despite a general background of slow economic growth, saw the birth in Ireland of a consumer society, in which middling and elite purchasers invested in a widening range of goods, and showed a new sensitivity to questions of style and fashion.[13] The peasant population itself had little contact with the money economy: they paid the rent for their small plots of land in labour, in livestock, or through some form of crop sharing. But their lives were nevertheless shaped by a market that efficiently sucked up the greater part of any surplus, beyond what was needed to maintain a bare subsistence, that they produced. Henry Boyle, no idealistic social

[11] For these and other comments see Connolly, *Religion, Law and Power*, 46.
[12] L. M. Cullen and T. C. Smout (eds.), *Comparative Aspects of Scottish and Irish Economic and Social History* (Edinburgh, n.d.), 5.
[13] This is the case argued in Barnard, *Making the Grand Figure*. Changing patterns of elite consumption are discussed later in this chapter.

reformer but speaker of the Irish Commons and for two decades the leading parliamentary manager for successive viceroys, admitted in 1747 that 'the bulk of the people in Ireland live so miserably that no two million of people besides of any country in Europe consume so little of the commodities which they raise themselves'.[14]

One vivid illustration of the extent to which the forces of commercialization reached into the lives of the rural poor is provided by the transformation of popular diet. The main food of the lower classes had long been milk and milk products. It was a diet made possible by the easy availability of grazing in a thinly populated landscape, and also by the absence of alternative sources of demand. By the early eighteenth century, on the other hand, more intensive and closely regulated use of land, rising internal demand for dairy products, and an expanding export trade in butter, all meant that milk, though still important in popular diet, was no longer so freely available. Instead what emerged was a new staple, the potato. Nutritious and easy to cultivate, yet low in status, difficult to transport, and hence of limited commercial value, it remained for the next century and a half the ideal food for a poor family in a rural economy dominated by external markets.[15]

Why did post-Restoration Ireland develop an economic system that so efficiently stripped the labouring population of so much of what they produced? One obvious answer would be the country's recent history of conquest and colonization. The Gaelic society overturned by the Tudor and Stuart conquest had itself been brutally exploitative. Nor is there any reason to believe that a victory for the Catholic Confederates in the 1640s, or the Jacobites in 1689–91, would have ushered in a golden age of the Irish peasant. In the Scottish Highlands the opportunities provided by expanding external markets, combined with the increased expenditure required by their integration into metropolitan elite society, transformed the indigenous elite from clan chiefs who measured their wealth in the number of followers they supported to capitalist landlords clearing their estates to make way for sheep. There is no evident reason to assume that a victorious Gaelic or Old English ruling class would have behaved any differently. Having said this, it remains likely that ethnic and religious divisions made New English landlords and middlemen even more ruthless than they would otherwise have been in their dealings with what they saw as a debased underclass.

A second, more speculative explanation would be that the sudden replacement of one economic system by another had left little room for the sort of customary entitlements that in other early modern societies protected the position of the rural poor. In Ulster English and Scottish tenantry, sharing with their landlords in the enterprise of creating a new society, or appealing to customs already

---

[14] 'Observations', *c*.1747 (PRONI D2707/A1/12/3).
[15] L. M. Cullen, *The Emergence of Modern Ireland 1600–1900* (London, 1981), 141–9.

existing in their region of origin, were able to establish a concept of 'tenant right', primarily recognition that a tenant possessed an interest in his holding that he was entitled to sell to a successor, but also implying a right to go on occupying the land concerned on reasonable terms.[16] Outside Ulster large tenants in some cases appealed to a similar concept, somewhat more loosely defined. Lower down the social scale, however, there is little indication that such customary restraints, or entitlements such as gleaning rights or access to woods and commons, played a significant role. Instead the rural poor were left exposed, to an unusual degree, to the full pressures of a rapidly developing market economy.[17]

The mass starvation of the years 1740–1 confirmed the continuing weakness of the Irish economy as it approached the mid-century. But it was nevertheless the result of an unusual concentration of ill luck. By the end of the 1730s there were in fact signs that Ireland was beginning to climb out of the depression that had produced such despair among thinkers like Swift and Berkeley. Total exports in 1740 were valued at £1.3 million, compared to £993,000 in 1730 and £815,000 in 1700. Thereafter this modest expansion gave way to a period of much more dramatic growth, continuing to the end of the century and beyond. Already by 1750 the value of exports had risen by nearly half, to £1.9 million. By 1770 the figure was over £3 million, and by 1790 it stood at £4.9 million.[18] Another calculation, inevitably somewhat speculative, suggests that between 1730 and 1776 national income more than doubled, rising from £15 million to £37.5 million, and that it was to double again, to £75 million, by 1815.[19]

One reason for this turnaround in Ireland's economic fortunes was the dramatic expansion of a new manufacturing industry, the spinning and weaving of linen from flax fibre. Sixteenth-century Ireland had already possessed an indigenous tradition of flax cultivation and market-oriented spinning and weaving. But it was the movement to Ulster of English and Scots settlers during the seventeenth century, bringing with them additional skills, capital, and commercial expertise, that provided the basis for commercial production, first evident on a significant scale in the 1670s and 1680s. In the period after 1688, at a time when the English parliament was able to use its increased power to force through legislation against Irish wool, linen had the great advantage that it threatened no major English interest; on the contrary British policy favoured a growth likely to reduce dependence on continental imports. In 1699 the treasury granted funds to the Huguenot émigré Samuel Lewis Crommelin to support a colony of weavers at Lisburn in County Antrim.[20] More importantly the English parliament agreed,

---

[16] M. W. Dowling, *Tenant Right and Agrarian Society in Ulster 1600–1870* (Dublin, 1999).

[17] This argument is developed in more detail in Connolly, *Religion, Law and Power*, 54–6.

[18] Unless otherwise stated, all figures on trade are taken from Cullen, *Anglo-Irish Trade*; Truxes, *Irish-American Trade*.

[19] Cullen in *NHI*, iv. 185–7.

[20] Crommelin's venture, once seen as laying the basis for the Ulster linen industry, has now been reassessed as a premature, though in the long run possibly valuable, attempt to promote the

in 1696, to remove the import duty on Irish linen. Over the next few decades this favoured status allowed Irish producers to take over the English market, eclipsing rival Dutch and German suppliers. Linen exports to Great Britain, accounting for more than 95 per cent of total Irish exports of the cloth, rose from 1.5 million yards in 1710 to 6 million by 1740, 20 million by 1770, and more than 33 million by 1790. Across the same period the share of total exports represented by hemp, flax, and linen rose from 8 to 57 per cent.

The second motor of Ireland's economic expansion, alongside an expanding English market for its linens, was the growth of the transatlantic economy. Here Ireland benefited from the specialization that accompanied an increasingly sophisticated pattern of exchange between constituent parts of the first British empire, and from the same framework of tight mercantilist regulation that had damaged its woollen industry. As European demand pushed up the price that West Indian planters could expect for their sugar, tobacco, and other colonial produce, it became uneconomic to divert land and labour to the production of food. Instead Irish exports of preserved beef, pork, butter, and fish became a staple part of the diet of the white population, while salted fish helped to meet the needs of the growing army of black slaves. Over time North American suppliers, geographically closer, took over much of the Caribbean food trade. But accumulated Irish expertise in pickling, salting, and packing perishable goods so as to survive the West Indian climate allowed its suppliers to retain a substantial share of the market for better-quality produce. In the North American colonies themselves, meanwhile, the high price of labour allowed imported cloth to compete effectively with the locally produced variety. The navigation acts of 1663 and after had limited Irish exports to the colonies to servants, horses, and provisions. But in 1705, in a hard-won concession, the English parliament legislated to permit direct exports of linen. A later act of 1717 allowed linen destined for America to enter England duty free, and the introduction from 1743 of a system of bounties on exports to the colonies ensured that the great bulk of Irish linen that crossed the Atlantic did so from English ports.

The huge growth of transatlantic trade, as the European powers built up their American colonies, was thus of central importance to what emerged as the two leading engines of Irish economic growth, the provisions trade and the linen manufacture. In the quarter-century up to 1776 transatlantic markets took 40 per cent of Ireland's beef exports, between 55 and 76 per cent of its pork exports, and 14 per cent of its butter. The proportion of linen exports crossing the Atlantic, likewise, rose from 11 per cent in 1751 to 21 per cent by the 1770s. In all shipments to the Caribbean and North America, whether sent directly from Irish ports or indirectly through England, accounted for around

manufacture of finer cloths: Brian Mackey, 'Overseeing the Foundation of the Irish Linen Industry: The Rise and Fall of the Crommelin Legend', in Brenda Collins and Philip Ollerenshaw (eds.), *The European Linen Industry in Historical Perspective* (Oxford, 2003), 99–121.

10 per cent of total Irish exports in the period 1732–56, and for around 16 per cent over the next two decades. This was significantly less than Ireland's trade with Great Britain, which accounted for more than half of all Irish exports in the 1740s and 1750s and more than three-quarters by the 1770s. On the other hand a significant proportion of the Irish beef, pork, and butter that was exported to France, Portugal, and Spain was also destined for these countries' overseas colonies. In particular the willingness of French planters, unlike their British counterparts, to include meat in the diet they allowed their slaves created a market for the poorest-quality Irish beef, from dairy cattle that had reached the end of their useful life. To these indirect exports via Europe, moreover, must be added the profitable trade developed by Cork and other southern ports in equipping and provisioning transatlantic shipping, as British and (in peacetime) other vessels took advantage of the last available landfall before the long voyage west.

The extent to which Ireland's improving economic fortunes depended on the wider framework provided by the British colonial system was evident also in the organization of this expanding overseas trade. London merchant houses and financiers provided much of the elaborate mechanism of credit and financial transfers essential to facilitate trade over such huge distances. The vessels involved were likewise mainly British. The navigation acts had been relaxed in 1731 to allow the direct import into Ireland of a range of colonial goods. But the main high-value Caribbean products, sugar and tobacco, could still be landed only in British ports, cutting off the possibility of a profitable two-way trade from Ireland. Instead the normal pattern was for British vessels to take on board provisions at Irish ports before making the westward leg of their voyage. The result was that the proportion of shipping using the country's ports that was registered in Ireland actually declined as overseas trade expanded, falling from just over a quarter in 1700 to just under an eighth in 1800. (The one noteworthy exception was the trade between Ulster and North America, where vessels carrying provisions and emigrants westward had a profitable return cargo in flaxseed, imported because the quality of linen produced in Ireland required that the plant be harvested before it had produced seed.) Here at least commercial restrictions can be seen to have had a real impact on Ireland's economic development. The wealth and resources of Ireland's merchant class should not be underestimated. The wealthiest Cork merchants, it has been calculated, gave their daughters dowries roughly equal to those common among the second rank of the region's landowners.[21] The leading commercial dynasties had an international reach, with members permanently established in the Caribbean, in Philadelphia or New York, or in the main ports of southern Europe. Some, like the La Touches of Dublin or the Blakes and Bellews of Galway, acquired their own slave plantations in the Caribbean.[22] But

---

[21] Dickson, *Old World Colony*, 163–6.
[22] Nini Rodgers, *Ireland, Slavery and Anti-Slavery 1612–1865* (Basingstoke, 2007), 159–60.

their role within the British commercial revolution remained a secondary, if well-rewarded one.

The centre of the provisions trade that lay at the heart of Ireland's economic expansion was a large crescent of rich grazing land, taking in substantial parts of the counties of Kerry, Cork, Limerick, and Waterford, with the port of Cork as its focal point. But the effects of Ireland's new role as larder for the Caribbean were felt far beyond this favoured hinterland, as its graziers bought in cattle reared in regions of poorer grassland to be fattened in preparation for slaughter. In County Sligo, for example, a local landlord later recalled that demand for store cattle from the grazing regions of south Munster had begun to be felt around 1720, creating new opportunities for profit, though only at the expense of clearing poor cottagers from their tillage-based smallholdings to make way for livestock. In the eastern counties, from Wexford up through Kilkenny and Kildare into Meath and Louth, the pattern of agriculture was different again, as a more favourable climate, combined with the expanding market provided by Dublin and other towns, encouraged a greater concentration on tillage. The growing interdependence of steadily more specialized agricultural zones was reflected in the increased volume of activity at fairs, and in the emergence of certain venues, such as Ballinasloe in County Galway and Mullingar in County Westmeath, as major centres of interregional exchange.

A parallel process of regional specialization accompanied the runaway growth of the linen manufacture. Like the provisions trade, this involved a variety of levels of economic activity. The raw material was flax, grown as a tillage crop, fermented under water ('retting'), then dried and beaten ('scutching') to extract the fibre. This heavy and malodorous work was done mainly by hand, although the first water-powered scutch mill opened near Belfast around 1740. The spinning of flax fibre into linen yarn was women's work, done on hand-driven spinning wheels. Weaving too was a home-based handicraft industry. The next stages of the process, by contrast, were large-scale industrial enterprises. The brown linen produced on handlooms was bleached white by being treated with chemicals and exposed to sunlight, then pounded ('beetling') over an extended period to produce a finish. From the 1720s water-powered beetling mills, along with engines for washing the cloth, began to replace hand finishing, contributing substantially to the huge increase in output achieved in the mid-eighteenth century. The technology of bleaching was also transformed, first from 1756 with the substitution of acid for soured buttermilk, then from 1785 by the use of chlorine gas, which for the first time allowed bleaching to continue all year round. Successive innovations thus placed the final stages of the process in the hands of an emerging class of substantial entrepreneurs deploying large amounts of fixed and circulating capital. But the enterprise also depended on a multiplicity of small-scale transactions as these entrepreneurs bought up the produce of independent weavers in the brown linen markets held across a large part of Ulster. To reduce the inevitable problems of quality control a state-run

Linen Board, created in 1711 and financed by the duties on imported linen and calico, employed sealmasters who inspected and stamped all linen offered for sale in public markets.[23]

The core of this increasingly important manufacturing enterprise lay in a relatively small region of east Ulster, comprising the northern half of County Armagh, with parts of adjoining counties. Half of the linen woven in late eighteenth-century Ulster, and most of the finer cloth, was produced in a triangle linking Belfast, Dungannon, and Armagh city. Weavers in this region were predominantly independent small producers, working up yarn produced in their own households or purchased on the market, then selling the finished product. However there were also journeymen weavers, employed in such households as extra hands, as well as poorer men reduced to weaving yarn supplied by a dealer who paid them by the piece.[24] Independent weavers commonly combined the trade with the holding of a small farm, as a means of insulating themselves against fluctuations in the price of both food and linen, so that over time Armagh and the surrounding district became a landscape of minutely subdivided holdings. Weaving was also important, though not dominant, in the economies of Counties Londonderry and Antrim, with the main centres of the trade in Londonderry and Ballymena.

If the weaving and finishing of cloth was largely confined to east Ulster, however, the spectacular rise of linen nevertheless transformed the economy of a much larger region. The labours of wives, daughters, and female servants in the cottages of the linen triangle soon failed to keep pace with the needs of the looms concentrated there. In addition there was from an early stage a large export trade in linen yarn. In response spinning, along with some weaving of coarse cloth, quickly spread into the other counties of Ulster, and also across the northern parts of both Connacht and Leinster. Arthur Young, visiting Leitrim in 1776, found six bleach greens in operation, and 'many weavers', while 'spinning is universal in all the cabins'. In neighbouring Sligo there was as yet 'very little weaving . . . but a little scattered spinning everywhere; the women earn 3d. or 4d a day, by a hank a day'.[25] Cash earnings on this scale permitted households to sustain themselves on what would otherwise have been inadequate holdings, and even allowed some modest consumption beyond the needs of bare subsistence. The work of the spinners in turn created a demand for flax, a labour-intensive tillage crop ideally suited to cultivation on small holdings, where it could be sown

[23] Compare the negative verdict of H. D. Gribbon, 'The Irish Linen Board 1711–1828', in Cullen and Smout, *Comparative Aspects*, 77–87, with the more favourable assessment of W. H. Crawford, 'The Evolution of the Linen Trade in Ulster before Industrialisation', *IESH* 15 (1988), 32–53.

[24] With the advent of machine spinning of linen yarn after 1826 weavers were increasingly to work under a putting-out system that reduced them to the status of employees on piece work. However Crawford rejects suggestions that this process was already under way to a significant degree in the eighteenth century ('Evolution of the Linen Trade', 32–7).

[25] Arthur Young, *A Tour in Ireland* (London, 1780), i. 238, 233.

in rotation with potatoes and oats. In addition agriculture in these peripheral counties benefited from the rising market for butter, beef, and oats in east Ulster, where the part-time labour of farmer weavers on their subdivided holdings was no longer sufficient to feed a densely concentrated population.

The self-evident benefits of a vibrant rural industry encouraged landlords and other would-be improvers, aided by the Linen Board, to look for ways of extending linen spinning and weaving into other regions, often by means of imported colonies of Ulster tenants, doubly attractive as skilled workers and as Protestants. The most celebrated example was at Monivea in County Galway, where the landowner, Robert French, imported workers from Ulster to establish a bleach green alongside the model village and charter school he had established on his estate. By 1776 there were 36 looms and 373 spinning wheels operating on his lands.[26] Such ventures attracted praise, but generally failed to make a significant impact on the regional economy. The one major exception was two regions on the south coast, Carbery in west Cork and Corkaguiny in Kerry, where flax became a major tillage crop, permitting the rapid growth in the second half of the century of both spinning and weaving. In the west Cork region alone some 2,000 looms were at work by 1815.[27] To contemporaries the concentration of profitable linen manufacture in Ulster was evidence of the superior industry and discipline of the region's mainly Protestant inhabitants. Modern accounts, by contrast, emphasize the greater attraction of linen in a region less well suited geographically to participate fully in the alternative business of the provisions trade. Seen in this light the concentration of linen weaving and finishing in east Ulster was a further example of the regional specialization that characterized a more developed Irish economy.

The contrast between the north-east and other regions should not in any case be overstated. Efforts to disseminate linen weaving may not have succeeded. But parts of the south developed their own important manufacturing enterprises. The provisions trade of Cork and other ports, with its giant slaughterhouses and packing factories, was itself an example of a significant industrial enterprise, whose efficiencies of scale and specialized techniques allowed it to retain its place against strong North American competition in the Caribbean market. Wool, though denied an export market after 1699, remained a major source of employment, spun into yarn in the countryside of Munster and Leinster and then either exported or sent to the towns to be woven into cloth for domestic consumption. Irish brewing in the first half of the century had been dispersed across a large number of small-scale enterprises, and its output had a poor reputation. By the end of the century, however, production was beginning to be concentrated in a smaller number of large-scale enterprises, of which the most important were

[26] Denis Cronin, *A Galway Gentleman in the Age of Improvement: Robert French of Monivea 1716–79* (Dublin, 1995), 28–33.
[27] Dickson, *Old World Colony*, 203–9, 396–8.

Beamish and Crawford in Cork, followed by the Dublin brewery established in 1759 by Arthur Guinness. Meanwhile rising urban demand, especially from Dublin, supplemented by new bounties on inland transport, had encouraged a major growth from the 1760s in flour milling. The new mills were substantial, three to five storeys high, and the machinery they employed represented the most extensive application of water power so far seen in Ireland.[28] In addition growing prosperity, particularly in the second half of the century, created a widening market for handicraft production of luxury goods: gold, silver, and glassware, coachbuilding, and the working of silk and other fine fabrics.

Flour milling and brewing, representing the application of large-scale factory production and advanced technology to the processing of agricultural produce, prefigured what were in the long term to be the main areas of strength of Irish manufacturing industry outside the north-east. What seized the public imagination in the late eighteenth century, however, was something different: the new technology of machine spinning that was laying the foundations for the development of factory-based mass production in England and Scotland. Flax fibre broke too easily to be spun by the machinery available at this stage. Instead the focus of the new technology, as in Great Britain, was to be cotton. The first water-powered spinning mills appeared in the 1770s. The early development of the industry was for a time distorted when parliament, concerned to reduce industrial unrest in the capital, offered financial support exclusively to factories located outside a ten-mile radius of Dublin. The most prominent product of the policy of diffusion was Prosperous in County Kildare, established around 1780. Its founder Richard Brooke secured grants and loans of £36,000 on a promise to resettle 2,000 Dublin artisans on the site, but the venture collapsed in 1786. Instead the main centres of the Irish cotton industry were Dublin, which took around half of all cotton wool and yarn imports in the 1790s, and Cork and Belfast, which took a quarter each. The Dublin and Cork enterprises, however, were mainly finishing and printing works, with manufacture concentrated in Belfast, which by 1800 had eight of Ireland's sixteen cotton-spinning mills. The mills were initially water powered. However a new spinning mill that opened in Lisburn in 1790 installed a steam engine soon after, and by 1811 there were fifteen steam-driven mills within a ten-mile radius of Belfast.

Despite this early promise, the Irish cotton industry was to have a short history. Output grew rapidly in the decade after 1800. Thereafter, however, the industry entered a period of growing difficulty. Even if cheaper Irish labour could compensate for the lack of local supplies of coal, the concentration of resources taking place in the cotton mills of Lancashire and western Scotland was by now producing economies of scale against which no adjacent region could compete successfully. For Belfast's cotton manufacturers, representing the best capitalized

[28] L. M. Cullen, 'Eighteenth-Century Flour Milling in Ireland', *IESH* 4 (1977), 5–25; Patrick Lynch and John Vaizey, *Guinness's Brewery and the Irish Economy* (Cambridge, 1960), 39–72.

and most technologically advanced section of the industry, rescue came in the form of new processes that made possible the machine spinning of linen as well as cotton, allowing them to transfer their capital and resources into an area in which they had a strong comparative advantage. Elsewhere the recession of 1825–6, following closely on the removal of the last tariffs on imports from Great Britain in 1821, largely wiped out Irish cotton spinning and printing. In the 1790s, however, none of this could be predicted. In the long run Ireland's potential as a centre of heavy industry was to be inescapably limited by its lack of significant deposits of coal and iron. At this stage, however, water power still greatly exceeded steam as the driving force of industrialization, and there seemed to be no reason why Ireland, with its wide rivers, abundant rainfall, and even more abundant supplies of cheap labour, should not be well placed to join in the new opportunities being opened up by the 'Manchester manufactories'.[29]

GRAIN AND POTATOES

The soaring agricultural exports, and the urban and industrial growth, of the mid- and late eighteenth century did not by any means eliminate the stark poverty that had so appalled earlier visitors to Ireland. The cabins of the labouring poor, Arthur Young reported in 1776, were 'the most miserable looking hovels that can well be conceived', single-roomed dwellings with walls of mud kneaded with straw, without either windows or a chimney to let out the smoke from the continuous turf fire. Many of their inhabitants went barefoot, and 'so ragged that their nakedness is scarcely covered'. Their diet consisted almost exclusively of potatoes and milk.[30] By this time, however, these labourers and smallholders were only one part of a more complex rural social structure. In the first half of the eighteenth century the dominant group, over most of the countryside, had been a labouring peasantry, renting land in partnerships which gave each family control of a few acres, and often paying all or part of their rents in labour. As agricultural profits rose, however, this uniform peasant class began to break up. On the one hand there emerged the independent small tenant, still directly involved in the hard toil of agricultural work, but possessing the livestock and other resources to take an individual holding of 25 acres or more and to pay rent in cash rather than labour. On the other there was a growing labouring class. Most continued to hold small plots of land. Some performed an agreed number of days' work

[29] J. J. Monaghan, 'The Rise and Fall of the Belfast Cotton Industry', *IHS* 3 (1942), 1–17; David Dickson, 'Aspects of the Rise and Decline of the Irish Cotton Industry', in Cullen and Smout (eds.), *Comparative Aspects*, 100–11. For the argument that the Belfast industry was competitive in terms of costs and the scale of capital investment, and that the transfer of resources to linen was in pursuit of comparative advantage rather than a confession of failure, see Frank Geary, 'The Rise and Fall of the Belfast Cotton Industry: Some Problems', *IESH* 8 (1981), 39–48.

[30] Young, *A Tour in Ireland*, ii. 47–8.

for a farmer or landlord in exchange for sufficient ground to provide a potato crop that would feed a family, and space to keep one or two cattle. Others, though working for cash, invested the greater part of their earnings in renting a similar small potato garden, under the system known as conacre. In both cases, however, their true position was of a rural proletariat, exchanging their labour for the means of subsistence. A further indication of the marginal position of this group in the new order was the appearance of the *spailpín* or migrant labourer travelling from regions such as west Cork and Kerry, Connemara, or Donegal, to seek seasonal employment in the richer lands further east.

Even for those at the lower levels of this more complex social hierarchy, conditions by the second half of the century had significantly improved. The labouring poor of the Irish countryside were still exceptionally deprived in terms of material consumption. But they no longer lived, as their grandparents had done, in the shadow of famine. There were further harvest failures, notably in 1755–6 and 1782–4, but these no longer led to widespread loss of life. Increased imports of grain compensated for local shortfalls, and improved communications permitted the transport of food to the worst-hit areas. Houses of industry and other official institutions, supplemented by private charity, provided emergency relief to the worst affected. Most important of all, more of the poor had sufficient resources of their own to allow them to survive a period of dearth. Already by 1760 the County Sligo landowner Charles O'Hara noted his own lack of concern at a wet season that fifteen years earlier would have caused 'dreadful apprehensions'. 'A family now has a better bottom than formerly. . . The lower class of people grow more above small accidents.'[31] Indeed the Irish poor, for all their material deprivation, may well have enjoyed greater physical well-being than the apparently more favoured labouring classes of other parts. A survey of Irishmen recruited in 1778–82 to the army of the East India Company, a brutal service attracting only the poorest on either side of the Irish Sea, shows that they were on average taller than their English comrades and reached full adult height at an earlier age.[32]

By the time of this survey Irish agriculture had entered a new phase of development, once again with significant long-term implications for the welfare, and ultimately the very survival, of the Irish poor. The dramatic economic expansion of the mid-eighteenth century, taking place at a time when Irish livestock products were excluded from Great Britain, had depended instead on rising demand in European and Atlantic markets. In 1768, however, the British

[31] Notes on the development of County Sligo by Charles O'Hara (NLI MS 20,397), *sub* 1760. For late eighteenth-century harvest failures and their management see David Dickson, 'The Gap in Famines? A Useful Myth?', in E. M. Crawford (ed.), *Famine: The Irish Experience* (Edinburgh, 1989), 96–111; James Kelly, 'Scarcity and Poor Relief in Eighteenth-Century Ireland: The Subsistence Crisis of 1782–4', *IHS* 38 (1992), 38–62.

[32] Joel Mokyr and Cormac Ó Gráda, 'The Height of Irishmen and Englishmen in the 1770s: Some Evidence from the East India Company Army Records', *ECI* 4 (1989), 83–92.

government, faced with increased demand and rising prices, lifted the ban on Irish
livestock, meat, and animal products. The initial response from Irish producers
was muted. In 1775 only one-fifth of Irish beef exports went to Great Britain.
From the 1780s, however, transatlantic demand began to weaken, as North
American producers made new inroads into Caribbean markets. Continental
demand seems also to have contracted, and from 1793 war between Britain and
France disrupted exports to mainland Europe. Positive and negative pressures
combined to produce a dramatic reorientation, in which Irish agricultural exports
became an important part of the support required by the urban and industrial
expansion beginning to take place in England, Wales, and Scotland. By 1800
83 per cent of beef, 79 per cent of butter, and 86 per cent of pork exported
from Ireland went to Great Britain. The change of market also brought a shift
in emphasis, from the cow to the pig. Beef exports in the 1790s were around
one-fifth lower than they had been in the 1760s, and butter had risen only
modestly. Pork exports, on the other hand, were three times what they had been
thirty years earlier.

The other novel feature of the switch to a predominantly British market
was the emergence of demand for grain as well as livestock. Ireland from the
1730s to the 1770s was a net importer of grain. By the 1750s, however, rising
demand both at home and abroad helped to make tillage more attractive. In
1758 parliament acted to secure the food supplies of the expanding capital by
instituting a system of bounties on the transfer of grain and flour to Dublin. In
1784 it supplemented already rising demand from the other side of the Irish Sea
with a corn law sponsored by John Foster, chancellor of the Irish exchequer, that
offered a subsidy to corn exports. Exports of cereal and flour rose from just under
10,000 tons in the five years to 1778 to 37,000 across a similar period twenty
years later. Observers in the first half of the century had frequently pointed to the
dominance of livestock as a prime cause of Irish poverty and underdevelopment.
Modern studies suggest that the swings between pasture and tillage were never
as extreme as alarmists suggested. But the displacement of small-scale cultivators
to make way for large-scale stock rearing undoubtedly constituted a negative
by-product of the agrarian growth achieved in the first half of the century. From
the 1750s, on the other hand, an expansion in arable farming, for both home
and external markets, boosted the demand for agricultural labour and improved
the prospects of the multiplicity of holdings too small to engage in efficient
stock rearing.

The late eighteenth-century revival of tillage was closely linked to two other
developments. The first was a sharp rise in population. In the mid-1740s,
following the demographic disasters of 1728–9 and 1740–1, population was
no higher, and probably slightly lower, than it had been three decades earlier.
By 1791, on the other hand, numbers had more than doubled, to almost 4.5
million. By the time of the first complete official census, in 1821, they would reach
6.8 million. The full causes of this growth, unparalleled in eighteenth-century

Europe, remain unclear. The average age at marriage was apparently low by European standards. But this seems to have been the case well before the population began to rise spectacularly. Instead limited parish register evidence suggests that the great change was a fall in mortality, in particular infant and child mortality, from mid-century. This may in turn have been due to rising living standards, to the reduced virulence of smallpox, thanks to the spread of the risky but effective practice of inoculation, or to a combination of the two. The result was to remove the lid from what had up to then been a classic 'high-pressure' demographic system of high birth rates balanced by equally high mortality. There may also have been a certain rise in fertility, as more intensive employment of women in farming reduced the contraceptive effect of extended breast-feeding.[33]

Rising population and expanded tillage in turn acted to consolidate the position of the potato in the diet of the poor. On the one hand grain was now priced beyond their reach. On the other the potato fitted neatly into a regime of intensive tillage. It was a means of preparing the soil for a corn crop. And it could also, when labourers received their wages in fallow land set aside as potato ground, allow under-capitalized tillage farmers to secure the extra labour needed on their holdings without having to pay cash. Agricultural technique, market forces, and population growth thus interacted in what was, for the moment, a benign circle. When the circle was broken, first with a further change in market forces after 1815, then, from 1845, with the collapse of the potato crop, the consequences were to be disastrous.

IMPROVEMENT AND ENLIGHTENMENT?

The surge of economic growth that began in the 1740s and continued into the early nineteenth century transformed the physical appearance of town and countryside alike. In the rural landscape the most immediately noticeable change would have been the enclosure, sometimes by stone walls but more commonly by hedge-topped ditches, of what had been previously open or only lightly partitioned countryside. Although the general nature of this process is clear, the details are often obscure. In the tillage areas of Munster and Leinster enclosure was already under way in the seventeenth century and was largely complete by the mid-eighteenth. In the main areas of medieval English settlement this new field pattern would have obliterated the large open fields parcelled out in long narrow strips that had been characteristic of manorial agriculture. The best

---

[33] For an up-to-date review of an often technical literature see William Macafee, 'The Pre-Famine Population of Ireland: A Reconsideration', in Brenda Collins, Philip Ollerenshaw, and Trevor Parkhill (eds.), *Industry, Trade and People in Ireland 1650–1950* (Belfast, 2005), 69–86. The precise importance of inoculation continues to be debated. For the latest assessment see Dickson, *Old World Colony*, 308–9.

grazing land in Munster and east Connacht was also enclosed early, though in larger fields than was common in tillage regions. There was no reason in principle why land so enclosed, in any of these areas, could not be taken in partnership by several small tenants, perhaps introducing their own temporary boundaries within the larger permanent demarcations. But in practice enclosure may well have been associated in many cases with a shift from such partnerships to a single occupying tenant. In large parts of the west and north, on the other hand, the holding of large tracts of land in partnership, with individual plots being allocated as tillage and meadow and shared access to rough pasture, remained common, being phased out only gradually during the late eighteenth and early nineteenth centuries.[34] In other cases again enclosure took place where areas of mountain or other marginal land had previously been left open but were now, in an era of more intensive exploitation, fenced off for individual use.

A second striking change was the creation of a fully developed road network. The first major improvement came with the development from the 1730s of a turnpike system, permitting road maintenance to be financed by a charge on users. However this mainly benefited the most commercial areas, extending northwards along the coast from Dublin into eastern Ulster, and west into the midlands and central Munster. The construction and maintenance of public roads was still the responsibility of individual parishes, relying on the six days' unpaid labour a year required from inhabitants under the highways act of 1615. From 1710, however, a series of acts allowed grand juries to order work on roads and bridges, paid for by a charge on the barony or county. An act of 1765 abolished the day labour system and transferred the main responsibility for construction and upkeep to the grand juries. Although contemporaries complained of jobbery in the placing of contracts, and vested interests in the siting of roads, county management permitted both a higher degree of planning and more intensive investment. Already by 1776 the density of the road network moved the normally censorious Arthur Young to something close to rhapsody: 'I will go here, I will go there; I could trace a route upon paper as wild as fancy could dictate, and everywhere I found beautiful roads without break or hindrance.' In fact most Irish roads, made of gravel and loose stones, were suitable only for pack horses, or light carts drawn by a single animal: Young himself, in a calmer moment, admitted that the loads taken by the carts of the Irish poor 'are such as an Englishman would be ashamed to take in a wheelbarrow', and even the genteel, away from major routes, normally went on horseback rather than by coach. Nevertheless much

---

[34] Discussion of this point is complicated by the argument that 'rundale', partnership farming practised by a group of families living together in a 'clachan', represented the survival into recent times of an ancient settlement pattern. The alternative view is that such arrangements were part of a much more varied and loosely defined set of adaptations to changing agrarian conditions in the eighteenth century itself. For a general review of the issues, see J. H. Andrews in _NHI_, iv. 241–5. For enclosures see F. H. Aalen, Kevin Whelan, and Matthew Stout (eds.), _Atlas of the Irish Rural Landscape_ (Cork, 1997), 134–44.

had changed since the time, not long past, when travellers could expect to have to ford rivers, and rely on local guides to find a passable way through tracts of open country.[35]

The first public transport networks further widened the opportunities open to travellers. By 1737 there were twice-weekly coach services from Dublin north to Drogheda, west to Athlone, and south to Kilkenny. A coach service to Belfast, taking two days in summer and three in winter, began in 1740 but did not survive. A regular service reached Newry only in 1760, and Belfast in 1788. From the following year, however, the first Irish mail coach services—instituted just five years after the English service had commenced—ran from Dublin to Cork and Belfast, with a service to Limerick following in 1791.

Eighteenth-century Ireland also tried enthusiastically to take its place in the canal age. The first venture, linking Newry to Lough Neagh, was completed in 1742, with the intention of allowing the Tyrone coalfield to supply the Dublin market. A ship canal completed in 1769 opened up Newry itself to heavy vessels. The Lagan navigation linked Belfast to Lisburn by 1763, although a planned extension to Lough Neagh was not completed until 1794. Other schemes followed, including works to open up the Shannon to inland navigation. Most of these projects never fulfilled the expectations vested in them, mainly because the high-priced ores and industrial goods they were expected to carry did not materialize. The most successful were the Lagan navigation, running through the densely settled linen-producing region, and the Barrow navigation, carrying the produce of a region of intensive tillage. By contrast the most ambitious project of the period, the Grand and Royal canals, completed only in 1805 and 1817, owed more to its symmetry on the map than to sound commercial reasoning.[36] Nevertheless these huge waterworks, with their apparatus of locks and bridges and associated buildings, were a major addition to an increasingly man-made landscape, while their very existence was evidence of the extent to which earlier pessimism had now given way to a sometimes uncritical belief in the possibility of economic improvement.

Economic expansion was clearly reflected in both the scale and the quality of urban living. Dublin continued its spectacular growth, from 112,000 inhabitants in 1744 to 154,000 in 1778 and 182,000 in 1800, by which time it was the sixth largest city in Europe. By this time, too, it had begun to live up to its status as the second city of the British empire, not just in size, but in appearance. To the east of the city centre, on both sides of the river, a succession of increasingly ambitious private developments created a new grid of straight streets and spacious squares, lined with three- and four-storey houses (Map 4). The area between St Stephen's Green and Trinity College was largely filled in during the 1720s. In 1745 the young earl of Kildare, Ireland's premier nobleman, confirmed the elite status

[35] Young, *A Tour in Ireland*, ii. 79, 81.
[36] See above, Ch. 8.

of the new development when he positioned his palatial new residence, more country mansion than town house in its proportions and scale, at the end of Molesworth Street. Two decades later development began further west again, on the huge suburban estate owned by the Viscounts Fitzwilliam of Merrion. Its showpiece was Merrion Square, intended to be 'the grandest and greatest square in Europe'. North of the river, meanwhile, Luke Gardiner drew on capital acquired both through his banking interests and through his management of official funds as deputy vice treasurer to buy up land for a series of developments. The most notable was Sackville Mall, today O'Connell Street, commenced in 1749, its unprecedented 150-foot width designed to incorporate an obelisk-lined central walk running its entire length.

Public building also played its part in the creation of a new city centre. The massive colonnaded forecourt of Edward Lovell Pearce's new parliament house, built between 1729 and 1731, gave monumental expression to the political aspirations of the Irish Protestant nation, while the construction between 1752 and 1759 of the great western façade of Trinity College closed off a second side of the irregular square of College Green, thus giving the new eastern quarter a distinctive focal point. A wide streets commission, created by act of parliament in 1757, played an important part in guaranteeing the symmetry and regularity of the new urban landscape, straightening and widening crooked medieval streets, and imposing standards on projected new developments. Initially, however, its work was dominated by a political feud between vested interests. To realize their full potential the new developments north and south of the river needed to be joined by a bridge. But this would make it necessary to relocate the Customs House further downstream, where it could still be reached by masted vessels. The city corporation, backed by John Ponsonby, first commissioner of the revenue and the government's leading political manager, concerned to protect existing property interests, remained determined to preserve the primacy of the traditional centre. Hence the first work of the wide streets commission was an imposing new avenue, Parliament Street, from the existing Essex Bridge to the Castle. The erection during the 1770s of Thomas Cooley's domed and colonnaded Royal Exchange, replacing the Tholsel erected in the 1680s, was a further reassertion of the primacy of the old city.

By this time, however, Ponsonby had been politically eclipsed by John Beresford, a relative by marriage of the Gardiners. With his support, a new Customs House, designed by James Gandon, was constructed well downriver between 1781 and 1791, opening the way to the construction in 1795 of Carlisle Bridge, at the bottom of an extended Sackville Street. Some of the more powerful opponents of the eastward move were conciliated by the erection closer to the traditional centre of Gandon's other masterpiece, the new courts of law or Four Courts, whose domed block became the city's signature in the way that Wren's St Paul's, a hundred years earlier, had become for London. But from the 1770s the wide streets commissioners, under new political management, turned their attention to the east. Dame Street (1778–84) ran from the Castle past the Royal Exchange to the Parliament House and Trinity College. Westmoreland and Dolier Street ran from the College to the new Carlisle Bridge and Lower Sackville Street, connecting to Sackville Mall. Lower Abbey Street, widened and straightened, provided an approach to the Customs House. Building along these new thoroughfares was left to private enterprise, but the leases issued by the commissioners specified ground-floor shops with residential quarters above. A visitor to Lower Sackville Street in 1810 complained of the juxtaposition of 'peers, pastry cooks and perfumers, bishops, butchers, and brokers in old furniture'.[37] But the architectural record is nevertheless of a successful attempt to combine the ordering of public space with provision for the commercial life of a thriving capital city.

The spacious elegance that characterized the eastwards extension of the city contrasted sharply with conditions in the old districts to the west. Here there was little expansion into the surrounding countryside. Instead development took the form of infill building and the subdivision of houses, as a growing labouring and artisan population crowded into the narrow lanes and crooked streets. Investigators in the early nineteenth century found multiple occupancy taken to shocking levels: in large houses 'each of these rooms is let to separate tenants, who again re-let them to as many individuals as they can contain, each person paying for that portion of the floor which his extended body can occupy'.[38] Those of intermediate rank sought respectable quarters either in the less expensive parts of the new developments, or in the more salubrious parts of the old city. But already by the mid-eighteenth century some in these middling groups had begun to retreat from the social extremes of the metropolis to villas in the proto-suburbs emerging around villages like Clontarf to the north and Rathmines to the south.

Dublin's growth and conspicuous if unevenly distributed wealth reflected its status as a national capital. It was the headquarters for a steadily expanding state, providing the base both for new government organizations like the Linen Board and for unofficial but prestigious bodies like the Dublin Society and later the Royal Irish Academy. The viceregal court, hampered by the poor accommodation available at the Castle, the lack of a country base, and the relatively miserly allowance paid to lords lieutenant, never achieved real magnificence.[39] But it nevertheless provided an important social focus. Meetings of parliament, now a seasonal rather than an occasional event, also played a part in bringing peers and gentry regularly to town. But even before the change from biannual to annual meetings from 1771 a distinct winter season had emerged, largely independent of parliamentary sessions, involving a lively round

---

[37] Quoted in Edel Sheridan-Quantz, 'The Multi-Centred Metropolis: The Social Topography of Eighteenth-Century Dublin', in Peter Clark and Raymond Gillespie (eds.), *Two Capitals: London and Dublin 1500–1840* (Oxford, 2001), 283.

[38] Warburton, Whitelaw, and Walsh's history of Dublin (1818), quoted ibid. 280.

[39] Barnard, *Making the Grand Figure*, ch. 1. For the deficiencies of the Castle as a centre of government see ch. 8.

of entertainments, visiting, and socializing that ran from November to March of each year and provided the custom for an expanding range of coffee houses, clubs, and other social facilities.[40]

Dublin's predominance also had an economic basis. In addition to its administrative and political functions, it was a major manufacturing centre, with large numbers employed in the manufacture of silk and woollen cloth, brewing and distilling, sugar refining, and a variety of luxury trades. Up to the 1790s it consistently accounted for more than half the customs duties collected in the kingdom. Its dominance was particularly striking in the case of linen. In the first half of the century three-quarters of all exports, though originating mainly in Ulster, were shipped through Dublin, where a White Linen Hall was erected, conveniently situated on the still less developed north side of the river, in 1721. From the 1740s Newry and Belfast began gradually to increase their share of the trade, but even in the last quarter of the century 47 per cent of all linen exports went through the capital.

Dublin's exceptional pre-eminence, economic as well as social and political, inevitably had implications for other urban centres. Yet there too the eighteenth century was a period of impressive growth. The most spectacular success story was that of Cork, whose position as an Atlantic port and centre of the provisions trade allowed population to grow from around 18,000 at the beginning of the century to 45,000 by 1760 and to 57,000 by 1796. But the next rank of towns, Belfast, Drogheda, Limerick, and Waterford, all with 5,000 inhabitants or less in the late seventeenth century, were also to grow between two- and threefold over the next hundred years. Cork's rapid expansion depended on a haphazard succession of private initiatives. A visitor in 1807 complained of its mixture of old and new façades, 'like red new buttons on an old blue coat'.[41] In Limerick, by contrast, Edmund Sexton Pery, a descendant of the early convert to the Reformation who had incurred the posthumous vengeance of the city's Old English elite,[42] directed an orderly expansion across lands owned by his family to the south of the traditional centre. His first development, during 1751–6, was a square still located within the city walls. But these were then demolished to facilitate a further grid of streets and squares that came to be known as Newtown Pery. In Belfast new building to reflect the town's growing commercial status was initially stalled by the problems of the local dynasty. The Chichester earls of Donegall had become absentees when the castle burned down in 1708, and the fourth earl, who succeeded in 1716, was mentally incapacitated. From 1757, however, his successor, the fifth earl, provided long building leases, accompanied by firm stipulations on size and quality, that laid the basis for the rebuilding of the town. By 1776 Arthur Young found Belfast 'a very well built town of brick',

---

[40] Tighernan Mooney and Fiona White, 'The Gentry's Winter Season', in David Dickson (ed.), *The Gorgeous Mask: Dublin 1700–1850* (Dublin, 1987), 1–16.

[41] Quoted in Dickson, *Old World Colony*, 420.   [42] Connolly, *Contested Island*, 193.

with 'broad and straight' streets and an elegant assembly room, established above the town Exchange, to provide a venue for what had become a lively urban culture of sociability.[43]

Outside these major towns, a variety of smaller centres also flourished. A survey of Armagh in 1770 reveals the diversity of economic activity to be found in a market town of just under 2,000 inhabitants. Nearly a third of employed persons worked in manufacturing, mainly leather, clothing, and metalwork, just over a quarter in transport or as dealers, while a further quarter provided services, a minority as clergy, teachers, lawyers, or doctors, the remainder as domestic servants. Enniscorthy, in County Wexford, provides a contrasting example of small-town prosperity based more closely on a rich agricultural hinterland. The iron works that had flourished in the seventeenth century survived, though at a diminished level, until 1792. But the main occupations were distilling, brewing, malting, and flour milling, as well as the manufacture of woollen cloth, carried on in workshops or weavers' houses. On this basis population rose steadily, from around 1,000 in 1660 to 1,500 by 1729 and 2,500 by 1785.[44]

Modest but cumulatively significant economic growth in the first half of the century, and a great surge in economic activity thereafter, affected the lives of all sections of the population. The largest share of the profits, in a mainly rural and deeply inegalitarian society, inevitably went to the aristocracy and gentry. At the beginning of the eighteenth century Irish landed society seemed to outsiders both economically and culturally backward. The resulting stereotype of a boorish, drunken, and quarrelsome gentry was to have a long life. But already by this time there were the beginnings of a huge programme of rebuilding that was to transform the domestic circumstances of the landowning class. The professional architect was still a rarity, and costs remained a constant constraint. But proprietors, armed with manuals illustrating the newly fashionable adaptation of classical and Renaissance styles, or advised by knowledgeable friends, rebuilt and adapted on a large scale. In laying out parks and gardens round these new houses, Irish men of wealth were more conservative than their English counterparts in their continued preference for formal, geometric patterns. Some, however, took up the new fashion for the artful adaptation of nature, planting trees where their ancestors had felled woodland, and converting streams into decorative lakes and cascades. Interiors too were transformed. The fashion for decorating walls with hanging tapestries survived into the eighteenth century, but by the 1750s had largely given way to paper. Paintings also became more common, providing the basis for a growing trade in originals and copies from Britain and the continent. Meanwhile rooms were more clearly differentiated by function and level of

---

[43] Young, *A Tour in Ireland*, i. 146.

[44] L. A. Clarkson, 'An Anatomy of an Irish Town: The Economy of Armagh 1770', *IESH* 5 (1978), 27–44; Kevin Whelan, 'Enniscorthy', in Anngret Simms and J. H. Andrews (eds.), *Irish Country Towns* (Cork, 1994), 71–82.

formality, becoming reception rooms, parlours, and sitting rooms adapted to more subtle gradations of social interaction.[45]

Newcomers and visitors in the early eighteenth century had been particularly struck by the unsophisticated quality of dining habits, with their emphasis on profusion over culinary refinement. The earl of Orrery, settling in Ireland in the early 1730s after an upbringing in England, recoiled in fastidious horror from his first social encounters.

Nonsense and wine have flowed in plenty, gigantic saddles of mutton and Brobdingnaggian rumps of beef weight down the table. Bumpers of claret and bowls of white wine were perpetually under my nose. . . . [Our entertainments] are esteemed according to the quantity, not to the quality, of the victuals. Be the meat good or bad, so that there is as much as would feed an army, the esquire thinks he comes off with honour.[46]

Here, too, however, change was under way. Tableware became more lavish, with silver and glass displacing pewter, tin, and wood. The widening range of specialized cutlery and dishes reflected the more elaborate succession of courses. Imports of porcelain cups and teapots testified to rising consumption of tea which, along with coffee and chocolate, supplemented (though by no means displacing) wine and spirits. In this and other areas new ideas of refinement were encouraged by experience of foreign travel, as a tour of suitable continental centres, formerly restricted to the sons of the truly great, became a normal way of rounding off the education of a wider section of the landed classes. Greater affluence also facilitated more frequent sojourns in England, again contributing to the penetration of a provincial society by metropolitan fashions and standards of behaviour.[47]

It would be wrong to suggest that social change was entirely in one direction. Duelling, in particular, seems from the evidence of newspaper reports actually to have increased during most of the eighteenth century, reaching a peak in the 1770s and 1780s. But then duelling was an ambiguous indicator. An undue readiness to quarrel was widely seen as an indicator of poor breeding or insecure status. Yet a willingness to defend one's reputation on the field of honour was everywhere recognized as an essential attribute of a gentleman. Rising numbers of reported duels may thus reflect the growing number claiming gentility—perhaps with an edge of insecurity that promoted aggression—in a rapidly expanding economy. Another, more practical reason for the rising number of engagements may have been the switch from sword to pistol, which reduced the proportion of reported duels leading to death from 69 per cent in the first half of the century to only 30 per cent by 1776–90 (although more than two-thirds of all

[45] All of these developments are covered in detail in Barnard, *Making the Grand Figure*. For other surveys see the chapters by J. H. Andrews and Anne Crookshank in *NHI*, iv.

[46] *The Orrery Papers*, ed. countess of Cork and Orrery (London, 1903), i. 215. See also Connolly, *Religion, Law and Power*, 69–73.

[47] Once again the key source is now Barnard, *Making the Grand Figure*.

duels in the later period nevertheless ended with a participant either dead or injured).[48]

The transformation of the material culture of the major landowners is the most visible consequence of the great economic expansion of the mid- and late eighteenth century. Its monuments remain in those great country mansions and Dublin town houses that survived the politically inspired indifference of post-independence Ireland. But this elite was outnumbered many times over by the holders of other forms of wealth, as expanding trade increased the size and riches of the commercial classes, while rising prosperity expanded the demand for professional services. For these groups too the eighteenth century brought a widening of access to material possessions. Religious inhibitions, particularly among those of dissenting backgrounds or affiliation, along perhaps with the greater need to protect a credit status not backed by landed acres, meant that some in this social group held back from ostentatious display. Where they chose to do so, however, the richest among them could boast of silver, china, and furniture easily equalling that of most landowners.

Lower down the social scale, among tradesmen, shopkeepers, or the larger farmers, ownership was more constrained. The range of clothes or household goods was narrower; pictures were engravings rather than oils; individual pieces of silver or china were prized possessions, protectively set apart rather than in daily use. But there too there is evidence of a gradual expansion in the range of possessions, and of a concern with fashion as well as utility. The County Limerick farmer and land agent Nicholas Peacock, who in 1748 purchased six spoons, paid for by instalments, after his new wife had introduced tea drinking into his household, stands as one small glimpse of a new world of consumption opening up for even the modestly prosperous.[49] A handbill printed three decades later for a grocer in the County Antrim town of Ballymena reveals a much richer range of goods: coffee mills, bread racks and nut crackers, necklaces, watch chains and snuff boxes, buckles, buttons, and hairpins. Much of this may have been for middle-class customers or the local gentry. But the labouring classes too were entering the world of goods. Account books from two farming households in the second half of the eighteenth century, one in County Tyrone and the other in County Down, show the live-in servants regularly obtaining small cash advances on their wages, not just for the purchase of basic items of clothing, but for refinements such as hair ribbons and handkerchiefs, as well as sweetmeats, books, and tea.[50]

---

[48] James Kelly, *'That Damn'd Thing Called Honour': Duelling in Ireland 1570–1860* (Cork, 1995), 73, 82, 120, 175.

[49] Barnard, *Making the Grand Figure*, 135–6.

[50] W. H. Crawford, 'A Ballymena Business in the Late Eighteenth Century', in John Gray and Wesley McCann (eds.), *An Uncommon Bookman* (Belfast, 1996), 24–6; Vivienne Pollock, 'The Household Economy in Early Rural America and Ulster: The Question of Self-Sufficiency', in

New venues likewise appeared for music and drama. Dublin's Smock Alley Theatre was rebuilt in 1735, in response to the challenge of a new theatre opened in Aungier Street the previous year, and the two remained in competition until their companies amalgamated in 1740. A music hall opened in Crow Street in 1731 was reconstructed as a theatre in 1758. The New Musick Hall, erected in Fishamble Street in 1741, provided the venue, a year later, for the first performance of Handel's 'Messiah', and remained for most of the next three decades the most important Dublin location for concerts and other musical events. In the winter of 1764–5 it provided the premises for 13 grand balls, 13 assemblies, 25 concerts, and an entertainment sponsored by the lord lieutenant.[51] Soon after, however, the Hall began to take second place to the Rotunda, the purpose-built concert hall and assembly rooms erected in 1767 to raise funds for the pioneering maternity hospital that stood at the top of Sackville Mall. Theatre also spread to the provinces. Belfast, for example, had a succession of venues from at least the 1730s to accommodate visiting companies of players. From 1771 the town was home to a permanent company that divided its time between there and Derry. In all by the end of the century permanent theatres existed in at least eight provincial towns, while others could count on periodic visits from Irish and British touring companies.

Expanded facilities for music and play-going did not in themselves imply either originality or discrimination. Where music is concerned, the preference of the Irish elite, as typified by a successful early performance of the *Beggar's Opera* at the Smock Alley Theatre in March 1728, was for the light entertainment of ballad opera. Performances of concert music, by contrast, were almost invariably linked to charitable purposes, to an extent that made clear that fashionable philanthropy was at least as important as musical taste. The celebrated première of the 'Messiah', for example, raised money for Mercer's hospital, an infirmary, and the relief of prisoners.[52] Theatre, similarly, relied on a mixture of classics and light entertainment. In Belfast, Shakespeare remained the most popular author performed, while two-thirds of pieces staged were comedies. Details of individual performances indicate a strong demand for spectacle rather than intellectual depth. In June 1770 audiences attending *The Rival Queens* were promised 'the grand triumphal entry of Alexander into Babylon with all the Grecian trophies, ensigns, banners, urns, vases and the triumphal car drawn by two captive kings'. Later the same year a production of more local interest, *Thurot, or the Taking of Carrickfergus*, involved 'a variety of new scenes particularly a view of Carrickfergus, Joy's paper mill, a landscape waterfall with cattle grazing, and an exact representation of a Patagonian man and woman

H. T. Blethen and C. W. Wood (eds.), *Ulster and North America: Transatlantic Perspectives on the Scotch Irish* (Tuscaloosa, Ala., 1997), 70–1.

[51] Mooney and White, 'The Gentry's Winter Season', 7.
[52] Harry White, *The Keeper's Recital: Music and Cultural History in Ireland 1770–1970* (Cork, 1998), 25–33.

brought from Patagonia by the *Dolphin* man of war in her voyage round the world'.[53]

Developments in printing and publishing also testified to the quickening of cultural and intellectual life. The collapse of the king's printer's monopoly in the late seventeenth century allowed printing and bookselling to develop rapidly in response to rising demand. By 1760 Dublin had 33 printers and 46 booksellers. In the second half of the century expansion was more rapid still. The number of book dealers rose from 70 in 1781 to 118 by 1793. By 1800 there were also printing presses operating in 34 centres outside Dublin. Much of this growth, particularly in the provinces, was linked to the rise of newspapers. The initial growth was fragile. Of 37 titles launched between 1704 and 1714, only 6 lasted long enough to be considered successful. Of 33 launched between 1714 and 1727, on the other hand, 15 were successes. All these were Dublin papers. The first attempt at a provincial paper, the *Cork Idler*, was as early as 1715. But of 17 titles launched outside Dublin up to 1760 only 3, the *Belfast Newsletter* in 1737, the *Limerick Journal* in 1739, and the *Cork Journal* in 1753, lasted more than one year. Within two years of its establishment, however, the Catholic-owned *Cork Journal* had a rival in the aggressively Protestant *Cork Evening Post*, reflecting the beginnings of what was to be a rapid growth of the provincial press. By 1788 there were 24 provincial papers.[54]

By far the greater part of this growing body of printed material consisted of imports or, more commonly, reprints of books published in England. English copyright did not extend to Ireland, and part of the impetus behind the rapid expansion of the Irish trade during the eighteenth century came from illegal but profitable exports of these pirated texts to England and America. There was also a limited but significant market for texts in other European languages. Theobald Wolfe Tone, despite his middle-class origins, famously felt himself hampered in his career as an international revolutionary by his lack of facility in French. But instruction in the language, along in some cases with German, Italian, or Spanish, was a standard part of education for the better off, whether in grammar schools or with private tutors. Imports of texts in these languages became more common across the century. In 1744 a minister serving the Dublin Huguenot community launched *A Literary Journal*, carrying news of mainland European publications, which continued, with an interruption, to 1752. Just over a third of the stock advertised by one Galway bookseller in 1799 was in French, with another 2 per cent in Italian.[55]

[53] J. C. Greene, *Theatre in Belfast 1736–1800* (London, 2000), 125, 129.

[54] For a comprehensive general survey see Raymond Gillespie and Andrew Hadfield (eds.), *The Oxford History of the Irish Book*, iii: *The Irish Book in English 1550–1800* (Oxford, 2006). See also W. G. Wheeler, 'The Spread of Provincial Printing in Ireland up to 1850', *Irish Booklore*, 4/1 (1978), 7–18. For newspapers, see Robert Munter, *The History of the Irish Newspaper 1685–1760* (Cambridge, 1967), 15–18, 132.

[55] Máire Kennedy and Geraldine Sheridan (eds.), 'The Trade in French Books in Eighteenth-Century Ireland', in Graham Gargett and Geraldine Sheridan (eds.), *Ireland and the French*

Such evidence of an openness to continental influences is important not only in its own right, as an indication of cultural change, but because it raises the question of how far the signs of a more active intellectual life from the early eighteenth century onwards can be seen as part of the broader European movement referred to as the Enlightenment. The question, however, has to be posed carefully. Modern work has moved away from the idea of a single, coherent intellectual movement radiating outwards from a presumed French centre of origin. Instead 'Enlightenment' is now recognized as a loose collection of related dispositions: in favour of religious toleration, free enquiry, and the rational pursuit of progress, opposed to arbitrary power, censorship, and prejudice. Enlightenment in this sense had no one source: even England, it is now recognized, had its Enlightenment, characterized by a commitment to pragmatic enquiry, individual self-realization, and social improvement.[56] Moreover Kant, answering his own famous question 'What is Enlightenment', made clear that what was involved was a process not a state: 'If it is now asked whether we at present live in an enlightened age, the answer is: No, but we do live in an age of enlightenment . . . the hindrances to universal enlightenment or to humankind's emergence from its self-incurred minority are gradually becoming fewer.'[57]

Where the dominant Protestant culture of eighteenth-century Ireland is concerned, the evidence for an Enlightenment, even by Kant's modest benchmark, is relatively weak. Library lists and booksellers' catalogues confirm the circulation, both in imported volumes and in local printed texts, of the work of the leading *philosophes*. In 1780 the Dublin bookseller Luke White ordered thirteen copies of the thirty-nine-volume reprint of the *Encyclopédie*. Yet there is little evidence for a serious intellectual challenge to traditional values and beliefs. Ireland produced one noted contribution to the early history of deism, John Toland, whose *Christianity Not Mysterious* appeared in 1696. But Toland was a marginal figure, a Donegal Catholic turned Protestant then sceptic who made his career mainly outside Ireland. Robert Clayton, bishop of Clogher, who died in 1758, caused outrage by expressing his doubts as to the divinity of Christ. But this heterodoxy sat alongside a close interest in Scripture-based millenarianism that makes it difficult to present him as the apostle of a new rationalism.[58] Another Church of Ireland bishop, George Berkeley, made a distinctive, not to say idiosyncratic, contribution to metaphysics. But his solution to the problem he himself posed—that nothing could exist except through being perceived—was the very antithesis of

Enlightenment 1700–1800 (Basingstoke, 1999), 185; Máire Kennedy, 'Foreign Language Books 1700–1800', in Gillespie and Hadfield (eds.), *The Irish Book*, 374.

[56] Roy Porter, *Enlightenment: Britain and the Creation of the Modern World* (London, 2000).

[57] 'An Answer to the Question: What is Enlightenment' (1784), in Immanuel Kant, *Practical Philosophy*, ed. Mary J. Gregor (Cambridge, 1996), 21.

[58] For an attempt to present Toland, Clayton, and others as constituting an Irish Enlightenment see David Berman and Patricia O'Riordan (eds.), *The Irish Enlightenment and Counter Enlightenment* (Bristol, 2002).

Enlightenment thinking, an appeal to faith in an all-seeing God. Jonathan Swift, Ireland's closest parallel to Voltaire in terms of a willingness to subject the institutions of his society to caustic criticism, was a dogmatic defender both of Christian orthodoxy and of the privileged position of his own church. And in the intellectual citadel of the Protestant establishment, Trinity College, Dublin, the traditional classics- and divinity-based curriculum continued untouched by new currents of European thought.

Where an Enlightenment element in Irish elite culture can be more convincingly suggested—in a form closer to the English concern with pragmatic and practical enquiry than to the French assault on repressive political and religious structures—is in the activities of two bodies concerned with social and economic development. The Dublin Philosophical Society reconvened in 1692 but ceased to meet in 1698, and an attempted revival in 1707–8 was short-lived. However it found a successor in the Physico-Historical Society, established in 1744 with a membership of over 200, drawn mainly from the Church of Ireland clergy and the professional classes. Like its predecessor, the new society collected information on topography and natural history, for both utilitarian and scientific purposes. But there was also, as a new element, a strong emphasis on the social progress achieved since the wars of the seventeenth century. These collective efforts led to the publication between 1744 and 1756 of valuable surveys of four counties, all compiled by Charles Smith, but by the time the last appeared the society had ceased to meet.[59]

A second body, the Dublin Society, established in 1731, was more successful, acquiring a charter in 1750 and going on to become the Royal Dublin Society in 1820. Where the two earlier bodies had concentrated on social and scientific enquiry, the Dublin Society was more directly interventionist, using grants and prizes to disseminate improved practice in farming, livestock breeding, land reclamation, and manufactures. From the mid-1740s it sponsored, again with an eye to the practical benefits to be expected from improved design, what became a group of schools of art. Leading members of the society also made important contributions to public debate. Thomas Prior, a founding member, was the author of the influential tract on absentees, and also wrote on issues of coinage. Arthur Dobbs, a County Antrim landlord who at the age of 65 embarked on an extraordinary second career as colonial governor in North Carolina, and Samuel Madden, a clergyman and nephew of William Molyneux, published pioneering works of social enquiry examining the causes of Ireland's underdevelopment and the possible remedies.[60] In doing so, it has been suggested, they laid the foundations for a wholly new concept of social improvement, sidestepping

---

[59] Eoin Magennis, ' "A Land of Milk and Honey": The Physico-Historical Society, Improvement and the Surveys of Mid-Eighteenth-Century Ireland', *PRIA*, C, 102 (2002), 199–217.

[60] Arthur Dobbs, *An Essay on the Trade and Improvement of Ireland* (Dublin, 1729); Samuel Madden, *Reflections and Resolutions Proper for the Gentlemen of Ireland* (Dublin, 1738).

the traditional preoccupation with Ireland's dependent constitutional status, and the restrictions on its trade, to develop instead a model of how an activist intellectual and social elite could create a prosperous and orderly society.[61]

A separate strand of Enlightenment interest can be detected in Ireland's other main Protestant culture. The steady stream of Ulster Presbyterians who travelled to Scotland for their advanced education, whether for the ministry or for a secular career, encountered there a dynamic intellectual environment, in which universities were centres of real creative thought, and where the experience of a rapid transition from poverty and isolation to a prosperous commercial society had inspired a distinctive concern with the human sciences. It was a Glasgow graduate, James Arbuckle, part of the circle loosely associated with Viscount Molesworth, who in 1725 launched the *Dublin Weekly Journal*, a self-consciously didactic journal, devoted to disseminating a classic Enlightenment vision of civility and civic virtue as the basis of social improvement. Nor was the intellectual influence all in one direction. Francis Hutcheson, born in County Down and during the 1720s master of a dissenting academy in Dublin, returned to Glasgow as professor of moral philosophy in 1730. His ideas on the social nature of moral virtue strongly influenced later Scottish thinkers, including Adam Smith. In America his insistence that government existed for the benefit of those governed (including the first formulation of the principle of the greatest good of the greatest number), with the corollary that rebellion was a legitimate last resort against tyranny, were also influential in shaping the thought of what became the revolutionary generation. In Ireland, likewise, exposure to the Scottish Enlightenment had important long-term effects, in the rise of New Light theology, and in the early emergence among some Ulster Presbyterians of a commitment to independent and reformist politics.[62]

The Scots were not, of course, the only group to leave Ireland for their advanced education. Aspiring Catholic priests routinely made the journey to colleges in Spain, France, or the Spanish Netherlands. Their return, typically after six or more years or study, was a further injection into all parts of Ireland of the languages, manners, and ideas of continental Europe. How far this particular stream of returned travellers contributed to an Irish Enlightenment is less clear. The career of the Dublin-born Luke Joseph Hooke, professor of theology at the University of Paris from 1742, provides one striking example of the influence on an academically inclined émigré of the new intellectual currents of Enlightenment France. Taking as his starting point the unity of all creation, Hooke sought to integrate human reason and desire, the laws of nature, and revealed religion, a bold intellectual synthesis that earned him the suspicion of ecclesiastical superiors and

---

[61] For this argument see James Livesey, 'The Dublin Society in Eighteenth-Century Irish Political Thought', *Historical Journal*, 47/3 (2004), 615–40.

[62] Michael Brown, *Francis Hutcheson in Dublin 1718–1730* (Dublin, 2002). For New Light theology see ch. 7. For the so-called 'Molesworth circle' see ch. 10.

led to several interruptions in his academic career.[63] For the most part, however, the attachments of the extensive Irish community abroad, comprising clergy, soldiers in the armies of the Catholic powers, and clients of the Jacobite court, were to the dynastic loyalties and confessional exclusiveness of the *ancien régime*. By the second half of the century Catholics within Ireland had begun to campaign for the removal of penal legislation affecting their property and political rights. But here it made more sense to rest their case on the native Whig cult of 1688, with its values of liberty and entitlement to representation, rather than on the writings of foreign intellectuals—especially since the bigotry and intolerance denounced by the leading *philosophes* was primarily that of the Catholic church.

OLD AND NEW WORLDS

In a period characterized by extensive movement across and between continents, the Irish of the seventeenth and eighteenth centuries stand out as an exceptionally mobile people. During the sixteenth, seventeenth, and eighteenth centuries perhaps three-quarters of a million Spaniards, up to twice that number of Portuguese, and about 420,000 English left their homelands for destinations in America, Africa, and Asia. Another million, about half from the Netherlands itself, the rest mainly German and Scandinavian mercenaries, sailed for the Dutch colonies. In comparison an Irish total of just under 350,000 emigrants between 1600 and 1800 might seem less remarkable. But from an island whose population was initially no more than a million, and came to exceed two million only from around 1750, it in fact represents a significant outflow. Mobility on this scale reflects the extent of the upheavals, political, cultural, and economic, visited across a period of two centuries on the population of what had previously been a peripheral and relatively static society. As with the other transformations of this period, what took place must be understood as a mixture of involuntary and often traumatic displacement and the active seizure of new opportunities.[64]

Of the different streams that made up this huge outward flow, the most long-standing was enlistment in the armies of Catholic Europe. The main recruiting

---

[63] Thomas O'Connor, *An Irish Theologian in Enlightenment France: Luke Joseph Hooke 1714–96* (Dublin, 1995).

[64] Figures calculated from the annual totals suggested by L. M. Cullen, 'The Irish Diaspora of the Seventeenth and Eighteenth Centuries', in Nicholas Canny (ed.), *Europeans on the Move: Studies on European Migration 1500–1800* (Oxford, 1994), 140. For the figures for other European countries see ibid. 64, 203, 265–72. Apart from Cullen's overview, the best introduction to recent work on the Irish overseas is in two volumes of essays: Thomas O'Connor (ed.), *The Irish in Europe 1580–1815* (Dublin, 2001); Thomas O'Connor and Mary Ann Lyons (eds.), *Irish Communities in Early Modern Europe* (Dublin, 2006). For transatlantic migration see Kerby A. Miller, Arnold Schrier, Bruce Boling, and David Doyle, *Irish Immigrants in the Land of Canaan: Letters and Memoirs from Colonial and Revolutionary America 1675–1815* (New York, 2003). Rodgers, *Ireland, Slavery and Anti-Slavery*, highlights a neglected but inescapable consequence of Ireland's close involvement in the international trade of both Old and New worlds.

power in the seventeenth century had been Spain, which had created its first Irish regiment in 1605. The 'Irish tercio' was abolished in the 1680s, but renewed warfare after 1701, and the availability of large numbers of displaced fighting men following the Williamite victory in Ireland, encouraged the creation of new regiments. Three of these, bearing the titles Irlanda, Ultonia, and Hibernia, remained in service up to 1818. Apart from one surge of activity during 1720–2, apparently in connection with a planned campaign in North Africa, Spain's Irish regiments made no sustained effort to recruit in Ireland itself, and it appears that already by the 1730s a large majority of the rank and file were of other nationalities. The officers, however, continued up to the 1790s to be of Irish birth or descent. Although Spain was no longer the main destination of the Irish military diaspora, some individuals achieved prominence in the service of what was still a large, if declining empire. Ricardo Wall, born in France in 1694, the son of an exiled Jacobite officer, served as a soldier in Italy and elsewhere and as a diplomat in Russia and London, before becoming minister for war between 1754 and 1763. The Irish-born Ambrose O'Higgins (1721–1801), having first come to Spain as a merchant, entered government service as a military engineer, rising to become governor of Chile and, by the time of his death, viceroy of Peru.[65]

For rank and file recruits, however, the main destination was now the new Great Power of France. The 20,000 or so Jacobite soldiers who withdrew there during or after the Williamite war had been organized into a new set of regiments which came to be referred to collectively as the Irish Brigade. Over the next half-century or more these units, unlike their Spanish counterparts, were replenished with new blood from Ireland. Recruitment depended heavily on the ability of well-born recruits to the officer class and of other members of propertied Catholic families, as well as possibly some Catholic priests, to raise volunteers and arrange their transport. Numbers leaving reached a peak of around 1,000 a year in the 1720s and 1730s, but by the 1750s had fallen to a trickle. There is evidence to suggest that the threat of official sanctions made surviving propertied families reluctant to risk recruiting. But Jacobite sympathies were in any case in decline during this period, and economic conditions at home had improved markedly. The men Morty Óg O'Sullivan had been recruiting around the time of his death in 1754, significantly, were deserters from the regular army rather than local peasants. Three Irish regiments, Dillon's, Berwick's (now incorporating the celebrated regiment of Clare), and Walsh's, survived to the Revolution, still officered almost entirely by men of Irish birth or descent, but with a rank and file in which 90 per cent or more had no connection with Ireland.

[65] Harman Murtagh, 'Irish Soldiers Abroad 1600–1800', in Thomas Bartlett and Keith Jeffery (eds.), *A Military History of Ireland* (Cambridge, 1996). See also Sam Scott, 'The French Revolution and the Irish Regiments in France', in David Dickson and Hugh Gough (eds.), *Ireland and the French Revolution* (Dublin, 1990), 14–27.

Side by side with this exodus of fighting men, and continuing longer, there was a growing movement of actual and would-be priests. In the seventeenth century only a minority of the priests serving in Ireland had received the formal seminary education prescribed by the Council of Trent. By the eighteenth century, however, it had become the norm for candidates to travel to Catholic Europe for a period of formal training, although a proportion, possibly more than half, were still ordained before departure, so that they could support themselves abroad by saying masses and performing other duties. The most popular destinations were the university of Paris, which may have taken up to a third of the total number of Irish émigré students, along with Nantes and Bordeaux. Outside France the leading destinations were Salamanca, Lisbon, Louvain, and Rome. There and elsewhere students found accommodation and supervision in dedicated Irish colleges, although their studies were generally at the university of the city concerned. The course of studies was a long one, lasting six years for those coming as ordained priests, and considerably more for those arriving in their teens. The number of students abroad at any one time was thus substantial, numbering perhaps 600 in the late eighteenth century. Although they were in theory being prepared for service in the Irish mission, the number who did in fact return to take up duties there may have been as low as a half. Most of the rest found careers for themselves in the French church, whether in France itself or, for the less lucky, in the arduous and unpopular role of chaplains to naval vessels or to colonial settlements.[66]

A third stream of migration was that of merchants and other entrepreneurs, following the lines of trade between Ireland and continental Europe. By the eighteenth century there were significant Irish communities at Nantes, Bordeaux, Cadiz, Lisbon, and other French and Iberian ports, with smaller groups in the Austrian Netherlands and the Dutch republic. Movement of this sort was driven by economic, rather than political or religious considerations. Protestant merchant families maintained houses in European centres, both Catholic and Protestant, just as some leading Irish Catholic merchant families had branches in London. But permanent residence south of the Netherlands inevitably posed fewer problems for Catholics. Indeed the mercantile diaspora, particularly in Spain and Portugal, had a somewhat archaic flavour, with families from the once great Old English trading strongholds of Galway, Limerick, and Waterford retaining a position of prominence, while Cork and Dublin, the main centres of an eighteenth-century economic growth focused more on transatlantic commerce, were less well represented. Even in the eighteenth century, however, trade with continental Europe still accounted for a substantial part of Irish commerce, and the émigré families at its heart commanded substantial resources. Antoine Walsh, the Nantes merchant who conveyed Charles Edward Stuart to Scotland

[66] L. W. B. Brockliss and P. Ferté, 'Irish Clerics in France in the Seventeenth and Eighteenth Centuries: A Statistical Study', in *PRIA*, C, 87 (1987), 527–72.

in 1745, had made his fortune in a succession of slaving voyages to Africa
and the Caribbean—calculations suggest that he was the fifth most successful
slaver in the France of his day—and was to retire to the plantation he bought
for himself on the island of St Domingue. Richard Hennessy, born in County
Cork around 1729, moved on from a short spell in the French army to become
one of several Irishmen who became prominent in the lucrative brandy trade,
although it was his French-born son James whose commercial acumen laid the
foundations for one of the industry's most enduring brands. At Ostend Thomas
Ray, son of a Youghal merchant, played a central role in opening up direct trade
between the southern Netherlands and the East Indies, and was mayor of the
town during 1728–38. In Cadiz there were nineteen Irish merchant houses by
1775, including among them the second and third largest traders in the port.[67]

Geography ensured that the main flow of Irish migrants was to western
Europe. A number, however, made their way further east. In 1629, with their
main house at Louvain seriously overcrowded, Irish Franciscans opened a college
in Prague, where the recently instituted Habsburg offensive against Bohemian
Protestantism ensured them official support. The medical faculty at Prague also
attracted Irish students excluded by religious tests from a professional training
at home, and an Irishmen, William MacNeven, was director of medical studies
there from 1754, as well as acting as personal physician to the Empress Maria
Theresa. The most significant Irish presence in the Austrian lands, however, was
that of soldiers. An account of the crushing of the Bohemian Protestant army at
the White Mountain in 1620 noted the presence in the imperial forces of 'Irish
Catholics, who hate all heresy from their hearts with a kind of inborn hatred'. Irish
officers also took a prominent part in the assassination of the celebrated general
Wallenstein and his associates, after he had lost the emperor's trust in 1634; one
of them, Walter Butler, was rewarded with a portion of Wallenstein's landed
estates. In the reign of Maria Theresa (1740–80) the Austrian army was said still
to 'swarm with the offspring of the best Roman Catholic families' of Ireland,
while as late as the Revolutionary and Napoleonic wars some 200 Irishmen held
Austrian commissions. The most prominent family among these Irish servants of
the Habsburgs was the Taaffes. Francis, son of Charles II's faithful companion
in exile and his successor as third earl of Carlingford, distinguished himself in
campaigns against the Turks in the 1680s. Nicholas Taaffe, from another branch
of the family, rose to the rank of lieutenant general, as well as becoming a

    [67] For surveys of Irish mercantile communities abroad see L. M. Cullen, 'Merchant Communities,
the Navigation Acts and Irish and Scottish Responses', in Cullen and Smout (eds.), *Comparative
Aspects of Scottish and Irish Economic and Social History*; idem, 'Apotheosis and Crisis: The Irish
Diaspora in the Age of Choiseul', in O'Connor and Lyons (eds.), *Irish Communities*; and other
essays there and in O'Connor, *The Irish in Europe*. For Antoine Walsh see Rodgers, *Ireland, Slavery
and Anti-Slavery*, 106–11, for Hennessy and others L. M. Cullen, *The Irish Brandy Houses of
Eighteenth-Century France* (Dublin, 2000), and for Ray Jan Parmentier, 'The Irish Connection: The
Irish Merchant Community in Ostend and Bruges during the Late Seventeenth and Eighteenth
Centuries', *ECI* 20 (2005), 38–43, 54.

count of the Holy Roman Empire and chamberlain to Maria Theresa. In 1766 the Catholic Committee sought to capitalize on his international reputation by publishing under his name a critique of the penal laws, *Observations on Affairs in Ireland*, although the text was largely the work of Charles O'Conor. The earldom of Carlingford became extinct in 1738, but the family continued to hold the title Viscounts Taaffe until 1917, when it was declared forfeit because the holder, continuing a 300-year tradition of service in the imperial forces, was in arms against the United Kingdom.[68]

Émigré soldiers, clerics, and merchants, spread across Catholic Europe, formed a cohesive ethnic and religious network. Irish priests provided religious services to merchants and soldiers, who in turn used their political influence to advance clerical careers. With the same leading Irish families prominent in the hierarchies of all three, there were ties of kinship, reinforced by intermarriage. The Jacobite court in exile, whose recommendations carried weight both with governments and with the papacy, was a shared point of reference. The extent to which a sense of Irish identity survived prolonged exile inevitably varied. In Seville the son of the Waterford-born merchant William White, who had emigrated there before 1711, became Guillermo Blanco, and married a Spanish rather than an Irish bride. He did not entirely forget his non-Spanish origins, but the expression they found was when in 1783 he became British vice-consul in the city.[69] In other cases émigrés seeking to make their way in the hierarchical and status-conscious world of the *ancien régime* often found it politic to retain a strong, if not necessarily scrupulously accurate, sense of their Irish birth, commissioning genealogies that would allow them to claim noble status in their new homeland. The support given to the Stuart expedition of 1745 by Antoine Walsh and others likewise testifies to the survival among those of Irish blood but continental birth of traditional political allegiances.

The other great movement out of Ireland, westwards across the Atlantic, was almost as old as the military exodus to continental Europe. One notable early venture was a colony on the Amazon for the production of tobacco and cotton, established in 1612 but by 1629 overrun by the Portuguese on whose territory it trespassed. More lasting success came in the islands of the Carribean, where Irish merchants and planters began to establish themselves from the 1630s, with Galway families such as the Blakes, Lynches, and Kirwans playing a particularly prominent part. The strongest Irish presence was on Montserrat, where in 1729

---

[68] Micheál MacCraith and David Worthington, 'Aspects of the Literary Activity of the Irish Franciscans in Prague 1620–1786', in O'Connor and Lyons (eds.), *Irish Migrants after Kinsale*, 119; Murtagh, 'Irish Soldiers Abroad 1600–1800', 301. For Taaffe's *Observations* of 1766 see Thomas Bartlett, *The Fall and Rise of the Irish Nation* (Dublin, 1992), 54–5.

[69] Martin Murphy, 'Varieties of Irishness in Eighteenth-Century Seville: Wisemans and Whites', in O'Connor and Lyons, *Irish Communities*. Guillermo's son was to go through yet another reinvention, as Joseph Blanco White, an Anglican clergyman, later a Unitarian, and a fierce campaigner against Catholicism.

eighteen of the thirty largest planters were Irish, all but one of Catholic origin and eight among them still Catholic. At a lower social level indentured servants, paying for their passage by agreeing to be disposed of on arrival for a fixed term of bound labour, had also begun making their way to the West Indies from at least the 1620s. These migrants came mainly from Munster ports, including both New English, a settler population on the move once again, and members of the pre-plantation population. Within a couple of decades Ireland was in fact the main source of white labour in a climate shunned by better-placed emigrants. By the end of the century the shift from tobacco to more labour-intensive sugar, and the associated surge in the import of African slaves, had put an end to this plebeian Irish migration. But Irish merchants and plantation owners, Catholic and Protestant, continued throughout the eighteenth century and beyond to play an active part in Caribbean commerce.[70]

The transatlantic flow in indentured servants from Ireland was never exclusively to the West Indies; a proportion, from the start, went to the American mainland, mainly to Virginia. However it was only in the eighteenth century that North America replaced what was now a slave-dominated Caribbean as the main destination. The first great surge in departures, mainly from the province of Ulster, came in 1717–20, at a time of economic crisis. Harvests were poor, there was recession in the linen industry, and farmers faced sharp increases in rents as the twenty-one-year leases on easy terms with which landlords had wooed tenants in the difficult 1690s came up for renewal. Modern estimates suggest that as many as 7,000 left. The outward flow continued in the decades that followed, with peaks and troughs broadly corresponding to changes in economic conditions. Estimates of the total number leaving rely mainly on newspaper reports of the number of vessels that sailed, supplemented by patchy evidence on arrivals from American sources. A pioneering study put the number leaving Ulster ports between 1717 and 1776 at between 100,000 and 120,000. Later, more speculative assessments suggest that the true total for Ulster was closer to 170,000–200,000, and that in addition 100,000 migrants left other Irish ports across the somewhat longer period from the 1670s. Other calculations, by contrast, push the totals sharply downwards, suggesting no more than 75,000 Ulster Protestant migrants, and fewer than 30,000 Catholics across the whole eighteenth century. Migration resumed as soon as the end of the Revolutionary War in 1783 permitted. The outward flow over the next three decades was normally between 3,000 and 5,000 a year, of whom 70 per cent came from Ulster.[71]

[70] Donald Harman Akenson, *If the Irish Ruled the World: Montserrat 1630–1730* (Liverpool, 1997); Rodgers, *Ireland, Slavery and Anti-Slavery*, chs. 2–4.

[71] The figure of 100,000 to 120,000 was suggested by R. J. Dickson, *Ulster Emigration to Colonial America 1718–1775* (London, 1966). The most detailed argument for a much higher total, and a much higher proportion of southern and Catholic migrants, is in David N. Doyle, *Ireland, Irishmen and Revolutionary America 1760–1820* (Dublin, 1981). A statistical appendix to Miller et al., *Irish Immigrants*, 656–78, endorses Doyle's revised figures. The lower estimate is that offered by Cullen,

The largest single group within this huge outflow, far out of proportion to their share of total population, were Presbyterians from Ulster. Landlords, anxious to deflect criticism of their own demands, and Whig and Presbyterian opponents of the sacramental test, sought to blame this exodus, damaging both to the economy and to the balance of Protestant and Catholic within Ireland, on the oppression dissenters suffered at the hands of the established church. The chronology of the emigrant flow, however, suggests that economic factors rather than religious grievances were paramount. Ulster Presbyterians were already a mobile group. Some of those leaving in 1717–20 may well have participated in the last great immigration of Scots in the 1690s, and there was also a history of significant movement by Scottish families within Ulster. Their high levels of literacy, and relative prosperity, made emigration in response to difficult times an easier option than it was for many others. Four-fifths of the first wave of emigrants, in 1717–20, paid for their passage, mostly involving a whole family. Later emigrants were poorer, for the most part going as indentured labourers, but by this time contacts with emigrants already settled in North America made emigration a self-sustaining process.

The exploits of these Presbyterian migrants as pioneers and frontiersmen were to become the basis of a self-congratulatory legend that still has a surprising resonance in Northern Irish Protestant mythology. But the geographical record confirms the broad picture of a migrant stream driven by aspirations to self-betterment, rather than a mere mobile labour force. A substantial part of the first wave of migrants in 1717–20 had gone to New England. Their successors, however, for the most part avoided both New England and New York, where land was already expensive and the social hierarchy established. There was likewise little to attract them to the south, with its plantation agriculture worked with slave labour. Instead their destination was the Middle Colonies. The main ports of entry were Philadelphia and its Delaware outports, their first main area of settlement western Pennsylvania. Later, as this region lost its frontier character, both newcomers and some longer-established settlers moved on, south into west Virginia and the Carolinas, or across the mountains into what would become Kentucky.

Arriving in America as a people who had only recently exchanged one European homeland for another, the settlers faced the task of defining their ethnic identity. Middle-class immigrants setting up in Philadelphia appear to have had no problem in seeing themselves as Irish. The Society of the Friendly Sons of St Patrick, established in Philadelphia in 1771, united Presbyterian, Anglican, and Catholic merchants in a shared commitment to conviviality and

'The Irish Diaspora', 127–8. For the revised total of 7,000 emigrants in 1717–20 (as compared to Dickson's partial total of 2,600 going to New England) see Graeme Kirkham, 'Ulster Emigration to North America 1680–1720', in Blethen and Wood (eds.), *Ulster and North America*, 96. For emigration after 1783 see Maldwyn A. Jones, 'Ulster Emigration 1783–1815', in E. R. R. Green (ed.), *Essays in Scotch-Irish History* (London, 1969), 46–68.

mutual aid, allied in most cases to support for a developing American patriotism. But this was the hyphenated-Americanism of a successful, well-integrated group. Less well-situated migrants, by contrast, confronted a strong negative stereotype, in which both 'Irish' and 'Scotch Irish' were used to imply drunken, violent, and lawless behaviour. In New Hampshire in 1719–20 a party from Londonderry who found themselves in dispute over land were dismissed by their opponents as 'poor Irish' squatters. Their minister protested that 'we are surprised to hear ourselves termed Irish people, when we so frequently ventured our all for the British crown and liberties against the Irish papists'. When, forty years later, the Paxton Boys, a militia raised in western Pennsylvania in the last stages of the Seven Years War, caused outrage by their massacre of two parties of unarmed Indians, another minister responded to criticism by insisting that these were not 'native Irish that trot in our bogs'.[72] By the nineteenth century the descendants of Ulster Presbyterian immigrants were to turn to the term 'Scotch Irish', now purged of its negative connotations, as a way of setting themselves apart both from the image of the 'wild Irish' inspired by their own often disorderly behaviour, and from the growing stream of poor Catholic Irish whose arrival had begun to inspire nativist alarm. At this earlier stage, however, they were still in the position, like a large section of the Protestant Ireland they had left behind them, of defining themselves primarily in terms of what they were not.

While the Presbyterians who numerically dominated migration to North America were later given a retrospective historical identity as Scots Irish, the Irish Catholics who made the same journey have been largely lost to view. There were exceptions. A branch of the Carrolls, descendants of a midlands Gaelic lordship who had retained their gentry status, migrated to Maryland in the 1680s. Their descendants were to include the only Catholic signatory to the Declaration of Independence, as well as a signatory to the federal constitution of 1787. The Carrolls, however, were the exception, gentlemen adventurers whose careers had more in common with the Irishmen who became merchants and army officers in *ancien régime* Europe than with the legion of indentured servants who contributed to the white labour force of the American colonies.[73] Without a larger body of potential leaders, and without the institutional support that would have been provided by a church organization (another Carroll was to become the new United States' first Catholic bishop, but not until 1789), these humbler migrants would appear to have lost any external markers of ethnicity as they

---

[72] Miller et al., *Irish Immigrants*, 435–51, 536–46; Patrick Griffin, *The People with No Name: Ireland's Ulster Scots, America's Scots Irish, and the Creation of a British Atlantic World 1689–1764* (Princeton, 2001), 172. Miller's account of the New Hampshire case is important in suggesting that the adoption of the label 'Scotch Irish' began before the era of mass Catholic migration, to which it is normally seen as a response.

[73] For the Carrolls see Rodgers, *Ireland, Slavery and Anti-Slavery*, ch. 9, to whom I owe the image of the American dynasty's founder as 'a wild goose blown off course by transatlantic winds' (p. 227). Also Miller et al., *Irish Immigrants*, 452–61.

became submerged in the wider white society. How far their experience in the New World was that of victims of economic forces beyond their control, and how far it represented the opening of possibilities that could never have existed in the land of their birth, must have depended on myriad accidents of personality and circumstance, all now beyond even the most committed historian's field of vision.

10

Imperial Crisis

When William Molyneux, in 1698, composed his statement of Ireland's claim to legislative independence, he paused briefly to consider and reject one particular argument, that Ireland was a colony of England:

Of all the objections raised against us, I take this to be the most extravagant; it seems not to have the least foundation or colour from reason or record. Do not the kings of England bear the style of Ireland amongst the rest of their kingdoms. Is this agreeable to the nature of a colony? Do they use the title of kings of Virginia, New England, or Maryland? . . . Have we not a parliament and courts of judicature? Do these things agree with a colony? This on all hands involves so many absurdities, that I think it deserves nothing more of our consideration.[1]

A sense of outrage at the demeaning comparison breaks through what is otherwise the even flow of legal and antiquarian argument. The Americans, however, did not take their dismissal to heart. Instead a succession of colonial reprints testifies to the interest they took in Molyneux's broader arguments on the issues of consent and legislative autonomy. Indeed it was from America that *The Case of Ireland* seems to have been reintroduced, from the 1770s, into Irish political literature, after some decades in which it had fallen partly out of sight.[2] By the time this rediscovery occurred, the comparison Molyneux had rejected would have seemed considerably less damaging to the Irish case. His popularity on the other side of the Atlantic had been one reflection of the development, over half a century or more, of a vigorous colonial commitment to the defence of their constitutional rights. As the confrontation with an increasingly intrusive British government escalated into armed revolt, some Irish patriots were to see in the American Revolution the inspiration to move forward to new forms of radicalism. Most, however, were to respond in a more parochial, and in many cases frankly opportunistic, manner.

Yet if Irish Protestants declined to see the parallels between themselves and settlers in more distant British territories, they were nevertheless affected by developments within that wider empire. During the first part of the eighteenth century, it has been suggested, it is possible to see the evolution in the American

---

[1] William Molyneux, *The Case of Ireland's Being Bound by Acts of Parliament in England Stated* (Dublin, 1698), 148–9.

[2] Patrick Kelly, 'William Molyneux and the Spirit of Liberty in Eighteenth-Century Ireland', *ECI* 3 (1988), 138–40.

and West Indian colonies of what was in effect an informal imperial constitution. Local representative assemblies increasingly gained the right to participate in the domestic government of the different colonies, while matters of defence and trade were controlled from London.[3] The rise from the 1690s of the Irish parliament, and the emergence of a partnership between British chief governors and Irish undertakers, on the basis of a division of patronage and influence, can be seen as part of the same development. From the 1760s, however, this network of understandings and mutual accommodation began to come apart. What destroyed it was the sharply rising cost of financing an extended empire at the height of Great Britain's century-long contest for supremacy with France. The Seven Years War of 1756–63, a worldwide conflict, fought in India, North America, and Africa, as well as in continental Europe and on the high seas, imposed unprecedented strain on all the major combatants. In Great Britain the response was an increased concern with the organization and financing of imperial defence. By seeking to impose new taxes on the North American colonies through the stamp act of 1765, and then by formally asserting their subordination to the London parliament by the declaratory act of 1766, London initiated a series of confrontations that was to culminate a decade later in armed revolt.

The specific issue of finance had less direct impact on Ireland than on other British territories. The kingdom already contributed substantially to imperial defence through a large reserve force supported as part of its military establishment but available for service overseas. A demand at the end of the 1760s that this establishment should be expanded to meet the empire's rising needs was to meet with resistance. Unlike the American case, however, this did not involve a point of political principle: the issue was rather how much Ireland should contribute, and what price the British government might have to pay local power brokers for any increase. Where the developing imperial crisis did affect Ireland's future was in influencing the way in which episodes of this kind were perceived in London. However much Irishmen might insist on their status as a kingdom, a substantial section of elite British opinion had always taken it for granted that their real place was as part of an empire that existed to serve the needs of Great Britain. Against this background the new concern with creating a more tightly controlled imperial system had implications for Ireland also. Already in the 1750s the money bill dispute had indicated the extent to which power had been allowed to slip into local hands. After 1763 the pretensions of the undertakers, and the restiveness of the Irish parliament, were easily interpreted as part of a wider pattern of central government weakness that needed urgently to be remedied if Britain was to remain a great power.[4]

[3] J. P. Greene, *Peripheries and Centre: Constitutional Development in the Extended Polities of the British Empire and the United States 1607–1788* (Athens, Ga., 1986).

[4] The only comprehensive survey of politics in the period 1760–1800 is R. B. McDowell, *Ireland in the Age of Imperialism and Revolution 1760–1801* (Oxford, 1979). This can be supplemented by a

TIME HAS ALMOST DESTROYED THE OLD MACHINE

On the evening of 3 December 1759 a crowd of some 3,000, some armed with clubs and swords, descended on the parliament house on College Green. Their arrival followed a protest two weeks earlier against heads of a bill to facilitate the rapid summoning of parliament during a period of adjournment. The stated purpose of the bill was to provide against emergencies such as a French invasion or a domestic insurrection. However there had been discussion over the preceding few years of the possibility of a union between Ireland and Great Britain, and the rumour now spread that the proposed bill's real object was to open the way for a legislative ambush that would rush through a union in a suddenly convened parliament. The chief secretary, in response to this hostile demonstration, had withdrawn his bill. But the crowd that assembled on 3 December remained unconvinced. Having taken possession of the parliament house they forced some fifty of the Lords and Commons to swear that they were 'for the country and against the union'. The whole episode had a double significance. At one level it indicated the extent to which the Dublin crowd now identified with the rhetoric of the parliamentary patriots, seeing the existence of a separate parliament as an essential guarantee of Irish political liberties. During the invasion members regarded as 'true to their country' were respectfully treated while others, including the attorney general, were roughly handled. At the same time the demeanour and actions of the crowd made clear that they had little respect for the political conduct of the generality of their betters. Among their actions was to place an old woman in the chair from which the lord chancellor presided over the House of Lords, 'with an English pipe in her mouth . . . alleging that many an old woman had sat there before her'.[5]

To British observers, the riot of December 1759, following hard on the money bill dispute of 1753–6, was evidence of the dangerously unstable character of Irish political life. The veteran Whig politician George Dodington found it 'a very striking and very shocking picture . . . to see a Protestant multitude attack a Protestant government, in a country where all together do not make a sixth of the whole, without any imaginable cause of complaint but because it is government'. His Dublin correspondent, the English-born lord chancellor John Bowes, who had himself been manhandled as he sought to enter the House of Lords (and dismissed, by implication, as an old woman), took a longer

---

series of monographs: M. J. Powell, *Britain and the Eighteenth-Century Crisis of Empire* (Basingstoke, 2003); M. R. O'Connell, *Irish Politics and Social Conflict in the Age of the American Revolution* (Philadelphia, 1965); James Kelly, *Prelude to Union: Anglo-Irish Politics in the 1780s* (Cork, 1992); as well as by the biographies of leading actors (Flood, Newenham, Fitzgibbon, Foster) cited below.

[5] Sean Murphy, 'The Dublin Anti-Union Riot of 3 December 1759', in Gerard O'Brien (ed.), *Parliament, Politics and People: Essays in Eighteenth-Century Irish History* (Dublin, 1989), 49–68.

view. Ireland since 1714 had been 'the most flourishing state in Europe'. Its inhabitants were now numerous and wealthy. They had no real grievances, but instead 'have been taught to think themselves injured by their present constitution'. In consequence 'time has almost destroyed the old machine by which this country was governed as a province, and till either that be restored or another framed, like uneasinesses will happen'.[6]

By the time Bowes had finished elaborating on these points, concern at the unmanageable state of Irish politics had been reinforced by a new dispute. Since the sole right controversy of the 1690s, the British government had been content to allow financial legislation to originate as heads of a bill in the Irish House of Commons. At the same time it continued to insist on certain symbolic performances to ensure that the crown's rights were not lost by default. One such, following the precedent established in 1695, was the inclusion of a token financial measure in the bills submitted to England for certification, as required by Poynings's Law, before a new parliament could be summoned. When the Irish lords justices applied in November 1760 for writs to be issued for the election of a new parliament, however, they submitted only two minor bills, neither of which concerned finance. When the English privy council demanded that they send a money bill 'agreeable to former precedents', a majority on the Irish side, including the three lords justices, Shannon, Stone, and John Ponsonby, refused. Their recalcitrance provoked a strong reaction. The English council, as it considered the matter, called for papers relating to Sidney's clash with the parliament of 1692. William Pitt, having initially opposed a confrontation, demanded a trade embargo to bring the Irish to heel. The duke of Devonshire, himself a former lord lieutenant, warned cabinet colleagues that the Dublin council's stand 'was one step towards throwing off their dependency on England which it was visible they were aiming at very fast'. Informed that the duke of Bedford was unwilling to return to his post as lord lieutenant, Devonshire declared that he acted wisely, 'for that country was come to such a pass that no man that was at ease or had any character to lose would care to go among them'.[7]

That Devonshire, an experienced Irish hand, should leap so quickly to the conclusion that the leaders of the Irish Protestant nation sought to cast off their dependency on England is eloquent testimony to the frustration, combined with a recurring unease, with which British politicians contemplated their Irish dependency. As a response to what, from the other side of the Irish Sea, seemed like an endless succession of provocations such sentiments were understandable. But it was nevertheless a serious misreading. In the first place it overlooked the

---

[6] Dodington to Bowes, 19 Jan. 1760 (HMC, *MSS of Miss M. Eyre Matcham* (1909), 73); Bowes to Dodington, 17 Apr. 1760, 25 Dec. 1760, 2 Feb. 1761 (ibid. 75, 77).

[7] *The Devonshire Diary: William Cavendish, Fourth Duke of Devonshire Memoranda on State of Affairs 1759–62*, ed. P. D. Brown and K. W. Schweizer, Camden Ser. 4/27 (London, 1982), 62, 78, 136.

extent to which the privy council's stand in 1760–1, like that of Boyle and his associates in 1753–6, employed patriot rhetoric to mask a variety of political calculations. Significantly it was Stone, the one-time self-appointed spokesman for the English interest now back in office through reinventing himself as the champion of popular and patriot causes, who argued most strongly that to transmit a money bill would violate the kingdom's constitution. By contrast the earl of Kildare, though considered a patriot, was still bitterly hostile to the primate, and so became the only leading figure to speak in favour of transmitting a bill as required.

Secondly, and more important, British ministers who muttered darkly of an Irish desire for 'independence' overlooked the wider political culture of which patriotism was a part. Lucas and others might make extravagant claims for Irish constitutional rights. But the basis on which they did so was largely the kingdom's claim to equal participation in what were thought of as specifically British liberties, developed across the centuries and reaffirmed in 1688. Over time, in fact, belief in the exceptional virtues of the British constitution became more prominent in Irish political rhetoric, superseding an older tradition in which England was just one of several homelands for an ancient 'Gothic constitution'.[8] To the sense of a shared tradition was added a lively sense of Great Britain and Ireland as sharing a common imperial destiny. In 1759, for example, the corporation of Dublin resolved to present the freedom of the city to William Pitt, celebrated both as the minister chiefly responsible for the recent string of naval victories and as living proof that a man could hold office without sacrificing his political principles. The corporation's address, significantly, was to the king's 'most disinterested and patriot minister'—a definition of patriotism clearly British and imperial rather than Irish in scope. Cork city, a decade later, paid its own tribute to Pitt when it installed a marble statue at the head of the staircase in the newly built mayor's residence.[9]

Attachment to the Hanoverian dynasty found further expression in regular public celebrations, marking royal marriages, births, and anniversaries, as soldiers fired volleys and fountains flowing with wine allowed the common people to drink loyally while their betters feasted. Military victories were another occasion for collective displays of a wider British patriotism. In March 1740, for example, news of Admiral Vernon's capture of the port of Porto Bello in modern Panama reached the medium-sized Ulster market town of Belfast:

The inhabitants flocked to the streets, and from thence to the Long Bridge, from whence, to their surprise, they saw the neighbouring country all, as it were, on a fire; for those who

---

[8] S. J. Connolly, 'Introduction', to idem (ed.), *Political Ideas in Eighteenth-Century Ireland* (Dublin, 2000), 14–15.
[9] Journal of the Sheriffs and Commons of Dublin, 14 Dec. 1759 (Dublin Municipal Library, C1/JSC/01, 389). For Cork see David Dickson, *Old World Colony: Cork and South Munster 1630–1830* (Cork, 2005), 366.

had not faggots cut, set the hedges of their fields afire, so that (as this town is encircled with a ridge of mountains) one could have counted upwards of one hundred bonfires on the adjacent hills.[10]

This, of course, was in north-east Ulster. It is unlikely that the fields of the Catholic south blazed with anything like the same fires, real or metaphorical. But for the Protestant population, Swift's whole people of Ireland, it is clear that an often prickly sense of their kingdom's rights and grievances coincided with a well-developed sense of its place in the Hanoverian dominions and its resulting share in a heritage of British liberties and pride in British imperial power.

The intransigence that so irritated Devonshire and others, then, did not arise from any rejection of the British connection. The problem lay rather in the way in which that connection was envisaged: the insistence on Ireland's status as equal partner in a union of crowns, and consequently on the absolute parity of the British and Irish parliaments. 'They have considered your house as the model', Bowes told Dodington, 'and in general think themselves injured in the instances wherein theirs upon the legal constitution must differ.' Sir Richard Cox, replying to Lucas, had commented on the folly of such pretensions. A graceful surrender to Ireland's subordinate status 'puts her into the most amiable light, of using her liberty so as not to abuse it'. By contrast only a madman 'would provoke a nation able without much labour to reduce us to our primitive nothing, to exert that power they have in order to convince us that we are dependent'. Two decades later, the chief secretary George Macartney, himself, unusually, an Irishman, was shouted down when he told the Commons that the passage of a government money bill at the start of each new parliament represented 'a kind of fine which we pay for the renewal of parliament', and that the British privy council was 'in some respect a branch of our legislature'. He went on to offer a more conciliatory image, that the passage of such a bill was 'a point of form . . . a courtesy which an affectionate younger sister has always paid to her elder'. But even this emollient domestic metaphor failed to win over a hostile Commons.[11]

The insistence of Irish Protestants on their status as part of what would later be called a dual monarchy had been a feature of debate since the 1690s. The underlying problem, that the personal rule of a monarchy was by this time a transparent political fiction, had been clear for almost as long. By the middle of the eighteenth century, however, other developments were giving this gap between rhetoric and political reality a new disruptive potential. When the privy council declined to transmit a money bill in preparation for a new parliament

---

[10] *Dublin Daily Post*, 29 Mar. 1740.

[11] Bowes to Dodington, 2 Feb. 1761 (HMC, *Eyre Matcham MSS*, 77); 'Anthony Litten' [Sir Richard Cox], *The Cork Surgeon's Antidote against the Dublin Apothecary's Poison* (Dublin, 1749), no. 2, p. 10; no. 3, p. 5; Macartney's speech in *A Comparative State of the Two Rejected Money Bills in 1692 and 1769, with Some Observations on Poynings' Act . . . by a Barrister* (Dublin, 1770), 72–3, 75. See also Thomas Bartlett, 'Ireland 1769–72', in Peter Roebuck (ed.), *Macartney of Lisanoure 1737–1806* (Belfast, 1983), 74.

in 1760, some individuals were playing factional politics. The main reason for their refusal to comply with precedent, however, was the imminence of a general election. Ireland had no equivalent to the English acts of 1694 and 1716 that had required elections every three, and then every seven, years. The only limit on the duration of parliament was the life of the monarch, and the general election of 1761 was in fact the first to take place since 1727. With the death of George II in October 1760, however, a new parliament became unavoidable, and it was clear to all concerned that neither the chief undertakers, Stone, Ponsonby, and Shannon, nor most other members of the privy council, were prepared to risk the electoral consequences of being seen not to take the popular and patriotic side.

By the time of this new money bill dispute, the quirk in the Irish constitution that had allowed the same parliament to sit for thirty-three years had itself become the subject of debate. The need for more frequent renewals of parliament's mandate had been taken up by the patriot opposition in the session of 1757–8: in November 1757 the Commons had voted unanimously for heads of a bill on the subject. When a general election did finally become necessary, just over three years later, the outcome was in some respects an anticlimax. Of 150 constituencies only 26, 9 counties and 17 boroughs, saw an electoral contest. But in several of these cases candidates appeared pledging themselves if elected to support a septennial bill, limiting the lifetime of a parliament to seven years; one, standing unsuccessfully in County Westmeath, went so far as to propose that parliament should back up this demand with a short money bill, in place of the usual two years' supply. A further indication of changing times was the election as MP for Dublin city of Charles Lucas, returned from exile and standing on a platform that included both a septennial bill and a reduction in the pension list.

The general election of 1761, like the popular agitation during the money bill dispute of 1753–6, and the anti-union riot of 1759, were evidence of the progressive widening that was taking place in the circle of political debate. Resistance to Wood's Halfpence in 1722–5 had come largely from within the political establishment; popular demonstrations on the subject were few and received no encouragement. Half a century later, by contrast, patriot issues brought crowds onto the streets, whether or not their betters wanted them there. In part the political elite had brought this new set of pressures from a politicized public opinion on themselves. This was particularly the case with Boyle and his associates, who during 1753–6 had blatantly turned a factional conflict within the political establishment into a patriot crusade. Yet it is doubtful whether elite manipulation alone can explain the quickening of popular politics evident in the 1750s and 1760s. By this time the effects were also being felt of a period of unprecedented economic growth. Where Dublin is concerned, a threefold increase in population between 1685 and 1760 meant that there was now the possibility of mobilizing truly formidable numbers, creating an urban crowd of the kind that had long been a factor in the politics of London and other European capitals. Rising levels of literacy, and the growth of the newspaper press, facilitated the circulation of ideas and information. Contemporaries commented with alarm on the spread of newspaper reading among the lower classes.[12] Meanwhile economic expansion, modest but cumulative up to the 1740s, rapid and far-reaching thereafter, had begun to increase the ranks of the economically independent if only moderately prosperous in both town and country, swelling the ranks of those with sufficient sense of their own consequence, and sufficient freedom of action, to demand a political voice. The reluctance of Ponsonby, Shannon, and others to comply with an empty formality formerly accepted without question was the response of a political elite that had helped to release forces it could no longer control, but that in any case could no longer take for granted that political debate could be contained within the restricted circle from which its members were drawn.

The extension of political argument and activity to a wider range of social groups had particular implications, perhaps, for one particular body, the Protestant dissenters. The idea that non-episcopal ecclesiastical structures were in themselves peculiarly conducive to an egalitarian spirit is probably misleading; the management of congregational and wider affairs by a partnership of ministers and lay elders, it has been pointed out, was generally oligarchic rather than democratic.[13] What is true is that the Ulster Presbyterians, the largest dissenting body, were heirs to a distinctive political tradition that set them apart from their Anglican counterparts. One element in Scottish political thinking of the sixteenth and seventeenth centuries, most fully developed by the Covenanters, had been a contractarian understanding of society, in which allegiance to the monarch was conditional on his proper discharge of his obligations. In 1688 Ulster Presbyterians, like their Scottish counterparts, had accepted the replacement of one king with another without any of the equivocation or mental torment seen among so many Anglicans. At the height of party conflict in the last years of Queen Anne, likewise, two of their ministers, John McBride and James Kirkpatrick, had responded to Tory attacks in pamphlets defending not only the rights of religious dissenters but the principle of limited monarchy and the legitimacy of resistance against tyrannical government.[14]

The radical potential of Ulster Presbyterian political thinking, particularly when fused with the developing culture of the Scottish Enlightenment, was

[12] McDowell, *Ireland in the Age of Imperialism and Revolution*, 229, quotes the excitable comments of the MP Edward Tighe: 'A labouring man now hardly goes to work until he has read the news.' For literacy levels see ch. 8.

[13] Ian McBride, *Scripture Politics: Ulster Presbyterians and Irish Radicalism in Late Eighteenth-Century Ireland* (Oxford, 1998), 91–2.

[14] McBride, *Scripture Politics*, 91–100; Pieter Tesch, 'Presbyterian Radicalism', in David Dickson, Daire Keogh, and Kevin Whelan (eds.), *The United Irishmen: Republicanism, Radicalism and Rebellion* (Dublin, 1993), 33–48. For the Scottish background see Claire Jackson, *Restoration Scotland 1660–1690: Royalist Politics, Religion and Ideas* (Woodbridge, 2003), 64–72.

likewise evident in the activities of a group of writers active in Dublin in the 1720s. These included the publishers John Smith and William Bruce, as well as James Arbuckle, editor of the *Dublin Weekly Journal*, and the moral philosopher Frances Hutcheson, all of them Ulster born and graduates of the university of Glasgow. They appear to have found a patron or mentor in Viscount Molesworth, a peer with estates in both Yorkshire and County Dublin and the author of a classic text, *The Principles of a Real Whig*, setting out a radical interpretation of the Revolution of 1688. Suggestions of a 'Molesworth circle' are perhaps an exaggeration. But the prevalence among them of advanced political ideas of the kind associated with his name is evident, particularly in the work of Hutcheson, whose arguments on the legitimacy of resistance to tyranny were to be influential on both sides of the Atlantic.[15]

Hutcheson, Arbuckle, and the rest were primarily thinkers and teachers. They were also, it must be recognized, a tightly interconnected group. Hutcheson, for example, was a cousin of William Bruce, and had studied at the academy at Killyleagh, County Down, founded by Bruce's father. His partner in the Dublin Academy was Thomas Drennan, the father of William Drennan, who decades later was to be a key figure in the emergence of the United Irishmen. There is an obvious risk of mistaking the shared assumptions of an extended family for the workings of a culture.[16] Occasional glimpses of the political culture of ordinary Presbyterians within Ulster itself, however, suggest that the advanced intellectual radicalism of Hutcheson and others did in fact have its roots in a deeper soil. The minister Alexander MacLaine, preaching in Antrim during the Jacobite rebellion of 1745, had no hesitation in presenting the Revolution of 1688 as both an exercise of the right of resistance and a precedent for future action:

Nobler principles upon which to act, and more generous motives, can never enter into the heart of man, than to deliver a nation from the chains of merciless tyranny and slavery, and to advance and effectually secure their happiness and prosperity. These were the motives upon which James the Second was resisted, and permitted to banish himself, and these are motives which will for ever justify resistance in the same circumstances.[17]

Commitment to advanced Whig principles was reinforced by practical grievances that set Presbyterians at odds with the political establishment. Economic friction between dissenting weavers and farmers and a predominantly Anglican landlord

[15] Ian McBride, 'The School of Virtue: Francis Hutcheson, Irish Presbyterians and the Scottish Enlightenment', in D. G. Boyce, Robert Eccleshall, and Vincent Geoghegan (eds.), *Political Thought in Ireland since the Seventeenth Century* (London, 1993), 73–99; Michael Brown, *Francis Hutcheson in Dublin 1719–1730* (Dublin, 2002), esp. ch. 1. The idea of a 'Molesworth circle' originated with Caroline Robbins, *The Eighteenth-Century Commonwealthman* (London, 1959). For discussion see Michael Stewart, 'John Smith and the Molesworth Circle', *ECI* 2 (1987), 89–103.

[16] For the close-knit nature of the group, and also the connecting influence of an involvement in freemasonry, see A. T. Q. Stewart, *A Deeper Silence: The Hidden Origins of the United Irishmen* (London, 1993).

[17] Alexander Maclaine, *A Sermon Preached at Antrim, December 18, 1745, Being the National Fast* (Dublin, 1746), 11–12, 14–18.

class took on the additional edge of denominational hostility, while Presbyterians of all classes resented paying tithes to support the episcopalian established church.

Presbyterian radicalism thus had a long intellectual history. Its practical political potential, however, was initially limited. The sacramental test excluded even wealthy dissenters from participation in urban government, while county politics remained the exclusive playground of what even in Ulster was a mainly Anglican aristocracy and gentry. With the rise of new forms of popular political participation, on the other hand, dissenters, with their generally higher level of prosperity, their greater literacy, and their tradition of radical political thought, were well placed to take a leading role. Presbyterian areas of Ulster were prominent in the agitation in support of Boyle and his associates during 1753–6; the Antrim Patriot Club had to respond directly to allegations that it represented a sectional dissenting interest, while at the same time defending 'that bulwark of the Protestant succession and the liberties of these kingdoms, the Protestants of the north of Ireland'.[18] Government awareness of the disruptive potential of dissent appeared again in the immediate aftermath of the 1759 riot, when the lord lieutenant sought to blame the disturbances partly on the presence among the weavers of the Liberty area in the west of the city of 'New Light Presbyterians' whose principles were 'totally republican and averse to English government'. His chief secretary, likewise, warned of the danger posed by a sect of Protestants descended from Cromwell's followers who remained hostile to both monarchy and the established church.[19]

At the same time that Presbyterians were thus beginning to emerge as a distinct political voice so too, much more hesitantly, were the Catholics. A first Catholic Association appeared in Dublin in 1756, through the efforts of Charles O'Conor, a landholder in County Galway and the most notable antiquarian writer of the mid-century, and John Curry, a medical doctor. Its early efforts were unimpressive: the clergy, and a substantial section of the laity, reluctant to court controversy, resisted O'Conor's attempts to organize a loyal address, much less to challenge a last attempt soon after to revive the idea of a registration system for priests. Their pessimism seemed vindicated when the Irish parliament over the next few years threw out by large majorities three separate bills that sought to permit Catholics to lend money against the security of landed property. From 1760 the Association had given itself a more representative character by organizing the election of nine members from the Dublin parishes, but three years later it had ceased to meet. In 1767, however, a new threat appeared. Catholic merchants and traders had for several decades contested attempts by the guilds which denied them membership to levy a charge, quarterage, in

---

[18] *Remarks on a Late Pamphlet Entitled, Advice to the Patriot Club of the County of Antrim* (Dublin, 1756), 4–6. I am grateful to Mr Gordon Rees for drawing my attention to this aspect of the pamphlet.
[19] Murphy, 'Dublin Anti-Union Riot', 59, 61.

exchange for permission to carry on their businesses. Between 1767 and 1775, following a court judgement in favour of Catholic tradesmen in Cork, supporters of the guilds made five attempts to introduce legislation legalizing quarterage. A revived Catholic committee organized a counter-campaign, engaging counsel in both Ireland and England and submitting addresses to government. The success of their agitation, directed against a self-avowed bastion of the Protestant interest but conducted with a vigour in sharp contrast to the timidity of only a decade earlier, was further evidence of a political system undergoing rapid and far-reaching change.

BRINGING GOVERNMENT BACK TO THE CASTLE

British ministers responded to the reluctance of the Irish council to submit a money bill in advance of the new parliament to be elected in 1761 with grim talk of a supposed push for independence, to be crushed with trade blockades or other drastic measures. But such bellicose language did not last. In the end the council agreed to accept a bill continuing certain exceptional duties voted in the last session of parliament—less than the vote of ordinary supply required by precedent, but at least a money bill. At the same time it reaffirmed its authority by approving Bedford's recommendation to dismiss Anthony Malone, who had headed the opposition to sending over a supply bill, from his position as chancellor of the Irish exchequer. As in 1756 and on other occasions both sides, once the posturing was over, opted for compromise over confrontation.[20]

If the undertakers had caused concern by their recalcitrance over the money bill, however, their subsequent performance hardly reassured. In the parliaments of 1761–2, 1763–4, and 1765–6 they duly delivered grants of the necessary additional revenue, for the usual period of two years in each case. But they proved either unable or unwilling to prevent the Commons from raising awkward constitutional issues. By this time Sexton Pery, up to now the leading spokesman for the independent or patriot interest, had been overtaken by a new star, Henry Flood, first elected for County Kilkenny in 1759. As a son of the lord chief justice of the King's Bench, Flood had initially supported government, but moved into opposition after the Ponsonbys declined to support his re-election for Kilkenny, forcing him to stand instead for the borough of Callan. The number of MPs prepared to support a frontal assault on the administration was

[20] For contrasting accounts see R. E. Burns, *Irish Parliamentary Politics in the Eighteenth-Century*, ii: *1730–1760* (Washington, DC, 1990), 298–312, who emphasizes the Irish council's successful defiance, and James Kelly, 'Monitoring the Constitution: The Operation of Poynings's Law in the 1760s', in David Hayton (ed.), *The Irish Parliament in the Eighteenth-Century: The Long Apprenticeship* (Edinburgh, 2001), 96–9, who emphasizes the extent to which London eventually got its way.

relatively small: patriot resolutions on issues such as the distribution of pensions and offices, the appointment of Englishmen to judicial office, and the operation of Poynings's Law were easily defeated. A much larger group, however, were prepared to follow the patriot lead on measures more of symbolic importance. During 1765–6 the Commons passed heads of bills formally to extend to Ireland the English law of habeas corpus, and to allow judges to hold office during good behaviour rather than at the king's pleasure. They also passed heads of a bill, in 1761 and again in 1765–6, limiting the duration of parliament to seven years. It is unlikely that most members had in fact any real desire to face the electorate more often. But they were clearly happy to pay lip service to a popular measure, confident that the government would take on itself the odium involved in not allowing the bill to proceed.

It is hardly surprising, given this background, that British politicians continued to believe that something needed to be done to bring the management of the dependent kingdom of Ireland under tighter control. But at a time of political instability in Britain, leading to a succession of short-lived ministries, policy failed to progress beyond a series of false starts. The earl of Halifax, who succeeded Bedford as lord lieutenant in 1761, took a tougher line with the undertakers than his predecessor. Meanwhile his chief secretary William Hamilton worked to build up a personal following in the Commons. There seems also to have been some suggestion that Halifax would further strengthen the lord lieutenant's direct control of affairs by remaining in Ireland beyond the period of the parliamentary session. In the event, however, he stayed only six months. His successor, the duke of Northumberland, came to Ireland only for the duration of the parliamentary session of 1763–4. Hamilton had, unusually, continued as chief secretary under the new viceroy, but in 1764 he was forced out of office when the undertakers made clear that they were not prepared to work with him. At a meeting on 1 February 1765 the British cabinet resolved that the next lord lieutenant appointed should be directed to reside 'constantly'. The deletion from the minutes of the preceding word 'almost' suggests a collective commitment to a real change in the viceroy's role. In fact the next appointee, Viscount Weymouth, never assumed office, since the ministry that appointed him collapsed a month later. His successor, the earl of Hertford, appointed by a different cabinet, followed the usual practice of coming to Ireland only for the parliamentary session of 1765–6. The earl of Bristol, appointed in October 1766, agreed to reside constantly, but resigned on an English political matter before taking up office. When George, fourth Viscount Townshend, accepted the lord lieutenancy in August 1767 there may have been some suggestion that he should be a resident chief governor. But nothing definite seems to have been settled by the time he left for Dublin two months later.[21]

[21] The question of what instructions Townshend initially received is crucial to an understanding of how far the subsequent shift to direct control by a resident viceroy was part of a long-term

If Townshend did not come to Ireland with instructions to be permanently resident as a means of bypassing the increasingly unsatisfactory undertakers, he nevertheless came with a mission. Since 1697 Irish taxes had supported an army fixed at a permanent establishment of 12,000 men. This was well beyond what was needed for the defence of the kingdom. Instead several thousand were at any one time stationed overseas, so that Ireland in effect provided a reserve garrison for the British dominions as a whole. In 1762–3, as they contemplated the huge cost of the Seven Years War just coming to an end, ministers considered increasing Ireland's contribution to imperial defence by expanding its military establishment to 18,000 or more. They abandoned the proposal, but the underlying problem of financing the defence of a growing empire in an age of global warfare did not go away. Indeed a direct result of the decision to leave the Irish military establishment untouched was the ill-fated attempt to impose stamp duties on the American colonies.

By 1767 ministers had decided that what was referred to as the 'augmentation' of the army should after all go ahead. To ease its passage the cabinet agreed that Townshend could promise concessions to patriot sensibilities: legislation to secure judges' tenure of office during good behaviour, a septennial bill, and a promise that proposals for a habeas corpus act and a revival of the militia (important to Irish Protestants in terms both of civic pride and of the opportunities for patronage it created) would be at least considered. Having duly announced the first of these measures, however, Townshend received instructions to insert a clause allowing judges to be removed at the will of the British as well as the Irish parliament. Then came orders to alter the promised septennial bill to an octennial one. The reasons were sound enough: it avoided the uncertainties that would arise if general elections in both kingdoms coincided, and an eight-year cycle better suited a parliament that met every second year. In each case, however, the effect was the dilution of a promised concession; the Irish Commons refused to amend the septennial act, so that the alteration had to be made by the English privy council.

Against this unpromising background, Townshend opened negotiations for the passage of the augmentation act. Stone and Shannon had both died in 1764. Townshend had thus to deal with two main figures: John Ponsonby, speaker of the Commons and now the dominant figure in the Irish parliament, and the

British strategy of establishing tighter control, and how far it was the unplanned consequence of the difficulties Townshend encountered. Thomas Bartlett, 'The Townshend Viceroyalty 1767–72', in Thomas Bartlett and D. W. Hayton (eds.), *Penal Era and Golden Age* (Belfast, 1979), 88–94, rejects suggestions that Townshend was from the start intended to be permanently resident, pointing in particular to a paper from February 1768 in which Townshend himself proposed, as a new principle, that lords lieutenant should in future reside constantly. Powell, *Britain and the Crisis of Empire*, 95–9 argues that Townshend was from the start intended to be a permanently resident chief governor. However his only explanation of the February 1768 memorandum is that 'shadows of doubt continued to surround Townshend's instructions', which would seem largely to concede Bartlett's point.

second earl of Shannon, married to Ponsonby's daughter but also head of an important political connection in his own right. By the beginning of 1768 it was becoming clear that neither undertaker was willing to support what was likely to be an unpopular measure, except in return for what the ministry regarded as unacceptable further grants of office. Without their backing the augmentation had no chance of success and in May 1768 the Commons rejected by 105 votes to 101 a request to increase the Irish military establishment.

Townshend's instinctive response to the undertakers' obstruction was to go on the offensive. His brother Charles Townshend, the recently deceased chancellor of the English exchequer, had given his name to a second unsuccessful attempt, between 1767 and 1770, to impose new taxes on the American colonies. Townshend himself spoke openly of the need to prevent Ireland both from succumbing to the English disease of factionalism and from shaking off its dependency. In February 1768 he wrote to London proposing that augmentation should be postponed while steps were taken to establish the crown's authority in Ireland. There should be a permanently resident lord lieutenant, a reorganization of the system of government patronage, and the installation as speaker of a reliable crown servant. The cabinet, however, refused to back such a new departure, and Townshend reluctantly agreed to go ahead with the augmentation proposal. A general election took place, in accordance with the recently introduced octennial act, in the summer of 1768, but the new parliament, according to the customary two-year cycle, did not meet until autumn 1769. When it did so Townshend was ready with concessions: he proposed economies to reduce the cost of the increased establishment, and also offered assurances that in normal circumstances 12,000 of the expanded force of 15,000 men would be stationed in Ireland—a concession that deprived the measure of much of its value as a contribution to imperial defence, and arguably encroached on the king's prerogative of controlling the armed forces. In this form the proposal passed the house on 27 November 1769. But this eventual success was overshadowed by a near simultaneous defeat. To obtain the writs for the summoning of a new parliament in 1768 the Irish privy council had once again had to transmit bills to England for approval, and these, as the government's interpretation of Poynings's Law required, had included a finance bill. When this bill then came before the Commons on 21 November members rejected it, on the grounds that it had not originated in that house.

The rejection of the money bill was not, as might be assumed, a calculated show of strength by the disgruntled undertakers. The initiative seems in fact to have come from a patriot grouping led by Flood and Pery, taking advantage of the general breakdown of parliamentary discipline. But the apparent new challenge to its authority helped to move the government towards a more aggressive response of the kind Townshend had already advocated. There was a brief but embarrassing delay until the ordinary supply bills had passed through both houses. Once these had been secured, however, Townshend, on direct orders from London, prorogued parliament on 26 December, having first entered a formal protest in the journals of the Lords against the behaviour of the lower house. The establishment the following month of a more stable and, on imperial issues, more assertive ministry under Lord North allowed the lord lieutenant to go further, dismissing Ponsonby from the revenue board, Shannon as master general of the ordnance, and both men from the privy council. Next Townshend, aided by his chief secretary Sir George Macartney, a County Antrim landowner recently returned from a controversial special embassy to Russia, set about building a Castle party in the Commons sufficient to ensure the passage of government business. To this end they single-mindedly employed every scrap of patronage available. One important tactical move was to divide the Revenue Board into separate customs and excise divisions, reducing the influence of any one officer while increasing the number of posts at the disposal of the lord lieutenant.

Townshend's victory over the undertakers was not instantly achieved. In a short parliamentary session between February and May 1771, he succeeded in obtaining a vote of thanks from the Commons for his continuance in office. Ponsonby, faced with the prospect of having formally to present the address at the Castle, resigned the speakership. However the election as his successor of the veteran troublemaker Edmund Sexton Pery represented at best a qualified victory. When parliament met again in the autumn, Flood was able to carry resolutions condemning the division of the Revenue Board. Meanwhile the opposition sought, as in 1753, to mobilize popular opinion against this latest attempt to subordinate Ireland to England. During 1770 Flood wrote a lengthy introduction to a new edition of Molyneux's *Case of Ireland*. This time, however, a more sophisticated public proved less responsive to such blatant use of the patriot card. Meanwhile Townshend and Macartney continued to consolidate their parliamentary majority. By the time the session ended in June 1772 it was clear that they had succeeded in their aim of replacing dependence on undertakers with a new system of direct management from the Castle.

Townshend's five years as lord lieutenant did not change the fundamental principles on which the Irish parliament was managed. His aim, he had explained to his chief secretary in February 1769, was that 'people may be taught to request through the person H[is] Majesty pleases to employ the favours of the crown, instead of wresting them by the menaces, intrigues, and bargains of a faction'.[22] Patronage, in other words, was still central to the whole process. Nor was it possible, in practice, to outlaw the 'bargains of a faction'. By the time he left Ireland, in fact, Townshend himself had concluded that a stable long-term settlement required that the earl of Shannon, able to control the return of up to nine members and with a total of eighteen to twenty followers in the Commons, be won back to the government side. In 1776 the earl duly returned to the privy council and accepted the office of muster master general. Thirteen years later,

[22] Townshend to Macartney, 9 Feb. 1769 (*Macartney in Ireland 1768–72: A Calendar of the Chief Secretaryship Papers of Sir George Macartney*, ed. Thomas Bartlett (Belfast, 1979), 4).

during another falling out with government, he set out the terms on which he would be willing to resume his parliamentary support: 'that he should always have the nomination of one bishop, one judge, and one commissioner of the Revenue, besides office for himself, inferior office for his dependants, and the whole patronage of the county and city of Cork'.[23] Townshend's viceroyalty, as so formidable a shopping list made clear, had not ended the ability of leading magnates to translate control of parliamentary seats into benefits for themselves and their clients. What had changed was not the degree of attention paid to their wishes, but the way in which such transactions were managed. The negotiations required to construct a parliamentary majority, formerly delegated to the undertakers, were now the responsibility of a resident lord lieutenant and chief secretary. The Castle, in effect, became the chief undertaker.

If Townshend's viceroyalty did not end the bargaining power of the great borough proprietors, neither did it end the reliance of English chief governors on Irish office holders. There was, however, an important change in the character of the crown's Irish servants. The undertakers, from Conolly to Shannon and Ponsonby, had been first and foremost parliamentary managers. Their successors, by contrast, were men of business, chosen for their administrative ability and skill in debate, rather than their command of parliamentary seats. John Beresford, who replaced Ponsonby as a commissioner of the revenue in 1770 and became first commissioner ten years later, was in fact a younger son from an important political dynasty, with lands in Waterford, Londonderry, and elsewhere. In 1791 the family controlled the return of nine members (although in four or even five of these cases their hold depended on their access to government patronage), and was reckoned to have influence over the votes of around twenty MPs. By contrast John Foster, owner of a medium-sized estate in County Louth and from 1785 speaker of the Commons, controlled only three seats: one of the two members for his county, and one each from the pocket borough of Dunleer and the open constituency of Drogheda. John Fitzgibbon, who became attorney general in 1784 and (as earl of Clare) lord chancellor in 1789, had no electoral interest of his own: having lost his Trinity College seat on becoming a government supporter, he failed to be returned for County Limerick, despite owning a substantial estate there, and sat instead for a friend's pocket borough of Kilmallock. Yet Foster and Fitzgibbon, along with Beresford, formed the core of what came to be spoken of as the Irish 'cabinet', a small group of office holders, their tenure continuing under successive viceroys, who exercised a significant influence over policy and who over time were to prove capable of dominating a weak lord lieutenant.[24]

---

[23] Quoted in E. M. Johnston, *Great Britain and Ireland 1760–1800: A Study in Political Administration* (Edinburgh, 1963), 261.

[24] For the Irish cabinet see A. P. W. Malcomson, *John Foster: The Politics of the Anglo-Irish Ascendancy* (Oxford, 1978), 64–70. For the limited importance in this connection of command of seats, see ibid., ch. 5. See also Johnston, *Great Britain and Ireland*, 71–4.

The shift from the beginning of the 1770s to the direct management of Irish political affairs through a resident lord lieutenant and chief secretary contributed to the emergence in the parliaments of that decade of a more coherent and organized patriot grouping. Opposition, where factional in origin or arising from political principle, was now more clearly opposition to a British government. One dramatic indication of a changing political climate was the election for County Antrim in 1776 of James Wilson, a naval officer independent of the main landed interests, who stood on a popular platform that included a habeas corpus bill, parliamentary reform, the exclusion from parliament of pensioners and some office holders, the modification of Poynings's Law, and a reform of the franchise. Overall this general election was reckoned to have increased the size of the patriot opposition from fifty to around seventy. The group had suffered a serious setback the previous year, when its leading spokesman, Henry Flood, joined the government, accepting the office of vice treasurer. By this time, however, they had found an important new supporter in the earl of Charlemont. Charlemont himself, a well-travelled aesthete disabled by nerves from speaking in public, was better equipped to be a patron than a leader. But in 1775 he offered one of the seats for his pocket borough of Charlemont in County Tyrone to a young Dublin lawyer, Henry Grattan, who over the next three years replaced Flood as the chief patriot spokesman in the Commons.[25]

A few years earlier Horace Walpole, son of the former prime minister but himself an observer from the political sidelines, offered a characteristically cynical characterization of the Irish patriots: 'those who had been too insignificant to be bought off, or whose demands had been too high—and a few well meaning men'. Townshend, in 1769, had referred equally dismissively to 'new purchasers into parliament, or adventurers, who must be patriots until provided for'.[26] Their cynicism was understandable. In the 1740s Malone and Sir Richard Cox had moved from patriot opposition to co-option into Speaker Boyle's political system. A few years later Robert French and Edmund Sexton Pery had apparently made the opposite journey, from supporting government as clients of Archbishop Stone to attacking it at the behest of a now disaffected primate. In late 1759, at the same time that he described the anti-union riot, Lord Chancellor Bowes reported the appearance in the Commons of a new orator, John Hely-Hutchinson, who had made his first speech within minutes of being sworn in and whose 'patriotic zeal has from the warmth of that house expanded itself since *de die in diem* [from day to day]'. His impractical proposal relating to the export of cattle had passed unanimously 'because the question was too popular to admit of opposition'. By the end of the following year, however, Hely-Hutchinson was the government's

---

[25] David Lammey, 'The Growth of the "Patriot Opposition" in Ireland during the 1770s', *Parliamentary History*, 7 (1988), 257–81.

[26] Walpole, quoted in F. G. James, *Ireland in the Empire 1688–1770* (Cambridge, Mass., 1973), 257–8; Townshend to Macartney, 9 Feb. 1769 (*Macartney in Ireland*, ed. Bartlett, 4).

prime serjeant. Thereafter his reputation was of a shameless jobber. 'There is no retaining him', the solicitor general observed despairingly in 1773, 'but by paying him as you do post boys on the road, for the length he goes; and he will go any length for pay.'[27]

A progress like Hely-Hutchinson's—a triumphant demonstration of the capacity to make trouble from the back benches, followed by a rapid acceptance of office—would seem to suggest that patriotism was not even the last, but rather the very first, refuge of a parliamentary scoundrel. But generalization remains hazardous. If some were content to establish the need to buy them off, others gave evidence of more consistent commitment. Malone, after all, was to forfeit his office for his resistance to the transmission of a money bill in 1761. Whatever encouragement Pery and French received from Stone, equally, their opposition in 1757–8 was no short-term opportunist gesture. French continued to sit as an independent member, frequently critical of the administration, until 1776, although he seems over time to have lost faith in the value of opposition politics. Pery, having led the patriot opposition throughout the 1760s, accepted government support to replace Ponsonby as speaker of the Commons in 1771, but did not cease to challenge the administration on issues such as the status of money bills and the restrictions on Irish trade. Like Cox before them, moreover, both men could point to other activities as proof that their declared commitment to improvement went beyond political rhetoric: Pery to his transformation of Limerick's urban landscape, French to his much-praised development of his Galway estate.

Against this background it becomes easier to understand the career of Henry Flood. In the negotiations that preceded his appointment as vice treasurer, he undoubtedly drove a hard bargain in terms of patronage and the promise of a future additional appointment. Yet he seems genuinely to have believed that there was no inherent conflict between patriotism and the acceptance of office: instead it should be possible to follow the example of Flood's own political hero, William Pitt the elder, and serve both king and country.[28] It was a well-established stance that can be traced back to the equally complex career, between the 1690s and the 1720s, of Alan Brodrick, later earl of Midleton. By the 1770s, however, times had changed. Once in office Flood discovered that there was no longer a place on the government benches for the independent politician; in the new political system inaugurated by Townshend admission to the inner circle of office holders, and the influence that went with it, could be acquired only by a wholehearted commitment to the administration and its measures. The readiness of his fellow patriots to condemn his defection, equally, reflected a new outlook, which for the first time rejected office as inherently compatible with the

---

[27] Godfrey Lill to Macartney, 23 Oct. 1773 (*Macartney in Ireland*, ed. Bartlett, 247).

[28] James Kelly, *Henry Flood: Patriots and Politics in Eighteenth-Century Ireland* (Dublin, 1998), esp. 68–9, 210–12, 216–17.

public interest. Over the next two decades, under the influence of two Atlantic revolutions and new political conflicts at home, the options of patriotism and office, which Flood had attempted to combine, were to become ever more clearly irreconcilable.

DRAGON'S TEETH

Townshend's contest with the undertakers, and the emergence over the next decade of a more coherent patriot grouping in parliament, took place against the background of a developing conflict in the American colonies. Some on the Irish side were ready, from an early stage, to see the two struggles as linked. In 1771 Benjamin Franklin visited Dublin to dine with Lucas and others whom he described as 'friends of America'. Such expressions of solidarity, however, were for the most part superficial. Irishmen might see the Americans and themselves as victims of the same high-handed treatment at the hands of British ministers. Their patriotism, however, was based on the principles first developed by Molyneux and obsessively elaborated by Lucas: Ireland was no colony but a kingdom, whose claims to legislative autonomy derived from long-established historical rights. Its case was thus, as Molyneux himself had proclaimed, radically different from that of the Americans. A much larger section of Irish opinion, meanwhile, remained largely indifferent to events on the other side of the Atlantic.

With the firing of the first shots at Lexington and Concord in April 1775 the American conflict could no longer be ignored. But Irish reactions remained ambivalent. When the Irish parliament, in October, passed resolutions condemning the revolt, it was noted that 28 of the 37 county MPs present, in other words those considered most likely both to reflect and to be responsive to public opinion, were among the 54 who voted against. The most common view, however, appears to have been that, even though the crown's ministers had badly mishandled the situation, it was nevertheless entitled to support in suppressing open rebellion. The opportunistic intervention on the American side of France in 1778 and Spain in 1779 further rallied Irish support for the crown. Even among the Presbyterians of Ulster, where heavy emigration across the Atlantic since the second decade of the century had created particularly close ties with the colonies, support for the revolt appears to have been more limited than has been claimed. Both Belfast and Derry celebrated the British capture of Charleston in South Carolina in May 1780 with illuminations, parades, and the ringing of bells.[29]

---

[29] The fullest analysis, largely followed here, is now Vincent Morley, *Irish Opinion and the American Revolution 1760–1783* (Cambridge, 2002), 32, 73, 115–25, 170–7, 249–50. See also M. J. Bric, 'Ireland, America and the Reassessment of a Special Relationship 1760–1782', *ECI* 11 (1996), 88–119. O'Connell, *Irish Politics and Social Conflict*, notes the votes of the county members (pp. 26–7), but on the whole sees Irish criticism of the government's American policy as largely

If the American revolt awakened only limited ideological resonances, its impact on Irish politics was nevertheless to be dramatic. One immediate consequence was the withdrawal from Ireland of the greater part of the regular army. This had been the standard response to earlier emergencies, such as the Jacobite risings of 1715 and 1745. On this occasion, however, the withdrawal was not to Great Britain but to the other side of the Atlantic, and with the entry of European enemies into the conflict Ireland stood dangerously exposed. In earlier decades, moreover, the militia, a part-time force in which the entire adult Protestant population were theoretically liable to serve, had provided a second line of armed defence. Since the 1760s, however, the government had allowed the militia to fall into disuse, and in 1776 had allowed the act for its upkeep to expire without renewal. Following the outbreak of war, it introduced a new militia act in 1778, but did not provide the funds that would be required to assemble and arm a significant body of men. The government's motives were pragmatic: a preference for a mobile force of regular soldiers under central government control rather than home-based amateurs organized on a local basis. For the emerging patriot movement, on the other hand, the issue was one of political as well as military significance. Protest against the running down of the militia allowed them to deploy the well-established theme of the superiority of the citizen soldier to the hired mercenary in the service of a proposal that was popular on account both of its lower cost and of the opportunities for patronage that it created.

The removal to America of the regular army, combined with the renewed threat of invasion by European rivals, transformed the nature of the debate. Even when the official militia had been fully operational there had also been independent companies, organized on their own account by local gentry, and the number had grown as the official force atrophied. A new set of such companies appeared during 1778, following the declaration of war with France, but it was not until 1779 that volunteering developed real momentum. By this time it was clear that the government was not going to implement the militia act, and the appearance of a French fleet near Bantry Bay in June highlighted the danger of invasion. By the end of the summer what had been individual companies had begun to organize themselves into battalions and regiments. The total number enlisted rose from around 15,000 in April 1779 to over 40,000 by the end of the year and to 60,000 by mid-1780. In July 1779 the government issued arms formerly stored for use by the militia to county governors for distribution to the Volunteers, though in terms worded so as to avoid giving the force formal recognition.

opportunistic. Neil Longley York, *Neither Kingdom nor Nation: The Irish Quest for Constitutional Rights 1698–1800* (Washington, DC, 1994), 102–6, 242–64, likewise emphasizes the lack of real mutual understanding behind superficial expressions of transatlantic solidarity. For a more positive assessment of Irish support for the Americans, see David Dickson, *New Foundations: Ireland 1660–1800* (Dublin, 1987), 141–4.

At the same time that the Volunteer movement was taking shape, the Irish economy was beginning to suffer from the effects of the American War. In February 1776, seven months after the first shots had been fired on the other side of the Atlantic, the government sought to ensure adequate supplies for its armed forces by imposing an embargo on the export of Irish beef, butter, pork, and other provisions. The parliamentary patriots attacked the proclamation on constitutional grounds. But with military and naval demand more than compensating for the loss of exports, their protests evoked limited interest. By 1778, on the other hand, a general economic recession due to wartime dislocation of trade had spread from Great Britain to Ireland. This time the patriots were able to focus rising discontent on the issue of the supposed damage inflicted on Ireland's economy by English commercial legislation. The British cabinet sought to defuse the issue by a Westminster bill removing some of the restrictions on Irish trade. However British manufacturing interests succeeded in having a number of the proposed concessions withdrawn, so that Irish opinion was inflamed rather than conciliated. In response the patriot press began from early 1779 to call for a boycott of British goods. The movement had little support in Ulster, where the strongly export-oriented linen trade had by now begun to revive. In the south, on the other hand, the non-importation movement spread rapidly, and by the end of the year it had begun to attract the support of the increasingly numerous and organized Volunteers.

The Volunteer movement that thus began to assume a political as well as a military role marked an important stage in the development of popular politics. Members were required to equip themselves with uniforms, muskets, and other equipment. They had also to be in a position to leave their normal occupations to attend what became an increasingly elaborate round of parades, reviews, and manoeuvres. It was thus not a movement open to the labouring classes of either town or country. Instead those recruited ranged from urban professional groups down to shopkeepers and independent tradesmen, as well as the more prosperous tenant farmers. These were the people that contemporaries would have referred to loosely as 'the middling sort'. But it was precisely the significance of the Volunteer movement that it helped to give that heterogeneous collection of social groups a stronger sense of shared identity. Assembled on parade, or for the field camps that by 1781 could last for two to three days, individual Volunteers could see themselves and their comrades as the true backbone of society: men of modest but definite substance gathered of their own volition to perform their patriotic duty as the citizen soldiers of real Whig and patriot rhetoric.

For formal leadership the Volunteers turned to their traditional superiors: most companies were commanded by landlords. But they also made increasingly clear in what direction they wished to be led. In County Tyrone James Hamilton, agent to the earl of Abercorn, complained of having been 'forced in amongst them' and of finding himself 'in a very disagreeable situation': 'those who they call their commanders must obey their orders; they are their constituents and their orders must be observed.' On occasion pressure from below turned into open class hostility. A correspondent in the *Dublin Evening Post* urged on freeholders in the same county 'the necessity of boldly throwing off your subjection to landlords', and insisted that a forthcoming meeting to nominate parliamentary candidates should not be 'a meeting of what are called gentlemen only'. At the same time that they made clear their rejection of unconditional deference to social superiors, however, the Volunteers demonstrated their own identity as the lesser propertied classes in arms. Units regularly turned out to pursue robbers, disperse riotous crowds, and otherwise preserve public order. When Dublin journeymen in June 1780 staged a demonstration opposing new legislation against trade unions, armed Volunteers took over the streets to contain any disturbances.[30]

The agitation for free trade, in the sense of the removal of British restrictions on Irish commerce, reached its peak towards the end of 1779. When parliament met, Barry Yelverton, one of the leading parliamentary patriots, proposed that the Commons should vote taxes only for six months, rather than the customary two years. On 4 November ten corps of the Dublin Volunteers, numbering around 900 men, staged a demonstration on College Green. 4 November was the birthday of William III, and the parade took place around his statue. A placard bore the legend 'A Short Money Bill—A Free Trade—or Else'.[31] Eleven days later a crowd estimated at 3,000–4,000 strong gathered outside parliament, forcing MPs as they arrived to leave their coaches and sedan chairs and to pledge their support for the same measures. Later a mob smashed windows in the house of the attorney general. When the Commons debated the issue of free trade nine days later, it was clear that the Castle had lost control. An amendment in favour of free trade proposed by Walter Hussey Burgh, a law officer since 1777 but now in the process of breaking with the administration, passed unanimously. Later, in the debate on supply, Burgh offered an extraordinary tribute to the Volunteers: 'England has sown her laws like dragon's teeth, and they have sprung up in armed men.'[32] The Commons supported by 170 votes to 47 a resolution by Grattan against granting new taxes; instead it voted to grant funds to meet the interest on the public debt for a period of just six months. Faced with this unprecedented level of agitation, uniting the Commons, the urban crowd, and an armed militia outside state control, the government gave way. In December the prime minister, Lord North, announced plans to remove the prohibition on the export of Irish glass and wool, and to allow Irish ships and merchants to participate without restriction in trade with the colonies.

---

[30] For Hamilton see his letter to Abercorn (5 Dec. 1779), printed in W. H. Crawford and Brian Trainor (eds.), *Aspects of Irish Social History* (Belfast, 1969), 167–8. Otherwise these two paragraphs draw on O'Connell's pioneering discussion in *Irish Politics and Social Conflict*, 88–98, 260–3.

[31] The versions of the placard given in secondary sources vary considerably. The one given here is from Morley, *Irish Opinion and the American Revolution*, 224, quoting the *Hibernian Magazine*.

[32] Quoted in O'Connell, *Irish Politics and Social Conflict*, 186.

The government's surrender on free trade was complete. Its only stipulation was the reasonable demand that Ireland would impose duties on the colonial produce it was now free to import to match those levied in Great Britain. Even this, however, was enough to give rise to a subsequent squabble about the level of protective tariffs that should be allowed to the Irish sugar-refining industry that patriots saw as one of the major potential benefits of free trade. A more serious problem for the government was that the prolonged controversy that had preceded the concession, culminating in a debate on Irish policy in the British parliament in November and December, had raised public awareness of the wider issue of Ireland's constitutional status. Between February and April 1780 meetings of the inhabitants of eighteen counties and five towns or cities called on their MPs to support the repeal of Poynings's Law. On 19 April Grattan moved a resolution 'that the king's most excellent majesty, and the Lords and Commons of Ireland, are the only power competent to make laws to bind Ireland'. His appeal was a strongly worded one. Ireland had gained 'commerce but not freedom'. So long as the declaratory act remained in force, it remained 'a colony without the benefit of a charter' and its parliament 'a provincial synod'. Grattan based his arguments in part on historical rights of the kind previously cited by Molyneux and Lucas. But he also appealed, in a bold antithesis, to the principles of the Glorious Revolution:

Every argument for the house of Hanover is equally an argument for the liberties of Ireland: the act of settlement is an act of rebellion, or the declaratory statute of the 6th of George the First is an act of usurpation; for both cannot be law.

To this he added warnings. Great Britain, defeated in America, had 'no policy left . . . but to cherish the remains of her empire and do justice to a country who is determined to do justice to herself'. MPs, likewise, should recognize that they had been instructed by their constituents 'in a style not the less awful because full of respect. They will find resources in their own virtue, if they have found none in yours.'[33]

Grattan's resolution was only the beginning of a determined assault on Ireland's constitutional subordination. Within a week another patriot spokesman, Barry Yelverton, had sought leave to bring in heads of a bill to modify Poynings's Law. Later Hussey Burgh introduced heads of a mutiny bill that provided the legal basis for the maintenance of discipline within the armed forces, a gesture that implicitly denied the insufficiency in Ireland of the British act. Grattan's motion was rejected by 136 votes to 97, and Yelverton's by 130 votes to 105, while the Commons voted by 117 votes to 80 to accept an amendment to the mutiny bill that removed any implication that a British act needed to be duplicated in Ireland. These were respectable enough divisions, from the patriot point of view. By the

---

[33] *The Speeches of the Right Hon. Henry Grattan*, ed. Daniel Owen Madden (Dublin, 1874), 38–51.

summer, however, the tide was running more strongly against them. When the British privy council amended heads of a bill to reduce the proposed tariff on imported sugar, the Commons refused to accept what was now an altered money bill. Having done so, however, they tamely voted, by 119 to 38, to bring in new heads of a bill imposing the reduced rate of duty. The same day they voted by 114 votes to 62 to accept the mutiny bill, even though the British privy council had amended it to a permanent measure, removing its constitutional function as a guarantee that parliament would meet regularly. When the Dublin Merchants' Volunteer Company published resolutions condemning this last vote, both Lords and Commons reacted angrily, threatening prosecution for contempt. Behind this growing resistance to patriot demands observers detected a concern on the part of the traditional political class to recover the ground lost in recent surrenders to popular pressure. William Eden, who took over in late 1780 as chief secretary to the new lord lieutenant, the earl of Carlisle, neatly summarized his perception of a changing political climate: '. . . the truth is that the toe of the peasant has lately pressed unpleasantly on the kibe [raw spot] of the aristocracy and gentry, and there is a general wish in the higher class to resume the old energy of good government.'[34]

Eden's assessment was largely borne out by the low political profile adopted by the Volunteers during 1781. The real test, however, would come when parliament met again in the autumn. Carlisle and Eden sought to prepare the ground by attracting supporters. One of their most important recruits was John Fitzgibbon, an able young lawyer of a convert background who had earlier supported the patriots on the short money bill, the mutiny bill, and the sugar duties. They also sought to conciliate moderate patriot opinion. London vetoed their proposal to include in the speech from the throne an acknowledgement of the services of the Volunteers, who during the summer had rallied promptly in response to reports of a possible Franco-Spanish invasion. However the administration allowed another long-standing patriot demand, an Irish habeas corpus bill, to proceed unopposed. More important, Eden and Carlisle reached an accommodation with Barry Yelverton. By doing so they not only detached one of the most able members of the opposition; they also made progress towards removing a central grievance. In December 1781 Yelverton, with government approval, introduced a measure allowing the Irish parliament to introduce bills that would be transmitted to London under the great seal of Ireland without interference by the Irish council. Meanwhile the Commons rejected a new address on legislative independence proposed by Grattan by a healthy majority of 137 to 68, and also voted down resolutions relating to the mutiny act and Poynings's Law.

---

[34] Quoted in O'Connell, *Irish Politics and Social Conflict*, 295. Eden's otherwise odd use of the term 'peasantry' to characterize the Volunteers is explained by his borrowing from the words of Shakespeare: Cf. *Hamlet*, v. i. 143–6.

It was against this background of an emerging accommodation between the administration and moderate patriot opinion that a meeting held at Armagh at the end of December 1781 denounced the failure of parliament to respond to their concerns and called for a convention of representatives from the province's Volunteer corps. On 15 February 1782 delegates assembled at Dungannon in County Tyrone to agree a series of resolutions drafted by Charlemont and other patriot leaders. The first item, reflecting recent challenges to the legitimacy of political agitation by the Volunteers, was a declaration that 'a citizen, by learning the use of arms, does not abandon any of his civil rights'. The convention went on to denounce as unconstitutional the claim of any body other than the parliament of Ireland to make laws for the kingdom, and to demand the reform of Poynings's Law, security of tenure for judges, and a mutiny bill of limited duration.[35]

The precise place of the Dungannon Convention in the political history of eighteenth-century Ireland remains uncertain. Representatives of only 143 companies, out of a total of up to 400 in Ulster at that time, attended the meeting, lending support to the suggestion that it should be seen as the last desperate throw of the militant patriots, rather than as the triumphant act of national self-assertion it became in later legend. But it also seems true that the organizers did in fact succeed in injecting new life into a flagging cause. Over the next few weeks grand juries and assemblies of electors in different parts of the country met to declare their concurrence with the resolutions, and call on their MPs to support them. How far the administration would have been able to face down this new surge of public opinion by the methods that had proved reasonably successful for most of the preceding two years will never be known. During March 1782, following news of military disaster in America, Lord North's government collapsed. It gave way to a Whig ministry headed by the marquis of Rockingham. The Rockingham Whigs, by their stand on Irish issues while in opposition, had already to a large extent committed themselves to meeting Irish demands. By the end of June the British parliament had repealed the declaratory act. During the following month Yelverton's modification of Poynings's Law received the royal assent, as did the habeas corpus act, a mutiny act limited in duration, and an act giving judges security of tenure during good behaviour.

A BUNGLING IMPERFECT BUSINESS

On 16 April 1782, as the Irish parliament reassembled under the new lord lieutenant appointed by the Rockingham administration, Grattan rose to propose

---

[35] Resolutions of the Dungannon Convention, printed in Edmund Curtis and R. B. McDowell, *Irish Historical Documents 1172–1922* (London, 1943), 233–5.

an amendment to the officially agreed address. A later published version of his speech began with some dramatic lines:

I am now to address a free people: ages have passed away, and this is the first moment in which you could be distinguished by that appellation.

I have spoken to you on the subject of your liberty so often, that I have nothing to add, and have only to admire by what heaven-directed steps you have proceeded until the whole faculty of the nation is braced up to the act of her own deliverance.

I found Ireland on her knees, I watched over her with a paternal solicitude; I have traced her progress from injuries to arms, and from arms to liberty. Spirit of Swift! spirit of Molyneux! your genius has prevailed! Ireland is now a nation! In that new character I hail her! and bowing to her august presence, I say, *Esto Perpetua*.[36]

Grattan's actual words on the occasion were quite possibly not as tautly elegant. But it is the published version that survives, offering both a classic expression of the high-flown rhetoric that now characterized Irish patriotism, and an unwitting insight into certain major contradictions that it had not resolved, or perhaps had not even recognized.

By the time of Grattan's speech, Irish Protestant patriotism was entering its golden age. For most of the eighteenth century its spokesmen had based their claims on the legal arguments for Ireland's status as an independent kingdom first systematically outlined by William Molyneux. These arguments retained their appeal. Grattan himself, proposing an earlier resolution on Ireland's legislative independence in February 1782, had treated his audience to a minutely detailed recitation of what had become the touchstones of the patriot case: the 'original compact' between Henry II and the Gaelic chiefs, the *Modus tenendi parliamenta* supposedly drawn up in the reign of Henry II, the 'Magna Carta' granted to the kingdom by Henry III, as well as a battery of lesser precedents and legal instruments.[37] Others appealed to the same historical touchstones with more enthusiasm than precision. In a debate on Poynings's Law in 1781 one speaker had referred proudly to 'the Modus Tenendi Parliamenta transmitted hither by Henry the 3rd', while another had cited 'our modus tenendi parliamenta sent us by our first English sovereign, Henry II'.[38] A few years later the myth of Ireland's ancient constitution was acknowledged even by the representative of the English crown. In 1789 the lord lieutenant, the marquis of Buckingham, commissioned the Italian Vincent Waldré to paint three ceiling panels in the hall of Dublin Castle. Alongside depictions of George II supported by liberty and justice, and

---

[36] Grattan, *Speeches*, ed. Madden, 70. Gerard O'Brien, 'The Grattan Mystique', *ECI* 1 (1986), 177–94, casts doubt on the evocation of Swift and Molyneux, pointing out that this version of the speech dates from 1822, and is not supported by earlier reports. However W. McCormack and Patrick Kelly, ibid. 2 (1987), 14–15, and 3 (1988), 142, offer evidence that Swift and Molyneux were in fact widely cited, by Grattan and others, at this time.

[37] Grattan, *Speeches*, ed. Madden, 58–60, speech of 22 Feb. 1782.

[38] *Parliamentary Register*, i (1781), 165, 173. For the actual date of the *Modus*, see above, Ch. 5 n. 34.

St Patrick converting the Irish to Christianity, stood Waldré's representation of *King Henry II Receiving the Submission of the Irish Chieftains*. The iconography was ludicrous: a clean-shaven figure, in a doubly anachronistic uniform of plate armour and a plumed helmet more reminiscent of depictions of ancient Rome, received a delegation clad in equally improbable draperies before a somewhat unsteady round tower. But the testimony to the staying power of Molyneux's distinctive Irish version of the original compact was nevertheless remarkable.[39]

Within this new climate of patriot enthusiasm, Grattan himself was the hero of the hour. The Commons that had repeatedly voted down his resolutions on legislative independence now awarded him a sum of £50, 000, sufficient for him to transform his social status from lawyer to country gentleman by the purchase of a landed estate in Queen's County and a country house in Wicklow. Within a short time, however, the mood of triumphant unanimity had disappeared. The immediate cause of discord was the intervention of Henry Flood. Flood, the outstanding opposition speaker of the early 1770s, had taken office in 1775, only to find himself forced to watch others, notably Grattan, assume the leadership of a suddenly triumphant patriotism. Unwilling to admit his error by resigning, he had repeatedly failed to support the administration in parliament until it at length dismissed him in November 1781. However he had been unable to regain anything like his former dominant position among the Castle's opponents. Immediately after his resignation the attorney general, John Scott, responded to Flood's motion for the repeal of the perpetual mutiny act with a devastating speech recounting the fable of Harry Plantagenet, king of all the animals in the royal forest, who had for a time entered the employment of the chief huntsman only to discover on returning to the woods that 'not a dog obeyed me, not a sportsman attended my call'. By May 1782, however, Flood had found the cause that had up to then eluded him. He joined with others in arguing that the simple repeal of the declaratory act was not a sufficient guarantee of Ireland's future liberty to make its own legislation; what was needed was a formal renunciation by the British parliament of all claims to make laws for Ireland.

The hair-splitting nature of this point adds weight to the inevitable suspicion that Flood's real motive was to regain the popular leadership that, as Scott had so unkindly pointed out, he had forfeited by taking office. However it has also been argued that he took up the issue out of genuine conviction; and indeed his overall career would support the view that he was probably motivated as much by an unshakeable faith in the superiority of his own judgement in complex constitutional matters as by a cynical hunger for power.[40] Although the

---

[39] Fintan Cullen, *Visual Politics: The Representation of Ireland 1750–1930* (Cork, 1997), 73–80. The hall was to be used for the investiture of members of the Order of St Patrick which Buckingham, during an earlier term of office, had created to give expression, under royal patronage, to Ireland's new constitutional status.

[40] For a general discussion of Flood's motives, see Kelly, *Henry Flood*, 311–25, and for Scott's speech ibid. 293–4. Flood's confidence in his own superior abilities had already been demonstrated

majority of the parliamentary patriots rejected the demand for renunciation as an unnecessary refinement, the campaign quickly built up out of doors, particularly among the Volunteers. The pressure was sufficient to force the government to rush through a British act, completed in April 1783, to acknowledge the exclusive legislative rights of the Irish parliament.

Flood's campaign for a renunciation act took off as it did because the issue became the focus for a wider series of popular grievances. Grattan's acceptance of a substantial financial reward for his services to the kingdom seemed to many inappropriate. In addition he, like other parliamentary patriots, now made no secret of his view that the Volunteers, having played their part in achieving 'the constitution of 1782', should quietly withdraw, leaving its implementation to their betters. There was particular resentment when the Commons voted in 1782 to raise a new body of Fencibles, a full-time force for home defence, in effect making Volunteering redundant. The Volunteer movement had from the start included elements unimpressed by, or even openly hostile to, the traditional political dominance of the landed elite. They and others looked back to the failure of the Commons, throughout the greater part of 1780–1, to respond to a vigorous public campaign for constitutional change as confirming its failure as a representative body. In September 1783, immediately following a general election that had once again demonstrated the dominance in all but a handful of constituencies of proprietorial interests over popular sentiment, a second Volunteer convention at Dungannon met to draw up proposals for a reform of the electoral system.

The emergence of parliamentary reform as the main focus of public agitation reflected the transformation that had now taken place in the terms of Irish political debate. In the first decades of the eighteenth century criticism of the workings of parliamentary politics had concentrated on the capacity of corruption to undermine constitutional checks and balances. In the 1760s attention had shifted to the need for more frequent elections. The proposals put forward at the second Volunteer convention at Dungannon duly demanded that parliaments were to be elected annually. But they also included novel demands for a reform of the machinery of representation. Seats were to be redistributed from small boroughs to the counties and larger towns. Office holders and pensioners were to be debarred from sitting in parliament. In place of the existing tangle of voting qualifications there was to be a uniform franchise, extending to those with property worth £20 in the counties and to householders paying £5 a year or more in rent. There was also to be a secret ballot.

The overall programme agreed at Dungannon, devised after a correspondence with leading English reformers, was a radical one. Not all of its individual components, however, had the same significance. The secret ballot and the

in his genuine outrage that Yelverton's amendment to Poynings's Law should be preferred to his own, more complex solution: ibid. 295–300.

widening of the franchise appealed to those who wished to curb the ability
of landlords and others to convert economic superiority into electoral interest.
But the reform campaign also gained support through what Charlemont later
described as 'the general desire of all such gentlemen as had no interest in
boroughs to gain additional influence by their being laid open'.[41] For those in
this category the most attractive proposals were measures like the redistribution
of seats, or, as proposed by the Irish Whig party in 1794, the extension of
the boundaries of each borough four miles in all directions from its centre.
Such reforms would widen the circle of men of property able to play a part
in electioneering. They would not, taken in isolation, reduce the influence of
property itself. Behind the superficial unanimity achieved at Dungannon and
other gatherings there thus lay seriously divergent interests and aspirations.

The conflict that now developed between different conceptions of reform was
also, from the start, a conflict between personalities. Flood had stayed away from
the Dungannon Convention, pleading illness. He was never wholly at ease with
the role of popular rather than parliamentary politician; moreover he was just
about to secure a seat at Westminster, and over the remaining eight years of his
life was to devote much of his energy to an unsuccessful attempt to establish
himself as a figure in English politics. Meanwhile a second, more flamboyant
leader had emerged. Frederick Augustus Hervey, third son of a prominent
English family, had entered the church long before unexpectedly succeeding
his two brothers as fourth earl of Bristol in 1779. He had become chaplain to
his brother, a short-lived and wholly non-resident lord lieutenant of Ireland,
who had appointed him bishop of Cloyne. Returning to Ireland after a period
as an absentee, possibly in response to the breakdown of his marriage, he had
accepted command of the Londonderry corps of Volunteers and now emerged
as an enthusiastic champion of reform.[42]

Grattan was by now openly at odds with the Volunteers. Instead Hervey's main
rival for control of the movement was Charlemont, still commander in chief but
now in what he considered a very difficult position. Charlemont firmly believed
in the necessity of parliamentary reform. He defined this, however, primarily in
terms of the elimination of 'paltry, decayed and depopulated boroughs', whose
owners predominated 'over the real representatives of the people'. The secret
ballot was in his view 'too democratical to be admitted in a constitution such
as the British'. More important, he had serious doubts as to the legitimacy of
the new campaign. Already before the Convention, he had recommended that
the Volunteers should confine themselves to declaring support for the principle
of reform, without prescribing specific measures, and he continued to worry
both about the propriety of their 'entering violently into a matter purely of
internal regulation', and about the 'civil contention' that might result if their

41 Charlemont, 'Memoirs of his Political Life' (HMC, *Charlemont MSS*, i. 111).
42 J. R. Walsh, *Frederick Augustus Hervey, 1730–1803* (Maynooth, 1972).

demands were refused. Against this background his leadership became a delicate balancing act. He himself later summed up his role as having been 'in regulating the irregular sallies of a set of men, brave and honest but, as must naturally be expected, rash and precipitate', their 'virtuous zeal easily inflamed by the machinations of the designing'. And from an early stage he had concluded that Hervey, proud, vindictive, hungry for popularity, and 'possessed of no one firm principle', fell firmly into that latter category.[43]

The next step in the reform agitation was a national convention, of delegates chosen by the Volunteers of each county and of a few urban centres, held in Dublin in November 1783. The event was a dramatic combination of pomp and paramilitary menace. The delegates paraded from the Royal Exchange to the Rotunda, along a route lined with armed Volunteers. Inside, they took their seats on tiered benches in an oblong square.

At the upper end, under the orchestra, upon an estrade, elevated by three steps, was placed a gilded chair, in the nature of a throne, for the president, beneath which was a table with seats for the two secretaries. The orchestra was filled with ladies, and the remainder of the room, outside the oblong square, was thronged with Volunteers, who were of right admitted, and with men of all ranks.[44]

Hervey had already attempted to set his mark on the proceedings by organizing a triumphal progress from Derry to Dublin. However the convention, despite its radical posturing, was dominated by men of property. The 186 delegates included no less than 59 MPs and 6 peers, and as chairman they elected, not Hervey, but Charlemont. Discussion of a reform bill initially became bogged down in a confusion of competing schemes. However Flood, co-opted to the drafting committee, succeeded in gaining agreement to a moderate set of proposals: a uniform franchise taking in freeholders and holders of thirty-one-year leases with at least ten years unexpired, the enlargement of borough boundaries, the restriction of voting in boroughs to those either resident or owning property there, a maximum period of three years between elections, the exclusion from the Commons of holders of government pensions, and a requirement that MPs taking office should seek re-election. It was a plan that fell well short of that put forward at Dungannon and elsewhere. In particular the committee rejected proposals for a secret ballot. However there was a good case for the view that only such a carefully toned down set of proposals had any chance of being accepted.

In the event even this moderate scheme was denied a hearing. On 29 November Flood and another convention delegate, William Brownlow, MP for County Armagh, took their seats in the Commons preparatory to seeking leave to introduce a bill. Both men, in what proved to be an unfortunate gesture, were wearing their Volunteer uniforms. The lord lieutenant, the earl of Northington,

---

[43] *Charlemont MSS*, i. 110–11, 121–4, 113–16, 94–5.   [44] Ibid. i. 123.

had lobbied members of the Commons to take a stand on the principle that parliament should refuse even to consider proposals laid before it by an armed association. In the debate itself Barry Yelverton, as attorney general, took the lead for the government. Only four years earlier, in November 1779, it had been Yelverton who proposed the short money bill that had provided the great Volunteer demonstration on College Green with its central political demand. Now, however, he told MPs that it was 'inconsistent with the freedom of debate for the legislature to receive a bill originating with an armed assembly'. Other members spoke in similar terms, and Flood's motion was defeated by a margin officially returned as 157 votes to 77. The convention reconvened briefly to agree on an address of protest to the king and a series of county meetings to continue the campaign, then quickly dissolved.[45] Over the winter of 1783–4 twenty-two counties and urban centres submitted petitions calling for parliamentary reform. But when Flood introduced another bill in March 1784 the Commons rejected it by 159 votes to 85.

Immediately after this second dismissal of parliamentary reform, the Commons spurned a second popular cause. In the autumn of 1783, against a background of industrial recession, an agitation had begun for protective tariffs to aid the development of Irish industries. At the end of March, however, the Commons voted by 123 votes to 36 against a proposal by Luke Gardiner to impose a heavy import duty on English cloth. The double rebuff inspired radical activists to launch a new campaign for what were now the linked causes of parliamentary reform and protection. In Dublin, the centre of the agitation, the two leading figures were John Binns and James Napper Tandy, both members of Dublin corporation. In the summer of 1784 they sought to promote a new campaign of boycott against imported goods and the shops that carried them, to be backed by a revitalized Volunteer movement. At the same time they called on the freeholders of the counties and major towns to elect delegates to a new reform convention to be held in October. The agitation had the support of the *Volunteer Journal*, edited by a young Catholic, Matthew Carey. This not only carried inflammatory attacks on leading office holders, notably John Foster, whom it lampooned as 'Jacky Finance'. It also wrote openly of the possibility that the Volunteers might be called on to use their arms, and advocated 'a total separation from England and Englishmen'.[46]

The combination of Volunteering and non-importation superficially recalled the heroic days of 1779. The free trade agitation of that year, however, had been

---

[45] Kelly, *Henry Flood*, 355–61. Kelly (p. 360 n. 227) notes an alternative report, in the *Belfast Newsletter*, putting the vote against Flood's motion at 163 to 78.

[46] These first stirrings of explicitly separatist thinking have not yet been studied in detail. For brief surveys see Thomas Bartlett, 'The Burden of the Present: Theobald Wolfe Tone, Republican and Separatist', in David Dickson, Dáire Keogh, and Kevin Whelan (eds.), *The United Irishmen: Republicanism, Radicalism and Rebellion* (Dublin, 1993), 12; R. B. McDowell, *Irish Public Opinion 1750–1800* (London, 1944), 113–17.

legitimized by the support of landlords, aristocrats, and parliamentarians. Since then, with the exception of the brief euphoria of 1782, these members of the traditional elite had been in steady retreat from radicalism. Binns and Tandy were men of middling, or at best ambiguous, status. Binns was a member of the weavers' guild. Tandy had been permitted by a good marriage to exchange his original business as an ironmonger for the more respectable occupation of land agent and rent collector. Yet Fitzgibbon, in 1784, was still able to ignore his challenge to a duel, on the grounds that he was no gentleman. During 1784 Volunteer corps in Dublin and elsewhere attempted to compensate for this withdrawal of elite support by broadening their social base, admitting both Catholics and poorer Protestants. But the result was further to increase the rupture between the movement and its former allies in parliament and among the propertied classes. It was against this background that Grattan, in January 1785, openly supported government moves to curb what he now described as 'the armed beggary of the nation'.[47]

The withdrawal of elite support left the administration free to respond to the radical challenge with increasingly aggressive counter-measures. In response to the inflammatory attacks of the *Volunteer Journal*, it introduced a libel act which was to become the basis of subsequent control of the liberal and radical press. Carey himself was imprisoned on a charge of having libelled Foster, and on his release left Ireland for America. For several months commencing in the summer of 1784 the authorities intercepted the correspondence of Edward Newenham, MP for County Dublin and a leading supporter of reform, and kept his house under surveillance, in the apparently genuine belief that he and Hervey were in treasonable correspondence with France.[48] Meanwhile the attorney general, Fitzgibbon, sought to hinder preparations for the October convention by threatening with prosecution sheriffs who responded to requests to arrange freeholders' meetings. These tactics helped to ensure that the assembly made a poor showing: only 40 of the 95 delegates proposed appeared. A second meeting in January was somewhat better attended, but could do little more than reiterate the demand for reform. By this time Charlemont, alarmed by signals that the government might be considering introducing a militia as a prelude to suppressing the Volunteers, had begun using his influence to withdraw the force completely from political agitation.

The reform agitation of 1784–5, led by men who were clearly from outside the ranks of the governing elite, and openly appealing to the authority of numbers rather than property, was an important new phase in the development of popular politics. It was also a training ground for a number of those who were to be prominent in the revived radical politics of the following decade. At

[47] James Kelly, *Henry Grattan* (Dublin, 1993), 22.
[48] Kelly, *Sir Edward Newenham MP 1734–1814: Defender of the Protestant Constitution* (Dublin, 2004), 200–3, 225–6.

the same time the outright rejection by parliament of even the modest electoral reform proposed by the national convention fatally compromised the claims made, by Grattan and others, for the constitutional changes so opportunistically snatched from a weakened British government in 1782. The Irish parliament could no longer be overridden by acts passed by its British counterpart. It could pass legislation without the restrictions embodied in Poynings's Law. But it remained, as Grattan himself was to complain in 1797, 'a borough parliament': three-quarters of its members sat for boroughs, in all but a handful of which the outcome of elections was decided by a patron. Against this background the main outcome of 1782 was to allow such patrons, answerable to no one but themselves, to drive even harder bargains with an administration for whom it had become more important than ever to maintain control of the Irish parliament. For one Irish radical, writing just under a decade later, 'the revolution of 1782 was the most bungling imperfect business that ever threw ridicule on a lofty epithet . . . a revolution which enabled Irishmen to sell, at a much higher price, their honour, their integrity and the interests of their country.' Another, writing during the reform campaign itself, was more concise: without parliamentary reform all that had been achieved was 'a transference of arbitrary power from despotism abroad to aristocracy at home'.[49]

IRELAND IS NOW A NATION

The demand for parliamentary reform raised one question about what it meant to say that the Irish were now a free people. A second, equally pressing, concerned the place within the new political order of the kingdom's Catholic majority. It was more than three-quarters of a century since Catholics had offered an armed challenge to the Protestant establishment. The laws restricting their religious organization and practice had long ceased to be even sporadically enforced. The severe restrictions on Catholic property rights, on the other hand, and their complete exclusion from political life, continued. In 1761 and again in 1764 the Commons rejected modest proposals to allow Catholics to lend money on the security of land, despite safeguards designed to ensure that they would not be able to convert unredeemed mortgages into direct control of landed property. By this time the spread of Enlightenment ideas might have been expected to work against the notion of imposing civil penalties on religious dissidents. But then Enlightenment thinkers generally saw Catholicism as a threat to civil and

---

[49] T. W. Tone, 'An Argument on Behalf of the Catholics of Ireland', in *Theobald Wolfe Tone: Memoirs, Journals and Political Writings*, ed. Thomas Bartlett (Dublin, 1998), 281; William Drennan, *Letters of Orellana, an Irish Helot* (Dublin, 1785), 19. For Grattan's comment, A. P. W. Malcomson, 'The Parliamentary Traffic of this Country', in Bartlett and Hayton (eds.), *Penal Era and Golden Age*, 137.

religious liberty. A more important influence in the direction of change was the ever-growing need for military manpower in the first age of global war.[50] Already in 1761, in the last stages of the Seven Years War, the government had shown interest in a proposal by Lord Trimleston to raise six regiments of Catholics to serve England's ally Portugal, only to have the Irish parliament reject the idea of arming papists, even overseas, as wholly unacceptable.

By 1778 Lord North's government, faced with a new imperial crisis, had come to believe that some measure of conciliation was now essential, as a means both of securing the loyalty of Irish Catholics and of making it possible to draw more easily on the huge reserve of potential cannon fodder they represented. Accordingly his government gave tacit support to the heads of a bill introduced by Luke Gardiner, the wealthy property developer and MP for County Dublin. Gardiner proposed that those Catholics who had taken a recently introduced oath of allegiance should be permitted to bequeath landed estates intact to a single heir, and to purchase land on equal terms with Protestants. The bill provoked a series of sharp debates. MPs objected in particular to the prospect of Catholics acquiring outright ownership of land, despite the continuing prohibition on their exercising the political rights that would go with it. An amendment substituting the right to take leases for up to 999 years—the economic equivalent of ownership, but not carrying the status of freeholder—passed by 111 votes to 108. In this modified form Gardiner's measure passed through the Commons and on to the Irish privy council, who transmitted it unaltered to London.

Ireland's other religious minority, the Protestant dissenters, also benefited from the government's sudden willingness to consider the relaxation of long-standing disabilities. During the debate on Gardiner's bill Edward Newenham and others added a clause repealing the sacramental test. Some of those involved, including Newenham, were genuine sympathizers with the claims of dissenters. Others hoped to sabotage the proposed concession to Catholics. The British privy council, however, removed the clause. When the amended bill came before the Commons MPs, including both Grattan and Fitzgibbon, protested at the slight given to Presbyterians at the same time that papists were favoured. But Gardiner's bill nevertheless passed by a majority of 129 to 89. When parliament next met, in October 1779, Newenham returned to the attack, with his own heads of a bill to repeal the test. By this time early military failures in America, and even more the rapid growth and particular concentration in Ulster of the Volunteers, made a further rebuff to the Presbyterians and other dissenters self-evidently unadvisable. Newenham's heads were approved by the Irish and British councils and the bill received the royal assent in May 1780. Further legislation in 1782 removed another Presbyterian grievance by giving full recognition to the marriages celebrated by their ministers, and also deferred to the scruples of the

---

[50] The military background to the Catholic relief acts is particularly emphasized in Thomas Bartlett, *The Fall and Rise of the Irish Nation: The Catholic Question 1690–1830* (Dublin, 1992).

Seceders by allowing them to take oaths in court without being required to kiss the Bible.[51]

Any hopes that the relief act of 1778 would ensure that the Catholic question did not become entangled in what was rapidly emerging as the Irish dimension of a wider imperial crisis were quickly disappointed. The patriot tradition had traditionally combined the symbolism of advanced Whiggery with a confidently exclusive Protestantism. A dinner in 1775 for the Free Citizens of Dublin, a radical club involving Tandy and others, had included toasts to the memory of William III, to the battles of the Boyne and Aughrim, to Culloden and the memory of the duke of Cumberland, and even to the execution of Charles I and the memory of Oliver Cromwell.[52] The early Volunteers fell into the same pattern, as was evident in their choice of 4 November, and the statue of King William, as the date and location of their great demonstration of November 1779. Already by this stage, however, Catholics in different counties had begun to offer addresses of support, in some cases accompanied by donations of money, to those mobilized to defend the kingdom. By the following year some Volunteer units, ignoring the still theoretically operative prohibition on papists bearing arms, had begun to admit Catholics into their ranks. There are indirect indications that the administration may have seen Gardiner's proposals for a new Catholic relief bill, announced in late 1781, as a means of dividing the Protestant reform movement. However patriot leaders such as Grattan and Charlemont openly spoke of the need to prevent the government using tactics of divide and rule, as they believed it had done in 1778.[53] Political calculation thus combined with what seems to have been a genuine enthusiasm, in some quarters, for a new sense of national unity transcending long-standing religious differences. The resolutions adopted at Dungannon in February 1782 concluded with a declaration that 'the relaxation of the penal laws against our Roman Catholic fellow subjects' was a measure 'fraught with the happiest consequences'. A few weeks later Gardiner brought forward heads of two bills, the first permitting Catholics to purchase land and removing most of the restrictions affecting bishops and other ecclesiastics, the second permitting Catholics who had taken the oath of allegiance to establish schools. In contrast to the acrimony expressed in 1778, both measures passed easily through the Commons.

To acclaim the removal of long moribund restrictions on bishops and regular clergy, and to remove the legal shackles restraining what was by now a vestigial Catholic landed interest, was, however, one thing. To consider ceding a share in political power to a body that outnumbered Protestants up to four to one was quite another. Even in the atmosphere of ostentatious good will cultivated in

---

[51] James Kelly, '1780 Revisited: The Politics of the Repeal of the Sacramental Test', in Kevin Herlihy (ed.), *The Politics of Irish Dissent 1650–1800* (Dublin, 1997), 74–92.

[52] Morley, *Irish Opinion and the American Revolution*, 126.

[53] Bartlett, *Fall and Rise of the Irish Nation*, ch. 6.

1782 the Commons had taken care to stipulate that the new freedom to purchase real estate should not extend to land in parliamentary boroughs. Several of the English reformers whose advice had been sought before the second Dungannon convention in September 1783 had taken it for granted that a commitment to civil liberty and equal representation must extend to the admission of Catholics to the franchise. Some Irish reformers agreed, the most prominent being William Todd Jones, a barrister who had been returned in 1783 as MP for Lisburn in an electoral revolt against the local landlord, Lord Hertford. By contrast all of the national leaders, while accepting the grant of property rights and freedom of worship, were at this stage convinced that the Protestant monopoly of political power must be maintained. Grattan was eventually to conclude that only complete equality would serve 'to make the Catholic a freeman and the Protestant a people'.[54] But that was not until 1792. Charlemont's conversion came even later, near his death in 1799. Newenham and Flood, on the other hand, never abandoned their belief that an extension of political rights to Catholics was incompatible with the survival of Protestant freedom. If Catholics should get the vote, Newenham explained to Benjamin Franklin in October 1783, no Protestant could expect to be elected in any county or free borough. Moreover they would use their dominance of parliament to reverse the seventeenth-century land settlement and 'serve us as the Scotch and American rebels intended to have served the friends of liberty in America, had tyranny prevailed over virtue'.[55]

Fears of this kind meant that any attempt to broaden the reform campaign to include an extension of political rights to Catholics was bound to be hugely divisive. The resolutions agreed at the Dungannon meeting in September 1783 held out the possibility that some Catholics would be enfranchised, but left it to the national convention to decide what categories among them would benefit. When the convention met George Ogle, a delegate from Wexford, claimed to have been assured that the Catholics themselves did not want the issue raised. The announcement, though immediately repudiated by the Catholic committee, was enough to allow a relieved majority among the delegates to agree that the whole question of Catholic rights should for the moment be set to one side. The reform movement of 1784–5, more radical in its assumptions and relying for support on a Volunteer movement that now contained a growing proportion of Catholics, had little choice but to go further. A Dublin meeting in June 1784 declared its support for the extension of the vote to Catholics 'still preserving in its fullest extent the present Protestant government of this country'.[56] It was a guarded statement, generally interpreted as implying the enfranchisement of a safe minority of wealthy Catholics. But it nevertheless went too far for many. A few months later Tandy tried unsuccessfully to persuade the Catholics themselves to renounce their claims.

---

[54] Kelly, *Henry Grattan*, 27.   [55] Quoted in Kelly, *Sir Edward Newenham*, 196.
[56] J. R. Hill, *From Patriots to Unionists: Dublin Civic Politics and Irish Protestant Patriotism 1660–1840* (Oxford, 1997), 176.

The Catholic leaders, however, declined to help the Protestant reformers escape the awkward conflict between their political principles and the realities of Irish sectarian divisions. At the same time they also resisted pressure from the government to dissociate themselves from the reform agitation. Their studied neutrality, winning them friends in neither camp, contrasts with the skill with which, less than a decade later, they were to play the same two sides off against one another.

A MERE CAKE OF WAX

Within a short time the euphoria that greeted the inauguration of 'the constitution of 1782' had thus given way to disputes over the relationships, between representatives and voters, and between Catholics and Protestants, that were to exist within the redefined political system. Grattan's initial insistence that he now addressed a free people reflected the extent to which he and other patriots saw all such matters as secondary to the great question of Ireland's relationship to the crown, government, and parliament of England. Following the fall of North's administration Rockingham, Fox, and the other members of the incoming Whig ministry had argued that the best way forward was a negotiated treaty that would spell out the rights and duties of both kingdoms. Grattan and Charlemont, however, had insisted on an immediate settlement removing what they saw as two illegitimate encroachments on Ireland's status as a parliamentary monarchy in its own right: the claim of the British parliament to pass legislation binding on Ireland, and the ability of the Irish privy council, under Poynings's Law, to suppress or amend legislative initiatives of which it disapproved. The resulting settlement—the repeal of the declaratory act, followed by the renunciation act, and the modification of Poynings's Law by Yelverton's act—left a number of apparent contradictions. Bills now went direct from the Irish parliament to the king. But when they returned with the royal assent they did so under the great seal of Great Britain. Warrants for official payments, equally, were countersigned by the lords of the British treasury. In theory such anomalies called into question the claim of a purely regnal union between two separate kingdoms. In practice they gave rise to little concern. Indeed John Foster, arguing against the necessity of an act of union in 1799, was to claim that the appending of the British seal to Irish legislation had been retained as a deliberate guarantee of the continuing union of the two kingdoms. When a group of radical lawyers, in 1792, mounted a legal challenge to the lord lieutenant's patent, arguing that the British great seal was, in Ireland, 'a mere cake of wax', the judges who threw out their case included none other than Barry Yelverton.[57]

---

[57] *Speech of the Right Honourable John Foster, Speaker of the House of Commons of Ireland, Delivered in Committee of the Whole House, on Thursday the 16th of April* (London, 1799), 57; McDowell, *Ireland in the Age of Imperialism and Revolution*, 290.

If seals could be taken as a harmless, or even valuable, symbol, however, the practical workings of 'legislative independence' presented more serious problems. Yelverton's act introduced two major changes: instead of mere heads of a bill emanating from one of its two houses, the Irish parliament would now produce its own bills, backed by the authority of both Lords and Commons, and these bills were to be transmitted unaltered to London. But there they had still to receive the approval of the king, signified by the attachment of the great seal of England. In theory this gave Irish statutes the same status as those of Great Britain, as the will of king, Lords, and Commons. In practice it raised once again the difficulties inherent in the patriot attempt to draw a clear line between allegiance to the crown of Great Britain and subordination to its parliament and government. The king, in the late eighteenth century, was not yet wholly a figurehead; but he exercised his routine functions on the advice of his ministers. Hence it was the British privy council that considered bills coming from Ireland, referring them to its law officers for scrutiny and retaining the power either to amend or to refuse any measure of which it disapproved. In practice a reluctance to aggravate Irish sensibilities ensured that this power was used sparingly. Only two bills are known to have been refused approval. Amendments, likewise, were rare, in most cases arising from the necessity, in the new circumstances of free Irish access to imperial trade, of avoiding discrepancies in the commercial legislation obtaining in the two kingdoms. But it was only this self-imposed restraint that concealed the limited nature of the legislative independence attained in 1782.[58]

British politicians of a wide range of political outlooks shared the perception that the settlement of 1782, dismantling the existing methods by which Ireland had been kept under political control while putting nothing in its place, had left the connection between the two kingdoms dangerously weakened. Over the next two years controversies over renunciation and parliamentary reform distracted attention from the unfinished business of defining a new constitutional relationship, while confirming the fears of those who believed that the existing connection was now dangerously weak. In 1784 the chief secretary, Thomas Orde, brought forward a series of propositions to regulate future commercial interchange. The immediate background was the aggressive Irish campaign for protective tariffs, raising the spectre of an Anglo-Irish trade war. But Orde's proposals attracted the personal interest of the prime minister, William Pitt, who saw in them not just an economic agreement but the basis of a new settlement of Anglo-Irish relations generally.

The prospects for Orde's proposals, worked out in consultation with the Irish executive's two financial experts, Foster and Beresford, at first seemed promising.

---

[58] These points were first explored in a pioneering article by J. C. Beckett, 'Anglo-Irish Constitutional Relations in the Later Eighteenth Century', first published in 1964 and reprinted in his *Confrontations: Studies in Irish History* (London, 1972), 123–41. The systematic investigation of the handling of Irish bills that Beckett called for at that time has still not been attempted. But see Kelly, *Prelude to Union*, 157–8, 222–3.

When the resulting series of eleven Commercial Propositions reached England in February 1785, however, industrial and commercial interests mobilized to force through a series of changes. By the time the much-amended proposals, now embodied in twenty resolutions, came before the Irish parliament in August, they had become the focus of a noisy campaign of resistance. The objection was in part to the revision, at English insistence, of points already agreed. There was also resentment at specific restrictions, especially the continued exclusion of Irish ships and merchants from trading with territories east of the Cape of Good Hope, the rich preserve of the East India Company. But opponents further maintained that the propositions infringed Ireland's legislative independence. In particular they objected to the fourth resolution, which committed the Irish parliament to replicating all acts passed in Great Britain relating to shipping and colonial trade. They also challenged the requirement—seen by Pitt as essential to the concept of a new understanding of the mutual obligations of the two kingdoms—that Ireland would contribute to the cost of imperial defence. The bill to implement the resolutions in fact passed its first reading by 127 votes to 110. But Pitt's aim had been to see Ireland voluntarily commit itself to a new relationship, and he abandoned the propositions rather than press ahead on this dubious basis.

The failure of the Commercial Propositions did not lead directly to any breakdown in relations between Ireland and England. Pitt's vision of a comprehensive settlement between the two kingdoms had been lost to a combination of real grievance and constitutional punctilio. But over the next few years a range of individual issues were resolved in a somewhat haphazard but amicable fashion. In 1787 the Irish parliament accepted without difficulty a navigation act replicating the provisions of an English law of the preceding year. In the same year the administration deferred to Irish sensitivities by laying before the Dublin parliament the terms of a new commercial treaty with France. In 1790, with England and Spain on the brink of war, Theobald Wolfe Tone, a young Dublin barrister on the fringes of the Irish Whig party, published a pamphlet calling for Ireland to remain neutral. Tone's argument rested in part on a radical interpretation of the way in which the connection between the two kingdoms had been redefined in 1782. Their union, as independent legislatures under one head, was not 'so complete an union of power or of interest' as to require either one to take up the other's quarrels. But he also drew attention to a less debatable point: if a decision of the English parliament could bring Ireland into a war then 'the charter of our liberties is waste paper'.[59] This, however, was an argument that few, on either side, wished to pursue. The Commons unanimously voted the supplies requested to support the war, as it did again in 1793, on the commencement of war with revolutionary France. In 1797 the lord lieutenant, after some hesitation, laid before parliament papers relating to Spain's defection to the French side and the failure of peace negotiations.

   [59] T. W. Tone, 'Spanish War', in *Wolfe Tone*, ed. Bartlett, 267, 270–1.

Some issues, however, could not be so easily resolved or glossed over. In November 1788 George III became mentally disturbed to the point of being incapable of ruling. Pitt and his colleagues faced the prospect of a regency by a prince of Wales openly hostile to them and a patron of their Whig opponents. Their strategy was to propose a bill that would give the prince limited powers, while hoping that the king would recover before it could be completed. The Whigs argued instead for an address calling on the prince to assume the regency by right and with full powers. But this left the question of how Ireland was to be dealt with. The lord lieutenant, the marquis of Buckingham, believed that he was taking account of Irish sensitivities by proposing that the Irish parliament should pass its own regency bill. When parliament assembled in February 1789, however, the two houses voted instead for an address to the prince requesting him to assume the regency of the kingdom immediately and without restrictions. The vote passed through the massed defection of government supporters. Buckingham complained in particular of the conduct of 'four great rats'—William Brabazon Ponsonby, who had just succeeded his father as head of the family's parliamentary connection, the second earl of Shannon, the duke of Leinster, and Viscount Loftus, a County Wexford landowner who up to then had used his control of seven borough seats to top up a modest landed income with extensive government patronage. When the lord lieutenant refused to transmit the address, the two houses appointed a deputation to present it directly to the prince. By the time the two peers and four MPs set out, however, the king had already shown signs of recovery, and they arrived in London on a mission that had become humiliatingly redundant.

Parliament's revolt over the regency bill cannot, any more than any other political transaction of the era, be taken at face value. The main concern of most Irish politicians was to attach themselves to what they assumed was the rising star of the prince and the Whigs. Some of the bargaining that took place was openly mercenary. Henry Agar, Lord Clifden, whose connection included his uncle Charles, the archbishop of Cashel, as well as four MPs, committed himself to the Whigs on the promise of succeeding his recently deceased father as joint postmaster general, something Buckingham had just denied him. John Scott, now Lord Earlsfort and chief justice of the King's Bench, remained loyal, but blatantly availed of Buckingham's difficulties to exchange an office worth £500 a year for one worth £800. The Ponsonbys, too, were widely believed to be concerned primarily with regaining the political primacy they had lost under Townshend. At the same time there was also a real constitutional issue. Opposition to the regency bill was led by Grattan, who called on the Commons to imitate the English Convention parliament of 1689, which had declared the crown vacant by the flight of James II and bestowed it on William and Mary. His argument, that to wait tamely for the decision of the English parliament was to admit that the Irish assembly was indeed a subordinate legislature, was the same as that raised a year later by Tone in connection with the Spanish War. Then it was to awaken no response, and served only to end Tone's brief career as a client of the Irish Whigs. But on the purely symbolic issue of the regency the appeal to national pride was clearly easier to accept.

The issue, however, was not wholly symbolic. In taking the stand they did in 1789, MPs and Lords were also asserting their right to make their own decision on the one fragile link, the crown, that now held two theoretically autonomous kingdoms together. The point was spelled out explicitly by the attorney general, Fitzgibbon. Members might today want only to assert themselves by conferring the regency a little more quickly than the British parliament, and on somewhat different terms. By doing so, however, they opened up the possibility that in some future succession crisis an Irish parliament might go further. 'If the address of both houses can invest the Prince of Wales with royal power in this country, the same address could convey the same power to Louis XVI, or to his Holiness the Pope, or to the right honourable mover of this resolution [Grattan].'[60] Fitzgibbon had by this time established himself as the gadfly of what he saw as an irresponsible (in his terms 'giddy') Irish assembly, and his speech was intended to be provocative. But his comments, and the episode that provoked them, nevertheless highlighted a real constitutional anomaly arising from the incomplete settlement of 1782.

The regency crisis also had a more permanent legacy. The English Whig leaders, notably Fox and the duke of Portland, had for some time shown an interest in the possibility of establishing their party in Ireland. To do so they could look partly to a shared concern with moderate reform linking them to figures like Charlemont and Grattan. There were also family connections: the duchess of Leinster was a daughter of the duke of Richmond and Fox's aunt, while the Ponsonbys were related by marriage to Portland. Up to 1789 neither ideology nor family had prevented both Leinster and the Ponsonbys from giving well-rewarded support to Pitt's administration. Their defection over the regency crisis, however, proved to be a turning point. During the summer of 1789 the Ponsonbys, Leinster, and Shannon came together with Grattan, Charlemont, and others to form a Whig party, in close contact with its British namesake, and declaring itself dedicated to the preservation of the Irish constitution as established in 1688 and 1782.

Precisely why the opportunistic defections of 1789 became the basis of a permanent realignment of political forces remains unclear. Once what had become the fiasco of the address to the prince was over, Buckingham had no choice but to swallow his rage and rebuild a government majority by accepting

---

[60] For Fitzgibbon's remarkable speech, which included the warning to 'the country gentlemen of Ireland' that their title to their estates rested on 'an act of violence' against the former Catholic proprietors, and that they weakened the connection with an English crown that could alone uphold it at their peril, see Ann Kavanaugh, *John Fitzgibbon, Earl of Clare* (Dublin, 1997), 146–50. The relevance of his remarks to the settlement of 1782 was first highlighted in E. M. Johnston, *Ireland in the Eighteenth Century* (Dublin, 1974), 161.

the return of both greater and lesser rats, including Clifden and Loftus. It is possible that he calculated that he could afford to indulge his resentment by excluding the Ponsonbys. Alternatively they themselves, along with Leinster, may have felt that they had gone too far with their English allies to withdraw while retaining any credit. Shannon also stayed in opposition, supposedly due to the influence of his wife, who reportedly 'raved like a madwoman' at the suggestion that he might desert her brother. A more recent analysis, however, suggests that this image of a henpecked magnate was more probably a fiction by Shannon himself, intended to minimize the offence he gave to the king by joining the opposition to his ministers.[61]

The extension to Ireland of British party divisions added further complexity to the already difficult situation created by the settlement of 1782. Irish parliamentary politics had always derived their particular character from the complete separation of the executive, a British-appointed lord lieutenant and his officers, from the legislature with which he had to deal. The problem had been resolved, first by the use of undertakers, then by direct management by a permanently resident lord lieutenant and chief secretary, relying heavily on the distribution of patronage. The settlement of 1782 made no difference in this respect: lords lieutenant, in theory the king's representative or viceroy, continued to be senior members of the British ministry of the day. The theoretical alternative, indeed the only manner in which the Irish parliament could have achieved the status it craved by becoming the real source of effective power, would have been to allow an Irish chief minister of some kind to emerge on the basis of whoever could demonstrate effective control of the Commons. Such a course was not even considered—although the earl of Abercorn, in 1791, had brief hopes of becoming the first Irish lord lieutenant since 1713, on the basis partly of his parliamentary following and partly of his personal friendship with Pitt. But that left the question of what was to happen when a shift in parliamentary power in England replaced one ministry with another.

Awareness of this point had been one reason why Irish allies of the English Whigs had initially failed to respond to invitations to form a sister party. Charles Francis Sheridan, brought into minor office in 1782, retained his place when Pitt displaced the Whigs and their allies two years later and gave the expected support to the new lord lieutenant, explaining to his brother that 'our subordinate situation necessarily prevents the formation of any party amongst us'.[62] In 1789, on the other hand, Sheridan opposed the administration on the regency issue and was dismissed. In his case the episode ended his political career. But the

---

[61] A. P. W. Malcomson, 'Introduction' to *Lord Shannon's Letters to his Son*, ed. Esther Hewitt (Belfast, 1982), pp. xxxix–xliv.

[62] Quoted in Denis Kennedy, 'The Irish Whigs, Administrative Reform and Responsible Government 1782–1800', *Eire-Ireland*, 8 (1973), 59 n. 8. Sheridan's brother was Richard Brinsley Sheridan, the celebrated playwright and a Whig MP in England.

decision of others to coalesce as a fixed party, linked to the British opposition, could only strengthen further an already developing sense that the management of Irish politics had become a dangerously precarious undertaking.

MEDITERRANEAN VISIONS

The slowly increasing prominence of patriot issues in popular and parliamentary politics took place alongside, and to some extent in connection with, an equally gradual reassessment of the vocabulary of national identity, and of attitudes to Gaelic culture and the Gaelic past. The use of 'Irish' as synonymous with 'Catholic' remained standard up to around 1720. Thereafter people more commonly spoke of 'Papists' or 'Romanists' or, if they wished to be unusually polite, of 'Roman Catholics'.[63] 'Irish' retained for some time longer its negative connotations. As late as 1738 Samuel Madden, a clergyman much concerned with patriotic schemes for the improvement of Ireland, argued that 'the children of those Englishmen who have planted in our colonies in America [may] be as justly reckoned Indians and savages, as such families who are settled here can be considered and treated as mere Irishmen and aliens'. For most of his contemporaries, however, 'Irish' was by now a looser term, employed to suggest provincialism and lack of civility. In 1723 the Queen's County landowner Pole Cosby, visiting an Irish monastery at Prague (where he was enthusiastically received as a fellow countryman), found the church richly ornamented but the other premises 'but ordinary and Irish all over, very dirty'. Edward Synge, bishop of Elphin, in 1751, dismissed the servant travelling with a guest as 'the errantest Irish trull you ever saw. It vexed me to have her put in one of my pretty beds.' (He had later to admit that she was in fact 'a Protestant, of an English family, and a very creditable one, though now low in condition'.) A decade earlier Letitia Bushe, the thirty-something daughter of a former official, adopted a similar, but more jocular, tone. A doctor who attended her was 'an Irish physician, and though a skilful man, yet absurd and entertaining by his manner of knocking words out of joint and a mixture of bad French, bad English, and good Irish, which he jumbles through each other'. She headed a letter written on 17 March with a piece of pseudo-Gaelic: 'Tuesday 17 and St Patrick's o hone'. She even described herself, during an illness, as 'no Roman-souled maid, but a poor, sneaking, Irish-hearted trollop'.[64]

---

[63] A Catholic writer of the early nineteenth century dated the first use of 'Roman Catholic' rather than papist in a parliamentary debate to 1764: Mathew O'Conor, quoted in Bartlett, *Fall and Rise of the Irish Nation*, 68.

[64] *A Discourse on the Woollen Manufactory of Ireland* (London, 1698), 11–12; Samuel Madden, *Reflections and Resolutions Proper for the Gentlemen of Ireland* (Dublin, 1738), 108; 'Autobiography

At the same time that the terminology of ethnic identity became gradually more muted, developments in the field of literature testified to the beginnings of a broader change in attitude. In 1723 Dermot or Darby O'Connor produced an English-language translation of the work the older Sir Richard Cox had so readily dismissed, Geoffrey Keating's early seventeenth-century history of Ireland. It appeared in a handsome volume, illustrated by a striking depiction of the eleventh-century ruler Brian Boru anachronistically but nobly attired in plate armour. The dedication was to the earl of Inchiquin, and the list of subscribers included the earl of Burlington and Cork, absentee head of the Boyle family, the duke of Grafton, then lord lieutenant, and Archbishop King of Dublin, as well as the exiled Jacobite peer Donough MacCarthy, credited with his full titles as earl of Clancarty and Viscount Muskerry. A Dublin newspaper proudly reported the 'esteem and favour' shown to O'Connor when he presented a copy of the work to the prince of Wales.[65] By this time too, themes from ancient Irish history had begun to find a place on the Dublin stage. In *Rotherick O'Connor* (1720) Charles Shadwell, son of a former English poet laureate but now Dublin's leading playwright, dramatized the twelfth-century conquest, presenting the English Strongbow as bringing order to a land of warring and arbitrary kings, but also allowing his heroine Eva, daughter of the king of Leinster, to praise the virtues of the Irish and lament their military subjugation. William Phillips's *Hibernia Freed* (1722) offered a more straightforward celebration of the defeat of the barbarous Vikings by the Gaelic kings of Ulster and Munster, though including a brief reference forward to another invasion, this time by a superior and benevolent civilization, still to come.[66] In 1721 there appeared a collection of compositions by Turlough O'Carolan, the most celebrated harpist of the day, the first of several collections making music from the native tradition (modified, in Carolan's case, by influences from European art music) available to polite society.[67]

An essential part of the background to this new interest in selected elements of the Gaelic cultural tradition was the collapse of the social order out of which it had emerged. As late as 1707 the Irish parliament thought it necessary to legislate

of Pole Cosby of Stradbally, Queen's County, 1703–37', *Kildare Archaeological and Historical Society Journal*, 5(1906–8), 97–8; *The Synge Letters: Bishop Edward Synge to his Daughter Alicia, Roscommon to Dublin 1746–52*, ed. M. L. Legg (Dublin, 1996), 300; S. J. Connolly, 'A Woman's Life in Mid-Eighteenth-Century Ireland: The Case of Letitia Bushe', *Historical Journal*, 43(2000), 443.

[65] *Dublin Intelligence*, 12 Jan. 1723. See Diarmaid Ó Catháin, 'Dermot O'Connor, Translator of Keating', *ECI* 2 (1987), 67–87.

[66] W. S. Clark, *The Early Irish Stage: The Beginnings to 1720* (Oxford, 1955), 170–4; J. Th. Leerssen, *Mere Irish and Fíor Ghael: Studies in the Idea of Irish Nationality, its Development and Literary Expression Prior to the Nineteenth Century* (Cork, 1996), 326–7. Christopher Morash, *A History of Irish Theatre 1601–2000* (Cambridge, 2002), 39–40, lays more emphasis on Shadwell's negative depiction of pre-conquest Ireland.

[67] Harry White, *The Keeper's Recital: Music and Cultural History in Ireland 1770–1970* (Cork, 1998), 13–25.

for the transportation as vagrants of 'such as pretend to be Irish gentlemen and . . . wander about demanding victuals and coshering from house to house amongst their fosterers, followers, and others'. But the image, with its echoes of Spenser and Davies, was already anachronistic. Observers continued for several decades more to comment on the respect shown by the common people in some areas to those known or believed to be the descendants of their former lords. But the massive land confiscations of the seventeenth century, accompanied by the imposition of a wholly new system of landlord–tenant relationships, had destroyed any potential to turn this lingering respect into a serious military threat. When two English travellers, visiting the fair at Callan, County Kilkenny, in the early 1740s, observed the 'extraordinary respect' paid to the impoverished descendant of a former proprietor as he rode through the town, they saw nothing sinister in the spectacle, only a quaint echo of former times. This was in sharp contrast to conditions in the Scottish Highlands, where the rebellion of 1745 was to confirm the continued ability of Jacobite chiefs to call out their human rent of armed followers recruited or impressed from among their tenants and clan members. One consequence was that the Highlander had to wait until the very end of the eighteenth century for his image to be transformed from that of bloodthirsty savage to idealized symbol of a noble simplicity of life and manners. The selective rehabilitation of Irish Gaeldom was already well under way several decades earlier.[68]

The first major contribution to that process was the work of Charles O'Conor, a member of an ancient family maintaining a precarious gentility on what remained of his family's lands in County Roscommon. His *Dissertations on the Ancient History of Ireland* (1753) set out to present early Gaelic Ireland in terms acceptable to the Enlightenment. It depicted an orderly society with a highly developed legal and intellectual tradition firmly based on the written word, and a system of government by the three estates of king, nobles, and commons. The appeal to educated Irish opinion of this new, more positive image was made evident a few years later, in the outraged response to the appearance in 1760–3 of MacPherson's *Ossian* poems, which revived the argument that the real centre of an advanced early Gaelic civilization had been Scotland, with pre-Christian Ireland as a mere cultural satellite. Yet if MacPherson's self-promoting excesses threatened Irish self-regard, they also helped to awaken public interest in an imagined past age of heroism and primitive simplicity, creating new publishing opportunities for Irish as well as Scottish authors. Joseph Cooper Walker's *Historical Memoirs of the Irish Bards* (1786), produced with the help of O'Conor and others, drew on MacPherson's work while strenuously rejecting his claims for Scottish cultural primacy. In 1789 Charlotte Brooke,

---

[68] [W. R. Chetwood]. *A Tour Through Ireland in Several Entertaining Letters* (Dublin, 1746), 147–8. For other comment on the respect shown to old proprietors see Connolly, *Religion, Law and Power*, 141–2. For the act of 1707 see *Irish Statutes*, 6 Anne, c. 11.

daughter of the pamphleteer and man of letters Henry Brooke, published her *Reliques of Irish Poetry*, in which original texts ranging in date from the early medieval period to the seventeenth century appeared accompanied by her own verse translations. Her preface drew attention to the 'various and comprehensive powers' of 'this neglected language', and offered her translations as evidence of 'manners of a degree of refinement totally astonishing at a period when the rest of Europe was nearly sunk in barbarism'.[69] The same period saw further attention paid to what survived of the indigenous musical tradition. In 1792 a committee based in Belfast brought together ten of the last surviving practitioners on the traditional Irish harp, six of them blind, in order to rescue 'some of the most ancient airs, now nearly obsolete'. The event inspired Edward Bunting, the 19-year-old organist of St Anne's church and one of the three conventional musicians employed to transcribe the airs, to begin what became a lifelong work, commemorated in the three volumes of his *A General Collection of the Ancient Irish Music*, published between 1797 and 1840.[70]

O'Conor, Brooke, and Bunting were all serious scholars. But the new enthusiasm for the Gaelic past also encouraged more colourful propagandists. Sylvester O'Halloran, by profession an optical surgeon in Limerick city, went well beyond the sources to imagine an ancient Ireland that had been the centre of European civilization. His *Introduction to the Study of the History and Antiquities of Ireland* (1772), and a subsequent *General History of Ireland* (1778), argued that the ideas of chivalry and knighthood current throughout medieval Europe as a whole had had their origin in an Irish heroic age. A second enthusiast, even more flamboyant in his claims, was Charles Vallancey, an English army officer of Huguenot origin who had made Ireland his adoptive home. Vallancey's particular concern was to demonstrate that the Irish language was closely related to that of the Phoenicians, thus confirming the status of Gaelic Ireland as a product of the advanced cultures of the ancient Mediterranean, and of its language as one of the oldest in the world. His enthusiastic speculations alarmed more serious scholars in the field. But he became joint secretary of the antiquities committee established in 1772 by the Royal Dublin Society. He was also a founder member of the Royal Irish Academy, established in 1785 to promote the study of science, polite literature, and antiquities.[71]

The new interest in the glories of the ancient Gaelic past was clearly linked to the rising spirit of political patriotism. The term 'patriot' appears several times in Brooke's poetic celebration of ancient Gaelic heroes. The first president

[69] Charlotte Brooke, *Reliques of Irish Poetry* (Dublin, 1789), pp. vi–vii.

[70] White, *The Keeper's Recital*, 37–43.

[71] The fullest account is now Clare O'Halloran, *Golden Ages and Barbarous Nations: Antiquarian Debate and Cultural Politics in Ireland c.1750–1800* (Cork, 2004). See also Leerssen, *Mere Irish*, 294–376; Norman Vance, 'Celts, Carthaginians and Constitutions: Anglo-Irish Literary Relations 1780–1820', *IHS* 22 (1981), 216–38.

of the Royal Irish Academy was the earl of Charlemont, commander in chief of the Volunteers. Henry Flood showed no more than a mild interest in Irish antiquarianism at any point in his complex progress from opposition to office holder and then to a reassumed patriotism. But when a family dispute left him anxious to disinherit his potential heirs, his solution was to bequeath the bulk of his estate to Trinity College for the purpose of supporting 'a professorship of and for the native Irish or Erse language', along with the purchase of printed books in Irish and other languages.[72]

An enthusiasm for Gaelic antiquities, increasingly linked to a political patriotism, had the potential to bridge the division between Catholic and Protestant. In 1773 Charles O'Conor and the Catholic archbishop of Dublin, John Carpenter, were invited to attend the select committee on Gaelic antiquities of the Dublin Society as corresponding members. O'Conor wrote enthusiastically to his son of 'a revolution in our moral and civil affairs the more extraordinary, as in my own days such a man [as Carpenter] would only be spoken to through the medium of a warrant and a constable'. Yet such acceptance was not to be taken for granted. O'Conor had initially published his *Dissertations* anonymously, putting his name only to a second edition, in 1766, from which some potentially contentious comment on the period of the Anglo-Norman invasion had been removed. And his correspondence with Protestant scholars seems to have retained throughout his life a tone of deferential anxiety.[73]

Nor was his caution necessarily misplaced. Despite the shared concern to create a positive image of the Irish past, the shadow of political and sectarian controversy was never wholly lifted. There were particular differences over the presentation of early Irish Christianity. Protestant writers, hunting out evidence that the heirs of St Patrick had resisted papal dictation in matters such as the dating of Easter, depicted a national church that in its golden age had remained free of the corruptions of Rome. Catholics, by contrast, emphasized the papal origins of Patrick's mission to Ireland, and the orthodox character of the church he had established.[74] On a broader front two Church of Ireland clergymen, Thomas Campbell and Edward Ledwich, led a sustained attack during the 1780s and 1790s on O'Conor's idealized image of the Gaelic past, reiterating instead Cox's vision of Gaelic barbarism. They also rejected Vallancey's thesis of Phoenician origins, and indeed the whole notion that the Irish had a distinct ethnic identity, presenting them instead as sharing the same northern European 'Gothic' ancestry as the British. The antipathy of both men to the myth of a glorious Gaelic past can in part be seen as politically motivated.

[72] Kelly, *Henry Flood*, 428–36.   [73] O'Halloran, *Golden Ages*, 37–8, 161–5.
[74] Clare O'Halloran, ' "The Island of Saints and Scholars": Views of the Early Church and Sectarian Politics in Late Eighteenth-Century Ireland', *ECI* 5 (1990), 7–20; Bridget McCormack, *Perceptions of St Patrick in Eighteenth-Century Ireland* (Dublin, 2000).

Ledwich expressed concern for the future of the Protestant establishment, while Campbell was a strong supporter of a union of Britain and Ireland. However it was not to be until after the shock of 1798 that most Irish Protestants were forced to have second thoughts regarding their enthusiasm for Gaelic antiquities.[75]

[75] J. P. Delury, 'Ex Conflicta et Collisione: The Failure of Irish Historiography 1750–1790', *ECI* 15 (2000), 9–37, sees a politically based fracture already fully developed in the late eighteenth century. O'Halloran, *Golden Ages*, 58–70, and Leerssen, *Mere Irish*, 348–9, are more cautious. For the very definite retreat from patriotic antiquarianism after 1798 see Joep Leerssen, *Remembrance and Imagination* (Cork, 1996), 73–7.

11

Revolution Contained

The 1790s are the hinge that connects, not just the eighteenth and nineteenth centuries, but early modern and modern Ireland. The rising violence of the decade, culminating in the bloody civil war of 1798, invites us to re-examine the preceding century of internal peace, and to consider the fault lines concealed behind a façade of apparent stability. But the violence was also the product of new political alignments that laid the foundations for developments that were to continue into the nineteenth century and beyond. Alongside the traditional patriot insistence on Ireland's status as a separate kingdom, joined to Great Britain by a shared monarch, there developed during the 1790s a new movement based on an explicitly separatist republicanism. The same decade saw Protestant radicals finally escape from the sectarian exclusiveness that had constrained the Volunteers and their ideological predecessors, from Lucas back to Molyneux, to seek an alliance of Catholic and Protestant behind shared political goals. In responding to their overtures, and committing themselves to the republican cause, Catholics too broke decisively with the dominant tradition of their political past, a commitment to the exiled Stuart dynasty as rightful rulers of the kingdoms of England, Scotland, and Ireland. Yet the new political departure was at best incomplete. The democratic republican coalition came under attack, both within and without, from the forces of a powerfully revived sectarianism, recasting in new terms the religious antagonisms that had dominated the seventeenth century. Modern Irish republicans may look back to the United Irishmen as the founders of their tradition. But the one present-day organization that can trace an unbroken descent from the 1790s is the Protestant supremacist Orange Order.

The long-term developments that contributed to the escalating violence of the years up to 1798 are, with the benefit of hindsight, easily summarized. The stability of early Hanoverian Ireland had been that of a society in which the dominance of property over numbers as the key to political power had been not just a generally accepted doctrine, but also a political reality. With their gentry and aristocracy stripped of their lands and in some cases driven overseas, and their church cowed into passivity, the Catholic majority, leaderless and disarmed, posed no real threat to the political order, despite the survival of a strong popular Jacobite tradition. By the second half of the century, on the other hand, new forces were at work. A Catholic middle class, expanding along with the general growth of commercial wealth from mid-century onwards, gradually began to assert itself. Rising living standards, improved literacy, and the growth of the urban population all provided the basis for a growth in popular political awareness. The commercialization of agriculture, along with the expansion of population, disrupted traditional economic relationships and created new social tensions in the countryside, reflected in the emergence of widespread movements of agrarian protest. Meanwhile developments at the level of high politics made their own contribution to the collapse of traditional structures of power. The self-interested appeal to public opinion of Boyle and his allies in the 1750s, and the increasingly bold attempts of parliamentary patriots in the 1770s and 1780s to mobilize mass support, encouraged the growth of an assertive popular radicalism. The actions of the British government, increasingly alienated from the Irish Protestant elite and openly willing to play off Catholic against Protestant in pursuit of its own long-term strategic interests, added a further element of instability, and in particular further encouraged a revival of sectarian animosities.

To these internal tensions must be added the impact of external events. Mainstream Irish patriotism may have been ambivalent, and ultimately opportunistic, in its response to the American Revolution. But the more radical political language evident by the mid-1780s, including as it does the first hints of separatism, must be seen as in part at least a reflection of the ideas that had taken shape on the other side of the Atlantic. The crisis of the French monarchy, commencing in 1789, expanded into a revolutionary upheaval that transformed politics across Europe. Its effect on Ireland may have been partly to bring to the surface existing conflicts, political, social, and sectarian. But then the same was true within France itself: one result of the revolution there was the emancipation of the Protestant minority, which in turn was to give a sectarian tinge both to counter-revolutionary revolt in the west and to the later white terror in the south. Elsewhere too, in Italy, in Spain, and even in Great Britain, the prospect of imminent radical change gave a new edge to existing conflicts between privileged and subordinate, rulers and ruled, initiating an increasingly violent cycle of protest and repression. Against this background, the claim that the events of the 1790s demonstrate the uniquely divided and exploitative nature of eighteenth-century Irish society must be treated with caution.

An awareness of the exceptional character of the 1790s is also important in assessing the claims that have been made for the new revolutionary movement to which the decade gave birth. Subsequent generations were to look back to the rising of 1798 as a vindication of their ideal of a nationalism that would transcend religious divisions. In the mid-1880s Gladstone was to appeal to the memory of the United Irishmen in his efforts to win over Ulster Presbyterians to his proposals for Home Rule.[1] More recently the bicentenary of the insurrection provided the

---

[1] R. F. G. Holmes, 'United Irishmen and Unionists: Irish Presbyterians 1791 and 1886', in W. J. Sheils and Diana Wood (eds.), *The Churches, Ireland and the Irish* (Woodbridge, 1997), 171–89.

occasion for a sustained campaign to promote the United movement as a model of pluralist, democratic nationalism that might provide the basis for a new Irish political identity.[2] What all such assessments must take into account, however, is, once again, the wider international background. Episodes of revolutionary upheaval, of the kind that existed in the 1790s, are by definition times when the pressure of events is intense, encouraging or imposing courses of action that would not otherwise be taken. They are also generally periods of excitement, or even euphoria, in which the normally unimaginable seems suddenly possible and within reach. The political alignments forged against such a background may well represent bold new departures. In Latin America, for example, the inhabitants of different colonies found themselves suddenly forced to look beyond long-standing animosities to the new possibilities opened up by the collapse of Spanish power across the region. But the kaleidoscope of alliances that emerged, involving creoles, natives, and an imported black population, were for the most part unstable, contingent, and often temporary.[3] A realistic account of the Ireland of the 1790s must recognize the euphoric sense of imminent transformation that led so many to believe that they could leave a divided past behind them. But it must also acknowledge the provisional and temporary nature of the alignments that emerged in that fevered atmosphere.

UNITED IRISHMEN

In November and December 1784 the *Belfast Newsletter* carried three anonymous letters signed with the pseudonym 'Orellana, an Irish helot' — a name circuitously derived from a character in a well-known Restoration novel.[4] Addressed to the seven Ulster counties that had failed to send delegates to the reform convention that had just met in Dublin, the letters spoke for the radicalized agitation that had arisen to challenge the deceptive consensus briefly achieved in 1782. There were glancing blows at Grattan, who had diminished his greatness by accepting a monetary reward for his services to the national cause, and at Charlemont, for his persistent advocacy of caution: 'Resolutions, resolutions, shall we never

---

[2] For the full astonishing story of this collaboration between academics and government publicists see R. F. Foster, *The Irish Story: Telling Tales and Making it up in Ireland* (London, 2001), ch. 12; Tom Dunne, *Rebellions: Memoir, Memory and 1798* (Dublin, 2004), 101–48.

[3] L. D. Langley, *The Americas in the Age of Revolution 1750–1850* (New Haven, 1996). For a fuller discussion of these parallels see S. J. Connolly, 'Tupac Amaru and Captain Right: A Comparative Context for Eighteenth-Century Ireland', in David Dickson and Cormac Ó Gráda (eds.), *Refiguring Ireland* (Dublin, 2003), 104–8.

[4] Aphra Behn's *Oroonoko* (1688) told the story of a prince of royal blood sold into slavery in Surinam. The two great rivers of South America, as A. T. Q. Stewart points out, were the Orinoco and the Amazon, also sometimes in that period referred to as the Orellana, after its Spanish discoverer. A. T. Q. Stewart, *A Deeper Silence: The Hidden Origins of the United Irishmen* (London, 1993), 134–5.

have done with resolutions?' But the author's scorn was primarily directed at the political establishment that had rejected the call for parliamentary reform. If the aggregate Dublin meeting that had initiated the campaign could be dismissed as 'the dregs of democracy', the fault lay with 'those rich, respectable honourable gentlemen . . . who came in so late [and] went out so early, and did not finish the work which they did *not* begin'. When the House of Commons had rejected the principle of reform, 'it becomes the business of the people who first formed the house to deliberate on the means of reforming it'. The convention was thus 'a constitutional and at the same time peaceable means of expressing with energy and affect the conjunct will of a royal people'.[5]

'Orellana' was the pen name of William Drennan, a 30-year-old doctor then practising in Newry. As the son of the Thomas Drennan who had taught with Francis Hutcheson in Dublin, he was the heir to a well-developed tradition of Presbyterian political radicalism. Yet Drennan's letters, published the following year in pamphlet form, were notable less as the continuation of an established line of thought and argument than as a break with much of what had gone before. His one brief reference to the cherished traditions of the Revolution of 1688 was couched in deliberately provocative terms: 'that glorious innovation on the customary rules of succession, which placed the crowns of three kingdoms on the head of a German elector'. Elsewhere he went out of his way to reject the proposition, central to the Whig tradition as it had developed since 1688, that liberty was to be preserved by creating a balance between the forces of monarchy, aristocracy, and democracy. 'Those that rest their liberties upon certain imaginary checks in the machinery of state, are more conversant in the constitution of a clock than that of a commonwealth.' He had equally little time for customary tributes to the supposed perfection of the balance between liberty and restraint achieved in the British constitution: 'the world is as yet too young in political experience to repose upon any plan of government with unbounded confidence.' Instead Drennan based his argument on 'first principles and self-evident truths, which are axioms in their nature' and which concerned 'those rights respecting life, liberty and property without which we cannot be free'.[6]

Orellana was not a wholly consistent political writer. An expanded version published in pamphlet form included among four additional letters a proposed address to the king, calling on him to take a lead in the renewal of the balance of the constitution, suddenly restored to its status as 'a pyramid of matchless workmanship'. Taken as a whole, however, the *Letters* illustrate the extent to which, already by the mid-1780s, before the French Revolution had

---

[5] The original letters appeared as [William Drennan], *Letters of Orellana, an Irish Helot, Republished by Order of the Constitution Society of Dublin* (Dublin, 1785). The expanded version was *Letters of Orellana, an Irish Helot, to the Seven Northern Counties not Represented in the National Assembly of Delegates held at Dublin, October 1784* (Dublin, 1785). For the passages quoted see this latter text, 46, 16–17, 28–9.

[6] *Letters of Orellana . . . to the Seven Northern Counties*, 30, 8–11.

begun to transform political fears and aspirations everywhere in the western world, Irish radicalism was beginning, however tentatively, to take a new and bolder direction. The key to political liberty, Drennan insisted, lay, not in any institutional balance between monarchy and parliament, but in the constant exercise of the popular will. 'The spirit of a nation able to be free must be a haughty and magnanimous spirit, strenuous, vigilant, vindictive, always impatient, often impetuous, sometimes inexorable.'[7] It was a language that owed more to the influence of recent events in America than to the real Whig tradition of Molyneux, Molesworth, and Lucas. At the same time Drennan, a man of literary ambitions who was later to coin the phrase 'the emerald isle', gave expression to another developing trend within Irish patriotism, when he signed his last letter from 'Rath-geltair mic Duach', a Gaelic name for Downpatrick.

If the address to the king revealed only an understandable hedging of bets, however, Orellana's fifth letter provided a more significant demonstration of the limits of even advanced Protestant radicalism. Drennan began by appealing to Anglicans, dissenters, and Catholics to unite in 'one grand association, one great fund of virtue', recognizing in the difference between their different churches 'the imperfection of all human institutions'. But this was avowedly an appeal to the enlightened few. The majority within each denomination, Drennan argued, were characterized by 'strong antipathies', a natural sentiment that shielded them against religious indifference. In this context the 'great misfortune' of the Catholic religion was that history had left its followers without sufficient of the 'men of weight and estimation' that in other denominations could act to counter the dangerous effects of such prejudices. Hence they were for the moment 'absolutely incapable of making a good use of political liberty'. The enlightened Catholic, Drennan concluded, would 'resign himself to the sentence of fate, and for a time be content to serve his brother'. Within a few years it was to become clear that he was prepared to do no such thing. But the events that followed were to demonstrate that fears regarding the 'leaven of intolerance and persecution' that existed on both sides of the religious divide, however opportunistic their deployment by Orellana, were by no means ill founded.

The collapse of the parliamentary reform movement of 1784–5 left radicals like Drennan temporarily without a political cause. After 1789 the creation of the Whig party encouraged a new alliance with dissident representatives of the governing class. In particular the two groups found a common cause in their campaign against the Dublin police act of 1786, which had replaced the traditional system of watchmen and constables with an armed force under the control of three commissioners.[8] Radicals and Whigs joined with the guilds and members of the Common Council of the corporation in attacking what they saw as an unacceptable extension of state control at the expense of both urban autonomy and civil liberties. When the Board of Aldermen in 1790 selected as

---

[7] *Letters of Orellana . . . to the Seven Northern Counties*, 23.			[8] Above, Ch. 8.

lord mayor William James, an alderman but also one of the police commissioners, the Common Council mounted a sustained campaign of resistance that forced his eventual resignation. In the general election of the same year Tandy took the lead in organizing an electoral committee that secured the return as MPs for the city of Grattan and Lord Henry Fitzgerald, a brother to the duke of Leinster.

The alliance of radicals and reform-minded parliamentarians was, like its predecessor of 1779–82, an inherently precarious juncture, and by 1791 divisions had begun to appear. In Dublin Tandy, who had been elected a member of the Whig Club in 1790, joined with others in March of the following year to form their own body, the Whigs of the Capital. Drennan, now living in Dublin, described them as 'a body made of good honest men but not so honourable as of the Whig club, and not so genteel as to gain admission there'. The Whig Club itself he denounced as 'literally an eating and drinking aristocratical society without any fellow-feeling with the commonalty'.[9] In Belfast there was similar dissatisfaction with the Northern Whig Club, set up in March 1790 by Dr Alexander Haliday, a close ally of Charlemont. A rival Belfast Whig Club appeared in the summer of 1791. By this time there was also another, more shadowy group: a 'secret committee' of eleven members, headed by Samuel Neilson, a successful linen merchant, and also including Drennan's brother-in-law, the chandler Samuel McTier, who had come together for the purpose of working behind the scenes to push a revived Volunteer movement in as radical a direction as possible.[10]

These political realignments took place against a background of increasingly dramatic news from France, where a so-far largely bloodless revolution had forced the king to hand over effective power to a National Assembly. The level of interest among Irish radicals was evident in the massive circulation of Thomas Paine's defence of the Revolution, *The Rights of Man*. By May 1791, two months after its appearance in London, there had been three Irish editions, and either extracts or the whole text had also appeared in three Dublin papers, as well as in the *Belfast Newsletter*. In June the Whigs of the Capital sponsored the publication of a cheap edition, priced at sixpence, reportedly running to 20,000 copies.[11]

[9] Drennan to McTier, 21 May 1791 (*The Drennan–McTier Letters 1776–1793*, ed. Jean Agnew (Dublin, 1998), 357). Drennan's comment in the same letter that he would like to see a new society 'instituted in this city having much of the secrecy and somewhat of the ceremonial of freemasonry . . . its general end real independence to Ireland, and republicanism its particular purpose' has led some to hail him as the real founder of the United Irishmen. But his clear reference to Dublin as the home of such a society makes the link a purely rhetorical one.

[10] The reference to 'a secret committee, who are not known or suspected of co-operating' appears in Tone's diary for 12 Oct. 1791 (*Theobald Wolfe Tone: Memoirs, Journals and Political Writings*, ed. Thomas Bartlett (Dublin, 1998), 119). For the fragmentary evidence on its origins see Stewart, *A Deeper Silence*, 153–6.

[11] David Dickson, 'Paine and Ireland', in David Dickson, Dáire Keogh, and Kevin Whelan (eds.), *The United Irishmen: Republicanism, Radicalism and Rebellion* (Dublin, 1993), 135–51.

The following month the Belfast Volunteers assembled to celebrate 14 July, the second anniversary of the fall of the Bastille, apparently with the intention of using the occasion to launch a new radical society. Drennan duly produced a flowery declaration to be laid before the meeting. But when he was asked to supplement this with a set of resolutions, he took offence at the short notice, and instead suggested the name of Theobald Wolfe Tone.

Tone, a barrister and the son of an initially prosperous Dublin artisan, was a young man in search of a cause. His first venture, in 1788, when he was 25, had been to lobby for a colonizing expedition, with himself as leader, to the Sandwich Islands. In later life he was to reflect on the very different career he might have followed if the government had accepted his proposal. Subsequently he had, like other radicals, put his hopes in the newly formed Whig party, for whom he wrote his first, undistinguished political pamphlet in 1790. However his second, far more original pamphlet, arguing against participation in the Spanish War, demonstrated how far he had progressed beyond reformist Whiggery, as well as cutting off any hopes of further preferment from that quarter. He now produced three resolutions, the first denouncing Britain's continuing influence over Irish affairs, the second calling for a complete reform of parliamentary representation, and the third advocating 'a complete internal union' that would abolish the differences that had long divided Irishmen. He also suggested a name for the proposed new organization, 'the Society of United Irishmen'. But when his handiwork reached Belfast the Volunteer corps agreed that, in the interests of unanimity, this last resolution, with its implicit call for the extension of political rights to Catholics, should be quietly dropped.[12]

This unexpected rebuff seems to have delayed the planned launch of the proposed society. But the setback was a temporary one. In August Tone, stung to action by the rejection of his third resolution, published *An Argument on Behalf of the Catholics of Ireland*, a vigorous statement of the reasons why Catholics must be included in any scheme for radical reform. The pamphlet was a runaway success, selling 6,000 copies by early 1792. In October, meanwhile, Neilson and others invited Tone to Belfast to join in discussions about the establishment of a new political society. It was 'very curious', Tone noted in his diary, 'how the thermometer of Blefescu has arisen as to politics'. Returning to the resolutions he had drawn up in July he found that passages in the first copy 'which were three months ago esteemed too hazardous to propose, are now found too tame'.[13] On 14 October members of the secret committee agreed to a new set of resolutions. Four days later Tone attended a meeting of the Society of United Irishmen, with

---

[12] For Tone's resolutions see Marianne Elliott, *Wolfe Tone: Prophet of Irish Independence* (New Haven, 1989), 125. For Tone's own comment see his diary entry for 14 July 1791 (*Wolfe Tone*, ed. Bartlett, 119).

[13] Journal, 12 Oct. 1791 (*Wolfe Tone*, ed. Bartlett, 119).

McTier in the chair and twenty-eight of the thirty-six members present.[14] On 9 November Tandy convened the first meeting of a sister society in Dublin.

The founding resolutions adopted by the new society constituted an uncompromising distillation of radical and patriot demands. Having begun by hailing 'the present great era of reform, when unjust governments are falling in every quarter of Europe', they went on to identify Ireland's central grievance: 'We have no national government; we are ruled by Englishmen, and the servants of Englishmen, whose object is the interest of another country, whose instrument is corruption; whose strength is the weakness of Ireland.' The only force capable of resisting that power was 'unanimity, decision, and spirit in the people', which could best be exerted through 'a complete and radical reform of the representation of the people in parliament'. The Dublin Society subsequently adopted the same resolutions verbatim. In a circular letter drawn up at the end of December, it added its own eloquent profession of faith:

In thus associating, we have thought little about our ancestors—much of our posterity. Are we forever to walk like beasts of prey, over fields which these ancestors stained with blood? In looking back, we see nothing on the one part but savage force succeeded by savage policy; on the other an unfortunate nation, 'scattered and peeled, meted out and trodden down.' . . . We see this and are silent. But we gladly look forward to brighter prospects.

Their rule of conduct, they added, had been 'to attend to those things in which we agree, to exclude from our thoughts those in which we differ'.[15]

The call to concentrate on what united made a fine manifesto. When it came to formulating particular policies, however, the differences in outlook became more difficult to ignore. This was most obviously the case, in the early years of the new society, in connection with their efforts to give specific form to the call for a 'complete and radical reform of the representation of the people in parliament'. A committee established by the Dublin society at the end of 1792 divided almost equally on whether to call for universal male suffrage or a more restricted franchise. The Dublin society as a whole, after a vigorous debate, rejected the secret ballot in favour of a continued system of open voting. Supporters of a property qualification could argue that the poorest voters were too vulnerable to pressure from social superiors to be entrusted with the vote. Even Tone had

[14] The literature on the United Irishmen is now enormous. For a comprehensive though highly partisan review of the literature see Kevin Whelan's introductions to successive sections of Thomas Bartlett, David Dickson, Dáire Keogh, and Kevin Whelan (eds.), *1798: A Bicentenary Perspective* (Dublin, 2003). Marianne Elliott's pioneering *Partners in Revolution: The United Irishmen and France* (London, 1982) remains valuable for its account of the United movement itself, as well as of its French links. Nancy Curtin, *The United Irishmen: Popular Politics in Ulster and Dublin 1791–1798* (Oxford, 1994) is important for its reconsideration of the relationship between the earlier and later phases of the movement. Dickson, Keogh and Whelan (eds.), *The United Irishmen* is an important earlier collection of essays.

[15] *Proceedings of the Society of United Irishmen of Dublin* (Philadelphia, 1795), 3–4, 11.

conceded that the enfranchisement of Catholics should be accompanied by a new franchise of £10, removing 'the wretched tribe of forty shilling freeholders, whom we see driven to their octennial market by their landlords'.[16] Opponents of the secret ballot could argue, perhaps less plausibly, that a system of open voting was both a school of civic virtue and a guarantee, through peer group pressure, against electoral venality. But in both cases the suspicion remains that the real issue was a continuing distrust of the capacity of the propertyless masses to use power other than destructively. There was also, possibly, a desire to ensure that Protestant property could continue to counterbalance Catholic numbers. The reform plan eventually published was unprecedented in its radicalism. Parliaments were to be elected annually, on the basis of 300 electoral districts of equal size, by an electorate comprising all males of 21 and over. But this was in January 1794, at a time when intensifying repression was pushing the society in a more radical direction. Even at this stage, moreover, the Dublin society did not commit itself to the abolition either of the monarchy or of the House of Lords.[17]

A second set of divisions was less obvious, but only because those involved thought it better not to bring them into the open. The initial programme of the United Irishmen went no further than the realization of the long-standing patriot model of sister kingdoms. Ireland was to be governed by its own properly representative parliament, without the interference of British officials or politicians, but there was no explicit challenge to the union of crowns. Yet the militant language of the *Volunteer Journal* seven years earlier had already made clear that separatism was no longer unthinkable. Tone wrote privately in July 1791 that a separation of Ireland and Britain would in his view be 'a regeneration for this country'. Since 'that opinion is for the present too hardy', however, he had not included in the resolutions 'one word that looks like a wish for separation'.[18] How many others shared this view, but retained the same politic silence, is impossible to say. What is clear is that even in the late 1790s, when the United Irish movement had committed itself, in a transformed political climate, to separation by force of arms, attitudes to the British connection still varied widely. Thomas Addis Emmet, one of the Dublin leaders, questioned before a secret committee of the Irish House of Lords in the summer of 1798, declared that 'if Ireland were separated from England, she would be the happiest spot on the face of the globe'. William James MacNeven, another Dublin-based United man, was more equivocal. Separation from England had become their

[16] *Wolfe Tone*, ed. Bartlett, 293.
[17] The divisions concealed behind the proclamation of a union of Catholics and Protestants under the common name of Irishman were first analysed in Maureen Wall, 'The United Irish Movement', in J. L. McCracken (ed.), *Historical Studies* (London, 1965), 122–36. Though clearly written as a polemic against certain simplistic notions current at that time, the article retains its relevance, particularly in the light of recent attempts to revive elements of the same tradition of uncritical celebration.
[18] Elliott, *Wolfe Tone*, 106–7.

object 'when we were convinced that liberty was not otherwise attainable'. He still believed that there could be a shared monarch, and 'a federal connexion advantageous to both countries', so long as Ireland had a free parliament and was not obliged to share in England's wars. And even if Ireland were to become an independent republic 'and Britain ceased to be formidable to us, our interest would require an intimate connection with her'.[19]

In other respects too attitudes within the new movement to issues of national identity varied widely. Some of those involved were enthusiastic supporters of the cultural nationalism that had by this time been grafted on to the patriot political tradition. Thomas Russell, who had come to Belfast as an army officer after service in India and had been one of the founder members of the society, took Irish lessons from a local teacher, Patrick Lynch. In 1795 the two collaborated in the first and only issue of a projected magazine *Bolg an sSolair* [Bag of Goods], printed by the United Irish newspaper, the *Northern Star,* and containing reprinted poems by Charlotte Brooke alongside elementary lessons in the Irish language. However there was no clear-cut connection between such cultural enthusiasm and political leanings. Although some of those who had organized the Belfast Harp Festival became United Irishmen, others took the loyalist side in the crisis that developed later in the decade. Tone, the early separatist, derided the festival ('strum, strum and be hanged', he noted in his diary), and showed no interest in Irish language or antiquities.[20] By contrast Drennan, an early defector as the movement became more radical, was a key figure in the rise of Irish literary nationalism.

In the year or so following the Belfast meeting of October 1791 there are scattered references to United Irish societies in a handful of other centres, including Lisburn and Armagh in the north, Limerick and Clonmel in the south. But the two main societies were those of Belfast and Dublin. The Dublin society was the more conspicuous of the two, with a large and quite broadly based membership. Of more than 400 members, 130 can be identified as Protestants and 140 as Catholics. They made up a reasonable cross-section of propertied society, including in their ranks around 30 country gentlemen, 56 attorneys and barristers, and 99 merchants or manufacturers involved in the textile trades. By contrast there were only two employees, both clerks. The presence of some 50 members who can be identified as living outside the capital indicates that the society functioned to some extent as a national body.[21] In terms of organization, the Dublin society held regular meetings of the whole membership, with little

[19] *Memoire or Detailed Statement of the Origins and Progress of the Irish Union,* 31, 69, 82. This printed document has no place or date of publication. Multiple copies may be found in NAI, Rebellion Papers 620/44/1. The background to its production is the post-rebellion agreement with the United Irish 'state prisoners' described below.

[20] Diary, 13 July 1792 (*Wolfe Tone,* ed. Bartlett, 132).

[21] R. B. McDowell, 'The Personnel of the Dublin Society of United Irishmen 1791–4', *IHS* 2 (1940), 12–53.

attempt at concealment. Indeed when Neilson visited them in January 1794 to warn that an informer was reporting their activities to Dublin Castle, and to recommend that they establish a twelve-man inner committee, the Dubliners indignantly refused.

The early Belfast United Irishmen were by contrast a more closed and tightly knit group, drawn from the Presbyterian middle classes of the town, and conducting their proceedings in secret. Stray references during 1792 indicate that by the autumn of that year there were four societies active in Belfast, coordinated by a small inner committee of some kind. Their aim at this stage was primarily to work behind the scenes to promote the revival of a broad radical movement, working in particular through a reinvigorated Volunteer movement. However there are occasional hints that already in these early years some of those involved were looking beyond political agitation to the likelihood that they would eventually have to resort to armed action.[22]

The central innovation of the United Irishmen was their commitment to the complete abolition of political distinctions based on religion. Tone's celebration of the changed political climate in Belfast was apparently borne out in January 1792 when a town meeting produced a strong declaration in favour of Catholic emancipation, rejecting an attempt by Haliday and another conservative Whig, the Revd William Bruce, to specify a gradual admission to political rights. But already in July, when Volunteers from other parts of Ulster assembled in the town for another Bastille Day celebration, the outcome was more precarious. Tone and his associates managed to carry a resolution in favour of full religious equality, but only after some anxious preliminary discussions, and after they had substituted the words 'Irishmen of all religious denominations' for the term 'Catholic'. The night before, observing the Volunteer rank and file as they assembled, Tone noted with alarm that 'some of the country corps [are] no better than Peep-of-day-boys', identifying them with the Protestant secret society that had for the past few years terrorized the Catholics of south Ulster.[23]

In committing themselves, despite such opposition, to the cause of Catholic equality, the United Irishmen were responding to clear political necessity. The defeats of 1782–5 had made clear the limitations of a radicalism that confined itself to the Protestant minority. The reformers of that period, Tone noted in his *Argument*, 'built on too narrow a foundation. . . . The exclusion of the Catholics lost the question under circumstances that must have otherwise carried it against all opposition.' In arguing that a different approach was now essential, he did not wholly deny charges that Irish Catholics were ignorant and bigoted, and that

---

[22] The contrast between the Dublin and Belfast societies was first emphasized by L. M. Cullen, 'The Internal Politics of the United Irishmen', in Dickson et al. (eds.), *The United Irishmen*, 176–96. The theme is developed in detail in Curtin, *United Irishmen*. For the hints of early moves towards a military structure see ibid. 98–9. Also Nancy Curtin, 'The Transformation of the Society of United Irishmen into a Mass Based Revolutionary Organisation 1794–6', *IHS* 24 (1985), 468–76.

[23] Diary, 13 July 1792 (*Wolfe Tone*, ed. Bartlett, 133).

the pope had more power in Ireland than was desirable. All this, however, was the result of persecution.

The emancipated and liberal Irishman, like the emancipated and liberal Frenchman, may go to mass, may tell his beads, or sprinkle his mistress with holy water; but neither the one nor the other will attend to the rusty and extinguished thunderbolts of the Vatican, or the idle anathemas, which, indeed, his Holiness is nowadays too prudent and cautious to issue.[24]

As proof Tone pointed to recent events in France, where the pope was now burnt in effigy. Other radicals too looked to the spectacle of a Catholic population rising up to overthrow the epitome of absolutism as evidence of a world transformed, in which old fears could at last be abandoned. Events, however, were to show that this confident Enlightenment optimism was not the ideal basis for the real business of constructing an alliance across long-standing lines of religious division.

Expediency was not all on one side. The Catholics themselves responded to the advances of the Protestant radicals with what proved to be considerable political dexterity. When the Catholic committee, largely dormant since 1784, had reformed in 1790, a new leader had emerged. This was John Keogh, a labourer's son who had amassed a fortune through brewing, textiles, and property dealing, and had been active in the reform agitation of 1784–5. In July 1791 Keogh and others waited on the chief secretary, Robert Hobart, to announce their intention of petitioning for a further relief bill. In September they demonstrated their intention of pressing their case forcefully by employing as their secretary Richard, son of Edmund Burke, the distinguished Irish-born spokesman for the English Whig party. The appointment was a carefully calibrated gesture. Burke senior was a long-standing advocate of political reform but also, more recently, the most eloquent British opponent of the French Revolution. In December the premier Catholic peer Lord Kenmare, alarmed at what he saw as the unduly assertive tone of the committee's proceedings, seceded along with a group of conservative supporters. Kenmare's caution had the support of the Catholic bishops, including the influential John Thomas Troy, archbishop of Dublin. But majority opinion was behind Keogh and his colleagues, and the secession served only to leave them in unchallenged control.

Having failed to dissuade the Catholics from pressing their case the lord lieutenant, the earl of Westmorland, insisted to London that their demands must be refused. His language, reflecting what was now a real sense of crisis, was remarkably frank: there could be no question of granting them political power in a country 'where everyone holds his estate and political consequence by dispossession of Catholics'. The British government, however, took a different view: that something had to be done to prevent any junction between the new

[24] *Wolfe Tone*, ed. Bartlett, 285, 290.

Catholic movement and the French-inspired radicalism already making alarming progress among sections of the Protestant population. Henry Dundas, the home secretary, ordered Westmorland to secure the repeal of all remaining restrictions on Catholic education and on entry into trades and professions, as well as of their exclusion from juries and the armed forces. He was also to make clear that, even if Catholics were not to be immediately admitted to the country franchise, 'the door should not be understood to be finally closed' against it. The Irish administration reluctantly complied, although it left it to a private member, Sir Hercules Langrishe, a long-standing supporter of Catholic relief, to introduce a relief bill in January 1792. This allowed Catholics to practise law, though not to serve as judges. It also repealed restrictions on foreign education and on the number of apprentices a Catholic tradesman could take, and removed the requirement for Catholic schoolmasters to have a licence from the Church of Ireland bishop. The proposal to remove the ban on Catholics bearing arms, on the other hand, was dropped, as was the proposal to admit them to juries. Meanwhile the Catholic committee had presented a petition requesting that they should also receive a share in the franchise. A few days after passing Langrishe's bill, the Commons voted by 208 votes to 25 to reject the petition. The overall message was clear. Catholics could seek the repeal of restrictions on their civil rights. But anything implying their admission to equal citizenship remained out of the question.[25]

The response of the Catholic committee to this rebuff was to move towards precisely that juncture with Protestant radicalism that the London government had been anxious to head off. Keogh and a number of others were already members of the Dublin United Irish society. Now, in July, they replaced Richard Burke with a very different secretary—Theobald Wolfe Tone. By this time they had also adopted an ambitious plan to give their movement a broader popular base, by calling on Catholics throughout the kingdom to collect signatures for a new petition, and to organize the election of delegates to a national convention. If a Protestant political nation had proclaimed itself in the Volunteer reviews and conventions of 1779–82, a Catholic political nation was now to use the same tactics. The establishment reacted with outrage. During the summer at least twenty-three county grand juries passed resolutions reaffirming what was now being widely referred to as 'Protestant ascendancy', and the government threatened legal action against the proposed assembly. But the Catholic leaders refused to be deflected. Tone, Keogh, and another Dublin leader, the retired merchant Thomas Braughal, travelled widely in Ulster and Connacht to spur local leaders into action. The clergy, in an anticipation of Daniel O'Connell's tactics thirty years later, provided crucial support at parish level, organizing the

---

[25] The fullest account of the relief acts of 1792–3 is Thomas Bartlett, *The Fall and Rise of the Irish Nation: The Catholic Question 1690–1830* (Dublin, 1992), chs. 8, 9. For Westmorland's and Dundas's comments see pp. 131, 138.

collection of signatures and the appointment of 'electors' who would in turn choose delegates to the convention.

On 3 December the Catholic convention, comprising over 200 members representing the Dublin parishes, the counties, and the larger cities and towns, came together in Dublin. They had initially sought to follow the Volunteers in using the Rotunda, but Charlemont intervened to have their application refused. Instead the convention met at Tailors' Hall in Back Lane, the same guild assembly hall used by the city's United Irishmen. Over the next five days it agreed a petition to the king requesting admission to full political rights. This, in a deliberate snub to Dublin Castle, was not to be submitted to the lord lieutenant. Instead the convention appointed five delegates to present their appeal directly to the king. In an important gesture Archbishop Troy, along with Francis Moylan, bishop of Cork, attended the first and last days of the proceedings. Both men had supported Kenmare's secession a year earlier, but had now recognized that popular feeling was too strong to be resisted.

The United Irishmen observed these proceedings with mixed feelings. A year earlier Drennan had offered his view of Catholic tactics. 'The truth was and is, the Catholics wish to have two strings to their bow, a *part* to treat with government, a *part* to ally with us, and if one string cracks, why try the other. This is a good and *perhaps* fair archery.'[26] Subsequent events were largely to confirm this jaundiced assessment. Tone's appointment as secretary was a useful signal of Catholic impatience. But it was important not to go too far, in terms either of provoking the government or of frightening off conservatives in their own ranks. By the time of the convention Tone himself was keeping his distance from fellow United Irishmen. The northern radicals did manage one important intervention in the proceedings. The original proposal had been to make two specific requests, admission to the franchise and the right to sit on juries. However Neilson and McTier had primed Luke Teeling, a wealthy Lisburn merchant and delegate for County Antrim, to press for full legal equality, and he intervened from the floor to propose that the convention should replace these specific demands with a prayer to be admitted to 'equal enjoyment of the blessings of the constitution'. Even here, however, Keogh insisted that the assembly take time to reflect, before accepting the proposal the following day. Meanwhile a delegation of Dublin United Irishmen who had attended to present an address of solidarity found themselves excluded on a series of pretexts. A few days later the delegates travelling to London made what was possibly the significant decision to sail to Scotland from the northern port of Donaghadee, rather than from Dublin to Liverpool. Their passage through Belfast allowed the northern radicals to stage a demonstration of support. At one point a crowd unhitched the horses from the carriage carrying the Catholic delegates so that they could be drawn in triumph across the Long Bridge out of the town. But on balance it seems more likely that

[26] Drennan to Samuel McTier, 7 Dec. 1791 (*The Drennan–McTier Letters*, ed. Agnew, 376).

the ostensible reason for their choice of route—that no boat had been ready to set out on the more direct passage from Dublin to Liverpool, and that the winds were unfavourable—was in fact genuine.[27]

The Catholic delegates returned from London in January 1793 without having received any firm commitment, but with a clear impression that major concessions were about to follow. Some may for a time have believed that complete civic equality was within reach. However Hobart quickly persuaded Keogh that this was not feasible.[28] Catholics were still to be excluded from the highest offices in central and local government, from the judiciary, and from both houses of parliament. However they were to be admitted to a wide range of offices, including municipal corporations, they would be permitted to bear arms, and they were to be allowed to vote. Even these concessions had to be got through a parliament that only a year before had voted overwhelmingly to reject the Catholic petition. This time, however, the administration permitted no ambiguity. The relief bill was introduced by Hobart and it was made plain that office holders were required to support it. Once it was clear that the government was determined to push through the enfranchisement of Catholics, members were in any case less ready to court unpopularity with what was about to be a new electorate. Indeed George Knox, acting on behalf of the earl of Abercorn, initiated what the undersecretary at Dublin Castle referred to as 'a race between Lord Abercorn and Lord Westmorland' by bringing forward an alternative proposal that Catholics should be admitted to full political rights.[29] The administration also helped to make the relief bill more palatable by coupling it with a series of concessions to opposition demands, including an act to exclude pensioners and holders of certain offices from the Commons, and to limit the overall cost of the pension list. Hobart's relief bill became law on 9 April. Soon after the Catholic committee wound up its operations, leaving only a small body to deal with educational matters. The Catholics did not abandon their Protestant radical allies too brutally; to the irritation of the Castle, they issued a final declaration in support of parliamentary reform. But it was clear that the alliance had served its purpose.

At the same time that the Catholic campaign was proceeding to a successful conclusion, the Belfast United Irishmen continued their strategy of seeking to promote a broader radical revival. In January 1792 they launched a newspaper, the *Northern Star*, edited by Neilson. Prominent reformers among the gentry

---

[27] See in particular the comments of Charlemont's correspondent Haliday on the good sense of the Catholic delegates in dissociating themselves from the violent tone of reporting in the United Irish newspaper the *Northern Star*: R. B. McDowell, *Ireland in the Age of Imperialism and Revolution 1760–1801* (Oxford, 1979), 412.

[28] The precise sequence of events at this point remains unclear, because of subsequent charges from rivals, hotly disputed by others, that Keogh had sold his coreligionists short. The most detailed account (Bartlett, *Fall and Rise of the Irish Nation*, 168–9) rejects suggestions that more could have been achieved in 1793.

[29] Quoted in Bartlett, *Fall and Rise of the Irish Nation*, 163.

and middle classes were initially sceptical or hostile, responding to Neilson's efforts to canvass support by questioning both the necessity and wisdom of promoting a radical alternative to the existing liberal paper, the *Belfast News Letter*. In fact the *Northern Star*, published at the low price of two pence and benefiting from the high levels of literacy among the Presbyterian population of the north-east, proved to be a massive popular success. Circulation quickly rose to over 4,000, equal to that of the most successful national papers in either Britain or Ireland. The society's effort to use the Volunteer movement as the vanguard of a new radical agitation was by contrast less successful. In February 1793 delegates from five Ulster counties met in convention at Dungannon, assembling at what Neilson described as the *mons sacer*, the Presbyterian church where a Volunteer convention eleven years earlier had opened the way to the triumph of 1782.[30] However the outcome was, from the point of view of advanced radicals, disappointing. The meeting passed resolutions in favour of Catholic emancipation and parliamentary reform. But it also declared its attachment to the existing constitution, repudiated any attempt to apply republican principles to Ireland, and rejected calls to condemn the war against revolutionary France that had commenced two weeks earlier, following the execution of Louis XVI.

At the same time that they discovered the lack of popular backing for their radical programme, the United Irishmen came under attack from the government. In autumn 1792 Tandy and other Dublin radicals had launched a new Volunteer corps, the first National battalion. The government's initial response was cautious. A proclamation on 8 December declared the new corps illegal, but carefully distinguished between it and the existing Volunteer movement. Over the next few weeks, however, civic authorities in Dublin used threats of arrest to disperse members of older Volunteer companies who attempted to parade. In Belfast there was a brief confrontation in early March, when troops angered by the playing of a French tune went on the rampage, smashing windows and shop signs. Several hundred Volunteers assembled in arms, but then obeyed an order to disperse. A proclamation two days later effectively banned Volunteer parades in Ulster. The previous month the Irish parliament had passed an act imposing restrictions on the importation and movement of gunpowder and firearms. In August it passed the convention act, making it illegal for any body claiming a representative character to meet for the purpose of seeking change in church or state; there were to be no more attempts to overawe or bypass parliament on the basis of a claim to superior legitimacy such as those made a decade before at the Rotunda, or more recently at Tailors' Hall. Side by side with this tightening of the legal noose, a series of prosecutions demonstrated the government's determination to silence radical critics. The proprietors of the *Northern Star* survived two indictments, in May and November 1792. But on 1 March Simon Butler and Oliver Bond, president and secretary of the Dublin society of United Irishmen, were fined

---

[30] Neilson to Drennan, 17 Dec. 1793 (*Drennan–McTier Letters*, ed. Agnew, 491).

and sentenced to six months imprisonment by the House of Lords for having questioned its authority. Shortly afterwards Tandy, threatened with a potentially capital charge of having conspired with the Defender secret society, fled the country, eventually going to America. At the beginning of 1794 Drennan and another prominent United Irishman, Archibald Hamilton Rowan, were tried for seditious libel on the basis of an address in support of the Volunteers following the proclamation of December 1792. Drennan was acquitted, but thereafter largely withdrew from political agitation. Rowan was sentenced to two years in prison.

The United Irishmen had originally sought to make use of the same tactics that had brought partial victory during 1778–82: widespread popular mobilization, including a revival of armed associations, on a scale that would make it impossible for either the Irish parliament or the British government to ignore their demands. The prosecutions of 1793, along with the suppression of Volunteering, made clear that no such campaign would be tolerated. The United Irish leaders themselves, after the debacle of 1798, were to emphasize the role of this repression in forcing them to turn from open if radical agitation to revolutionary conspiracy. In fact there are clear indications that some, particularly in Ulster, had already been willing to contemplate the eventual use of armed force. The government's crackdown, bringing a brutal end to what had seemed like a triumphant new beginning, may well have converted others from constitutional to revolutionary methods. But overall the events of 1793–4 are best seen, not as transforming the character of the United Irishmen, but as shifting their centre of gravity, as more timid or conservative individuals like Drennan dropped out of the movement, and the bolder and more militant came to the fore.[31]

That the willingness of some among the early United Irishmen to contemplate moving beyond radical street politics to revolutionary conspiracy was not solely the invention of a repressive government was evident in the circumstances that led to the suppression of the Dublin society. The first contact with France had in fact taken place as early as November 1792, involving Henry Sheares, already recognized as one of the most radical members of the Dublin society, and Lord Edward Fitzgerald, younger brother of the duke of Leinster, not yet a member for family reasons but nevertheless a close associate. In May 1793 a French agent held talks with, among others, Butler, Bond, and Rowan. In April 1794 a second agent, William Jackson, arrived in Dublin. Irish born, Jackson had been ordained in the Church of England but had never held a benefice, instead living as a journalist, initially conservative, then pro-American, and more recently a propagandist for Pitt. He may indeed have gone to France initially as a British agent. Most of the Dublin United Irishmen treated him with understandable wariness. However Rowan, whom he visited in prison, spoke freely of the

---

[31] The image of a clear transition from constitutional to revolutionary methods in response to government repression receives its clearest modern statement in Elliott, *Partners in Revolution*. It is most explicitly challenged in the work of Cullen and Curtin (n. 23 above).

prospects of a republican rising, and had Tone draw up a paper on the subject for transmission to France. What neither man knew was that Jackson, though himself apparently a genuine convert to the revolutionary cause, had come to Ireland accompanied by a friend who was in fact a government spy.

The consequences for individuals were not as drastic as they might have been. The main victim was Jackson, who was tried for high treason in April 1795, and committed suicide in the dock, by poison, before sentence could be passed. Rowan, the government's main target among the United Irishmen, was allowed a conjugal visit to his home on his wedding anniversary and seized the opportunity to flee to France. Tone was by comparison small fry, and the case against him was weak; moreover his family had influential friends, including the attorney general, Arthur Wolfe. He was allowed to sail for America, having first submitted a confession sufficient to hang him should he return without permission. The real importance of the affair was that it legitimized another, decisive strike against the United Irishmen. On 23 May, the high sheriffs raided a meeting of the Dublin society and seized its papers. The leaders debated whether to revive the society along clandestine lines, as suggested by Henry Sheares, or to challenge the action of the sheriffs in the courts. In the event they did neither, and the society of United Irishmen disappeared, for the moment, from public view.

PROTESTANT ASCENDANCY

The long shadows cast by the conflicts of an earlier era were evident in the political and religious literature of Hanoverian Ireland. Every 23 October, as directed by government, clergymen of the Church of Ireland delivered sermons commemorating the massacre of Protestant settlers that had taken place in the autumn of 1641. The more important performances, normally those delivered before members of the two houses of parliament, were frequently published, to become a permanent part of the corpus of religious polemic. Sir John Temple's inflammatory history of the same events, first published in 1646, was reprinted at least ten times between then and 1812. The timing of new editions confirmed the book's relevance, in the eyes of readers, to contemporary affairs: 1713, 1714, 1724, and 1746 were years when events gave fear of Jacobitism an additional edge, while a Cork edition in 1766 reflected the tensions arising from the first great Whiteboy agitation. In 1747 John Curry, a Catholic soon to be active in the Catholic committee, published the first of a series of works challenging the black legend of 1641. But his arguments provoked a scathing response, under the title *Fiction Unmasked*, from the Protestant antiquarian Walter Harris. In 1773 Thomas Leland, a Church of Ireland clergyman and former fellow of Trinity College, published what he hoped would be accepted as a 'philosophical' history of Ireland, offering a generally accepted resolution of old conflicts such as had recently been achieved for Scotland and England by David Hume. In the event he pleased no one. Protestants resented his concession that Catholics in the reign of Charles I had genuine grievances, and that some of their leaders had behaved honourably and with restraint; Catholics were appalled at his insistence that atrocities against Protestants had nevertheless taken place in 1641 and after.[32]

What relationship did these literary or historical controversies have to the day-to-day interaction of Catholic and Protestant? Antagonisms did not necessarily receive explicit expression. The state of the law made direct demonstrations of hostility by Catholics a dangerous undertaking, while providing possible Protestant aggression with a mask of legality. But a range of instances provide glimpses of the potential for conflict. In Dublin, for example, it was reported in 1731 that Trinity College students going in procession to church had taken to carrying weapons, following attacks by what they claimed was a hostile Catholic crowd. At Timahoe, County Kildare, in 1740 local people burnt down the Quaker meeting house, following reports that its users had burnt an effigy of the Virgin Mary, as well as of the Pretender, at a celebration of 4 November, the birthday of William III. Three years later arsonists destroyed a newly erected meeting house near Crossmaglen in south County Armagh, apparently in protest at Presbyterian migration into what had previously been an exclusively Catholic district. Earlier, in 1723, an itinerant preacher, William Smith, attracted large crowds in County Londonderry and elsewhere with his inflammatory preaching, allegedly telling hearers that if they rose up to 'crush the heretics . . . the papists would flourish and be restored to all their former dignities, abbeys, temples, and monasteries'. Another part of his tirade testified to the longevity of popular historical memory, reminding his hearers of the death of the martyred archbishop Oliver Plunkett, and assuring them that if they died fighting for their church their souls would immediately ascend to heaven. Smith was an oddity, a Catholic layman who claimed to have spoken to the Virgin Mary in a trance. But the authorities took him seriously enough: convicted of blasphemy, he was whipped, pilloried, and branded on the face before being transported to America.[33]

Against such indications of the potential for sectarian hostility must be set examples of distinctly more relaxed attitudes between acquaintances or neighbours. A bundle of affidavits collected in 1745 to clear a County Clare priest

---

[32] T. C. Barnard, 'The Uses of 23 October 1641 and Irish Protestant Celebrations', *English Historical Review*, 106 (1991), 889–920; idem, '1641: A Bibliographical Essay', in Brian MacCuarta (ed.), *Ulster 1641: Aspects of the Rising* (Belfast, 1993), 173–86; Joseph Liechty, 'Testing the Depth of Catholic/Protestant Conflict: The Case of Thomas Leland's "History of Ireland" 1773', *Archivium Hibernicum*, 42 (1987), 13–28.

[33] P. J. Larkin, ' "Popish Riot" in South Co. Derry, 1725', *Seanchas Árdmhacha*, 8 (1975–6), 97–110. For Trinity College, *Dublin Intelligence*, 16 Mar. 1731. For the other incidents see Connolly, *Religion, Law and Power*, 125–6. There are also suggestions that the long-standing feud between the predominantly Protestant weavers of the Liberties area of Dublin and the predominantly Catholic butchers of the Ormond market, on the south bank of the river, had a partly sectarian basis. However James Kelly, *The Liberty and Ormond Boys* (Dublin, 2005), 33–4, points to the lack of evidence to support this hypothesis.

charged with having been involved in recruiting for the Spanish army reveal a network of contacts. A Protestant innkeeper had seen him at his sister's funeral and helped him to refreshments; a turnpike keeper deposed that he and the priest 'very often ate and drank together'; on one occasion, when a Church of Ireland clergyman was not available, a Protestant family had even called him to baptize a dangerously ill child.[34] Intermarriage, though not common, was also possibly more frequent than has been recognized. A visitation of the parish of Navan in County Meath around 1733 found thirty-six Protestant families, and no less than twelve Protestant women married to Catholics. The census carried out by Church of Ireland clergy in the western diocese of Elphin in 1749 did not systematically record interchurch marriage. But where individual incumbents did note their presence, they seem to have accounted for around 3 per cent of all unions.[35]

By the second half of the eighteenth century there were clear signs that day-to-day relations between Catholics and Protestants were becoming more relaxed. Enlightenment ideas of religious toleration may have played a part, although it is important to remember that the culture of the Enlightenment was itself unashamedly hostile towards Catholicism as the enemy both of political liberty and of freedom of thought and speech. A stronger and more direct influence was almost certainly the growing sense, encouraged by accumulating decades of internal peace, that Catholics presented no direct threat. Their subordination to a foreign power, the papacy, meant that they still could not be trusted with political rights. But they themselves were no longer assumed to be malevolently bent on the overthrow of the constitution. Eaton Stannard, recorder of Dublin, caught the new attitude precisely in a pamphlet of 1749. The Catholics, from 'a grateful and proper sense of the mildness and moderation of our government', had behaved well during the recent Jacobite revolt: 'not a man of them moved tongue, pen or sword.' And so long as they continued to behave with due allegiance 'I shall hold them, as men, in equal esteem with others in every point—but one'.[36] The resistance offered, in the 1760s, to the first attempts to relax the restrictions on Catholic landed property made clear that there were still strict limits to what such tolerant sentiments might mean in practice. On the other hand the passage of the relief acts of 1778 and 1782, even allowing for the influence in both cases of the British government, seemed to provide clear evidence of changing public attitudes.

[34] PRO, SP63/407/52–71, 109–32.
[35] Visitation of the diocese of Meath, *c.*1733 (Representative Church Body Library, Dublin, GS 2/7/3/10, 48); *The Census of Elphin 1749*, ed. Marie-Louise Legg (Dublin, 2004). The statistical analysis offered in this printed edition, by Brian Gurrin, comes up with a very low total of 144 interchurch marriages or 0.9 per cent of a total of 16,841 households. However his count is incomplete, and his assumption that all such marriages were recorded is almost certainly wrong. See my review in *IHS* 35 (2006).
[36] Eaton Stannard, *The Honest Man's Speech* (2nd edn. Dublin, 1749), 14–15.

By this time, moreover, some vocal sections of Protestant opinion were willing, not just to disavow any hostility towards their Catholic countrymen, but to offer public demonstrations of good will. In June 1784 the Belfast Volunteers paraded in full uniform at the mass held in the first Catholic place of worship to be erected in the town, and subscribed generously to a collection towards the cost of the building work. Such gestures were in keeping with what was by this time the radical phase of the Volunteer movement. But the previous year a more broadly based body, the corporation of Derry, had contributed £50 towards the building of the first Catholic church in that former bastion of Protestant exclusiveness. Five years later the Catholic bishop reciprocated by appearing, with his clergy, to take part in the celebration of the centenary of the closing of the gates of the town against the earl of Antrim's Jacobite army. In 1791 the bishop of Killaloe reported to his Roman agent that the grand jury of County Clare had made a generous subscription to a school he had set up in Ennis, an example of 'what liberal sentiments at present subsist betwixt Roman Catholics and Protestants'.[37]

Such public demonstrations of tolerance, and even good will, explain why Tone and others concluded that the time had come for Ireland to abandon long-standing divisions. Other Protestants, however, viewed the weakening of religious distinctions with alarm. The execution of Nicholas Sheehy and others in Tipperary during the first Whiteboy outbreak had demonstrated how easily traditional fears could be reawakened. The Rightboy movement of 1785–8 gave rise to no similar judicial outrages. But the launching of a direct attack on the tithes payable to the established church, coming as it did so soon after the relief acts of 1778 and 1782, produced a strong polemical reaction. Patrick Duigenan, a professor at Trinity College, Dublin, and MP for County Armagh, writing under the pen name Theophilus, claimed that the tithe issue was exploited by 'agitating friars and Romanish missionaries, sent here for the purpose of sowing sedition'. By contrast *The Present State of the Church of Ireland*, published in 1786 by Richard Woodward, bishop of Cloyne, avoided crude polemic. It began, in fact, with the author's apology to 'the two respectable bodies of his fellow citizens', Catholics and Presbyterians, for the 'unreserved manner' of his comments. But the argument was nevertheless uncompromising. 'Truths, which in happier seasons should rest in oblivion for the preservation of general harmony, must now be brought forward to public notice.' In almost every European country the ecclesiastical and civil constitutions were inextricably linked. Arbitrary monarchies retained popery, while republics favoured 'the levelling principle of the Presbyterian church'. Only Protestant episcopacy, of the kind established in both Ireland and Great Britain, could give wholehearted

---

[37] Michael Peter MacMahon to Thomas Bray, 15 Nov. 1792 (Cashel Diocesan Archives, Thurles, Bray Papers, 1792/22, consulted on microfilm in NLI).

support to the principles of order and freedom that characterized the constitution of the two kingdoms.[38]

Woodward's pamphlet was a huge success, passing through six editions in a fortnight, and nine in all during 1786–7. One reason for its success was the way in which it skilfully recast traditional arguments in an acceptable contemporary form. The problem with Catholics was no longer their idolatrous religious doctrines, or their potential as the fifth column of what was by now an unlikely pan-Catholic crusade, but rather the incompatibility of their principles with those of Britain's cherished mixed monarchy. Yet in elaborating the reasons why no assurances that they offered to prove the contrary could be trusted, Woodward was able to rehearse some comfortably familiar themes: the oath taken by bishops binding them to persecute heretics, and the teaching that faith need not be kept with non-Catholics. The bishop also helped to popularize a potent new entry into the lexicon of Irish politics. Upholders of the established order had for some time talked of 'the Protestant interest'. In 1782, however, Sir Boyle Roche, while supporting the Catholic relief act, had emphasized the need to uphold 'the Protestant's ascendancy'. Four years later, in February 1786, the strongly anti-Catholic George Ogle told fellow MPs that 'the landed property of the kingdom [and] . . . the Protestant ascendancy' were under threat from the Whiteboys. Woodward, writing later that year, made use of the same term, reminding the landowner 'that the security of his title depends very much (if not entirely) on the Protestant ascendancy'. He also anticipated what was to be one of the great debates of the decade that followed, warning dissenters that any gains they could expect from joining in the attack on the establishment would be strictly temporary: 'They can have nothing then before them, but an option of the ascendancy of either the church of Ireland, or the church of Rome.'[39]

At the same time that Woodward was reformulating the case for what he called Protestant ascendancy, humbler men were beginning to offer their own, more direct response to the dismantling of traditional structures of inequality. From 1784 reports began to circulate of a series of clashes between Protestants and Catholics in County Armagh. Commencing in Markethill, in the centre of the county, the violence spread, particularly into the south of Armagh, from where it extended into parts of the neighbouring counties of Down and Louth. Although precise details are sparse, the reaction of the authorities in the first years of the violence indicates that they saw the Protestants as the aggressors and the Catholics primarily as victims. Peep-of-Day boys, noted by Arthur Young

---

[38] Richard Woodward, *The Present State of the Church of Ireland* (4th edn., Dublin, 1787), 3, 10, 14, 18. For the wider background, including Duigenan's contribution and the origin of the phrase 'Protestant ascendancy', see James Kelly, 'The Genesis of "Protestant Ascendancy": The Rightboy Disturbances of the 1780s and their Impact upon Protestant Opinion', in Gerard O'Brien (ed.), *Parliament, Politics and People: Essays in Eighteenth-Century Irish History* (Dublin, 1989), 93–127.

[39] Woodward, *Present State of the Church of Ireland*, 17, 78.

in 1780 as an agrarian society similar to the Oakboys or Hearts of Steel, now became the name of a Protestant society engaged in attacks on Catholic homes. Before long, however, the Catholics of the county had formed their own society, the Defenders, and had begun to retaliate in kind. In one particularly savage incident, in January 1791, Catholics in Forkhill, in the south of the county, attacked the house containing Alexander Barkley, a Protestant schoolmaster, his wife, and her 14-year-old brother. They cut out the tongues of all three, sliced off the calf from one of the boy's legs, and hacked off some of the fingers of both Barkley and his wife, who later died of her injuries. A Catholic pamphleteer claimed soon after that Barkley had been attacked because his brother-in-law had given evidence leading to the hanging of one Defender and the transportation of another, and was also alleged to have vandalized the vestments and chalice belonging to a local priest.[40]

Discussion of the origins of the Armagh troubles is unavoidably speculative.[41] A localized vendetta, confined to the lower orders, attracted little initial attention. By the time its wider significance was recognized, most observers had a partisan position to uphold. Armagh's religious geography clearly played some part in its emergence as the birthplace of a new type of sectarian warfare. The county was roughly evenly divided between Catholic and Protestant, with three broad zones of settlement. The richest, to the north, was predominantly occupied by members of the Church of Ireland. Presbyterians, unusually for Ulster, were a less prosperous group, located on poorer lands in a central zone, creating the dangerous combination of a population less amenable than Anglicans to

---

[40] *An Impartial Account of the Late Disturbances in the County of Armagh* (Dublin, 1792), printed in David Miller (ed.), *Peep O'Day Boys and Defenders: Selected Documents on the County Armagh Disturbances 1784–96* (Belfast, 1990), 102–5. The author of this contemporary account uses the name J. Byrne, and was initially identified as the John Byrne who sat on the Catholic committee as a representative for Armagh in 1790 (ibid. 4–6). However later evidence suggests that he may have been James Quigley, a Catholic priest executed for treason in 1798 and believed to have been an important link between the United Irish and Defender movements. See D. W. Miller, 'Politicisation in Revolutionary Ireland: The Case of the Armagh Troubles', *IESH* 23 (1996), 3–4.

[41] Writing on the origins of the sectarian conflict in south Ulster has gone through several phases. The first academic study, Hereward Senior's *Orangeism in Ireland and Britain 1795–1836* (London, 1966), relied on what was soon to become the outdated assumption of a land system characterized by constant conflict, although Senior also noted plebeian Protestant resentment of the relaxation of legal restrictions on Catholics, and the role of the Volunteers in giving a new relevance to the issue of the right to bear arms. Subsequent studies sought alternative explanations rooted in a more accurate depiction of the local economy. Peter Gibbon, *The Origins of Ulster Unionism: The Formation of Popular Protestant Politics and Ideology in Nineteenth-Century Ireland* (Manchester, 1975) emphasized developments within linen manufacturing, though in a rather schematic and thinly documented study. D. W. Miller ('The Armagh Troubles 1784–95', in Samuel Clark and James S. Donnelly (eds.), *Irish Peasants: Violence and Political Unrest 1780–1794* (Madison, 1983), 155–91) emphasized the weakening of familial control, and the symbolic importance of the right to bear arms, outlined below. More recently Cullen and others have argued that sectarian conflict should be seen instead as a by-product of high politics, and as largely promoted from above. These arguments rest on what is now known to be a seriously misleading image of the early Orange Order: see n. 79 below. In any case, they relate to developments in the mid-1790s, leaving it unclear how the initial surge of sectarian feuding a decade earlier is to be explained.

landlord control, resentful of their inferior status within the Protestant polity, and with strong anti-Catholic religious traditions not mellowed as elsewhere by economic prosperity. The south of the county, where the conflict became most vicious, had been one of Ireland's last lawless regions, overwhelmingly Catholic and Irish speaking, a base for tory activity well into the eighteenth century. In the middle decades of the century landlords anxious to bring the region under control, and boost their rent rolls, had pursued a policy of active colonization, by importing Protestant tenants from other parts. The burning of the Presbyterian meeting house at Crossmaglen in 1743 is one indication of the extent to which such policies may have kept alive, to a degree not general elsewhere after the seventeenth century, some of the tensions of a frontier society.[42]

Armagh was also, by this time, the centre of Ulster's linen industry. Sectarian tension may in part have reflected the entry of growing numbers of Catholics into spinning and weaving. At a time when the earnings of existing weavers were being pushed down by competition from the mechanized cotton industry, the arrival of new recruits was inevitably resented. Moreover cash earnings from linen allowed Catholics to compete more vigorously with Protestants as potential tenants of the smallholdings with which weavers liked to supplement their earnings. Both grievances help to explain why attacks by the Peep-of-Day Boys seem frequently to have involved economic sabotage, by raiding the houses of Catholic weavers to cut the elaborate web of threads that had to be assembled before a loom could be put into operation. Another possibility is that independent earnings from weaving liberated young men from the control of both family and landlord, thus making it possible for what began as essentially factional brawling to escalate out of control. To this can be added the impact on relationships at local level of the Volunteer movement. The willingness of some corps to support Catholic claims was deeply alarming to those who wished to uphold traditional boundaries. More immediately the admission in some places of Catholics to the ranks of the self-proclaimed citizen soldiers ignored the long-standing prohibition, still theoretically in force, on their bearing arms. The raids on Catholic houses to seize firearms that were a frequent feature of Peep-of-Day activities can thus be seen, not just as a pragmatic tactic to disarm an enemy, but as the aggressive defence by plebeian Protestants of an increasingly precarious token of their supremacy over a despised underclass.

Against this contradictory background, in which assertions of a new spirit of tolerance existed side by side with a revival of both elite and plebeian anti-Catholicism, a reformed Catholic committee, during 1791–3, launched its bold campaign for a new relief bill. The nationwide agitation to secure signatures to a Catholic petition, and the return of delegates to what was denounced as the

---

[42] L. M. Cullen, *The Emergence of Modern Ireland 1600–1900* (London, 1981), 206–8. For the religious demography of the county see D. W. Miller, 'The Origins of the Orange Order in County Armagh', in A. J. Hughes and William Nolan (eds.), *Armagh: History and Society* (Dublin, 2001), 583–5.

popish parliament at Tailors' Hall in December 1792, provoked an outraged response. One consequence was the consolidation in public parlance of the phrase Woodward had picked up six years earlier. In September 1792 the corporation of Dublin issued a public letter to the Protestants of Ireland denouncing the Catholic agitation and offering a comprehensive definition:

And that no doubt may remain of what we understand by the words Protestant ascendancy, we have further resolved, that we consider the Protestant ascendancy to consist in—a Protestant king of Ireland—a Protestant parliament—a Protestant hierarchy—Protestant electors and government—the benches of justice—the army and the revenue—through all their branches and details Protestant.

Several months earlier Edmund Burke, in a private communication clearly intended for publication, had commented sarcastically on the currency of what he presented as a new coinage, 'lately struck in the mint of the Castle of Dublin; thence it was conveyed to the Tolsel or city hall, where, having passed the touch of the corporation, so respectably stamped and vouched, it soon became current in parliament'.[43]

At the same time that the rhetoric of Protestant conservatism was taking shape, resentment at the new assertiveness of the Catholics was also beginning to assume a more sinister form. In October 1793 authorities in County Meath arrested John Fay, a Catholic mill owner who had acted as local secretary to the Catholic committee. The charge was complicity in the recent murder of a Protestant gentleman who had been active against the Defenders. In January three Catholic merchants from Drogheda were likewise charged with instigating Defender attacks in County Louth. Both prosecutions seem to have been at least in part the work of John Foster, MP for County Louth and speaker of the House of Commons. As foreman of the Louth grand jury Foster had earlier sponsored a strong anti-Catholic resolution, denounced by Edmund Burke as 'Mr Foster's declaration of war'. He had also, despite his position as an office holder, been the leading parliamentary opponent of the 1793 relief bill. Both Fay and the Drogheda merchants were acquitted. But the laying of capital charges against Catholics, reminiscent of the fate of Sheehy and others in Tipperary, was eloquent testimony to the ruthlessness of an elite on the defensive, and confirmed Foster's reputation as the chief spokesman of Protestant reaction.[44]

[43] Quoted in W. J. McCormack, 'Eighteenth-Century Ascendancy: Yeats and the Historians', *ECI* 4 (1989), 174–5. McCormack first identified 'Protestant ascendancy' as a new term of the late eighteenth century in *Ascendancy and Tradition: Anglo-Irish Literary History from 1789 to 1939* (Oxford, 1985), 61–89, tracing it to 1792. He has been reluctant to accept that Kelly and others have since uncovered a longer history, reaching back at least to the early 1780s. The rather sterile debate that has resulted can be followed in successive issues of *ECI*.

[44] For Foster's opposition to the relief act see A. P. W. Malcomson, *John Foster: The Politics of the Anglo-Irish Ascendancy* (Oxford, 1978), 66–7. For his role in the 1794 prosecutions James Smyth, *The Men of No Property: Irish Radicals and Popular Politics in the Late Eighteenth Century* (Basingstoke, 1992), 106–7.

The violence of the Protestant response to the Catholic challenge must be understood, not just in terms of developments within Ireland, but also in the context of the changing stance of the British government. In forcing through the relief act of 1793, contrary to the advice of its own lord lieutenant and against the wishes of the local elite, ministers made a clear choice of priorities. The urgent necessity, at the start of a new war with France, of preventing any junction between Irish Catholics and Protestant radicals, and the possibility of drawing more freely on the huge potential reserve of military manpower within Catholic Ireland, took precedence over the desire of the Protestant establishment to preserve its local supremacy. Dundas's summary of the position to Westmorland, at the beginning of 1793, was brutally frank:

If it is a mere question of whether one description of Irishmen or another are to enjoy a monopoly of pre-eminence, I am afraid that is not a question which [the British government] would feel either their passions or their interests so materially concerned in as to justify any application of the reserves of Great Britain in the decision of it.[45]

Irish Protestants were thus not only confronted with a Catholic agitation of unprecedented boldness. It was also clear that, in this crisis, they could count on no support beyond their own efforts.

The bitterness surrounding the passage of the 1793 relief act was evident, not just in political rhetoric, but in the changed tone of relations between classes. In the same month that the act became law another measure received the royal assent. This was the militia act, creating a local defence force under central government control to replace the suppressed Volunteers. Its introduction provoked widespread riots during the spring and summer of 1793. Protest arose mainly from the detail of the scheme, in particular from the provision that a quota of men was to be raised by ballot from each district. When, after a few weeks, the ballot was dropped, and when better provision was subsequently made for the families of those enlisted, protest died away and the government in fact encountered no difficulty in filling up the ranks of the new force with voluntary recruits. But the disturbances, while they lasted, were marked by a new bitterness. The death toll, it now seems, may not have been as high as was once claimed, and the violence that did occur was in part a continuation of a wave of protest, associated in particular with the Defender movement, that was already under way before balloting for the militia began. At the same time there were indications that plebeian Catholics saw the imposition of compulsory service in the militia as the Protestant elite's revenge for the recent relief act—or perhaps as the price of that concession, agreed behind their backs by their own upper-class leaders. The elite, for its part, alarmed by further evidence of Catholic insubordination,

---

[45] Quoted in Thomas Bartlett, 'The Origins and Progress of the Catholic Question in Ireland', in T. P. Power and Kevin Whelan (eds.), *Endurance and Emergence: Catholics in Ireland in the Eighteenth Century* (Dublin, 1990), 15.

and bitter at its betrayal by London, showed a new willingness to resort to force in the face of protest, calling out soldiers to fire on unruly crowds. Even the lower figure of 100 deaths now offered (as compared to a previous estimate of 230) stands in sharp contrast to a total of perhaps 50 killed as a result of agrarian protest in the whole of the preceding three decades.[46]

The suppression of Volunteering, providing the background to the militia act, also had direct implications for plebeian Protestant politics. One of the ways in which, during the late 1780s, landlords had sought to contain the rising sectarian violence spreading across south Ulster had been by organizing their Protestant tenants into revived Volunteer corps. By doing so they provided a legitimate form of self-defence while at the same time imposing some discipline on their activities. This revival of Volunteering as a domesticated form of Protestant paramilitarism helps to explain Tone's reference in July 1792 to 'Peep-of-day-boys'.[47] The suppression of Volunteering in the early months of 1793, however, closed off this outlet. As Defender attacks continued Protestants in south Ulster began to find themselves in danger of losing an increasingly brutal sectarian war. Their response was to seek alternative ways of combining to defend themselves. In 1793 James Wilson, a farmer from the Dyan in County Tyrone, had organized a group called the Orange Boys, and there are scattered references to similar groups elsewhere.

The turning point in this plebeian Protestant mobilization came in County Armagh in the autumn of 1795. In the early 1790s, as Defenderism spread into adjoining Ulster counties and south into parts of Leinster, Armagh itself had been relatively quiet, partly, it seems, as a result of the hanging of at least seven troublemakers, from both sides of the conflict, during 1790–1. In the spring and summer of 1795, however, violence once again flared. On 12 June Protestants assembled for a dance at Dan Winter's inn at the Diamond, a crossroads near Loughgall, exchanged shots with Catholics gathered for a wake on a nearby hill. The encounter seems to have been ritualized, with both sides keeping their distance. In September, however, Peep-of-Day Boys and Defenders gathered near the same location for a more serious confrontation, with both sides drawing reinforcements from a wide surrounding area. The Defenders were encamped on a fortified hill top, but the Protestants, still equipped with the arms of former Volunteer corps, won an easy victory. An eyewitness, William Blacker, son of a local gentleman and at that time a student at Trinity College, put the number

---

[46] The significance of the militia riots was first emphasized in Thomas Bartlett, 'An End to Moral Economy: The Irish Militia Disturbances of 1793', in C. H. E. Philpin (ed.), *Nationalism and Popular Protest in Ireland* (Cambridge, 1987), 191–218. A more recent study emphasizes the close geographical correlation between the riots and Defenderism, suggests a lower overall death toll, and also suggests that the abandonment of the ballot was due more to the inefficiency of the system than to the protests described by Bartlett: I. F. Nelson, ' "The First Chapter of 1798"? Restoring a Military Perspective to the Irish Militia Riots of 1793', *IHS* 33 (2003), 369–86.

[47] Above, n. 23.

of Defenders killed at around 30. The victory was the signal for what seems to have been a concerted attempt to clear the northern half of the county of Catholics by a wave of night-time attacks. The 'wrecking' continued over the winter, spreading into adjacent counties. Hundreds of families fled their homes. One north Connacht landlord estimated in November 1796 that as many as 4,000 refugees had arrived in the region from Ulster.

Meanwhile those directly involved in the skirmish had followed up their victory by laying the foundations for a new organization. Meeting immediately afterwards at a second inn near Loughgall, this time belonging to James Sloan, they agreed to create a body to be known as the Orange Society. One later historian of the movement, R. H. Wallace, claimed that the new society consciously modelled itself on Wilson's earlier Orange Boys. As an acknowledgement of its primacy he cited the allocation to the Dyan of the very first warrant authorizing the raising of a local lodge, conferring what was to become the prized title of Loyal Orange Lodge No. 1. By contrast R. M. Sibbett, in the first full official history, insisted that the Orange Boys in fact continued as a separate movement after September 1795. The contrast between these accounts, both written a century after the event, is easily explained. Wallace sought to incorporate the first bearers of the Protestant standard into a single tradition; Sibbett was more concerned to distance the emerging Orange Society from the explosion of sectarian aggression that immediately followed its creation. Where the matter of warrants is concerned, Blacker's contemporary account indicates that the first ten or a dozen warrants were in fact allocated by lot. Other evidence, notably the high fee of £1 2s. 6d. charged for warrants, suggests that the Orange Society was intended to be a new beginning. In place of both the Peep-of-Day Boys and the Orange Boys there was to be a respectable and disciplined society that would secure for the Protestant side in the continuing sectarian war the patronage of the gentry and the civil authorities. On the other hand it is hard to believe that some Peep-of-Day Boys did not find their way into the new movement, or that individual members of the new society did not play a part in the anti-Catholic violence of the months that followed.[48]

DELIRIUM OF THE BRAVE

By the end of 1794 the Irish government had at first sight successfully negotiated a potentially dangerous crisis. Faced with the threat of a Catholic radical alliance,

---

[48] For Wallace's account see *The Formation of the Orange Order 1795–1798* (Belfast, 1994), 25–9, and for Blacker, ibid. 16. For the contrary view, R. M. Sibbett, *Orangeism in Ireland and Throughout the Empire* (Belfast, 1914–15), i. 216–19. The suggestion that the new society was a conscious attempt to create a more respectable body that would attract elite patronage is a central theme of Senior, *Orangeism*.

it had responded with what proved to be a successful, if partly fortuitous, blend of conciliation and repression. Some Catholics may have been disappointed to be denied the full political rights that had seemed briefly within reach. Most, however, saw the relief act of 1793 as a satisfactory instalment. The most effective way of securing what had been withheld, as Keogh told one of his critics, was through what had been granted, the right to vote. Meanwhile the government had also seized the opportunity to mollify other strands of reformist opinion. In addition to the place and pensions bills that had accompanied Catholic relief, the session of 1793 introduced legislation to give juries more discretion in cases of libel, thus granting the press a somewhat greater freedom of expression, and to exempt poorer houses from the payment of the hearth tax. Having thus isolated the intransigent radicals from their Catholic and reformist allies, the government was then able, during 1793–4, to suppress Volunteering and put down the society of United Irishmen.

This apparent triumph was, however, in several respects deceptive. The Dublin United Irishmen, radicalism's public face, had been cowed into inactivity. But their Ulster associates went on quietly with what may well have been from the very start their more dangerous projects. The continuing conflict between Catholic and Protestant in south Ulster, reaching a fresh peak of violence in 1795, introduced a new element of instability. Most important of all the Defender movement had by this time developed into something altogether more formidable than its origins as the Catholic wing of a sectarian feud suggested. By the summer of 1792 it had spread from south Ulster into the north Leinster counties of Louth and Meath. By 1794 Defenders were also active in north Connacht, in the counties of Leitrim, Longford, Roscommon, and Sligo. A digest of intelligence prepared for the government in mid-1795 summarized their activities: 'the burning of turf and rooting up of the potatoes belonging to persons who refuse to be sworn, and to join them; the cutting down of plantations of trees to make handles for pikes; digging up meadows; levelling banks; houghing cattle; robbing and setting fire to houses; ravishing, murder etc.' One clergyman claimed that in eight months there had been 147 'robberies, rapes and murders' in County Longford and immediately adjacent districts. In one particularly violent incident, in April of the same year, Defenders surrounded eleven revenue officers who had seized materials relating to illicit distillation near Carrick-on-Shannon in County Leitrim, set fire to the house in which they took refuge, then hacked them to death with pikes, scythes, and pitchforks as they tried to escape.[49]

The Defenders were alarming, not just for their violence and the growing scale of their organization, but for their ideology. Earlier popular movements, from the Houghers to the Rightboys, had presented a challenge to law and order. Their

---

[49] Thomas Bartlett (ed.), 'Select Documents XXXVIII: Defenders and Defenderism in 1795', *IHS* 24 (1985), 373–94.

aims, however, had been limited and defensive, concerned with the preservation of an existing way of life. The Defenders too pursued pragmatic grievances. As the movement spread from its original home in south Ulster, its concerns broadened to include agitation on such issues as rents, tithes, wages, and the occupation of land. Underlying agitation on these traditional grievances, however, was not just the militant Catholic sectarianism out of which Defenderism had been born, but also increasingly clear aspirations to both social and political revolution. As early as January 1793 Westmorland reported to Pitt that the movement 'swear the whole country to be true to the Irish nation, . . . they have been frequently heard to declare that the king was not the Catholic king—they look upon or talk of the English settlers as not of their nation.' A paper posted at a Catholic church in County Cavan proclaimed: 'All men were born equal; we have no king but the Almighty.' A man overheard speaking after mass in the town of Roscommon put the message more directly: 'we have lived long enough upon potatoes and salt; it is our turn now to eat beef and mutton.'[50] Buoyed up by such expectations, Defenderism proved alarmingly resistant to repression. A conscious attempt to set 'an awful example' at the spring assizes of 1793, with twenty-one Defenders sentenced to death and thirty-seven more transported, failed to check the spread of the movement. The undersecretary at Dublin Castle, struck by the defiant attitude of thirteen apprentices hanged in Dublin in September 1795, confessed that 'Defenderism puzzles me more and more—there is an enthusiasm defying punishment.'[51]

Where did this enthusiasm come from? The Defenders were clearly aware of recent events in France. 'The French Defenders will uphold the cause', one password ran, 'and Irish Defenders will pull down the British laws.' A paper found on a man hanged at Carrick-on-Suir in 1795 contained a more elaborate recognition code:

Are you concerned? I am. To what? To the National Convention. What do you design by that cause? To quell all nations, dethrone all kings and plant the true religion that was lost since the Reformation. What do you fall by? Sin. What do you rise by? Repentance. Where did the cock first crow that all the world heard? France.[52]

If the French inspiration is clear, however, its precise nature is not. The intermingling of references to the national convention and the dethroning of kings with an invocation of the true religion lost at the Reformation suggests a certain fusion of traditions, in which France's long-standing role as the patron of Catholic Ireland merged with its new role as the beacon of universal liberation. In the same way it seems likely that elements of a new political language that rejected hierarchy and privilege in favour of universal rights blended easily in many minds with an older motif, inherited from the Jacobite tradition, of a people deprived of their lands and freedom by alien conquerors.

---

[50] Ibid. 376, 385.   [51] Elliott, *Partners in Revolution*, 44; Senior, *Orangeism*, 16.
[52] Bartlett (ed.), 'Defenders and Defenderism', 390.

More recent developments within Ireland also contributed to the rising atmosphere of revolutionary excitement. The Catholic committee's campaign of 1791–3 had both mobilized the masses and raised their expectations. Westmorland, in November 1792, commented on the 'insolence' of the lower orders: 'they have been taught that the elective franchise will improve their condition, and they connect with it the non-payment of rents, tithes and taxes.'[53] The militantly anti-Catholic rhetoric employed by opponents of the relief bill had also contributed to a new polarization along religious lines, evident in the violence associated with the militia riots of 1793. The militia act itself also played a part. From an early stage there was concern that the new force, recruited mainly from the Catholic lower classes, was infected by Defenderism, and the transfer of regiments from one region to the next was one means by which the movement spread into new geographical areas. Accounts of the sectarian conflict in south Ulster, disseminated by Catholic refugees from Protestant violence, further contributed to the sense of grievance underpinning an assertion of militant Catholic solidarity. So too did the blatantly partisan handling of those disturbances by some local magistrates, as well as the increasingly violent response of the authorities elsewhere to the alarming spread of the Defenders themselves. In a familiar pattern, popular disaffection and harsh repression became the mutually reinforcing elements in a cycle of atrocity and reprisal.

The appearance of the Defenders marks an important stage in the politicization of the Catholic lower classes. The example given by the Catholic committee's campaign of 1791–3 undoubtedly contributed something to the growth of the movement, and to its development of a more political edge. Indeed there are indications that both Catholic activists like Keogh and Richard McCormick, and Protestant radicals like Tone, Russell, and Tandy, established links of some kind with the Defenders during the same period.[54] In this sense the government's attempts to implicate its political opponents in treasonable conspiracy were not necessarily wholly fictitious. But Defenderism itself was a firmly plebeian movement. A report from County Meath identified those involved as 'alehouse keepers, artisans, low schoolmasters, and perhaps a few middling farmers'.[55] As such it testified to the changes that had taken place since mid-century in the character of Irish society. Several decades of sustained economic growth had produced a new plebeian class, Catholic as well as Protestant, literate, exposed to external political influences, and able to look beyond the defensive concerns of a Whiteboy or an Oakboy to the possibility of radical change. The two best-documented Defenders of the mid-1790s were both fit representatives of this new popular culture. Lawrence O'Connor, executed in Kildare in 1795 for administering an oath 'to

---

[53] Westmorland to Dundas, 18 Nov. 1792 (NAI, Westmorland Papers, 69).

[54] The most ambitious attempt to trace these links, on what remains at best circumstantial evidence, is in Smyth, *Men of No Property*, 66–70.

[55] Bartlett, 'Defenders and Defenderism', 394. The additional claim that 'inferior Roman Catholic priests' were 'its principal instigators' is more open to question.

be true to the French', was a schoolteacher. Arthur 'Switcher' Donnelly, who commanded the Defenders at the battle of the Diamond, was a dancing master, described as being of 'very great address, good choice of words, and fluency of speech'.[56]

Although popular disaffection thus had its own dynamic, developments at the level of high politics also played a part in the loss of control on the part of government that had become evident by 1795. In July 1794, following a split in the English Whig party, the more conservative faction, headed by the duke of Portland, entered a coalition government with Pitt and his followers. As part of their agreement the second Earl Fitzwilliam, nephew of Rockingham and brother-in-law of George and William Ponsonby, took over from Westmorland as lord lieutenant of Ireland. On arrival in Ireland in January 1795 he set about a purge of office holders. The attorney general, Arthur Wolfe, the solicitor general, John Toler, the first commissioner of the revenue, John Beresford, and the two undersecretaries at Dublin Castle were all to be removed, and their places taken by the Ponsonbys and their followers. On 12 February Grattan introduced a bill for the removal of all remaining Catholic disabilities, and Fitzwilliam wrote to London demanding permission to support the measure. On 20 February, however, the cabinet instructed him to oppose the relief bill. Three days later Portland wrote ordering him to withdraw from the government, leaving lords justices in charge.

Exactly how the Fitzwilliam crisis had come about remains open to debate. In the aftermath all parties, anxious to avoid inflaming Irish opinion, denied that he had been recalled because of his stand on the Catholic question. Instead, his critics claimed, the problem lay with his unauthorized removal of Beresford and others, violating a prior agreement that his appointment to Ireland was not to mean the introduction of a 'new system'. And indeed it seems to have been the case that Fitzwilliam failed to understand the peculiar character of the Irish executive, in which office holders like Beresford saw themselves more as civil servants than as politicians tied to a particular administration. (Alternatively he may simply have let himself be unduly swayed by what contemporaries regarded as the shameless office seeking of the Ponsonbys.) Yet it is hard to believe that the Catholic question was not in fact the key issue. Fitzwilliam's instructions, agreed in cabinet in November 1794, were to try to prevent the question being raised, and in any event to do nothing to commit the government without fresh instructions from London. He himself was a firm supporter of Catholic rights. In particular he believed that the only solution to the growing problem of public disorder was a full measure of emancipation, clearing the way for the creation of a new defence force, the yeomanry, in which loyal Catholics could be enlisted to defend the constitution. By the time he arrived in Ireland Grattan, whether with direct encouragement or on his own initiative, had already assured Keogh

[56] Smyth, *Men of No Property*, 115–16.

and Byrne that Fitzwilliam was pledged to their cause and preparations for a new relief bill were under way. Fitzwilliam could possibly claim that he was not responsible for the issue being raised. But he clearly made no attempt to discourage the agitation. Instead he tried to use its advanced state as a lever with which to extract London's consent to the measure.[57]

Fitzwilliam's recall caused widespread outrage. When his successor, the earl of Camden, reached Dublin in April, crowds armed with knives and firearms rioted in the streets, dispersing only after the soldiers called out to control them had killed two men. Suggestions that the episode was the turning point that set Ireland irretrievably on the road to civil war are questionable. There was nothing in Fitzwilliam's programme that would have satisfied the aspirations that were by this time being articulated by the Defenders, or indeed those of the United Irishmen. Yet the way in which the prospect of radical change, symbolized by the purge of the Castle clique, had been raised then snatched away undoubtedly helped to strengthen perceptions that worthwhile reform was not to be achieved without extreme measures. More particularly Fitzwilliam's viceroyalty undid much of what had been achieved by the relief act of 1793. Catholics who had at the time accepted the franchise and other gains as a reasonable instalment had been encouraged to focus instead on what was still denied them, and were unlikely to go back to being satisfied with what they had.

The tone set by Fitzwilliam's successor helped further to reinforce this alienation of both radicals and Catholics. Camden did not wholly abandon the policy of seeking to conciliate Catholic opinion. In particular he went ahead with a proposal, developed under Fitzwilliam, for the establishment of a state-supported seminary for the training of Catholic priests, located at Maynooth, County Kildare, on land provided by the duke of Leinster. Such a commitment of public funds to the training of Catholic priests was striking evidence of how far policy had come since the repeal less than twenty years earlier of the bishops' banishment act. In this particular case, however, the pragmatic arguments were overwhelming. The dispatch of these potentially influential figures to acquire their intellectual formation in institutions controlled by Britain's continental rivals had always been an anomaly. With the repeal of the laws restricting Catholic education within Ireland, it also became an anachronism. More immediately the French Revolution had led to the closure of the seminaries at Paris and elsewhere that had supplied most of the priests required in Irish dioceses. In other respects Portland's instructions to Camden were clear. Catholics could not be admitted to power. Therefore it was essential to 'rally the friends of the Protestant interest'.[58]

---

[57] For the argument that Fitzwilliam's failure was in his understanding of the nature of the Irish executive, see E. M. Johnston, *Great Britain and Ireland 1760–1800* (Edinburgh, 1963), 104–16. For the role of the Ponsonbys, David Wilkinson, 'The Fitzwilliam Episode 1795: A Reinterpretation of the Role of the Duke of Portland', *IHS* 29 (1995), 315–39. For the Catholic issue see in particular Bartlett, *The Fall and Rise of the Irish Nation*, 193–201.

[58] Quoted in Bartlett, *Fall and Rise of the Irish Nation*, 207.

Camden quickly reinstated Beresford and the others dismissed by Fitzwilliam. He also threw the government's weight against Grattan's relief bill, which was duly defeated on 5 May by 155 votes to 84; a few office holders who voted for the measure subsequently lost their places. The message was thus clear. In 1793 strategic considerations had dictated a substantial concession to Catholic demands. Now, however, the interests of the British state were best served by firmly identifying with what was by this time openly defined as the Protestant ascendancy.

The early months of the new administration saw Irish radicalism take a decisive new direction. The first step was the adoption by the United Irishmen of Ulster, in May 1795, of a revised constitution and organizational structure. The already more clandestine nature of the Ulster movement had allowed it to survive the government clampdown of 1793–4. But the new constitution formalized its existence as a secret society. Members were bound by an oath of secrecy and organized in tightly knit groups of no more than thirty-six, with baronial and county committees sending delegates to a provincial and national executive. Within three months there were 8,000 members of the new society, in the counties of Antrim, Down, Armagh, and Tyrone. Their aim was to establish an Irish republic, independent of England. Two weeks after the adoption of the new constitution Tone arrived with his family in Belfast, from where he was to sail to begin his agreed exile in Philadelphia. During a round of farewells with Neilson and other United Irish associates it was agreed that he should go secretly from America to France, to solicit support for an insurrection. The former leaders of the Dublin society of United Irishmen were not yet members of the new organization. But Tone, before leaving Dublin, had already discussed the same plan with Thomas Addis Emmet, Russell, and the brothers John and Henry Sheares.

Although the new United Irish movement was designed as a secret society, its activities as it spread across Ulster during 1796 were a curious mixture of the public and the clandestine. Members collected weapons, trained in military drill, and developed a repertoire of secret signs and passwords. But they also offered open demonstrations of their numbers and organization. In particular they turned the funerals of deceased members, or indeed mock funerals staged for the purpose, into major shows of strength, assembling in force and marching in formation. During the autumn they also staged a series of potato diggings, where large crowds of United men gathered to harvest the crops of imprisoned or incapacitated comrades. Such theatrical gestures served both to keep up morale and to cow opponents. By the early months of 1797, however, they had given way to more direct forms of intimidation. Reports multiplied of gentlemen's houses raided for arms, whole stands of trees cut down to provide handles for pikes, and loyalists threatened or assaulted. A Church of Ireland clergyman, writing from County Armagh in April, reported a collapse of social order. Juries refused to convict United Irish prisoners. The gentry had fled their homes for the safety of the towns. Wealthy linen merchants had taken the United oath in order to save their property, 'which being very much exposed would certainly be destroyed. . . . Terror seems to be the order of the day.'[59]

A second major development was the coming together of the new United Irish society and the Defenders. The details and chronology of their union remain unclear, but two separate processes seem to have been involved. In Ulster, according to the later testimony of Emmet, what took place was the coming together of two parallel movements. Many Catholics had from the start been members of both societies. Protestant United Irishmen had then also joined the Defenders, in a conscious effort to end their 'exclusively Catholic appearance'. Eventually the Defenders as a body, 'by specific votes in their own societies', agreed to take the United oath, so that the two movements 'merge[d] into the broadest and best concerted institution'.[60] In Dublin and the surrounding counties, by contrast, the reshaped United Irish organization appears to have been belatedly grafted onto an already active popular radicalism. By 1795 the Defenders were well established in the city. There was also a variety of radical clubs, including a Telegraphic Society, a Philanthropic Society, a Shamrock Society, and Jacobin clubs, all composed mainly of shopkeepers, artisans, and apprentices, and linked in some cases to the Defenders. Some of the more radical members of the disbanded Dublin society of United Irishmen, such as the Sheares brothers and Oliver Bond, had also remained politically active, in a society known as the Strugglers. However it was not them, but two emissaries from Belfast, James Hope and James Metcalf, who in the summer of 1796 negotiated an alliance with the Defenders and other working-class groups in the capital.

The juncture with the Defenders allowed the United Irish leaders to transform a radical club based in Belfast and the surrounding countryside into a mass revolutionary movement. In October 1796 the movement claimed just over 38,000 members in Ulster, of whom 26,000 were in Antrim and Down. By February 1797 the number had risen to 69,000, and by May to 118,000, with particularly rapid growth in Armagh, Londonderry, and Tyrone. Outside Ulster the United Irish organization was at this stage still fairly limited. Another return, a few weeks earlier, showed a total of 16,000 members in the five Leinster counties of Louth, Meath, Westmeath, Kildare, and Dublin. Over the next year, however, the United Irish movement gradually strengthened its organization in these Leinster counties. Meanwhile evidence from Cork and other parts of

[59] C. Warburton to Richard Archdale, endorsed 12 Apr. 1797 (NAI, Rebellion Papers 620/29/242).

[60] T. A. Emmet, 'Part of an Essay Towards the History of Ireland', in William James MacNeven, *Pieces of Irish History* (New York, 1807), 117–20. For Dublin see Smyth, *Men of No Property*, ch. 6; Thomas Graham, 'The Transformation of the Dublin Society of United Irishmen into a Mass-Based Revolutionary Organization 1791–6', in Bartlett et al (eds.), *1798: A Bicentenary Perspective*, 136–46.

Munster suggests that a United Irish organization began to develop from the early months of 1797. By this time United Irish emissaries were also active in Connacht, although it was to remain the province in which the movement was weakest.[61]

The rapid spread during 1796–7 of the combined United Irish-Defender movement built on the widespread disaffection already evident in the first half of the decade, as well as on the resentment created by the increasingly repressive response to that disaffection of the authorities at both central and local level. Economic conditions contributed further to the growth of unrest. By the 1790s the effects of several decades of rising population were evident both in the decline in real wages and in growing competition for land. In 1797 the rising cost of wartime defence led the government to impose a new tax on salt, and to cancel the bounties on the inland transport of grain to Dublin, hitting in particular the tillage agriculture of the south-east. Taxation was a lesser burden on the Irish poor than either rents or tithes. But it was one that it suited United Irish propagandists to emphasize, as evidence of the practical benefits that would follow from a radical reform of the political system.[62]

To political, religious, and economic grievances must be added the capacity of a popular conspiracy, with its alluring paraphernalia of oaths, passwords, and secret signs, much of it borrowed from what was already a widespread masonic movement, to develop its own momentum. A saddler's apprentice in Carlow town, looking back in embittered old age, wrote caustically of the lighthearted manner in which he and others entered the United movement. 'It became the fashion and people would laugh as heartily at what was going forward as they would at any other piece of amusement.' He particularly derided the 'most ridiculous and nonsensical fashion' of wearing close-cropped hair in the French fashion, which he equated with wearing a label stating 'I am a United man'.[63] Membership of a secret society also held out the prospect both of conviviality and of fraternal support. A servant sworn into the Defenders at Ballyshannon, County Donegal, in July 1795, was told that he 'would have brothers and friends enough, that [he] would soon find the good of it, and see a great alteration in the world'.[64]

The creation of this new cross-class alliance, extending far beyond their original base in Belfast and Dublin, forced the United Irish leaders significantly

[61] For membership figures see Curtin, *United Irishmen*, 69; Thomas Graham, '"An Union of Power": The United Irish Organisation', in Dickson, Keogh, and Whelan (eds.), *The United Irishmen*, 246–7. For Munster David Dickson, *Old World Colony: Cork and South Munster 1630–1830* (Cork, 2005), ch. 12.

[62] David Dickson, 'Taxation and Disaffection in Late Eighteenth-Century Ireland', in Clark and Donnelly (eds.), *Irish Peasants*, 37–63.

[63] *Carlow in '98: The Autobiography of William Farrell of Carlow*, ed. Roger McHugh (Dublin, 1949), 30, 66.

[64] Information of Thomas Mulheran, 27 July 1795 (NAI, Frazer MSS 2/1).

to modify their original political message. The commitment to an independent Irish republic, and the primacy of political reform, remained. But United Irish propaganda now placed a greater emphasis on the additional prospect of social change. It had always been part of their strategy to emphasize the practical advantages, in terms of a reduction in taxation, a more equitable justice system, and a general increase of prosperity, that would follow from the elimination of political corruption and the overthrow of a self-interested oligarchy. From the mid-1790s this element in their propaganda became more prominent. The United Irish leaders still insisted that property rights would be protected in the new republic. But by emphasizing that the estates of those who opposed the liberation of the country would be forfeit they were nevertheless able to hold out the prospect of a significant redistribution of land and wealth. One pamphlet, *The Poor Man's Catechism*, published in 1796, went further. 'The Almighty', it proclaimed, 'intended all mankind to lord the soil.' Hence great estates would be broken up in order to give 'to every person without exception a competent share to enable him or her to get a comfortable livelihood'.[65] There are also indications that middle-ranking and local United Irish organizers were more willing than the national leadership to encourage their popular following with images of social as well as political revolution. Bartholomew Warren, dispatched from Belfast to County Mayo in February 1797, swore local men 'to be true to all republicans and particularly the French', and told those he recruited that 'when the French would land, that properties would be divided and given to those that took the oath'.[66]

The requirements of popular mobilization also led the United Irishmen to compromise to some extent their secular radicalism. From the mid-1790s their propaganda made free use of the Armagh wrecking, and of other instances of Orange terror, to arouse the resentment of the Catholic masses and persuade them of the need to mobilize in their own defence.[67] More striking still was their circulation, alongside the conventional political propaganda of the *Northern Star*, of a set of prophecies attributed to the medieval saint Colmcille, detailing the signs and wonders that would precede some great transformation within Ireland. Nor was it only Catholics who were catered for in this way. A parallel set of prophecies circulated in Presbyterian areas, attributed to the seventeenth-century Scottish Covenanter Alexander Peden. Their appearance is a reminder that the rapid growth of support for the principles of democratic republicanism was not necessarily linked, as might have been expected, to the rationalist principles of New Light theology. Many New Light Presbyterians were indeed led to commit

[65] James Quinn, 'The United Irishmen and Social Reform', *IHS* 31 (1998), 198–9.

[66] Information of Bernard Mulholland and Edward Pue, 17 Feb. 1797 (NAI, Rebellion Papers 620/28/279). On this theme see also J. S. Donnelly 'Propagating the Cause of the United Irishmen', *Studies*, 69 (1980), 21.

[67] For examples of this use of the Orange bogey see Allan Blackstock, 'The Irish Yeomanry and the 1798 Rebellion', in Bartlett et al. (eds.), *1798: A Bicentenary History*, 339–40.

themselves to an alliance with Catholic Ireland by the same Enlightenment ideal of religious toleration, combined with an optimistic faith in the universal triumph of reason, that had inspired Tone's *Argument*. But the United Irish movement also attracted Old Light Presbyterians, whose goal was less a secular republic on French lines than the much older ideal of a covenanted society, where justice and true religion would flourish. For some of these theological conservatives, it appears, the coming political conflict was to be understood in millenarian terms, as the long-prophesied conflict against the forces of the Antichrist that would precede the reign of the saints [68] The alliance with Catholics, in this perspective, became conceivable because the French Revolution, overthrowing the very personification of popish absolutism, meant that the downfall of popery itself was now at hand.

This combination of political radicalism and Presbyterian millenarianism was just one part of the kaleidoscope of allegiances and aspirations brought together beneath the banner of a widely disseminated United movement forced to operate under conditions of secrecy that militated against any real degree of central control. The propaganda and organizational efforts of the United Irishmen undoubtedly furthered the dissemination at popular level of a political ideology that combined democratic republican principles with commitment to the ideal of an independent Ireland. But this existed side by side with the articulation of more immediate economic and social grievances, and also with a strong sense of sectarian solidarity. The Reverend George Knipe, a clerical magistrate in County Meath, reported in February 1797 that 'the French militia, as they now style themselves', active on the borders of Meath, Kildare, and King's County, 'make one dreadful distinction between Protestant and Papist: the latter they only rob, but they former they not only rob, but endeavour to murder'. When Knipe himself was assassinated two months later, the leader of his attackers, known only as Captain Fearnought, 'fired a shot at the body with a holster pistol, saying there lies the body of a heretic which I hope to have the nation shortly quelled of and become republicans'.[69] Notes relating to United Irish activities in Dublin city in January 1798 included the claim that 'the great men in coaches will soon be settled . . . in a couple of months there will be but one religion and we will be the owners of the soil.' A private in the Tipperary militia, inducted into the United movement in Carlow town, later testified that he had been sworn 'to be true to the Catholic religion and to assist the French should they land in this kingdom'. Other oaths revealed a similar combination of loyalties. In Clare in September 1798 men were sworn 'to be true and faithful to the Roman Catholic religion

[68] D. W. Miller, 'Presbyterianism and "Modernisation" in Ulster', in Philpin (ed.), *Nationalism and Popular Protest*, 93–102. For the circulation of millenarian prophecies see also Donnelly, 'Propagating the Cause of the United Irishmen', 15–20.

[69] Knipe to Pelham, 23 Feb. 1797 (NAI, Rebellion Papers 620/28/293); trial of John Kelly, ibid. 620/5/61/12.

and . . . to be true also to the convention of France'. In Cork, two months later, the oath was 'to be true to their religion, or the tenets of the White boys'.[70]

In the southern counties a middle-class radical leadership, combining Catholic and Protestant, placed itself at the head of an overwhelmingly Catholic mass following. In Ulster, on the other hand, the key question was the response to the call to arms of plebeian Protestants. The outcome revealed sharp regional variations. Protestant support for the United Irish movement was consistently strongest in County Antrim and the northern part of County Down. But these were areas in which Catholics made up a quarter or less of the population. In more evenly divided Armagh the Defender–United Irish alliance was strongest in the predominantly Catholic south, while the mainly Church of Ireland north was dominated by the aggressive loyalism of the Orange Order. The Presbyterians of the county had been the main supporters of the Peep-of-Day Boys, but for the moment they held aloof from Orangeism and some at least joined the United Irish movement.[71] A detailed report, from around 1797, on the state of Tyrone and Londonderry depicted a more intricate patchwork of allegiances. The area immediately south of Dungannon was 'mixed, abounding with Protestants (temperate Orangemen) and united Irishmen, composed of the Old Defenders and new sans culotte Protestants now associated'. In Dungannon itself a majority were 'violent reformists, enemies to government and also to French equality, and who will probably sit still and let them decide the contest between themselves'. Further north, along the west shore of Lough Neagh, lay 'the most violent and unanimous United Irish country I know'.[72] In Tobermore, only a few miles further west, on the other hand, a satisfied magistrate could report in January 1797 that 'the monstrous union of the two religions' had dissolved into 'a complete schism', after the Catholic side had seized all the arms in the county for themselves, leading the excluded Presbyterians to clamour for admission to the yeomanry. A clergyman in Donegal commented that disaffection in the county was confined to a fertile region immediately south of Derry city, in which 'the dissenting power and interest' was strongest. The predominantly Anglican region to the south, and the mainly Catholic territory to the west, remained quiet.[73]

As the United Irishmen built up their revolutionary organization, others were working to secure the French intervention on which their plans for armed revolt depended. Tone, following preliminary negotiations with the French minister in Philadelphia, arrived in Paris in February 1796. Despite his initially shaky command of French, he proved to be a capable diplomat, gaining access to

---

[70] 'Michael Edwards, 28 Jan. 1798' (ibid. 620/35/71); information of Daniel McCarthy, 5 May 1798 (ibid. 620/37/27); court martial of John Begley, 6 Sept. 1799 (ibid. 620/5/59/9); testimony of Daniel O'Sullivan, Cork, 19 Apr. 1799 (ibid. 620/5/60/25).

[71] Miller, 'Origins of the Orange Order in County Armagh', 596–8.

[72] Undated letter signed 'WK' (or 'WM') (NAI, Rebellion Papers 620/54/98).

[73] R. G. Hill to Beresford, 16 Jan. 1797 (NAI, Rebellion Papers 620/28/102); Revd William Hamilton to Edward Cooke, 15 Feb. 1797 (ibid. 620/28/269).

Lazare Carnot, a member of the five-man ruling Directory. Two months later Lord Edward Fitzgerald and Arthur O'Connor travelled to Hamburg, where they too pressed the Irish case in talks with French representatives. Circumstances favoured both missions. Britain's role in promoting the bloody insurrections by the conservative peasantry of the west of France that had erupted in 1793 had been bitterly resented. Carnot, along with Lazare Hoche, France's leading general, saw in the proposal for an Irish expedition an opportunity to pay the enemy back in kind. There were numerous delays and false starts, as the government sought to balance competing strategic priorities. But on 16 December a fleet of some fifty ships left Brest, carrying 14,450 troops and over 40,000 stand of arms. It was an expedition on a scale that recalled the great Spanish seaborne offensives, against both Ireland and Great Britain, of the 1580s and 1590s. And the outcome, despite two centuries of progress in techniques of navigation and seamanship, was no more successful. Storms carried a number of vessels, including Hoche's flagship, away from the main fleet. The remainder, thirty-six ships, arrived off Bantry Bay, on the coast of County Cork, on 22 December, but continued bad weather made it impossible for the troops they carried to attempt a landing.

The French mission to Bantry Bay was a disastrous moment in the development of the Irish revolutionary movement, not so much on account of its failure as because of the sheer scale of the resources that had been committed to it. Such visible proof that French military aid was a real possibility created a surge of confidence among radicals. Its effects were seen in the dramatic growth in United Irish numbers, rising threefold in Ulster between October 1796 and May 1797, and in the sharp increase in popular aggression evident in the early months of 1797. The expedition, however, had not arrived off the Ulster coast. It had chosen a point in the far south-west, where the United Irish organization had not as yet begun to spread. Government supporters commented, with a mixture of relief and triumph, on the loyal behaviour of the population. In places, it was claimed, peasants had willingly cleared snow from the roads to hasten the passage of government troops. Such accounts cannot be taken wholly at face value: there was neither time nor opportunity for an unprepared population to react much differently. To the French, however, the lack of response suggested that their United Irish allies had exaggerated the revolutionary potential of Ireland. They continued to see the island as Britain's weak spot. But any further action would have to wait until the Irish themselves had given proof of their readiness to fight. And France was never again to commit resources comparable to those it invested in December 1796.

In the period since Fitzwilliam's departure the combination of radical conspiracy and Defender outrages had already led the administration to adopt new measures of repression. In the autumn of 1795 the commander in chief of the Irish army, the second earl of Carhampton, sent to restore order in the western counties, had initiated the practice, imitated by other magistrates, of rounding up suspects and sending them, without trial, to serve in the navy.[74] These arbitrary proceedings caused outrage. In a striking display of the persistence of historical memory, vandals desecrated the grave of Carhampton's grandfather, the Henry Luttrell who had allegedly caused the defeat at Aughrim. An insurrection act in 1796 made the administering of an unlawful oath a capital offence. It also empowered the lord lieutenant to proclaim a district as in a state of disturbance, giving magistrates wide powers to search and detain, and authorizing justices of the peace, sitting without juries, to send 'idle and disorderly persons' to serve in the king's fleet. An indemnity act of the same year, the first of five that were to cover the whole period 1795–1801, implicitly acknowledged the extra-legal proceedings of magistrates and other officials by granting them immunity for acts committed while checking insurrection. A third act, in October 1796, partially suspended habeas corpus, by allowing the lord lieutenant or chief secretary to order the detention of persons suspected of treason. In fact even before this date the authorities had begun to arrest and imprison radical agitators, mainly in Ulster. On 16 September soldiers raided the offices of the *Northern Star* in Belfast and sent a group of prisoners to Dublin.

In addition to these security measures, the government had by this time created a new peacekeeping force. Camden had inherited plans for a yeomanry, a part-time force for peacekeeping and civil defence, from Fitzwilliam's administration. He was at first reluctant to proceed, because of fears that any locally raised force might pursue its own political ends, as the Volunteers had earlier done. But it was also becoming clear that the other locally raised line of defence, the militia, had been extensively penetrated by the Defenders. During 1796 Thomas Knox, MP for Dungannon, campaigned vigorously for the creation of a loyalist force, coining the slogan 'the first up will carry the day'. In October, as militant disaffection continued to spread, the government introduced legislation for the raising of a yeomanry. A first levy, in 1796, raised 20,000 men, and by 1798 numbers had increased to 39,000. The new force, in keeping with the terms of the relief act of 1793, was theoretically open to loyal citizens of all denominations. In the south some Catholics did in fact become yeomen. In Ulster, on the other hand, the new force was overwhelmingly Protestant, and more particularly was composed mainly of members of the established church. In some cases, indeed, Protestant recruits came forward only on condition that no Catholics were admitted to the same corps.

The arming of an overwhelmingly Protestant force to contain the threat of the United Irishmen and Defenders raises the question of the relationship between the government and the landed elite on the one hand, and the forces of Protestant sectarianism, as represented in particular by the Orange Order, on the other. The

---

[74] Although some accounts speak of hundreds of suspects being dispatched to the fleet, recent research suggests that the number was around 200. See L. M. Cullen, 'The Politics of Crisis and Rebellion 1792–1798', in Jim Smyth (ed.), *Revolution, Counter-Revolution and Union: Ireland in the 1790s* (Cambridge, 2000), 32.

new Orange Society had from the start the active patronage of a few local landed families, of which the most prominent was the Verners of County Armagh. Other men of property, however, regarded the appearance of an armed plebeian movement of any description with alarm, and their misgivings were shared by leading figures in the Dublin administration. The brutal and indiscriminate campaign of 'wrecking' that followed on the battle of the Diamond contributed further to such reservations. At the end of December the grand jury of County Armagh, summoned by the governor, Viscount Gosford, denounced the recent attacks on Catholics and promised to deal impartially with all those who broke the law. But in practice complaints of the partisan administration of justice continued in the months that followed. On 12 July 1796 Gosford himself, ignoring instructions from Dublin to discourage potentially provocative parades, allowed Orangemen to march through his demesne, appearing in person to take the salute as they passed. Thomas Knox, the earlier champion of a loyalist yeomanry, likewise presented the Orange Society as a necessary ally, though by no means a wholly desirable one. Its members, he wrote in August 1796, must not be 'entirely discountenanced . . . for with all their licentiousness on them we must rely for our lives and properties'.[75]

All this was at a time when revolutionary conspiracy was at a fairly early stage of development. By 1797, with the Defender–United Irish movement apparently dominant across a large part of south Ulster, and following the frighteningly narrow escape of December 1796, the arguments for distinguishing between Orange and Catholic violence were even stronger. A central figure at this stage in the development of official policy was John Knox, commander of the army at Dungannon and a brother of the MP. In May he made two key decisions: that the task of searching for arms should be entrusted to the local yeomanry, and that they should disarm only United Irish supporters, tacitly ignoring illegal weapons held by Orangemen. The aim, he admitted frankly, was less military than political: 'to increase the animosity between the Orangemen and the United Irishmen . . . Were the Orangemen disarmed or put down, or were they coalesced with the other party, the whole of Ulster would be as bad as Down or Antrim.'[76] As the crisis deepened the Dublin administration, though nervous of the possible implications of mobilizing Protestant sectarianism, largely allowed local figures like Knox to take the initiative. But even in the early months of 1798, with armed confrontation increasingly likely, it stopped short of accepting proposals to arm the Orangemen as a body, outside the at least partial discipline imposed by the yeomanry system. Instead what one minister called 'this dangerous species of ally' were to be kept in reserve.[77]

[75] Quoted in McDowell, *Ireland in the Age of Imperialism and Revolution*, 470.
[76] Quoted in Blackstock, 'The Irish Yeomanry and the 1798 Rebellion', 335.
[77] The role of the state and the landed elite in promoting the growth of Orangeism remains a disputed topic. For recent attempts to restate the conspiratorial thesis that Orangeism was

Interpretations of the relationship between the Irish political and social elite and plebeian Orangeism have long been distorted by one colourful but bogus piece of evidence. In March 1798 eighteen members of the Orange Society met in Dublin to discuss ways of coordinating the movement at national level. The establishment as a result of what became the Grand Lodge of Ireland has been taken as the moment at which the grandees of Protestant Ireland took command of the movement for their own political purposes. The Grand Lodge, it has been claimed, became 'the most powerful club in Dublin'.[78] This account, however, depends mainly on two histories of the movement published in 1825 and 1859 by the Wexford Orangeman Ogle Gowan, whose father had, by his son's account, been a key figure in these early years, introducing the first Orange lodge into Wexford in February 1798. Recent research in the newly opened archives of the Grand Lodge indicates that Gowan's history is a fabrication, probably intended to further his own political career by creating an attractive legend of Orange origins in which his father had played a leading part. The first members of the Grand Lodge were in fact drawn from the same respectable but middling social groups that had taken control of the emerging movement in Armagh itself. Of the 18 present at the first Dublin meeting, at least 15 served in the militia or yeomanry, but of these 11 were of non-commissioned rank. The gentry and aristocracy of Protestant Ireland did indeed come to see Orangeism as a necessary ally in the war on radicalism. But they did not at this stage assume direct control through the Grand Lodge.[79] Nor was there, as has been claimed, a grand strategy of 'implanting' Orange lodges throughout the counties of Leinster as part of a concerted campaign of counter-revolution. The first warrant for a lodge in Wexford came, not in February 1798, as Gowan claimed, but on 4 December, when the United Irishmen had already risen and been suppressed.[80]

By the time of Brigadier Knox's accommodation with Orangeism the government, stirred to action both by the growing boldness of the Defender–United Irish alliance and by the alarm of December 1796, had launched a concerted offensive against the radical movement in Ulster. In March 1797 Camden ordered the commander there, General Gerard Lake, to disarm the province. His orders, the lord lieutenant told Portland, were 'not to suffer the cause of

deliberately promoted as a means of splitting the Catholic–Protestant alliance see Kevin Whelan, *The Tree of Liberty: Radicalism, Catholicism and the Construction of Irish Identity 1760–1830* (Cork, 1996), ch. 3; Smyth, 'The Men of No Popery: The Origins of the Orange Order', *History Ireland*, 2 (1995), 48–53. Both authors, in this as in other respects, owe much to hints first thrown out by L. M. Cullen. See Cullen, 'The Political Troubles in County Armagh: A Comment', *IESH* 23 (1996), 18–23. Allan Blackstock, 'The Irish Yeomanry and the 1798 Rebellion', restates the argument, first developed in Senior, *Orangeism*, that Camden and military commanders sought to ensure that the juncture with Orangeism was 'as limited a link-up as they could make it' (p. 341).

[78] Senior, *Orangeism*, 76.
[79] James Wilson, 'Orangeism in 1798', in Bartlett et al., (eds.) *1798: A Bicentenary Perspective*, 345–62.
[80] Ibid. 349. For 'implanting' see Whelan, *Tree of Liberty*, 123.

justice to be frustrated by the delicacy which might possibly have actuated the magistracy'.[81] Lake took his superior at his word. When ordinary searches failed to uncover sufficient arms, his troops began burning the houses of suspected radicals as a means of forcing their surrender. Complaints quickly multiplied of indiscriminate violence against civilians. In one incident in June a detachment of Welsh Fencibles fired on a crowd at Newry said to consist mainly of women, children, and old men, killing between ten and twenty. Meanwhile, in June, soldiers in Belfast smashed up public houses used by the United Irishmen, and wrecked the offices and printing equipment of the *Northern Star*. By September 1796 an estimated 500 to 600 radicals had been taken into custody across Ulster, and Newgate prison in Dublin had come to be jocularly referred to as 'the Belfast hotel'.[82]

The turn to measures of exceptional repression did not go wholly unopposed. The Irish Whig party had supported the declaration of war on revolutionary France, and had largely distanced itself from the United Irishmen, the one exception being the lawyer John Philpot Curran, who had acted as defence counsel for a number of accused radicals. After the disappointment of Fitzwilliam's recall, however, the party divided. The Whig grandees, Thomas Conolly, the duke of Leinster, and even Charlemont, allowed themselves to be persuaded to support the new yeomanry. On the other hand Grattan and the Ponsonbys came out openly in opposition to government policy. In the spring of 1797, with the aid of United Irishmen and other radical activists, they organized a series of county meetings to demand political reform and an end to repression. They also seem to have negotiated with United Irish leaders on the details of a bill for parliamentary reform that William Ponsonby introduced in May. But the attempt to revive the alliance of 1778–85 was unsuccessful. The radicals had come too far to follow the lead of even the more advanced Whigs. Within parliament, meanwhile, the Whigs themselves were a diminished force. The Commons rejected Ponsonby's reform bill by 117 votes to 30. In the same month Grattan, after an angry speech comparing what was happening to the disastrous policies that had provoked the American Revolution, withdrew from parliament with a few followers.[83]

Disquiet at the new security policy was not confined to political opponents. In October 1797 Sir Ralph Abercromby, a highly regarded Scottish soldier, replaced

[81] Quoted in Thomas Bartlett, 'Defence, Counter-Insurgency and Rebellion: Ireland 1793–1803', in Thomas Bartlett and Keith Jeffery (eds.), *A Military History of Ireland* (Cambridge, 1996), 270.

[82] McDowell, *Ireland in the Age of Imperialism and Revolution*, 572–3. McDowell's rather muted account of the disarming of Ulster must be set against Bartlett's account of much harsher proceedings. See also Blackstock, ''The Irish Yeomanry and the 1798 Rebellion', 336–7.

[83] The fullest account of this phase of Whig policy is Danny Mansergh, *Grattan's Failure: Parliamentary Opposition and the People in Ireland 1779–1800* (Dublin, 2005), which lays particular emphasis on the dealings of Grattan and others with the United Irishmen, but does not always seem to be sufficiently alive to the dangers of relying too heavily on the evidence of informers and the allegations of political opponents.

Carhampton as commander in chief. He quickly made clear his disapproval of
the current state of affairs. In general orders issued on 24 December he insisted
that soldiers must remain within the laws of the land. Before long Foster, the earl
of Clare, and other leading members of the Dublin political establishment were
clamouring for his removal. The immediate focus of their protest was a second
general order, issued on 26 February. Outraged by an incident in County Cork in
which two lieutenants were found to have raped a servant girl taken into custody
as witness in a murder case, Abercromby denounced the armed forces in general
as being 'in a state of licentiousness which must render it formidable to everyone
but the enemy'. The real issue, however, was a wider debate on military tactics.
Abercromby deplored the dispersal of soldiers in small units to support the civil
power, as both bad for discipline and dangerous in the event of an invasion.
Where troops had to be used for counter-insurgency, moreover, his policy was
'free quarters': the billeting of the soldiers concerned on the inhabitants of the
area concerned, an arbitrary act of collective punishment, but more defensible
than house burning or random violence. With Abercromby's resignation in
late April, and his replacement by Lake, the pacifier of Ulster, the debate was
resolved. With the north now intimidated into quiescence, the army began a
reign of terror in the second main centre of radical organization, the counties
round Dublin. This time their methods extended not just to house burning but
also to torture, in a way that apparently had not been systematically employed
in Ulster.[84] The main method used was the standard military punishment of
flogging, continued until the victim broke. But other suspects were subjected to
the repeated strangulation of half-hanging, or to the pitchcap, smeared over their
heads and then set on fire.

By the end of 1797, with the majority of the northern leadership in custody,
the direction of the United Irish movement had passed to Dublin. There
were deep divisions on strategy. A conservative group, headed by Emmet and
MacNeven, insisted that any attempted rising had to wait for the French—not
solely to ensure military success, but in order to minimize the risk that a popular
revolt would develop either into a religious civil war or a general attack on
property. On 12 March 1798 the Dublin police, acting on the evidence of an
informer, raided the home of Oliver Bond and arrested twelve leaders of the
Leinster Directory. Emmet and MacNeven were seized elsewhere on the same
day. The imprisonment of these more cautious spirits left the leadership in radical
hands. However tactical disputes continued. Within the new five-man National
Directory Lord Edward Fitzgerald and Samuel Neilson, recently released from

[84] Bartlett, 'Defence, Counter Insurgency and Rebellion' refers to 'house burnings, floggings
and mass arrests' (p. 270). However Lecky points out that Lord Moira, denouncing government
methods in the Irish House of Lords in February 1798, was able to cite only one instance of torture
from Ulster, involving a Downpatrick blacksmith accused of manufacturing pikes who had been
picketed and possibly half-hanged: W. E. H. Lecky, *A History of Ireland in the Eighteenth Century*
(London, 1898), iv. 45.

prison, now set about planning an insurrection, to commence on 23 May. The brothers John and Henry Sheares, on the other hand, argued for an alternative strategy of a revolt by United Irish and Defender elements within the militia. On 19 May Dublin police officers tracked Lord Edward to a house in Dublin. He was arrested after a vicious struggle, and was to die of his wounds on 4 June. Almost immediately afterwards the Sheares brothers fell victim to their enthusiasm for the militia as the key to the Irish revolt. Having responded eagerly to the feigned disaffection of a militia captain they had met by chance in a bookshop, they were arrested on 21 May. A fourth conspirator, Neilson, was intercepted two days later, on 23 May, near Newgate prison, where Fitzgerald and others were being held. Contemporary accounts suggest that he was drunk. A more recent analysis argues, from circumstantial evidence, that he was in fact engaged in a risky but rational attempt to liberate key leaders in advance of a nationwide rising due to begin that night.[85]

The competing readings of Neilson's escapade are symptomatic of the very different assessments that have been offered of the wider events of which it formed a part. On the night of 23 May an estimated 10,000 men mobilized in arms in the counties of Dublin, Kildare, and Meath. Older accounts emphasize the uncertain and ineffective movements of the rebels, implying a movement deprived of direction by the arrest of the national leaders. More recent work suggests that their rising was in fact part of a coherent strategy, in which their role would have been to converge on Dublin after insurgents had seized the city in a surprise attack. But the arrest of Neilson disrupted the plan, and last-minute information on the imminent rising allowed the government to flood the streets with troops and yeomanry. One account spoke of lanes and alleys in the manufacturing districts to the west of the Castle littered with pikes and muskets, discarded as the potential insurgents melted away. The failure of Dublin to rise left the country detachments to maraud aimlessly, while crown forces prepared their counter-attack. On 26 May troops engaged several thousand men encamped on the hill at Tara, killing 350 and dispersing the remainder. In Kildare a large body of insurgents surrendered and laid down their arms but were then attacked, in disputed circumstances, by troops who killed around 200 of them. Meanwhile the rebellion had also spread to Carlow, where a United Irish attack on the town was bloodily defeated on 26 May.

If old and new stories of what happened in Dublin and the surrounding counties differ significantly, the same is even more true of events in County Wexford. Traditionally the revolt that began in the south-east on 27 May has been seen as 1798 without the United Irishmen: a spontaneous popular uprising,

---

[85] Thomas Graham, 'Dublin in 1798: The Key to the Planned Insurrection', in Dáire Keogh and Nicholas Furlong (eds.), *The Mighty Wave: The 1798 Rebellion in Wexford* (Dublin, 1996), 74; Liam Chambers, 'The 1798 Rebellion in North Leinster', in Bartlett et al. (eds.), *1798: A Bicentennial Perspective*, 122–35.

largely independent of prior clandestine organization, but provoked instead by the ruthless terror tactics employed during preceding weeks by local loyalists. More recent accounts dismiss this image of a largely apolitical rising as a later fabrication. In the period after the rebellion, supporters of a conciliatory policy towards Catholics had every reason to depict a fundamentally loyal peasantry driven to revolt by unnecessarily harsh measures. Later, during the centenary celebrations in 1898, constitutional nationalists and the Catholic church authorities, anxious to prevent the anniversary from being captured by militant republicans, sought to divert the focus from Dublin and Belfast to Wexford, and to present a Catholic peasantry engaged, under the leadership of their priests, in a defensive rising against a vicious sectarian onslaught. In contrast recent work emphasizes Wexford's radical credentials. It was a prosperous county, dominated by commercially oriented tillage farming rather than peasant agriculture. It was predominantly English speaking, with relatively high levels of literacy. It had a prehistory of political mobilization, in the Catholic campaign of the early 1790s and in subsequent radical agitations. There was also a United Irish organization, whose leaders included a number of Protestant gentry, such as Beauchamp Bagenal Harvey and John Henry Coclough.[86]

Pre-1798 Wexford was also a county marked by particularly sharp religious divisions. The northern part of the county, along with south Wicklow, had been the scene of minor but quite effective plantation schemes during the first half of the seventeenth century. The result was a stronger Protestant element than elsewhere in rural Leinster, amounting in some parishes to between 20 and 30 per cent of the population. This Protestant population were well established among the more substantial tenant farmers, and in the towns, while the labourers and smallholders of the countryside were predominantly Catholic. To these inequalities, inherited from the plantation period and sustained by the discriminatory practices of local landlords, there was added a more specific conflict between two groups of middlemen, Catholic and Protestant, in competition for the declining economic opportunities open to them as landlords began to reassume direct control of their estates. The tensions that resulted can be glimpsed in the long-standing feud between the father of Miles Byrne, one of the most active insurgent leaders of 1798, and Hunter Gowan who, if he did not play quite the prominent role in early Orangeism that his son was later to claim for him, was nevertheless active in the local war against radicalism. It is significant that one of the clearest references to the traditional theme of the reversal of the seventeenth-century confiscations to be found in connection with 1798 occurs in Byrne's much later memoirs,

---

[86] The new interpretation of the Wexford rising is set out in Keogh and Furlong (eds.), *The Mighty Wave*. Much of this work takes its inspiration from the writings of L. M. Cullen. See in particular 'The 1798 Rebellion in Wexford: United Irish Organisation, Membership, Leadership', in Kevin Whelan (ed.), *Wexford: History and Society* (Dublin, 1987).

where he describes how his father had often 'shown me the lands that belonged to our ancestors, now in the hands of the sanguinary followers of Cromwell'.[87]

Wexford, then, was a more likely participant in a political revolt than was once recognized. The precise origins of what became the most serious military challenge to the state to be offered at any point during 1798 are less clear. The traditional account is of a spontaneous popular rising, turning for leadership to a local priest, Father John Murphy. More recent analyses present a concerted mobilization by units of United Irishmen, possibly in response to a message brought from Dublin by John Hay, a former officer in the French army, who arrived by mail coach on the afternoon of the 26th, dismounting at Oulart on the Dublin–Wexford road. Much of the new account, however, is extrapolated from circumstantial and sometimes questionable evidence, and many details remain unclear. There is disagreement, for example, over whether Murphy, the priest who assumed initial command, had been part of the prior United Irish movement.[88] In either case the turning point in the revolt was an unexpected victory on 27 May, when insurgents defeated a force of militia and yeomanry at Oulart Hill, killing 100 of them. The following day they moved on to Enniscorthy, where the garrison retreated after a short engagement. On 30 May government troops in Wexford, demoralized by the ambush and defeat of a relief force approaching from Duncannon fort, abandoned the town to its fate. The insurgents now controlled the entire county, and Wexford became for the next three weeks the headquarters of an improvised revolutionary government. Their south-eastern corner of the island, however, remained a cage. The insurgents attacked New Ross to the west on 5 June, and Arklow to the north four days later, but in each case were beaten back with heavy losses. Thereafter they could only wait while the government massed its forces for a counter-attack, defeating the rebels at Vinegar Hill on 21 June and retaking Wexford the following day.[89]

The nature of this short-lived revolutionary regime is central to any assessment of the character of the south-eastern rising. As the rebel force gained ground Bagenal Harvey and other gentry leaders, arrested on the eve of the rising, were released from custody and assumed overall command. Their success in maintaining order in Wexford town and the surrounding countryside, and in mounting a formidable military effort against crown forces, indicates a significant level of both commitment and discipline among their followers. At the same

---

[87] Cullen, *Emergence of Modern Ireland*, 226. Cullen's pioneering examination of the background to religious conflict in Wexford is now supplemented by Daniel Gahan, 'Class, Religion and Rebellion: Wexford in 1798', in Smyth (ed.), *Revolution, Counter Revolution and Union*, 83–98.

[88] Brian Cleary, 'The Battle of Oulart Hill: Context and Strategy', in Keogh and Furlong (eds.), *The Mighty Wave*. Cleary's account of Hay's arrival (p. 80), for example, comes from oral testimony, often second hand, collected more than four decades later by a local historian and Carmelite friar Luke Cullen. For Murphy, compare Cleary's introduction of him on p. 80 with Whelan's on p. 21 of the same volume.

[89] The fullest narrative of the Wexford rising is now Daniel Gahan, *The People's Rising: Wexford 1798* (Dublin, 1995).

time some of the more extravagant claims made for 'the Wexford republic', such as the existence of a Senate of 500 citizens, appear to be without foundation.[90] Moreover discipline was not complete. Wexford was the scene of two particularly brutal outrages. At Scullabogue on 5 June rebels shot more than 30 prisoners, then herded up to 100 more, including women and children, into a barn which they set on fire. A list of 126 known dead included 11 Catholics, but all of these seem to have been imprisoned because of their connections with local Protestants. Two weeks later 93 Protestants held in Wexford town were dragged from their prison, cursorily tried by an improvised court martial, then taken to the bridge where they were piked to death and their bodies thrown in the river. Both episodes had a context. Scullabogue followed on the rebel defeat at New Ross (although claims that it was direct retaliation for the burning by government troops of a hospital packed with rebel wounded cannot be substantiated).[91] The killings on Wexford Bridge took place as defeat loomed and the grip of the leaders weakened. But these were not isolated incidents. Accounts by Protestant survivors repeatedly told of being threatened as 'Orangemen' or as 'heretics', whose deaths would see them instantly consigned to hell. At the main rebel camp on Vinegar Hill, outside Wexford, between 300 and 400 Protestant loyalists were executed after summary trials. Reports of prisoners being invited to save their lives by converting to Catholicism provide a startling echo, in the age of the Enlightenment, of the events of 1641.[92]

In Ulster, the original base of the United Irish movement, the southern risings produced no immediate response. Many of the most active leaders were still in custody, and the violent repression of the previous year had left others demoralized. In the days that followed, however, there appears to have been a revolt by lower-ranking United officers against the caution of their leaders. On 6 June Henry Joy McCracken, a member of one of Belfast's leading commercial families, assembled a force on Donegore Hill and went on to capture Randalstown

---

[90] For the Senate see Whelan, 'Reinterpreting the 1798 Rebellion in County Wexford', in Keogh and Furlong (eds.), *The Mighty Wave*, 25, and a more elaborate account by Brian Cleary, 'Wexford in 1798: A Republic Before its Time', in Cathal Póirtéir (ed.), *The Great Irish Rebellion of 1798* (Dublin, 1998), 101–14. The only source for this claim is the propagandist account of the Revd George Taylor, a Methodist minister whose purpose was to emphasize the kinship between the Wexford rebels and what he saw as the worst excesses of French democracy. See Dunne, *Rebellions*, 118–24.

[91] Dunne, *Rebellions*, 131–2, 227–9. For a detailed review of the evidence relating to the number and identity of those killed at Scullabogue see ibid. 247–57.

[92] Whelan seeks to minimize the significance of the Scullabogue and Wexford Bridge killings, as part of his general argument that sectarianism was primarily a creation of the state and the Protestant elite. See 'Reinterpreting the 1798 Rebellion in County Wexford', 25; idem, *Tree of Liberty*, ch. 3. For the evidence that anti-Protestant rhetoric and violence was in fact widespread during the revolt see J. S. Donnelly, 'Sectarianism in 1798 and in Catholic Nationalist Memory', and Thomas Dunne, 'Resistance and Rebellion in the Gaelic Literary Tradition from 1798 to 1848', both in L. M. Geary (ed.), *Rebellion and Remembrance in Modern Ireland* (Dublin, 2001). For invitations to convert to Catholicism see J. D. Beatty (ed.), *Protestant Women's Narratives of the Irish Rebellion of 1798* (Dublin, 2001), 15.

nearby. There were also risings further north, where insurgents seized Ballymena and established a committee of public safety, and along the east coast. However McCracken's attack on Antrim town was beaten back in a bloody battle. In County Down a rising began on 9 June under Henry Munro, a linen dealer who claimed to be a direct descendant of the Scottish general who had controlled the area during the 1640s. Munro's men occupied Lord Moira's estate at Montalto near Ballynahinch, where government troops defeated them in a pitched battle on 13 June.[93]

The Ulster risings were a more significant challenge than is often recognized. One calculation suggests that a minimum of 27,000 men took part. Mobilization on this scale, despite the repression and disarming of the previous year, testifies to the depth of radical commitment in the north-east. The religious composition of the insurgents remains unclear. Contemporary and later reports suggested that the Defenders in many cases failed to turn out, and that where they did the two sides cooperated uneasily. Presbyterians and Catholics in the attack on Randalstown were reported to have carried different flags, and to have fallen out later as they celebrated their victory. It is difficult to tell how far such accounts have their origin in loyalist propaganda designed to discredit the radical alliance.[94] But the failure of the more Catholic south of County Down to rise alongside the predominantly Presbyterian north lends support to the view that the union of Irishmen, even in its place of origin, was at best an imperfect one.

The last act in the confrontation between the Irish establishment and the forces of revolution began with the arrival on 22 August of the long-awaited French expedition. In the early summer of 1798 the attention of French military planners was directed east rather than west, towards a projected offensive in Egypt. News that Ireland had at last risen in arms led them to revive plans for an invasion, involving three separate fleets. The force that arrived at Killala, however, comprised just three ships. Their commander, General Jean Joseph Amable Humbert, had lost patience with the delays hindering the main expedition and had set out on his own with just 1,019 men. By this time the last straggling parties of insurgents in Leinster, apart from a small number still holding out in the Wicklow mountains, had been hunted down or induced to surrender. However the appearance of the French at Killala encouraged some 3,000 local volunteers to flock to their support.

As at Bantry Bay two years earlier, the French choice of a landing site ignored the political geography of the island. Connacht, physically isolated, still largely Irish speaking, and dominated in its western counties by an impoverished peasantry living close to subsistence level, was the province in which the United

---

[93] The most recent analysis of the Ulster rising is Curtin, *United Irishmen*, ch. 10. A. T. Q. Stewart, *The Summer Soldiers: The 1798 Rebellion in Antrim and Down* (Belfast, 1995) is a lively narrative.

[94] See for example Curtin, *United Irishmen*, 269–70, 276, whose examples come entirely from the later 'annals' of the firmly loyalist antiquarian Samuel McSkimin.

Irish organization had made least progress. Humbert was able to find enough local notables to create a provisional government headed by John Moore, son of a local Catholic merchant and landowner. However he and his officers were taken aback by the indiscipline and lack of political awareness of the common Irish who joined their army. One much-quoted account described local people brandishing rosaries and scapulars as they welcomed the representatives of the atheistic French republic in terms that looked back to the France of Louis XIV, traditional ally of Catholic Ireland, rather than to the new era of liberty, equality, and brotherhood: they were saviours, 'come to take arms for France and the Blessed Virgin'.[95] On 27 August Humbert's seasoned troops defeated a mixed force of yeomanry, militia, and Fencibles at Castlebar, giving him temporary control of the greater part of Connacht. But his strategic options were limited. He set off east, in what seems to have been a desperate attempt to strike at a relatively unprotected Dublin. But on 8 September vastly superior forces surrounded his army at Ballinamuck in County Longford. They accepted the surrender of the French regulars, but slaughtered their Irish allies, both on the field and in the subsequent reconquest of Connacht, without mercy.

The insurrection of 1798 was a brutal and bloody business. Yet the violence was not quite on the scale that has sometimes been claimed. An early estimate of 30,000 deaths in the course of the fighting has been revised downwards, in more recent work, to around 10,000.[96] This is one-and-a-half times the number believed to have been killed at the single battle of Aughrim in 1691, and well below the death toll for the war of 1689–91, much less that of 1641–53. The subsequent repression was also less harsh than might have been expected. In the immediate aftermath crown forces and loyalist irregulars continued the indiscriminate violence that had been so widely used before the revolt, burning houses and Catholic churches, hanging prisoners or flogging them half to death after perfunctory courts martial, and in some cases slaughtering civilians out of hand. In June 1798 the marquis of Cornwallis replaced Camden as lord lieutenant, while also assuming direct command of the army. The new lord lieutenant was no mild humanitarian. As commander of the encircled British forces at Yorktown, in the closing stage of the American War, he had driven his black auxiliaries into no man's land to starve or be cut down, in order to preserve supplies for his regular troops.[97] But his mission in Ireland was to end a dangerous internal conflict as quickly as possible. He did not wholly succeed in suppressing unofficial reprisals, especially in the south-east, where chapel burning and other outrages by loyalists continued for at least another three

---

[95] Quoted in Elliott, *Partners in Revolution*, 224.

[96] Thomas Bartlett, 'Clemency and Compensation: The Treatment of Defeated Rebels and Suffering Loyalists after the 1798 Rebellion', in Smyth (ed.), *Revolution, Counter Revolution and Union*, 100 n. 6, citing unpublished calculations by L. M. Cullen.

[97] Henry Wiencek, *An Imperfect God: George Washington, his Slaves and the Creation of America* (London, 2004), 247–8.

years.[98] However he acted decisively to curtail the scale of official retribution, reviewing all trials by court martial and refusing to confirm death sentences except where murder had been clearly proved. Incomplete records suggest that in all around 1,450 persons were sentenced by either military or civilian courts for their part in the rebellion. Of 850 convicted by courts martial, where the records are most complete, 330 were sentenced to death, and 430 to transportation, although an unknown proportion of these sentences would have been commuted or remitted.[99] Many of the leaders escaped more lightly. The Sheares brothers were executed, as were McCracken in Antrim, Munro in Down, and Bagenal Harvey in Wexford. Tone, captured on board a French vessel in September, cut his throat in prison after being sentenced to hang. The members of the Leinster Directory arrested in March 1798, however, were in custody well before the fighting began and the evidence against them was of uncertain weight. Under an agreement concluded in July, MacNeven, Emmet, and O'Connor put their names to a detailed statement on the rise of the United Irish organization, later supplemented by oral evidence to two parliamentary committees. The prisoners were then transferred to Fort George in Scotland until the temporary peace with France in 1802, when they were allowed to leave the country.

The rising of 1798 may not have rivalled that of 1641 in bloodshed. But it too was a war of many parts. In some respects—in the Defender movement, in the rallying of the Connacht peasantry to Humbert, and to some extent in the Wexford insurrection—what took place can be seen as a last revolt of traditional Catholic Ireland against the new order created by the seventeenth-century confiscations. In Ulster the participation of Old as well as New Light Presbyterians suggests a last round of the conflict between English and Scot, conformist and dissenter, whose foundations had likewise been laid more than one hundred years earlier. In other respects, however, the conflict fought out in 1798 arose from conflicting responses to more recent changes in politics and ideology. It pitted Protestants willing to carry the assumptions of patriotism to their logical conclusion, and to look beyond the preservation of existing religious distinctions to the new ideals of democratic republicanism, against those who believed that their only security as a threatened minority lay in the preservation of the existing constitutional order. The Catholics too were divided. Some of those active in the Catholic committee of the early 1790s, like Keogh and McCormick, subsequently allied themselves with Protestant radicals in the United Irish movement. Others, however, held aloof. A few Catholic priests, particularly in the south-east, were either United Irish supporters already or decided at the moment of crisis that their place lay with their parishioners. But

---

[98] Troy to Castlereagh, 5 Aug. 1800 (NAI, Rebellion Papers 650/58/100). See J. G. Patterson, 'White Terror: Counter-Revolutionary Violence in South Leinster 1798–1801', *ECI* 15 (2000), 33–53.

[99] McDowell, *Ireland in the Age of Imperialism and Revolution*, 675–7. See also Bartlett, 'Clemency and Compensation', 99–119.

the Catholic bishops, and the majority of the lower clergy, remained firmly opposed to the revolutionary movement.[100] Nor were they alone. Some United Irish leaders had expected the militia, predominantly Catholic and penetrated by the Defenders, to turn on their officers and become the spearhead of the revolt. In the event, however, the militia did not mutiny. They were not always reliable soldiers, as was demonstrated at Castlebar. But that was the response, seen also among the yeomanry and the local allies of the French, of inexperienced combatants suddenly exposed to the horrors of an eighteenth-century battlefield. And in many key engagements Catholic fought Catholic, just as Protestant fought Protestant, in a brutal and many-sided civil war.[101]

AN ACT OF UNION

The outbreak of revolt in Ireland led directly and with surprising speed to a decision to put an end to Ireland's two-and-a-half centuries of existence as a separate kingdom. On 28 May, the day after receiving the first news of the insurrection, Pitt wrote to Camden that its suppression should be followed by negotiations for a union. Over the next few days he discussed the project intensively with colleagues, notably the foreign secretary, Lord Grenville. George III, likewise, saw the rebellion less as a mortal threat to the security of his dominions than as an opportunity to resolve long-standing constitutional anomalies. On 13 June, with Wexford still in arms and other areas only just brought under control, he observed to Pitt that Cornwallis, about to replace Camden as lord lieutenant, 'must not lose the present moment of terror for frightening the supporters of the Castle into an union'.[102]

The speed with which discussion moved from rebellion to union lent apparently credibility to later accusations, from figures such as Daniel O'Connell and the son and biographer of Henry Grattan, that Pitt's government had deliberately provoked insurrection in Ireland in order to impose a union.[103] In reality what it confirmed was the extent to which events over the past three decades or more

[100] Dáire Keogh, *The French Disease: The Catholic Church and Radicalism in Ireland 1790–1800* (Dublin, 1993).

[101] Thomas Bartlett, 'Indiscipline and Disaffection in the Armed Forces in Ireland in the 1790s', in P. J. Corish (ed.), *Radicals, Rebels and Establishments* (Belfast, 1985), 115–34. See also Bartlett's contribution to Bartlett and Jeffery (eds.), *Military History of Ireland*, 247–93.

[102] Patrick Geoghegan, *The Irish Act of Union: A Study in High Politics 1798–1801* (Dublin, 1999), 2, 10–12. Geoghegan's detailed account now supplements G. C. Bolton's classic study *The Passing of the Irish Act of Union* (Oxford, 1966). See also Dáire Keogh and Kevin Whelan (eds.), *Acts of Union: The Causes, Contexts and Consequences of the Act of Union* (Dublin, 2001), and Michael Brown, Patrick Geoghegan, and James Kelly (eds.), *The Irish Act of Union: Bicentennial Essays* (Dublin, 2003).

[103] James Kelly, 'The Historiography of the Act of Union', in Brown, Geoghegan, and Kelly (eds.), *The Irish Act of Union*, 13–14, 17–18.

had destroyed the faith of the British political class in existing constitutional arrangements. In rejecting the commercial propositions the Irish parliament had spurned proposals to resolve the anomalies created by the settlement of 1782. The regency crisis had demonstrated the fragility of the remaining link between the two kingdoms. The linking of party politics in the two kingdoms following the establishment of the Irish Whig party in 1789 had added further to the sense of an unstable system that could at any stage become unmanageable. There were also other difficulties. By 1798 the Irish administration had become incapable of financing the rising cost of the war, and was kept from bankruptcy only by large subsidies from England. In addition there had been growing concern in London at the rising level of disorder. The eruption in May 1798 of the long-awaited popular revolt seemed to provide the final confirmation that Ireland could no longer be safely left to manage its own affairs, even under the supervision of a British lord lieutenant.

The replacement of Camden was an important part of the new strategy. He had already declared himself weary of his Irish posting, and the state of open rebellion that now prevailed arguably required the hand of a military rather than a civilian governor. But Camden was also too closely associated with the clique of Castle office holders, such as Foster and Beresford, whose policy of indiscriminate repression was now being blamed for the breakdown of order, and whose excesses Pitt believed it was essential to curb so that tranquillity could be restored. Cornwallis, by contrast, was an experienced commander who could be counted on to combine firmness with restraint. In addition he was known to be sympathetic to the further extension of Catholic political rights that Pitt and others at this stage envisaged as part of the union package. Yet the very qualities that made Cornwallis a more reliable instrument of Pitt's new policy undermined his capacity to carry it through. Almost from the start his determination to bring an end to loyalist reprisals, both official and unofficial, put him at odds both with senior office holders within the Irish executive and with Protestant opinion in general. In addition it quickly became clear that the new lord lieutenant had little taste or aptitude for political management. His chief associate in that task was the chief secretary, Robert Stewart, Viscount Castlereagh. Castlereagh was the eldest son of the earl of Londonderry, a one-time standard bearer of Presbyterian independent politics in his native County Down, but now a Castle supporter. Appointed to succeed the ailing Thomas Pelham as chief secretary in March 1798, despite doubts about the wisdom of allowing an Irishman to occupy this key post, the younger Stewart had ahead of him a career as a senior British statesman. But at this stage of his career he was 29 years old, inexperienced, over-confident, and seriously lacking in both charm and oratorical ability.

The work of thrashing out the details of the union, and of canvassing support in Ireland, continued during the autumn of 1798. The first step in the public campaign was the publication in November of a pamphlet by Edward Cooke, undersecretary at the Castle, ably setting out the main arguments for a union.

Within the executive Lord Clare, the former John Fitzgibbon, long-term critic of the pretensions of his fellow parliamentarians, was an immediate supporter, as was John Beresford, first commissioner of the revenue. A major early failure, however, was the refusal of John Foster, speaker of the Commons, to give his support. His subsequent prominence in resistance to the measure suggests that his opposition was deep rooted. But tactless handling by Cornwallis, Castlereagh, and also Pitt ruled out any possibility there might have been of an accommodation. The lord lieutenant and chief secretary also blundered in failing to quash promptly a damaging report in December 1798 that there were to be no reprisals against office holders who did not support the measure. It was not until just before parliament met on 22 January that Cornwallis did something to restore discipline by dismissing the chancellor of the exchequer, Sir John Parnell, and the prime serjeant, James Fitzgerald. At this point Castlereagh still believed that it would be possible to secure a majority for the union proposal. In the event, however, the king's speech, referring guardedly to 'some permanent adjustment' to the relationship between the two kingdoms, was carried only by the disastrously small margin of 107 to 105. Then, on 27 January, the Commons voted by 109 votes to 104 to delete from its address of thanks a paragraph hinting at the possibility of a union.

The debate that was now under way was in part conducted in terms of the practical advantages and disadvantages to be expected from the creation of a single kingdom. Supporters emphasized the mortal threat posed by revolutionary France, and the consequent need for the closest possible coordination of defence and security. They also pointed to the economic and other advantages that Ireland would derive from a closer connection. Opponents argued that Ireland would lose the ability to promote its own economic development, and warned of the dangers of overtaxation and of the loss to the kingdom of its resident aristocracy and gentry. But supporters of the union also brought into the open the view, long privately held by many on the British side of the Irish Sea, that the constitutional settlement of 1782 was fundamentally unsatisfactory. Cooke, in the first major statement of the pro-union case, suggested that the existing arrangements 'have all the disadvantages without the advantages of an union'.

The king of Ireland, as the king of Scotland before the union, resides in another kingdom. The counsels for the government of Ireland are framed in the British cabinet; the government of Ireland is actually administered by a British lord lieutenant, who distributes the patronage of the crown; the Irish parliament is supposed to be in a great degree subject to British influence, and near one million of the rents of the kingdom are annually exported to absentees. The jealousies upon these points are great and unavoidable, and form the perpetual topic for inflaming the minds of the people.[104]

---

[104] [Edward Cooke], *Arguments for and against an Union between Great Britain and Ireland Considered* (4th edn., Dublin, 1799), 10–12.

Pitt put the point more simply: 'You abolished one constitution, but you forgot to form another.' Grattan, in response, offered a detailed defence of 'the constitution of 1782' as a 'final adjustment' in the relationship between the two kingdoms.[105] George Ponsonby, moving an anti-union amendment in the first major debate, insisted on 'the undoubted birthright of the people of Ireland to have a free and independent legislature, as it was asserted by the parliament of this kingdom in 1782, and acknowledged and ratified by his majesty and the parliament of Great Britain'.[106]

Grattan emphasized the finality of the 1782 settlement in order, not just to emphasize Ireland's constitutional rights, but to meet the point that the connection with Great Britain was somehow insecure. He described in detail how the Irish parliament had, at his instigation, rejected British proposals that the repeal of the declaratory act should be accompanied by the negotiation of a new compact between the two kingdoms. Once that act had been unconditionally repealed, however, it had been agreed that there were to be no further constitutional claims on either side. Instead Great Britain and Ireland were to be pledged to one another on 'the eternal principle of unity of empire, and separation of parliament'. But that left the question of how precisely those two principles were to be reconciled in practice. Cooke, pressing home his case, had been able to point to the parallels with America, where Adams and Washington had belatedly recognized that the United States could not function as a conglomeration of autonomous units but required a federal constitution. *Imperium in imperio* [sovereignty within sovereignty] had likewise been the downfall of Poland and the United Provinces. Grattan, on the other hand, could only assert that the use of the term 'final' in 1782 somehow guaranteed that no future conflict of interests would get out of hand.

Grattan's continued commitment to the principle of absolute legislative autonomy for Ireland can be contrasted with the case made against the union by a politician of very different outlook and background, John Foster. Where Grattan was the quintessential opposition politician, eloquent on the floor of the house but quickly at sea on the rare occasions when he was required to involve himself in matters of administrative detail, Foster had for the best part of two decades been one of the government's most prized men of business.[107] For him the whole point of the settlement of 1782 was that it did not in fact amount to 'leaving the connection a bare junction of two kingdoms under one sovereign'.

[105] Speech of 15 Jan. 1800, in *The Speeches of the Right Hon. Henry Grattan*, ed. D. O. Madden (Dublin, 1874), 226–9. Pitt is quoted ibid. 230.
[106] Quoted in Geoghegan, *Irish Act of Union*, 62.
[107] For Grattan's incapacity as an administrator see Malcomson, *John Foster*, 396. See also Frederick Jebb's indictment of a man 'who, impracticable himself, would give to our politics the same inflexibility which characterizes his own mind': Frederick Jebb, *Considerations Submitted to the People of Ireland . . . in Answer to a Pamphlet lately Entitled 'Observations on the Money Bill' etc* (Dublin, 1781), 7.

The stipulation that acts of the Irish parliament should be ratified under the great seal of England was both a symbolic and a practical safeguard. It made 'the British minister answerable to the British nation' if any law passed in Ireland should prove damaging to the empire, and so secured 'union and confederation on a firm and lasting basis'. Since issues of peace and war, and the conclusion of treaties, were wholly in the hands of the executive, moreover, there could be no question of Ireland pursuing a separate foreign policy. The most its parliament could do was refuse to contribute to the financing of a war, a stance in which it would be unlikely to persist since it would have no way of avoiding the war itself.[108] Pragmatic arguments of this kind provide a glimpse of the way in which the settlement of 1782 might have been made to work. By contrast Grattan's uncompromising claims can only have confirmed ministers in their belief that its removal offered the only reliable hope of long-term stability.

Foster's emergence as a leading anti-union spokesman was a reflection of the extent to which the issue of union had split the Irish Protestant establishment. Others too accepted dismissal from office rather than support the measure. John Beresford's son, John Claudius, for example, disagreed with his father about the union, and saved both him and the government embarrassment by voluntarily resigning his minor positions of inspector general of exports and imports, and registrar general of tobacco. Recent work has emphasized the extent to which opposition to the union from men who had been pillars of the Protestant establishment was due to a suspicion, understandable in the light of the relief act of 1793 and other concessions, that English ministers could not be counted on to preserve what remained of Protestant political privilege. And it is indeed the case that some sections of the Orange Order, nominally neutral on the issue of the union, openly campaigned against it. There were even fears that the yeomanry might emulate the Volunteers of two decades earlier by opposing the measure. Yet it would be wrong to assume that opposition, even from men who had been reliable servants of successive British lords lieutenant, rested solely on vested interest. Foster rejected as 'idle talk' references to the improvement in manners and customs that would follow a union. 'Much as I admire Britain, I am not ready to give up the Irish character, or to make a sacrifice for the change.' He likewise responded to attempts by the pro-union side to secure Catholic support with a passionate counter-appeal:

Your country is in danger, a desperate attempt is on foot to seduce you to surrender the independence of your parliament. You are . . . bound by every tie of duty to yourselves, your country, and your posterity; to preserve it join all hands and hearts together, bring the vessel into port, forget all family differences, all local or partial jealousies, and save Ireland, save your country.[109]

---

[108] *Speech of the Right Honourable John Foster, Speaker of the House of Commons of Ireland, Delivered in Committee of the Whole House, on Thursday the 11th of April* (London, 1799), 22–3, 53–7.
[109] Ibid. 65, 110.

Foster's principles, and those of others like him, prevented him from taking the logical further step of seeking to outbid the British government by promising the Catholics full political rights at the hands of an Irish parliament. But his language was nevertheless evidence of the extent to which an emotional commitment to the idea of an Irish kingdom was by no means confined to the self-defined patriots.

The unexpected defeat of January 1799 brought home to Cornwallis and Castlereagh the necessity of more decisive action. In order to be carried through, Cooke had warned an English correspondent the previous October, a union would have to be 'written-up, spoken-up, intrigued-up, drunk-up, sung-up and bribed-up'.[110] The lord lieutenant and chief secretary now belatedly took his advice. During 1798 both pro- and anti-union forces exerted themselves to organize demonstrations of support, arranging meetings of the freeholders in counties and towns, organizing petitions, and seeking a vote on the issue by the grand juries, representing the property holders of each county. The results of such orchestrated displays of public opinion cannot be taken wholly at face value. But the general impression is that politically articulate opinion was divided, with pro-union sentiment most evident in the south and west, and also in Antrim and Down, while anti-union sentiment was stronger in Dublin and in other parts of Ulster. Such a geographical pattern could be interpreted as reflecting the greater strength of Protestant sectarianism, and particularly of the Orange Order, in more religiously mixed areas. Alternatively it could be seen as reflecting the greater strength in the east and parts of Ulster of the Volunteer tradition.

The grand juries and freeholders' meetings, however, were still disproportionately organs of Protestant opinion. By 1799 it was no longer possible, as it had been for Swift in 1724, to take Irish Protestants as 'the whole people of Ireland'. The Catholics were now a well-organized interest group, and their open opposition, in the name of four-fifths of the population, would nullify any attempt to claim that the union was legitimized by popular support. On the other hand one of the arguments that could be made for a union was that it would permit a final settlement of Ireland's destructive religious divisions. Within a united kingdom, Cooke argued in his pamphlet of November 1798, Catholics could safely be admitted to what would still be a predominantly Protestant imperial parliament. At the same time the British government, currently 'not pledged upon any specific principle to support one sect in Ireland more than another', would be committed to maintaining a Protestant church establishment within a unitary British and Irish state.[111] His comments reflected the initial view of both Pitt and Grenville that the union should also include the admission of Catholics in both Great Britain and Ireland to seats in parliament. In addition

---

[110] Quoted in Geoghegan, *Irish Act of Union*, 21.   [111] Cooke, *Arguments*, 27.

they proposed that the Catholic clergy in Ireland should, like their Presbyterian counterparts, receive a contribution towards their maintenance from the state. This, it was argued, would make priests more independent of their congregations and hence both free and willing to uphold principles of loyalty rather than disaffection. It would also help to defuse the contentious issue of the tithes still paid to the established church.

By the autumn of 1798 the cabinet had retreated from this bold initial strategy. Grenville, in particular, seems to have changed his mind on the issue, and his defection, along with energetic lobbying by Lord Clare, by this time the union's most committed Irish supporter, led Pitt to decide that a decision on the Catholic question should be postponed until after the union had been completed. Cornwallis and Castlereagh, on the other hand, remained strongly committed to the view that full equality for Catholics was the only means by which permanent stability could be brought to Ireland. At a cabinet meeting in November 1799, with another meeting of the Irish parliament imminent, Castlereagh delivered a forceful report: with the government's parliamentary majority 'composed of very doubtful materials', and Protestant opinion divided, 'the measure could not be carried if the Catholics were embarked in an active opposition to it'. In response the cabinet gave Cornwallis new, and carefully qualified, instructions: to avoid if possible making any specific promise to Catholic leaders, but at the same time to make clear to them that they could expect a united parliament to look sympathetically at their case. Those present did not, however, keep the usual formal minute of their meeting. The reason, reflecting what was to be the fatal flaw in Pitt's strategy for a final solution to the Irish problem, was that they were not yet ready to reveal this part of their planning to the king.

Not all Catholics responded to Cornwallis's overtures. The 25-year-old Daniel O'Connell, nephew and heir to one of the surviving Catholic landowners in County Kerry, having already passed from the fringes of the United Irishmen to the yeomanry, made his first formal political appearance with a passionate speech declaring that in preference to a union he would accept 'the re-enactment of the penal code in all its pristine horrors'.[112] The majority, however, had little cause to regret the passing of a parliament that had introduced the penal laws and had repealed them only under heavy pressure from London. Against this background Cornwallis's private assurances were enough to induce the main body of Irish Catholics either to support the union or to remain quietly neutral. In the century that followed Catholic nationalism was to confront Protestant unionism. But in 1799–1800 the government successfully invoked Catholic loyalism, if only that of a silent majority, to counter a vociferous Protestant defence of Ireland's constitutional autonomy.

---

[112] Oliver MacDonagh, *The Hereditary Bondsman: Daniel O'Connell 1775–1829* (London, 1988), 93.

The administration's concern to organize displays of support by Protestants, and secure at least the neutrality of Catholics, is testimony to the extent to which the political life of late eighteenth-century Ireland, for all its inequalities and downright absurdities, was never solely about the naked exercise of power. When Cornwallis in October 1799 made a tour of the northern counties, for example, he was happy to accept pro-union addresses from the corporations of Dundalk and Armagh, despite admitting privately that these had been obtained by the dominant influence there of the earl of Roden in the first case and the archbishop of Armagh in the second. In Belfast, however, the corporation was too notoriously the sole possession of the marquis of Donegall. This made it necessary to resort instead to a public dinner, organized behind the scenes by Donegall's father-in-law and chief man of business, at which 150 leading inhabitants declared their support for the union.[113] Despite such efforts, however, and the careful calculations that underlay them, the battle for public opinion was never central. All that was required, on the government side, was to ensure that it could not be charged with imposing a settlement against the clear will of the nation. The real issue was to be decided at the next meeting of the Irish parliament. Ignoring the protests of the opposition, Cornwallis and Castlereagh made clear that office holders were to be required to support the union. Those who persisted in their opposition, like Foster, were removed during 1799. Later, in February 1800, the government, in what many thought a shocking departure from the regard that should be shown to a territorial magnate, dismissed the marquis of Downshire as governor of County Down and colonel of the county militia, for the offence of having circulated an anti-union petition in his regiment.

Meanwhile the full range of favours in the government's gift—promotions in the church, army, and judiciary, appointment to sinecures and offices, pensions and peerages—were deployed to win over MPs or the patrons of parliamentary seats. As late as 1804 the first post-union lord lieutenant, the earl of Hardwicke, complained that he had not been able to dispose of a single church living worth more than £100 a year for any purpose other than the settlement of the long list of 'union engagements' he had inherited on taking office three years earlier.[114] In addition more than £32,000 was diverted from the secret service fund to finance the Castle's campaign. The number of MPs who actually changed their vote was not large. Between twelve and twenty members who had opposed the union in January 1799 voted in favour twelve months later. Even then, their change of side was balanced by that of three others who switched from support to opposition. Instead what the government most commonly secured, by one means or another, was the resignation of anti-union MPs and their replacement

[113] Cornwallis to Portland, 22 Oct. 1799 (*Correspondence of Charles, First Marquis Cornwallis,* ed. Charles Ross (London, 1859), iii. 139).

[114] Michael MacDonagh (ed.), *The Viceroy's Postbag: Correspondence Hitherto Unpublished of the Earl of Hardwicke, First Lord Lieutenant of Ireland after the Union* (London, 1904), 38–9.

by others willing to vote for the measure. In all 75 out of 300 parliamentary seats changed hands between 22 January 1799 and 7 June 1800.

The vigorous behind the scenes dealing that went on between the two sessions of parliament stretched contemporary conceptions of the legitimacy of patronage as a tool of political management to their limit. Whether it went beyond that limit is less clear. It was openly accepted that parliamentary support for the government and its measures brought entitlement to a reasonable level of reward. In a system thus constituted, MPs and borough patrons who consented to the permanent dissolution of the Irish parliament surrendered a valuable asset, and could expect to be rewarded for doing so. Castlereagh referred to the need 'to buy out and secure to the crown forever the fee simple of Irish corruption'.[115] Cornwallis's announcement that the crown would pay cash compensation to those borough proprietors whose seats were to be abolished was an open acknowledgement of the same principle, as well as an essential move in the drive to insure against another parliamentary defeat.

When the Irish parliament reassembled in January 1800, the results of the Castle's labours quickly became evident. An anti-union amendment to the Commons address was defeated by 138 votes to 96. On 15 February the Commons voted by 158 votes to 115 to accept a message from the lord lieutenant recommending a union, and a series of opposition motions over the next few weeks were defeated by comfortable margins. The Irish and British parliaments proceeded to pass parallel acts creating, from 1 January 1801, a United Kingdom of Ireland and Great Britain. Ireland was to be represented at Westminster by 100 MPs, two from each county and the remainder from the more substantial boroughs, as well as by four bishops of the Church of Ireland and twenty-eight representative peers sitting in the House of Lords. Each country was to retain its own financial system, with Ireland contributing two-seventeenths of the cost of imperial expenditure. Tariffs on the movement of goods between Great Britain and Ireland were to be progressively reduced, with complete free trade from 1824. There was talk of abolishing the separate Irish executive, in favour of the same direct rule from London that sufficed for Scotland and Wales. In the event, however, a lord lieutenant and chief secretary were to remain at Dublin Castle for a further century and a quarter.

Faced with the two terminal events of the eighteenth century, the rebellion of 1798 and the act of union, historians have offered radically different assessments. The rebellion is taken as marking the inauguration of a political tradition, physical force republicanism. The union is seen as a flawed measure, doomed to failure from the moment of its passage. Both judgements are perverse. The crude Catholic separatism of the Defenders survived into the 1820s and 1830s in the Ribbon movement. The democratic republicanism of the United Irishmen reappeared briefly in 1848, and somewhat more credibly in the Fenian movement

---

[115] Quoted in Bolton, *Passing of the Irish Act of Union*, 162 n 1.

after 1858. But the mainstream of Irish nationalism, from O'Connell's repeal movement in the 1830s to the Home Rulers of the Edwardian era, remained conspicuous above all for their willingness to negotiate a position for Irish Catholics within the structures of the British state. The United Irish ideal of a union of Protestant and Catholic behind shared political goals, meanwhile, has continued only in the imaginations of a handful of idealists. The act of union, on the other hand, was undoubtedly a flawed settlement. In particular, the opportunity to make a real difference to the political future of Ireland was forfeited when Pitt and his colleagues bowed to the prejudices of George III and abandoned any plans to accompany the union with full Catholic emancipation. But the union nevertheless had the great merit of lifting effective power out of the hands of the contending parties within Ireland. It was also a flexible settlement, which across a century was to accommodate the widening of the franchise, a radical reform of the land system, and the progressive dismantling of institutionalized religious discrimination.[116] By doing so it provided the framework within which the island was governed for 120 years—half as long again as the modern Irish state has so far endured.

[116] The argument for a more positive assessment of the act of union is developed more fully in S. J. Connolly, 'Varieties of Britishness: Ireland, Scotland and Wales in the Hanoverian State', in Alexander Grant and Keith J. Stringer (eds.), *Uniting the Kingdom? The Making of British History* (London, 1995), 206–7; idem, 'Reconsidering the Irish Act of Union', *Transactions of the Royal Historical Society*, 10 (2000), 399–408.

12

The Common Name of Irishman

In August 1796 Theobald Wolfe Tone compiled a short memoir of his political life, charting the progress that had taken him from Dublin to political exile in revolutionary Paris. What he had sought to achieve, he wrote, had been 'to unite the whole people of Ireland, to abolish the memory of all past dissensions, and to substitute the common name of Irishman in place of the denominations of Catholic, Protestant and Dissenter'.[1] Tone, as on other occasions, displayed his talent for phrase making, and his words were to enter the rhetoric, if rarely the practice, of Irish nationalist politics. Taken as a reflection on the political developments of the preceding three centuries, however, his comments were as striking for what they took for granted as for what they chose to emphasize.

For Tone the self-evident alternative to the sectarian divisions that he saw as the curse of his country was acceptance of a shared Irishness. Yet he would only have had to look briefly at some features of the Ireland that he had recently left behind him to observe clear traces of what had once been quite different lines of division. During his close involvement in the affairs of the Catholic committee, for example, he would have dealt with John Thomas Troy, archbishop of Dublin from 1786 until 1823. If he had chosen to enquire into the matter, he would have found that Troy's four predecessors, dating back to 1734, had borne even more clearly English or Old English names: Linegar, Lincoln, Fitzsimons, Carpenter. He might, if so minded, have compared this record with that of another Catholic archbishopric, Armagh, occupied between 1707 and 1818 by three MacMahons and two O'Reillies. (The unhappy career there of the one exception to this succession of Gaelic surnames, a Blake from the former Old English stronghold of Galway, tells its own story.) When he sat in the gallery of the House of Commons, a hungry political outsider absorbed in its proceedings, he would have noted a very different range of surnames, whose associations were most frequently with the age of warfare and plantation that had extended from the reign of Elizabeth to that of Cromwell. At the same time he would also have been able to note certain striking exceptions, reminders of the divergent paths that individuals and families had taken over the preceding 300 years: an O'Hara sitting for County Sligo, an O'Neill for County Antrim, an O'Donnell

---

[1] *Life of Theobald Wolfe Tone: Memoirs, Journals and Political Writings*, ed. Thomas Bartlett (Dublin, 1998), 46.

for County Donegal, not to mention the tell-tale Anglo-Norman prefix to the surname of John Fitzgibbon who, as lord chancellor and earl of Clare, had taken the lead in engineering Tone's own involuntary departure.

In reality, of course, there is no reason to think that Tone noticed any of these things. He was not, despite his politics, a great student of Irish history. And in any case no one, by these last decades of the eighteenth century, spoke in terms of native Irish, Old English, and New English. When Lord Edward Fitzgerald, younger brother of Ireland's premier peer, emerged as one of the most militant of the United Irish leaders, no observer bothered to link his action to the rebellion almost three centuries earlier with which his distant ancestor, Thomas, Lord Offaly, had unwittingly set in train what was to become the Tudor conquest of Ireland.[2] In this sense Tone's appeal to the common name of Irishman testified, not just to new political aspirations, but to the obsolescence of a whole earlier vocabulary of identity.

What had replaced that vocabulary, with its blending of ethnicity and religion, was, as Tone's comments made clear, a more straightforward division between Catholic and Protestant. This was the line that, by Tone's lifetime, and indeed for most of the century in which he had been born, separated both a John Foster and a John Fitzgibbon from a John Carpenter, as well as from a Hugh MacMahon. For a time, in the 1770s and 1780s, it had been possible to believe that old animosities had been softened by the passage of time, and that formerly hostile groups could unite behind shared national aspirations. It was an argument to this effect that had given Tone his first great success as a political writer, in 1791. Even as he wrote that work, however, the continuing conflict between Orange and Defender societies, and the appearance in political debate of the novel slogan 'Protestant ascendancy', testified to the growth of new forms of sectarian conflict. In less than a decade the bloody events at Scullabogue, Wexford Bridge, and elsewhere were to demonstrate even more horribly just how far Ireland was from leaving its religious conflicts behind it.

The sectarian fears and animosities that regained vitality in the late eighteenth century continued to shape Irish political life in the decades that followed. The failure of Pitt's original plans to accompany the union with the admission of Catholics to full political rights was in this respect disastrous. Catholic emancipation came only in 1829, at the end of a mass agitation that brought Ireland to the brink of civil war. A whole generation of Catholics had their first experience of organized political activity in the context of a burning religious grievance. For Protestants, equally, the spectacle of the Catholic masses organized as a disciplined electoral army, officered by their clergy, confirmed their worst fears of the uses to which any power they conceded would be put. The emancipated Catholic, Tone had prophesied, would cease to base his politics on religion. The experience of the 1820s, 1830s, and 1840s seemed to prove the

[2] Connolly, *Contested Island*, 76–90.

exact opposite. By this time, too, religion itself had become a disruptive force, as the rise on one side of Protestant evangelicalism, and on the other of a more militant Catholicism, made both education and pastoral work a battleground for opposing zealots.[3]

The rise of sectarian animosity during the first half of the nineteenth century is undeniable. Yet other forces were also at work, helping to shape the character of political life. The same relationships of clientage and deference that in the seventeenth and eighteenth centuries had sometimes cut across lines of religious and social division continued to operate after 1800. In county and borough politics, as soon as the debris of the rebellion had been cleared away, landed families were able to resume their electoral pursuit of local and factional rivalries, taking for granted the compliance of their armies of tenant voters, now Catholic as well as Protestant. O'Connell's mobilization of the Catholic electorate, between 1823 and 1847, presented a powerful short-term challenge. But landlord power was dented, not overthrown. In fact the 1850s and 1860s, following the collapse of the repeal movement and against a background of improved economic conditions, were to be a last golden age of landlord-dominated politics in the counties. Borough elections, during the same period, revolved around a more varied mix of personality, localism, and a patronage that frequently shaded into straightforward bribery. Nor were political alignments yet organized along strictly denominational lines. O'Connell's parliamentary following in the 1830s and 1840s relied heavily on the willingness of Protestant gentlemen, blessed with the means others lacked to finance their own return to parliament, to enlist under his banner.[4] Following his death and the collapse of the repeal movement, the majority of these, along with their Catholic counterparts, moved without undue difficulty into the Irish Liberal party, which became the new vehicle for cooperation between Catholics and reform-minded Protestants. In County Cavan, for example, the future Unionist leader Edward Saunderson was returned as Liberal MP in 1865 by the votes of a mainly Catholic electorate, on the basis of his reputation as a mildly progressive landlord.[5] The rise of the Home Rule movement during the 1870s reduced the scope for local and personal politics of this kind. But the new party initially attracted substantial Protestant support, based partly on a continuing tradition of patriotism and partly on outrage at the latest outcome of direct rule by a British government, the disestablishment of the Church of Ireland. It was not in fact until the Home Rule crisis of 1885–6 that Irish politics came to be organized round a clear division between Catholic and Protestant.

---

[3] For a fuller discussion of these issues see S. J. Connolly, 'Mass Politics and Sectarian Conflict', in W. E. Vaughan (ed.), *A New History of Ireland*, v: *Ireland under the Union, Part 1, 1801-70* (Oxford, 1989), 74–107.

[4] J. H. Whyte, 'Daniel O'Connell and the Repeal Party', *IHS* 11 (1958–9), 297–316.

[5] Alvin Jackson, *Land and Loyalty in Victorian Ireland: Colonel Edward Saunderson* (Oxford, 1985), ch. 1.

These points are worth making because they highlight the continued relevance of the central themes developed in this study. Throughout both the present volume and its predecessor, the emphasis has been on the fluid and contingent nature of allegiances and aspirations, and on the capacity of personal, local, and strategic alliances to cut across seemingly intractable lines of ethnic, political, or religious division. It would be easy to assume that in the nineteenth century, the great age of political ideology, these ceased to be features of Irish life. But in fact they remain central to the political world of mid-Victorian Ireland, as they were to its early modern predecessor.[6] Nor should their eventual supersession by the tight polarity of Catholic nationalist and Protestant unionist be seen as predetermined. Perceptions of the union as a settlement doomed by its inner contradictions do not do justice to the flexibility of the structures it created, or indeed to its longevity as a framework for government. The unprecedented strains created by the First World War may eventually have brought about its collapse. But it was by no means clear, in the 1850s or the 1860s, that the majority of Irish Catholics would not complete their journey towards joining the Scots and the Welsh, as well as the English nonconformists and the representatives of organized labour, in the broad anti-establishment coalition that was British Liberalism. In the event they did not do so. In the event, also, Irish Protestants came to see ideas of Irish self-determination that many of them would earlier have supported as a threat to their very existence. But all this came about through yet another hectic period, the Home Rule crisis of the mid-1880, that once again, as in the 1640s or the 1790s, saw old identities shed and new ones assumed or constructed.

'Are we forever to walk like beasts of prey, over fields which these ancestors stained with blood?' The hint of despair in the language of the Dublin United Irishmen is understandable. The history of the preceding three centuries had indeed been a bloody and destructive one. What was misleading, however, was the implication of a single conflict recurring without change across the generations. From the ethnically and culturally mixed forces that clashed at Knockdoe in 1504 to the slaughter of Protestant by Protestant and Catholic by Catholic on the battlefields of 1798, conflict was often brutal, but rarely simple. If the long-term tensions arising from conquest and colonization are undeniable, so too is the ability and willingness of the different components of a diverse society to redefine allegiances and relationships in response to changing circumstances. Those involved, whether border lords like the earls of Kildare,

---

[6] For the fluid nature of political allegiances in the 1850s and 1860s see in particular K. T. Hoppen, *Elections, Politics and Society in Ireland 1832–1881* (Oxford, 1984). For the contingent nature of the late nineteenth-century outcome see in particular R. V. Comerford, *The Fenians in Context: Irish Politics and Society 1848–1882* (Dublin, 1985), as well as Comerford's contribution to Vaughan (ed.), *New History of Ireland*, v, chs. 20–3. There is, of course, a well-developed alternative tradition of interpretation that would emphasize instead the consistency of sectarian antagonisms across the nineteenth century and the long-term roots of the nationalist and unionist movements that took shape in the 1880s.

balancing the need to maintain their credibility as local magnates against the requirement for at least minimal compliance with the demands of a distant crown, or late eighteenth-century Irish Protestants weighing their dissatisfaction with an unresponsive political regime against an uneasy awareness of their exposed position within a predominantly Catholic Ireland, made difficult and dangerous choices. In doing so they were unavoidably influenced by historical memory and inherited tradition. But they did not act out a script written for them by their ancestors. Nor, indeed, did they leave such a script as their legacy to future generations.

Maps

Map 1. Main places mentioned in the text

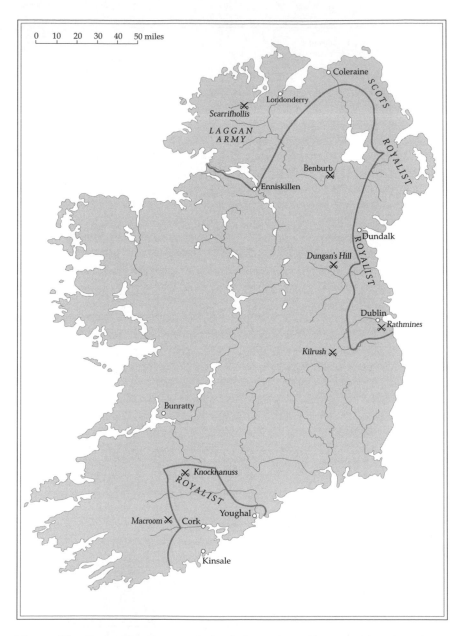

Map 2. The Contending Forces in Ireland, September 1643, with Selected Battlesites 1642–50

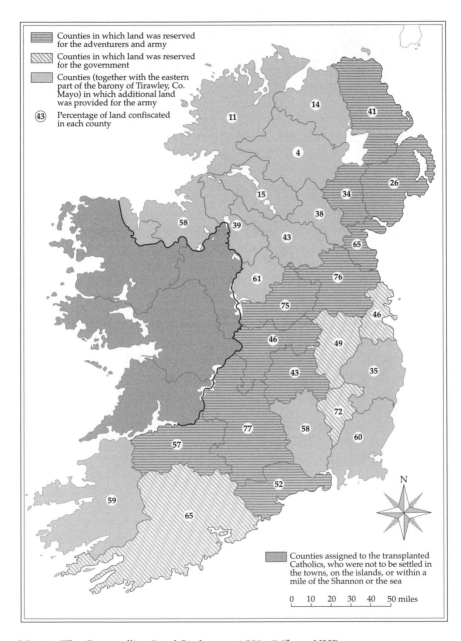

Counties in which land was reserved for the adventurers and army

Counties in which land was reserved for the government

Counties (together with the eastern part of the barony of Tirawley, Co. Mayo) in which additional land was provided for the army

(43) Percentage of land confiscated in each county

Counties assigned to the transplanted Catholics, who were not to be settled in the towns, on the islands, or within a mile of the Shannon or the sea

0 10 20 30 40 50 miles

N

Map 3. The Cromwellian Land Settlement 1652–7 (from *NHI*)

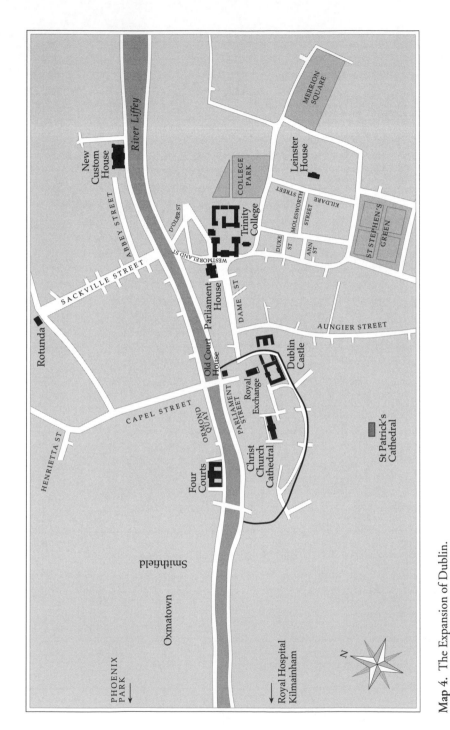

Map 4. The Expansion of Dublin.

Note: This is a selective sketch, designed to show: (a) the medieval city, as marked by the walls; (b) major Restoration developments—Capel Street, Aungier Street, Ormond Quay, St Stephen's Green; (c) some landmarks in the subsequent eastwards expansion of the city.

Index

Abbreviations: abp archbishop; bp bishop; LD Lord Deputy; LL Lord Lieutenant; C of I Church of Ireland; RC Catholic; Pres. Presbyterian